The EU and the WTO: Ever the Twain Shall Meet

The EU and the WTO: Ever the Twain Shall Meet

Liber Amicorum Marco Bronckers

Edited by

Freya Baetens

Stefaan Van den Bogaert

Wolters Kluwer

Published by:
Kluwer Law International B.V.
PO Box 316
2400 AH Alphen aan den Rijn
The Netherlands
E-mail: lrs-sales@wolterskluwer.com
Website: www.wolterskluwer.com/en/solutions/kluwerlawinternational

Sold and distributed by:
Wolters Kluwer Legal & Regulatory U.S.
920 Links Avenue
Landisville, PA 17538
United States of America
E-mail: customer.service@wolterskluwer.com

ISBN 978-94-035-4876-0

e-Book: ISBN 978-94-035-4886-9
web-PDF: ISBN 978-94-035-4896-8

Editors

Freya Baetens is a professor of public international law (Faculty of Law, University of Oxford), Head of Programmes at the Bonavero Institute of Human Rights and fellow at Mansfield College, Oxford. She is also affiliated with the PluriCourts Centre (Faculty of Law, Oslo University) and the Europa Institute (Faculty of Law, Leiden University). As a member of the Brussels Bar, she regularly acts as counsel or expert in international and European disputes.

Stefaan Van den Bogaert is a professor of European law, director of the Europa Institute and vice-dean of Leiden Law School.

Contributors

Carl Baudenbacher is a partner at the Zurich/Brussels-based law firm of Nobel Baudenbacher. From 2003 to 2017, he was president of the EFTA Court, of which he was a judge from 1995 to 2018. He is a visiting professor at the London School of Economics and a professor emeritus at the University of St. Gallen.

Frederik Behre is a lawyer at the Legal Service of the European Commission, Brussels. At the time of writing, he was a postdoctoral researcher at the Europa Institute of Leiden Law School. He defended his PhD on national constitutional limits to EU fiscal integration in October 2021 at Leiden University. His research centres around the interaction between national constitutional law and EU law employing the comparative constitutional methodology.

Jacques Bourgeois is an *advocaat* at the Brussels Bar and senior advisor of Sidley Austin, assisting clients in EU competition and trade matters. He is a former director of the European Commission Legal Service. He is an honorary professor of the College of Europe and a guest professor at the University of Ghent.

Mielle Bulterman is Head of the European Law Division, Ministry of Foreign Affairs, The Netherlands. After studying law at Leiden University, she obtained a PhD at Utrecht University. From 1998 to 2008, she lectured on EU law at the Europe Institute at Leiden University.

James Crawford† AC, FBA took up his position as Judge of the International Court of Justice in February 2015 and served on the bench until his untimely death on 31 May 2021. Previously he was Whewell Professor of International Law at the University of Cambridge and a Professorial Fellow of Jesus College; he also held chairs at Adelaide, Sydney and LaTrobe Universities in Australia and was Chang Jiang Distinguished Professor at Xi'an Jiaotong University, PRC. During his practising career, he was involved as counsel or expert in many cases before the ICJ and other international tribunals, in addition to multiple appointments as arbitrator in inter-State and investor-State proceedings.

Armin Cuyvers is Professor of European Law at Leiden University, where he holds the chair in EU Constitutional Law and Comparative Regional Integration. He is the director of CompaRe, the Leiden Jean Monnet Centre of Excellence on Comparative Regional Integration and the faculty teaching director for legal Masters.

Isha Das read for her undergraduate in Law in India, after which she received her LLM from University College London (2018-2019). She is a Teaching and Research Assistant to the Chair of Constitutional and Administrative Law, European Law and European and International Economic Law at the University of Passau, Germany. She is also a lecturer of International Economic Laws at Jindal Global Law School in India.

Daniela Gómez Altamirano is a private sector specialist at the World Bank focusing on investment policy and a PhD candidate at Leiden University. She previously worked at the Permanent Mission of Mexico to the WTO, the Legal Service of the European Commission, and as editor of the *Journal of International Economic Law* at Georgetown University.

Giovanni Gruni is an Associate Professor at ESADE Law School in Barcelona and visiting professor at Georgetown Law School. He holds a PhD in Law from the University of Oxford and an LLM from the European University Institute.

Bernard M. Hoekman is Professor and Director of Global Economics at the Robert Schuman Centre for Advanced Studies, European University Institute. A CEPR Research Fellow, he is a graduate of the Erasmus University Rotterdam and holds a PhD in economics from the University of Michigan. His research focuses on international trade and global governance

Robert Howse is the Robert Lloyd C. Nelson Professor of International Law at NYU Law School. For several years, he served as an advisor to the Renewable Energy and International Law Project of REEP, a consortium of the private sector and other actors.

Richard Jiang is Assistant Professor at the China University of Political Science and Law. He studied law in Shanghai (LLB 2009) and the Netherlands (Leiden University, LLM 2014, PhD 2020). He interned with the WTO in 2018 and the United Nations ESCAP in 2017.

Joris Larik is Assistant Professor of Comparative, EU and International Law at Leiden University. His research has been acknowledged with several awards, including NATO's Manfred Wörner Essay Award and the EUI's Mauro Cappelletti Prize. In 2022, he was appointed to the Committee on European Integration of the Dutch Advisory Council on International Affairs and the European Commission's pool of arbitrators for disputes in the framework of bilateral trade agreements.

Richard H. Lauwaars was Professor of European Organizations at the Free University in Amsterdam from 1972 until 1979. During the academic year 1979-1980, he was a Visiting Professor at the University of Michigan Law School at Ann Arbor (US). From 1980 until 1994, he taught European Union Law at the University of Amsterdam. From

1994 to 2008, he was a member of the Netherlands Council of State. On 4 June 1985, he had the pleasure of being Marco's *promotor* at the University of Amsterdam.

Rick Lawson is Professor of European Human Rights Law at the Europa Institute of Leiden Law School; he was dean of Leiden Law School in 2011-2016. Currently, he serves as a member of the Management Board of the EU Fundamental Rights Agency.

Sarah Levin is a graduate of NYU Law School. She was previously a Vice President at Goldman Sachs in the Business Intelligence Group. After graduation from Law School, she clerked at the Court of International Trade.

Petros C. Mavroidis is Professor of Law at Columbia Law School and has acted as Chief Reporter for the American Law Institute study 'Principles of International Trade: the WTO'.

Tom Ottervanger is Professor Emeritus of European and Competition Law at Leiden University; he is a former partner of the law firm Allen & Overy; former (deputy) justice at the Court of Appeal of The Hague; visiting Professor at LUISS University, Rome; Chairman of the Board of Advisors of the Jean Monnet Center 'CompaRe'.

Reinhard Quick studied law at the Universities of Mannheim (PhD 1983) and Michigan (LLM 1984). From 1984 until 2016, he worked as a lobbyist at the German and European Chemical Industry Associations. In 2006, Reinhard Quick was appointed honorary professor of international economic law at Saarland University.

Ben Smulders is the Deputy Director General responsible for State aid control in DG Competition of the European Commission. In addition, he is a Professor of International and European Competition law at the Free University of Brussels as well as a Visiting Professor of Law at the College of Europe in Bruges, Université Paris 2 and the Collegio Europeo di Parma. He was educated at Leiden University and the London School of Economics.

Christian Tietje is University Professor of Public Law, European law, and International Economic Law at Martin Luther University Halle-Wittenberg and the former Rector of that university (2018-2022).

Christa Tobler is Professor of European law at the Universities of Basel (Switzerland) and Leiden (the Netherlands). Her research specializations are legal equality and discrimination as well as the EU-Swiss agreements, seen against the background of other external relation regimes of the EU, in particular, association agreements.

Anne Vallery is a partner with the law firm WilmerHale, specializing in antitrust and competition, with 25 years of experience in defending international and local companies before national Courts, national regulatory and competition authorities, the European Commission and the European Courts.

Peter Van den Bossche is director of studies of the World Trade Institute and professor of international economic law at the University of Bern, Switzerland; President of the

Society of International Economic Law (SIEL); and former Member and Chair of the Appellate Body of the World Trade Organization, Geneva, Switzerland (2009-2019).

Yves Van Gerven was a practising lawyer at the Brussels Bar for almost 25 years and specialized in all areas of European and Belgian competition law (1989-2016). He was a member of the Competition College of the Belgian Competition Authority (BCA) from 2013 to 2018. He served as *référendaire* at the Court of Justice (1995-1998) and the General Court of the EU (2016-2018). He obtained his Bachelor of Laws from KU Leuven (1986) and holds a DESS in Finance at Aix-Marseille III (1988) and a Master of Laws (LLM) from Harvard Law School (1989). Currently, he is the Director of Legal Affairs of the BCA.

Summary of Contents

Table of Contents

Preface

In November 2022, our colleague and friend, Professor Marco Bronckers, retired from his position as Professor of WTO and EU Law at the University of Leiden, where he had been a highly-valued member of the Europa Instituut for many years: a charismatic teacher, whose lectures were consistently greatly appreciated by his students from the Advanced Master in European and International Business Law; a dedicated supervisor to his LLM and PhD students; an excellent scholar, author of many innovative and thought-provoking legal contributions to the academic debate in his fields of expertise; a gifted speaker at national and international fora; and above all an open, smart, genuine, warm and engaging colleague in the workplace.

We would like to honour him with this *Liber Amicorum*. The title and unifying theme of the book is *The EU and the WTO: Ever the Twain Shall Meet*. As well as having an internal coherence with respect to the development of international and European economic law, the proposed topics reflect some of the areas in which Professor Bronckers has made an outstanding intellectual contribution, recognized by legal practitioners and scholars all over the world.

The European Union (EU) and the World Trade Organization (WTO) are becoming ever more important players on the international legal scene, as well as points of reference for the development of similar institutions elsewhere. What initially began for both institutions as a relatively small and well-delimited trade-focused mandate, has been significantly expanded over the past decades so that there are few legal issues today that are not, in some way, affected by the EU or, perhaps to a lesser extent, WTO law. Finally, the EU and the WTO interact on a global scale as rule-makers and -enforcers, with repercussions for the entire world's population.

Nevertheless, they are currently also undergoing a backlash, as demonstrated, in particular, by Brexit in the framework of the EU and the deadlock concerning the WTO Appellate Body. For this reason, the book takes a macro-approach looking at the EU and the WTO in a broader context, as well as a micro-approach analysing specific high-profile issues. Both institutions are likely to undergo major reform in the next years: the book scrutinizes current proposals and makes an educated attempt at predicting the format of the EU and the WTO in the next decades.

Contributors to the book are first and foremost friends, (former) PhD fellows and colleagues of Marco, active in legal academia, in international legal practice, or both. The editors have strived to make this book as appealing and relevant as possible through their selection of a diverse group of proposed contributors in terms of subject specialisation, geographic origin and theoretical methodology. This approach ensures a broad and thoughtful evaluation of the topics. As such, a variety of audiences stands to benefit from its discussion and proposed solutions: legal practitioners, scholars and students of international and European law; as well as related disciplines, such as political science and economic theory. The book is aimed at a worldwide audience, with particular appeal to those who know Marco personally.

A final word on the cover image: those who have had the pleasure of being invited to Marco's home in Brussels know that Jonathan Laskers' 'For Boys and Girls' (2000, oil on linen, 254 × 191 cm) takes up pride of place in the middle of his living room. Dominique, Marco's wife, ensured us that this is his favourite painting, so we could not think of a more fitting cover image for this book – with special thanks to Mr Lasker for giving us permission to use it.

Retirement (or 'ascending to emeritus status') is not an end but a new beginning – *ut vivat, crescat, valeat*!

Freya Baetens & Stefaan Van den Bogaert
Oxford & Leiden, 2022

PART I The European Union

CHAPTER 1

Next Generation EU: Bridge over Troubled Water

Stefaan Van den Bogaert & Frederik Behre[*]

Next Generation *EU, the European Union's (EU) EUR 750 billion COVID-19 recovery strategy, is a significant achievement that alters the EU's economic governance. Not only have Member States empowered the Union for the first time to engage in large-scale borrowing to frontload Next Generation investments. But the Union has also embraced the opportunity to connect recovery efforts with its own green-digital policy priorities, thereby incentivizing a transformation of European economies. This contribution traces the political context and legal design that ensured the adoption of Next Generation EU. It furthermore explores how the Commission could continue to block funding to Member States that violate EU foundational values. And finally, it considers the unanswered question of repayment of the issued EU debt. Despite remaining uncertainties, Next Generation EU constitutes a solid, ingeniously construed bridge which may lead the EU and its Member States over socially, economically and politically troubled water into a more integrated Europe for the future generation.*

1 EVERY INCH A GENTLEMAN

In Leiden, it is common practice that young, newly appointed professors are informally assigned to an elder, more experienced professor, who can lend them their ear and offer

[*] The author is a European Commission official. All views expressed in this article are strictly personal and do not in any way bind that institution.

them some good advice. When I, a young, inexperienced Belgian, was appointed to the chair of European law at the Law School in the summer of 2009, Marco Bronckers became my confidant. At that time, he was a practising lawyer in Brussels and a part-time professor of World Trade Organization and EU law at the Europa Institute in Leiden, the position from which he now retires. Our first one-on-one meeting was in a restaurant, coincidentally, or perhaps rather appropriately called *Grand Café De Vriend*, in the Doezastraat in the city centre, not far away from the Kamerlingh Onnes Building where the law school is established. Since that first lunch, many more have followed, usually once or twice a year, always in the same place. And, now that I think of it, almost always the same lunch as well, even when it officially was no longer on the menu. In the beginning, we mainly talked about work. Later on, the emphasis in our conversations gradually shifted to other topics as well, such as life or the status quo in the European Union (EU). Invariably, our talks were pleasant and insightful. Marco is such an incredibly kind, charming, genuine, intelligent and wise person. Working with him at the Europa Institute all these years was a true pleasure. Unfortunately, that will come to an end now. We will lose a charismatic teacher, a committed PhD supervisor, an excellent scholar, and a gentleman ambassador for the Europa Institute. I wish him all the best for the future. I do hope we stay in touch. We can perhaps even have lunch in another place.

2 INTRODUCTION

The outbreak of the severe acute respiratory syndrome coronavirus 2 (SARS-CoV-2) was first identified in Wuhan in China, in December 2019. When efforts to contain it failed, the virus spread across the globe with breathtaking speed, prompting the World Health Organization (WHO) to declare it a public health emergency of international concern already on 30 January 2020 and a pandemic on 11 March 2020. As of 9 February 2022, COVID-19 had caused more than 400 million cases and almost 6 million deaths, making it a human tragedy of biblical proportions. The virus certainly didn't spare Europe. In the spring of 2020, the old continent was the epicentre of the pandemic. Italy was the first country worldwide to impose a national lockdown. In March 2020, more than 250 million people in Europe were confined to their homes. Public life had come to a halt. Even schools were closed.

Confronted with this health crisis, arguably the largest in Europe since the Spanish flu in 1918, at first, chaos reigned in the EU headquarters as individual Member States put their own national needs first in the desperate hunt for sufficient supply of medical equipment for their national population and enacted various national restrictions on freedom of movement to that effect. National borders were closed, and in no time, the internal market, one of the undisputed major achievements of the EU integration project, was in complete disarray. Parallels could be drawn from the Union's initially hesitant and reluctant reaction to the outburst of the sovereign debt crisis in 2009.[1] This time around, though, the tide quickly turned. In the spirit of Benjamin Franklin, who famously commented at the time of the signing of the Declaration of Independence, 'We must all hang together, or, most assuredly, we shall all hang separately', the Member States and the EU institutions rose to the challenge and decisively responded to the pandemic and its disastrous socioeconomic effects with a wide array of emergency measures. Striking examples of successful Union action in the health sphere are the centrally negotiated agreements for the delivery of COVID-19 vaccines, the operational EU-wide vaccination passport that facilitates movement between the Member States and the coordination of national health policies at the EU level.[2] More generally, however, the measure that stands out in this respect and that will constitute the focus of this contribution is *Next Generation EU (NGEU)*, the Union's recovery plan, which provides financial support to Member States that are particularly affected by the pandemic. At the same time, it aspires to do so much more, as it is also perceived to be a 'once in a lifetime' opportunity to emerge stronger from the pandemic, transform our economies and incentivize Europe to become 'greener, more digital and more resilient'.[3]

In terms of structure, we will start by sketching the legal background and the political circumstances which led to the adoption of this ambitious recovery package, already described as a paradigm shift in the EU integration process. Notably, it departs from the traditional approach of loan-based, conditional EU support for Member States and includes substantial non-repayable grants through which Member States can finance structural reforms and the transition into a green, digital future,[4] therefore hailed by some as a 'Hamiltonian moment' for the EU.[5] Subsequently, we will analyse the complex legal framework that underpins Next Generation EU. Third, our focus will turn to the spending issue: how the available funds are allocated to the Member States and which conditions are attached. Special attention in this respect will be dedicated to the fierce opposition from Poland and Hungary against the Conditionality Mechanism for its reliance on respect for the rule of law. Fourth, we will tackle the thorny issue of who will ultimately 'pay the bill'. We will conclude with some thoughts on the potential wider significance of this recovery-plus plan for the future of the EU.

1. Borger, *The Currency of Solidarity: Constitutional Transformation During the Euro Crisis* (CUP, 2020).
2. *See, inter alia*, Editorial Comments, 'Charting deeper and wider dimensions of (free) movement in EU law', 58 *Common Market Law Review* (2021), 969-986.
3. As the European Commission announces on the NGEU's website, cf. ec.europa.eu/info/strategy/recovery-plan-europe_en (accessed 20 February 2023).
4. Bekker, 'The EU's recovery and resilience facility: A next phase in EU socioeconomic governance?', 9 *Politics and Governance* (2021), 175-185, at 177.
5. Editorial Comments, 'Compromising (on) the general conditionality mechanism and the rule of law', 58 *Common Market Law Review* (2021), 267-284, at 274; Fabbrini, 'The legal architecture of the economic responses to COVID-19: EMU beyond the pandemic', 60 *Journal of Common Market Studies* (2022), 186-203, at 194; Celi, Guarascio and Simonazzi, 'A fragile and divided European Union meets COVID-19: Further disintegration or "Hamiltonian moment"?', 47 *Journal of Industrial and Business Economics* (2020), 411-424, at 419.

3 LEGAL BACKGROUND AND POLITICAL CONTEXT

Before the proposal for a comprehensive recovery plan for Europe was tabled by the European Commission in May 2020, a myriad of measures had already been taken by the EU institutions to address the socioeconomic consequences of the pandemic. To mention some prominent examples, the European Commission adopted a temporary State aid framework to enable Member States to make full use of flexibility foreseen under the State aid rules to support the economy.[6] The Commission also triggered the establishment of a European instrument for temporary support to mitigate unemployment risks in an emergency (SURE) following the COVID-19 outbreak. Financial assistance, up to a maximum of EUR 100 billion financed out of the EU's own resources, is provided by the Union to Member States through loans to complement national measures intended to preserve jobs and mitigate the direct economic, social and health-related effects of the pandemic.[7] Furthermore, the Commission activated the general escape clause from the Stability and Growth Pact, allowing Member States, in a coordinated and orderly fashion, to temporarily deviate from the normal budgetary requirements for all Member States and incur extra expenditure.[8] Intrinsically related to this, the European Central Bank (ECB) launched the Pandemic Emergency Purchase Programme (PEPP), allowing the ECB to buy private and public sector securities on the financial markets up to EUR 750 billion.[9] In June 2020, the ECB Governing Council increased the initial PEPP envelope by EUR 600 billion and by another EUR 500 billion in December 2020, leading up to a total of EUR 1.850 billion. Finally, the Board of Governors of the European Stability Mechanism (ESM) stepped in, approving the establishment of the Pandemic Crisis Support Facility, enabling all ESM members to obtain loans under attractive interest rates, subject only to the condition to spend the money on direct and indirect health sector costs, linked to the pandemic.[10]

Significant and important as these measures may be, according to some, they still did not go far enough. In an open letter published in several newspapers all over Europe, Spanish Prime Minister Sanchez urged the EU to do more:

> Europe is enduring its worst crisis since the second world war. ... The EU is facing a different war from those we have successfully averted over the past 70 years: a war against an invisible enemy that is putting the future of the European project to the test. ... We need unwavering solidarity. ... Europe must build a wartime economy and promote European resistance, reconstruction and recovery. It must start doing so as soon as possible with measures to support the public debt that many states, including Spain, are taking on. And it must continue to do so when

6. De Witte, 'The European Union's COVID-19 recovery plan: The legal engineering of an economic policy shift', 58 *Common Market Law Review* (2021), 635-682, at 638.
7. Fabbrini, *supra* note 5, at 189.
8. Ladi and Wolff, 'The EU institutional architecture in the COVID-19 response: Coordinative Europeanization in times of permanent emergency', 59 *Journal of Common Market Studies* (2021), 32-43, at 36.
9. Vanhercke and Verdun, 'The European semester as goldilocks: Macroeconomic policy coordination and the recovery and resilience facility', 60 *Journal of Common Market Studies* (2021), 204-223, at 206.
10. De Witte, *supra* note 6, at 640.

> this health emergency is over, to rebuild the continent's economies by mobilising significant resources through a plan we are calling the new Marshall plan and which will require the backing of all of the EU's common institutions. ... The challenge we face is extraordinary and unprecedented. It calls for a single, united, radical and ambitious response to preserve our economic and social system and protect our citizens.[11]

His plea did not fall on deaf ears. A group of nine Eurozone countries – Belgium, France, Greece, Ireland, Italy, Luxembourg, Portugal, Slovenia and Spain – called for the creation of a common debt instrument 'issued by a European institution to raise funds on the market on the same basis and to the benefit of all Member States'.[12] The idea of introducing 'Eurobonds', however, was met with vehement opposition from the 'Frugal Four' States – Austria, Denmark, the Netherlands and Sweden – as well as Germany. As a result, no consensus was found during the European Council (video) meetings in March 2020. Eventually, the deadlock was broken when Germany, confronted with the devastating impact of the pandemic, remarkably let go of its traditional resistance against debt mutualization or a 'transfer union' and agreed to support, in a joint effort with France, 'an ambitious, temporary and targeted Recovery Fund in the framework of the next [Multiannual Financial Framework]'.[13] Under the Franco-German proposal, the Commission would have been entitled to borrow EUR 500 billion on the financial markets and distribute it, not as loans, but as budgetary expenditure, to the EU countries most heavily impacted by the economic fallout of the pandemic. This initiative paved the way for the presentation, just 10 days later, of an own ambitious recovery plan by the Commission called *Next Generation EU*, a set of legislative proposals intended to allow recovery from the pandemic and prepare the Union for the next generation. In essence, the proposal consisted of an increase in the next Multiannual Financial Framework and, linked to this, the establishment of a EUR 750 billion recovery fund. Two-thirds of the money would have been allocated to the Member States as grants, the remaining EUR 250 billion as loans. Ultimately, it was only after five (!) days of long and often acrimonious discussions that the July European Council managed to secure a deal on the establishment of Next Generation EU, together with the approval of the 2021-2027 Multiannual Financial Framework (MFF), the main features of which were outlined in 65 (!) pages of EU Council conclusions. To obtain the necessary support from all Member States, including the frugal ones, the division between grants and loans had to be changed from the

11. Sánchez, 'Europe's future is at stake in this war against coronavirus', *The Guardian*, 5 April 2020, theguardian.com/world/commentisfree/2020/apr/05/europes-future-is-at-stake-in-this-war-against-coronavirus (accessed 20 February 2023).
12. euractiv.com/section/economy-jobs/news/nine-member-states-ask-for-eurobonds-to-face-coronavirus-crisis (accessed 20 February 2023). The text of the letter can be found here: governo.it/sites/new.governo.it/files/letter_michel_20200325_eng.pdf (accessed 28 April 2022).
13. French-German initiative for European recovery from the coronavirus crisis, 18 May 2020, available at: diplomatie.gouv.fr/en/coming-to-france/coming-to-france-your-covid-19-questions-answered/coronavirus-statements/article/european-union-french-german-initiative-for-the-european-recovery-from-the (accessed 20 February 2023).

originally foreseen EUR 250-500 billion to EUR 360-390 billion.[14] The remaining months of 2020 were used to specify the details in legal texts reflecting the terms of the agreement. In this context, a major hiccup occurred in November 2020, when Poland and Hungary threatened to make use of their veto and block the entry into force of the new Multiannual Financial Framework and Next Generation EU over a disagreement on the Conditionality Mechanism, which subjects financial assistance to a number of conditions, amongst which respect for the rule of law.[15] It required a modification of this mechanism before eventually the new MFF and Next Generation EU could finally be approved.

4 THE LEGAL FRAMEWORK OF *NEXT GENERATION EU*

The legal architecture of Next Generation EU is complex. It consists of three separate elements. First, Regulation 2020/2094 establishes a European Union Recovery Instrument (EURI) to support the recovery in the aftermath of the COVID-19 crisis.[16] This Instrument provides the overarching legal infrastructure for Next Generation EU.[17] It binds together the revenue side with the expenditure side of the recovery package by allocating the available funds of EUR 750 billion to various support programmes. Second, the revenue side is established by the amended EU Own Resources Decision 2020/2053 (ORD).[18] This decision specifies that the Commission is empowered to borrow funds of up to EUR 750 billion on the capital markets for the sole purpose of addressing the consequences of the pandemic. It stipulates that up to EUR 360 billion of the funds borrowed may be used for providing loans, and up to EUR 390 billion may be used for providing grants. All liabilities of the Union incurred by the exceptional and temporary empowerment of the Commission to borrow funds shall be fully repaid by 31 December 2058. Repayment of these funds is secured through an extraordinary temporary increase of the own resources ceilings by 0.6 percentage points, as well as, possibly, through the introduction of new own resources.[19] Third, the expenditure side of Next Generation EU comprises the Recovery and Resilience Facility (RRF), a new instrument established by Regulation 2021/241,[20] as well as six existing spending programmes, which receive a temporary increase in funding.[21] The RRF has an overall budget of EUR 672.5 billion and thus takes up the lion's share of the entire EU recovery

14. Ladi and Wolff, *supra* note 8, at 37.
15. Editorial Comments, *supra* note 5, at 268-270.
16. Council Regulation EU 2020/2094 establishing European Union Recovery Instrument (EURI) to support the recovery in the aftermath of the COVID-19 crisis, O.J. 2020, L 433 I/23.
17. Fabbrini, *supra* note 5, at 191.
18. De Witte, *supra* note 6, at 637; Heber, 'Europarechtliche Grenzen für den Wiederaufbaufonds', 56 *Europa-Recht* (2021), 416-454, at 418-419.
19. Article 6 ORD 2020/2053.
20. Regulation EU 2021/241 of the European Parliament and the Council establishing a Recovery and Resilience Facility, O.J. 2021, L 57/17.
21. EU Council Conclusions July 2020, A14: ReactEU receives EUR 47.5 billion, Horizon Europe EUR 5 billion, InvestEU EUR 5.6 billion, Rural Development EUR 7.5 billion, the Just Transition Fund EUR 10 billion and RescEU EUR 1.9 billion.

package. It is intended to provide Member States with financial support with a view to achieving the milestones and targets of reforms and investments as set out in their national recovery and resilience plans. These plans require endorsement by the European Commission and approval by the Council.[22] The available funds are distributed based on a complex spending key that benefits particularly less strong EU economies.[23]

It is, of course, remarkable that recourse was had to such a complex legal architecture, albeit within the framework of the European Treaties, to set up Europe's comprehensive recovery plan. From a legal perspective, it would have been more straightforward to increase the EU budget in the Multi-Annual Financial Framework with EUR 750 billion and to increase the own resources ceilings in the ORD with the same amount, especially since the discussions about the new MFF for 2021-2027 were still ongoing at the time. That one did not choose this option can only be explained by the fact that Member States were not prepared to take on such an extra financial contribution to the EU at this moment of universal crisis. And thus, an alternative legal design had to be found, which had to do justice to the exceptional, temporary and one-off nature of the proposed recovery plan. This truly required legal ingenuity, as Next Generation EU is evidently much more than a 'mere' recovery plan; it is also about resilience, with its expressed intention to prepare the EU for the next generation and its focus on, especially, green transition, digital transformation and social inclusion. The three-way legal solution finally adopted is firmly rooted within the Treaty framework, which in itself is worthy of being noted nowadays. To make this possible, however, creative use had to be made of the legal bases chosen to underpin the legal architecture.

First, the most far-reaching aspect of Next Generation EU arguably is the explicit empowerment of the Commission to borrow the required funds for the foreseen investments on the financial markets and thereby allow the EU to temporarily indebt itself.[24] In fact, it is still partly disputed whether the EU actually has the general competence to do this. The relevant EU Treaty provisions in Title II on Financial Provisions remain silent on this issue.[25] In the past, the EU has borrowed (more limited) funds to provide financial assistance to its Member States, for example, during the 1970s oil crisis, or, more recently, during the eurozone crisis through the European Financial Stability Mechanism.[26] The most recent example is the SURE programme, which provides back-to-back loans to Member States, thereby passing on the favourable credit rating of the EU to the Member States.[27] These examples suggest that the Union is competent to borrow funds on the financial markets to finance its policies, as

22. De Witte, *supra* note 5, at 676.
23. Notably, in absolute numbers Italy and Spain are projected to receive around 41% of the available grants under the RRF; cf. Annex IV of RRF Regulation 2021/241.
24. Ladi and Tsarouhas, 'EU economic governance and COVID-19: Policy learning and windows of opportunity', 42 *Journal of European International* (2020), 1041-1056, at 1045-1046.
25. Heber, *supra* note 18, at 423-424; Ruffert, 'Europarecht für die nächste Generation – Zum Projekt Next Generation EU', 39 *Neue Zeitschrift für Verwaltungsrecht* (2020) 1777-1780, at 1778.
26. De Witte, *supra* note 5, at 647-648; Schorkopf, 'Die Europäische Union auf dem Weg zur Fiskalunion – Integrationsfortschritt durch den Rechtsrahmen des Sonderhaushalts "Next Generation EU"' 73 *Neue Juristische Wochenschrift* (2020), 3085-3091, at 3088.
27. De Witte, *supra* note 5, at 648.

the EU Treaties do not exclude this possibility. This time, however, the situation is not entirely comparable in terms of scale and mode of allocation: the borrowed amounts are much larger, and almost half of them are allocated as grants – instead of loans only under previous practices.

To overcome possible legal concerns, the European Commission, backed by the European Council, proposed to explicitly enshrine the ability of the EU to borrow the required funds to finance Next Generation EU in the amended ORD, which is based on Article 311 Treaty on the Functioning of the European Union (TFEU), and to increase the national own resources ceilings by 0.6% of national Gross National Income (GNI) for the period until 2058 to secure the repayment of EU debts.[28] Importantly, the borrowed funds are *not* labelled as own resources under Article 2 ORD 2020/2053, but rather as 'specifically assigned revenue' that may only be used to finance Next Generation EU, as established in Article 5(1) ORD 2020/2053 and further specified in Article 21(2)(a) Regulation 2018/1046.[29] This emphasizes the exceptional and temporary nature of these 'other' sources of revenue. In case these funds had simply been labelled as 'own resources' in the sense of Article 2 ORD 2020/2053, it would have been (politically) more challenging to remove them in the future from the own resources list, and these funds would have been assigned to the general EU budget – instead of to Next Generation EU only.[30] This would have been difficult to square with the principle of budgetary balance in Article 310 TFEU. Furthermore, the fact that Article 311 TFEU requires not only unanimous Council support for the amended ORD but also approval by the Member States in accordance with their national constitutional requirements probably played a role in the decision to empower the EU to issue the necessary debts to finance Next Generation EU in the ORD.

Second, Regulation 2020/2094, which sets up the EU Recovery Instrument, is based on Article 122 TFEU. Interestingly, however, it is not specified which of the two sub-paragraphs constitutes the precise legal basis.[31] According to Article 122(1) TFEU, the EU is empowered to adopt, 'in a spirit of solidarity between Member States', appropriate measures to address the prevailing economic situation. The wording of this provision already indicates its broad scope and the wide discretion enjoyed by the Council when adopting measures based on Article 122(1) TFEU.[32] In contrast, Article 122(2) TFEU allows the EU to grant financial assistance in case 'a Member State is in difficulties ... caused by natural disaster or exceptional occurrences beyond its control'. The wording of this provision suggests that its application is more limited, as it specifically requires the existence of an exceptionally difficult situation beyond the

28. As established in Article 6 ORD 2020/2053; Cf. as well: Schorkopf, *supra* note 26, at 3087.
29. Ruffert, *supra* note 25, at 1779.
30. Heber, *supra* note 18, at 422.
31. Schorkopf, *supra* note 26, at 3087.
32. Bandilla, 'Art. 122 AEUV – Maßnahmen bei gravierenden Schwierigkeiten', in Grabitz, Hilf and Nettesheim (Eds), *Das Recht der Europäischen Union – Kommentar* (C.H. Beck 2021), pp. 10-12; Heber, *supra* note 18, at 419.

control of the Member State. Furthermore, the provision refers to 'a Member State', as opposed to 'Member States', and it specifically allows (only) financial assistance.[33]

It would appear that each of these two legal bases, taken in isolation, did not provide a sufficient foundation for Regulation 2020/2094. Article 122(2) TFEU would constitute the more specific legal basis as it allows explicitly for financial assistance, which is the core idea behind the EU Recovery Instrument. However, the provision's wording suggests that it can only be employed as legal basis for financial assistance addressed to a single Member State and not to the Union as a whole, as is the case with Next Generation EU.[34] In addition, this financial assistance should be limited to the recovery from the shock that led to the support, whereas Next Generation EU is clearly not limited to recovery but also contains a future-oriented resilience component.[35] Article 122(1) TFEU is less specific than Article 122(2) TFEU, but it provides an appropriate legal basis for a solidarity-based scheme that covers all Member States and for the funding side that underpins the EU Recovery Instrument, as set out in the ORD.[36] These considerations probably prompted the Council to base Regulation 2020/2094 on Article 122 TFEU in general, similar to the approach of the European Commission in relation to SURE.[37] Obviously, a combination of both legal bases is, from a procedural point of view, possible, as both provisions prescribe adoption by the Council upon a proposal from the European Commission, and therefore both adoption procedures are compatible (or, in fact, identical).[38] A different, arguably rather wide, reading of the choice of legal basis in relation to the EU Recovery Instrument could be that Article 122 TFEU, taken as a whole, could constitute a legal basis for EU acts that concern EU-wide financial assistance that includes not only recovery from an emergency but also a connected resilience ambition.

Third, Regulation 2021/241, which provides for the creation of the Recovery and Resilience Facility and which administers almost 90% of the available funds, is based on Article 175(3) TFEU. This provision enables the EU to set up additional action outside the established EU cohesion funds under Title XVIII on Economic, Social and Territorial Cohesion. In this respect, it is again interesting to observe that the scope of the RRF is linked to 'policy areas of European relevance' that are structured in six pillars, only two of which refer explicitly to economic and social cohesion policy. This broad reading of Article 175(3) TFEU suggests that it can also be used as legal basis to

33. As specifically emphasized in the German-speaking comments, cf.: Meyer, 'Next Generation EU – Neues Eigenmittelsystem weist in eine Fiskalunion', 32 *Europäische Zeitschrift für Wirtschaftsrecht* (2021), 16-22, at 19; Schorkopf, *supra* note 26, at 3087; Ruffert, *supra* note 25, at 1778.
34. Schorkopf, *supra* note 26, at 3088; Ruffert, *supra* note 25, at 1778.
35. De Witte, *supra* note 5, at 655; Schorkopf, *supra* note 26, at 3088.
36. De Witte, *supra* note 5, at 654.
37. Cf. Council Regulation 2020/672 on the establishment of a European instrument for temporary support to mitigate the unemployment risks in an emergency (SURE) following the COVID-19 outbreak, O.J. 2020, L 159/1; De Witte, *supra* note 5, at 654.
38. On the notion of two-fold legal basis, cf. Case C-43/12 *Commission v. European Parliament and Council (Traffic Offenses)*, ECLI:EU:C:2014:298, para. 30; Case C-300/89 *Commission v. Council (Titanium Dioxid)* ECLI:EU:C:1991:244, para. 18.

regulate cohesion policy in a broad sense which connects to other EU policy fields, such as green transition, digital transformation, health or education.[39]

Member States were clearly willing to take extraordinary measures to deal with the exceptional circumstances and were also willing to look beyond the recovery from the pandemic and make projections for a stronger future for the Union. Instead of going for the seemingly simpler solution of increasing the MFF and the own resources ceilings in the ORD, however, they opted for the alternative of a complex legal design for Next Generation EU, consisting of three separate components, which was made possible within the framework of the Treaty only by a broad and creative reading of Articles 122, 175(3) and 311 TFEU. Evidently, Member States were closely involved in the drafting of Next Generation EU. In the first place, crucial political decisions were taken within the setting of the European Council. Subsequently, also the decision to make the amended ORD the backbone of the recovery plan by empowering the European Commission to issue debt and generate the necessary financial resources on the capital markets, proved quintessential, as the entry into force of the ORD required ratification at national level. This ensured additional (political) legitimacy to the chosen legal construct.

5 ALLOCATION OF FUNDS, ASSESSMENT AND THE RULE OF LAW

But with Next Generation EU, the EU does not only enter into uncharted territory from a legal point of view. As already indicated, it adopts a modified approach to the allocation of available funding, providing assistance not only in the form of loans but also as non-repayable grants. Moreover, the available *Next Generation funds* are not only intended to mitigate the impact of the crisis but also to contribute to specific Union policy objectives in order to boost the overall recovery within the EU.[40] Under the RRF, Member States are required to invest the available funds at least to 37% into green transition and at least to 20% into digital transformation.[41] The remaining funding has to be invested in one of the categories defined by the RRF Regulation.[42] Hence, the EU directs and guides the national recovery efforts in order to match its own policy ambitions and objectives. As ECB President *Christine Lagarde* noted, this indicates that the recovery crafted under Next Generation EU moved beyond strictly 'preserving the status quo' and instead focused on 'transforming the economy'[43] – which seems indicative of a new approach to EU economic governance.[44] The prescribed investment

39. De Witte, *supra* note 5, at 658.
40. Dorn and Fuest, 'Next generation EU: Chancen und Risiken des europaöischen Fonds fuör die wirtschaftliche Erholung nach der Corona-Krise', 101 *Wirtschaftsdienst* (2021) 78-81, at 79; Alcidi and Gros, 'Next generation EU: A large common response to the COVID-19 crisis', 55 *Intereconomics* (2020), 202-203, at 203.
41. Recital 23 as well as Articles 16(2)(b)(i) + (ii) and 18(4)(e) RFF Regulation; cf. as well De Witte, *supra* note 5, at 675.
42. As projects under the national recovery and resilience plans have to fall within the scope defined in Article 3 RFF Regulation according to Article 17(1) RFF Regulation.
43. Lagarde, 'Europe's response to the crisis', 2020 ecb.europa.eu/press/blog/date/2020/html/ecb.blog200723~c06fafabb6.en.html (accessed 20 February 2023).
44. Fabbrini, *supra* note 5, at 194; Ladi and Tsarouhas, *supra* note 24, at 1050.

targets require Member States to design their national recovery efforts in line with the objectives of the EU as a whole in order to receive the available funds. The EU hence acquired fiscal space to promote its own policy priorities through Next Generation EU.

A separate - and politically contested - matter is the process of allocation of NGEU funds to the Member States, in particular under the RRF. The underpinning Regulation 2021/241 determines allocation rules and specifies the available funding per Member State. Member States wishing to receive a financial contribution under the RRF must submit a recovery and resilience plan to the European Commission.[45] These national recovery and resilience plans must be duly reasoned and substantiated along the terms and conditions of Article 18(4) RRF Regulation 2021/241. These national plans have to hit certain investment targets and have to be linked to the country-specific recommendations issued by the European Commission as part of the European Semester.[46] The Commission is charged with assessing the national plans according to Article 19 RRF Regulation 2021/241. If the assessment of the Commission is positive, the national plans are approved by the Council by a qualified majority vote as established in Article 20 RRF Regulation 2021/241. Hence, an endorsement by the Commission is a *conditio sine qua non* for the available NGEU funds to be allocated to the Member States.[47]

Political disagreement on the application of the rules arose in 2021 as the Commission initially refused the approval of the Polish and Hungarian recovery and resilience plans based on rule of law concerns. This had major financial implications for Poland, in particular, as it needs the money to recover from the pandemic. The country may not be the biggest beneficiary of NGEU funding - these are, in absolute numbers, Spain and Italy, which each receives around EUR 69 billion of the EUR 338 billion in available RRF grants (current prices) - the Polish funding package is nevertheless substantial. Poland may receive up to EUR 24 billion in grants and up to EUR 34 billion in loans under the RRF.[48] According to experts, the additional funding and the expected economic transformation could boost the Polish gross domestic product (GDP) in the long run by an additional 2%-2.5%.[49] Therefore, the Commission's initial refusal to approve the Polish plan - together with the unsuccessful Polish challenge against the Conditionality Mechanism[50] and the Commission's decision to withhold Polish EU funds to recover unpaid fines resulting from decisions of the Court of Justice of the European Union (CJEU)[51] -put arguably domestic economic and political pressure on the Polish Government. Although the Hungarian and the Polish recovery and resilience plans are by now approved by the Council of Ministers upon

45. Article 18(1) RRF Regulation 2021/241.
46. Vanhercke and Verdun, *supra* note 9, at 5.
47. De Witte, *supra* note 5, at 676.
48. Annex IV RFF Regulation 2021/241; cf. dw.com/en/will-the-eus-tight-squeeze-on-aid-rein-in-poland-and-hungary/a-59170734 (accessed 20 February 2023).
49. *Ibid.*
50. Regulation (EU, Euratom) 2020/2092 of the European Parliament and of the Council of 16 December 2020 on a general regime of conditionality for the protection of the Union budget, O.J. 2020, L 433 I/1; cf. Case C-156/21, *Hungary v. European Parliament and Council*, ECLI:EU:C:2022:97; Case C-157/21, *Poland v. European Parliament and Council*, ECLI:EU:C:2022:98.
51. nytimes.com/2022/02/08/world/europe/eu-poland-fine.html (accessed 20 February 2023).

the Commission's endorsement, it is insightful to consider the (legal) prerogatives of the Commission under the RRF Regulation to refuse the initial allocation of NGEU-funds specifically when rule of law concerns prevail. Under the applicable framework, the Commission has to evaluate the national plans based on the assessment criteria established in Article 19 RRF Regulation 2021/241. These are divided into four groups that correspond to the principles of the Better Regulation guidelines: relevance, effectiveness, efficiency and coherence.[52] The RRF Regulation further specifies that no funds should be allocated to Member States in case their national plans do not 'satisfactorily address the assessment criteria'. Although the primary focus of these criteria rests on whether national recovery plans deliver on the six pillars of the EURI Regulation and thus ensure sustainable economic recovery in line with the EU's cohesion, environmental and digital objectives, the criteria also include safeguards for the proper national management of allocated funds. This is emphasized in Article 22 RRF Regulation 2021/241, which requires that the funds are soundly administered by the Member States in order to protect the Union's financial interests. All in all, in light of the broad phrasing of the assessment criteria, it can reasonably be argued that the Commission enjoys a margin of discretion when assessing national recovery plans.

In relation to Poland and Hungary, the concerns of the Commission related to the independence of the judiciary and to corruption, respectively.[53] Both concerns could affect the sound administration of NGEU funds in these Member States, thereby threatening to undermine the effectiveness and efficiency of the national recovery and resilience plans. This was invoked by the Commission to reject the initial approval of national recovery plans under Article 19 RRF Regulation 2021/241 until these concerns were finally sufficiently remedied, thereby delaying the adoption of the required implementing decision of the Council until June 2022 for Poland and even December 2022 for Hungary. A final consideration in relation to Poland that might have impacted the Commission assessment is the outright rejection of core EU law doctrines, including the supremacy of EU law, in the constitutional judgment K 3/21.[54] Given the uncertainty that stemmed from this rejection, the risk emerged that Polish authorities would not comply with their EU law commitments and potentially spend, for example, the allocated funds on different projects than the ones specified within the national recovery plans. Once adopted, the Commission would then only retain limited possibilities to intervene and recover transferred funds, as Polish authorities could have rejected compliance with, for example, judgments of the CJEU. Therefore, the Commission concluded that the proper administration of NGEU funds ran into serious uncertainty, which ultimately justified the highlighted rejection of the Polish recovery

52. Article 19(3) RFF Regulation 2021/241; Corti and Núñez Ferrer, 'Steering and monitoring the recovery and resilience plans:- Reading between the lines', 2 CEPS Recovery and Resilience Reflection Paper (2021), at 6.
53. euractiv.com/section/economy-jobs/news/gentiloni-eu-recovery-fund-idea-could-be-used-aga in-if-it-is-a-success-now (accessed 20 February 2023).
54. Polish Constitutional Tribunal, 7 October 2021, Case K 3/21, Assessment of the conformity to the Polish Constitution of selected provisions of the Treaty on European Union; Editorial Comments, 'Clear and present danger: Poland, the rule of law & primacy', 58 *Common Market Law Review* (2021), 1635-1648.

and resilience plan until June 2022 to safeguard the financial interests of the Union as a whole. It should also be noted that in order to further mitigate any remaining potential risk for the EU's financial interest, it was ultimately agreed that the disbursement of NGEU-funding to Poland and Hungary remains connected to the fulfilment of so-called important rule of law 'milestones'.[55]

This illustrates that the Commission could directly rely on the RRF Regulation to block the allocation of most Next Generation EU funding to Poland without even having to rely on the Conditionality Mechanism. The latter only becomes relevant now as the Polish recovery and resilience plan is implemented following the approval of the Council, and it is also of relevance for Next Generation funding that is channelled through the existing EU programmes. After the CJEU's confirmation of the Conditionality Mechanism,[56] the Commission has already triggered this new EU law instrument against Hungary and it will certainly assess the need to employ the instrument in other circumstances in the future as well.

Finally, for the record, it should be pointed out that besides Poland and Hungary, the endorsement of the Bulgarian, Dutch and Swedish recovery and resilience plans was also delayed to 2022 due to both specific national reasons as well as EU concerns. Taken together, this means, however, that by now all 27 Member States' plans are endorsed and that all Member States are thus currently set to receiving financial assistance under the Facility to implement these national recovery and resilience plans.

6 REPAYMENT OF EU DEBT AND THE LEGAL SPACE FOR INTRODUCING NEW OWN RESOURCES

An open question – the metaphorical elephant in the room – is the repayment of the issued EU debt. Until now, the primary focus of Next Generation EU rested on economic recovery after COVID-19 by financing investments in the Member States. The repayment of the issued debt is only envisaged for the period between 2028-2058 and thereby pushed to the future. Clearly, the European Council opted to postpone the politically most inconvenient question. As it stands, three ways to repay the EU debts incurred can be envisaged. First, as the repayment is arranged through the general EU budget, it could theoretically be an option to reduce all other EU expenditures in order to cover the costs for debt repayment. Second, the Member States' national contributions to the Union could be extraordinarily and temporarily increased by 0.6 percentage points, on top of the ordinary 1.4% of Member States' GNI annually due to the own

55. Even called "super milestones" in relation to the Hungarian plan, cf. Council of the EU, "NextGenerationEU: Member states approve national plan of Hungary"(12 December 2022), < https://www.consilium.europa.eu/en/press/press-releases/2022/12/12/nextgenerationeu-member-states-approve-national-plan-of-hungary/ > (accessed 20 February 2023).

56. Case C-156/21, *Hungary v. European Parliament and Council*, ECLI:EU:C:2022:97; Case C-157/21, *Poland v. European Parliament and Council*, ECLI:EU:C:2022:98; *see also*: Pech, 'No More Excuses – The Court of Justice greenlights the rule of law conditionality mechanism', *Verfassungsblog*, 16 February 2022 verfassungsblog.de/no-more-excuses (accessed 20 February 2023).

resources of the EU,[57] for the sole purpose of covering all liabilities of the Union resulting from the borrowing on the capital markets until all liabilities have ceased to exist.[58] Third, new EU own resources could be introduced.[59]

While the first option is practically bound to remain merely a theoretical possibility, and the second option would entail entering a political minefield, bearing in mind most Member States' reluctance to increase national contributions to the EU budget, the third option to introduce new own resources appears to be the most viable solution that could both secure the debt repayment and at the same time equip the EU with more fiscal and budgetary autonomy. The EU has two different legal options to introduce these new own resources, which will be considered in turn.

First, the amended ORD explicitly mentions several levies that could be introduced as new own resources to feed into the EU budget. In its Recital 8, the Decision mentions a carbon border adjustment mechanism, a digital levy, an amendment of the EU Emission Trading System, as well as a financial transaction tax, which could be introduced as new own resources of the EU. The options for the EU to introduce these different levies or taxes are, however, limited by the Treaties, as the Union does not enjoy a general taxation competence.[60] Instead, the Council can decide to either approximate national taxation measures following Articles 113 and 115 TFEU or to introduce EU measures of a fiscal nature in the field of environment following Article 192 TFEU. In a subsequent step, the revenue generated from these EU acts can then be assigned to the EU as own resources under the ORD. This first option thus involves a two-step procedure that requires the introduction of (harmonized) taxes or levies and the subsequent allocation of the revenue to the Union.[61]

Second, a different approach was chosen by the EU in relation to the new levy on non-recycled plastic packaging, which was introduced by the amended ORD in its Article 2(1) (c). Notably, this levy is based on Article 322(2) TFEU and hence not on the traditional legal bases under the outlined two-step approach. Instead, Member States are required to contribute specified amounts to the EU budget, but EU law does not enter into more detail as to how Member States are expected to generate the required funds. Member States are thus free to decide whether they introduce national levies to finance this EU contribution or whether they rather pay these contributions from their general budget.[62] This provides Member States with wide discretion on how to source the funds required to comply with their commitments under the ORD. Moreover, and similarly to the GNI-based national contribution, it requires Member States to act in order to identify additional revenue streams to fund these contributions. This might, in fact, increase tax differences amongst Member States, which Articles 113 and 115 TFEU

57. Article 3 ORD 2020/2053.
58. Article 5 ORD 2020/2053.
59. De Witte, *supra* note 5, at 665-666; Meyer, *supra* note 33, at 17.
60. Heber, *supra* note 18, at 421.
61. Schratzenstaller and Krenek, 'Tax-based own resources to finance the EU budget', 54 *Intereconomics* (2019), 171-177, at 174-175; cf. as well: Heber, *supra* note 18, at 448.
62. Reichert et al., *The 'EU Plastic Tax' – Greenwashing New Revenue for the EU Budget* (cepInput, 2021), at 5.

aim to reduce and could ultimately have a negative impact on the functioning of the internal market.

Until now, the crucial question of 'who is going to pay the bill?' remains unanswered. In a way, it is understandable that primarily, most legal efforts went into soundly establishing Next Generation EU and ensuring that the desperately needed financial assistance was provided, as well as the essential investments for recovery were initiated. At the same time, however, as long as it remains uncertain how the debt is going to be repaid, the assessment of whether the common NGEU debt amounts to a 'fiscal transfer' is rendered impossible.[63] Arguably, it is of great importance to address the repayment question in due time in order to avoid difficult political and legal negotiations – especially in light of high public deficits and debt rates in most EU Member States. In any event, the amended ORDs clearly outline the contours of the timeframe within which repayment is due: repayments shall start before the end of the MFF 2021-2027 period. And all liabilities incurred shall be fully repaid at the latest by 31 December 2058.[64] Ultimately, it remains to be seen how much money available under Next Generation EU is effectively disbursed and whether Member States that have made use of the NGEU-credit-line will be able to fully repay their obligations. In light of these uncertainties, the ambition to equip the EU with new, genuine own resources appears desirable, as this would reduce the regularly recurring and well-known tensions surrounding the MFF adoption and would make the EU less dependent on the goodwill from the Member States to increase their national contributions to the EU. The creation of limited fiscal autonomy at the EU level would, of course, potentially amount to a game-changer in the integration process of the EU. The Commission has initiated the debate by presenting a roadmap for introducing new own resources. It will be very interesting to observe how the Member States will react to this.[65]

7 CONCLUSION: NEXT GENERATION EU AS A BRIDGE OVER TROUBLED WATER

Confronted with the devastating consequences of the COVID-19 pandemic, the EU has risen to the occasion. Mindful of Churchill's motto, 'Never let a good crisis go to waste', the Member States and the Union proved capable of devising an ambitious recovery strategy. To make this happen, EU institutions and the Member States set up a complex legal framework consisting of three interconnected elements. Member States have empowered the Union through the amended ORD to engage in large-scale borrowing on the capital markets. The available funds are allocated to the Member States in the form of loans and grants, mostly through the new RRF. The legal basis of the EU Recovery Instrument, the overall framework that ties the expenditure and revenue sides of the rescue plan together, underscores that the entire Next Generation EU scheme is also based on solidarity amongst the Member States. This solidarity is

63. De Witte, *supra* note 5, at 678; cf. as well: Schorkopf, *supra* note 26, at 1779.
64. Article 5(2) ORD 2020/2053.
65. euractiv.com/section/economy-jobs/news/gentiloni-eu-recovery-fund-idea-could-be-used-again-if-it-is-a-success-now (accessed 20 February 2023).

particularly visible in the allocation of available funds: almost 41 % of RRF grants are allocated to Spain and Italy. At the same time, Next Generation EU is not only focusing on economic recovery, but it also aims to *build back better*, in the interest of all Member States, by integrating an environmental, digital and socially inclusive focus. In their national recovery and resilience plans, Member States are required to hit targets in order to achieve a sustainable recovery in line with other prominent EU policies, such as the EU Green Deal. This not only provides a considerable (financial) booster for these EU policies, but it also constitutes a paradigm shift in the EU's economic governance and results in new fiscal space for the implementation of Union priorities.[66]

Evidently, this does not mean that suddenly all is well in a crises-riddled Union now. The negotiations towards Next Generation EU revealed a considerable political divide on the future direction of the Union. For months, Poland and Hungary did not eschew politically hijacking the Union by threatening to reject the amended ORD, which would have effectively blocked the adoption of Next Generation EU in its current form.[67] Although a compromise was finally agreed upon, the rule of law crisis in both Member States continues to cast a dark shadow on the Union. Specifically because of these rule of law crises, the endorsement of both countries' recovery and resilience plans was delayed to June 2022 for Poland and December 2022 for Hungary. Now, the disbursement of financial assistance under NGEU is strictly tied to compliance with (super) milestones related to the rule of law, thereby requiring both Member States to adhere to this foundational EU principle. And beyond, it should also be emphasised that Poland and Hungary were certainly not the only Member States that caused problems in the lead-up towards the establishment of Next Generation EU. The Frugal Four States, together with Finland, toughly negotiated for a reduction of the amount of grants distributed through the recovery plan. Also, on this issue, a compromise may have been found, but the still unanswered question of 'who will ultimately pay the bill' could bring back concerns from these Member States against any major redistribution effects. Therefore, the current phase should be used to establish a solid own resources system which provides the Union with sufficient financial means independent from higher national contributions. The amended ORD outlines several possible new sources of EU revenue. Now would be the moment to introduce (some of) them in order to secure the required funds for the repayment of the issued EU debts. In case the Member States were to agree to implement the proposed new system, this would equip the Union with fiscal autonomy and could be therefore considered a real game-changer in the context of the European integration process.

All in all, Next Generation EU nicely illustrates that when the going gets tough, the EU is tough enough to get going. The EU Treaties provided sufficient legal space to establish the ambitious recovery strategy. Important in this regard was the political support for the chosen approach, both at the EU and national levels. Also, initial constitutional concerns could be overcome, for example, in Finland,[68] and the recent

66. Fabbrini, *supra* note 5, at 194.
67. Editorial Comments, *supra* note 5, at 278.
68. Finnish Constitutional Law Committee Case PeVL 14/21 vp Ratification of the Own Resources Decision (II.) [2021]; Cf. as well: Leino-Sandberg, 'Who is ultra vires now? The EU's legal U-turn

verdict from the German Constitutional Court on Next Generation EU displays that even the German Court did not identify an insurmountable conflict between the EU's recovery strategy and the German Constitution.[69] The devil is, of course, in the details. The plan may not be completely watertight yet, as the crucial issue of repayment still needs settling. Regardless, it seems absolutely fair to say that Next Generation EU constitutes a solid, ingeniously construed, temporary bridge which may ultimately lead the EU and its Member States over socially, economically and politically troubled water into a more integrated Europe for the future generation.

in interpreting Article 310 TFEU', *Verfassungsblog*, 18 June 2020 verfassungsblog.de/who-is-ultra-vires-now-the-eus-legal-u-turn-in-interpreting-article-310-tfeu (accessed 20 February 2023).

69. Bundesverfassungsgericht, Case 2 BvR 547/21 and 2 BvR 798/21, Final Judgment on the Act Ratifying the EU Own Resources Decision and Next Generation EU, judgment of 6 December 2022, ECLI:DE:BVerfG:2022:rs20221206.2bvr054721; Cf. also the interim decision: Bundesverfassungsgericht, Case 2 BvR 547/21, Interim Decision on the Ratification of the Own Resources Decision (NGEU), judgment of 15 April 2021, ECLI:DE:BVerfG:2021:rs20210415.2bvr054 72.

CHAPTER 2

Articulating Environmental Sustainability in EU Competition Law: The 'Sustainable' Consumer Welfare Test

Yves Van Gerven & Anne Vallery

Climate change is a growing concern for international, public and private organizations around the world. While the focus will be on regulation, European Union (EU) competition law can play a role in the fight against global warming. This chapter examines different ways in which the 'constitutional' requirements of sustainability and protection of the environment can be articulated in the competition rules. Sustainable business conduct can be excluded from the scope of the competition rules altogether; the notion of restriction of competition of Article 101(1) Treaty on the Functioning of the European Union (TFEU) can be interpreted narrowly, and sustainable conduct can be more easily exempt on the basis of Article 101(3) TFEU. Furthermore, sustainability can be given a place in the notions of abuse and objective justification in Article 102 TFEU. By doing this, the competition rules will be a shield to permit business practices that favour environmental sustainability. Also, the competition rules can be used as a sword to attack business cooperation and dominant conduct that restricts competition and harms the environment. Overall, this chapter submits that the objective warranting the intervention of competition law should include the well-being of intermediate and final consumers that seek sustainable consumption. This standard of the "sustainable" consumer will produce efficient and fair outcomes for society as a whole.

1 INTRODUCTION

Climate change poses a great threat to humankind. Society as a whole faces a 'climate emergency.' Action must be taken urgently on all fronts. In July 2021, the European Commission presented the Green Deal, a package of measures ranging from cutting greenhouse gas emissions to investing in infrastructure and research and innovation and to preserving natural environment.[1] Regulation will be the main tool in fighting the climate crisis. However, regulation and competition law have complementary roles, and competition policy should play its part. In the words of Commissioner Vestager, 'every one of us – including competition enforcers – will be called on to make a contribution to the change'.[2] Future business initiatives will be key in environment-friendly manufacturing and marketing of products, and competition enforcers will have to review them.

Some commentators see an obvious friction between competition law and environmental sustainability. On the one hand, the need for sustainable development and environmental protection is anchored in the European Union (EU) Treaties. Article 3(3) Treaty on European Union (TEU) declares that the Union shall work for the sustainable development of Europe and a high level of protection and improved quality of the environment, and Article 11 Treaty on the Functioning of the European Union (TFEU) prescribes that environmental protection requirements must be integrated into the Union's policies and activities. Article 37 of the Charter of Fundamental Rights also requires the integration of a high level of protection and improved quality of the environment in the Union's policies and activities. On the other hand, the Union courts define the goal of the competition rules as the protection of competition on the market.[3] For the European Commission (DG COMP), the protection of competition is a means of enhancing consumer welfare.[4] Therefore, it could be argued that competition rules neither pursue sustainability nor protect the environment, should consumer welfare only be based on financial considerations and increasing revenues and profits. However, we submit that this position does not correspond to the 'constitutional' provisions of the Treaties. The concept of consumer welfare can and should include sustainable development and environmental protection considerations. Competition authorities must integrate these considerations in their policies and in the competition law assessment of business initiatives that seek to remedy market failures responsible for unsustainable growth and environmental harm.

1. COM(2019)640 final, 'The European Green Deal'.
2. Speech by Commissioner Vestager, conference in Brussels on competition law and sustainability, October 2019, available at ec.europa.eu/newsroom/comp/items/661165.
3. Case C-52/09, *Konkurrensverket v. TeliaSonera Sverige AB*, ECLI:EU:C:2011:83, para. 22; Joined cases C-501/06 P, C-513/06 P, C-515/06 P and C-519/06 P, *GlaxoSmithKline v. Commission* and *Commission v. GlaxoSmithKline* and *EAEPC v. Commission* and *Aseprofar v. Commission*, ECLI:EU:C:2009:610, para. 63.
4. *See, e.g.*, Guidelines on the application of Article 81(3) of the Treaty, O.J. 2004, C 101/97, para. 13.

The 'constitutional' requirements of sustainability and protection of the environment can be articulated in various ways in the competition rules. As many commentators have explained: we can exclude sustainable business conduct from the scope of EU competition rules altogether; we can interpret the notion of restriction of competition of Article 101(1) narrowly and exempt sustainable conduct under the criteria of Article 101(3); and we can include sustainability in the notions of abuse and objective justification in Article 102 TFEU. By doing this, we use the competition rules as a shield to permit business practices, both cooperation and dominant conduct, that favour environmental sustainability. Furthermore, the competition rules can be used as a sword to attack business cooperation and dominant conduct that restricts competition *and* harms the environment.[5] We deal with the competition rules first as a sword (section 2), then as a shield (section 3). We end with a short conclusion (section 4).

2 BUSINESSES PRACTICES HARMING ENVIRONMENTAL SUSTAINABILITY

2.1 Anticompetitive Agreements Which Harm Environmental Sustainability

Competition authorities can apply the cartel ban to agreements that restrict competition in a way that harms environmental sustainability. An often-cited example is the Consumer Detergents decision in which the European Commission fined three producers of household laundry detergents for agreeing to achieve market stabilization and price coordination in the context of the trade association's environmental initiative to promote more sustainable consumption of these products in the EU. The environmental initiative, endorsed by a Commission recommendation,[6] led to dosage and weight reductions of detergent powder and accompanying packaging. However, the producers sought to achieve that none of them would use the environmental initiative to gain a competitive advantage over the others and that market positions and prices, in spite of the more compacted products and downsized quantities, would remain unchanged as compared to prior to the environmental initiative.[7] In other words, anticompetitive conduct was pursued to restrict competition made possible by the environmental initiative.

Even more in point is the recent decision of the Commission imposing heavy fines on three German car manufacturers for restricting competition in emission cleaning for new diesel passenger cars. European legislation introduced minimum standards for nitrogen oxide emissions ('Euro 5' and 'Euro 6' norms). The manufacturers had

5. As regards the terminology sword/shield, *see* Nowag and Teorell, 'Beyond balancing: Sustainability and competition law', *Concurrences* No. 4 (2020), at 9-14 and Holmes, 'Climate change, sustainability, and competition law', 8 *Journal of Antitrust Enforcement* (2020), 354-405.
6. Commission Recommendation of 22 July 1998 concerning good environmental practice for household laundry detergents, O.J. 1998, L 215/73.
7. Commission decision of 13 April 2011, COMP/39579 – Consumer Detergents. *See* Monti, 'Four options for a greener competition law', 11 *Journal of European Competition Law & Practice* (2020), 124-132, at 126-127.

developed new emission cleaning technology to meet the EU norms but agreed not to compete on exploiting it to its full potential. Although they had the technical possibility to clean better than required by law and compete on this important parameter relevant for consumers, they decided to collude by indicating to each other that none of them would aim at cleaning above the minimum standard required by law. The Commission considered that any attempt to restrict competition to the detriment of innovation would make it more difficult to meet the Green Deal objectives.[8]

We make two observations. First, the last decision is an important reminder that innovation is an essential parameter of competition. As the Commission points out, this is the first time that it finds that cooperation on purely technical elements, as opposed to price fixing or market sharing, amounts to cartel behaviour. Economic literature shows that competition is a key driver to innovation, and innovation is key to tackling the climate crisis.[9] In future, given the crucial role of new technologies to combat climate change, one can expect more cases that focus on 'restriction of innovation' as a theory of harm: competitors cannot agree on not exploiting the full potential of new technologies at their disposal. Second, these decisions also show that there are boundaries to the lobbying exception. The competition rules permit normal lobbying activity for the adoption of environmental legislation and standards carried out by an industry association or the companies themselves in order to protect and promote their interests.[10] However, these companies should not agree not to engage in environment-friendly activities beyond this legislation and standards.

2.2 Abusive Practices Which Harm Environmental Sustainability

Competition authorities can also challenge behaviour of dominant companies that is non-sustainable and impairs effective competition. For example, unsustainable business practices that lead to unfair selling prices or unfair purchase prices can be caught by Article 102 TFEU, provided all conditions of this article are fulfilled. Conversely, Article 102 TFEU will also apply to unilateral practices of dominant companies pursuing laudable sustainability objectives, where they have exclusionary or other negative effects on the ability of rivals to compete.

However, we consider that the scope of Article 102 TFEU should not be stretched to create a new category of abuse that encompasses non-sustainable business practices, irrespective of any effects on competition.[11] Practices that 'push the planet beyond a safe and just operating space' or 'make production inputs cheaper than they

8. European Commission – Statement 21/3583, 8 July 2021. *See also* Monti, *supra* note 7, at 127.
9. *See* Peeperkorn, 'Competition and sustainability: What can competition policy do?', *Concurrences* No. 4 (2020), at 15-17.
10. Case T-432/05, *EMC Development AB v. Commission*, ECLI:EU:T:2010:189, paras 81-82.
11. *See* Iacovides and Vrettos, 'Radical for whom? Unsustainable business practices as abuses of dominance', in Holmes, Middelschulte and Snoep (Eds), *Competition Law, Climate Change, and Environmental Sustainability* (Concurrences, 2021), pp. 91-103; Thomas, 'Exploring the Sustainability of Article 102', in *ibid.*, p. 113; Holmes, *supra* note 5, at 384-387; and also the Hellenic Competition Commission's staff discussion paper 'Competition Law & Sustainability', available at epant.gr/en/enimerosi/competition-law-sustainability.html, at 36-37.

ought to be' without impeding competition would, in principle, not be caught by Article 102 TFEU. Indeed, for Article 102 TFEU to apply, one must show that there is an anticompetitive effect, or at the very least a potential anticompetitive effect, attributable to the dominant firm's impugned conduct.[12] In other words, Article 102 cannot be used as a catch-all provision to prohibit any non-sustainable or unlawful action by a dominant company. Competition law aims at protecting free competition and prohibiting practices that restrict or eliminate competition. Therefore, unsustainable business practices should only be caught by Article 102 TFEU if they have anticompetitive effects.

3 BUSINESS PRACTICES FAVOURING ENVIRONMENTAL SUSTAINABILITY

3.1 Sustainability Cooperation Which Would Fall Outside of the Scope of Article 101(1) TFEU

3.1.1 Agreements Which Do Not Restrict Competition Within the Meaning of Article 101(1) TFEU

Competition authorities may decide that cooperation between firms serving environmental sustainability does not constitute a restriction of competition within the meaning of Article 101(1) TFEU. In the recently published 2022 draft revised horizontal guidelines, the European Commission looks favourably at sustainability agreements which it defines as any type of horizontal cooperation that genuinely pursues one or more sustainability objectives.[13] Such agreements will often not have an anticompetitive object because they may aim to overcome a particular type of market failure, i.e., the existence of negative externalities,[14] as expressly acknowledged by the Commission.[15] The cost of environmental pollution and greenhouse gas emissions are generally not included in the price of products.[16] Sustainability agreements may seek to internalize these costs imposed on society in the price. In that setting, the price increase of the products for the consumer is not the result of an agreement pursuing the

12. Case T-612/17, *Google and Alphabet v. Commission*, ECLI:EU:T:2021:763, paras 438 and 441; *see also* Case C-457/10, *AstraZeneca AB and AstraZeneca plc v. Commission*, C-457/10, ECLI:EU:C:2012:770, para. 199.
13. Draft for a Communication from the Commission, Guidelines on the applicability of Article 101 TFEU to horizontal cooperation agreements, 1 March 2022 (hereinafter 'Draft Revised Horizontal Guidelines 2022'), points 547 and 548.
14. Gassler, 'Sustainability, the Green Deal and Art 101 TFEU: Where we are and where we could go', 12 *Journal of European Competition Law & Practice* (2021), 430-442, at 436 (referring to Case C-238/05, *Asnef-Equifax*, ECLI:EU:C:2006:734, paras 47 and 48 on information asymmetry between lenders and borrowers regarding non-payment risks and available guarantees) and Dolmans, 'Sustainable competition policy and the 'polluter pays' principle', in Holmes, Middelschutte and Snoep (Eds), *supra* note 11, pp. 18-19.
15. Draft Revised Horizontal Guidelines 2022, cited *supra* note 13, point 545.
16. *See* Dolmans, *supra* note 14, at 18.

objective of restricting competition,[17] and it leads to efficient market outcomes as the 'polluting' consumer will have the incentive to reduce the relevant consumption.[18] The Commission confirms that an agreement which genuinely pursues a sustainability objective will not restrict competition by object.[19]

Sustainability agreements will therefore often require an effects analysis, i.e., whether competition has in fact been restricted to an appreciable extent.[20] In the past, the European Commission provided guidance to industry for self-assessing the effects on competition: first in the 2001 horizontal guidelines (now revoked), which included a separate chapter on environmental agreements, and later in the 2010 horizontal guidelines that assessed environmental agreements in the respective chapters on R&D, production, commercialization and standardization agreements.

Similarly, the Commission states in the chapter on 'sustainability agreements' of the 2022 draft revised horizontal guidelines that sustainability agreements corresponding to agreements in these other chapters will be assessed according to the principles laid out in these chapters.[21] Furthermore, the Commission proposes to create a 'soft safe harbour' for competitors that agree to adopt and comply with certain sustainability standards for products, production methods and trading processes ('sustainability standard agreements').[22] These agreements will be deemed unlikely to produce appreciable negative effects on competition if the following cumulative conditions are met: (i) the procedure for developing the sustainability standard is transparent and all interested competitors can participate in the process leading to the selection of the standard; (ii) there is no obligation to comply with the standard for undertakings not wishing to participate in the standard; (iii) participating undertakings remain free to adopt for themselves a higher sustainability standard than the one agreed with the other parties to the agreement; (iv) there is no unnecessary exchange of commercially sensitive information; (v) effective and non-discriminatory access to the outcome of the standardization procedure is ensured; (vi) the sustainability standard does not lead to a significant increase in price or to a significant reduction in the choice of products available on the market; and (vii) there is a mechanism or a monitoring system in place to ensure that undertakings that adopt the sustainability standard comply with the requirements of the standard.[23] These conditions should ensure that the sustainability standard does not foreclose innovative alternative standards, nor exclude or discriminate against other undertakings and ensures an effective access to the standard. However, failure to comply with one or more of these conditions will not create a presumption that competition is restricted. Rather, an effects analysis of the agreement

17. However, the fact that an agreement pursues a legitimate objective does not preclude that agreement from being regarded as having an object restrictive of competition where it pursues at the same time another anticompetitive objective (*see* Case C-67/13 P, *Groupement des cartes bancaires (CB) v. Commission*, ECLI:EU:C:2014:2204, para. 70).
18. Van den Brink and Ellison, 'Article 101(3) TFEU: The roadmap for sustainable cooperation,' in Holmes, Middelschutte and Snoep (Eds), *supra* note 11, p. 46.
19. Draft Revised Horizontal Guidelines 2022, cited *supra* note 13, paras 559-560.
20. Case C-67/13 P, *CB v. Commission*, para. 52.
21. Draft Revised Horizontal Guidelines 2022, cited *supra* note 13, paras 556-558.
22. *Ibid.*, paras 561-567.
23. *Ibid.*, para. 572.

must then be conducted, taking into account the market coverage of the products incorporating the standard.[24] Where sufficient competition exists from alternative sustainability standards or from products produced conventionally (i.e., outside standards), there should be no appreciable anticompetitive effects. If market coverage of the agreement is significant, the restraining effect of potential competition may still be sufficient where the agreement is limited to establishing a label, leaving the participating firms free to also operate outside the label.[25]

However, for environmental standards to have a real impact on the environment, they would often need to be mandatory and phase out non-complying products across the market, excluding genuine alternatives. In that case, they are likely to have restrictive effects on competition in terms of reduced product choice and price increases for products covered by the standard.[26] Another example is the creation of a joint venture between competitors to combine their R&D efforts to improve the production and performance of an existing vehicle component that reduces consumption of fuel and emits less carbon dioxide (CO_2). If the joint R&D effort is not aimed at a completely new product, the parties continue to manufacture and sell the components separately, and several competing technologies exist in the market, it is unlikely that the joint venture will restrict competition.[27] However, where the parent companies hold large market shares and the joint venture involves the combination of production facilities and supply of components to them, the joint venture may have restrictive effects on competition, even if production of these components has wider environmental benefits for society. These two examples show that, in spite of a positive approach towards sustainability, environment-friendly business cooperation may still fall under Article 101(1) TFEU.

3.1.2 *Agreements Which Contain Restrictions of Competition Inherent to the Policy Objective It Pursues*

Many authors have identified the *Wouters* and *Albany* case law as a suitable route to assess sustainability agreements. Pursuant to this case law, '[n]ot every agreement between undertakings ... which restrict the freedom of action of the parties or of one of them necessarily falls within the prohibition laid down in Article [101](1) [TFEU]'.[28] To determine whether those restrictions fall within the scope of Article 101(1) TFEU, an account should be taken of the overall context in which the agreement was concluded and of the objectives it pursues. More particularly, certain restrictions of competition can be inherent to the agreement and objectively justified by the legitimate public

24. *Ibid.*, paras 573-574.
25. *Ibid.*, para. 575.
26. *See* the example discussed in the contribution of the Commission to the OECD Policy Roundtable, Horizontal Agreements in the Environmental Context, 2010, DAF/COMP(2010)39, at 123.
27. OECD Policy Roundtable, report cited *supra* note 26, at 124.
28. Case C-309/99, *J. C. J. Wouters, J. W. Savelbergh and Price Waterhouse Belastingadviseurs BV v. Algemene Raad van de Nederlandse Orde van Advocaten*, ECLI:EU:C:2002:98, para. 97; Case C-519/04 P, *David Meca-Medina and Igor Majcen v. Commission*, ECLI:EU:C:2006:492, para. 42.

policy or superior objective pursued by the agreement.[29] If the restrictions do not go beyond what is necessary in order to ensure the realization of the public objectives pursued, they will fall by virtue of their nature and purpose outside the scope of 101(1) TFEU.[30]

It results from this case law that an agreement, which pursues a legitimate objective of public interest or of public policy, could fall outside the scope of Article 101(1) TFEU, even if it contains provisions which restrict competition, provided these restrictions are inherent in, objectively justified by and proportionate to the objective pursued. In that way, the case law has opened the door to a balancing test whereby restrictions of competition may be justified not only by a weighing-off against economic benefits (i.e., consumer welfare) but also against 'non-economic' objectives of public interest.

It is undisputed that environmental protection and sustainable development are superior non-economic goals recognized as EU constitutional goals. Therefore, cooperation agreements pursuing these goals are obvious candidates to benefit from the ancillary restraints doctrine and could fall outside the scope of 101(1) TFEU, even if they contain restrictions of competition. These restrictions must, however, be inherent in and proportionate to these objectives: without the restrictions, the agreement would not have been concluded, and the restrictions must be necessary to carry out the realization of the objectives.[31] The chances to convince competition authorities of the objective necessity of the cooperation would increase should the national or EU legislator have set the particular objectives that the business conduct also seeks to achieve (e.g., the Green Deal).

An example[32] is an agreement between airlines that commit to investing an amount equal to the social cost of their combined greenhouse gas emissions in the R&D of innovative tools to decrease these emissions. This agreement restricts the commercial freedom of the participants and might result in a price increase for consumers should some airlines decide to increase airfares by passing on the costs to the 'polluting' consumer. However, this will not necessarily be the case as the solution for covering this investment will not have been exchanged, discussed or agreed upon between the participants, and other airlines might decide to internalize the costs. By applying the case law on ancillary restraints, the agreement would not fall within the scope of Article 101(1) TFEU, as it would be inherent to the objectives of sustainable development and environmental protection pursued by the agreement and would be limited to achieving these goals. Also, it would leave room for manoeuvre for the airlines to assimilate or pass on the costs to the consumer. Furthermore, should the costs be passed on to the polluting consumer, this will be an incentive for the consumer to reduce his/her contribution to greenhouse gas emissions.

29. Case C-67/96, *Albany International BV v. Stichting Bedrijfspensioenfonds Textielindustrie*, ECLI:EU:C:1999:430, paras 62-64.
30. Case C-67/96, *Albany*, paras 59-60.
31. Holmes, *supra* note 5, at 370; Dolmans, *supra* note 14, at 28-30.
32. Dolmans, *supra* note 14, at 26 and 30.

The difficulty in applying the ancillary restraints doctrine to environmental sustainability agreements is that it may exempt agreements from the scope of the competition rules without clear environmental benefits (greenwashing). It will therefore be important to subject the application of this doctrine to well-defined limits. First, the agreement should aim at the achievement of public interest objectives that include widespread benefits to society as a whole, such as the reduction of CO_2 emissions and unclean air (negative externalities). Again, this public interest condition will evidently be easier to meet where the agreement contributes to concrete environmental goals that have been detailed in secondary EU or national legislation. This includes sustainability agreements that transcend the specific relationship between the firm and the users of the product in question and creates benefits for society. Moreover, in order to avoid that, firms and consumers will free ride on declared green ambitions, the proportionality test should be applied strictly: the agreement should provide incentives to 'polluting' firms and consumers to reduce non-sustainable production and consumption by internalizing negative externalities' costs (suitability test)[33] and price increases resulting from the agreement should be strictly related to these costs (necessity test).

In its 2022 draft revised horizontal guidelines, the Commission does not retain the *Wouters* route. Agreements that restrict competition could not 'escape the prohibition of Article 101(1) for the sole reason that they are necessary for the pursuit of a sustainability objective'.[34]

3.2 Sustainable Cooperation Which Could Be Exempted under Article 101(3) TFEU (Cost-Benefit Analysis)

The third route consists of including environmental benefits from inter-firm cooperation in the cost-benefit test of Article 101(3) TFEU. Cooperation can not only benefit the environment but also have appreciable restrictive effects on competition. Examples are, as mentioned above, industry-wide collaboration to phase out unsustainable production processes or products, and joint R&D, investment and production regarding sustainable new technologies and products. In these cases, production costs and, therefore, prices may increase, and buyers' choices may be restricted because cheaper yet more pollutive products or processes disappear from the market. Exemption under Article 101(3) is then required.

The inclusion of environmental benefits in the cost-benefit analysis, however, requires a rethinking of the present state of the law. In the 2004 guidelines on Article 101(3),[35] the Commission interprets the exemption in accordance with the consumer welfare standard. The agreement must offer 'economic' benefits, i.e., efficiency gains, both cost efficiencies or qualitative efficiencies (new, improved or higher quality products) (first condition of application of Article 101(3)), and consumers must receive

33. *See*, with regard to the cost-benefit analysis of Article 101(3) TFEU, Van den Brink and Ellison, *supra* note 18, at 46-47. *See also* Dolmans, *supra* note 14, on the polluter pays principle.
34. Draft Revised Horizontal Guidelines 2022, cited *supra* note 13, para. 548.
35. European Commission Guidelines Article 101(3) TFEU (hereinafter 'Guidelines Article 101(3) TFEU').

a fair share of these gains generated by the agreement (second condition of application of Article 101(3)).[36] The notion of a 'consumer' is strict: it includes only direct or indirect users of the products covered by the agreement.[37] In other words, only in-market benefits are considered: 'efficiencies generated by the restrictive agreement within a relevant market must be sufficient to outweigh the anticompetitive effects produced by the agreement within that *same* relevant market. Negative effects on consumers in one geographic market or product market cannot normally be balanced against and compensated by positive effects for consumers in another unrelated geographic market or product market'.[38] And: 'the net effect of the agreement must at least be neutral from the point of view of those consumers directly or likely affected by the agreement. If such consumers are worse off following the agreement, the second condition of Article 101(3) is not fulfilled'.[39] Consumers must be fully compensated for the anticompetitive harm caused to them by the agreement.

This interpretation will often not be an obstacle to taking into account environmental considerations. Environmental agreements will often offer qualitative efficiency gains, such as a more sustainable product that is extra valued by consumers (first type of benefits). However, these agreements can also be aimed, even exclusively, at reducing negative external environmental effects, e.g., greenhouse gas emissions, waste and other pollutants (second type of benefits), and create non-economic benefits to society as a whole. These 'non-economic' and 'out-of-market' benefits are not included in the cost-benefit analysis of Article 101(3) TFEU.

Therefore, we consider that the current scope of Article 101(3) TFEU might be revisited for the following reasons.

First, as already explained, consumer welfare should not be limited to pure financial benefits but also include broader non-economic benefits, such as sustainability and environmental considerations and well-being.

Second, the text of Article 101(3) TFEU does not prevent the inclusion of non-economic and out-of-market benefits in the cost-benefit analysis, even more so when the objective of protection of competition as a means of enhancing consumer welfare should be interpreted broadly. The concepts of 'technical progress' and 'economic progress' are broad.[40] And Article 101(3) only requires a 'fair share' of the resulting benefit for the consumer, which is not the same as full compensation for the anticompetitive harm. Also, the case law of the Union Courts, while not making explicit

36. Goals pursued by other Treaty provisions can only be taken into account in so far as they can be subsumed under the conditions of Article 101(3) (Guidelines Article 101(3) TFEU, para. 42).
37. Guidelines Article 101(3) TFEU, paras 84 and 87. *See* Gassler, *supra* note 14, at 438.
38. Guidelines Article 101(3) TFEU, para. 43. However, the same point also states: 'where two markets are related, efficiencies achieved on separate markets can be taken into account provided that the group of consumers affected by the restriction and benefiting from the efficiency gains are substantially the same'.
39. *Ibid.*, para. 85. However, the same paragraph also states: 'Moreover, society as a whole benefits where the efficiencies lead either to fewer resources being used to produce the output consumed or to the production of more valuable products and thus to a more efficient allocation of resources.'
40. *See, e.g.*, Dolmans, *supra* note 14, at 31: 'technical progress' includes development and implementation of new sustainability technology; 'economic progress' is anything that provides a higher living standard, including access to both market and non-market goods.

statements on the question, does not exclude the inclusion of such benefits.[41] Some case law suggests that non-economic benefits might be included in Article 101(3) analysis,[42] and the courts have not limited the goal of competition law to the pursuit of consumer welfare only.[43] As to out-of-market benefits, the General Court accepts to take into account benefits of the agreement not only for the relevant market but for every other market on which the agreement in question might have beneficial effects and, in a more general sense, for any service the quality or efficiency of which might be improved by the existence of that agreement.[44]

Third, a revision of the scope of Article 101(3) would not be at odds with the Commission's position taken in a number of exemption decisions prior to the decentralized application of the EU competition rules.[45] A case in point is the CECED decision, where the Commission exempted a sector-wide agreement among manufacturers of washing machines to cease the production of machines that did not meet energy efficiency standards. The Commission found that the expected increase in production costs and price of the remaining, more energy-efficient types of washing machines was outweighed by consumers' savings on electricity bills (individual economic benefits) and by savings in marginal damage from avoided carbon dioxide emissions that it estimated as a monetary value per ton of carbon dioxide (collective environmental benefits). The benefits to society brought about by the agreement were

41. For an analysis of the case law as to whether as to whether it allows out-of-market benefits, *see also* ACM Legal Memo, 'What is meant by a fair share for consumers in Article 101(3) TFEU in a sustainability context?', 27 September 2021.
42. *See, e.g.*, Case 26/76, *Metro SB-Großmärkte GmbH & Co. KG v. Commission*, ECLI:EU:C:1977:167, para. 21 (the powers of the Commission under Article 101(3) allow to reconcile the requirements of workable competition with the safeguarding of 'objectives of a different nature') and Joined Cases T-528/93, T-542/93, T-543/93 and T-546/93, Metro*pole télévision SA and others v. Commission*, ECLI:EU:T:1996:99, para. 18 (the Commission may base itself on considerations connected with the pursuit of the public interest in order to grant exemption under Article 101(3)).
43. Case C-52/09, *Konkurrensverket v. TeliaSonera Sverige AB*, ECLI:EU:C:2011:83, para. 22 (the function of the competition rules is 'to prevent competition from being distorted to the detriment of the public interest, individual undertakings and consumers, thereby ensuring the well-being of the European Union') and Case C-501/06 P, *GSK and others*, para. 63 (the competition rules 'aim to protect not only the interests of competitors or of consumers, but also the structure of the market and ... competition as such. For a finding that an agreement has an anticompetitive object, it is not necessary that final consumers be deprived of the advantages of effective competition in terms of supply or price').
44. Case T-86/95, *Compagnie générale maritime and Others v. Commission*, ECLI:EU:T:2002:50, para. 343.
45. *See* Brook, 'Struggling with Article 101(3) TFEU: Diverging approaches of the Commission, EU Courts and five competition authorities', 56 *Common Market Law Review* (2019), 121-156 (explaining that when the Commission still had the monopoly to adopt exemption decisions, it took into account non-economic benefits in the analysis under Article 101(3) TFEU, notably environmental, employment and industrial policy benefits) and Murray, 'Antitrust and sustainability: globally warming up to be a hot topic', Kluwer Competition Law Blog, 18 October 2019, available at competitionlawblog.kluwercompetitionlaw.com/2019/10/18/antitrust-and-sustainability-globally-warming-up-to-be-a-hot-topic/ (mentioning Commission decisions *Exxon/Shell* (IV/33.640), O.J. 1994, L 144/20 and *Philips-Osram* (IV/34.252), O.J. 2004, L 378/37 dealing with joint ventures having, amongst other benefits, a favourable impact on the environment and the reduction of negative externalities).

found to be many times higher than the increased purchase costs of more energy-efficient washing machines. The Commission concluded that '[s]uch environmental results for society would allow consumers a fair share of the benefits even if no benefits accrued to individual purchasers of machines'.[46]

Fourth, in view of the need to combat the climate change crisis on all fronts, competition authorities find in the cost-benefit analysis of Article 101(3) TFEU a balanced tool to include environmental considerations in the equation. There is a change in the mindset, with the Dutch competition authority (ACM) as a front-runner adopting draft guidelines in early 2021[47] and the European Commission taking position in the 2022 draft revised horizontal guidelines.[48] Both authorities clarify the conditions of application of Article 101(3) TFEU to environmental sustainability agreements.

As regards the first condition, both regulators are willing to interpret it broadly. Thus, the ACM accepts that sustainability agreements can offer benefits for both the users and society. They can relate, first, to the reduction of negative externalities in production and consumption, using in that way scarce natural resources in a more efficient manner and, second, to other efficiency gains, such as production at lower costs or easier introduction/distribution on the market of sustainable products, or better information of consumers. The ACM defines the concept of efficiency gains broadly and includes de facto non-economic environmental benefits (e.g., reduction of harmful emissions).[49] The Commission also recognizes that sustainability agreements can produce efficiencies, such as the use of cleaner production or distribution technologies, less pollution, improved conditions of production and distribution, more resilient infrastructure or supply chains, better quality products, etc. Furthermore, the agreements can avoid supply chain disruptions, reduce the time it takes to bring sustainable products to the market and can help to improve consumer choice by facilitating the comparison of products.[50] The Commission therefore accepts that sustainability benefits may constitute efficiency gains covered by the first condition. While cost efficiencies remain relevant, qualitative efficiencies are notably important in the sustainability context.[51]

As regards the second exemption criterion in particular, both regulators step away, to some extent, from the consumer welfare standard in its traditional meaning. The ACM is ready to deviate for a specific type of agreement, i.e., 'environmental damage agreements', from the rule that users in the relevant market must be fully

46. Commission Decision *CECED* (IV.F.1/36.718), O.J. 2007, L 187/47. It has been rightly recalled that the reference to collective benefits is obiter dictum because the individual economic benefits were in themselves sufficient to outweigh the anticompetitive effects of the agreement (Peeperkorn, *supra* note 9, at 20).
47. ACM, Second Draft Guidelines Sustainability Agreements, 26 January 2021 (hereinafter 'ACM Draft Guidelines'). *See* the discussion by Van Dijk, 'A new approach to assess certain sustainability agreements', in Holmes, Middelschutte and Snoep (Eds), *supra* note 11, pp. 55-68; Brook, *supra* note 45 (explaining that ACM incorporated already prior to the draft guidelines sustainability considerations in individual decisions and positions).
48. Draft Revised Horizontal Guidelines 2022, cited *supra* note 13, paras 577-614.
49. ACM, Second Draft Guidelines, paras 35-37.
50. Draft Revised Horizontal Guidelines 2022, cited *supra* note 13, para. 578.
51. Murray, *supra* note 45.

compensated for any anticompetitive harm. The ACM defines an environmental damage agreement as an agreement (i) pursuing the reduction of environmental damage (negative externalities) and (ii) helping to comply with an international or national standard or to realize a concrete policy goal to prevent such damage. Incidentally, this closely resembles the 'public interest' standard in the ancillary restrictions doctrine discussed above. For these agreements, out-of-market benefits may be taken into account because 'it can be fair not to compensate users fully for the harm that the agreement causes because their demand for the products in question essentially creates the problem for which society needs to find solutions' and 'they enjoy the same benefits as the rest of society.'[52] With regard to other sustainability agreements, only in-market benefits are considered: users must still be fully compensated for the anticompetitive harm they suffer.[53]

The Commission's approach in the 2022 draft revised horizontal guidelines is again more cautious. It repeats the position in the 2004 guidelines on Article 101(3) that the claimed sustainability benefits have to be related to the consumers of the products covered by the agreement, i.e., consumers in the relevant market.[54] The Commission identifies three types of benefits. First, 'individual use value' benefits which result for the consumer from the use of the product covered by the agreement. Such benefits may result from the consumption of a sustainable product (e.g., healthier products or reduced plastic packaging) in the same way as they result from the consumption of any other product. These benefits constitute in-market benefits that may outweigh the harm caused by the price increase or the reduction in choice caused by the sustainability agreement.[55] Second, 'individual non-use value' benefits which do not result for consumers from the use of the sustainable product prescribed by the agreement but from the consumers' appreciation of the impact of their sustainable consumption on others (society). These benefits will accrue to consumers within the relevant market via their personal/individual valuation of the effect on others, including on non-users outside the relevant market.[56] From this perspective, these benefits are also in-market.

52. ACM Draft Guidelines, para. 48.
53. *Ibid.*, para. 49: 'First, this concerns agreements that are not related to the reduction of environmental damage, but that do fall under the broader definition of sustainability agreements. Second, it can concern agreements that do relate to the reduction of environmental damage but that are not necessary for achieving a standard or concrete policy objective. Think of product standards or environmental standards that are more ambitious than the standard or the policy objective.' These are assessed similarly as the 'other sustainability agreements'. These other sustainability agreements concern, for instance, working conditions, animal welfare, social sustainability and human rights (para. 50).
54. Draft Revised Horizontal Guidelines 2022, cited *supra* note 13, paras 588-589.
55. *Ibid.*, paras 590-591 and 593 (mentioning that an agreement between competitors requiring that vegetables are grown with the help of organic fertilizers will create health benefits for consumers outweighing the harm caused by the price increase charged to these consumers in the relevant market, or that an agreement to reduce packaging will also reduce production and distribution costs, and ultimately lead to a lower price that outweighs reduced consumers' choice in the relevant market).
56. *Ibid.*, paras 594-596 (mentioning the example of consumers who may be ready to pay a higher price for furniture made from wood that is grown and harvested sustainably not because of the better quality of the furniture but because consumers want to stop de-forestation and loss of natural habitats to the benefit of society).

Third, collective benefits which occur irrespective of the consumers' individual appreciation of the product and objectively can accrue to the consumers in the relevant market if the latter are part of the larger group of beneficiaries (society).[57] In nuancing the principle of full compensation of consumers for the anticompetitive harm, the Commission states: 'where consumers in the relevant market substantially overlap with, or are part of the beneficiaries outside the relevant market, the collective benefits to the consumers in the relevant market occurring outside that market, can be taken into account if they are significant enough to compensate consumers in the relevant market for the harm suffered'.[58] Hence, the Commission is only willing to take collective benefits into account if the parties to the agreement demonstrate that the 'consumers in the relevant market substantially overlap with the beneficiaries or are part of them' and 'demonstrate what part of the collective benefits occurring or likely to occur outside the relevant market accrue to the consumers of the product in the relevant market'.[59]

On the third criterion (indispensability of the cooperation), the message is double when looking at environmental sustainability agreements. On the one hand, sustainability can be seen as a quality of the product and, therefore, a parameter of competition. No cooperation will be needed between competitors where there are enough consumers willing to pay the extra price for a more sustainable product. Sustainable and non-sustainable products will compete and be part of the same relevant market.[60] According to the Commission in the 2022 draft revised horizontal guidelines, cooperation agreements are not indispensable as there is demand for sustainable products.[61] On the other hand, the situation may be such that companies seeking to introduce more sustainable products will suffer from first-mover disadvantages, for example, because consumers are not willing to pay the extra price and switch to other less sustainable products. In that case, the indispensability test is normally met.[62] The same would apply when investments in sustainable technology and

57. Draft Revised Horizontal Guidelines 2022, cited *supra* note 13, para. 601.
58. *Ibid.*, para. 603.
59. *Ibid.*, para. 606. The Commission illustrates its proposal with the following example where collective benefits can be taken into account: ' [D]rivers purchasing less polluting fuel are also citizens who would benefit from cleaner air, if less polluting fuel is used. To the extent that a substantial overlap of consumers (the drivers in this example) and the beneficiaries (citizens) can be established, the sustainability benefits from cleaner air are in principle relevant for the assessment and can be taken into account if they are significant enough to compensate consumers in the relevant market for the harm suffered' (para. 604). However, collective benefits cannot be taken into account in the following example: 'consumers may buy clothing made of sustainable cotton that reduces chemicals and water use on the land where it is cultivated. Such environmental benefits could in principle be taken into account as collective benefits. However, there is likely no substantial overlap between the consumers of the clothing and the beneficiaries of these environmental benefits that occur only in the area where the cotton is grown. Therefore, it is unlikely that these collective benefits would accrue to the consumers in the relevant market' (para. 604).
60. Van Dijk, *supra* note 47, at 66.
61. Draft Revised Horizontal Guidelines 2022, cited *supra* note 13, para. 582.
62. Van Dijk, *supra* note 47, at 66-67.

production capacity would require a minimum scale to be economically viable.[63] The Commission also takes this view in the 2022 draft revised horizontal guidelines.[64]

The fourth criterion (no elimination of competition) is also important as it is meant to confirm the true environmental goals of the participants by guaranteeing that sufficient effective competition subsists in the market. However, assuming all three other conditions are fulfilled, this fourth condition should normally not prevent a sustainability agreement from benefitting from the exemption under Article 101(3) TFEU.[65]

Fifth, we consider that the proposed revision of the consumer welfare standard offers a balanced approach to the concept of 'fair share to the consumer'. On the one hand, the consumer welfare standard will continue to fully apply to all agreements that are only aimed at offering efficiency gains (the vast majority) or environmental benefits (e.g., more sustainable products) for direct and indirect users of the product.[66] On the other hand, the rule that users of the product must be fully compensated for the competitive harm from the agreement is not applied to agreements that create general benefits to society as a whole beyond the confines of a particular market, such as agreements to reduce negative externalities (e.g., reduction of CO_2 emissions and environmental pollution).[67] In that case, as the ACM position shows in an example, agreements between producers of a semi-finished product sold primarily in the Netherlands, making their manufacturing process carbon-neutral and leading to a price increase of the semi-finished product are justified, provided that total environmental benefits for society are large enough to offset the price increases in the Netherlands. Direct efficiency gains for users of the product may exist and be included in the cost-benefit calculation. However, even if no such direct gains exist, environmental benefits (reduction of CO_2 emissions) can be taken into account in the example, and the ACM is willing to include the total benefits for Dutch society in the calculation even if the buyers of the end-product represent merely 30% of the Dutch population and the environmental benefits accruing to them alone are not large enough to offset the price increase of the product.[68] The buyers of this product are, however, part of the wider group (society at large) that benefits from the agreement[69] and can therefore be deemed to obtain a fair share of the benefits. In the 2022 revised horizontal guidelines, the Commission, though relaxing somewhat the traditional reading of Article 101(3) TFEU, expressly requires that consumers in the relevant market substantially overlap with the larger group of beneficiaries (society) or be part of them and that out-of-market collective benefits are significant enough to compensate consumers in the relevant market for the harm suffered. Regardless of the specificities of the approach, the inclusion of collective benefits in the assessment under Article 101(3) TFEU is now clearly in the minds of antitrust regulators. In our view, this amendment to the

63. Middelschulte, 'Article 101 TFEU in the decisive decade', *Concurrences* No. 4 (2020), at 49.
64. Draft Revised Horizontal Guidelines 2022, cited *supra* note 13, paras 584-585.
65. *Ibid.*, paras 610-614.
66. Van Dijk, *supra* note 47, at 56-57.
67. *Ibid.*, at 57.
68. ACM Draft Guidelines, para. 58 and example 5.
69. *Ibid.*, para. 60.

consumer welfare standard, which one may call the 'polluting' or 'sustainable' consumer welfare standard, is justified because buyers of the product enjoy the benefits of the product, and it is then fair that they also bear the costs of the price increase resulting from an agreement between competitors that provides environmental benefits to society (of which they are part) by reducing negative externalities from the manufacturing of the product. It is also efficient as the internalization of the pollution or emission costs in the price will be an incentive for the consumer to adapt his/her consumption behaviour.[70]

Sixth, we consider that the inclusion of environmental sustainability considerations in the cost-benefit analysis of Article 101(3) TFEU can be put into effect without creating unsurmountable problems of practical application. Many authors have pointed out that there is well-established environmental economics literature on valuing environmental benefits[71] and that authoritative independent estimates exist on the economic costs of emitting carbon dioxide.[72] This should help to avoid the inclusion of external environmental effects in the cost-benefit analysis, which leads to slow, costly and unpredictable outcomes and therefore undermines the effective application of the competition rules.[73] Also, by requiring that the value of environmental benefits be taken into account in the cost-benefit analysis is based on scientific evidence, the risk that national interests are introduced in the application of Article 101(3) could be contained.[74]

In that regard, it is useful to refer again to ACM's suggestions for the practical application of the cost-benefit analysis for sustainability agreements. The ACM advances a mere qualitative assessment if the parties have a limited combined market share (< 30%) or if, based on a rough estimate, the harm to competition (price increase/reduction in choice) is manifestly smaller than the benefits (cost savings, reduced emissions).[75] Where a quantitative assessment is necessary, the ACM proposes for environmental damage agreements that the total benefits for consumers and non-consumers (members of society) are weighed against the harm to competition. The ACM will use the concept of 'environmental prices', i.e., the value that society assigns to the harm of environmental damage caused by pollutive emissions.[76] These prices estimate the reduction in emissions and, therefore, the benefits to members of society, regardless of whether they are a consumer of a particular product.[77] By including these out-of-market environmental benefits to society as a whole in the cost-benefit calculation, the agreement may meet the fair share test (second criterion)

70. Van den Brink and Ellison, *supra* note 18, at 46-47.
71. Kingston, 'Competition law in an environmental crisis', 10 *Journal of European Competition Law & Practice* (2019), 517-518, at 518.
72. Van den Brink and Ellison, *supra* note 18, at 44.
73. This risk has been underlined by Peeperkorn, *supra* note 9, at 21.
74. *See* on the latter point Brook, *supra* note 45, pp. 121-156.
75. ACM Draft guidelines, paras 55-56.
76. *Ibid.*, para. 58: These prices can be estimated on the basis of either damage costs to humans and the environment or prevention costs, i.e., the costs needed to achieve a concrete policy objective. *See* on the damage cost method and the abatement cost method: Van Dijk, *supra* note 47, at 62-64.
77. ACM Draft guidelines, para. 59.

even if these benefits to the consumers (buyers) of the product are not large enough to compensate for the harm to competition.[78] For other sustainability agreements, ACM proposes the use of willing-to-pay studies to estimate the value that users assign to a certain product or product feature, such as improvement in terms of environmental or animal friendliness.[79] These studies estimate what extra price consumers are willing to pay for a more sustainable product. If these in-market benefits are not enough to compensate for the price increase resulting from the agreement, the second condition of Article 101(3) is not met. This echoes the well-known *Chicken of Tomorrow* case, where the ACM used a willing-to-pay study to quantify the value that consumers attach to animal welfare and concluded that consumers were not ready to pay the price increase of the chicken meat resulting from the arrangements between supermarkets to buy and sell only chickens produced according to certain sustainability standards. The exemption under Article 101(3) was therefore refused.[80]

3.3 Justified Unilateral Sustainable Business Practices (Article 102 TFEU)

A dominant firm's behaviour may have an important impact on the way products are produced and sold on the market, with obvious consequences for the environment. The question arises whether a dominant company could invoke an 'environmental stainability' defence to justify its actions and escape the application of Article 102 TFEU.

As recently recalled, a dominant undertaking can provide a justification for behaviour that is liable to fall under Article 102 TFEU by demonstrating either that its conduct is objectively necessary or that the anticompetitive effects of the conduct may be counterbalanced by efficiencies that also benefit consumers.[81] We submit that, as for Article 101 TFEU, a dominant undertaking may be able to rely on these two lines of defence to justify conduct on the basis of environmental protection and sustainability considerations.

First, according to the case law, the dominant company can raise a plea based on objective necessity when its conduct is objectively necessary for legitimate technical or commercial considerations.[82] In particular, the case law accepts that allegedly abusive conduct can be justified by legitimate commercial considerations, such as protection against unfair trade practices, protection of commercial interests,[83] and also by

78. *Ibid*. These consumers of the product are considered to be also part of the wider group (society at large) that benefits from the agreement and therefore enjoy these benefits as much as the rest of society (ACM Draft guidelines, para. 60).
79. ACM Draft guidelines, paras 61-62.
80. ACM's analysis of the sustainability arrangements concerning the 'Chicken of Tomorrow', ACM/DM/2014/206028, consultation document, 26 January 2015.
81. Case C-209/10, *Post Danmark A/S v. Konkurrencerådet*, ECLI:EU:C:2012:172, paras 40-41.
82. Case 311/84, *CBEM Télémarketing v. CLT and IPB*, ECLI:EU:C:1985:394, para. 26.
83. Case 27/76, *United Brands Company and United Brands Continentaal BV v. Commission*, ECLI:EU:C:1978:22, para. 189.

legitimate technical justifications, such as technical efficiencies due to superior technical performance.[84] In both cases, the conduct must be proportionate to the objective to be achieved.[85]

So far, the case law has never applied the objective necessity justification in environmental matters. However, as sustainable development and environmental protection belong to the constitutional goals of the Union and these goals must be integrated into all EU policies and activities, an objective justification based on these considerations could be envisaged.[86] The chances of a positive result would obviously increase should the national or EU legislation have already identified and/or imposed the particular goals pursued by the business conduct concerned. Take the example of a dominant company that invokes objective necessity to justify charging different prices to different customers, depending on the sustainable use of the product, or to justify a refusal to buy products from suppliers with unsustainable business practices. Such conduct may possibly fall outside the scope of Article 102 TFEU provided that it does not eliminate competition, aims at achieving genuine sustainability and environmental protection and is proportionate and necessary (i.e., no less restrictive means can be applied) to achieve these goals. This is obviously a sensitive and delicate area, and competition authorities will be cautious as this could lead to private policing of commercial relationships. In its Article 102 TFEU Guidance Paper, the Commission accepted that 'exclusionary conduct may be considered objectively necessary for health or safety reasons related to the nature of the product in question'. However, it also said that 'proof of whether conduct of this kind is objectively necessary must take into account that it is normally the task of public authorities to set and enforce public health and safety standards' and that '[i]t is not the task of a dominant undertaking to take steps on its own initiative to exclude products which it regards, rightly or wrongly, as dangerous or inferior to its own product'.[87] This arguably leaves some room for taking into account goals of sustainable development and environmental protection (i.e., more sustainable products; reduction of negative externalities). In any event, competition should not be eliminated, and a strict application of the objective necessity test and the principle of proportionality will be required. This approach may find support in the future with the adoption at the national and EU levels of the Due Diligence Acts, which will impose obligations on big corporations to establish and effectively implement a due diligence strategy and to adopt 'all proportionate and commensurate policies and measures' to cease, prevent or mitigate potential or actual adverse impacts on human rights, the environment and good governance.[88]

84. Case T-201/04, *Microsoft Corp. v. Commission*, ECLI:EU:T:2007:289, paras 1144, 1146 and 1159.
85. Case 27/76, *United Brands*, para. 190.
86. Holmes, *supra* note 5, at 370; Thomas, *supra* note 11, pp. 105-116. *See also* HCC Staff Discussion Paper, *supra* note 11.
87. Guidance on the Commission's enforcement priorities in applying Article 82 of the EC Treaty to abusive exclusionary conduct by dominant undertakings, O.J. 2009, C 45/7. *See also* Case T-30/89, *Hilti AG v. Commission*, ECLI:EU:T:1991:70, paras 118-119; Case T-83/91, *Tetra Pak International SA v. Commission*, ECLI:EU:T:1994:246, paras 83-84 and 138.
88. For example, European Parliament Resolution of 10 March 2021 with recommendations to the Commission on corporate due diligence and corporate accountability (2020/2129(INL)).

Second, a dominant company can also invoke an efficiency defence under current law. Under the efficiency defence, a dominant company can provide justification for its behaviour by establishing that the anticompetitive effects produced are outweighed by advantages in terms of efficiency that also benefit consumers.[89] In particular, the dominant company would need to demonstrate that (i) the efficiency gains 'likely to result from the conduct under consideration counteract any likely negative effects on competition and consumer welfare in the affected markets'; (ii) 'those gains have been, or are likely to be, brought as a result of that conduct'; (iii) 'such conduct is necessary for the achievement of those gains in efficiency'; and (iv) 'it does not eliminate effective competition by removing all or most existing sources of actual or potential competition'.[90]

Hence, similarly to the cost-benefit analysis under Article 101(3) TFEU, Article 102 TFEU includes a balancing test where the negative effects of the dominant firm's conduct on competition and consumer welfare are weighed against efficiencies that also benefit consumers. In a sustainability context, one might apply the concept of efficiencies, first, and this is not new, to give appropriate attention to qualitative efficiencies (i.e., more innovative sustainable products) and, second, to include environmental benefits, e.g., the reduction of negative externalities (e.g., decrease of CO_2 emissions) as an efficient use of natural resources. Qualitative efficiencies will normally benefit the same consumers that are harmed by the anticompetitive effects of the firm's behaviour (in-market efficiencies). The second type of efficiencies (reduction of negative externalities) might benefit society as a whole. The question is then again whether, as for the fair share for the consumer in Article 101(3) TFEU, the dominant firm's behaviour could be justified on the basis that even if the direct consumers of the product are not being fully compensated, total environmental benefits for society (of which consumers are part) are enough to counteract the negative effects on competition. In any event, the strict conditions for relying on the efficiency defence as defined in the case law mentioned will have to be met, including the maintenance of effective competition, which as a result of the very presence of the dominant firm, is already weakened. Should a dominant undertaking be able to establish the existence of such efficiency gains outweighing the anticompetitive effects resulting from its conduct without eliminating effective competition in the market, such conduct could then be acceptable under Article 102 TFEU.[91]

This possible interpretation of the two defences against allegations of abusive behaviour puts into effect the constitutional provisions of the Treaty on sustainable development and environmental protection when assessing environment-friendly conduct of a dominant company. However, it will be up to the dominant company to establish that its conduct is objectively justified or will lead to substantial efficiencies outweighing any anticompetitive effects. The goals of sustainable development and

89. Case C-209/10, *Post Danmark*, para. 41; Case T-612/17, *Google and Alphabet*, para. 551. *See also* Commission guidance on Article 82, cited *supra* note 87.
90. Case C-209/10, *Post Danmark*, para. 42; Case T-612/17, *Google and Alphabet*, para. 553; *see also* HCC Staff Discussion Paper, *supra* note 11.
91. HCC Staff Discussion Paper, *supra* note 11.

environmental protection cannot give 'carte blanche' to dominant companies to escape their special responsibility under Article 102 TFEU. In particular, relying on these goals cannot be a pretext for dominant companies to impair genuine undistorted competition.

4 CONCLUSION

We conclude that sustainable development and environmental protection can be integrated into competition law, being constitutional goals of the EU.

While this might require a limited shift in competition policy and in the approach by competition authorities, the existing paradigms of competition law allow for such an approach. Consumer welfare is not only a pure financial standard based on revenues and profits but can be enlarged to include the benefits for society as a whole and take less economic considerations such as sustainability and environmental protection into consideration. According to the 'polluter pays principle', this will also lead to efficient outcomes as the 'sustainable' consumer will bear the environmental costs of the consumption of products he/she enjoys and adapts his/her behaviour in consequence.

That does obviously not mean a 'blank check' for companies which allegedly pursue sustainability or environmental protection goals. Competition law should, in the first place, be focused on the protection of competition. The fulfilment by competition authorities of this mission will in itself greatly contribute to these goals. Competition is a key driver of innovation, and innovation is key to tackling the climate crisis. However, competition law is not the solution for all problems in society and should not cover unsustainable practices which do not have any anticompetitive effects.

CHAPTER 3

From 'Muted Dialogue' to 'Shouting Matches': The Role of the Court of Justice in Post-Brexit Relations

Joris Larik

This chapter applies the insights from Marco Bronckers' seminal 2008 article 'From "Direct Effect" to "Muted Dialogue"' in the context of Brexit and the new legal international framework that governs European Union (EU)-United Kingdom (UK) relations. Even though a lot has happened since 2008, the major legal trends identified by Bronckers have carried on. In particular, the Court of Justice of the EU has continued to find other ways to give effect to international law beyond direct effect. This is particularly salient in post-Brexit-legal arrangements, as the Trade and Cooperation Agreement (TCA) between the EU and the UK cannot be relied upon by individuals for the most part. By contrast, the Withdrawal Agreement represents a significant new exception to what is now the rule of excluding the direct effect of international agreements in the EU's external relations. Post-Brexit law also evinces other forms of muted and not-so-muted dialogues, building on previous practices, such as under the European Economic Area (EEA). Last but not least, as trade wars between the EU and its former Member State have become a real possibility, this should encourage us to resuscitate debates about compensating those who suffer damages for the 'greater good'.

1 INTRODUCTION

This chapter is, first and foremost, a token of appreciation for the profound and lasting impression that Marco Bronckers' scholarship has made on the fields of European Union (EU) and international law - and on me personally. I started reading his texts first while I was a trainee at the European Commission's Legal Service and later at the World Trade Organization (WTO) Appellate Body Secretariat. I read them again during my doctoral studies at the European University Institute, where they played a formative role early on in my thinking about the Common Commercial Policy and the EU's approach to international law and international courts, also outside of the WTO context.[1] To this day, the analysis, concepts, and recommendations put forward by Bronckers remain a valuable resource for scholars, students, and practitioners.

One particularly insightful piece of his scholarship is the article 'From "Direct Effect" to "Muted Dialogue"', which was published in the *Journal of International Economic Law* in 2008.[2] The concept of 'muted dialogue' and Bronckers' reflections about the role of the Court of Justice of the EU (CJEU) regarding international law and international courts have stayed with me ever since, and doubtlessly many other scholars.

The main argument put forward in Bronckers' article was to caution against equating giving 'direct effect' to international law in the EU's legal order with giving 'effect' to international law more broadly, including through implementation at the domestic level. As Bronckers demonstrated, 'there are different and sometimes rather subtle ways for the European courts to grant domestic law effect to a treaty'.[3] He emphasized the doctrine of consistent interpretation, the direct review of EU measures in cases where there was a clear legislative intent to implement WTO law (the *Fediol* and *Nakajima* exceptions; also known as the 'implementation principle'[4]), and 'muted dialogue' with the WTO Appellate Body. A 'muted dialogue', according to Bronckers, takes place when the CJEU does not 'refer to the WTO ruling in its findings, but its judgment can be read as an effort to avoid inconsistencies with the WTO Appellate Body'.[5] One prominent example he gives is from the 'zeroing' disputes regarding the calculation of anti-dumping duties.[6]

1. *See*, respectively, Larik, 'Much more than trade: The common commercial policy in a global context' in Evans and Koutrakos (Eds), *Beyond the Established Legal Orders: Policy Interconnections Between the EU and the Rest of the World* (Hart Publishing, 2011), pp. 13-46; and Larik, 'Two ships in the night or in the same boat together: How the ECJ squared the circle and foreshadowed Lisbon in its *Kadi* judgment', 13 *Yearbook of Polish European Studies* (2010), 149-173.
2. Bronckers, 'From "direct effect" to "muted dialogue": Recent developments in the European Courts' case law on the WTO and beyond', 11 *Journal of International Economic Law* (2008), 885-898. The term 'muted dialogue' was originally used in Bronckers 'Private appeals to WTO Law: An update', 42 *Journal of World Trade* (2008), 245-260, at 258.
3. Bronckers, *supra* note 2, at 897.
4. Gáspár-Szilágyi, 'The relationship between EU law and international agreements: Restricting the application of the *Fediol* and *Nakajima* exceptions in *Vereniging Milieudefensie*', 52 *Common Market Law Review* (2015), 1059-1077, at 1061.
5. Bronckers, *supra* note 2, at 890.
6. Case C-351/04, *IKEA v. Commissioners of Customs & Excise*, ECLI:EU:C:2007:547, paras 55-56; not referencing but arguably being influenced by WTO Appellate Body Report, *European*

Fifteen years after the publication of Bronckers' seminal article, we find ourselves in a time of 'shouting matches',[7] where the acrimonious negotiations over the withdrawal of the United Kingdom (UK) from the EU have given way to a rocky post-membership relationship. Yet, these negotiations have resulted in a new 'sophisticated legal structure'[8] with various roles being accorded to the CJEU. This structure has opened a sizeable field of research and analysis for legal scholars. This chapter provides one such analysis through the lens of Bronckers' concepts and predictions as voiced in 'From "Direct Effect" to "Muted Dialogue"'.

The chapter proceeds as follows: Section 2 situates the article in its time and contrasts it with the situation in 2023, highlighting the development of the relevant case law in the meantime. Section 3 outlines the role of the Court of Justice in the emerging field of 'post-Brexit law'.[9] Section 4 critically discusses this role in light of Marco Bronckers' article and wider scholarship. Section 5 provides a conclusion.

2 FROM 2008 TO 2023: FROM PRE-LISBON TO POST-BREXIT

The world of 2008, when 'From "Direct Effect" to "Muted Dialogue"' was published, differs in important respects from the world of 2023. Admittedly, there is always a danger of excessive nostalgia when looking at the past, but important changes have taken place with regard to the EU and its position on the global stage, of which five are highlighted here.

First, when 'From "Direct Effect" to "Muted Dialogue"' came out, the Lisbon Treaty still lay 'dormant'.[10] It entered into force on 1 December 2009, bringing about important changes to the way the EU works,[11] including its external relations.[12] Bronckers already put his finger on an important new substantive provision, i.e., what is now Article 21 of the Treaty on European Union (TEU), which states that the EU's 'action on the international scene shall be guided by the principles which have inspired its own creation, development and enlargement' and that it 'shall promote multilateral solutions to common problems, in particular in the framework of the United Nations'.[13]

Communities – Anti-Dumping Duties on Imports of Cotton-Type Bed Linen from India (EC – Bed Linen), WT/DS141/AB/R, adopted 12 March 2001.

7. euronews.com/my-europe/2018/03/13/brexit-shouting-match-in-european-parliament (last visited February 2023).
8. Van Elsuwege, 'A new legal framework for EU-UK relations: Some reflections from the perspective of EU external relations law', 6 *European Papers* (2021), 785-799, at 787.
9. For this term, *see* Larik and Wessel, 'The EU-UK post-Brexit Trade and Cooperation Agreement: Forging partnership or managing rivalry?' in Łazowski and Cygan (Eds), *Research Handbook on Legal Aspects of Brexit* (Edward Elgar, 2022), pp. 122-147, at 125.
10. Bronckers, *supra* note 2, at 893, note 39.
11. *See* Piris, *The Lisbon Treaty: A Legal and Political Analysis* (CUP, 2012).
12. Cardwell (Ed.), *EU External Relations Law and Policy in the Post-Lisbon Era* (Springer, 2021); Wouters and Ramopoulos, 'Revisiting the Lisbon Treaty's constitutional design of EU external relations' in Rossi and Casolari (Eds), *The EU after Lisbon: Amending or Coping with the Existing Treaties?* (Springer, 2014), pp. 215-239; Van Elsuwege, 'EU external action after the collapse of the pillar structure: In search of a new balance between delimitation and consistency', 47 *Common Market Law Review* (2010), 987-1019.
13. Article 21(1) TEU.

These principles include democracy, the rule of law, human rights and fundamental freedoms, and respect for the principles of the United Nations Charter and international law. Bronckers made the point that EU citizens should be able to expect that the EU 'abide by the rule of law', including its international legal commitments.[14]

In the years that followed, the CJEU used Article 21 TEU and the similar provision in Article 3(5) TEU, which stresses that 'the strict observance and the development of international law' is part of the EU's foreign policy objectives, in its case law. In particular, the Court relied on it as the primary legal argument for reasoning that the EU is bound by customary international law[15] and that the maintenance of international peace and security needs to be done in a manner that respects international law.[16]

Second, at the time of Bronckers' article, the CJEU's case law that denies, except for some narrow exceptions, direct effect to the WTO agreements and rulings of WTO panels and the Appellate Body was still seen as an exception to a generally more open and friendly approach to international agreements.[17] After all, the CJEU had accorded direct effect not only to association agreements such as the one with Turkey but also to the partnership agreement with Russia and the Lomé Convention.[18] Bronckers, presciently, remarked that 'WTO case law may become a trend setter for the way European courts will want to deal with key international agreements',[19] pointing to the then-recent judgment in which the CJEU applied its more restrictive approach to the United Nations Convention on the Law of the Sea.[20]

This trend has ever since been confirmed in the case law of the CJEU.[21] Bronckers, moreover, noted the Council Decision concluding the WTO Agreements, which 'declared that these agreements are not of such a nature that they can be relied on directly before national or Community courts'.[22] This foreshadowed a related trend, with both Council decisions and the text of the agreements foreclosing directly effect in explicit terms.[23]

14. Bronckers, *supra* note 2, at 893.
15. Case C-366/10, *Air Transport Association of America*, ECLI:EU:C:2011:864, para. 101.
16. Joined Cases C-584/10 P, C-593/10 P and C-595/10 P, *Commission v. Kadi*, ECLI:EU:C:2013:518, para. 103.
17. Bronckers, *supra* note 2, at 894.
18. Respectively, Case 12/86, *Demirel*, ECLI:EU:C:1987:400; Case C-265/03, *Simutenkov*, ECLI:EU:C:2005:213; and Case C-469/93, *Chiquita Italia*, ECLI:EU:C:1995:435.
19. Bronckers, *supra* note 2, at 897.
20. Case C-308/06, *Intertanko*, ECLI:EU:C:2008:312.
21. Case C-366/10, *Air Transport Association of America*, ECLI:EU:C:2011:864, where the CJEU denied direct effect to the Kyoto Protocol, though the CJEU did accord certain provisions of the EU-US Open Skies Agreement direct effect; *see* further Ghazaryan, 'Who are the "gatekeepers"?: In continuation of the debate on the direct applicability and the direct effect of EU international agreements', 37 *Yearbook of European Law* (2018), 27-74.
22. Bronckers, *supra* note 2, at 886. Council Decision 94/800/EC of 22 December 1994 concerning the conclusion on behalf of the European Community, as regards matters within its competence, of the agreements reached in the Uruguay Round multilateral negotiations (1986-1994), O.J. 2004 L 336/1, final preambulatory clause: 'Whereas, by its nature, the Agreement establishing the World Trade Organization, including the Annexes thereto, is not susceptible to being directly invoked in Community or Member State courts.'
23. *See*, for example, Council Decision (EU) 2017/38 of 28 October 2016 on the provisional application of the Comprehensive Economic and Trade Agreement (CETA) between Canada, of the one part, and the European Union and its Member States, of the other part, O.J. 2017, L

Third, at the time of 'From "Direct Effect" to "Muted Dialogue"', the WTO Appellate Body was still fully operational. Described as the 'lynchpin'[24] of the international trading system, its reverse-consensus rule allowed for a rich stream of case law to emerge. Following long-standing criticisms of the Appellate Body by the United States (US), the Trump administration succeeded in putting the Appellate Body out of service through its consistent refusal to appoint new members (something that is not decided by reverse consensus) or to allow for consensus for renewing the terms of sitting members.[25] Ever since, WTO members' appeals disappear 'into the void' for the foreseeable future. The Biden administration, as of the time of writing this chapter, has not reversed this policy.

Fourth, Bronckers notes that the EU 'does not appear to have felt the need so far to initiate formal dispute settlement proceedings under its bilateral agreements, and also has not had to defend itself against complaints from its bilateral partners under such proceedings'.[26] This would remain true for another decade, fitting with a general trend of dispute settlement mechanisms under bilateral agreements not being used.[27]

However, since 2018 there have been several disputes under bilateral agreements of the EU. All of these have been initiated by the EU, respectively, under the EU-Algeria Association Agreement and the EU-Korea Free Trade Agreement, the Economic Partnership Agreement between the EU and the Southern African Development Community, and the EU-Ukraine Association Agreement.[28] This may be explained, on the one hand, by the WTO Appellate Body being rendered dysfunctional and, on the other hand, by the EU positioning itself in a more 'assertive' way internationally,[29] including a preparedness 'to initiate bilateral dispute settlement' under its preferential trade agreements.[30]

Fifth, the UK was still a Member State of the EU in 2008. As Bronckers relates in his article, there were 'practitioner scholars' who argued that if the CJEU accorded direct effect to international agreements, this would 'circumscribe the EC's growing negotiating power too much'.[31] Through its economy, but also its diplomatic and

11/1080, final perambulatory clause; and Comprehensive Economic and Trade Agreement (CETA) between Canada, of the one part, and the European Union and its Member States, of the other part, O.J. 2017, L 11/1079.

24. Jackson, *The World Trading System: Law and Policy of International Economic Relations*, 2nd ed. (MIT Press, 1997), at 124.
25. *See* Creamer, 'From the WTO's crown jewel to its crown of thorns', 113 *American Journal of International Law Unbound* (2019), 51-55.
26. Bronckers, *supra* note 2, at 895.
27. *See* generally Vidigal, 'Why is there so little litigation under Free Trade Agreements? Retaliation and adjudication in international dispute settlement', 20 *Journal of International Economic Law* (2017), 927-950.
28. *See* ec.europa.eu/trade/policy/accessing-markets/dispute-settlement/bilateral-disputes/ (last visited February 2023).
29. JOIN(2021)3 final, 'Joint communication to the European Parliament and the Council on strengthening the EU's contribution to rules-based multilateralism', 17 February 2021, at 1.
30. COM(2021)654 final, 'Report from the Commission to the European Parliament, the Council, the European Economic and Social Committee and the Committee of the Regions on Implementation and Enforcement of EU Trade Agreements', 27 October 2021, at 14.
31. Bronckers, *supra* note 2, at 895; referring to Bronckers and Kuijper, 'WTO law in the European Court of Justice', 42 *Common Market Law Review* (2005), 1313-1355, at 1317-1323.

military clout, the UK contributed significantly to the EU's power as an increasingly prominent actor on the international stage. Rather than a contributor to the EU's power, the UK has now become an 'object of EU external action'[32] and thus its (remaining) negotiating power. Their relations are now governed by international law, including dispute settlement procedures.

3 AN OVERVIEW OF POST-BREXIT DISPUTE SETTLEMENT ARRANGEMENTS

Given that, first, post-Brexit law is international law, second, that it features different forms of involvement of the CJEU, and, third, that parts of it are clearly inspired by the WTO's dispute settlement mechanism, it serves as a fresh terrain for legal research that can benefit from Bronckers' scholarship. Before applying a 'Bronckersian' lens to post-Brexit law, this section provides a brief overview of its dispute settlement arrangements.

Post-Brexit law consists chiefly of the Trade and Cooperation Agreement (TCA)[33] and the Withdrawal Agreement,[34] of which the contested Protocol on Ireland/Northern Ireland is an integral part.[35] Both are 'non-mixed' agreements, meaning that they have been concluded by the EU and UK, without the EU Member States as parties. These international agreements now governing EU-UK relations have created a set of institutions and interlocking dispute settlement arrangements. The following paragraphs outline the main similarities and differences between the post-Brexit agreements on the one hand, and the WTO and bilateral trade agreement concluded by the EU on the other. It should be noted that the dispute settlement provisions in the Withdrawal Agreement and TCA contain many special rules and exceptions, which are beyond the scope of this chapter.[36]

Both the Withdrawal Agreement and the TCA have an institutional setup that strongly resembles that of other trade agreements the EU concluded with external

32. Larik, 'EU external relations law and Brexit: "When Pluto was a planet"', 4 *Europe and the World: A Law Review* (2020), 1-18, at 2.
33. Trade and Cooperation Agreement between the European Union and the European Atomic Energy Community, of the one part, and the United Kingdom of Great Britain and Northern Ireland, of the other part, O.J. 2021, L 149/10 (hereinafter: TCA).
34. Agreement on the withdrawal of the United Kingdom of Great Britain and Northern Ireland from the European Union and the European Atomic Energy Community, O.J. 2020, L 29/7 (hereinafter: Withdrawal Agreement).
35. Article 182 Withdrawal Agreement. The Protocol will hereinafter be referred to as Northern Ireland Protocol. The Withdrawal Agreement also contains Protocols on the UK's sovereign base areas in Cyprus and on Gibraltar. The former provides for the CJEU's jurisdiction (Article 12 Protocol on the UK's Sovereign Base Areas in Cyprus). The latter does not.
36. *See* for detailed analyses on the Withdrawal Agreement, Peers, 'The end: Or a new beginning? The EU/UK Withdrawal Agreement', 39 *Yearbook of Economic Law* (2020), 122-198, at 181-197; and Larik, 'Decision-making and dispute settlement', in Fabbrini (Ed.), *The Law and Politics of Brexit: Volume II – The Withdrawal Agreement* (OUP, 2020), pp. 191-210; on the Northern Ireland Protocol, Wouters, 'Dispute settlement', in McCrudden (Ed.), *The Law and Practice of the Ireland-Northern Ireland Protocol* (CUP, 2022), pp. 55-65; and on the TCA, Levrat, 'Governance: managing bilateral relations', in Fabbrini (Ed.), *The Law and Politics of Brexit: Volume III – The Framework of New EU-UK Relations* (OUP, 2021), pp. 219-239.

partners. There is an overarching governance body called the 'Joint Committee' in the Withdrawal Agreement and the 'Partnership Council' in the TCA, followed by various specialized committees. These bodies include representatives from both sides.[37] Decisions are made by mutual consent.[38]

Regarding the dispute settlement procedures under the Withdrawal Agreement and the TCA, both exhibit similarities to the WTO's Dispute Settlement Understanding (DSU)[39] and other EU trade agreements. Disputes are first to be resolved through consultations in the political apex bodies 'with the aim of reaching a mutually agreed solution'.[40] If the dispute cannot be resolved through consultations, each party can request the dispute to be taken to arbitration.[41]

In case the arbitral tribunal confirms that obligations under the respective agreement have been breached, the tribunal can impose 'a lump sum or penalty payment'[42] (in the words of the Withdrawal Agreement) or 'temporary compensation'[43] (in the words of the TCA) on the respondent party. In case of continued non-compliance, the complaining party may suspend obligations under the respective agreement that are 'proportionate to the breach of obligation concerned'[44] (in the words of the Withdrawal Agreement) or to a 'level equivalent to the nullification or impairment caused by the violation' (in the words of the TCA).[45] A notable exception is Part Two of the Withdrawal Agreement on citizens' rights, which may not be suspended.[46] Similarly, only certain parts of the TCA belong to the 'covered provisions' to which the general dispute settlement procedures,[47] including the possibility to adopt suspensions,[48] apply. If the respondent party considers the level of suspension excessive, it may challenge the measures taken by the complaining party before the arbitral tribunal.[49]

37. Article 164(1) Withdrawal Agreement (for the Joint Committee); Article 7(1) TCA (for the Partnership Council). There are also possibilities to include Member State representatives on the EU's side, and representatives from the UK's devolved administrations.
38. Article 10(2) Withdrawal Agreement (for the Partnership Council and Committees); Article 166(3) TCA (for the Joint Committee).
39. Uruguay Round of Multilateral Trade Negotiations (1986-1994) - Annex 2: Understanding on Rules and Procedures Governing the Settlement of Disputes (WTO), O.J. 1994, L 336/234 (hereinafter: DSU). Unlike in the DSU, neither EU trade agreements, nor the Withdrawal Agreement or the TCA provide for an appellate body-type organ.
40. Article 169(1) Withdrawal Agreement; Article 738(1) TCA. The continued possibility to resolve a dispute by mutually agreed solution throughout the dispute settlement process is explicitly mentioned in Article 699 TCA. A similar reference is not included in the Withdrawal Agreement. The arbitral panel under the TCA should even 'provide adequate opportunities' for the parties to develop such a solution, Article 742(c) TCA, which is very similar to Article 11 DSU. A similar reference to that effect is similarly missing from the Withdrawal Agreement.
41. Article 170(1) Withdrawal Agreement; Article 739(1) TCA.
42. Article 178(1) Withdrawal Agreement.
43. Article 749 TCA.
44. Article 178(2)(2) Withdrawal Agreement.
45. Article 749(5) TCA.
46. Article 178(2)(a) Withdrawal Agreement.
47. Article 375(2) TCA. Importantly, Part Two of the TCA on trade, transport, fisheries and other arrangements is part of the 'covered provisions'.
48. Article 749(4) TCA.
49. Article 178(3) Withdrawal Agreement; Article 749(11) TCA.

Notably, post-Brexit law also provides the possibility of suspending obligations under the TCA for violations of the Withdrawal Agreement. In cases of persistent non-compliance with obligations under the Withdrawal Agreement, the complainant can opt for suspending 'parts of any other agreement between the Union and the United Kingdom under the conditions set out in that agreement'.[50] While the possibility of 'cross-retaliation' is well known in the WTO context,[51] it acquires special significance in the post-Brexit arrangements since the Withdrawal Agreement is not a trade agreement. Restricting market access is used here to enforce different types of obligations, including citizens' rights and the Northern Ireland Protocol.

Regarding the Withdrawal Agreement, there are some marked differences with 'traditional' dispute settlement in the style of the WTO and trade agreements. This is not surprising given that the Withdrawal Agreement is not a traditional trade agreement but instead, an agreement of a peculiar and unprecedented type, being the first to be negotiated under Article 50 of the TEU with a view to ensuring an orderly exit from the EU while protecting certain pre-existing rights, notably those of EU citizens that were already living in the UK, and British subjects already living in the EU (to which Part Two of the Withdrawal Agreement is dedicated).

What is perhaps surprising is the continued role of the CJEU under the Withdrawal Agreement and, in particular, the Northern Ireland Protocol. During the transition period, which lasted from 1 February until 31 December 2020, the CJEU, alongside other EU institutions and bodies, continued to wield powers over the UK to a very large extent as if the latter were still a Member State,[52] even though it was no longer represented in the EU's institutions. This included the continued jurisdiction of the CJEU, with the possibility for UK courts to submit requests for preliminary rulings and the possibility for the European Commission to launch infringement proceedings against the UK. Beyond the transition period, the CJEU retains jurisdiction in certain respects. This includes jurisdiction to give preliminary rulings on Part Two of the Withdrawal Agreement on citizens' rights for eight more years after the end of the transition.[53]

The position of Northern Ireland and the preservation of the peace process under the Good Friday Agreement was one of the most contentious points in the negotiations.[54] The Northern Ireland Protocol reflects this, with the region having left the EU together with the rest of the UK and being explicitly named a part of the UK's customs

50. Article 178(2)(1)(b) Withdrawal Agreement.
51. Article 22(3)(c) DSU, which allows cross-retaliation only if the complaining party 'considers that it is not practicable or effective to suspend concessions or other obligations with respect to other sectors under the same agreement, and that the circumstances are serious enough'. The Withdrawal Agreement (Article 178(2)(2) demands that the complainant first consider whether the suspension of parts of the Withdrawal Agreement 'would be an appropriate response to the breach' and that any suspension be 'proportionate'. Under the TCA, only 'covered provisions' of the TCA listed in Article 735 TCA can be suspended during dispute settlement proceedings, *see* Article 749(2) TCA, with additional conditions stipulated in Article 749(3) TCA.
52. Article 131 Withdrawal Agreement.
53. Article 158 Withdrawal Agreement.
54. Terhechte, 'Strukturen und Probleme des Brexit-Abkommens', (2020) NJW, 425-430, at 426; *see* further Doyle and Connolly, 'Brexit and the Northern Ireland question', in Fabbrini (Ed.), *The Law and Politics of Brexit* (OUP, 2017), pp. 139-159.

territory.[55] At the same time, it remains part of the EU's single market for goods. According to the Protocol, the relevant EU legislation, which is referenced in the annexes to the Protocol, continues to be applicable to Northern Ireland. To make sure of this, 'the institutions, bodies, offices, and agencies of the Union shall in relation to the United Kingdom and natural and legal persons residing or established in the territory of the United Kingdom have the powers conferred upon them by Union law'.[56] This includes the continued jurisdiction of the CJEU. Even though only the jurisdiction to provide preliminary rulings is mentioned explicitly, seeing the wording of the provision, it is plausible that this should also include the right of the European Commission to bring infringement proceedings against the UK.[57]

The Northern Ireland Protocol is designed to be of indefinite application. Only in case the Northern Ireland Assembly votes to withhold democratic support from it, which it can do at first in 2024, then the relevant provisions will be suspended.[58] Ever since its adoption, the UK government has pushed for the Protocol to be amended. In particular, the continued role of the CJEU is to be scrapped.[59]

4 THE CJEU IN POST-BREXIT LAW: A 'BRONCKERSIAN' ANALYSIS

It becomes apparent from the above overview that post-Brexit law evokes core themes of Bronckers' reflections on the idea of giving effect to international law beyond direct effect and of the role of the CJEU vis-à-vis international courts. Hence, the present section conducts what could be called a 'Bronckersian' analysis to post-Brexit law as a new subgenre of EU external relations and international law binding the EU. The main themes are direct effect (and lack thereof), consistent interpretation, 'muted dialogue', and claims for damages.[60]

55. Article 4(1) Northern Ireland Protocol.
56. Article 12(4) Northern Ireland Protocol.
57. Wouters, *supra* note 36, at 56; Larik, 'Governance and dispute settlement', in Fabbrini (Ed.), *The Law and Politics of Brexit: Volume IV – The Protocol on Ireland / Northern Ireland* (OUP, 2022), pp. 211-230. The European Commission already commenced, but later paused, infringement proceedings against the UK under the Protocol in March 2021, *see* European Commission, Letter from Vice-President Šefčovič to David Frost, Brussels, 15 March 2021, commission .europa.eu/system/files/2021-03/lettre_to_lord_frost_1532021_en.pdf (last visited 2023).
58. Article 18 Northern Ireland Protocol.
59. HM Government, 'Northern Ireland Protocol: the way forward', CP 502, July 2021, at point 67: 'It is highly unusual in international affairs for one party to a treaty to subject itself to the jurisdiction of the institutions of the other, all the more so when the arrangements concerned are designed to mediate the sui generis relationship between the EU and its Member States. The UK refused to accept this in the negotiations on the Trade and Cooperation Agreement, and only agreed to it in the Protocol because of the very specific circumstances of that negotiation.'
60. In the 2008 article, Bronckers also uses the category 'other substantiation' of EU law principles, Bronckers, *supra* note 2, at 890-891. However, for the present analysis, this scenario can be considered to be covered by the section on 'muted dialogue'.

4.1 Direct Effect (and Lack Thereof)

Bronckers' suspicion that the WTO agreements would not remain the exception to the CJEU's doctrine of denying direct effect has already been vindicated in general terms. Post-Brexit law, however, sends a mixed message.

The TCA generally denies direct effect. With two exceptions:

> nothing in this Agreement or any supplementing agreement shall be construed as conferring rights or imposing obligations on persons other than those created between the Parties under public international law, nor as permitting this Agreement or any supplementing agreement to be directly invoked in the domestic legal systems of the Parties.[61]

The two exceptions are individual rights protected by the Protocol on Social Security Coordination[62] and the TCA's Part Three on law enforcement and judicial cooperation in criminal matters, but only with regard to the EU. This confirms the prior trend that both multilateral and bilateral trade agreements concluded by the EU lack direct effect. At the same time, the TCA creates an exception to the exception for non-trade parts of the TCA.[63]

By contrast, the possibility for direct effect is the rule for the Withdrawal Agreement:

> The provisions of this Agreement and the provisions of Union law made applicable by this Agreement shall produce in respect of and in the United Kingdom the same legal effects as those which they produce within the Union and its Member States.
>
> Accordingly, legal or natural persons shall, in particular, be able to rely directly on the provisions contained or referred to in this Agreement which meet the conditions for direct effect under Union law.[64]

This does not mean that the Withdrawal Agreement as a whole has direct effect. The conditions under EU law for a provision needing to be 'unconditional and sufficiently clear and precise'[65] apply. Still, the 'nature and board logic' of the Withdrawal Agreement is thus such as to allow for direct effect. This is perhaps not entirely surprising given that the agreement is about 'disentangling legal orders',[66] which were characterized by direct effect and hence need, to some extent, continued protection. As the EU-UK Withdrawal Agreement is the first of its kind, being negotiated under Article 50 TEU, this is a significant development as a new category of

61. Article 5(1) TCA. Article 5(2), furthermore, states that a 'Party shall not provide for a right of action under its law against the other Party on the ground that the other Party has acted in breach of this Agreement or any supplementing agreement.'
62. Article 67 Protocol on Social Security Coordination (SSC).
63. By way of comparison, the EU-Ukraine Association Agreement does not include parts of either social security or law enforcement and judicial cooperation.
64. Article 4(1) Withdrawal Agreement. Article 4(2) clarifies that the UK 'shall ensure compliance with paragraph 1, including as regards the required powers of its judicial and administrative authorities to disapply inconsistent or incompatible domestic provisions, through domestic primary legislation'.
65. Case 9/70, *Franz Grad v. Finanzamt Traunstein*, ECLI:EU:C:1970:78, para. 9.
66. Odermatt, 'Brexit and international law: Disentangling legal orders', 31 *Emory International Law Review* (2017), 1051-1073.

international agreements exempted from the broader trend of denying direct effect (though, of course, the EU will not intend to launch a series of such agreements in the future).

An important case of 'Union law made applicable by this Agreement' is the Northern Ireland Protocol. The Protocol contains provisions on the region's continued participation in the EU's single market for goods. This concerns chiefly rules on the movement of goods and customs, technical regulations and certificates, value added tax and excise, the single electricity market and State aid.[67] For each of these areas, the Protocol includes an annex with references to EU legislation that continue to apply to Northern Ireland. Regarding the provisions of the Protocol and EU law applicable by virtue of it, the Protocol affirms the possibility of direct effect.[68] As the Protocol specifies, this includes the CJEU's jurisdiction.

Of course, these are the treaty provisions as agreed upon by the EU and UK. Case law from the CJEU would have to confirm the granting and denial of direct effect of provisions of these agreements. Seeing, however, how the CJEU in the past has referred to Council decisions on the conclusion of international agreements and the text of agreements in its determination of whether provisions of an agreement can produce direct effect,[69] it is likely to follow the explicit language from the agreements on these points.

4.2 Consistent Interpretation

In post-Brexit law, consistent interpretation may open the possibility for private litigants to reap benefits from international commitments that lack direct effect. Furthermore, the question about its relationship with WTO law, to which both the EU and the UK remain bound, is raised. In addition, post-Brexit law also shows how this doctrine can be flipped, i.e., prompting international tribunals to interpret the EU-UK agreements as much as possible in conformity with EU law and CJEU case law.

Bronckers defined consistent interpretation as a willingness of the CJEU to interpret EU law 'as much as possible in conformity with WTO law',[70] though it can also be applied to international law binding the EU in general. Bronckers refers to CJEU rulings in the context of the WTO and of other international agreements, where explicit reference to international legal obligations and the need to interpret EU law in conformity with them is made.[71] The CJEU still espouses this doctrine,[72] even though its explicit references to WTO case law are not so frequent.

67. Articles 5 and 7-10 Northern Ireland Protocol.
68. Article 12(5) Northern Ireland Protocol.
69. Case C-149/96, *Portugal v. Council*, ECLI:EU:C:1999:574, para. 48; and Opinion 1/17 *CETA*, ECLI:EU:C:2019:341, para. 198.
70. Bronckers, *supra* note 2, at 888.
71. *Ibid.*; *see, e.g.*, Case C-286/90, *Poulsen and Diva Navigation*, ECLI:EU:C:1992:453; and Case C-245/02, *Anheuser-Busch v. Budvar*, ECLI:EU:C:2004:717, at para. 49 (interpreting national trademark law consistently with the Agreement on Trade-Related Aspects of Intellectual Property Rights (TRIPS Agreement)).
72. Casolari, 'Giving indirect effect to international law within the EU legal order: The doctrine of consistent interpretation', in Cannizzaro, Palchetti and Wessel (Eds), *International Law as Law of the European Union* (Brill | Nijhoff, 2012), pp. 395-415.

In the TCA, EU law and the CJEU are virtually absent.[73] Here, the classic questions of giving it effect in the EU's legal order in the absence of direct effect and its relationship to WTO law re-emerge. Given the explicit denial of private rights under most of the TCA, private litigants, especially from the business community, may still be able to benefit to a certain degree from the commitments made by the EU and UK under the TCA due to the CJEU's doctrine of consistent interpretation.

Concerning the relationship with WTO law, the TCA establishes a free trade area between the EU and the UK in the sense of Article XXIV of the General Agreement on Tariffs and Trade 1994 and Article V of the General Agreement on Trade in Services (GATS).[74] The EU and the UK 'affirm their rights and obligations with respect to each other under the WTO Agreement and other agreements to which they are party'.[75] For disputes relating to obligations under the TCA 'and of a substantially equivalent obligation under another international agreement to which both Parties are party, including the WTO Agreement', the EU and the UK need to choose and stick with one forum.[76]

Regarding Part Two of the TCA, which focuses on trade, the TCA notes that the 'interpretation and application of the provisions of this Part shall take into account relevant interpretations in reports of WTO panels and of the Appellate Body adopted by the Dispute Settlement Body of the WTO as well as in arbitration awards under the Dispute Settlement Understanding'.[77] Thus, consistent interpretation of the TCA also means ensuring consistency with WTO law and case law.

Under the Withdrawal Agreement, in addition to the explicit possibility for direct effect mentioned above, the CJEU will be able to interpret EU law consistently with its provisions. The Court has referred to the Withdrawal Agreement already in several judgments in cases still covered by the transition period, which extended the CJEU's jurisdiction in general.[78] As the CJEU retains jurisdiction beyond the transition in important areas such as citizens' rights (for eight years) and parts of the Northern Ireland Protocol, the emergence of more CJEU case law and, thus, opportunities for practising consistent interpretation are likely.

In addition, the Withdrawal Agreement provides obligations and mechanisms to ensure its provisions are interpreted consistently with relevant EU law. Article 4 of the Withdrawal Agreement stipulates that provisions 'referring to Union law or to concepts or provisions thereof shall be interpreted and applied in accordance with the methods and general principles of Union law'.[79] Furthermore, these provisions 'shall in their

73. The only time the CJEU is mentioned in the TCA is in Article 728 concerning recovery and enforcement of financial interests.
74. Article 514 TCA.
75. Article 515 TCA.
76. Article 737(1) and (2) TCA.
77. Article 516 TCA. *See* for additional references to WTO law also Article 220 TCA on the TRIPS Agreement and Article 378 TCA with a reference to the GATS.
78. *See, e.g.*, Case C-276/19, *Commission v. United Kingdom*, ECLI:EU:C:2020:368; *see* further Peers, *supra* note 36, at 182-183.
79. Article 4(3) Withdrawal Agreement.

implementation and application be interpreted in conformity with the relevant case law of the Court of Justice of the European Union handed down before the end of the transition period'.[80] The UK's 'judicial and administrative authorities shall have due regard'[81] to case law handed down after the end of the transition period.

Furthermore, even in the Withdrawal Agreement's dispute settlement mechanism based on arbitration, the Court of Justice 'makes a surprise comeback'[82] in the service of such consistent interpretation with EU law, including CJEU case law. Where a dispute brought to arbitration:

> raises a question of interpretation of a concept of Union law, a question of interpretation of a provision of Union law referred to in this Agreement ... the arbitration panel shall not decide on any such question. In such case, it shall request the Court of Justice of the European Union to give a ruling on the question. The Court of Justice of the European Union shall have jurisdiction to give such a ruling which shall be binding on the arbitration panel.[83]

It is for the arbitral panel to make the request. The EU (or the UK, for that matter) cannot force it to do so.[84] However, the panel must provide a reasoned assessment for not making such a request if prompted to do so by either party. Parties can ask the panel to review its assessment.

These provisions on what could be called 'reverse consistent interpretation' are not dissimilar from the ones under the Agreement on the European Economic Area (EEA), which perhaps even inspired the TCA's. First, there is the obligation that provisions of the EEA Agreement that are identical in substance to those under the EU Treaties and secondary legislation, 'in their implementation and application, be interpreted in conformity with the relevant rulings of the Court of Justice ... given prior to the date of signature of this Agreement'.[85] Later CJEU case law shall be given 'due account'.[86] Second, the CJEU 'can be asked to interpret the relevant rules' of EU law.[87] However, an important difference here is that such an issue is first brought before the EEA Joint Committee as a diplomatic forum. Only if the dispute cannot be resolved in a timely manner there, then the 'Contracting Parties to the dispute may agree to request the Court of Justice ... to give a ruling on the interpretation of the relevant rules.'[88] In other words, mutual consent is required to bring in the CJEU under the EEA Agreement. Under the Withdrawal Agreement, this decision is at the discretion of the arbitral tribunal and cannot be blocked by either the EU or the UK.

80. Article 4(4) Withdrawal Agreement.
81. Article 4(5) Withdrawal Agreement.
82. Wouters, *supra* note 36, at 62.
83. Article 174(1) Withdrawal Agreement.
84. Larik, *supra* note 36, at 207.
85. Article 6 Agreement on the European Economic Area, O.J. 1994, L 1/3 (hereinafter: EEA Agreement).
86. Article 3(2) Agreement between the EFTA States on the Establishment of a Surveillance Authority and a Court of Justice, O.J. 1994, L 344/1.
87. Bronckers, 'The relationship of the EC Courts with other international tribunals: Non-committal, respectful or submissive?', 44 *Common Market Law Review* (2007), 601-627, at 607.
88. Article 111(3) EEA Agreement.

With regard to the Northern Ireland Protocol, post-Brexit law even reproduced a turbocharged version of homogeneity compared to that of EEA law. As noted above, large parts of EU law are made applicable through the Protocol. Whenever this legislation is amended, in the process of 'dynamic alignment',[89] the amendments become directly applicable under the Protocol without intervention or a possibility of blocking by the UK.[90] By contrast, under the EEA Agreement, the non-EU countries are accorded a decision-shaping role, and consensus within the EEA Joint Committee is required to realign EEA law with developments in EU legislation.[91]

4.3 Muted Dialogue

The concept of 'muted dialogue' developed by Bronckers captures cases where the CJEU does not explicitly rely on relevant WTO rulings when interpreting EU law but where 'it seems a fair guess' that it has been influenced by WTO rulings and implicitly strives 'to avoid inconsistencies'.[92] Bronckers named examples where CJEU judgments 'can be read as an effort to avoid inconsistencies with the WTO Appellate Body'.[93]

Ever since Bronckers' article, the CJEU seems to have continued this type of muted dialogue with the WTO Appellate Body – at least while the latter was still issuing reports before it was rendered dysfunctional in December 2019 by the US. A more recent case of muted dialogue is that of *Philips Lightning*. The Advocate General in the case had argued for consistent interpretation, using specific references to relevant Appellate Body reports.[94] The Court adopted the same interpretation but without these references.[95]

In post-Brexit law, muted dialogue remains a possibility. However, there are two caveats. First, it would require a body of case law from the arbitral tribunals under the Withdrawal Agreement and TCA that could actually influence CJEU rulings without the CJEU making explicit reference to it. While this is difficult to predict, there are some signs making the emergence of such case law plausible. There is the above-mentioned turn by the EU towards a more active approach when it comes to using dispute settlement mechanisms under bilateral trade agreements. In addition, in the context of the disputes over the Northern Ireland Protocol, the European Commission had already taken the first step towards arbitration (alongside infringement proceedings) in March 2021. Whether, however, the post-Brexit framework will generate enough case law by

89. Hayward, 'The Committees of the Protocol', in McCrudden (Ed.), *supra* note 36, pp. 44-54.
90. Article 13(3) Northern Ireland Protocol. By contrast, for new legislation which the EU would like to become applicable with regard to Northern Ireland, the UK's consent in the Withdrawal Agreement's Joint Committee is necessary, *see* Article 13(4) Northern Ireland Protocol.
91. Articles 99-104 EEA Agreement; *see* further Holter, 'Legislative homogeneity', in Baudenbacher (Ed.), *The Fundamental Principles of EEA Law* (Springer, 2017), pp. 1-17, at 8-10.
92. Bronckers, *supra* note 2, at 889.
93. *Ibid.*, at 890.
94. Case C-511/13 P, *Philips Lighting*, Opinion of AG Bot, ECLI:EU:C:2015:553, para. 132.
95. Case C-511/13 P, *Philips Lighting*, ECLI:EU:C:2015:553, para. 72. *See* Zang, 'Shall we talk? Judicial communication between the CJEU and WTO dispute settlement', 28 *European Journal of International Law* (2017), 273-293, at 286-287.

arbitral tribunals for the CJEU to engage in a sustained 'muted dialogue' rather than an occasional 'muted nod' remains to be seen.

The second caveat concerns case law from arbitral tribunals under the Withdrawal Agreement in particular. Since, as noted above, there is a built-in mechanism for involving the CJEU on questions of EU law, the CJEU is arguably dialoguing with itself here, with the arbitral tribunal as the intermediary. Hence, the question can be raised why such a dialogue would remain muted. With the arbitral tribunal being bound by the interpretations furnished by the CJEU, the CJEU could simply acknowledge that explicitly in its own case law involving interpretations of EU law in line with the Withdrawal Agreement. If, by contrast, the CJEU simply referred to its own case law without acknowledging arbitral tribunal rulings, which have taken the interpretations it furnished on board, this would hardly qualify as a dialogue at all.

4.4 Actions for Damages

Next to claims for invalidating or reinterpreting secondary EU law that is inconsistent with international law obligations, the possibility of claiming financial damages for both contractual and non-contractual liability has been raised.[96] Whether businesses that suffered economic damage from US tariffs adopted as part of a dispute with the EU, in which the latter was found to be in violation of its WTO obligations, can claim such damages, came to a head in the *FIAMM and Fedon* case.[97] This case was still 'very recent'[98] at the time of Bronckers' article but is now part of the canon of EU external relations law. According to the CJEU, no such right to being compensated exists.

In the post-Brexit framework, this question has gained new salience as 'innocent bystanders'[99] across the EU and the UK could find themselves in the crossfire of trade wars between the two. As noted earlier, these are possible not only under the TCA's 'covered provisions' but also under the Withdrawal Agreement, as persistent non-compliance with the latter can also lead to suspension of parts of the TCA.

Bronckers put forward that even where the EU is acting lawfully under international law, compensation for damages suffered by trade restrictions 'for the benefit of the public good as a whole' might be justifiable under what is called the *Sonderopfertheorie* in German and *égalité devant les charges publiques* in French.[100] Advocate General Maduro had proposed a number of conditions for qualifying for compensation in a 'no-fault' liability scenario in his opinion in *FIAMM and Fedon*.[101]

96. Article 340(1) and (2) Treaty on the Functioning of the European Union (TFEU).
97. Joined Cases C-120/06 P and C-121/06 P, *FIAMM and Fedon*, ECLI:EU:C:2008:476.
98. Bronckers, *supra* note 2, at 891.
99. Dani, 'Remedying European legal pluralism: The *FIAMM* and *Fedon* litigation and the judicial protection of international trade bystanders', 21 *European Journal of International Law* (2010), 303-340, at 309.
100. Bronckers, *supra* note 2, at 892.
101. Joined Cases C-120/06 P and C-121/06 P, *FIAMM and Fedon*, Opinion of AG Poiares Maduro, ECLI:EU:C:2008:98, paras 57-63.

In the post-Brexit context, this idea is worth being rediscovered. For instance, given the tenacity of disputes over Northern Ireland, an escalating dispute between the EU and the UK could lead to importers and consumers across the EU, who may have no link whatsoever to Northern Ireland, suffering damages through trade restrictions. While the EU would be acting here in the service of 'higher goods' such as the protection of its internal market and safeguarding the peace process under the Good Friday Agreement, it might be both just and politically wise to indemnify 'innocent bystanders' with a view to protecting EU cohesion and solidarity in its approach to the UK. Nevertheless, to the extent that the EU is already providing financial assistance to offset damages caused by Brexit, such as the Brexit Adjustment Reserve,[102] a legally enforceable right would not be necessary.

5 CONCLUSION

Brexit and its legal aftermath are one of the areas where Marco Bronckers' scholarship will remain of the utmost relevance and usefulness, as this chapter has attempted to demonstrate. The world of 2023 is different from that of 2008 in several key respects. The European Community is no more, having been absorbed by the post-Lisbon EU, the WTO Appellate Body is out of operation, and the UK has left the EU. In February 2022, large-scale interstate war returned to Europe with Russia's war of aggression against Ukraine, making reflections on both the EU's international position and contributions to the international legal order even more urgent.

At the same time, the major trends identified by Bronckers have continued. In particular, the CJEU has continued to find other ways to give effect to international law beyond direct effect. In the context of the post-Brexit legal arrangements, this ought to be remembered as the TCA, which is supposed to create 'an area of prosperity and good neighbourliness characterised by close and peaceful relations based on cooperation'[103] between the EU and the UK, cannot be relied upon by individuals in court for the most part.

By contrast, the Withdrawal Agreement and its Northern Ireland Protocol provide a wide-ranging grant of direct effect and CJEU jurisdiction. Therefore, they represent a significant new exception to what is now the rule of denying direct effect to international agreements. Post-Brexit law also brings in other forms of muted and not-so-muted dialogues, building on, and learning from, previous practices such as the EEA Agreement. The UK's authorities and the international arbitral tribunals are bound to respect CJEU case law in important instances. The CJEU can furnish binding interpretations of questions of EU law. Last but not least, in the post-Brexit world, trade wars between the EU and its former Member State, which is also a large economy, have become a real possibility that should prompt us to resuscitate debates about

102. Regulation (EU) 2021/1755 of the European Parliament and of the Council of 6 October 2021 establishing the Brexit Adjustment Reserve, O.J. 2021, L 357/1.
103. Article 1 TCA.

compensating those who suffer damages for the 'greater good'. All of these are good reasons to keep studying, pondering, and applying the works of Marco Bronckers for many years to come.

CHAPTER 4

Trade and Sustainable Development Chapters in EU Free Trade Agreements: Just Best Efforts?*

*Jacques Bourgeois***

In a number of free trade agreements (FTAs) concluded by the European Union (EU) parties entered into commitments on trade and sustainable development (TSD). Linking non-trade values to the EU trade policy raises some questions, as does their effect on trade. In addition, the nature of these commitments and their enforcement call for comments. And is there any role for private parties?

A friendship that goes back to the 1980s allowed me to appreciate Marco Bronckers' sharp mind, intellectual rigour and a clear eye for what Lon Fuller called the 'internal morality' of the law – the requirements which determine the efficacy of a legal system –while at the same time being mindful of the 'external morality' of the law – how well a legal system expresses the substantive aims of the law.[1] He follows this approach in his dual capacity as a scholar and as a practising lawyer. He did so as a member of the Brussels Antitrust Group and continues to surprise the Working Group on the Law in International Economic Relations with revealing insights and challenging statements.

* This contribution was submitted in March 2022.

** The view expressed in this contribution are exclusively those of the author and do not necessarily reflect those of Sidley Austin LLP and its partners. This contribution has been prepared for academic purposes and does not constitute legal advice. The information it contains is not intended to create, and the receipt of it does not constitute, a lawyer-client relationship. Readers should not act upon this without seeking advice from professional advisers.

Celia Challet, teaching assistant at the College of Europe and doctoral candidate at the University of Ghent, provided invaluable assistance for which I am extremely grateful. Errors are mine.

1. Fuller, *The Morality of Law* (Yale University Press, 1969).

This *liber amicorum* for Marco Bronckers offers me the opportunity to highlight these qualities by commenting on some of the issues which Marco analysed with Giovanni Gruni in two seminal articles on labour standards and sustainability standards in European Union (EU) free trade agreements (FTAs).[2]

1 INTRODUCTION

This contribution is simply putting some touches on the picture both authors painted in these two articles. I will select some of the issues addressed and proposals made in these two articles. I will refer only to the Trade and Sustainable Development (TSD) clauses in 10 of the 11 'new generation' EU trade agreements,[3] leaving aside the EU-UK Trade and Cooperation Agreement.[4] They have generated much literature from academics and policy analysts.[5]

I will first deal with specific TSD clauses – their object, their inclusion in the EU's common commercial policy and their legal nature. I will then comment on their enforcement – the dispute settlement mechanism (DSM) and (the absence of) sanctions to end up with private parties' involvement.

2. Bronckers and Gruni, 'Taking the enforcement of labour standards in the EU's free trade agreements seriously', 56 *Common Market Law Review* (2019), 1591-1622; Bronckers and Gruni, 'Retooling the sustainability standards in EU free trade agreements', 24 *Journal of International Economic Law* (2021), 25-51. These contributions will be referred to as, respectively, Bronckers and Gruni (2019) and Bronckers and Gruni (2021).
3. Free trade Agreement between the European Union and its Member States, of the one part, and the Republic of Korea, of the other part, O.J. 2011, L 127/1 (EU-Korea FTA); Agreement establishing an Association between the European Union and its Member States, on the one hand, and Central America on the other, O.J. 2012, L 346/3 (EU-Central America FTA); Trade Agreement between the European Union and its Member States, of the one part, and Colombia and Peru, of the other part, O.J. 2012 L 354/3 (EU-Colombia and Peru FTA); Association Agreement between the European Union and its Member States, of the one part, and Ukraine, of the other part, O.J. 2014, L 161/3 (EU-Ukraine AA); Association Agreement between the European Union and the European Atomic Energy Community and their Member States, of the one part, and Georgia, of the other part, O.J. 2014, L 261/4 (EU-Georgia AA); Association Agreement between the European Union and the European Atomic Energy Community and their Member States, of the one part, and the Republic of Moldova, of the other part, O.J. 2014, L 260/4 (EU-Moldova AA); Comprehensive Economic and Trade Agreement (CETA) between Canada, of the one part, and the European Union and its Member States, of the other part, O.J. 2017, L 11/23; Strategic Partnership Agreement between the European Union and its Member States, of the one part, and Japan, of the other part, O.J. 218, L 216/4 (EU-Japan Strategic Partnership Agreement (SPA)); Free Trade Agreement between the European Union and the Republic of Singapore, O.J. 2019, L 294/4 (EU-Singapore FTA); Free Trade Agreement between the European Union and the Socialist Republic of Viet Nam, O.J. 2020, L 186/3 (EU-Vietnam FTA).
4. Trade and Cooperation Agreement between the European Union and the European Atomic Energy Community, of the one part, and the United Kingdom of Great Britain and Northern Ireland, of the other part, O.J. 2021 L 149/10 (TCA).
5. Suffice it to refer to the literature cited by Bronckers and Gruni (2019 and 2021), *supra* note 2. *See also* LSE, 'Comparative Analysis of TSD Provisions for Identification of Best Practices to Support the TSD Review', September 2019, trade.ec.europa.eu/doclib/docs/2021/september/tradoc_159810.pdf.

2 TSD CLAUSES IN THE NEW GENERATION EU FTAs

2.1 Object of the Clauses

In analysing the patchwork of the various environmental and labour standards in the 'new generation' FTAs, Marco and Giovanni have done a very useful exercise in classifying them. They separate them into three groups: obligations based on existing international agreements, obligations relating to existing domestic legislation and obligations referring to a higher level of protection.

Within the category of obligations based on existing international agreements, the authors identify different sub-groups of different obligations: (a) to ratify specific international agreements on labour and environmental protection (no EU FTA includes an obligation to ratify multilateral environmental agreements), (b) to respect, promote and realize fundamental principles, even where a party has not ratified the agreement elaborating such principles - this applies to International Labour Organization (ILO) conventions - and (c) to effectively implement the multilateral labour and environmental agreements which the FTA parties ratified.[6] Their classification is Ariadne's thread of the following comments.

2.2 TSD Obligations as Part of the EU's Trade Policy

In a great many communications, reports and even non-papers, the European Commission makes a case for 'linking values' to the EU's trade policy.[7] It describes this in terms of leveraging the strength of that policy to create incentives for FTA parties to implement non-trade values in their policies,[8] restore the support of civil society and other stakeholders in trade liberalization,[9] and create a level playing field by reducing the disparities between the costs of producing goods and services in each of the parties.[10] There is a debate on the wisdom of such linkage,[11] which is left aside here. The linkage, as such, raises some legal questions. Among these questions, I will leave

6. Bronckers and Gruni (2019), *supra* note 2, at 1595-1597; Bronckers and Gruni (2021), *supra* note 2, at 2-4. A disaggregated description is also provided in LSE, report cited *supra* note 5.
7. Starting with COM(2006)567 final, 'Global Europe: Competing in the world', to the latest trade policy review: COM(2021)66 final, 'Trade Policy Review - An Open, Sustainable and Assertive Trade Policy'.
8. *See*, in particular, 'Non paper - Feedback and way forward on improving the implementation and enforcement of Trade and Sustainable Development chapters in EU Free Trade Agreements', 26 February 2018; 'Strategic Plan 2020-2024 - Directorate-General for Trade', available at trade.ec.europa.eu/doclib/docs/2020/november/tradoc_159104.pdf; COM(2021)66 final, report cited *supra* note 7; COM(2021)654 final, '2021 Report on Implementation and Enforcement of EU Trade Agreements', at 17-20.
9. *Ibid.*
10. *See*, in particular, Commission Strategic Plan 2020-2024, cited *supra* note 8. For a recent example of the EU's commitment to ensuring such a level of playing field, *see* the TCA, recital 9.
11. *See* Pelkmans, 'Linking values to the EU trade policy - A good idea?', 26 *European Law Journal* (2020), 391-400 where, while being generally critical, the author argues that the linkages have to be much more carefully considered, justified and circumscribed. *See also* the literature cited in Mancini, 'Fundamental rights in the EU's external trade relations: From Promotion "through" trade agreements to protection "in" trade agreements', in Kassoti and Wessel (Eds), *EU Trade*

aside the justification under the Treaty on the Functioning of the European Union (TFEU) for pursuing non-trade values with the EU's trade policy powers[12] and limit myself to two questions.

The *first* one is to which of the specific obligations of the TSD chapter of the FTAs the trade link applies. The introductory provision of the TSD chapter of the EU-Korea FTA states that '[e]xcept as provided in this Chapter, this Chapter applies to measures adopted or maintained by the Parties affecting trade-related aspects of labour and environmental issues'.[13] The specific provisions on the obligation relating to existing domestic legislation contain explicit 'trade' language. The obligation is breached when a party fails to effectively enforce environmental and labour standards 'in a manner affecting trade or investment between the Parties'[14] or where a party weakens or reduces the environmental or labour protection to encourage trade and investment 'in a manner affecting trade and investment'.[15] Such explicit reference is absent where parties 'commit to respecting, promoting and realising the fundamental principles concerning the fundamental rights' of the ILO.[16] An explicit link to trade does not appear either in the clause on the obligation to 'make continued and sustained efforts towards ratifying the fundamental ILO Conventions'[17] and on the obligation of 'effective implementation of the multilateral environmental agreements to which they are party'.[18]

The Panel of Experts on the EU's complaint against Korea was faced with the apparent inconsistency between the introductory provision generally stating that the TSD chapter concerns measures affecting trade-related aspects, except as provided in that chapter (Article 13.2.1) and specific clauses in that chapter that contain a requirement on affecting trade. Why repeat it in certain specific clauses and leave it out in another clause (Article 13.4.3)? It may well have been a 'constructive ambiguity' of negotiators to allow the negotiation to proceed without agreement on this specific point. The Panel resolved this by construing Article 13.4.1 as an exception to the

---

Agreements and the Duty to Respect Human Rights Abroad, CLEER Paper 2020/1 (Asser Institute, 2020), footnotes 57 and 58.

12. *See*, among others, the 'unpacking' of the combined reading of Articles 207 TFEU, 21(1) Treaty on European Union (TEU) and 3(5) TEU by Mancini, *supra* note 11, at 115; Vedder, 'Linkage of the Common Commercial Policy to the general objectives of the Union's external action', in Bungenberg and Hermann (Eds), *Common Commercial Policy after Lisbon* (Springer, 2013), pp. 115-144; Cooreman and Van Calster, 'Trade and sustainable development post-Lisbon', in Hahn and Van der Loo, *Law and Practice of the Common Commercial Policy* (Brill | Nijhoff, 2020), pp. 187-205.
13. Article 13.2.1 EU-Korea FTA. There is no such introductory provision in the other 'new generation' EU FTAs.
14. Article 13.7.1 EU-Korea FTA; Article 291.3 EU-CA FTA; Article 277.2 EU-Colombia and Peru FTA; Article 296.1 EU-Ukraine AA; Article 12.12.2 EU-Singapore FTA. Interestingly, several other FTAs use a different wording and specify that 'a party shall not, through a sustained or recurring course of action or inaction, fail to effectively enforce its environmental and labour law, as an encouragement for trade or investment' (Article 371 EU-Moldova FTA; Articles 23.4 and 24.5 CETA; Article 13.3 EU-Vietnam FTA). The EU-Japan SPA does not contain either of the wordings.
15. Article 13.7.2 EU-Korea FTA; Article 296.2 EU-Ukraine AA.
16. Article 13.4.3 EU-Korea FTA.
17. Article 13.4.3 EU-Korea FTA.
18. Article 13.5.2 EU-Korea FTA.

general rule of Article 13.2.1. Relying on the text read in context, in light of the object and purpose of the TSD Chapter, it concluded that Article 13.4.3. applies to measures irrespective of their affecting trade-related aspects.[19] This is doubtlessly the most significant outcome of the Panel Report, which 'confounded expectations'[20] by asserting that the Panel had jurisdiction to consider a breach of core labour standards.

The *second question* is how the 'trade' language is to be interpreted. As Marco and Giovanni demonstrate in relation to the non-regression and the not-weakening clause,[21] the '(affecting) trade' language puts the interpreter between a rock and a hard place. On the one hand, proving a low threshold could have a far-reaching impact on the policy space parties may need to adapt their labour or environmental laws when faced with certain overriding public needs. And this is while the FTAs do not generally make exceptions to the TSD obligations in order to protect such public needs. Some refer to (part of) Article XX GATT,[22] while others contain a wording that echoes the same principles.[23] On the other hand, proving a high threshold may render the obligations illusory.

Some guidance can perhaps be found by ascertaining the purpose behind the inclusion of the '(affecting) trade' language.[24] Is it designed as a condition to which the inclusion in the FTAs is subject? This appears, for example, to be the case for obligations relating to the activities restricting competition 'as far as they may affect trade'.[25] Or is the trade effect one of the elements defining the obligation itself? This is, for instance, the case for the obligation on subsidies - other than export subsidies - which are prohibited by the World Trade Organization (WTO) Agreement on Subsidies and Countervailing Measures (SCMA) if they cause qualified adverse effects to the interests of other WTO Members.[26]

---

19. Report of the Panel of Experts, Proceeding constituted under Article 13.5. of the EU-Korea Free Trade Agreement, 20 January 2021 (EU-Korea Panel Report), available at trade.ec.europa.eu/doclib/docs/2021/january/tradoc_159358.pdf, paras 63 et seq.
20. Novitz, 'Enforceable social clauses in trade agreements with "bite"? Implications of the EU-South Korea Panel of Experts Report of 20 January 2021' (ETUI Policy Brief, 2021).
21. Bronckers and Gruni (2021), *supra* note 2, at 31.
22. For instance, Article 158 EU-Central America FTA explicitly mentions Article XX(b) General Agreement on Trade in Services (GATS) and specifies that it is 'incorporated into and made an integral part of this Agreement'. Article 154 EU-Moldova AA contains a similar wording and makes explicit reference to Articles XX and XXI GATS. Finally, CETA (Article 28.3), the EU-Japan SPA (Article 2.22), the EU-Singapore FTA (Article 2.14) and the EU-Vietnam FTA (Article 2.22) contain a direct reference to Article XX GATS.
23. Article 6.1.g. EU-Korea FTA provides that 'measures to facilitate trade shall not prejudice the fulfilment of legitimate policy objectives, such as the protection of national security, health and the environment'. Article 106 of the EU-Colombia and Peru FTA mentions the possibility for the Parties to adopt measures that are necessary to the protection of the environment.
24. On the possible purposes of the 'affecting trade language' *see* Banks, 'Fit for purpose? The extent and enforcement on international trade agreement labour obligations after the *Guatemala – Labour Obligations* decision', 52 *Georgetown Journal of International Law* (2021), 639-677.
25. Article 11.11 EU-Korea FTA.
26. WTO-GATT Agreement on Subsidies and Countervailing Measures, O.J. 1994, L 336/156, Article 5.

As for other matters in the TSD chapter, so far, there does not appear to be guidance on how the '(affecting) trade' language is to be interpreted. Such guidance is overdue on this complex and divisive question.[27]

2.3 The Legal Nature of the Commitments

The TSD chapters of the 'new generation' FTAs contain commitments whose legal nature varies according to the distinct sub-groups identified by Marco and Giovanni. Among the many questions which the legal nature of these commitments raises, two are dealt with here.

The *first question* is how legally binding these commitments are. With respect to the first sub-group on ratifying international labour and environmental agreements, the FTAs generally formulate these as a best endeavours obligation. An example is the Parties' obligation in the EU-Korea FTA to make 'continued and sustained efforts' towards ratification.[28]

The EU-Korea Panel found that the FTA imposes ongoing obligations to make efforts[29] and that 'Korea's efforts are less than optimal'.[30] Yet, it concluded that Korea had not acted inconsistently with its obligation. It is unclear whether the Panel did reach that conclusion in light of the, albeit minimal, efforts of Korea or because Korea did not commit to a specific time frame, of which 'the Panel is mindful'.[31] In the latter hypothesis, it would seem that the Panel confused an obligation of conduct ('continued and sustained efforts') with an obligation of result (ratify the ILO conventions),[32] although the EU made the distinction in its submissions and the Panel in its analysis.[33] In the former hypothesis, one can disagree with the Panel's assessment of Korea's efforts yet support it for having carried it out. According to Marco and Giovanni, ratification deadlines would be preferable.[34] However, will parties be prepared to accept such obligation of result? In any event, the conclusion reached by the Panel is likely to further reduce the chances of private parties obtaining recognition that a third State has not complied with its obligation to ratify. This is all the more so that the notion of 'continued and sustained efforts' towards ratification of the ILO Convention remains undefined and likely to be subject to fluctuating interpretations.

The second sub-group – the obligation to respect, promote and realise the principles concerning fundamental ILO rights – initially seemed to Marco and Giovanni

27. As shown by the comments on the *Guatemala – Labour Obligations* Panel Report described by Banks, *supra* note 24, footnote 8.
28. Article 13.4.3 EU-Korea FTA.
29. EU-Korea Panel Report, cited *supra* note 19, para. 278.
30. *Ibid.*, para. 291.
31. *Ibid.*
32. This distinction is well established in public international law. *See* Draft articles on Responsibility of States for Internationally Wrongful Acts, *Yearbook of the International Law Commission*, 2001, vol. II, Part Two, comment 11 on Article 12. I thank Prof. Tom Ruys for our discussion on this point.
33. EU-Korea Panel Report, cited *supra* note 19, paras 272-276.
34. Bronckers and Gruni (2021), *supra* note 2, at 27.

as a soft law obligation.[35] I consider it a hard and binding obligation, as it was persuasively construed by the EU-Korea Panel. The Panel interpreted the relevant clause, Article 13.4.3 of the EU-Korea FTA, properly and at length in accordance with the interpretation rules of the Vienna Convention on the Law of Treaties (VCLT)[36] and addressed the objections raised by Korea. It dealt in particular with Korea's argument that the EU's interpretation would be tantamount to requiring it to adhere to the core ILO Conventions, which it had not ratified. The Panel considered that the FTA 'has incorporated these (existing) obligations (of the Parties under the ILO Constitution) ... as separate and independent obligations under Chapter 13 of the Agreement'.[37] It stated correctly, as I see it, that the commitment in Article 13.4.3 is one of the new obligations that the Parties assumed when they concluded the FTA.[38]

The obligations forming part of the third sub-group identified by Marco and Giovanni - to implement the ratified multilateral environmental and labour agreements - are formulated as 'reaffirm their commitment to effectively implement'.[39] They are, according to Marco and Giovanni, obligations of conduct. The added value of including such obligations in the FTAs is to allow them to be sanctioned under the (admittedly weak) DSM of the FTAs.[40]

The *second question* is how and against what standards compliance with this obligation is to be assessed. This question appears to be particularly relevant to the obligation to effectively implement the Paris Agreement. Under this agreement, a Party is to 'prepare, communicate and maintain successive nationally determined contributions that it intends to achieve'.[41] There does not appear to be any process in the Paris Agreement for determining whether the nationally determined contributions (NDCs) are such as to 'effectively implement' the agreement. Neither the Enhanced Transparency Framework nor the Article 15 Committee is designed to do so.[42] A Party to an EU FTA - and, for that matter, a possible dispute settlement panel - will have to make its own assessment of whether a Party complied with the obligation to achieve its NDCs. That Party and a possible dispute settlement panel will thus have to develop standards on their own against which to assess whether NDCs have been achieved. This could be a rather challenging task.

35. *Ibid.*, at 27.
36. VCLT, 1155 UNTS 331.
37. EU-Korea Panel Report, cited *supra* note 19, para. 107.
38. *Ibid.*, para. 122.
39. On labour protection, *see*, for instance, Article 23.3.4 CETA or Article 13.4.3 EU-Korea FTA. On environmental protection, *see*, for instance, Article 24.3.4 CETA and Article 13.5.2 EU-Korea FTA.
40. *See* Bronckers and Gruni (2021), *supra* note 2, at 28-29, for the example of the Paris Agreement and Mercosur.
41. Paris Agreement on Climate Change, United Nations Treaties Series, Ch. XXVII, 7.d, Article 4.2.
42. Gu, Voigt and Werksman, 'Facilitating implementation and promoting compliance with the Paris Agreement under Article 15: Conceptual challenges and pragmatic choices', 9 *Climate Law* (2019), 65-100, at 83. A measure such as a statement of non-compliance was intentionally excluded from the Enhanced Transparency Framework. I thank Jake Werksman not only for drawing my attention to this article but also for discussing it with me.

3 ENFORCEMENT

3.1 Compliance Mechanism

3.1.1 Nature of the Compliance Mechanism

For the TSD obligations, the FTAs introduce a specific compliance mechanism. It relies on monitoring processes, dialogues and cooperative actions, such as capacity building, an institutional involvement of civil society through Domestic Advisory Groups (DAGs) at national level and Civil Society Fora (CSFs) at the EU and FTA partner level and separate 'cooperative' DSM.[43] This mechanism follows the managerial model advocated by scholars in the context of international law enforcement. It has been described in a 2016 paper of the *Kommerskollegium*, the Swedish National Board of Trade, in connection with the enforcement of the TSD provisions of the FTAs.[44] This approach focuses on actual causes of non-compliance and on managing them through positive means, consisting of a blend of transparency, dispute settlement and capacity building. The Commission justifies this compliance mechanism by the specific challenges of complying with trade and sustainable commitments, which often involve tackling long-standing and deeply rooted domestic issues and different policy priorities and call for a long-term perspective on implementation.[45] This mechanism should be looked at against the background of the compliance record.

3.1.2 The Compliance Gap

The expectation that the TSD provisions would effectively improve the labour and environmental standards in the FTA partner countries has been unfulfilled in the main. This compliance gap has been analysed in various studies.[46] It has recently been confirmed by the extensive RESPECT research project investigating the factors that support or inhibit attainment of non-trade objectives of the EU trade agreements. The RESPECT report does not find evidence of a causal relationship between the inclusion of non-trade policy provisions in the EU FTAs and improvement in non-trade indicators while noting that there is evidence for a positive relationship between realization of non-trade policy objectives and foreign direct investment flows into partner

43. For a more complete description, *see* Prévost and Alexovičová, 'Mind the compliance gap: managing trustworthy partnerships for sustainable development in the European Union's free trade agreements', 6 *International Journal of Public Law and Policy* (2019), 236-269, at 244-248.
44. Swedish National Board of Trade, 'Implementation and Enforcement of Sustainable Development Provisions in Free Trade Agreements – Options for Improvement' (2016), available at kommerskollegium.se/globalassets/publikationer/rapporter/2016-och-aldre/publ-implementa tion-and-enfocement-of-sustinability-provisions-in-ftas.pdf, at 4; this paper refers to Chayes and Handler Chayes, *The New Sovereignty: Compliance with International Regulation* (HUP, 1998).
45. COM(2020)705 final, 'Commission Report on the implementation of EU Trade Agreements for the year 2019', at 28.
46. For example, the literature cited by Prévost and Alexovicova, *supra* note 43, in footnote 43.

countries.[47] The yearly Commission FTA implementation reports show that the TSD compliance mechanism has been actively used but that it has delivered few concrete results. Such outcome is all the more problematic that, by contrast with US FTAs, the countries that have signed FTAs with the EU are more likely to enhance their environmental performance during the implementation phase.[48] An effective compliance mechanism is thus even more crucial in the case of EU FTAs.

3.1.3 Compliance Gap and Deficiencies of the Compliance Mechanism

The European Parliament is of the view that the 'cooperative approach' is insufficient to close the compliance gap. In a 2016 resolution, it recalled, *inter alia*, earlier requests that the TSD chapters be covered by the general DSM of the FTAs, that social partners and civil society be given the possibility to appeal through a complaints procedure and that effective deterrent measures be provided.[49] The Commission is aware of this. From the consultation on its 2017 Non-paper, it concluded in its 2018 Non-paper that compliance needed to be stepped up and improved. It outlined 15 actions to be taken.[50]

However, the Commission limits itself to improvements to the cooperative aspects of the compliance mechanism. Some of the weaknesses of the compliance mechanism as it stands are probably due to insufficient reliance on other instruments, such as regulatory cooperation and development assistance to some FTA partner countries. This calls for some brief comments on whether the current specific TSD DSM is an appropriate compliance tool and whether it should be replaced by the regular DSM of the FTAs, completed by appropriate sanctions and an effective private complaint procedure.

3.2 Dispute Settlement

3.2.1 Separate but Unequal

The TSD chapter of the FTAs provides for a separate DSM (TSD DSM). Among the features that set it apart from the general DSM of the FTAs are the possibilities for DAGs to be heard in the dispute settlement process, the mandatory consultation of the ILO and Multilateral Environmental Agreement (MEA) Secretariats in disputes involving these instruments and the possibility for DAGs and the CSF to communicate their views

47. Hoekman, 'Realizing European Soft Power in External Cooperation and Trade: Final Project Report' (RESPECT 2021), available at respect.eui.eu/wp-content/uploads/sites/6/2021/RESPECT_final report.pdf, at 2.
48. LSE, report cited *supra* note 5, at 11. According to the report, 'the US sanction-based approach is more likely to have an impact *ex-ante* (before ratification), while the EU's soft approach is said to yield greater results *ex-post* (after ratification)'.
49. European Parliament Resolution of 5 July 2016 on implementation of the 2010 recommendations of Parliament on social and environmental standards, human rights and corporate responsibility, P8_TA (2016)0298), para. 21.
50. Commission Non-Paper, Feedback and Way Forward on Improving the Implementation and Enforcement of Trade and Sustainable Development Chapters in EU Free Trade Agreements (2018, http://trade.ec.europa/doc-lib/docs/2018/February/tradedoc156618.pdf_.

on the implementation of a panel report.[51] Certain technical arguments have been made against subjecting TSD obligations to dispute settlement proceedings: the TSD obligations are less clear, and compliance with them is difficult to assess; the reference to non-trade instruments, such as MEAs and ILO Conventions, requires a systemic assessment of these instruments; quantifying the damage caused by non-compliance faces practical challenges.[52] These arguments point to difficulties but are hardly persuasive, as demonstrated by Marco and Giovanni.[53]

One feature stands out. The TSD DSM provides, following a panel report, for 'a discussion by the Parties of actions or measures to resolve the matter in question, taking into account the panel's final report and its suggestions'.[54] The panel of experts is thus considered a stage in the cooperative compliance process. Including the implementation of panel findings in the dispute settlement process is one thing. Treating these findings as one of the elements to be taken into account in a discussion by the parties about appropriate implementing measures is another thing. It means that the panel of experts is considered a stage in the cooperative compliance process. It turns a panel report into some sort of advisory opinion, merely an element in the parties' ongoing attempts to conciliate their dispute.[55] This is misguided. It signals that the obligations at stake in the report are not to be unconditionally enforced and that they are less valuable than other FTA obligations that deserve binding panel reports.

3.2.2 Keep Third-Party Adjudicators and Private Parties Out?

One of the Commission Non-Papers states that the dispute settlement proceedings should be launched without hesitation, should the results of the various actions of the cooperative approach not be satisfactory and compliance concerns persist.[56] In view of the compliance gap concerning the TSD obligations, one would expect the EU to initiate a number of dispute settlement proceedings. Yet, the EU has launched only one, the proceeding against Korea.[57] It took it six years to decide to do so. This reluctance to have recourse to the TSD DSM may be explained by the priority given to the cooperative approach, the technical difficulties faced by panels (referred to earlier) or the absence of sanctions. This is not convincing. Recourse to the DSM does not exclude, nor is it an alternative to, the cooperative approach. It complements it. Why would the absence of sanctions lead to avoiding the TSD DSM, while the regular FTA DSM, which does provide for sanctions, is also avoided? There is bound to be another

51. For a good description of the TSD DSM, *see* Prévost and Alexovicova, *supra* note 43, at 249-251.
52. Swedish National Board of Trade, report cited *supra* note 44, 13(30).
53. Bronckers and Gruni (2021), *supra* note 2, at 12-13.
54. Article 16.18.6 EU-Japan SPA.
55. Bronckers and Gruni (2021), *supra* note 2, at 13.
56. Commission Non-Paper, cited *supra* note 50, at 7-8.
57. In that regard, it should be noted that this state of fact does not seem to apply solely to the EU. As stressed by Cooreman and Van Calster, *supra* note 12, at 202, the aforementioned US dispute with Guatemala on labour is so far the only 'sustainability' dispute brought by the US. It took the US nine years to initiate the dispute settlement process. The EU's current dispute settlement proceedings record thus seems to reflect a more widespread attitude towards the implementation of TSD obligations.

explanation for this manifest reluctance to have recourse not only to the TSD DSM but also to the regular DSM applying for trade obligations.

The EU - and not only the EU - has always been disinclined, if not averse, to submit disputes with its partners to adjudication, with the notable exception of disputes under the WTO. This attitude extends to judicial review by the EU courts of the EU's international agreements. It is noteworthy that in one or other form - be it in decisions on the conclusion of such agreements or agreeing to express clauses to that effect in such agreements - the EU makes clear that the FTAs are not to be construed as conferring rights or imposing duties which may be directly invoked by private parties. Marco recalled (and disputed) the various arguments in support of excluding the right of private parties to invoke international agreements in the EU courts and in the Member States' courts, such as the need to leave policy space to the EU, the absence of reciprocity, or the concern to avoid flooding courts with spurious claims.[58]

Excluding an international tribunal as an ultimate arbiter has its mirror image in the blocking by the EU political institutions of the access by private parties to courts in matters involving international agreements. This reflects the same concern of the EU's political institutions not to be hamstrung in these matters by the EU courts and Member State courts.[59] Be it as it may, avoiding dispute settlements, even in their cooperative TSD form, suits the EU political institutions and their diplomats and officials in charge of managing the often contrasting expectations of the various stakeholders and the wider external relations implications of administering international agreements. Understandable but wise? Apart from leaving persistent compliance gaps unattended, this approach does not assist stakeholders and, in particular, businesses. In the absence of agreed guidance by the parties, a policy of avoiding dispute settlement deprives stakeholders of the clarification of TSD provisions and, thus, of a modicum of legal certainty when striving to adjust their conduct and business plans to the public policy objectives pursued by these TSD provisions. Dispute settlement proceedings may clarify the meaning and scope of TSD provisions. If parties to FTAs have reservations about the interpretations of a dispute settlement panel, they have the option to amend the TSD provision as interpreted by the panel. This is how Canada, Mexico and the US proceeded following the panel report in the Guatemala-Labour Obligations dispute.

58. Bronckers, 'Schizophrenia in the EU about International Law', *Leiden Law Blog*, 27 January 2015, leidenlawblog.nl/articles/schizophrenia-in-the-eu-about-international-law.

59. This attitude goes back at least to the 1980s when in Case 270/80, *Polydor Ltd and RSO Records Inc. v. Harlequin Records Shops Ltd and Simons Records Ltd*, ECLI:LEU:C:1982:43, five of the then nine EC Member States intervened to argue against conferring direct effect to the 1972 Agreement between the EEC and Portugal. They referred to the traditional procedures provided by that agreement for resolving disputes ensuring that the agreement is duly implemented and argued in diplomatic terms that the Court should stay out of a matter to be handled by the EC political institutions alone. To note that the European Court of Justice goes through a three-step analysis for determining whether a provision of an international agreement may be relied upon by a private party. For a careful, detailed and extensive review of the case law of the EU courts, *see* Lenaerts, 'Direct applicability and direct effect of international law in the EU legal order', in Govaere, Lannon, Van Elsuwege and Adam (Eds), *The European Union in the World: Essays in Honour of Marc Maresceau* (Brill | Nijhoff, 2013), pp. 45-64.

They agreed on an amendments protocol of the United States-Mexico-Canada Agreement.[60]

3.3 Sanctions

Marco and Giovanni defend the position that sanctions add an extra layer to the agreements to secure compliance.[61] They argue that the EU has the right under international law to take countermeasures and that the FTAs TSD DSM does not exclude this right. In their view, unilateral trade retaliation can be a necessary enforcement option in case all other efforts to promote compliance with the FTA rules have failed.[62] I will not dwell on this point. In light of the position taken so far by the Commission on the inclusion of sanctions in the TSD chapter of FTAs,[63] it appears highly unlikely that the EU would have recourse to the unilateral tool of countermeasures. The inclusion of sanctions of some sort in the TSD chapters of the FTAs has been rejected with a number of arguments. Some are linked to the 'cooperative approach', which is said to be more effective than sanctions in closing the compliance gap.[64] Sanctions, it is also argued, would not fit easily with the 'EU model'.[65] These arguments miss the point that sanctions would be the *ultimum remedium*, which comes into play when the properly followed 'cooperative approach' fails to produce results.

Sanctions could hardly be less effective than the 'cooperative approach' in light of the current compliance gap. Quite the contrary, the 'sanctions-based' approach with labour and environmental commitments in the FTAs of the US and Canada has been advocated as producing more results than the EU's cooperation and dialogue approach.[66] Other arguments are of a more technical nature, as illustrated by comments in one of the Commission non-papers along the following lines: sanctions included in trade agreements are a means to compensate parties for quantifiable economic damage resulting from a failure to comply with the agreement; if included in the TSD Chapter it would mean that the EU would be 'compensated' for such a breach; but it would be difficult to 'translate' a breach of social or environmental standards into economic compensation and to quantify it.[67] This line of argument is hardly relevant in light of the very purpose of such sanctions. Rather than be designed to compensate for the economic damage caused by a breach of a TSD obligation, sanctions would aim at bringing the offending party into compliance with this obligation. In this connection,

60. For more details on this, *see* Banks, *supra* note 24, at 642.
61. Bronckers and Gruni (2021), *supra* note 2, at 16-18.
62. *Ibid.*, at 20.
63. *See* mlexmarketinsight.com/news/insight/eu-new-zealand-push-to-bridge-last-trade-deal-gaps-ahead-of-french-election, referring to the ongoing EU-New Zealand negotiations for an FTA in which New Zealand proposes a sanctions-bases system for enforcing TSD provisions and the EU does not appear ready to embrace a more stringent enforcement system.
64. Prévost and Alexovicova, *supra* note 43, at 242.
65. Commission Non-Paper, cited *supra* note 50, at 3.
66. Prévost and Alexovicova, *supra* note 43.
67. Commission Non-Paper, cited *supra* note 50, at 3.

one can refer to the arguments Marco and Freya Baetens put forward in support of financial sanctions in another context.[68]

Once the principle of sanctions is accepted, the various procedural and substantive conditions could and should be addressed. On substance, financial sanctions for breaches of TSD obligations should be based on such elements as the importance of the interests protected, the seriousness of the breach, the conduct of the offending party and its ability to pay and be subject to the proportionality principle. Such financial sanctions would be a necessary and appropriate complement to the compliance mechanism of the TSD obligations. By proposing it to its FTA partners, the EU would demonstrate that it is taking its own TSD commitments seriously.[69]

3.4 Private Parties' Involvement

As mentioned earlier, the parties to the FTAs have found innovative ways of involving civil society in the implementation of TSD obligations. On the national level, DAGs have an advisory role in the implementation of these obligations.[70] In government-to-government consultations, a party may request the communication of the DAGs' position.[71] In examining how to resolve a disagreement between parties, the intergovernmental Committee on TSD established by the TSD chapter may seek the advice of DAGs.[72] The Panel of Experts should seek information and advice from DAGs.[73] On the international level, the members of DAGs meet in the CSF.[74] Its views, opinions or findings can be submitted to the Parties.[75] These attempts to involve civil society have not been successful for various reasons,[76] which are not discussed here.

On the EU side, this has led to a number of initiatives. One of them is the appointment of a Chief Trade Enforcement Officer (CTEO), charged, *inter alia,* with managing a new complaint system available to stakeholders. Guidance is given to complainants, including detailed instructions on key information to be provided.[77] These initiatives should be welcomed for accepting the principle of complaints and for offering some (dis)comfort to complainants about the Commission's priorities in dealing with complaints. These initiatives fall short of the concrete proposals of Marco

68. Bronckers and Baetens, 'Reconsidering financial remedies in WTO dispute settlement', 16 *Journal of International Economic Law* (2013) 281-311.
69. Bronckers and Gruni (2021), *supra* note 2, at 26.
70. Article 13.12.5 EU-Korea FTA.
71. Article 13.4.1 EU-Korea FTA.
72. Article 13.14.4 EU-Korea FTA.
73. Article 13.15.1 EU-Korea FTA.
74. Article 13.13.1 EU-Korea FTA.
75. Article 13.13.3 EU-Korea FTA.
76. Prévost and Alexovicova, *supra* note 43, at 247-248; Drieghe, Orbie, Potjomkina and Shahin, 'Participation of civil society in EU trade policy making: How inclusive is inclusion?', 27 *New Political Economy* (2022), 581-596.
77. For a description of these initiatives, *see* the following Commission documents: Operating guidelines for the Single Entry Point and complaints mechanism for the enforcement of EU trade agreements and arrangements (2021); Working approaches to the enforcement and implementation work of DG Trade (2020).

and Giovanni to amend the Trade Barriers Regulation (TBR)[78] so that it can be used by private parties against violations of labour standards.[79] Such amendment of the TBR would remedy the defects of the new TSD complaint procedure devised by the Commission. These defects mostly relate to the absence of a formal Commission decision on the admissibility of a complaint (standing of the complainant, prima facie evidence of a violation of environmental or social obligations), the absence of time limits for initiating the investigation and for concluding it, and the absence of indications on how to seek compliance with the findings of the investigation. They affect all stages of the current TSD complaint procedure. If these defects are not remedied, it is doubtful that private parties will go through the trouble and cost of filing complaints.

Even if these effects are remedied in this way, the TBR still offers a rather limited scope for private parties' actions. It subjects both the decision to initiate the examination procedure and the adoption of measures following that procedure to an assessment by the Commission of the EU interest. In any case, and in particular as regards labour-related issues, one can only take note of the contrast between the current state of use of private complaint mechanisms based on FTAs and what has been described by Henner Gött as a proliferation of individual complaint mechanisms outside the FTA context over the past decades.[80] The fact that many of these mechanisms are not specifically dedicated to labour issues does not prevent labour-related cases from being filed under a number of them.[81] Examples provided by Gött include the International Covenant on Civil and Political Rights, the International Covenant on Economic, Social and Cultural Rights, the European Convention on Human Rights, the European Social Charter, the American Convention on Human Rights or the ILO supervisory mechanism.[82] The author concluded by stressing that 'compared to these other mechanisms, the limited role of individuals as mere petitioners under contemporary FTAs lags behind'.[83] On the face of it, that may be right.

4 CONCLUSION

The TSD commitments examined here represent binding obligations, either of conduct or of result. The better interpretation of the 'affecting trade' and comparable wording used in connection with most of these obligations is that 'affecting trade' is a condition to be fulfilled for these obligations to apply rather than a constituent element of the obligations themselves. When implementing the TSD obligations examined here, FTA

78. Regulation (EU) 2015/1843 of the European Parliament and of the Council of 6 October 2015 laying down Union procedures in the field of the common commercial policy in order to the exercise of the Union's rights under international trade rules, in particular those established under the auspices of the World Trade Organization, O.J. 2015, L 272/1.
79. Bronckers and Gruni (2019), *supra* note 2, at 1599-1609.
80. *See*, in particular, Gött, 'An individual labour complaint procedure for workers, trade unions, employers and NGOs in future free trade agreements', in Gött (Ed.), *Labour Standards in International Economic Law* (Springer, 2018), pp. 185-209, at p. 187.
81. *Ibid.*, at 187.
82. *Ibid.*
83. *Ibid.*

Parties face many complex situations, great difficulties and considerable obstacles. Yet, the Parties entered into commitments and accepted a compliance mechanism. This mechanism has proved to be deficient so far. The Parties should be prepared to strengthen it by subjecting these obligations to the FTA DSM and by adding financial penalties. The EU should insist on such strengthening in its negotiations of new FTAs and propose to its current FTA partners the necessary arrangements to that effect. Private parties should have the possibility to file complaints in the framework of proper formal procedures. The EU should render its new complaint procedure more operational and meaningful for private parties for whom it is designed by inserting it in the TBR.

Businesses are apparently not sufficiently aware of the disadvantages the current mechanism of compliance with TSD obligations entails for them. They should support strengthening compliance by governments, including the application of the FTA DSM and the addition of financial penalties. They have at least two reasons for doing so. First, such strengthening would contribute significantly to clarifying the substance of the Parties' obligations. Businesses need such clarification in their constant efforts to adapt their strategies to the way States handle their TSD obligations. The second, perhaps more important, reason is related to the Commission's proposal on sustainable corporate governance with new duties for businesses to act against environmental and labour abuses in companies' supply chains.[84] The legitimacy of such partial shifting of the burden of pursuing the TSD objectives away from the public sector to the private sector would be less questionable if compliance by governments with their TSD commitments were appropriately strengthened.

*

* *

This contribution was submitted in March 2022.

84. COM(2022)71 final, 'Commission Proposal for a Directive of the European Parliament and of the Council on Corporate Sustainability Due Diligence and amending Directive (EU) 2019/1937', 2022/0051 (COD).

CHAPTER 5

Can Paris Strike Back? On the Paris Agreement's Inability to Cope with Unilateral Trade-Related Carbon Measures Such as the European Commission's CBAM-Proposal

Reinhard Quick & Isha Das

Environmental degradation through soaring temperatures caused by greenhouse gas (GHGs) emissions pose an existential threat to humanity. The Paris Agreement, with a combination of (i) demanding commitments from all Parties and not just Annex I developed countries and (ii) with a more flexible approach than the Kyoto Protocol's legally binding targets, was hailed as a monumental triumph. However, Parties' conduct is still insufficient to meet the Paris objectives. In order to take firm and effective steps towards attaining the Paris goals, and achieving carbon neutrality by 2050, the European Commission has proposed a Carbon Border Adjustment Mechanism (CBAM-Proposal). This article examines the CBAM-Proposal's compatibility with the Paris Agreement and finds that the proposal is not compatible with the European Union's (EU) Paris obligations. In the second part, the Agreement's approach to dispute settlement is discussed. Arguably, the lack of a mandatory dispute settlement process allows the EU to adopt allegedly Paris-incompliant provisions without being held accountable. This lack puts a heavy burden on the World Trade Organization (WTO). It remains to be seen whether bilateral, plurilateral and multilateral negotiations could help to ease tensions of conflicting CBAM legislations most likely to be adopted by several countries because of the EU's unilateral legislative initiative.

Anecdote

Our friendship started with a shock. When Professor John H. Jackson introduced me to Marco Bronckers in September 1983 in Ann Arbor, he mentioned that my PhD thesis on Voluntary Export Restraint Agreements and Article XIX General Agreement on Tariffs and Trade (GATT) had just been published. Since Marco was about to finish his PhD thesis on GATT Article XIX this information did not go down well with him. This rough start was the beginning of a long friendship. After we both moved to Brussels, we discovered many common interests apart from international economic law, spent time together at conferences, dinners and holidays and most importantly enjoyed music and art. Now that Marco has moved from active professional life into retirement it is a great pleasure for me to honour him with a contribution in this *liber amicorum*. I am grateful to Ms Isha Das who has contributed as co-author and, knowing how interested Marco is in parting his knowledge to the young generation, I am certain he will appreciate it.

1 INTRODUCTION

The Paris Agreement,[1] hereafter the Agreement, was hailed as a 'monumental triumph'.[2] After the many controversies around the Kyoto Protocol and the repeated failures of the climate conferences leading to Paris, the international community was finally able to agree on a comprehensive approach towards climate protection involving all Parties. Notwithstanding the many disagreements among developed countries (Annex I countries) and between developed and developing countries, a compromise could at last be found. This compromise reflected a combination of legal obligations and more flexible approaches respecting sovereignty, differentiation, local conditions, and development, while also requiring an adequate contribution from each Party to achieve the long-term temperature goals, i.e., holding the temperature increase to below 2°C from pre-industrial levels with a preference to limit it to 1.5°C. By adopting a new, more flexible approach than the Kyoto Protocol's legally binding targets for Annex I countries the Agreement offers the Parties more freedom to implement domestic climate protection measures while expecting gradually increasing ambitions over time. This flexibility bears the potential of disagreements on how to achieve the Agreement's goals and hence protracted controversies over compliance.

Currently, Parties' conducts are considered insufficient to achieve the Agreement's temperature goal. Notwithstanding the recent announcements by many G20 Members on net-zero emission goals by 2050, the United Nations Environment Programme Emission Gap Report 2020 shows a considerable discrepancy between the ambitions under the Agreement and the combat measures taken so far by the big

1. Paris Agreement to the United Nations Framework Convention on Climate Change (2015), 21st Conference of Parties, 12 December 2015, O.J. 2016, L 282/4. Articles without any additions are those of the Paris Agreement.
2. news.un.org/en/story/2015/12/517982-cop21-un-chief-hails-new-climate-change-agreement-monumental-triumph (last visited 2 December 2021).

greenhouse gas (GHG) emitters.[3] Some Parties adopting more ambitious climate protection measures are critical of other Parties' lack of will to follow suit, whereas others criticize these measures for their negative effect on them.[4] A pertinent example of a contentious, yet ambitious, climate protection measure is the legislative proposal by the European Commission for the establishment of a carbon-border adjustment mechanism (CBAM).[5] The proposal identifies certain carbon-intensive products[6] and mandates European Union (EU) importers to pay a carbon price equivalent to the price imposed by the EU Emission Trading System (ETS) for importing the product. In practice, importers would have to purchase CBAM certificates for every ton of carbon emitted during the production process of these products, would need to submit declarations on the amount of the embedded emissions, and would have to surrender the corresponding CBAM certificates on an annual basis. The European Commission justifies its CBAM-Proposal as a climate measure to avoid 'carbon leakage',[7] arguing that an increase in the EU's climate ambitions coupled with less stringent requirements in third countries could result in EU industries' investing in third countries with lower climate protection laws and/or by replacing 'green' EU-products with more carbon-intensive imports. While the Juncker Commission raised some doubts on the compatibility of CBAMs with the EU's World Trade Organization (WTO) obligations and its obligations under the Agreement,[8] the Von der Leyen Commission insists that the CBAM-proposal is both WTO and Paris compliant.[9]

---

3. UNEP Emission Gap Report 2020, p. 7, www.unep.org/emissions-gap-report-2020 (last visited 27 November 2021). The 2021 UNEP Emission Gap Report confirms this tendency in principle acknowledging though the more ambitious actions undertaken by the Parties: *see* unep.org/resources/emissions-gap-report-2021 (last visited 27 November 2021). Over the last decade, the G20 accounted for 78% of all GHGs. Even if the Paris temperature goal will not be achieved by the end of the century, Crawford defends the Agreement, arguing that even if the current NDCs are insufficient the world is nevertheless better off with the Agreement than without it. Crawford, 'The current political discourse concerning international law', 81 *Modern Law Review* (2018), 1-22, at 20.
4. *See, e.g.*, the Commission's Communication 'Stepping up Europe's 2030 Climate Ambition', COM(2020)562 final, at p. 23, in which the Commissions 'asks ... all countries and notably G20 members to come forward with much more ambitious actions ... and suggests that ... in the absence of comparable increases in ambition by our partners, as the EU increases its climate ambition, the Commission will propose a carbon border adjustment mechanism'. *See also* Joint Statement, 30th BASIC Ministerial Meeting on Climate Change, 8 April 2021, in which India, Brazil, China and South Africa 'expressed grave concerns regarding the proposal for introducing trade barriers, such as unilateral carbon border adjustment, that are discriminatory and against the principles of Equity and CBDR-RC', point 19. environment.gov.za/mediarelease/basic_ministerialmeeting_climatechange_india (last visited 2 December 2021).
5. Proposal for a Regulation of the European Parliament and of the Council establishing a carbon-border adjustment mechanism, COM(2021)564 final (CBAM-Proposal). For a description of the proposal and a critical analysis *see* Chase and Pinkert, 'The EU's Triangular Dilemma on Climate and Trade', GMF Policy Brief September 2021.
6. Covered product sectors are cement, electricity, fertilizers, iron and steel, and aluminium, *see* Annex I CBAM-Proposal.
7. Article 1(1) CBAM-Proposal.
8. 'In-Depth Analysis in Support of the Commission Communication COM(2018)773, A Clean Planet for all, A European long-term strategic vision for a prosperous, modern, competitive and climate neutral economy', 28 November 2018, p. 263.
9. CBAM-Proposal, p. 2.

In this article, we will not discuss the issue of WTO compatibility of CBAMs[10] rather, we will concentrate on the CBAM-Proposal's compatibility with the Agreement. We begin by reiterating the Agreement's central requirements including the Oversight System, thereafter, we analyse the CBAM-Proposal's critical Paris issues, such as differentiation, a carbon dioxide (CO_2) price, response measures and its silence on trade issues. We have come to the preliminary conclusion that the CBAM-Proposal is not compatible with the EU's Paris obligations. Notwithstanding its reliance on sovereign decisions to combat climate change, unilateral impositions of domestic climate measures on others, as well as self-declarations on other Parties' Paris compliance, potentially violate the letter and the spirit of the Agreement.

In the second part of the article, we will discuss the Agreement's approach to dispute settlement. We brutally ask the question of whether compliance with the Agreement matters at all. The Agreement's lack of mandatory dispute settlement allows the EU to adopt allegedly Paris-incompliant provisions without being held accountable. Arguably, a carefully drafted CBAM legislation could be considered WTO-compliant if one interprets the GATT provisions in a lenient and climate-friendly way, yet even a successful WTO defence does not provide for an answer on how other Parties might react to the CBAM-Proposal. It is an open issue whether the EU will succeed in convincing other Parties to adopt more ambitious climate protection policies and hence avoid CBAMs or whether these parties will adopt a patchwork of different carbon-border adjustment provisions with no guidance coming from the Agreement.

2 POTENTIAL INCOMPATIBILITIES OF THE CBAM-PROPOSAL WITH THE EU'S OBLIGATIONS UNDER THE PARIS AGREEMENT

2.1 The Agreement's Central Requirements

Article 2 of the Agreement sets out the temperature goals and establishes the context for implementation for all Parties by referring to 'equity' and to 'common but differentiated responsibilities and respective capabilities (CBDRRC), in the light of different national circumstances'. The CBDRRC-principle is not the same as the United Nations Framework Convention on Climate Change's (UNFCCC)[11] differentiation principle (Article 3(1) UNFCCC and Article 10 Kyoto Protocol) in so far as the Agreement requires some contribution from each Party regardless of whether the Party is a developed (Annex I), developing or least developed (Non-Annex I) country. It is a central element for implementation as it considers specific national circumstances.[12] Parties are free to self-determine the CBDRRC-scope since Article 2.2 neither identifies

10. On the issue of WTO compatibility *see* Quick, 'Carbon border about adjustment' 4 *Zeitschrift für Europarechtliche Studien* (2020), 549-597. *See also* Pauwelyn and Kleimann, 'Trade related aspects of a carbon border adjustment mechanism: A legal assessment', *EP Briefing*, 14 April 2020, europarl.europa.eu/thinktank/en/document.html?reference=EXPO_BRI(2020)603502 (last visited 4 January 2022).
11. United Nations Framework Convention on Climate Change, 9 May 1992, 1771 UNTS 107.
12. Rajamani, 'Guiding principles and general obligation, Article 2.2 and Article 3', in Klein et al. (Eds), *The Paris Agreement on Climate Change: Analysis and Comments* (OUP, 2017), p. 133.

the actors nor specifies the actions the Parties must undertake to fulfil these temperature goals.[13] Article 3 contains the overarching obligation to undertake ambitious efforts pursuant to Articles 4, 7, 9, 10, 11 and 13 and to increase them progressively. Its reference to the articles on mitigation, adaptation, finance, technology, and capacity building, sets the scene for all Parties to collectively achieve the Paris goals and indicates that mitigation contributions are not the only efforts to be undertaken.[14] In setting out the guiding principles and general obligations, Articles 2 and 3 already give an indication of the tensions between self-determination, differentiation, ambition, and progression.

Article 4 contains the central obligation with respect to mitigation. Contrary to the Kyoto Protocol's[15] top-down approach of defined quantified emission limitation and reduction commitments (Article 3 Kyoto Protocol), the Agreement builds on the UNFCCC's preambular reference to sovereignty[16] and leaves the exact contribution of each Party to a sovereign, self-determined decision reflecting national standards and circumstances. Article 4(2), first sentence establishes the procedural commitment of each Party to prepare, communicate and maintain Nationally Determined Contributions (NDCs) and the second sentence adds the obligation to pursue domestic mitigation measures 'with the aim of achieving the objectives of such contributions'. Parties are obliged to communicate their NDCs every five years and are informed about the outcomes of the global stocktake (Article 4(9)). Since this bottom-up approach carries the danger of insufficient ambition,[17] it is coupled with other requirements aiming at ensuring that the Parties' contributions can achieve the Agreement's goal(s). The first requirement contained in Article 4(1) links the global temperature goals with specific mitigation goals to be achieved collectively by the Parties. It establishes the collective aim of rapid reductions of GHG emissions after reaching a peak noting that peaking will take longer for developing Parties. Peaking and reduction should achieve a balance between anthropogenic emissions by sources and removals by sinks of GHGs in the second half of this century taking equity, sustainable development, and poverty eradication into account. Though leaving the specific mitigation commitments to the Parties, paragraph 1 requires ambitious NDCs to be adapted to the specific conditions of the Parties including zero net carbon emissions.[18] As the exact timeframe for zero net carbon emissions is not foreseen,[19] the Agreement recognizes that different Parties will adopt different time frames (e.g., EU 2050, China 2060, India 2070).[20] The second

13. *Ibid.*, at 133.
14. Bodansky, Brunée and Rajamani, *International Climate Change Law* (OUP, 2017), p. 218. They point out that the progression requirement of Article 3 also applies to adaptation and support but question whether this is an individual or a collective requirement.
15. Kyoto Protocol, 10 December 1997, 37 ILM 22.
16. UNFCCC, Preamble: 'Reaffirming the principle of sovereignty of States in international cooperation to address climate change.'
17. Ghaleigh and Verkuijl, 'Article 3: Aims, Objectives and Principles', in Van Calster and Reins (Eds), *The Paris Agreement on Climate Change: A Commentary* (Edward Elgar, 2021), point 3.10.
18. Bodansky, Brunée and Rajamani, *supra* note 14, p. 230.
19. Mayer, 'Article 4: Mitigation', in Van Calster and Reins, *supra* note 17, point 4.06, p. 112.
20. As confirmed by the Glasgow Climate Pact which speaks about 'net zero around mid-century', Decision-/CP.26 p. 17.

requirement contained in Article 4(3) introduces the concept of progression for mitigation: Parties are expected to increase the ambition of their NDCs in each successive cycle. The paragraph reflects the general concept of progression already contained in Article 3[21] but does neither specify the form nor the content of such progression. Each Party will therefore decide for itself on how to translate progression into future NDCs. There are conflicting elements to be considered in this exercise: the 'highest possible ambition' versus 'CBDRRC', economy-wide absolute emission reduction targets versus the absence thereof (Article 4(4)) and the fact that progression also depends on the level of support received by developing countries (Article 9(3)). All these elements might render an assessment of the NDCs difficult,[22] except for the situation when the transparency process of Article 13(7) requiring information from each Party on the implementation and achievements of their NDCs were to lead to a clear indication that the NDC was unable to meet the stated objectives.[23] Relevant in this context is also Article 4(11) which allows for the adjustment of NDCs to enhance the Party's ambitions.[24] The third requirement relates to differentiation in mitigation: Article 4(4) recommends economy-wide absolute emission reduction targets for developed Parties and encourages developing Parties to move over time towards these targets. Before committing to those more ambitious targets, developing countries can choose a variety of measures for their NDCs such as economy-wide or intensity targets, reductions from a business-as-usual-scenario or just a set of policies and actions.[25] This paragraph reflects the Agreement's nuanced CBDRRC-concept: the recommendation for absolute emission reduction targets for developed countries follows the UNFCCC's traditional approach to differentiation, whereas the expectation for developing countries to contribute introduces the new differentiation element. These countries should continue enhancing their mitigation efforts and eventually move towards absolute emission reduction targets given their national circumstances. Relevant in this context is also Article 4(6), which allows least developed countries and small island developing states further flexibility in mitigation.[26] As NDCs fall into the sovereign domain of each Party, so does the determination of differentiation. No details are given as to when developing countries are supposed to adopt absolute reduction targets. Yet, these details matter[27] since the lack of precision might lead to arguments between the Parties on the effectiveness of their respective NDCs. The fourth requirement contained in Article 4(7) recognizes mitigation co-benefits from other measures such as adaptation actions or economic diversification plans which Parties are supposed to communicate

21. The concept of progression in Article 3 goes beyond mitigation and also relates to adaptation and support, *see* Bodansky, Brunée and Rajamani, *supra* note 14, p. 234.
22. Mayer, *supra* note 19, point 4.23.
23. Winkler, 'Mitigation: Article 4', in Klein et al., *supra* note 12, p. 148.
24. For a discussion on whether downward adjustments are permissible *see* Mayer, *supra* note 19, points 4.24 to 4.26, opposing the arguments made by Rajamani and Brunée, 'The legality of downgrading nationally determined contributions under the Paris Agreement: Lessons from the U.S. Disengagement', 29 *Journal of International Environmental Law* (2017), 537-551.
25. Mayer, *supra* note 19, point 4.18.
26. For a discussion on whether this paragraph exempts these States from the para. 4 requirements, *see* Mayer, *supra* note 19, point 4.20 and Winkler, *supra* note 23, p. 152.
27. Winkler, *supra* note 23, p. 151.

as part of the NDCs. The fifth requirement contained in Article 4(8) calls on Parties, when submitting NDCs, to provide 'the information necessary for clarity, transparency and understanding'. They must account for their NDCs in order 'to promote transparency, accuracy, completeness, comparability and consistency, and ensure the avoidance of double counting' as stipulated in paragraph 13. Due to the self-determination of NDCs, paragraph 8 introduces some guidance on how to compare divergent NDCs and provides for methodologies on their assessment. Decision 1/CP.21 of the Agreement's Conference of Parties (COP) in point 27 lists elements which Parties 'may' include under this paragraph such as quantifiable information, timeframes and periods of implementation, assumptions, methodological approaches and, most importantly, information on how the NDC contributes towards achieving the objectives of the Agreement in light of national circumstances. Further guidance can be found in Decision 4/CMA.1 of the COP which is less discretionary than Decision 1/CP.21:[28] when communicating their second and subsequent NDCs Parties are obliged ('shall') to provide the required information contained in Annex I. The guidance on accounting is contained in Annex II of Decision 4/CMA.1: Parties are required to use the methodologies developed by the Intergovernmental Panel on Climate Change (IPCC) and must ensure methodological consistency between the communication and the implementation of their NDCs. The sixth requirement contained in Article 4(19) invites the Parties to communicate their long-term strategies for low GHG emissions. As it is a discretionary requirement, these strategies are not obligatory and will not be considered in the transparency framework nor the global stocktake.[29]

Summing up, Article 4 requires the Parties to:

- take and communicate domestic mitigation measures through NDCs (Article 4(2));
- provide the necessary information on NDCs for clarity, transparency and understanding (Article 4(8));
- account for their NDCs (Article 4(13));
- adopt ambitious NDCs and improve them over time (Article 4(3));
- communicate the NDCs every five years from 2020 (Article 4(9));
- consider the impact of their response measures on other parties (Article 4(15)).

Furthermore, developed countries 'should' adopt stronger mitigation measures than developing countries (Article 4(4)) and 'shall' provide support to the latter for the implementation of their obligations arising under the Agreement (Article 4(5)).

In the run-up to the Paris Conference, the EU and other countries asked for binding commitments from Parties to achieve their NDCs to ensure effective implementation and compliance. Other countries, including the United States, China and India, were opposed to this request citing domestic (constitutional)[30] or participatory

28. Point 7 Decision 4/CMA.1.
29. Mayer, *supra* note 19, points 4.14, 4.16.
30. Crawford, *supra* note 3, 18-21; Bodansky, 'The Paris climate change agreement: A new hope?', 110 *American Journal of International Law* (2016), 288-319, at 297.

reasons[31] and arguing that an agreement with too demanding obligations risks not being adhered to. The compromise finally agreed (Article 4(2)) does not oblige the Parties to achieve the NDCs, yet requires them to comply with the above-mentioned procedural requirements (first sentence) plus the pursuance of domestic mitigation measures (second sentence); it therefore privileges 'participation over substance'.[32] Its opaque language also triggered a controversial discussion about its legal nature. Some argue that the achievements of the NDCs remain voluntary[33] or that NDCs 'are expectations and not binding obligations'[34] whereas others consider this article to create an obligation of conduct, 'an obligation to exercise due diligence towards an intended outcome, without necessarily guaranteeing the achievement of the outcome'.[35] Its second sentence adds a further difficulty since the wording 'Parties shall' refers to a collective obligation which is generally considered less legally demanding.[36] The Agreement does not give any guidance as to the precise legal character of the requirements contained in Article 4(2). It rather avoids such positioning and introduces a unique structure enabling implementation through a combination of procedural commitments, voluntary and transparency requirements, expert advice and peer pressure without clearly separating voluntary and binding commitments.

The different requirements contained in Article 4 combine self-determination with ambition and accountability and allow the Parties to submit NDCs tailored to their specific national circumstances. The individual contributions may also reflect carbon sinks (Article 5) and the transfer of emission reductions through voluntary cooperation (Article 6). Other requirements are included in Article 7 (adaptation), Article 8 (loss and damage) and Article 9 (finance); they all form an integral part of the Parties' responses to climate change. Given the Agreement's relative silence on issues of practical implementation, the Parties had to negotiate implementation guidelines – the so-called Paris Rulebook.[37] The rulebook encompasses not only the many mitigation issues just mentioned and how to track progress in emission reductions, but it also

31. *See generally* Bodansky, Brunée and Rajamani, *supra* note 14, p. 231.
32. Falk, 'Voluntary International Law and the Paris Agreement', richardfalk.org/2016/01/16/voluntary-international-law-and-the-paris-agreement (last visited 25 November 2021).
33. Falk, *ibid.*; Crawford, *supra* note 3, p. 21; Bodansky, *supra* note 30, p. 304.
34. Rajamani, 'Reflection on the US withdrawal from the Paris Climate Change Agreement', *EJIL:Talk!*, 5 June 2017, ejiltalk.org/reflections-on-the-us-withdrawal-from-the-paris-climate-change-agreement (last visited 13 December 2021).
35. Mayer, *supra* note 19, point 4.49.
36. While Mayer considers this sentence as creating an obligation of conduct notwithstanding its collective character (*see* Mayer, *supra* note 19, point 4.49), Bodansky, Brunée and Rajamani, *supra* note 14, p. 253, classify it as a cross-cutting obligation; they consider that only those norms which are phrased in mandatory terms and which contain a clear and precise normative content without any qualifying or discretionary elements as 'hard law' that can be assessed for compliance; *ibid.*, p. 213.
37. Most of the implementation guidelines have been agreed at COP24 at Katowice in December 2019. *See* unfccc.int/process-and-meetings/the-paris-agreement/katowice-climate-package#eq-9 (last visited 9 December 2021). The decisions on Article 6 and on the timelines for the submissions of NDCs have only been agreed upon at COP26 in November 2021; *see* ec.europa.eu/commission/presscorner/detail/en/ip_21_6021 (last visited 9 December 2021).

contains guidelines on adaptation, finance, transparency, and the global stocktaking.[38] It is supposed to make the Agreement operational.

2.2 How Does the Agreement Address Compliance?: The Oversight System

The Agreement addresses adherence to its provisions through an Oversight System comprising the following three prongs: (1) a transparency framework to hold each party accountable for their individual domestic action; (2) a periodical assessment of collective contributions of all Parties towards attaining the goals of Article 2; and (3) a facilitative compliance with, and implementation of, the mandates of the Agreement. These are embodied respectively in Articles 13, 14 and 15.

The three prongs of the Oversight System work together and establish a mechanism aimed at enabling the attainment of the central goals of the Agreement in a facilitative, non-intrusive, non-adversarial, non-punitive manner, and without a specific timeline for Parties to achieve the goals.[39] It is noteworthy that the international environmental law regime had found it challenging to implement the traditional, adversarial approach in international law to address situations of non-compliance.[40] Consequently, this facilitative system has been heralded as an important step towards encouraging adherence to the Agreement's mandate in a friendly manner.[41]

2.2.1 Transparency Framework

The first prong of the Oversight System is the transparency framework. The transparency framework is contained in Article 13 and establishes a three-part process: (i) reporting through national communications and biennial reports;[42] (ii) technical expert review of the information provided by the Party in these communications and reports;[43] and (iii) assessment of the Party's performance with respect to their NDCs regarding the Article 2 goals.[44]

Article 13 recognizes differences in domestic capacities and provides built-in flexibilities for developing and least developed countries.[45] While acknowledging the need for these flexibilities, the Agreement mandates participation in the transparency

38. For a discussion of the various elements of the Paris Rulebook *see* www.wri.org/paris-rulebook (last visited 7 December 2021).
39. Articles 13, 14 and 15.
40. Wang and Wiser, 'The implementation and compliance regimes under the climate change convention and its Kyoto Protocol', 11 *Review of European, Comparative & International Environmental Law* (2002), 181-198; Bodansky, *The Art and Craft of International Environmental Law* (HUP, 2010), pp. 245-50.
41. Van Asselt and Kulovesi, 'Article 13: Enhanced transparency framework for action and support', in Van Calster and Reins, *supra* note 17, p. 305.
42. Article 13(4)-(10).
43. Article 13(11).
44. Article 13(12).
45. Article 13(3); Van Asselt and Kulovesi, *supra* note 41, p. 305.

framework by all Parties – and not just Annex I developed countries.[46] The objective is clear: all Parties must participate in the framework to build mutual trust and confidence and to promote effective implementation of the Agreement. Mandating a reporting requirement for all Parties was an essential improvement from previous environmental agreements where this mandate was imposed only on Annex I countries. This system helps build confidence that the burden of taking mitigation action is not only borne by Annex I countries but also, to a certain extent, by developing countries.

Article 13 mandates each Party's report to contain information on (i) national GHG inventories of anthropogenic emissions by sources and removals by GHG sinks,[47] (ii) all information found relevant by the concerned Party to enable the expert review committee to track their progress in attaining their NDCs.[48] Further, Parties 'should' report information related to climate change impacts and their adaptation under Article 13(7) including relevant national circumstances, institutional arrangements and governance along with legal and policy frameworks available.[49] Further, if the reporting Party is a developed country, then it must provide information on its provision of financial, technological and capacity-building support to developing country Parties.[50] In case of developing or least developed countries, their reports should contain information about their financial, technological and capacity building needs as well as the support they have received so far.[51]

Importantly, while there is a mandate for reporting relevant information transparently, the language of Article 13 is soft and facilitative. This indicates the lack of any legal repercussions for not complying with this requirement. Hence, the Agreement relies on the Parties to report information accurately. This has implications during the review and assessment process, as these processes rely solely on the reports of the concerned Party.

Further, the Agreement provides that the review be conducted by a Technical Expert Review Committee (TER Committee) in a facilitative and multilateral manner.[52] In the multilateral assessment, other Parties can pose questions about the concerned Party's actions. Additionally, the review is to account for the flexibilities accorded to select Parties in this regard, especially in terms of national circumstances and capabilities. This reiterates that the transparency framework imbibes the CBDRRC in its functioning.

The TER Committee's review of each Party's action considers that Party's report, and other supplementary relevant information. Based on this information, an outcome of the technical review is prepared. Hence, the TER Committee relies entirely on what

46. Article 13(1).
47. Article 13(7)(a).
48. Article 13(7)(b).
49. Article 13(8); UNFCCC Decision 4/CMA.1, Further Guidance in Relation to the Mitigation Section of Decision 1/CP.21; UN Doc FCCC/PA/CMA/2018/3/Add.1 (19 March 2019) Annex I, para. 106; Van Asselt and Kulovesi, *supra* note 41, p. 316.
50. Article 13(9); Van Asselt and Kulovesi, *supra* note 41, p. 308.
51. Article 13(10); Van Asselt and Kulovesi, *supra* note 41, p. 308.
52. Article 13(11); Van Asselt and Kulovesi, *supra* note 41, p. 319.

the Party reports and no questions can be raised on the veracity of information provided.

Based on its review, the TER Committee identifies the areas of improvement for the concerned Party, keeping in mind the built-in flexibilities.[53] The TER Committee report is to be made available to all other Parties. The technical expert review has been welcomed as an extremely important step serving functions like adding clarity on each Party's domestic actions, encouraging improved action, enhancing confidence among Parties of each other's actions and collating the most accurate information by the Secretariat.[54] However, the Agreement is silent on the obligations of the Party to act on areas of improvement identified by the TER Committee. These concerns must be addressed for the transparency mechanism to realize its full potential.

2.2.2 Global Stocktake

Article 14 mandates a global stocktake to (i) assess the overall progress of implementation and to achieve long-term goals of all Parties; and (ii) strengthen NDCs over time.[55] The stocktake process requires Parties to communicate their (updated) NDCs every five years.[56] Its stated aim is 'to inform Parties in updating and enhancing, in a nationally determined manner, their actions'.[57]

Article 14 imposes two types of obligations: (i) on the COP to take stock of collective action and (ii) on Parties to use its outcomes to update their climate actions to better attain the objectives of the Agreement.[58] It does not prescribe how the stocktake must be carried out; the only guidance offered is that the COP must carry out the process in the light of 'equity' and 'best available science'.[59] The Rulebook on the Global Stocktake (adopted in 2018) has thrown more light on conducting the process.[60] First, 'equity' and 'best available science' is to be considered in a 'Party-driven and cross-cutting manner.'[61] This indicates that Parties have an important role in determining equity and best available science, and the decision does not rest entirely on the Secretariat. However, the Rulebook does not establish set criteria to determine equity and best available science. Second, the Rulebook elaborates on the steps involved in the stocktake procedure by establishing three components: (i) information collection and preparation, (ii) technical assessment and (iii) consideration of outputs.[62]

For information collection, the Rulebook provides that an 'open source of input of information' shall exist. This implies that apart from reports by each Party (as per

53. Article 13(12); Van Asselt and Kulovesi, *supra* note 41, p. 319.
54. Dagnet and Levin, 'Transparency: Article 13', in Klein et al., *supra* note 12, p. 311.
55. Article 14(1).
56. Article 4(9).
57. Article 14(3).
58. Friedrich, 'Global Stocktake: Article 14', in Klein et al., *supra* note 12, p. 321.
59. Article 14(1).
60. Peeters, 'Article 14: Global stocktake', in Van Calster and Reins, *supra* note 17, p. 330.
61. *Ibid.*, p. 339.
62. *Ibid.*, pp. 341-342.

Article 9), other sources of information including the reports of the Intergovernmental Panel on Climate Change, and reports of relevant non-government actors and major think-tanks can also be considered.[63] This is in contrast with the transparency framework discussed above, wherein information from sources other than the concerned party could not be presented. Hence, for the stocktake process, the Secretariat can rely not solely on the Party's own information but also on information from other sources leading to a balanced result.

The stocktake is to be conducted with the assistance of the Subsidiary Body of Scientific and Technical Assistance (SBSTA) and the Subsidiary Body of Implementation (SBI) in a 'flexible and appropriate manner'. Here too, the language suggests a wide discretion conferred to the bodies in the method of conducting the stocktake. However, the Rulebook does specify what information should be considered at the collective level, thereby somewhat restricting the discretion SBSTA and SBI have in this regard.[64]

Based on the outcome of the stocktake, Parties are to update and enhance their actions to achieve the goals of the Agreement and fulfil the obligations under their NDCs.[65] However, the facilitative text of the Agreement again precludes any legal consequences from non-compliance with this mandate.

Notably, the global stocktake process is an important step towards an overall assessment of the contribution of Parties and to enable better mitigation action to achieve the goals of the Agreement. However, the wide discretions and open-ended language of Article 14 and the Rulebook water-down the mandate of global stocktake. The first global stocktake is to be conducted in 2023[66] and only thereafter it will become evident how effective the process is.

2.2.3 Compliance and Implementation Mechanism

The compliance and implementation mechanisms are established under Article 15 which states that an Expert Committee is to be responsible for facilitating implementation and compliance with the Agreement.[67] Importantly, according to Article 15(2), this compliance and implementation must be facilitated in a non-adversarial and non-punitive manner.[68] This indicates that questions on compliance and implementation may not be subject to any dispute under the Agreement. In fact, compliance and implementation have been explicitly excluded from dispute settlement under the Katowice Guidelines of 2018.[69] Further, the soft and facilitative language indicates that any finding of non-compliance by the Expert Committee cannot be used to authorize

63. *Ibid.*, p. 342.
64. *Ibid.*, p. 342.
65. Article 14(3).
66. Article 14(2).
67. Article 15(1).
68. Article 15(2).
69. Katowice Guidelines, FCCC/PA/CMA/2018/3/Add.2.; Benjamin, Haynes and Rudyk, 'Article 15: Compliance and implementation', in Van Calster and Reins, *supra* note 17, p. 353.

any legal action, such as legal retaliation, against the non-compliant party. Article 15 accommodates other flexibilities too. Article 15(2) mandates that while conducting a compliance and implementation assessment, respective national circumstances and capabilities be paid special attention to. This guides the overall procedure for conducting the compliance and implementation assessment.

Article 15 does not establish a set procedure for determining and facilitating compliance and implementation, meaning that a wide discretion is conferred to the Committee. This discretion was delimited by the Katowice Guidelines, which have now established a procedure for initiating the compliance mechanism. This can be done in one of the three following ways:

(i) Party initiation in relation to itself: Paragraph 20 of the Katowice Guidelines allows Parties to initiate the compliance mechanism only in relation to their own measures. This means that Parties can seek discussions and guidance from the Expert Committee regarding their own measures. However, they cannot use this mechanism to initiate discussions regarding the measures of other Parties. Thus, Parties are precluded from submitting counter-notifications even under the compliance mechanism, just like under the transparency framework. This has implications on the information which the Compliance Committee can examine to determine compliance and consequently, in enabling better implementation.
(ii) Independent Committee: Paragraph 22(a) of the Katowice Guidelines permits the Compliance Committee to initiate an examination regarding compliance of the concerned Party, on its own accord. Under this provision, the Compliance Committee can initiate compliance examination only under the following situations: (a) where a Party does not commit or maintain their NDC according to Article 4; (b) where a Party does not submit a mandatory communication; or (c) where a Party does not participate in multilateral consideration of the concerned Party's individual progress.[70]
(iii) Committee initiation based on expert review teams' recommendations: herein, the Compliance Committee initiates a compliance review based on the expert review teams' recommendations, only upon the consent of the concerned Party.

Further, Article 15(2) mentions the necessity of compliance and implementation to be made in a transparent manner. In this regard, the transparency framework under Article 13 comes into play.[71] Notably, while the Compliance Committee has been assigned the task of facilitating compliance and implementation of obligations of the Agreement, they are not directed to do so exclusively. Hence, just as under the stocktake mechanism, for compliance and implementation purposes, the Committee

70. Benjamin, Haynes and Rudyk, *supra* note 69, p. 356.
71. *Ibid.*, p. 352.

may consider reports of non-parties and even non-state actors, including non-governmental organizations.[72] This is unlike the framework under Article 13 wherein the TER Committee is bound to make their reports by exclusively considering the concerned country's own reports.

Thus, the compliance and implementation mechanism are facilitative and non-punitive, just like the transparency and global stocktake frameworks. As mentioned earlier, the benefit of facilitative and collaborative mechanisms is that any concerns can get addressed in a cooperative manner. It protects political relationships, while also highlighting any concerns which may arise from a Party's actions.

Some Parties have faltered in fulfilling their obligations under the transparency framework by either not submitting a biennial report at all or submitting it extremely late. It is worth noting that, without the biennial report, the process under the transparency mechanism cannot be initiated.[73] Additionally, given that the transparency framework relies solely on the information provided by the concerned Party, there is no way of determining whether and to what extent the information provided is accurate. This may cast doubt on the veracity of the transparency mechanism. Not subjecting any aspect of the Oversight System to a mandatory dispute settlement means that a stringent mechanism to ensure adherence to the obligations of the Agreement is lacking.

2.3 Critical Paris Issues

2.3.1 Common but Differentiated Responsibilities and Respective Capabilities

The pertinent feature of the CBAM-Proposal is the purchase of CBAM certificates by importers of covered products for every ton of carbon emitted during the production process of these products. The European Commission contends that since the European installations are subject to a carbon price assessed on their actual emissions via the EU ETS, the imported products should also be assessed on their actual GHG emissions. The price of the CBAM certificates will be determined by the European Commission (Article 21 CBAM-Proposal). The Commission considers that this price needs to reflect closely the price of EU ETS allowances to avoid carbon leakage and explains in detail the differences between EU ETS and CBAMs in general and the differences between the CBAM certificates and the ETS allowances in particular.[74] The

72. Dagnet and Northorp, 'Compliance and implementation: Article 15', in Klein et al., *supra* note 12, p. 349; Dannenmaier, 'The role of non-state actors in climate compliance', in Brunnée, Doelle and Rajamani (Eds), *Promoting Compliance in an Evolving Climate Regime* (CUP, 2012), pp. 149-176.
73. Countries like Pakistan, the Philippines, Nepal, Nicaragua have never submitted a biennial report. Serbia has not submitted a biennial report since 2016. After 2018, Saudi Arabia has not submitted a report at all. Indonesia did not submit a biennial report after 2018, until December 2021, which was delayed by a whole year. The next report was due in 2020, but the report was submitted only in December 2021. *See* unfccc.int/BURs (last visited 10 January 2022).
74. CBAM-Proposal, Explanatory Memorandum, notes 17 to 23, 43.

most striking differences between the two systems are the following: first, the price of EU ETS allowances is set by the market and that of CBAM certificates by the Commission (and not by the market!) with the additional restriction that the latter cannot be traded; second, their effect on the reduction of GHG emissions: while EU ETS leads to a GHG emission reduction in the EU, the CBAM-Proposal does not lead to any reduction in the exporting country,[75] it rather amounts to a payment at the border.[76]

The embedded GHG emissions in the imported goods are determined by either the actual emissions or by default values, if the actual emissions cannot be obtained correctly (Article 7 and Annex III CBAM-Proposal); default values will either be based on the average emission intensity of each exporting country for the covered goods or, if not possible, on the average emission intensity of the 10% of the worst performing EU installations of the covered goods. The payment obligations for importers will not begin until 2026, with a transition period running from 2023 until 2025 in which importers will have to comply with the Regulation's reporting requirements on the embedded emissions of the covered products.

The CBAM-Proposal applies to imported products independent of their origin, therefore affecting the exports of developed[77] and developing countries[78] alike. Commissioner Gentiloni has characterized it as an environmental policy tool applying to products and not as a tariff tool applying to countries.[79] The European Commission assumes that all potential exporting countries, except for those mentioned in Article 2(3) CBAM-Proposal, do not have policies in place that 'result in the same level of climate ambition as the Union'.[80]

This justification is surprising. The Agreement does not require all Parties to adopt the same climate protection policies as the EU, rather, by relying on the

75. Such a reduction would only occur if the installation reduced its production or introduced a more climate friendly production technology. Recital 18 of the CBAM-Proposal claims that 'both systems [CBAMs and ETS] are justified by the need to curb GHG emission'. This claim is incorrect since the EU has no influence on the GHG emissions of specific production facilities in third countries.
76. The differences between ETS and CBAMs could be relevant in a WTO case regarding the characterization of CBAMs under GATT, i.e., a border measures or domestic measures applied at the border and, in case of the latter, regarding the interpretation of less favourable treatment under GATT Article III:4; *see* Quick, *supra* note 10, pp. 563 et seq.
77. Erixon, 'Europe's carbon border adjustment mechanism: Time to go back to the drawing board', *ECIPE Policy Brief* 14/2021, p. 9.
78. An IEEP study refers to Mozambique, Guinea, Sierra Leone and Cameroon for aluminium, Zimbabwe and Zambia for steel, and Algeria, Egypt and Trinidad and Tobago for fertilizers; *see* IEEP, 'What can Least Developed Countries and other climate vulnerable countries expect from the EU Carbon Border Adjustment Mechanism (CBAM)?', iisd.org/publications/europe-union-carbon-border-adjustment-mechanism (last visited 15 December 2021). *See also* Marcu, Mehling and Cosbey, 'Border carbon adjustments in the EU: Sectoral deep dive', *ERCST*, 2021 which, *inter alia*, refer to cement from Colombia.
79. ec.europa.eu/commission/presscorner/detail/en/SPEECH_21_3724 (last visited 30 July 2021). Article 2(3) CBAM-Proposal contains an exception for countries which are already subject, or fully linked, to the EU ETS Regulation such as Iceland, Norway, Switzerland and Liechtenstein (Annex II Section A). Further countries could be added to this Annex provided that the 'agreements concluded ensure a higher degree of effectiveness and ambition to achieve decarbonisation of a sector' (CBAM-Proposal, Explanatory Memorandum, pp. 2-3).
80. CBAM-Proposal, Explanatory Memorandum, p. 1.

fundamental principles of 'equity' and 'CBDRRC', it requires developed countries to adopt stronger climate protection policies than developing countries (Article 4(3) and (4)), a requirement which is underscored by the fact that many developing countries have lower per capita emissions than developed countries.[81] The European Commission suggests that the CBAM-Proposal does not put into question the Agreement's underlying principles and argues that it merely 'ensures that goods imported into the EU will follow the same rules as the goods produced in the EU without interfering with the policy choices in third countries'.[82] This assumption might be relevant in a WTO context concerning non-discrimination: the EU can, for example, rightfully impose on imported chemicals the same domestic health, safety, and environment requirements as it imposes on domestically produced chemicals.[83] Yet is it also relevant in a Paris context? The Agreement's underlying objective is to achieve the temperature targets with ambitious self-determined national contributions in the light of the different national circumstances of the Parties. The Agreement allows developing countries' NDCs more leeway than those of developed countries and does not even require the former to adopt economy-wide absolute emission reduction targets. Hence, it accepts asymmetrical contributions by the Parties which can lead, in extremis, to the situation where a developing country could legally produce cement in a climate unfriendly way while at the same time being Paris compliant.

Despite this argument, the European Commission rejects a preferential treatment for developing countries; it says that 'such a mechanism will encourage LDCs to increase their level of emissions and would run counter to the overarching objectives of CBAM' and that 'no country has an interest in fostering carbon-intensive industries'.[84] In other words, the European Commission fears that developing Parties would increase their GHG emissions by exporting more ('dirty') products to the EU if they were exempted from the CBAM-Proposal. This assumption, based on carbon-leakage considerations, can hardly be reconciled with the Agreement's differentiation principles. The Agreement requires developed countries to take the lead and it accepts that 'peaking' will take longer for developing countries (Article 4(1)) with the inherent consequence that these countries can emit (in relative terms) more GHG than developed countries. Over time their emissions will decrease because of the progression requirement and the Oversight System, but the pace of this decrease will be different than that of developed countries. The European Commission will probably argue that

81. data.worldbank.org/indicator/EN.ATM.CO2E.PC?most_recent_value_desc=true (last visited 20 November 2021).
82. SWD(2021)643 final, 'Impact Assessment Report Accompanying the Proposal for a Regulation of the European Parliament and of the Council Establishing a Carbon Border Adjustment Mechanism', p. 8.
83. A hypothetical example might show the boundaries on non-discrimination: Suppose the EU were to introduce a 'product import regulation' which would require from importers to pay at the border the difference in social security costs between imported and domestically produced products? Here again the EU could argue that goods imported into the EU would follow the same rules as the goods produced in the EU, yet such a 'product'-regulation would be clearly WTO-incompatible.
84. CBAM Impact Assessment, *supra* note 82, p. 30.

it has the sovereign right to self-define the CBDRRC-requirement which can be interpreted in various conflicting ways.[85]

In our view, the Agreement's obligations limit the scope for such a self-determination. Developed countries should take the lead to combat climate change and the measures which they adopt must be compatible with the Agreement's other obligations. The CBAM-Proposal interferes, in an extra-territorial way, with the right of developing countries to prescribe factory-specific emissions levels. Its intention is to induce these countries through a border payment to adopt policies that result in the same level of climate protection as the EU's. If one were to follow Cosbey's position,[86] one would elevate the avoidance of carbon leakage to an overarching principle of the Agreement to which all other obligations must be subordinate. Such argumentation renders the differentiation requirement nugatory. Instead, we believe that the avoidance of carbon leakage must relate to the Agreement's other obligations and cannot overrule them.

The European Commission is aware of the negative consequences of its proposal for developing countries. Yet instead of introducing a preferential treatment, it suggests a 'targeted' approach to support developing countries, such as 'technical assistance, technology transfer, extensive capacity building and financial support, with the objective to develop industrial production structures that are compatible with long-term climate objectives'.[87] These explanations are an implicit admission that the CBAM-Proposal is inconsistent with the CBDRRC requirements; they also disregard the fact that the EU is already obliged under other provisions of the Agreement (e.g., Article 4(5), 9, 10 and 11) to adopt such a targeted approach. The differentiation requirement cannot be substituted with a targeted approach, it could, however, be reflected in an agreement between the EU and the developing country concerned regarding the exact scope of the EU's contribution towards the improvement of the industrial production structures in the country from a climate protection point of view.[88] In the absence of such an agreement, the proposal contravenes the CBDRRC-requirement.[89] Yet even with such an agreement, the exports of the country concerned could be subject to CBAMs in case of a CO_2-price difference between the exporting country and the EU.

2.3.2 *Can Parties to the Agreement Impose a Carbon Price on Others?*

Within the EU, the producers of carbon-intensive products are subject to EU ETS. EU ETS sets a limit on carbon emissions (cap) which decreases over time, issues

85. Mayer, *supra* note 19, point 4.17. Cosbey points out that the principle of CBDRRC also requires developed countries to show leadership in reducing emissions and draws the surprising conclusion that 'it is hard to see how they might do so [show leadership] if they do not take measures to avoid leakage'; Cosbey, 'Counting carbon: The implications of border carbon adjustment on developing countries', 14 December 2021, p. 8 hinrichfoundation.com/research/article/sustainable/border-carbon-adjustments (last visited 9 December 2021).
86. Cosbey, *supra* note 85, p. 8.
87. CBAM Impact Assessment, *supra* note 82, p. 30.
88. *See* Recitals 53 to 55 of the CBAM-Proposal.
89. *See also* Dadush, 'The EU's carbon border tax is likely to do more harm than good', Policy Center for the New South, June 2021, p. 3.; policycenter.ma/publications/eu%E2%80%99s-carbon-border-tax-likely-do-more-harm-good (last visited 30 November 2021).

allowances corresponding to the cap and allocates these allowances to the installations subject to the system. The installations, therefore, pay the price for their carbon emissions. The CBAM-Proposal also reflects the concept that imported products should pay the price for their carbon content, yet the European Commission has decided, for a variety of reasons,[90] not to extend EU ETS to imports but has chosen instead a different mechanism: the European Commission will set a price for CBAM certificates which mirrors the price of EU ETS allowances. Importers of the covered products will have to pay on the verified embedded GHG emissions[91] of the imported products the carbon price which they would have to pay had these products been produced in the EU. The focus on EU-carbon prices is justified with carbon-leakage-reasons[92] requiring that imported products 'bear a comparable carbon price to domestically produced products'.[93] Carbon-pricing mechanism of exporting countries can be credited in so far as importers can reduce the number of CBAM certificates to be surrendered by the respective 'carbon prices' of those countries (Article 9 CBAM-Proposal). The CBAM-Proposal defines carbon prices narrowly: only a carbon tax or an ETS can be credited (Article 3(23) CBAM-Proposal), other climate policy actions of the exporting country cannot be credited due to the 'conceptual difficulties in determining the equivalence between carbon-pricing and non-price regulatory measures'.[94]

In sum, the CBAM-Proposal, if adopted, would impose a European carbon price on covered imported products. It would also influence the production processes in third countries by indirectly imposing, through the price, European climate production standards. As mentioned by some commentators,[95] the proposal represents a paradigm shift on how to regulate the decarbonization process which raises several Paris issues.

2.3.2.1 A Carbon Price in General

The Agreement is silent about a price of carbon. It does not oblige its Parties to adopt specific mitigation measures, leaving them the choice and freedom to adopt, for example, an ETS, a carbon tax, an emission-related command and control regulation, other regulations concerning housing or transportation, a prohibition of coal for energy production or heating or a massive reforestation exercise. The Parties decide which commitments contribute best to their 'highest possible ambition ... in the light of different national circumstances'. While most of these measures eventually influence the final price of products, only a few of them are directly related to the product as

90. For an explanation of why the European Commission considered it inappropriate to extend EU ETS to CBAMs, *see* CBAM Impact Assessment, *supra* note 82, p. 32. *See also* Recitals 18-23 of the CBAM-Proposal. It should be noted that these explanations and justifications might play an important role in a WTO dispute settlement case against the EU.
91. *See* Article 7 and Annex III CBAM-Proposal. Embedded emissions are established by using actual emissions or if those are not possible default values.
92. Recital 21 CBAM-Proposal.
93. CBAM Impact Assessment, *supra* note 82, p. 26.
94. *Ibid.*
95. Marcu, Maratou, Mehling and Cosbey, 'The EU Carbon Border Adjustment Mechanism (CBAM): Preliminary analysis of the European Commission Proposal for a Regulation Establishing a Carbon Border Adjustment Mechanism', *ERCST*, July 2021, p. 4.

such.[96] The European Commission recognizes the difference between carbon-pricing and non-price regulatory measures,[97] yet does not accept, for reasons of administrative convenience, the contribution of these measures to the achievement of the Agreement's goals since otherwise it would have to allow the crediting of those measures under Article 9 CBAM-Proposal. The EU is free to argue that carbon should have a price;[98] it can also adopt a domestic pricing mechanism and argue that it is 'an essential toolbox to meet the objective of a climate-neutral Union by 2050', yet it cannot claim that the application of this price to imports is in line with the Agreement.[99] The Agreement does not require the adoption of a carbon price even if such a policy tool is widely accepted as an efficient way to reduce emissions,[100] rather it accepts a myriad of ways of compliance including the position not to opt for a carbon price at all.[101] By not accepting non-price regulatory measures the CBAM-Proposal deprives other Parties of their freedom of choice and imposes on them a European pricing mechanism if they want to continue to export the covered products to the EU. Such a mechanism contravenes the Agreement since it wrongly assumes that only a carbon price ensures compliance, and it could also be considered as 'punitive'.

It remains to be seen which effect the CBAM-Proposal will have on the mechanisms contained in and whether it will hinder or promote cooperative approaches on the international transfer of mitigation outcomes (Article 6(2)) or on emission reduction offsets that another Party can use to fulfil its NDCs (Article 6(4)); both procedures have been extremely controversial,[102] their operational guidelines were only adopted in November 2021.[103] IMF economists have recently suggested to create an international carbon price floor arrangement with prices of USD 75, 50 and 25 for advanced, high-, and low-income countries.[104] This suggestion demonstrates that if a carbon price were introduced internationally such a price would reflect the Agreement's differentiation requirement.

---

96. The WTO, for example, allows the adjustment of indirect taxes on products at the border. It also allows the adoption of domestic health, safety, and environmental regulations at the border but only in respect of product regulations. The cost of an environmental command and control regulation, such as an emission-, waste- or soil regulation of an installation have to be borne by the producer and cannot be adjusted at the border.
97. CBAM Impact Assessment, *supra* note 82, p. 26.
98. ec.europa.eu/commission/presscorner/detail/en/SPEECH_20_1655 (last visited 11 November 2021).
99. Recital 9 of the CBAM-Proposal.
100. Gaspar and Parry, 'A proposal to scale up global carbon pricing', *IMF Blog*, 18 June 2021, p. 2 blogs.imf.org/2021/06/18/a-proposal-to-scale-up-global-carbon-pricing (last visited 20 December 2021).
101. Developing countries in particular have not set a carbon price due to the lack of statistical and administrative capabilities to manage such a policy tool, *see* Dardush, *supra* note 89, p. 3.
102. *See generally* Wemaere, 'Article 6: Voluntary cooperation', in Van Calster and Reins, *supra* note 17, points 6.06 et seq. and points 6.31 et seq.
103. For a comment on these guidelines *see* Andrei Marcu, 'Article 6 Rulebook: A post COP26 assessment', *ERCST*, November 2021.
104. Gaspar and Parry, *supra* note 100, p. 5.

2.3.2.2 *The EU Price, in Particular*

Suppose a Party adopts an ETS as part of its NDCs and further suppose that the industrial structure of the country is different from the EU's. Based on the specific national circumstances, the market in this country will determine the carbon price which, almost certainly, will be different from the EU-carbon price.[105] Although the Agreement is silent about carbon prices, it accepts them as a contribution to its temperature goals if they are part of the NDC. Given its reliance on different national circumstances, the Agreement also accommodates a difference in carbon prices.[106] By imposing a carbon price on imports which mirrors the EU's own carbon emission levels and decarbonization efforts, the European Commission fails to recognize that lower carbon prices of other Parties might constitute as much a valid contribution to the Agreement's goals as the EU's carbon price.[107] This 'gold-plating'[108] of the value of carbon emissions up to the EU price seems to be compatible with the EU's NDC, yet it is not in line with the Agreement's requirements on how other Parties are supposed to meet their climate goals.[109]

2.3.2.3 *Paris Compliance: A Related Issue*

The European Commission argues that an EU price of CBAM certificates is necessary given the EU partners' lack of climate ambition. If the CBAM-Proposal is adopted, the EU will, therefore, unilaterally judge the appropriateness and sufficiency of the commitments and actual climate actions of its trading partners. This judgment stands in contrast to the Agreement's Oversight System which aims at helping the Parties to comply with their obligations in a non-intrusive and non-punitive way. As mentioned above, this system introduces a facilitative, non-adversarial structure aimed at improving NDCs in a prospective way instead of punishing Parties for having taken insufficient actions retrospectively. In case the ambition of a Party is deemed insufficient, both the transparency and/or the compliance exercises of Articles 13 and 15 will result in suggestions of more ambitious NDCs while the global stocktake will result in more ambition collectively in case the parties are found not to achieve compliance collectively. The Oversight System is an innovative response to the Kyoto Protocol's failure to impose legally binding commitments,[110] it promotes cooperation and facilitates

105. Crochet, 'CBAM enters with a BANG: The European Commission puts forth its carbon border adjustment mechanism proposal', ielp.worldtradelaw.net/2021/07/cbam-enters-with-a-bang-the-european-commission-puts-forth-its-carbon-border-adjustment-mechanism-pr.html (last visited 17 December 2021).
106. *See* Pirlot, 'Carbon border adjustment measures: A straightforward multi-purpose climate change instrument?', 34 *Journal of Environmental Law* (2022), 25-52, at 33.
107. *See, e.g.*, the discussion on the South Korean ETS at icapcarbonaction.com/en/?option=com_etsmap&task=export&format=pdf&layout=list&systems%5B%5D=47 (last visited 13 December 2021). Despite having a carbon-pricing system, importers of covered products from South Korea might nevertheless have to buy CBAM certificates when importing into the EU.
108. Crochet, *supra* note 105, p. 4.
109. Pirlot, *supra* note 106, p. 9.
110. Savasan, *Paris Climate Agreement: A Deal for Better Compliance* (Springer, 2019), p. 227.

compliance through a structured process, accepts peer pressure, yet is hostile to punitive measures. By imposing a 'penalty' on the imports from alleged 'climate laggards', the CBAM-Proposal contravenes the Agreement's Oversight System; the EU cannot unilaterally decide that almost all its trading partners are not complying with the Agreement's requirements before the Oversight System has even become operational. One would expect the EU to wait for a confirmation by the oversight exercises that the climate commitments of its trading partners are not deemed sufficient.[111]

2.3.3 *The Impact of Response Measures*

The Agreement is silent on trade issues and does not contain any specific provisions on whether unilateral trade restrictions resulting from mitigation measures are acceptable or not. The climate agreements and the climate community leave this topic to the WTO even if there has been a constant debate on the issue in climate fora – a debate which only will accelerate because of the expected more ambitious climate actions.[112] The UNFCCC contains a reference to trade issues in Article 3(5)[113] which borrows the chapeau language of GATT Article XX; however, its application *mutatis mutandis* in the Paris context is controversial[114] since the relationship between the Agreement and UNFCCC remains unclear.[115] An indirect reference to trade can be found in Article 4(15) and in the Preamble (Recital 7), both of which refer to the impact of response measures on other Parties. At issue here is the question of whether the CBAM-Proposal, if adopted, would result in unjustifiable discrimination against other Parties and whether by not considering this effect the EU's measures would be incompatible with Article 4(15). This argument is, however, far-fetched since Article 4(15) does not specify which actions Parties would have to carry out to comply with this requirement.[116] The EU, for example, could not only refer to its obligation under Article 4(2) stating that CBAMs are domestic mitigation measures adopted with the aim of achieving the objective of its NDC, but could also argue that it has taken Article 4(15) requirements into account by conducting an exhaustive impact assessment of its proposal. The Forum on the impact of the implementation of response measure originally established under UNFCCC[117] and authorized by Decision 1/CP.21 to also

111. Pirlot, *supra* note 106, p. 9.
112. Bodansky, Brunée and Rajamani, *supra* note 14, p. 348.
113. Article 3.5 UNFCCC: 'Measures taken to combat climate change, including unilateral ones, should not constitute a means of arbitrary or unjustifiable discrimination or a disguised restriction on international trade.'
114. Bacchus, 'What is a Climate Response Measure? Centre for International Governance Innovation', CIGI Papers No. 220, July 2019, p. 9.
115. There is no agreement between the Parties on the meaning of the language of Article 2(1) 'enhancing the implementation of the Convention': some consider that the Agreement flows from UNFCCC and that it should therefore be interpreted in light of it, others see it as distinct; *see* Galeigh, 'Article 2: Aims, objectives and principles', in Van Calster and Reins, *supra* note 17, point 2.14 with further references.
116. Mayer, *supra* note 19, point 4.41.
117. For a history of the climate negotiations on response measures *see* Bacchus, *supra* note 114, pp. 7 et seq. *See also* Marcu and Stoefs, 'The role of response measures in ensuring the sustainable transition to a low-GHG economy', *ICTSD Policy Brief*, January 2017, pp. 3 et seq.

serve the Agreement has been unable to develop a proposal on acceptable response measures due to the unsurmountable disagreements between developing and developed Parties. Developed countries insist on a 'safety net' for both the social and economic impacts of their mitigation measures,[118] while developing countries would rather outlaw unilateral trade measures for climate purposes but have failed to do so in the conferences preceding the Paris meeting.[119] Bacchus suggests that the silence of the Agreement on this issue can be seen as a tacit acceptance of some form of unilateral trade restrictive climate measures[120] and calls for the development of a non-exhaustive list of acceptable response measures. He considers that the WTO Appellate Body's jurisprudence concerning the chapeau of GATT Article XX could be used as guidance for the development of such a list.[121] The *CBAM* case is an illustrative example of the difficulties in arriving at such a list: if the CBAM-Proposal were to violate a GATT provision it could be justified with GATT Article XX. Such justification requires a country-by-country analysis, given the chapeau's insistence on taking the specific situation of the country concerned into account. If a WTO Member/Party were able to demonstrate that its climate change policies were compatible with the requirements of the Agreement, a justification under GATT Article XX would not be possible. Consequently, the CBAM would be considered an arbitrary or unjustifiable discrimination since it did not take the specific situation in the country concerned into account.[122] If, however, the EU could demonstrate non-compliance with the Agreement by the complaining WTO Member/Party, the analysis under the chapeau could be concluded in favour of the EU. Hence, compliance with the Agreement would become the decisive factor in a WTO case against the CBAM-Regulation. An inclusion of CBAMs into the non-exhaustive list of acceptable response measures would therefore require a proviso that the CBAM can only be applied to countries not complying with their obligations under the Agreement – an assumption which the EU summarily and wrongfully makes.[123]

2.4 Preliminary Conclusions

The Agreement's reliance on 'equity' and 'CBDRRC' reflects the notion that the historic responsibility for climate change lies with developed countries. If developed countries accept this responsibility and adopt ambitious climate mitigation measures which go

118. Marcu and Stoefs, *supra* note 117, p. 6.
119. Bacchus, *supra* note 114, p. 11; *see also* Chan, 'The "new" impacts of the implementation of climate change response measures', 25 *Review of European, Comparative & International Environmental Law* (2016), 228-237, at 233.
120. Bacchus, *supra* note 114, p. 11.
121. *Ibid.*, p. 13.
122. *See* Quick, *supra* note 10, p. 583.
123. On 30 March 2021, Executive Vice-President Timmermans, made the following statement at an FT climate conference: 'If there is a serious risk of carbon leakage, if we take measures to comply with (the Paris Agreement) and others don't, and it leads to a disadvantage to our industries, I will have no hesitation whatsoever to introduce carbon border adjustment mechanism.' *See* ft.com/content/d31ec6c9-453a-4705-b47b-1c9e46de817a (last visited 27 November 2021).

beyond what other Parties are supposed to do, they find themselves in a dilemma. The European Commission believes that Europe can only comply with its Paris obligations by adopting very ambitious climate protection measures which require in parallel the protection of the domestic industry. Hence a system which elevates the avoidance of carbon leakage to an overarching principle of climate protection and applies nothing but a European CO_2 price on imports. Such a system is incompatible with the provisions of the Agreement though, which accepts an asymmetry of contributions to achieve the temperature goals. A European CO_2 price imposed on imports defies the Agreement's acceptance that Parties can apply a variety of measures and still be compatible with the Agreement. The EU claims that other Parties are not doing enough to comply with the Agreement, yet its claim cannot be verified given the 2018 Katowice Guidelines' exclusion of compliance and implementation issues from dispute settlement.[124] Other Parties could argue that the CBAM-Proposal is incompatible with the EU's Paris obligations, yet the non-adversarial Oversight System will not provide any answers on such unilateral action. And even if a negative comment on the CBAM-Proposal was made in this context, Parties are under no obligation to act on suggestions made on their action, as mentioned above.[125]

3 DIPLOMACY VERSUS ADJUDICATION: THE PARIS AGREEMENT BEGGARS ITS WTO NEIGHBOUR

3.1 Does Incompatibility with Paris Matter?

Could the Agreement's dispute settlement mechanism contained in Article 24 be used to find answers to the legal issues raised above?

Article 24 states that the dispute settlement provisions of the UNFCCC (Article 14 UNFCCC)[126] apply *mutatis mutandis* to the Agreement. Any dispute concerning the interpretation and application of the Agreement could therefore be handled under the UNFCCC dispute settlement mechanism. Procedurally, Article 14(1) UNFCCC (and Article 24) allow Parties to seek a settlement through negotiations or any other peaceful means of their choice. Further, Article 14(2) UNFCCC (and consequently Article 24) permit redressal of disputes by submitting the matter before the ICJ, arbitration or conciliation processes. Article 14(2)(b) UNFCCC and Article 24 respectively envisage the COP to adopt an arbitration procedure as an annex. However, to this date, no such procedures have been adopted or annexed.[127]

In view of the fact that the COP has not taken action to give effect to Article 14(2)(b) UNFCCC, the arbitration mechanism under the Agreement is rendered

124. Katowice Guidelines, FCCC/PA/CMA/2018/3/Add.2.; Benjamin, Haynes and Rudyk, *supra* note 69, p. 353.
125. *See supra* notes 54 and 69.
126. Article 14(1) UNFCC.
127. Cantley-Smith, 'Article 24: Settlement of disputes under the Paris Agreement', in Van Calster and Reins, *supra* note 17, point 24.05; Bacchus, *supra* note 114, p. 4.

ineffective and meaningless.[128] Further, the ICJ's jurisdiction has not been invoked to settle disputes under the Agreement till date.[129] Hence, it is safe to say that so far, Parties have not used the fora available to them to raise and resolve any disputes arising from the interpretation or application of the Agreement.[130] This begs the question, given the effective absence of a dispute settlement mechanism, whether inconsistency with the Agreement matters at all?

We argue that without a dispute settlement system to ensure adherence to the provisions of the Agreement, allegedly inconsistent Parties may be able to escape scot-free. First, no authoritative body would exist to give a finding of inconsistent conduct of a Party.[131] Second, even if the Oversight System establishes inconsistent conduct of a party, there would be no legal repercussions: if anything, inconsistent Parties may only be subject to political condemnation. Hence, the combination of self-determination and the non-adversarial Oversight System with its facilitative and cooperative mechanism to address any concerns may not be adequately effective in achieving the goals of the Agreement and an action on dispute settlement might become unavoidable.[132]

3.2 The Agreement's Lack of Guidance Puts the WTO Dispute Settlement System under Severe Stress

CBAMs are here to stay. As Parties aim to achieve net zero targets around 2050, some of them (for example, Canada, the United States and the United Kingdom) also contemplate the adoption of carbon adjustment for imports of some sorts[133] and others will probably follow suit. Arguably, the social and economic impacts of stricter domestic climate protection measures are too important to stop Parties from adopting these measures because of potential incompatibilities with international obligations. Carbon-border adjustments measures will therefore be regulated by the different authorities in different ways and importers will have to cope with divergent regulations. Given this bleak outlook, it is with good reason that commentators urge for the

128. Bacchus, *supra* note 114, p. 4. Only the Netherlands has made a statement accepting the means of dispute resolution under Article 14(2) UNFCC and repeated this statement also with respect to Article 24. *See* Amirfar and Write, 'The Paris Agreement's conciliation annex: If not now then when?', 25(17) *ASIL Insights* (2021), p. 2.
129. Cantley-Smith, *supra* 127, point 24.12.
130. Bacchus, referring to Lassus Saint Genie, considers the Agreement as 'lightly legalized' which has 'generally adopted a managerial rather than an enforcement approach to compliance', Bacchus, *supra* note 114, p. 4.
131. At European level, it is unlikely that the ECJ will accord the Agreement direct effect, given the flexible and discretionary nature of its obligations. For a more cautious approach *see* Ruiz Fabri, 'Is there a case – Legally and politically – For direct effect of WTO obligations?', 25 *European Journal of International Law* (2014), 151-173.
132. Amirfar and White suggest a mandatory conciliation process as a non-binding form of out of court settlement to deal with potentially upcoming Paris disputes and urge the Conference of the Parties to adopt an Annex on conciliation, Amirfar and White, *supra* note 128, pp. 3 et seq.
133. *See* Cosbey, 'Principles and best practice in border carbon adjustment', IISD Trade and Sustainability Review, September 2021, p. 1, iisd.org/articles/principles-border-carbon-adjustment-modest-proposal (last visited 12 December 2021). Cosbey notes that 63 Parties by now have communicated net zero targets.

adoption of principles and best practices or for an exhaustive list of acceptable response measures.[134] Yet so far, neither the WTO nor the Agreement have taken up the issue and have started negotiations in earnest on which unilateral actions to protect the climate should be allowed.

164 of the 192 Parties to the Agreement are members of the WTO. For the time being, WTO dispute settlement is all the 164 WTO members can resort to, if they want to have clarity on CBAMs or similar trade-related climate measures. CBAM disputes will arrive at the WTO at a time when the dispute settlement system is only half-functioning given the demise of the Appellate Body. As the many WTO rulings on trade and environment show, the Appellate Body has not shied away from giving guidance on difficult legal and political issues, its rulings have often compensated for the lack of will of the membership to agree on new rules or to react to new developments by adopting interpretative guidance.[135] Yet, it is exactly this activism which triggered the Appellate Body's crisis albeit in a different area (trade remedies). A half-functioning dispute settlement will probably not be able to provide clarity given the constant threat of 'appeals into the void'. Also, it remains to be seen whether the WTO Multi-Party Interim Appeal Agreement (MPIA) will follow the footsteps of the Appellate Body and whether it will have the courage to interpret the GATT the way climate advocates propose.

A WTO dispute settlement case concerning the CBAM-Regulation presents a myriad of legal issues which will not be addressed in this paper. Instead, we will concentrate on how the Agreement might influence a WTO ruling. We are mindful that in a WTO case against the CBAM-Regulation the Agreement will not be applied as such; it will, however, influence the interpretation of GATT Article III:4 or of the chapeau of GATT Article XX. The European Commission has characterized the CBAM-Proposal as a 'product'-legislation intending thereby to exclude the interpretation that CBAMs are border measures potentially incompatible with GATT Article II 1 (b), second sentence.[136] As domestic product legislation applied at the border, the CBAM-Regulation will be scrutinized under the criterion 'treatment less favourable' on whether it modifies the conditions of competition in the relevant market to the detriment of the imported products. In other words, if the domestic producers under EU ETS were 'better off' than importers, the CBAM-Regulation would be seen as a violation of GATT Article III:4. The proposed methodologies for the assessment of the embedded emissions (are they 'punitive'?), the setting of the price for CBAM certificates (arbitrary?) as well as the carbon-pricing issues in general, and in particular the EU price will influence the findings of the WTO panel. Were the CBAM measure found to be inconsistent with GATT Articles III:4 (or with GATT Articles I or II (1) b, alternatively), it could be justified with GATT Article XX. The analysis of the chapeau concentrates on the way the CBAM is applied: is it an arbitrary or unjustifiable discrimination or is it a

134. Cosbey, *supra* note 133, p. 3, Bacchus, *supra* note 114, p. 13. Both differ, however, on whether to develop such guidance under the auspices of the Agreement or the WTO.
135. *See generally* Quick, 'Do we need trade and environment negotiations or has the appellate body done the job?', 47 *Journal of World Trade* (2013), 957-983.
136. *See* Quick, *supra* note 10, pp. 577-579.

justified measure? In the *US – Shrimp*, the Appellate Body considered the measure at issue to be a single, rigid and unbending requirement whose coercive effect on the policy decisions of other WTO members had been intentional and confirmed arbitrary and unjustifiable discrimination. It said:

> However, it is not acceptable, in international trade relations, for one WTO Member to use an economic embargo to require other Members to adopt essentially the same comprehensive regulatory program, to achieve a certain policy goal, as that in force within the Member's territory, *without taking into consideration different conditions which may occur in the territories of those Members.*
>
> We believe that discrimination results not only when countries in which the same conditions prevail are differently treated, but also when the application of the measure at issue does *not allow for any inquiry into the appropriateness of the regulatory program for the conditions prevailing in those exporting countries.*[137]

The climate-relevant conditions of the Parties and the appropriateness of their regulatory programmes are governed by the Agreement. First, the Agreement leaves Parties a choice of action, notably it does not require them to introduce a carbon price. Second, the Agreement mandates differentiation, which allows developing countries to adopt less onerous measures than developed countries and to produce the covered products in a less climate friendly way provided their regulatory programme is, overall, in compliance with the Agreement. Third, the Agreement calls upon the Parties to implement its provisions in a 'facilitative, non-intrusive and non-punitive way' and repeats this language also with respect to compliance. Furthermore, the whole concept of implementation and compliance is based on the prerogative that it is not up to individual Parties to decide on the adequacy of other countries' climate actions, but it is up to the Oversight System to help Parties implement the Agreement and comply with it. When relating these points to the application of the CBAM-Regulation, one could argue that the measure is arbitrary: the EU does not take the exporting Party's compliance with the Agreement into account; it insists on an EU-carbon price without adjustments of non-price regulatory measures or without inquiring whether the carbon price applied in the exporting country achieves, together with the other mitigation commitments, the goals submitted in the NDC; rather the EU imposes a punitive measure with a coercive effect on exporting parties. The EU, however, will argue that the Appellate Body has recognized the Member's right to protect the global commons and that the balance to be found under the chapeau of GATT Article XX 'is not fixed and unchanging', but rather that the 'location of the line of equilibrium … moves as the kind and the shape of the measures at stake and as the facts making up specific cases differ'.[138] The EU could refer to the urgency of ambitious climate protective measures and the many scientific studies supporting this fact; it could cite the Agreement's obligation to achieve the temperature goals, the self-determination of NDCs and the requirement of increased ambition. From all this, it could draw the conclusion that the

137. Appellate Body Report, *United States – Import Prohibition of Certain Shrimp and Shrimp Products*, WT/DS58/AB/R 1998, paras 164-165 (emphasis added).
138. *US – Shrimp*, para. 159.

Agreement covers measures against carbon leakage and that, overall, its measure constitutes a bona fide application of GATT Article XX.

The essential element for a positive or a negative finding in the context of the chapeau of GATT Article XX is, in our view, analysing whether the climate-related activities of the complainant are in line with its Paris obligations. On this specific issue, the WTO cannot rely on any guidance from the Agreement, rather the WTO panel must come to a decision based on the submissions of the members. If the panel were of the view that the complaining member does not comply with its obligations under the Agreement, it could decide the case in favour of the defendant, even if the disputed measure contains elements incompatible with the Agreement. The Agreement's silence on trade and climate issues, its inability to decide on justifiable response measures and its overall lack of a mandatory dispute settlement takes its toll. It seems that the Parties to the Agreement accept that the WTO takes control and that trade and climate disputes are decided on the evaluation of an issue which lies beyond trade competences. This control comes at a price, though: if the panel interprets the chapeau of GATT Article XX conservatively, the climate community will complain and politically attack the WTO as being insensitive to climate protection issues; if, on the other hand, the panel interprets the chapeau of Article XX creatively, this will perpetuate the dispute settlement crisis of the WTO (too much judicial activism), will lead to appeals into the void and will increase the scepticism towards a multilateral dispute settlement process. If the Parties want to exercise control on climate issues within the Agreement, they need to consider giving authoritative guidance or accepting a mandatory dispute settlement system. Such activity would, in turn, allow for better functioning of the WTO dispute settlement system since WTO Panels could rely on authoritative guidance from the competent body on climate protection.

4 CONCLUSIONS

Does the CBAM-Proposal constitute a 'disruptive innovation' which will trigger the paradigm shift necessary to solve the climate crisis or is it a unilateral measure which will only trigger protectionist responses? The answer to this question will not depend on an isolated WTO case against CBAMs but on Europe's negotiation strategy with affected trading partners. Will the EU accept the underlying principle of the Agreement that the Parties can choose their climate protection policies and are not obliged to follow the EU's way if their measures are in line with the Agreement's temperature goals or will it impose its position on them? The European Commission has started this process by defying the rule of law in international relations: the CBAM-Proposal contravenes the letter and the spirit of the Agreement[139] and is, arguably, incompatible with the EU's WTO obligations. After the conclusion of the Uruguay Round, it was generally accepted that such power-oriented bullying policies should be overcome. On the one hand, power-oriented politics have become more popular over the past years and the European Commission's 'disruptive innovation' reflects the political mood in

139. As predicted by the Juncker Commission, *supra* note 8.

Europe concerning climate change. Furthermore, the EU will not be held accountable for its Paris-inconsistent proposal given the absence of a mandatory dispute settlement process in the Agreement; besides, any decision taken by the WTO will lack authority due to the demise of the Appellate Body and a potential appeal into the void.[140] WTO members might not even use the dispute settlement process but could just adopt other forms of carbon-border adjustment which could be even more creative than the CBAM-Proposal – just imagine a CBAM calculated on per capita CO_2 emissions. On the other hand, the CBAM-Proposal is not yet in force and anyway foresees a transition period which demonstrates Europe's readiness for dialogue and negotiations.[141] It looks as if the European Commission wants to use the instrument as a leverage to arrive at more ambitious climate protection measures by its trading partners; in such case, CBAMs would become redundant. This approach is not without risk, though. It is an open question whether the proposal will lead to the above-mentioned paradigm shift or whether it will end in failure and then lead to divergent and contradicting CBAMs and countermeasures applied by the Parties – a situation in which the 'disruptive innovation' would become a nightmare which reminds of Goethe's *Zauberlehrling* who could no longer control the 'spirits' which he called for:

> Herr, die Not ist groß, die ich rief, die Geister, werd' ich nun nicht los!
> (I have need of Thee, from the spirits that I called, deliver me!)

It will depend on the negotiating skills of the European Commission to demonstrate that Europe can control the 'spirits' invoked by the CBAM-Proposal.

We would like to end our deliberations with a remark on mandatory dispute settlement in Multilateral Environmental Agreements (MEAs). Like the Paris Agreement, most of these instruments have opted for a diplomatic instead of a mandatory resolution of disputes. They contain obligations which, unless enforced domestically (which is rather the exception), can eventually be breached without being held accountable. Not being held accountable, however, allows for power politics. It is an invitation for 'heavyweights' to impose their views on others. Should the countries participating in an MEA, therefore, not prefer a rules-based over a power-based system? It seems to us that the Parties to these agreements still do not see the need to have the agreed rules enforced with a mandatory dispute settlement.

140. Only 24 WTO members other than the EU have accepted the alternative MPIA system, *see* ec.europa.eu/trade/policy/accessing-markets/dispute-settlement (last visited 1 November 2021).
141. *See* CBAM-Proposal, p. 22, notes 50-55.

CHAPTER 6

A Few Thoughts on the Future Structure of the European Union

Richard H. Lauwaars[*]

The hard core of this chapter is a revival of the so-called plan Maudling, that is to say, the proposal to make the European Economic Community (EEC), as such, a member of the 'European Free Trade Area (FTA)', later re-baptized in the 'European Economic Association'. I do not go into the trade law aspects of this case; what I did like to revive is the idea of making one international organization, in addition to the other Member States, a member of another international organization. To place this idea in its context, I first discuss the Attali report of 1999, which mentions three models to cope with the problems of an enlarged European Union (EU). Thereafter I mention the Humboldt speech held by Joschka Fischer and the Commission's White Paper on the Future of Europe. My own proposal is, retaking Mr Maudling's ideas, to create two Unions: a 'Union 1', consisting of, for example, the euro States, which as such will become a member of 'Union 2', consisting of the 'Union 1' Member States and the others. 'Union 2' will correspond to the present EU, but with this difference, the Union of, say, the euro States (Union 1) will be the 28th member and will replace the euro States in the fields which fall under its (Union 1's) competences. Two obvious advantages will be: (1) the 'Union 1' Member States can further integrate and will not be hindered by unwilling colleagues; (2) the 'Union 2' Member States will be able to stay on their lower level of integration and nevertheless

* The author wishes to thank Mr A.J. Faughnan for translating this text.

maintain the quality of 'Union Member State' which they will not be willing to lose.

1 INTRODUCTION

The European Union (EU) has had 27 members since 1 February 2020. That figure could potentially grow to somewhere between 35 and 40 in the coming years.[1] It should be obvious that the EU's current structure is not cut out for this. In this article, I will explore how that structure might be organized to accommodate that many members, the ostensible absorption capacity.[2] For that, I will first look back to the years 1956-1958 when, in the Maudling Committee, plans were made for a 'European Economic Association' comprising the European Economic Community (EEC) and the other Organization for European Economic Cooperation (OEEC) countries.[3] I will then move on to the Attali report of 1999, Joschka Fischer's speech at the Humboldt University in Berlin, and conclude the overview with an account of the European Commission's 2017 White Paper on the Future of Europe. In the concluding chapter, I will recapitulate the proposals most pertinent to my argument and then give my thoughts.

2 THE MAUDLING PLAN

2.1 Working Party (19 July 1956-16 October 1957)

The 'Maudling Plan' refers to the United Kingdom's (UK) proposal to establish a free trade area (FTA) that would include the EEC itself, on the one hand, and the other 11 Member States of the OEEC, on the other: the so-called European FTA.[4] This proposal was discussed on 17 October 1957 in the Maudling Committee, an intergovernmental committee chaired by the British minister Reginald Maudling.

The proposal started to gain traction in the spring of 1956, once the UK had abandoned its hostile attitude vis-à-vis the (future) EEC. In a 5 July 1956 speech to the House of Commons, Sir Edward Boyle, Economic Secretary to the Treasury, indicated that the British Government was interested in an FTA between the UK and the customs

1. *See* the annex to this article for potential new members.
2. *See* De Zwaan, 'De toekomst van de Europese Unie – samenwerking', 60 SEW (2012), 438-450, at 441.
3. Originally the 'European FTA', it was later renamed the 'European Economic Association' – *see* Camps, *Britain and the European Community 1955 – 1963* (OUP, 1964), at 150 and 158. Euratom was excluded, given the UK's insurmountable reservations about Euratom's monopoly on the production and distribution of certain fissile materials (Camps, at 94).
4. The OEEC was succeeded, by treaty of 14 December 1960, by the OECD, with effect from 30 September 1961; *see* Ribbelink, *Opvolging van internationale organisaties* (T.M.C. Asser Press, 1988), at 124-140.

union of the Six, albeit not through direct negotiation, but within the OEEC framework.[5] On 19 July 1956, the OEEC Council of Ministers decided to set up a Special Working Group to consider the possibility of a multilateral association between the EEC and the other Member States.[6] This Working Group issued reports on 22 December 1956 and 10 January 1957, concluding that an FTA in the form of a joint agreement with the customs union of the Six was technically possible.[7] Based on that report, the OEEC Council decided, on 15 March 1957, to set up three working parties, the most important of which was Working Party No. 21, which was instructed to commence negotiations 'to determine the conditions under which a European Free Trade Area associating, on a multilateral basis, the European Common Market with the other Member countries, could be brought into being'.[8] This Working Group's chair issued a report on 11 July 1957.[9] Among the 'key problems' facing the Working Group was the type of treaty that would be chosen to embody the FTA and the nature of the association between the EEC and the other Member States: a facsimile of the Treaty of Rome or a trade treaty with as few rules as possible.[10]

2.2 Intergovernmental Committee (19 October 1957-15 January 1959)

In response to this report, the OEEC Council adopted two resolutions on 17 October 1957. The first resolution expressed the Council's intention 'to secure the establishment of a European Free Trade Area'.[11] The second established an intergovernmental committee, which chose Reginald Maudling to be its chair.[12]

Although the Treaty of Rome came into effect on 1 January 1958, for which reason the Commission should have taken over the negotiations (Article 228 EEC), the governments of the six Member States stayed put. The Commission did, however, increasingly assert itself in the negotiations. This notwithstanding, it was a committee of representatives of the Six, chaired by the Belgian Permanent Delegate to the OEEC,

5. Camps, *supra* note 3, at 95-96.
6. *See* the Resolution of the Council of 19 July 1956, concerning the study of the relationship between the proposed European Customs Union and Member countries not taking part therein, C(56)196, in: *Negotiations for a European Free Trade Area*, Documents Relating to the Negotiations from July 1956 to December 1958, Cmnd. 641 (hereinafter: the Documents), at 7.
7. Report by Special Working Party No. 17 of the Council on the possibility of creating a Free Trade Area in Europe, C(57)5, not included in the Documents, but discussed by Camps, *supra* note 3, at 110-111.
8. *See* the Resolution of the Council of 15 March 1957 concerning the arrangements for negotiations on a European FTA and problems linked therewith, Documents cited *supra* note 6, at 8.
9. Camps, *supra* note 3, at 125-126.
10. *See* the Report of the Chairman of the Working Party to the Chairman of the Council dated 11 July 1957, Documents cited *supra* note 6, at 10 et seq., paras 11 and 15.
11. *See* Resolution of the Council of 17 October 1957 on the European Free Trade Area and problems linked therewith, C(57)221, Documents cited *supra* note 6, at 48.
12. *See* Resolution of the Council of 17 October 1957 concerning an Inter-Governmental Committee on the establishment of a European Free Trade Area, C(57)222, Documents cited *supra* note 6, at 49; also *see* Camps, *supra* note 3, at 136.

Roger Ockrent, who was tasked with formulating a joint position.[13] The report in question was presented to the other OEEC countries on 17 October 1958.[14]

Regrettably, at the end of a 14 November 1958 meeting of the Maudling Committee, the French Information Minister, Jacques Soustelle, declared that it would be impossible to establish an FTA of the kind desired by the British.[15] This put an end to the negotiations on an FTA (although, according to Miriam Camps, they could have succeeded).[16]

3 THE ATTALI REPORT (19 JULY 1999)

3.1 The Proposal

The Attali Report was written at the behest of Hubert Védrine, the then French Foreign Minister under the presidency of François Mitterrand, and it comprises former President of the European Bank for Reconstruction and Development Jacques Attali's *réflexions personnelles* on the future of the Union.[17] Attali assumes in the first sentence of his report that the Union will have at least 35 members by 2020; towards the end of the introduction, he mentions a figure of 35 to 40.[18] The report was written after the Treaty of Amsterdam was concluded (2 October 1997) and published shortly after it entered into force (1 May 1999). In the annex to this article, I list the countries that Attali had in mind when he expressed his expectations for the future. In addition to the Union's then 27 Member States, the first to be mentioned are the five remaining federal republics of the former Federal Republic of Yugoslavia. Then come Albania, Moldova, Belarus (if it did not merge with Russia), Ukraine, and Switzerland. And, finally, Turkey, Georgia, and Armenia (for a total of 40 countries). Russia ought to be admitted to the Union as an associate member; in Attali's opinion, the West's worst nightmare is a Russia that has grown once again belligerent because it feels left out.[19]

Attali then gives five possible scenarios for managing this process, two of which at first only involve the then 15 Member States (at the time the report was written, the Eastern and Central European States, as well as Malta and Cyprus, had yet to join); the other three scenarios involve a more or less major expansion. I briefly discuss each of these scenarios below.

13. *See* Camps, *supra* note 3, at 147-148 and 157.
14. The report is included in Documents cited *supra* note 6, at 96-104. Chapter XII on 'Institutional Problems' is particularly relevant; according to para. 33, the Community aims 'to act as a unit within the Association'.
15. *See* Camps, *supra* note 3, at 164.
16. *See ibid.*, at 169.
17. Attali, *Europe 2020: Pour une Union plurielle,* Rapport au Ministre des Affaires Etrangères, which should be available at www.attali.com but was not to be found there. The library of the European Parliament in Luxembourg does have a copy, fortunately.
18. *Ibid.*, at 8.
19. *Ibid.*, at 19.

3.1.1 A Federal Union

In this scenario, the expansion would be preceded by intensification. This would be expressed primarily through the election of a European President under a European Constitution and a European government consisting of the Commission and Council of Ministers under the leadership of the President, for a total of 15 members. The candidate Member States would be kept on hold until all the above was accomplished. Attali believed that the chances of this scenario becoming a reality were slim at best; nothing like it had been achieved since the Treaty of Maastricht, not even by the Treaty of Amsterdam.[20]

3.1.2 A Sovereign Union

Monetary issues and the rise of populist parties foment resistance to new transfers of financial resources and powers to EU institutions. Resistance to inevitable change simultaneously gains traction in the candidate Member States. This scenario cannot be ruled out entirely: *l'acquis n'est pas acquis.*[21]

3.1.3 A Hazy Union (*l'Union floue*)

The most likely scenario would be successive waves of expansion, with no substantial changes made to the rules governing the Union's functioning or negotiating methods. The new members will have the same rights as the old ones, and changes made by the accession treaties will be limited to numerical adjustments to how the institutions are configured. Attali is convinced that the Union will become unmanageable once it crosses the threshold of 20 members. This will spell the end of the Union; some members will form new factions outside the Union, with most turning their attention to the United States.[22] This brings us to the fourth scenario.

3.1.4 An Atlantic Union

In this scenario, the Union would become an extension of the Atlantic Alliance. The Union would have to transfer its economic competences to North Atlantic Treaty Organization (NATO) in exchange for a transfer of defence competences from NATO to the Union. Were this proposal to be presented, the United States would immediately be seen as a *future member* of a larger entity, and it would influence the development of the Union in much the same way that EU candidate members currently immerse themselves in the present Member States' decision-making. The euro would become an

20. *Ibid.*, at 24.
21. *Ibid.*, at 26.
22. *Ibid.*, at 28-29.

extension of the US dollar. According to Attali, this scenario can rely on the widest support.[23]

3.1.5 *A Multiform Union*

In this scenario, Member State majorities would not, on the one hand, be constrained by minorities; on the other hand, those minorities would be able to launch special projects of their own. Attali refers to this as *géométrie multiple*, which he describes as the regularization of the Enhanced Cooperation set out in the Treaty of Amsterdam.[24]

This would bring about a polycentric Union; the Union would no longer be cast as a hierarchical pyramid but as a collection of factions in which anyone and everyone are welcome to participate. To avoid having this multiform Union devolve into an impromptu assortment of disparate projects, with the most powerful Member States locking themselves into ever-closer collaborative structures, one would also need to establish new areas of and mechanisms for loyalty and protection aimed at strengthening democracy.[25]

3.2 The Programme

3.2.1 *Treaty of Nice (2000-2001)*[26]

This treaty, according to Attali, would have to specify the minimum conditions for the preparations for future accessions.[27] Attali specifically advocates replacing the unanimity requirement with a qualified majority in as many areas as possible, as well as changing the relative weight of votes cast by members of the Council. In addition, the General Affairs Council would have to be split up into two bodies: one for the administration of the Union and the other for foreign policy.[28]

3.2.2 *Treaty of Lisbon (2007)*[29]

When the Treaty of Amsterdam was concluded, a second intergovernmental conference was already in the works (aside from the one that led to the Treaty of Nice). According to Protocol No. 11, a new Intergovernmental Conference (IGC) shall be convened '[a]t least one year before the membership of the European Union exceeds

23. *Ibid.*, at 29-31.
24. *Ibid.*, at 32.
25. *Ibid.*, at 32-33.
26. The Treaty of Nice was ratified on 26 February 2001 and came into force on 1 February 2003.
27. Attali, *supra* note 17, at 34.
28. *Ibid.*, at 35.
29. The Treaty of Lisbon was concluded on 13 December 2007 and it came into force on 1 December 2009.

twenty'.[30] Attali does refer to this and then goes on to note that this IGC should lead to the ratification of a new European Constitution or a new treaty. It should provide for:

(a) the formation of country factions (*circonscriptions*) to limit the Commission and the Councils of Ministers to no more than 20 members each; the same would have to apply to the European Central Bank's (ECB) Board of Governors. New members would have to be required to join one of the factions. Attali backs this up with explicit references to the International Monetary Fund (IMF) and the World Bank. Twenty was opted for in light of the provision quoted from Protocol No. 11; beyond that, the institutional system would require a substantial overhaul.[31] On an earlier page, he creates the impression that the 20 factions would be formed by the 15 countries that were already members of the Union by 1999, plus the 5 that the European Council of 12/13 December 1997 had accepted as candidate members. In the annex to the report, he outlines, as a means of illustration, a division of the 41 countries he had mentioned earlier into 20 factions.[32] As far as the IMF and the World Bank are concerned, it is true that the members of their non-plenary bodies represent groups of countries aside from the representatives of the largest contributors. Schermers and Blokker note that, in 1994, out of the IMF's 24 Executive Directors, 5 were appointed by the members with the largest quotas, with the remaining 19 elected by the organization's general congress, i.e., the Board of Governors; those 19 directors represented 164 Member States;[33]
(b) alternatively, the following solution could be opted for if (a) is beyond reach: Divide the Commission into 15 parts, each represented by a coordinating vice president; the meeting of the vice presidents and the president would effectively serve as the Union executive. Make qualified majority the rule in the Council, and the concept of enhanced cooperation commonplace, especially in the case of the countries in the Eurozone;[34]
(c) transfer essential functions from the Commission to the executive agencies;
(d) merge the presidencies of the Commission and the European Council into one post: EU President; and
(e) merge the Council of Ministers for European Affairs with the Commission.[35]

30. Treaty of Amsterdam - Protocol on the institutions with the prospect of enlargement of the European Union, Article 2, O.J. 1997, C 340/111.
31. Attali, *supra* note 17, at 38.
32. These factions diverge from the earlier premise on p. 37; for example, in the annex he mentions a faction consisting of Russia, Serbia, and Belarus, a faction consisting of Turkey, Bosnia, Albania, and Kosovo, and a faction consisting entirely of Ukraine.
33. *See* Schermers and Blokker, *International Institutional Law: Unity within Diversity*, 3rd ed. (Martinus Nijhoff, 1995), at 212-213 (paras 290-291), citing the earlier edition of this book, para. 235.
34. Attali, *supra* note 17, at 38-39.
35. *Ibid.*, at 39.

4 THE FISCHER SPEECH

Joschka Fischer's famous speech at Humboldt University echoes a point made in the Attali report, i.e., Attali's argument that the second IGC should culminate in the ratification of a European Constitution.[36] But that is not how the speech began. Fischer started by proposing the creation of a European federation, with a European Parliament and a European government as its respective legislative and executive branches.[37] Given the continued existence of the nation-States, he was not advocating the creation of a federation to replace them but one based on a division of sovereignty between Europe and the nation-States. The European Parliament would have to represent both a Europe of nation-States and a Europe of citizens. Fischer, therefore, proposed the institution of a bicameral European Parliament, with one chamber of directly elected members who are also members of their respective national parliaments and a second chamber (*Europakammer*) of senators or representatives directly elected by the States along the lines of Germany's *Bundesrat*.[38] Fischer saw two options for the European executive: either a transformation of the European Council into a European government or a directly elected president with extensive executive powers.[39] The nation-State would nevertheless continue to exist, given its irreplaceable role in ensuring the legitimacy of a union of citizens and States.[40]

None of this would be possible without a new *European Constitution*. And if a majority of Member States were unwilling, a smaller group of Member States could embark on it anyway, implying the formation of a 'centre of gravity' of Member States that stubbornly adhered to the European ideal and were in a position to take further steps towards political integration.[41] Fischer then set out a roadmap for the future development of European integration. First step: expansion and enhanced cooperation between those Member States willing to engage in it (cf. Economic and Monetary Union (EMU) and Schengen). Second step: the creation of a centre of gravity (*Kerngruppe Europas*) of Member States to ratify a new European framework constitution that lays the groundwork for the federation's constitution; the framework constitution would

36. *Ibid.*, at 36.
37. Fischer, 'Rede des Bundesministers des Auswärtigen Joschka Fischer am 12. Mai 2000 in der Humboldt-Universität in Berlin', *Bulletin* 29-1, 24 May 2000, available at bundesregierung.de/breg-de/service/bulletin/rede-des-bundesministers-des-auswaertigen-joschka-fischer-808150 (last visited 9 October 2022), at 9.
38. The term *Europakammer* is taken from a speech that Fischer gave on 14 January 2014 at The Hague Institute for Global Justice (available at youtube.com/watch?v=3_biN--Ysj8). The proposal is reminiscent of the Dutch Council of State's information campaign of 18 January 2013 on parliamentary involvement in, and monitoring of, the (formation and implementation of) regulations in the areas of financial, commercial, and monetary administration in the European context; *Parliamentary Papers I* 2012/13, 33454, No. AB. There, the Council of State advocates the creation of a new parliamentary body consisting either of members of the European Parliament elected in the countries of the Eurozone or members of the those countries' national parliaments, or a combination of the two.
39. Fischer, *supra* note 37, at 10-11.
40. *Ibid.*, at 11.
41. Fischer spoke only of a *Kerngruppe Europas* and not of the other countries in the EU or its neighbours; *see* De Zwaan, *supra* note 2, at 450, who criticizes this while nonetheless advocating a much broader approach.

contain provisions establishing the federation's institutions, a government that speaks with one voice within the Union, a powerful parliament, and a directly elected president. Third and final step: the creation of a European federation.[42]

5 THE COMMISSION'S WHITE PAPER (1 MARCH 2017)[43]

Before I get to the White Paper, I would like to offer an interim conclusion. We began with the so-called Maudling Plan, which assumed, among other things, that the EEC would, *as such*, become part of a wider free trade zone, i.e., several Member States would become part of a greater entity in the guise of an international organization. Although not directly applicable to the EU, the plan is based on the intriguing notion of there being two types of membership: in the international organization and the individual Member States. The Attali plan, on the other hand, sought a solution to the problem of increased membership by limiting the number of members in the Commission and the Council through the creation of country factions. Fischer advocated an abrupt move forward, i.e., the formation of a European confederation, which would mean that even defence and foreign affairs would be placed entirely under Union control. Now, however, we move on to the Commission's White Paper of 1 March 2017, which aims to map out the 'drivers of change in the next decade'[44] and to present 'a range of scenarios for how Europe could evolve by 2025'. Aside from the 'drivers of Europe's future',[45] the paper posits the following five scenarios: Scenario 1: 'Carrying on', i.e., 'the European Union focuses on delivering its positive reform agenda'; Scenario 2: 'Nothing but the single market', i.e., 'the European Union is gradually re-centred on the single market'; Scenario 3: 'Those who want more do more', i.e., 'the European Union allows willing Member States to do more together in specific areas'; Scenario 4: Doing less more efficiently, i.e., 'the European Union focuses on delivering more and faster in selected policy areas while doing less elsewhere', and Scenario 5: 'Doing much more together', i.e., 'the European Union decides to do much more together across all policy areas'.

There are two annexes to the paper: Annex 1 is a now-outdated timetable, and Annex 2 is a political overview of the five scenarios, which I revisit below. The first institution to respond to the White Paper was the European Parliament, in its resolution of 17 January 2019 on differentiated integration.[46] In that resolution, the Parliament made the following notable statements. In paragraph 3, it notes that 'Europe does not work to a one-size-fits-all approach'; differentiated integration is, at most, according to paragraph 4, a 'second best option and not a strategic priority'. Paragraph 6 is particularly relevant to my topic: 'any form of differentiation initiative that leads to the

42. Fischer reiterated these proposals in his The Hague speech referred to in footnote 38.
43. COM(2017)2025 final, 'White Paper on the future of Europe: Reflections and scenarios for the EU27 by 2025', 1 March 2017.
44. *Ibid.*, at 3.
45. With the Commission listing: Europe's geopolitical position, a profoundly transformed economy and society, heightened external threats, and trust and legitimacy.
46. European Parliament resolution of 17 January 2019 on differentiated integration, P8_TA (2019)0044.

creation of first- and second-class Member States of the Union (...) would be a major political failure'. According to paragraph 14, those countries unwilling to commit to full compliance with primary Union law and which either will not or cannot join the Union should be offered 'some form of partnership'; they would then have to contribute to the budget and respect the Union's fundamental values, the rule of law, and the four freedoms of the internal market. Finally, paragraph 18 mentions a 'future European institutional framework' that 'should include ineluctable European Pillars on political, economic, social and environmental rights'.

6 WHAT NOW?

6.1 Lessons from the Preceding Chapters

While making my way down the path that led from the Maudling plan to my proposal for the future of the EU, I stumbled upon the following, if you will, stepping stones, i.e., ideas and proposals, each of which led me to more or less the same direction. First of all, Attali's multiform and multi-geometric Union model, with a Union consisting of a complex of factions in which one and all would be welcome to participate. Fischer came very close to the concepts that I outline below with his proposal to establish a centre of gravity (*Kerngruppe Europas*) under a new European framework treaty.

Of the Commission's proposals, it is mainly the third scenario that matters: certain Member States want to do more in common. Among the areas in which certain Member States could do more together, the Commission cites defence, internal security, taxation, and social matters.[47] In Annex 2 to the White Paper (a policy overview), it adds that the *progressive Member States in question* should allocate additional resources for those areas for which they decide to do more. This scenario involves various factions of progressive Member States, i.e., one faction for defence, another for security and justice, etc. The Commission does conclude, in Annex 2, that this will entail increasingly complex decision-making.

6.2 My Proposal: Two Unions

I am not in favour of the idea that the Union, an edifice built on a common foundation, should be allowed to collapse into diverse and sundry alliances. I do agree that the Member States should be divided up – however, an idea which is to be found in all the plans discussed here. If it were up to me, the dividing line would run between those countries prepared to form a fully comprehensive economic and monetary union, or even a European economic government, of, say, the 19 countries in the Eurozone on the one hand, and the other Member States on the other. Unlike Fischer, I am not yet ready to consider a European federation, as this would imply that even defence and foreign affairs would have to be fully integrated into the competences of the Union

47. COM(2017)2025 final, cited *supra* note 43, at 10.

without, in this way, anticipating any conclusions which might be drawn from the present situation (Ukraine).

I will refer to the alliance of these, say, 19 countries as 'Union 1'. This Union would be eligible, *in that capacity*, for membership in the overall alliance, i.e., the current 27 Member States, which I will refer to as 'Union 2', thus harkening back to the so-called Maudling Plan discussed at the beginning of this article. 'Union 2' would be identical to the current Union, except that the Union of 19 Eurozone countries would join as the 28th member, so to speak, standing in for those 19 Eurozone countries in the areas that lie within its competence.[48]

But then again, 'Union 1' could never entirely take the place of the 19 Eurozone countries, given that there are still important policy areas that lie outside the competence of that Union, for example, the conduct of foreign policy and cooperation in criminal law and police affairs.[49] Accordingly, the treaty by which 'Union 1' accedes to 'Union 2' would have to be a 'mixed treaty' since not only 'Union 1' would be a party to it, but also its Members States.[50] 'Union 2' would itself need to be underpinned by an entirely new treaty, barring which an amendment of the current Union Treaty would be required, thereby incorporating 'Union 1' and making the necessary institutional arrangements. I am aware that this adds yet another layer to the already multi-layer European legal order; sandwiched between 'Union 2' (the current Union) and the domestic legal orders of the Member States would be a new 'Union 1', which I think would inevitably have to entail all the rules and decisions that jointly affect its Member States.

7 CONCLUSION

The purpose of this article is to propose a solution to the looming and, in my view, inevitable problem of managing a Union made up of 35 to 40 Member States. I have borrowed from the OEEC model proposed in the 1950s, whereby an alliance of States would accede, as a unit, to a larger organization. I was not prepared to endorse the subsequently discussed Attali, Fischer, and European Commission proposals, although they did reassure me that the Member States can no longer be lumped together and must be split into factions, albeit that, rather than have a plethora of potential alliances, I would prefer to see them *divided in two*.

I also hope that this chapter will redress an imbalance in the run-up to Marco's doctoral defence, the point being that the four articles that Marco had ready for his dissertation were, in my opinion, in need of a fifth. After considerable debate, this resulted in a 110-page article entitled 'Private Response to Foreign Unfair Trade Practices – US and EEC Complaint Procedures', which was published in, besides the

48. Cf. the European Union's role in the World Trade Organization (and before that, the General Agreement on Tariffs and Trade).
49. These areas are mentioned by De Zwaan, *supra* note 2, at 444-445 and 446, respectively.
50. *See*, in that connection, Lauwaars and Timmermans, *Europees recht in kort bestek*, 6th ed. (Kluwer, 2003), at 345.

dissertation,[51] the renowned *Northwestern Journal of International Law & Business*.[52] I am optimistic that I will be able to correct the imbalance with this (modest) contribution to the satisfaction of the erstwhile PhD candidate!

Annex

Future members, aside from the (then) 28 Member States:[53]

Second cluster

Bosnia and Herzegovina, Serbia, Montenegro, Macedonia, Albania and Kosovo; and further: Switzerland, Moldova, and possibly Belarus.

Third cluster

Ukraine, Russia, and Turkey. Forty members in total (Attali mentions a total of 41;[54] that figure does not include Kosovo but includes Georgia and Armenia). No mention is made of the Member countries of the European Economic Area (Iceland, Norway, and Liechtenstein).

51. Bronckers, *Selective Safeguard Measures in Multilateral Trade Relations: Issues of Protectionism in GATT, European Community and United States Law* (Kluwer / T.M.C. Asser Press, 1985), at 157-144.
52. Bronckers, 'Private response to foreign unfair trade practices – United States and EEC complaint procedures', 6 *Northwestern Journal of International Law & Business* (1984), 651-759.
53. Attali, *supra* note 17, at 18 and at 27-28.
54. *Ibid.*, at 18.

Part II The World Trade Organization

CHAPTER 7

Reassessing the Safeguards Mess

*Bernard M. Hoekman & Petros C. Mavroidis**

The WTO Agreement on Safeguards was hailed as an important achievement of the Uruguay round, rightly so, given that it managed to outlaw the use of voluntary export restraints. Intended to facilitate the use of transparent, temporary, and non-discriminatory instruments to assist domestic industries injured by import competition, World Trade Organization (WTO) jurisprudence undermined the realization of this objective. Worse, erratic case law created negative externalities, ranging from greater recourse to more discriminatory trade practices and use by the United States (US) of the types of managed trade that the Agreement of Safeguards was meant to abolish. As in the classic bootlegger-Baptist metaphor in the literature on regulation, the unintended consequence of WTO jurisprudence on safeguards has been more rather than less selective protection (discriminatory trade policies). As, if not more important, it made it more difficult for WTO members to use an instrument intended to assist governments in sustaining political support for an open trade regime. In this chapter, we describe the source of discomfort and suggest ways to address it in a meaningful manner.

1 SAFEGUARDS: FORTY YEARS AND TICKING

Safeguards are trade policy instruments used to protect domestic industries injured by import competition. They involve a government increasing protection for imported products beyond bound levels for a temporary period. Bronckers, in two papers,

* We are grateful to Chad P. Bown, Bill Davey, and Alan O. Sykes for helpful comments.

provided an excellent account of the legal treatment of safeguards, focusing on the applicable rules under the General Agreement on Tariffs and Trade (GATT) Article XIX (Emergency Action on Imports of Particular Products).[1] He underlined the 'incompleteness' of the legal disciplines embodied in Article XIX, pointing to the holes and loopholes in the agreement, an issue that also occupied his astute reviewer, Koulen.[2] Bronckers did not limit his observations to the legal discipline but also considered the behaviour of GATT Contracting Parties in the realm of safeguards and the extant dispute settlement practice. There was not much on the latter, reflecting the limited invocation of Article XIX to impose safeguard measures.

GATT required safeguards to be temporary (i.e., time-bound) protectionist measures that applied to all sources of supply, i.e., on a non-discriminatory basis, conditional on a finding that a domestic industry was seriously injured by import competition that, in turn, was the result of unforeseen developments. While there is a solid normative economic rationale for these criteria,[3] in practice, countries have always shown a revealed preference for what Bronckers called selective measures. Bronckers' major point was his concern that the GATT safeguard clause would, absent flexibility in its application, only see its relevance eviscerated. He was writing in the 1980s, against the background of readily available information to the effect that many GATT Contracting Parties were using so-called grey area measures such as the notorious voluntary export restrictions (VERs) and anti-dumping actions instead of global safeguards.

VERs clearly were not in conformity with the GATT. Anti-dumping actions were, in principle, permitted if they satisfied GATT procedural and substantive rules for their imposition. A common feature of both VERs and anti-dumping was that they were 'selective' – a neutral term that Bronckers privileged to denote actions targeting imports originating in specific countries. Safeguards, so the argument Bronckers engaged with, were not intended to provide relief against specific sources. VERs were source-specific and not transitory – they involved importing nations 'persuading' exporters to reduce the volume of exports. Compared to transparent, temporary tariffs applied to all imports of the products concerned, the welfare implications of VERs from a multilateral perspective were nefarious, as they did not generate revenue for the importing countries concerned and did more to restrain the ability of the most efficient exporters to contest the market than would be the case if tariffs were used.

1. Bronckers, 'The non-discriminatory application of Article XIX GATT: Tradition or fiction?', 8 *Legal Issues of Economic Integration* (1981), 35-76; Bronckers, *Selective Safeguard Measures in Multilateral Trade Relations: Issues of Protectionism in GATT, European Community and United States Law* (Kluwer, 1985).
2. Koulen, 'The non-discriminatory application of GATT Article XIX: A reply', 10 *Legal Issues of Economic Integration* (1983), 87-111, and the rejoinder: Bronckers, 'Reconsidering the non-discrimination principle as applied to GATT safeguards measures: A rejoinder', 10 *Legal Issues of Economic Integration* (1983), 113-137.
3. *See, e.g.*, Hoekman and Leidy, 'Policy responses to shifting comparative advantage: Designing a system of emergency protection', 43 *Kyklos* (1990), 25-51.

Bronckers pointed to ambiguities in the GATT text that could provide a legal basis to justify selectivity in the application of safeguards.[4] In a compelling response, Koulen (1983) took a different view, largely based on the negotiating record. That was then, before the Uruguay round and the new Agreement on Safeguards. The World Trade Organization (WTO) agreement on safeguards was a less incomplete contract than its GATT predecessor, explicitly closing the door to VERs.[5] However, it left open two sizeable windows: (i) it allowed for quota modulation in Article 5.2(b), whereby importers could weigh the impact of their measures and hit 'mavericks' the hardest (i.e., permitting some selectivity); and (ii) it did not endow the WTO membership with policing powers over VERs.[6] We do not know if the number of VERs has increased or decreased following the advent of the WTO because we have no information on the number of VERs in place during the GATT years. What we do know is that the WTO Appellate Body, presented with a more complete contract than panels during the GATT years, managed to confuse the membership with its rulings on safeguards-related disputes.

The persuasive analysis of WTO case law on safeguards by Alan Sykes is well summarized by the title of his 2003 article – 'The Safeguards Mess' – which says it all.[7] The legislative confusion that Bronckers pointed to in his work on safeguards in the GATT period was meant to be addressed through a new WTO Agreement on Safeguards. Instead, we now observe a discomposure because of the (failed) efforts of the Appellate Body to interpret the text that was negotiated in the Uruguay Round. In this chapter, we discuss the consequences of the Appellate Body's (re-)construction of the key provisions of the Agreement on Safeguards. We pick up the trail from where Bronckers (GATT) and Sykes (WTO) left it and discuss the impact that the Appellate Body case law had on the use of trade protective action by WTO members. Our argument is that, by tightening the screws and making recourse to the WTO safeguard clause onerous, the Appellate Body contributed to greater use of selective instruments

4. *See* Bronckers, *supra* notes 1 and 2. Bronckers has consistently taken the view that greater flexibility to apply safeguards on a selective basis would make this instrument more salient in the arsenal of commercial policy available to governments. Thus, e.g., he argues that if selective safeguards were to be accepted under the WTO Agreement on Safeguards this would remove the perceived need for à la carte mechanisms such as the specific safeguards included in China's protocol of accession to the WTO. *See* Bronckers, 'Non-discrimination in the WTO Safeguards Agreement: A European perspective', in Bagwell, Bermann and Mavroidis (Eds), *Law and Economics of Contingent Protection in International Trade* (CUP, 2010), pp. 367-373.
5. Vermulst, Pernaute and Lucenti, 'Recent EC safeguards policy: Kill them all and let God sort them out?', 38 *Journal of World Trade* (2004), 966-984, discuss this issue in some detail. Sykes, *The WTO Agreement on Safeguards: A Commentary* (OUP, 2006) offers an excellent overview of the WTO Agreement.
6. If both exporters and importers are incentivized to conclude VERs, they are likely to do so in a non-transparent manner. Mavroidis and Wolfe, 'From sunshine to a common agent: The evolving understanding of transparency in the WTO', 21 *The Brown Journal of World Affairs* (2015) 117-130, have argued that the WTO membership should empower its Secretariat to actively search for VERs. In the absence of such a mandate, independent initiatives, notably the Global Trade Alert have helped to fill the gap. See https://www.globaltradealert.org/.
7. Sykes, 'The safeguards mess: A critique of the WTO jurisprudence', 2 *World Trade Review* (2003), 261-295. A critical analysis of Sykes is offered by Lee, *Safeguard Measures in World Trade: A Legal Analysis* (Edward Elgar, 2014).

(anti-dumping) and de facto selective safeguards because of the expectation that measures justified under the Agreement on Safeguards would be found to be inconsistent with the agreement by the Appellate Body no matter the type of safeguard that was applied. While prima facie, the Appellate Body arguably acted in a manner that undercut the intention of negotiators as reflected in the text of the Agreement on Safeguards, the stance that was taken can be characterized by the bootlegger-Baptist metaphor in the literature on the political economy of regulation: the strict interpretation of the applicable regulations by the Appellate Body ('Baptists') had the effect of supporting those governments ('bootleggers') that prefer to pursue selective protection.[8]

There are good economic arguments in favour of introducing a safeguards clause in an agreement like the GATT/WTO. *Ex ante*, because of the flexibility introduced, it incentivizes participants to make more meaningful concessions, whereas *ex post*, it permits governments to offer domestic industries unable to confront import competition with a breathing space in which to adjust, thus helping to sustain (mobilize) political support for maintaining an open trade regime.[9] Economists recognize that using trade policy to address adjustment pressures generated by international competition is unlikely by itself to be sufficient – other domestic policies are needed[10] – but if safeguards are used, they should be transparent, time-bound, price-based (tariffs, not quotas) and apply to all sources of supply. Governments have rarely abided by these prescriptions. Historically, the revealed preference has been for discrimination (selectivity). VERs benefitted import-competing industries by reducing competition and allowed importing country governments to reap political gains while (partially) compensating exporters by permitting them to capture monopoly rents.[11]

Post-WTO, contingent protection has taken the form of anti-dumping, albeit at levels that are lower than during the GATT years in the case of Organisation for Economic Co-operation and Development (OECD) countries, subsidies of different kinds, most of which are designed to benefit domestic industries and, often, domestic

8. The concept is due to Yandle, 'Bootleggers and Baptists: The education of a regulatory economist', 7 *Regulation* (1983), 12-16.
9. There is an extensive economics literature analysing both the rationale for and design of safeguards provisions in trade agreements. *See, e.g.*, Corden, *Trade Policy and Economic Welfare* (OUP, 1974); Deardorff, 'Safeguards policy and the conservative social welfare function', in Kierzkowski (Ed.), *Protection and Competition in International Trae: Essays in Honour of W. M. Corden* (Blackwell, 1987), pp. 22-40; Horn and Mavroidis, 'What should be required of a safeguard investigation? *US–Lamb*', in Horn and Mavroidis (Eds), *The WTO Case Law: The American Law Institute Reporters' Studies* (CUP, 2007), pp. 85-127; and the contributions collected in Bown (Ed.), *The WTO, Safeguards, and Temporary Protection of Imports* (Edward Elgar, 2006).
10. The fundamental need is reflected in Spence's guidance that policy should aim to 'save people, not jobs': *see* Spence, *The Next Convergence* (Farrar, Straus and Giroux, 2011).
11. *See, e.g.*, Finger, Hall and Nelson, 'The political economy of administered protection', 72 *American Economic Review* (1982), 452-466 and Smith and Venables, 'Counting the cost of voluntary export restraints in the European market', in Helpman and Razin (Eds), *International Trade and Trade Policy* (MIT Press, 1991), pp. 187-220.

firms.[12]Under the Trump Administration, there was a shift back to explicitly managed trade by the United States to address situations that should have been addressed through global safeguards - which may in part have been a consequence of the Appellate Body case law on safeguards. While it is impossible to determine the counterfactual, the Appellate Body case law can be regarded as implicitly supporting the revealed preference of governments for selectivity (discrimination) by not encouraging the use of non-discriminatory safeguard actions - an example of bootlegger-Baptist dynamics at work. In contrast to the GATT period analysed by Bronckers, where textual ambiguity cast doubt on the usefulness of the safeguard instrument, it is the agents this time, and not the principals, that inflicted the damage. The Appellate Body, through its case law, contributed to the confusion, and not the WTO framers who managed to iron out some of their differences during the Uruguay round negotiations.

The remainder of the chapter proceeds as follows. In section 2, we discuss briefly what went wrong in the case law. Section 3 details our argument regarding the policy-substitution and policy-dilution effects of the case law. We end in section 4 with a few thoughts about prospects for return to the original (Uruguay Round) equilibrium.

2 WTO JUDICIARY DOES NOT PLAY TO THE TUNE

As mentioned, Alan Sykes has developed a very comprehensive critique of the way the Appellate Body interpreted the various provisions of the Safeguards agreement.[13] He argues that by re-introducing the 'unforeseen developments' criterion and requiring that investigating authorities 'cut the cloth according to the coat' and avoid imposing safeguards to counteract the precise amount of injury suffered (which in any event is calculated based on a range of elasticities and does not yield a precise number), the Appellate Body made it quite difficult for those imposing safeguards to prevail in case of litigation.

Numbers tell their own story. Under the GATT, there were only two formal safeguards disputes. Using the definition on the WTO webpage,[14] there have been 62 disputes on safeguards submitted so far, of which:

(i) Thirty never reached the stage where a panel report was issued:
  - in two cases, the panel's authority lapsed;[15]
  - in the remaining cases, the panel was either not formed or consultations were ongoing.[16]

12. The pattern of use of subsidies since 2008 is documented in Evenett and Fritz, *Subsidies and Market Access: Towards an Inventory of Corporate Subsidies by China, the European Union and the United States*, 28th Global Trade Alert report (CEPR, 2021).
13. Sykes, *supra* notes 5 and 7.
14. wto.org/english/tratop_e/dispu_e/dispu_agreements_index_e.htm (last visited April 2022). *See also* Ahn, 'Restructuring the WTO safeguard system', in Matsushita, Ahn and Chen (Eds), *The WTO Trade Remedy System: East Asian Perspectives* (Cameron May, 2006).
15. DS 351; DS 356.
16. DS 78; 133; 164; 214; 220; 223; 226; 230; 260; 274; 278; 303; 328; 428; 446; 544; 545; 546; 547; 548; 552; 554; 556; 562; 564; 568; 573; 595.

(ii) One was appealed 'into the void' because there no longer was a functional Appellate Body to adjudicate.[17]
(iii) Five cases were settled.[18]
(iv) In the remaining 26 cases, a report was issued in which the complainant prevailed. In fact, there is not one single case where the respondent managed to successfully defend its position.[19]

As Sykes was the first to point out, not even the most sophisticated agencies managed to prevail before the Appellate Body.[20] Complainants have a 100% record in litigation, a substantially higher percentage than the mean of 60% documented by Hoekman, Mavroidis, and Saluste for WTO disputes for the 1995-2020 period.[21] This win rate is unheard of in WTO litigation.

Besides the legally questionable interpretations of the agreement by the Appellate Body that Sykes has chastised, there is a policy consideration as well. Safeguards, if one plays by the book, are meant to provide temporary relief only – there is a 'dynamic use constraint'.[22] A peace clause introduced in the agreement obliges WTO members that impose safeguards for four or six years to remove the trade barriers and refrain from re-imposing them for an equal period in the sector concerned. Moreover, safeguards imposed for more than three years must be accompanied by the payment of compensation to affected trading partners. Compared to anti-dumping duties, this is the preferred option from a cosmopolitan perspective, as the balance of rights and obligations remains unaffected. There is no obligation to compensate when anti-dumping duties are imposed, and they can be imposed for a long time since sunset clauses merely oblige members to initiate a new investigation every five years, not to remove duties. Also salient here is that the Appellate Body has eviscerated much of the original thinking in the Anti-dumping Agreement regarding sunset clauses by hollowing out the requirements for a lawful sunset investigation.[23]

3 FACING THE MUSIC

Increasing the burden of proof for lawful imposition of safeguards risks contributing to the proliferation of anti-dumping duties, which are characterized by substantially higher transaction costs (since investigation takes place both in the importing as well as the exporting market), and punishes exporters for allegedly practising 'unfair' trade

17. DS 518.
18. DS 228; 235; 326; 550; 551.
19. DS 98; 121; 166; 177; 178; 202; 207; 238; 248; 249; 252; 252; 253; 254; 258; 259; 415; 416; 417; 418; 438; 444; 445; 468; 490; 496.
20. Sykes, *supra* note 7.
21. Hoekman, Mavroidis, and Saluste, 'Informing WTO reform: Dispute settlement performance, 1995-2020', 55 *Journal of World Trade* (2021), 1-50.
22. *See* Bagwell and Staiger, 'Enforcement, private political pressure, and the General Agreement on Tariffs and Trade/World Trade Organization escape clause', 34 *Journal of Legal Studies* (2005), 471-513.
23. For a detailed discussion of these issues, *see* Mavroidis, *The Regulation of International Trade*, vol. 1 (MIT Press, 2016), pp. 128 et seq.

without compensating them. On paper, safeguards have a function that is distinct from the other two contingent protection instruments, anti-dumping- and countervailing duties. From a legal perspective, the latter two measures purportedly address 'unfair' trade, whereas the former 'fair' trade. 'Unfair' means that export prices are lower than those in the home market, either because of a private decision by exporting firms to price discriminate, or because of a subsidy that a WTO member has bequeathed its national industry. From the perspective of economics, there is nothing unfair about dumping as similar behaviour - price discrimination - may also occur (and often does) in the domestic market.

In practice, the distinction between "fair" and "unfair" trade is more like a line in the sand than set in stone. Countervailing duties are a world apart since they presuppose state action, which might or might not exist. When it exists, there is no point in initiating a safeguarding investigation and document increased imports. By pointing to the subsidy paid, one needs to show price or quantity effects to show injury. Assuming the subsidy covers the price differential, it should be all downhill. If no state action is involved, it is impossible to impose countervailing duties. The instrument-substitutability nexus thus applies across two instruments: anti-dumping and safeguards.

With this in mind, we should also note that investigating authorities enjoy enough latitude to come up with a dumping margin, especially when they make recourse to "best information available." If invocation of safeguards becomes harder, then the obvious candidate for protective action is the imposition of anti-dumping duties. The difference between anti-dumping and safeguards is that the former is selective by design. The WTO member concerned can target the maverick and hit it with duties. This is not to suggest that the two instruments are complete substitutes. One important difference is that demonstration of injury is a mere procedural requirement in anti-dumping. If dumping is one factor contributing to injury, duties can be imposed to address all of the injury suffered. Conversely, as already explained, safeguards can address only the amount of injury caused by increased imports. All we want to suggest here is that the two instruments can be used interchangeably. It is because of this property that making it more difficult to use one may increase the frequency of use of the other.[24]

24. For an elaboration of the argument and evidence for the early WTO period, *see* Bown, 'Why are safeguards under the WTO so unpopular?', 1 *World Trade Review* (2002), 47-62. We recognize that the net effect post-WTO may nonetheless be positive from a welfare perspective because anti-dumping actions are more transparent (visible) than VERs and involve tariffs (price-based instruments) as opposed to quotas. Conversely, because anti-dumping is less effective in protecting a domestic industry than a global safeguard would be - unless most major sources of supply are targeted - the policy-substitution outcome may give rise to policy dilution: a shift to measures that actively undermine the rules-based trade order. As discussed below, the invocation of GATT Article XXI by the Trump Administration to justify higher tariffs on steel and aluminium is a prominent example, as is the rapidly increasing use of subsidies since 2009; *see* Evenett and Fritz, *supra* note 12.

3.1 Pushing Towards Anti-dumping

Industries can remain protected for long periods of time, with the instrument of protection changing over time.[25] A country that has imposed safeguards to protect say, its automotive sector, cannot keep safeguards in place forever under the Agreement on Safeguards. After four to six years, it must withdraw the measure for at least an equal period. What next? If the automotive lobby is politically powerful, it may exert pressure to maintain protection through other instruments, such as subsidies. If the industry wishes to keep tariffs in place, it can initiate an anti-dumping investigation. Of course, the incentive for this is increased given the likelihood that the government will lose the argument on the use of safeguards before WTO adjudicating bodies considering the case law record noted above.

Each of the three WTO contingent protection instruments was negotiated in a self-contained manner. The time-bound nature of safeguard actions, the dynamic use constraint, and the removal of the need to offer compensation to affected exporters during the first three years of safeguard imposition were laudable elements incorporated into the WTO agreement on safeguards that sought to encourage the use of safeguards relative to anti-dumping and countervailing duties. No one could have anticipated that WTO case law would evolve to reduce the usefulness of safeguards to those seeking temporary relief or that case law on anti-dumping would evolve the way it did, e.g., with regard to sunset clauses, increasing the scope for anti-dumping to provide long-term protection. Finger and Nogues point to substitution between anti-dumping and safeguards in the case of Mercosur countries.[26] Anti-dumping, in their analysis, was used by Mercosur partners to support liberalization of trade between themselves. In the minds of policymakers, anti-dumping was not a sanction against 'unfair' trade but was regarded to be the best available functional (de facto) safeguard, because 'real' safeguards had become dysfunctional following the Appellate Body case law. This gave rise to perceptions of a consequent risk that the attitude towards safeguards taken by the Appellate Body might be adopted in the Mercosur context as well. Case law in safeguards thus appears to have contributed towards incentivizing users to shift to other contingent protection instruments. An under-appreciated corollary risk for the trading system associated with this outcome is that the notion that trade is unfair becomes more entrenched over time and less attention is given to the need for industries to adapt to a more competitive environment.

3.2 Along Came the Trump Administration

An additional problem with the case law is that it might provide users with perverse incentives to instruments other than the three discussed above to address import

25. This pattern has been documented by Mansfield and Busch, 'The political economy of non-tariff barriers: A cross-national analysis', 49 *International Organization* (1995), 723-749.
26. Finger and Nogues (Eds), *Safeguards and Antidumping in Latin American Trade Liberalization: Fighting Fire with Fire* (World Bank, 2006).

competition. Section 232 of the US Trade Act[27] provides for the possibility to impose trade restrictions in the interest of national security. The Trump Administration conducted a series of investigations in the field of steel and aluminium products originating in various WTO members.[28] This provoked a hostile reaction in various quarters. The argument raised was that the legal basis invoked was arguably ill-suited to promote national security. What followed was a flurry of disputes by various members of the WTO, namely DS 544, 547, 548, 550, 551, 552, 554, 556, and 564. Canada and Mexico (DS 550 and 551, respectively) have settled their dispute with the US in the meantime. The remaining complainants are entangled in a legal battle with the US before WTO panels.

It is not our purpose here to assess whether the complaints introduced are well-founded. What is clear is that the US has consistently invoked Section 201 of the US Trade Act of 1974[29] whenever it initiated an investigation to impose safeguards. Consistently that is, until the actions by the Trump Administration are described above. What explains the change? It may be that the US authorities anticipated that if they had acted within the four corners of Section 201 and invoked only Article XIX of GATT and the Safeguards Agreement of the WTO and were subsequently challenged before a WTO panel, they would suffer yet another defeat. Invoking national security as a defence could tilt the balance in its favour since WTO panels have consistently applied a deferential standard in disputes where a respondent invoked national security.

The only case in the GATT history where the national security exception was discussed concerned the US embargo following the accession of Sandinistas to power in Nicaragua. As Pinchis-Paulsen explains, the panel dealing with the matter was lame even before its inception, as the US stated it would not accept an unfavourable outcome since, in its view, the national security exception was self-referential and non-justiciable.[30] All in all, national security concerns were never comprehensively litigated during the GATT era. Even though differing opinions regarding the justiciability of Article XXI (the provision discussing national security) were expressed, there was an implicit consensus that adjudication in this area could be prejudicial to the GATT system as such.

Opening the door to panels to adjudicating national security concerns comes, of course, close to a 'wrong case', in the sense that, absent a very careful judgment, the risk of a false positive looms large. As written, Article XXI does not bar justiciability (for fear of abuse of the provision) but endorses a highly deferential standard of review. With the advent of the WTO, it was impossible to keep the 'wrong cases' out anymore, and cases were brought. Largely because of the passage to negative consensus, but also because of the fact that fewer and fewer WTO members shared an understanding of the

27. The full text is reproduced in govinfo.gov/content/pkg/USCODE-2015-title19/pdf/USCODE-2015-title19-chap7-subchapII-partIV-sec1862.pdf (last visited June 2022).
28. *See* fas.org/sgp/crs/misc/IF10667.pdf (last visited June 2022).
29. *See* govinfo.gov/content/pkg/STATUTE-88/pdf/STATUTE-88-Pg1978-2.pdf (last visited June 2022).
30. Pinchis-Paulsen, 'Trade multilateralism and U.S. national security: The making of the GATT security exceptions', 41 *Michigan Journal of International Law* (2020), 109-193.

'wrong case' – a result of the increasing heterogeneity of the WTO membership – cases pertaining to national security found their way into the docket: DS512 and DS567 are illustrations, but not the only ones; DS547, 548, 551, 552, 554, 556, 564 mentioned above, all concern trade barriers justified by invoking the national-security exception. Whereas the European Union (EU) and the US managed to resolve the first national-security-related dispute in the WTO-era bilaterally (DS38), the same has not happened with the cases that we have cited above.

So, we are squarely in the realm of the standard of review and how deferential it is. In DS512 (*Russia – Measures Concerning Traffic in Transit*), the panel advanced a series of good points to support an approach in favour of deference, assuming the facts of the case support that a threat to national security exists. These are tough cases for any adjudicator. Even in deep-integration regimes like the EU, courts are not prepared to meddle with definitions of national security, adopting a highly deferential standard of review in this regard.[31] Pushing the frontier of the coverage of Article XXI of GATT so as to include the actions in the steel and aluminium sectors was thus, quite likely, a conscious attempt by the Trump Administration to benefit from a deferential standard of review, possibly because of fear of another failure before the WTO had it decided to defend its measures under the current safeguards-regime.[32]

3.3 Taking Stock

The Appellate Body case law in the realm of safeguards has been criticized for being overly restrictive, and the number of successful complaints against safeguard actions provide a prima facie veneer of confirmation to this effect. Those interested in providing breathing space to an ailing industry can more easily rely on recourse to anti-dumping. A plausible argument can be made to the effect that, by tightening the screws when adjudicating disputes under the Agreement on Safeguards, the Appellate Body contributed to the increased use of anti-dumping. Furthermore, there is a potential moral hazard issue as well, as the marginal effort to attempt to get it right when imposing safeguards is unlikely to be associated with a pay-off in the form of reducing the likelihood of being found to be at fault if a targeted country contests the safeguard measures.

Bronckers' worst fears regarding the policy-relevance of the safeguards agreement have materialized, but this time thanks to an unlikely source: the Appellate Body case law. Of course, all is not lost, as case law can always be reversed. The WTO legal order, as is, does not know of stare decisis (binding precedent). We advance a few thoughts to this effect in what follows.[33]

31. Mavroidis, *supra* note 21, vol. 1, pp. 477 et seq.
32. In Hoekman, Mavroidis and Nelson, Geopolitical Competition, Globalization and WTO Reform, *EUI RSC Working Paper 2022/67*, we suggest alternatives to formal dispute settlement to address the use of trade policy justified by national security concerns.
33. WTO panels ruled against the US in the disputes on steel and aluminium, and subsequently appealed 'into the void', as there is no functional Appellate Body to entertain its claim. See https://www.wto.org/english/tratop_e/dispu_e/cases_e/ds550_e.htm. The panels that dealt

4 SAFEGUARDING SAFEGUARDS

There is a key difference between safeguards on the one hand and the other two instruments of contingent protection on the other. The reason for intervening against dumping and countervailing subsidies originates in the behaviour of a foreign party that is dumping (exporting firms) or subsidizing (governments). Safeguards are predicated on serious injury to a domestic industry, which might occur even if growth rates at home have led domestic consumers to consume more. The intended function of each of the three instruments differs, with each supposed to fulfil a specific role. The intended balance across the use of these instruments has been undone, in part through the case law of the Appellate Body.

We have underscored why safeguards are a sensible instrument to include in a trade agreement like the WTO. Unlike anti-dumping, for example, which has been criticized for many good reasons,[34] contract flexibility through the inclusion of a safeguards clause facilitates concessions and allows WTO members to assist industries in adjusting to greater import competition by temporarily raising tariffs. This can help sustain domestic political support for a gradual process of trade integration and an open trade regime. Anti-dumping can do the same, albeit in a less straightforward and potentially more costly way – and one that is less accessible to developing countries given the administrative bureaucracy and expertise needed. One important policy and practical advantage of global safeguards is that they are easier to apply.

All this suggests that a strategy of making safeguards redundant through interpretation of the legal text is unwise from a systemic perspective. Understanding the negotiating intent is key for WTO adjudicators, who must also correct misconceptions about its interpretative exercise. Ideally, WTO members should rethink the type of adjudicators they would like to see appointed in the WTO courts. The membership can also take a decisive step through a targeted legislative amendment to bring the safeguard clause more in tune with its intended function. We take these issues in turn.

4.1 What Was the Negotiating Intent?

The negotiating record of the WTO Safeguards Agreement reveals heated discussions between (especially) Southeast Asian and Transatlantic nations regarding the issue of selective safeguard measures (VERs).[35] This was probably the single most important issue that occupied the minds of negotiators, and its resolution through the advent of quota modulation and the ban on VERs was a well-thought compromise. While

with the steel and aluminium disputes held that the US imposition of trade measures did not constitute a safeguard action and that the matter at hand concerned the legality of invoking the GAT national security clause.

34. There is an extensive literature on this score – *see, e.g.*, Finger, *Antidumping: How It Works and Who Gets Hurt* (University of Michigan Press, 1993) and Prusa, *Economic Effects of Antidumping* (World Scientific, 2021).
35. A comprehensive overview and discussion of the negotiations is provided by Brilliant, 'Safeguards', in Stewart (Ed.), *The Uruguay Round: A Negotiating History (1986-1992)* (Kluwer, 1993).

safeguards would be, in principle, non-discriminatory, their bite could be modulated to hit some exporting nations harder. A requirement to offer compensation for safeguards that lasted for more than three years imposed a dynamic use constraint.

Our understanding of the compromise reached in the Uruguay round negotiations is that the aim was to design an agreement that would be functional and workable. The Tokyo round agreement had shown its limits when practice moved to new pastures, notably VERs. This is what the new WTO agreement aimed to avoid in the future. It is a more realistic construct, as it tries to strike a balance between non-discrimination and acceptable selectivity while limiting the negative spillovers to 'tolerable' levels through the compensation requirement for longer-lasting safeguard actions. Unfortunately, the negotiating intent not only was not reflected in WTO dispute settlement rulings, but the Appellate Body made safeguards an almost unworkable instrument.[36]

4.2 Why Did the Appellate Body Get It Wrong?

WTO adjudicators are called to interpret one incomplete contract (the WTO) through another incomplete contract (the Vienna Convention on the Law of Treaties (VCLT)).[37] The latter mentions a few elements that must be considered without assigning weights to them. This is already a problem. Probably thinking that the safest way to avoid undoing the balance of rights and obligations struck by the Uruguay round negotiators was to insist on the words used, WTO courts became extreme textualists. Words are not a-contextual. Mistakes happened. 'Unforeseen developments' is not mentioned in Article 2 of the Safeguards Agreement, which explains under what conditions safeguards can be imposed. And yet, the Appellate Body saw room to include this requirement through an interpretation of Article 1 of the same agreement, entitled 'General Provision', which mentions Article XIX of GATT (which contains the 'unforeseen developments' requirement) but which simply refers to the type of measures covered and not to the conditions for their lawful imposition.

Why not look to the negotiating record, and see how this issue was debated there? Because the Appellate Body has also taken the view that considering the negotiating history is a matter of discretion for adjudicators under Article 32 of VCLT. In practice, the word 'may' appearing in Article 32 of VCLT, denoting that recourse to the negotiating record is optional, has been understood as 'not'. In cases where the argument could be made in two distinct ways, the Appellate Body picked one, satisfying itself that it was all clear.

In the early GATT days, detail did not matter much. The GATT was a relational contract among like-minded countries. In relational contracts, incompleteness is less of a problem. Good faith substituted for missing words. Disputes often were settled. But

36. *See* Stewart and Dwyer, *WTO Trade Remedy Disputes: The First Six Years (1995-2000)* (Transnational Publishing, 2001) on dispute adjudication in the realm of safeguards and its inconsistency with the negotiating intent.
37. Article 3.2 of the DSU states that WTO judges must clarify the agreements through recourse to customary rules of interpretation. In its very first report (DS2), the Appellate Body equated this reference to the VCLT.

things changed as membership expanded. The WTO is much less of a relational contract, and thus incompleteness generates greater costs. As the WTO contains overwhelmingly 'standards' and not 'rules', and because standards invite more discretion, WTO adjudicators are agents with substantial room to interpret the WTO agreements. Their attitude regarding the negotiating record will influence the extent of exercise of discretion. Practice shows that they opted for more rather than less discretion by consistently disregarding the Uruguay round negotiation.

In a dialogue between Oliver Wendell Holmes and Learned Hand, two giant figures in US judicial history and legal thinking in general, Hand reports saying to Holmes when the latter departs after a meeting:

> 'Well Sir, goodbye. Do justice!' He [Holmes] turned quite sharply, and he said: 'Come here. Come here.' I answered: 'Oh I know, I know.' He replied: 'That is not my job. My job is to play the game according to the rules.'[38]
>
> The rules are observed not by simply reading them but by asking what they are supposed to achieve. Part of the answer lies in the element the Appellate Body has consistently overlooked: the negotiating record.

4.3 Hercules in Geneva

Ronald Dworkin constructed an ideal judge, Hercules, who based judgments on 'fit and substance', debating the originalist Hermes, another fictional judge.[39] Negotiation can help but is not a panacea. More is required. What should the WTO Hercules look like? As already stated, she/he should know where the agreements originated. With this knowledge in mind, the WTO Hercules could/would ask what their intended function was and interpret the terms in light of their intended function. The purpose of the WTO is to liberalize trade as agreed by the parties. Trade liberalization is expressed in legal language but is a welfare-enhancing economic ideal. Indeed, some of the agreed institutions cannot be meaningfully interpreted absent some input from economic analysis. How can one understand likeness in the marketplace absent an understanding of cross-price elasticity? Is it possible to decide whether dumping, among many other factors, has caused injury absent an empirically informed analysis? How can the counterfactual be constructed when calculating the permissible level of retaliation without such knowledge? And so on and so forth.

Holmes observed, '[f]or the rational study of the law the black-letter man may be the man of the present, but the man of the future is the man of statistics and the master of economics'.[40] Over one hundred and twenty years later, Holmes' future has not arrived. We understand, of course, that our WTO Hercules is a multi-persona, a Renaissance woman/man, and it is undeniably rare to come across people who combine these talents. Perhaps the membership should try to mix talents and stop typecasting its adjudicators *à l'image de* proverbial WTO delegates. A change in this

38. Learned Hand, 'A personal confession', reproduced in Dilliard (Ed.), *The Spirit of Liberty: The Papers and Addresses of Learned Hand*, 3rd ed. (Alfred A. Knopf, 1974), p. 307.
39. Dworkin, *Law's Empire* (HUP, 1986).
40. Holmes, 'The path of the law', 10 *Harvard Law Review* (1897), 457-477, at 474.

respect might enhance the intellectual coherence of future WTO dispute settlement reports, assuming the Appellate Body crisis is resolved.

4.4 A Gap to Fill

There are two rationales behind safeguards, as we have noted above, an *ex ante* function to support the making of commitments, and an *ex post* function, to provide a breathing space to industries in WTO members that have suffered because of a greater volume (and lower price) of imports that compete with local production. The latter gives rise to a conundrum. Measures are imposed to provide relief, but if nothing changes, relief can only be temporary and maybe even a curse. While exporters continue to operate in a globally competitive environment and become more efficient, local producers will have a few years in the sun with no obligation to change their behaviour. If at all, they might be incentivized to lobby a few years later for anti-dumping duties or other forms of support.

And yet, many WTO members do use the breathing space in order to address the ultimate cause (increased imports being the proximate cause) of injury. From attempts to improve productivity to re-training workers (the German *Umschulung*) to become employed in activities for which there is demand, international practice reveals dozens of policy initiatives in this regard. To request that specific action be undertaken during the period when a safeguard is in place, in terms of a WTO obligation, would be doubly wrong: the world community would lose gains from innovation (in an area where a lot can be gained), and it would be perceived as an undue intrusion into national sovereignty. And we know from past experience that efforts to pierce the sovereignty veil have been consistently rebuffed.

This is where we would like to introduce a distinction between an obligation of action and an obligation of a specific action. The WTO could require those imposing safeguards to undertake some corrective action, as imports are only the proximate and not the ultimate cause of injury. The WTO should not be imposing a specific action but appropriate action. When a safeguard has been imposed, WTO members should be called on to address the causes behind a loss in competitiveness reflected in expanding import market shares. If safeguards aim to provide a breathing space, breathing spaces will come and go unless something more is done. Worse, we will return to the vortex of constant protection, where anti-dumping duties will be succeeding safeguards, in turn, succeeded by anti-dumping duties, and so forth. And as noted above, there may well be worse outcomes, insofar as large players return to a world of VERs, voluntary import expansions, motivate specific trade measures under the umbrella of national security and use instruments that are not or only partially subject to WTO rules.

Moving in this direction will be beneficial for the WTO in other ways as well. WTO members will be in a position to show those left behind that the WTO is not their enemy. In fact, a safety net will be available, and it will be up to individual societies to weave it to their liking. This could also be a way to bring in a discussion about labour in the WTO, which seems to be a priority for the current United States Trade Representative.[41]

These are subjects that have engaged Marco Bronckers over the course of a long and productive career, revealing his ability to be 'ahead of the curve'.[42] This is certainly illustrated by developments on the safeguard front in the almost 40 years since he wrote his papers arguing for greater flexibility in the use of selective safeguards. Looking back, the salience of the systemic worries he expressed at the time has become ever clearer. So has the need for approaches that recognize the political economy realities of sustaining an open global trade regime.

41. *See* reuters.com/article/usa-trade-tai-wto-idUSL2N2NS26V (last visited June 2022).
42. *See, e.g.*, Bronckers, 'More power to the WTO?', 4 *Journal of International Economic Law* (2001), 41-65.

CHAPTER 8

Injecting Valuable Flexibility into the WTO's De Facto Precedent System

Richard Jiang

The Biden administration has ended the deadlock over the World Trade Organization's (WTO) Director-General. This is a good start for revitalizing the WTO, including the Appellate Body (AB), but the precedential value of the AB's decisions will likely remain the subject of debate. In the past 20 years, the AB has never explicitly departed from its prior decisions. This raises the concern that incorrect interpretations would be exacerbated by the de facto stare decisis regime underlying the WTO's dispute resolution mechanisms. A complete dismissal of the precedential value of the AB's decisions, however, would inevitably undermine their capacity to clarify WTO law, thereby further risking inconsistent interpretations. Following precedent is common in international jurisdictions, even if these international tribunals are not formally obliged to comply with precedent. In support of a jurisprudence constante regime in the multilateral trading system, this contribution proposes judicial and political options to inject valuable flexibility into the WTO's de facto precedent system. It provides a comparative perspective by taking into account the practices of international tribunals, including the International Criminal Tribunal for the former Yugoslavia (ICTY), the International Court of Justice (ICJ), the European Court of Human Rights (ECtHR), and the Court of Justice of the European Union (CJEU), all of which offer experiences for the AB's departure from previous decisions. The next consideration is the likelihood that a political correction could modify settled jurisprudence in light of treaty provisions concerning the adoption of amendments, waivers, or authoritative interpretations.

1 INTRODUCTION

In his recent article about the WTO reform, 'Trade Conflicts: Whither the WTO?', Marco Bronckers argues that the starting point of this reform is not to repair the Appellate Body (AB).[1] Although the AB crisis has drawn much attention, Bronckers acutely points out that the problems associated with dispute settlement are a 'symptom', which appears to be a sign of 'the cause of the crisis bedevilling the WTO'.[2] The crucial issue here is to update 'the rules that govern the core function of the WTO: levelling the playing field between its members'.[3]

Although the discussions on how to address the root cause might be ongoing, WTO members have not yet made much progress in this regard – at least not publicly. The present contribution, thus, in Bronckers's honour, proposes a moderate treatment to alleviate one of the symptoms of the WTO crisis, namely how to provide WTO's de facto precedent system with valuable flexibility in order to avoid 'an undue adherence to precedent'.[4] It first rejects the idea endorsed by the United States (US) to completely deny the precedential value of AB reports. The following section shows that it is a common practice for international tribunals to follow precedents even if they are not formally obliged to do so.

That being said, however, it is equally important to acknowledge the need to temper the rigidity of WTO's de facto precedent system. It is noteworthy that the AB has never, in its more than 20 years of jurisprudence, explicitly reversed itself though it has made a few controversial decisions that are worth reconsideration. For instance, Bronckers argues that the AB could have chosen 'a much wiser outcome' when it comes to denying China 'the mere right to invoke generally accepted public policies' in *China–Raw Materials*.[5] Subsequently, a comparative perspective is provided by taking into account the practices of tribunals at various levels, including the International Criminal Tribunal for the former Yugoslavia (ICTY), the International Court of Justice (ICJ), the European Court of Human Rights (ECtHR), and the Court of Justice of the European Union (CJEU), all of which may throw light on judicial options for the AB's departure from previous decisions. The feasibility of conceivable political corrections is discussed, namely the adoption of amendments, waivers, authoritative interpretations, or a more flexible alternative. Finally, this contribution concludes with a proposal of

1. Bronckers, 'Trade conflicts: Whither the WTO?', 47 *Legal Issues of Economic Integration* (2020), 221-244.
2. *Ibid.*, at 234.
3. *Ibid.*, at 242.
4. *See* the farewell speech of the last US member of the Appellate Body, Thomas R. Graham, on 5 March 2020, at wto.org/english/tratop_e/dispu_e/farwellspeechtgaham_e.htm (last visited 10 April 2022).
5. Bronckers and Maskus, '*China–Raw Materials*: A controversial step towards evenhanded exploitation of natural resources', 13 *World Trade Review* (2014), 393-408, at 400-402. In early 2014, when I was an LLM student in his class at Leiden University, Marco encouraged me to look into this problematic decision from a Chinese perspective. This marked the start of my exciting PhD journey for the next six years in Europe. Thanks to his continuing support and excellent supervision, I finalized my thesis in 2020 which was published by Routledge in July 2021. *See* Jiang, *Environmental Protection, China and International Trade: Greening the WTO Ban on Chinese Export Duties* (Routledge, 2021).

the possible judicial and political options to enable the AB to balance the precedential value and the flexibilities to modify settled jurisprudence.

2 DENYING COMPLETELY THE PRECEDENTIAL VALUE OF AB REPORTS IS UNDESIRABLE

The AB is no longer operational because the Trump Administration blocked new appointments as well as renewals of AB members. This obstructionism was explained with reference to 'systemic concerns' over the 'adjudicative approach and proper role' of the AB in certain cases.[6] For instance, a 2016 US statement blocking the reappointment of an AB member raised concerns regarding both the *obiter dicta* in AB reports and the AB's approach to reviewing WTO members' domestic laws.[7]

Regardless of the merits of such concerns, the US also fears that the AB's allegedly incorrect interpretations would be further exacerbated by the de facto *stare decisis* regime underlying the WTO's dispute resolution mechanisms.[8] In other words, owing to the approach to precedent in the WTO, what the US fears is that one 'problematic' report could impact all future cases concerning a particular point of law. Given the reluctance of the AB to self-correct in the past 20 years, the rigidity of WTO's precedent system appears to have provoked the US to completely deny the precedential value of AB reports.[9]

It is, however, one thing to acknowledge the need to temper the rigidity of WTO's de facto precedent system but quite another to completely deny the precedential value of AB reports. The latter one is undesirable even for the US as it has correctly recognized that AB reports 'can provide valuable clarification of the covered agreements'.[10] Indeed, the common practice of WTO members has gradually coalesced into the de facto *stare decisis* regime in WTO dispute settlement. Under the General Agreement on Tariffs and Trade (GATT) 1947 system, as noted by the AB in *Japan-Alcoholic Beverages*, panel reports were 'often considered by subsequent panels' because they create 'legitimate expectations' among members.[11] For the same reason,

6. Statement by the United States at the Meeting of the WTO Dispute Settlement Body Geneva, 23 May 2016, wto.org/english/news_e/news16_e/us_statment_dsbmay16_e.pdf (last visited 10 April 2022).
7. *Ibid.*
8. Payosova, Hufbauer and Schott, 'The dispute settlement crisis in the World Trade Organization: Causes and cures', March 2018, piie.com/system/files/documents/pb18-5.pdf (last visited 10 April 2022).
9. 'The DSU does not assign precedential value to panel or Appellate Body reports adopted by the DSB, or interpretations contained in those reports.' *See* Statements by the United States at the Meeting of the WTO Dispute Settlement Body Geneva, 18 December 2018, geneva.usmission.gov/wp-content/uploads/sites/290/Dec18.DSB_.Stmt_.as-deliv.fin_.public.pdf (last visited 10 April 2022).
10. Office of the United States Trade Representative, '2018 Trade Policy Agenda and 2017 Annual Report', March 2018, ustr.gov/sites/default/files/files/Press/Reports/2018/AR/2018%20Annual%20Report%20FINAL.PDF (last visited 10 April 2022), at 28.
11. It continues: 'and, therefore, should be taken into account where they are relevant to any dispute'. Appellate Body Report, *Japan-Taxes on Alcoholic Beverages*, WT/DS8/AB/R, WT/DS10/AB/R, WT/DS11/AB/R, adopted on 1 November 1996, at 14.

the AB in *US-Stainless Steel (Mexico)* required that subsequent panels should not be 'free to disregard the legal interpretations and the *ratio decidendi*' contained in previous AB reports unless 'cogent reasons' were presented for departing from them.[12]

The development of the WTO's de facto precedent system is certainly not unique in itself. As noted by the AB in *Japan-Alcoholic Beverages*, the ICJ and its predecessor have also treated previous judgments in a similar manner,[13] although Article 59 of the ICJ's Statute clearly states that an ICJ judgment 'has no binding force except between the parties and in respect of that particular case'.[14] Relevant in this context is the holding of the ICJ in the *Cameroon-Nigeria* case that it could depart from its own precedent if 'there is cause not to follow the reasoning and conclusions of earlier cases'.[15] Similarly, while the ICTY Statute is silent on the issue of *stare decisis*, the ICTY Appeals Chamber in the *Aleksovski* case supported the rules of de facto *stare decisis* by emphasising the 'interests of certainty and predictability' to follow its previous judgments.[16] At the regional level, the ECtHR has developed rules of de facto *stare decisis* for 'the interests of legal certainty', 'the orderly development of the Convention case-law' and 'foreseeability and equality before the law'.[17] The CJEU also supports the rules of de facto *stare decisis* as 'there are passages in the judgments where the weights and the number of the previous decisions seen almost to be felt to be such as to make them binding in fact, if not in theory'.[18]

It is thus fair to say that even if international tribunals are not formally obliged to follow precedents, in practice, they commonly choose to develop de facto precedent systems. The reason behind such common practice is rather self-evident: 'the maintenance of security and stability' as a primary function of law.[19] Therefore, WTO members, including the US, have frequently cited AB reports in their submissions in what amounts to a clear recognition of their precedential value in ensuring that clarifications remain consistent. In this sense, a complete dismissal of the precedential value of the AB's decisions would inevitably undermine the AB's capacity to clarify

12. Appellate Body Report, *United States-Final Anti-Dumping Measures on Stainless Steel from Mexico*, WT/DS344/AB/R, adopted on 20 May 2008, paras 158-160.
13. 'It is worth noting that the Statute of the International Court of Justice has an explicit provision, Article 59, to the same effect. This has not inhibited the development by that Court (and its predecessor) of a body of case law in which considerable reliance on the value of previous decisions is readily discernible.' *See* AB Report, *Japan-Taxes on Alcoholic Beverages*, footnote 30.
14. The ICJ has developed rules of de facto *stare decisis* by 'closely following its earlier judgments', *see* Reinisch, 'The proliferation of international dispute settlement mechanisms: The threat of fragmentation vs. the promise of a more effective system? Some reflections from the perspective of investment arbitration', in Buffard, Crawford, Pellet and Wittich (Eds), *International Law between Universalism and Fragmentation: Festschrift in Honour of Gerhard Hafner* (Brill, 2009), pp. 107-126, at p. 123.
15. *Land and Maritime Boundary between Cameroon and Nigeria (Cameroon v. Nigeria: Equatorial Guinea intervening)*, ICJ Rep. 1998, 275, para. 28.
16. *Prosecutor v. Zlatko Aleksovski*, IT-95-14/1, Appeals Chamber judgment of 30 May 2001, paras 107-108.
17. ECtHR, *Cossey v. United Kingdom*, Appl. No 10843/84, judgment of 29 August 1990, para. 35.
18. Beck, *The Legal Reasoning of the Court of Justice of the EU* (Hart Publishing, 2013), p. 238.
19. AB Report, *US-Stainless Steel (Mexico)*, footnote 313.

WTO law, thereby further rendering interpretation inconsistent.[20] This result would certainly be contrary to the mandate of the WTO's dispute settlement system, which calls for 'providing security and predictability to the multilateral trading system'.[21]

That being said, it is equally important to acknowledge the need to temper the rigidity of WTO's de facto precedent system. The next section thus provides a comparative analysis of the practices of the ICTY, the ICJ, the ECtHR, and the CJEU to depart from previous decisions. The aim here is to throw light on the use of judicial options for AB's departure from previous decisions.

3 JUDICIAL OPTIONS TO LOOSEN THE GRIP OF PRECEDENT

The issue of how to balance the precedential value and the flexibility to modify settled jurisprudence is not unique to the WTO dispute settlement system. This section discusses the two major options, namely overruling and distinguishing, applied by the ICTY, the ICJ, the ECtHR, and the CJEU to depart from previous decisions. The advantages and limitations of these techniques are also assessed.

3.1 Overruling

With regard to the ICJ, the Court has never explicitly departed from a prior judgment. Instead, when necessary, it prefers to implicitly overrule a previous judgment. Such practice is observed in a series of ICJ judgments concerning alternative methods of maritime delimitation.[22] One approach, often referred to as the equidistance method, requires that maritime boundaries between states follow a median line, every point of which is equidistant from the nearest points on the respective coasts. In contrast, a second method, which is result-oriented, requires the application of equitable principles in order to achieve equitable results. In other words, tribunals are not bound by the aforementioned equidistance method and thus enjoy 'a significant degree of discretion which, however, comes at the cost of consistency and predictability'.[23] In its 1969 *North Sea Continental Shelf* ruling, the ICJ delimited the continental shelf in accordance with the second approach by 'taking account of all relevant circumstances', including geological factors.[24] The result-oriented approach seems, however, to have caused uncertainty regarding maritime delimitation.[25]

20. Lester, 'What is the precedential value of appellate body reports?', 1 March 2018, worldtradelaw.typepad.com/ielpblog/2018/03/what-is-the-precedential-value-of-appellate-body-reports.html (last visited 10 April 2022).
21. Article 3.2 DSU.
22. Guillaume, 'The use of precedent by international judges and arbitrators', 2 *Journal of International Dispute Settlement* (2011), 5-23, at 11.
23. Kaczorowska-Ireland, *Public International Law*, 5th ed. (Routledge, 2015), p. 325.
24. *North Sea Continental Shelf Cases (Federal Republic of Germany/Denmark and Netherlands)*, ICJ Rep. 1969, 3, para. 101.
25. 'The law appeared increasingly uncertain and even arbitrary'; Guillaume, *supra* note 22, at 11.

The ICJ became aware of the problems and implicitly 'reversed its jurisprudence' by merging both methods.[26] This began with the 1985 *Libya-Malta* case in which the ICJ considered the equidistance line as the starting point for marine delimitation.[27] The result of the equidistance method could be adjusted if such a correction is justified by geographic or other circumstances in order to achieve equitable results.[28] The large discretion conferred by the result-oriented approach is thus constrained by the preliminary use of equidistance method. This implicit overruling was confirmed and further generalized in the 2001 *Bahrain v. Qatar* and 2009 *Romania v. Ukraine* cases.[29] As a result, the ICJ 'abandoned' the original approach adopted in 1969 by 'successive strokes without recognizing its original mistake'.[30]

In comparison, the ICTY Appeals Chamber has practised explicit overruling in the past. In *Kordić and Čerkez*, for instance, the Appeals Chamber explicitly overruled its judgments in *Vasiljević* and *Krstić* about the permissibility of cumulative convictions based on the same act.[31] In the latter cases, the Appeals Chamber held that the same conduct should not be accused of both murder and persecution under Article 5 of the Rome Statute of the International Criminal Court (ICC Statute) because the offence of murder is subsumed by that of persecution.[32] This finding was considered to incorrectly apply the legal test relating to cumulative convictions as set out in the *Čelebići* case, which permitted multiple convictions on the basis of the same conduct provided that this conduct related to distinct crimes of which each one under a provision of the ICTY Statute contains 'a materially distinct element not contained in the other'.[33] Thus, through the correction of the *Vasiljević* and *Krstić* judgments, the Appeals Chamber further clarified the standards of the *Čelebići* test, emphasizing the legal elements of each crime at issue rather than on the underlying conduct of the accused for the purpose of 'ensuring that the convictions entered fully reflect his criminality'.[34]

A more recent example is the 2013 *Perišić* case, in which the majority of the Appeals Chamber held that 'specific direction remains an element of the *actus reus* of aiding and abetting liability' and that 'no conviction for aiding and abetting may be entered if the element of specific direction is not established beyond reasonable doubt'.[35] Judge Liu offered a dissenting opinion and, one year later, as presiding judge joined with other judges in the 2014 *Šainović et al.* case to explicitly overrule the *Perišić*

26. *Continental Shelf (Libyan Arab Jamahiriya/Malta)*, ICJ Rep. 1985, 13, para. 40.
27. *Ibid.*, para. 42.
28. Kaczorowska-Ireland, *supra* note 23, at 326.
29. Guillaume, *supra* note 22, at 12. *Maritime Delimitation and Territorial Questions between Qatar and Bahrain (Qatar v. Bahrain)*, ICJ Rep. 2001, 40; *Maritime Delimitation in the Black Sea (Romania v. Ukraine)*, ICJ Rep. 2009, 61.
30. Guillaume, *supra* note 22, at 12.
31. *Prosecutor v. Dario Kordić and Mario Čerkez*, IT-95-14/2, Appeals Chamber judgment of 17 December 2004, para. 1040.
32. *Prosecutor v. Mitar Vasiljevic*, IT-98-32, Appeals Chamber judgment of 25 February 2004, para. 146; *Prosecutor v. Radislav Krstic*, IT-98-33, Appeals Chamber judgment of 19 April 2004, para. 231.
33. *Kordić and Čerkez*, cited *supra* note 31, para. 1033.
34. *Ibid.*
35. *Prosecutor v. Momčilo Perišić*, IT-04-81, Appeals Chamber judgment of 28 February 2013, para. 36.

Appeal Judgment, stating that the finding, namely specific direction is an element of the *actus reus* of aiding and abetting liability, in the *Perišić* judgment is 'in direct and material conflict with the prevailing jurisprudence on the *actus reus* of aiding and abetting liability and with customary international law in this regard'.[36]

At the regional level, it has been argued that the ECtHR 'was extremely reluctant to expressly overrule established interpretations of the Convention' in the early stage.[37] The option of implicit overruling was thus applied in a number of old cases. For instance, the Court in *Huber* held that providing district attorneys with multifarious roles of investigator, authorizer of detention, and prosecutor was inconsistent with Article 5(3) of the Convention regarding the independence of judicial officers.[38] This conclusion is sharply contrary to a prior judgment, namely *Schiesser*, according to which another district attorney in a similar situation was found consistent with Article 5(3).[39] The Court thus implicitly overruled *Schiesser* by not expressly acknowledging that they were overruling their earlier case law. Another example is the *Borgers* case, in which the participation of the Belgian *avocat general* (a member of the Attorney General's department) in the deliberations of the Court of Cassation was found inconsistent with the fair trial commitments under Article 6(1) European Convention on Human Rights (ECHR),[40] despite that such practice was permitted according to the prior judgment of *Delcourt v. Belgium*.[41]

Currently, the ECtHR appears more willing to adopt the option of explicit overruling. For instance, it has explicitly overruled precedent 'to ensure that the interpretation of the Convention reflects societal changes and remains in line with present-day conditions'.[42] Illustrative in this context is the *Christine Goodwin* case, which concerned Article 8 of the Convention on respect for private life. The applicant in the case argued that the government of the United Kingdom had violated this provision by failing to recognize her gender reassignment.[43] The relevant precedents, such as the *Rees* judgment of 1986, suggested that the government's refusal to alter the register of births or to issue new birth certificates updating individuals' gender status could not be considered a prohibited interference with the right to respect for private life under Article 8.[44] However, after recognizing that 'it should not depart, without good reason, from precedents laid down in previous cases', the Grand Chamber in 2002 held that its interpretation must also take into account 'the changing conditions' within the Contracting States and ensure that the rights under the Conventions continued to be

36. *Prosecutor v. Nikola Sainovic, Nebojsa Pavkovic, Vladimir Lazarevic and Sreten Lukic*, IT-05-87, Appeals Chamber judgment of 23 January 2014, paras 1649-1651.
37. Mowbray, 'An examination of the European Court of Human Rights' approach to overruling its previous case law', 9 *Human Rights Law Review* (2009), 179-201, at 183.
38. ECtHR, *Huber v. Switzerland*, Appl. No. 18990/91, judgment of 18 February 1997, para. 43.
39. ECtHR, *Schiesser v. Switzerland*, Appl. No. 7710/76, judgment of 4 December 1979.
40. ECtHR, *Borgers v. Belgium*, Appl. No. 12005/86, judgment of 30 October 1991.
41. ECtHR, *Delcourt v. Belgium*, Appl. No. 2689/65, judgment of 17 January 1970, para. 29.
42. ECtHR, *Goodwin v. United Kingdom*, Appl. No. 28957/95, judgment of 11 July 2002, para. 60.
43. *Ibid.*, para. 60.
44. ECtHR, *Rees v. United Kingdom*, Appl. No. 9532/81, judgment of 17 October 1986; ECtHR, *Cossey v. United Kingdom*, Appl. No 10843/84, judgment of 29 August 1990.

'practical and effective' by maintaining 'a dynamic and evolutive approach'.[45] Thus, looking at the 'present-day conditions',[46] the Grand Chamber explicitly overruled its precedents by holding that the appropriate interpretation and application of the Convention should favour the applicant in the present case and found that the respondent government was in violation of its obligation under Article 8.[47]

With regard to the CJEU, a good example of an express overruling is the change in the doctrine of common origin from the *HAG I* case to the *HAG II* case. *HAG 1* concerned the 'Hag' trademark on decaffeinated coffee that was registered by the German firm Hag AG in both Germany and Belgium in the early twentieth century; a Belgian 'Hag' trademark was subsequently assigned to a Belgian subsidiary of the German firm, namely Hag SA. After the Second World War, Hag SA was seized by the Belgian government, and the Belgian 'Hag' trademark was assigned by Hag SA to Van Zuylen Frères. When Hag AG began to export its German 'Hag' decaffeinated coffee to Luxembourg in 1972, Van Zuylen Frères, defending its Benelux 'Hag' trademark, brought a case in Luxembourg to stop the import of the German product. Seeking to promote the free movement of goods, the Court in *HAG I* held that a prohibition based solely on identical marks having a common origin would be incompatible with European Union (EU) law, an approach often referred to as the doctrine of common origin.[48]

Years after the *HAG I* judgment, CNL-Sucal, the successor of Van Zuylen Frères, began to export its 'Hag' decaffeinated coffee from Belgium to Germany. In the *HAG II* case, Hag AG sought to exercise its German trademark rights in order to prohibit imports of Belgian 'Hag' decaffeinated coffee into Germany. This time, the Court held 'it necessary to reconsider the interpretation' in *HAG I* 'in the light of the case-law which has developed with regard to the relationship between industrial and commercial property and the general rules of the Treaty, particularly in the sphere of the free movement of goods.[49] Subsequently, the Court found that the doctrine of common origin did not apply to situations in which the event separated a trademark from its original owner without the owner's consent. Thus, the *HAG II* judgment explicitly

45. *Goodwin v. United Kingdom*, para. 74.
46. *Ibid.*, para. 75.
47. *Ibid.*, para. 93: 'While the Court is not formally bound to follow its previous judgments, it is in the interests of legal certainty, foreseeability and equality before the law that it should not depart, without good reason, from precedents laid down in previous cases (*see, e.g.*, *Chapman v. the United Kingdom* [GC], no. 27238/95, ECHR 2001-I, § 70). However, since the Convention is first and foremost a system for the protection of human rights, the Court must have regard to the changing conditions within the respondent State and within Contracting States generally and respond, for example, to any evolving convergence as to the standards to be achieved' (para. 74).
48. Case 192/73, *Van Zuylen frères v. Hag AG ('HAG I')*, ECLI:EU:C:1974:72.
49. Case C-10/89, *S SA CNL-SUCAL NV v. HAG GF AG ('HAG II')*, ECLI:EU:C:1990:359, para. 10: 'Bearing in mind the points outlined in the order for reference and in the discussions before the Court concerning the relevance of the Court's judgment in Case 192/73 *Van Zuylen v. HAG* [1974] ECR 731 to the reply to the question asked by the national court, it should be stated at the outset that the Court believes it necessary to reconsider the interpretation given in that judgment in the light of the case-law which has developed with regard to the relationship between industrial and commercial property and the general rules of the Treaty, particularly in the sphere of the free movement of goods.'

repeals the *HAG I* judgment by replacing the doctrine of common origin with the doctrine of 'consensual' common origin.[50] A possible reason behind this overruling is that 'the ruling in *HAG I*, which had been delivered sixteen years earlier, was out of step with subsequent developments in the case law on intellectual property rights and out of step with the evolving perception of the internal market'.[51]

These examples provide the AB with support to adopt implicit or explicit overrulings. The former option, however, is controversial because it may undermine legal certainty. Such practice, for instance, was criticized by one dissenting judge in *Borgers* for failing 'to do what a court that overrules an important judgment should do: it failed to state its reasons for doing so clearly and convincingly'.[52] In contrast, the latter one, namely an explicit overruling, would generate greater clarity in the existing body of case law. In this sense, when necessary, the AB may also bravely alter a previous decision.

The use of explicit overruling has limitations. If a tribunal overrules a very recent decision, it may sometimes generate confusion and raises doubt about its direction and decisiveness. A classic example is the *Šainović et al.* case, where the ICTY Appeals Chamber in 2014 found that the *Perišić* Appeal Judgment, which was made by a different bench the previous year, was wrong and explicitly overruled it. Given this conflict between the different benches of the Appeals Chamber, it has been claimed that the ICTY jurisprudence on certain legal issues 'remains in a state of flux and fragmentation' based on which the result of a future case 'will very much depend on which judges get assigned to their Appeals Chamber'.[53] Indeed, as a former Advocate General at the CJEU once stated: express departures from earlier cases are 'as few as they are celebrated'.[54] To explore other options, the following discussion discusses the practice of international tribunals to apply the technique of distinguishing.

3.2 Distinguishing

A common reason not to follow a precedent is that the reasoning in an earlier case does not apply in the present case due to a relevant distinction between them, which is often referred to as distinguishing. In a more obvious form of distinguishing, if two cases are materially different, the earlier one is not really a precedent to the later one. In contrast, and more relevant to this contribution, is the subtler form of distinguishing, namely

50. Smith, 'The unresolved tension between trademark protection and free movement of goods in the European Community', 3 *Duke Journal of Comparative & International Law* (1992), 89-118, at 122: 'Reviewing the case law of the ECJ and stressing the importance of the economic function of trademarks, Advocate General Jacobs proposed that the doctrine of common origin lacked any foundation in the EEC Treaty. Insofar as the facts of *Hag II* were concerned, the EC agreed.'
51. Tridimas, 'Precedent and the Court of Justice: A jurisprudence of doubt?', in Dickson and Eleftheriadis (Eds), *Philosophical Foundations of European Union Law* (OUP, 2008), pp. 307-330, at p. 317.
52. *Borgers v. Belgium*, dissenting opinion of Judge Martens, para. 1.
53. Milanovic, 'The self-fragmentation of the ICTY Appeals Chamber', *EJIL:Talk!*, 22 January 2014, ejiltalk.org/the-self-fragmentation-of-the-icty-appeals-chamber/ (last visited 10 April 2022).
54. Jacob, *Precedents and Case-Based Reasoning in the European Court of Justice* (CUP, 2014), p. 159.

'where a court departs from a precedent by making a particular ruling depend on the presence of a more extensive range of material facts'.[55]

In *Croatia v. Serbia*, the ICJ appeared to distinguish a previous judgment when there were certain situations in which realism and flexibility were called for to determine the jurisdiction.[56] With regard to the ICTY, for instance, by emphasizing the 'particular circumstances' concerning the offences at issue, the Trial Chamber once distinguished the *Čelebići* test and found that the conduct at issue would only lead to the conviction of destruction or wilful damage of cultural property for 'the interests of justice and the purpose of punishment'.[57]

At the regional level, Chambers of the ECtHR once adopted the option of distinguishing in the *Kopecký* case, which concerned an applicant's claim for the restitution of coins belonging to his father.[58] A Chamber of the ECtHR held that the 'present case should be distinguished from the case law' in which the applicants 'were excluded from the very beginning from the possibility of having the property restored' and on which the claims 'did not amount to a legitimate expectation'.[59] In the present case, however, a 'genuine dispute' was found to exist regarding whether the applicant could meet the requirements of the measure at issue, and thus the Court found that the applicant had a 'legitimate expectation' of obtaining effective enjoyment of the property right at issue.[60] In the view of the Chamber, the use of distinguishing in this case aimed to prevent the protection of the rights under the European Conventions on Human Rights and its protocols from being revealed as 'ineffective and illusory'.[61] Another example is the *Keck* case in which the CJEU chose to distinguish its earlier judgments in order to limit the scope of concerning measures equivalent to quantitative restrictions (MEQRs) under Article 34 Treaty on the Functioning of the European Union.[62]

Moreover, even the AB itself once appeared to distinguish its long-established sequence of analysis under GATT Article XX in *Indonesia – Import Licensing Regimes*. In this case, Indonesia requested the AB to reverse the panel's findings under Article XX because the panel had not followed the 'well-established sequence of analysis under Article XX' by assessing the chapeau of Article XX without first examining the

55. *Ibid.*, p. 115.
56. *Application of the Convention on the Prevention and Punishment of the Crime of Genocide (Croatia v. Serbia)*, ICJ Rep. 2008, 412. For further information, *see* Xue, *Jurisdiction of the International Court of Justice* (Brill, 2009), p. 152.
57. *Prosecutor v. Pavle Strugar*, IT-01-42-T, Trial Chamber judgment of 31 January 2005, para. 455.
58. ECtHR, *Kopecký v. Slovakia*, Appl. No. 44912/98, judgment of 7 January 2003, para. 27.
59. *Ibid.*, para. 27.
60. *Ibid.*: 'In this respect the present case should be distinguished from the cases of *Malhous* v. *the Czech Republic* and *Gratzinger and Gratzingerova* v. *the Czech Republic* referred to above or the case of *Brezny & Brezny* v. *Slovakia* ... in which the Court and the Commission respectively found that the applicants' claims for restitution of property did not amount to a legitimate expectation in the sense of the Court's case-law. In those cases the applicants were excluded from the very beginning from the possibility of having the property restored as it was obvious either that they failed to meet the relevant requirements or that their claim clearly fell outside the relevant law.'
61. *Kopecký v. Slovakia*, para. 29.
62. Joined Cases C-267/91 and C-268/91, *Keck and Mithouard*, ECLI:EU:C:1993:905.

applicable paragraphs, namely paragraphs (a), (b), and (d) in the present case.[63] The sequence of analysis under Article XX was first set out in *US-Gasoline*, in which the AB held that the analysis was two-tiered: first, provisional justification under the applicable paragraphs; second, further appraisal under the chapeau of Article XX.[64] This two-tiered sequence was highlighted in *US-Shrimp* as reflecting 'not inadvertence or random choice, but rather the fundamental structure and logic of Article XX'.[65] Thus, the panel in *Indonesia-Import Licensing Regimes*, choosing to only examine the measure under the chapeau of Article XX, appears to be inconsistent with the AB's prior decisions.

However, rather than reversing the panel's findings, the AB held that it was, in principle, to first examine the applicable paragraphs. This 'normal sequence' aimed to provide panels with the 'necessary tools to assess the requirements of the chapeau'.[66] To distinguish between normal and 'particular' circumstances, the AB held that a panel might deviate from the 'normal sequence' in the 'particular circumstances of the case' provided that the panel had made findings under the applicable paragraphs in order to complete the analysis of the chapeau.[67] In this way, the AB effectively altered the sequence of analysis under Article XX by allowing a deviation under certain circumstances. However, just like an express overruling, the use of distinguishing also has limitations. Although a tribunal could use distinguishing to alter a precedent by adding conditions, these conditions should be based on a material distinction between the precedent and the present dispute. After all, 'the judge who tries to distinguish cases on the basis of materially irrelevant facts is likely to be easily found out'.[68] Given the limitations of judicial options, the next section explores political options to temper the rigidity of the WTO's de facto precedent system.

4 POLITICAL OPTIONS TO LOOSEN THE GRIP OF PRECEDENT

The WTO Agreement gives great power to its decision-making body, which consists of the Ministerial Conference and the General Council. The former, as the organization's most authoritative body, has the power to settle all matters involving any of the

63. Appellate Body Report, *Indonesia-Importation of Horticultural Products, Animals and Animal Products*, WT/DS477/AB/R, WT/DS478/AB/R, and Add.1, adopted on 22 November 2017, para. 5.86.
64. In *US-Gasoline*, the AB stated: 'In order that the justifying protection of Article XX may be extended to it, the measure at issue must not only come under one or another of the particular exceptions – paragraphs (a) to (j) – listed under Article XX; it must also satisfy the requirements imposed by the opening clauses of Article XX. The analysis is, in other words, two-tiered: first, provisional justification by reason of characterization of the measure under XX(g); second, further appraisal of the same measure under the introductory clauses of Article XX.'
65. Appellate Body Report, *United States-Import Prohibition of Certain Shrimp and Shrimp Products*, WT/DS58/AB/R, adopted on 6 November 1998, para. 119.
66. *Indonesia-Importation of Horticultural Products*, para. 5.99.
67. *Ibid.*, para. 5.101.
68. Jacob, *supra* note 54, at 114.

multilateral trade agreements;[69] since it normally meets only every other year, day-to-day business is conducted by the latter.[70] This section assesses the advantages and limitations of relying on the decision-making body to inject valuable flexibility into the WTO's de facto precedent system.

4.1 An Amendment as a Formal Correction and a Waiver as a Stopgap Measure

An amendment can formally correct a precedent by directly altering the relevant WTO rules. Under ordinary rules, 'any Member' may submit a proposal for an amendment to the Ministerial Conference, which then has 90 days to try to reach a consensus on it.[71] If no consensus is forthcoming, the Conference may decide, by a two-thirds majority vote, to submit the proposal to the WTO membership for acceptance. Amendments take legal effect only if at least two-thirds of WTO members have deposited formal instruments of acceptance with the Director-General, a process that can result in considerable delays;[72] for example, it took almost 12 years for the amendment to the Agreement on Trade-Related Aspects of Intellectual Property Rights (the TRIPS Agreement) to enter into force.[73]

The issue concerning the effectiveness of amendments could alternatively be addressed through a waiver releasing WTO members from certain legal obligations under the WTO agreements.[74] In the aforementioned case of the amendment to the TRIPS Agreement, members that have not accepted the amendment can refer to the 2003 waiver decision regarding access to affordable medicines from a third country.[75] In practice, WTO members rely more heavily on waivers than amendments as a means to deviate from agreed-upon trade disciplines. Thus, while only two amendments have been approved since the organization's establishment in 1995, in 2017 alone, the General Council granted eight waivers.[76]

Waivers have one major disadvantage that amendments do not: they are granted only on a time-bound basis and can be modified or terminated by a simple majority of WTO members during annual reviews. For this reason, WTO members seeking a permanent and definitive reduction of their obligations cannot rely on waivers alone.

69. Article IV:1 WTO Agreement. Two plurilateral agreements set out in Annex 4 to the WTO Agreement are subject to different rules according to Article IV:8 of the WTO Agreement.
70. *See* wto.org/english/thewto_e/gcounc_e/gcounc_e.htm (last visited 10 April 2022).
71. The Ministerial Conference must receive a proposal for an amendment by a Member or one of the three specialized Councils.
72. Article X:7 WTO Agreement.
73. *See* wto.org/english/news_e/news17_e/trip_23jan17_e.htm (last visited 10 April 2022). The Protocol (2001) Amending the Annex to the Agreement on Trade in Civil Aircraft amended a plurilateral agreement.
74. ACWL, 'Giving Legal Effect to the Results of the Doha Round: An Analysis of the Methods of Changing WTO Law', Background Paper for ACWL Members and LDCs (2006), at 9.
75. 2003 waiver decision regarding access to affordable medicines from a third country, 1 September 2003, WT/L/540 and Corr.1.
76. WTO Secretariat, 'The WTO 2018 Annual Report', 31 May 2018.

Therefore, waivers can only serve as an interim instrument to temper the rigidity of the WTO's de facto precedent system.

4.2 An Authoritative Interpretation or a More Flexible Alternative

An authoritative interpretation, which was not part of the GATT 1947, would appear to be a necessary instrument amid the checks and balances of judicial interpretation adopted by the AB.[77] The space for judicial interpretations has increased owing to the differing systems of checks and balances that distinguish the GATT from the WTO.[78] Under the GATT dispute settlement system, individual members could veto the adoption of a judicial interpretation. In contrast, under the existing WTO dispute settlement system, a consensus is required to block the adoption of such an interpretation. The formation of this sort of consensus is unlikely, however, because the victorious party in a dispute can be expected to refuse to join in blocking a report favourable to itself. In this context, an authoritative interpretation could have been widely used to correct judicial interpretation because Article IX:2 of the WTO Agreement only requires a three-fourths supermajority of members for the adoption of an authoritative interpretation that binds all of them, including those who voted in opposition.

However, only one request has been made as of yet for an authoritative interpretation. This single request by the EU was for a clarification of the relationship between Articles 21.5 and 22 of the Dispute Settlement Understanding (DSU).[79] The US objected that the requested interpretation would have contradicted the final sentence of Article IX:2 of the WTO Agreement, which states that an authoritative interpretation 'shall not be used in a manner that would undermine the amendment provisions of Article X'.[80] This argument may explain why authoritative interpretations are unpopular in practice; namely, WTO members try to avoid the discussion of the demarcation line with amendments. As an alternative, the Ministerial Conference could take a decision under Article IV:1 of the WTO Agreement.[81] This decision could arguably constitute a subsequent agreement on the interpretation of a provision of a WTO agreement within the meaning of the Vienna Convention on the Law of Treaties (VCLT) Article 31(3)(a).

Indeed, Ministerial Decisions or Declarations have been found to qualify as subsequent agreements in *US-Clove Cigarettes* and *Australia-Tobacco Plain Packaging*.

77. Ehlermann and Ehring, 'The authoritative interpretation under Article IX:2 of the Agreement Establishing the World Trade Organization: Current law, practice and possible improvements', 8 *Journal of International Economic Law* (2005), 803-824, at 812.
78. Steinberg, 'Judicial lawmaking at the WTO: Discursive, constitutional, and political constraints', 98 *American Journal of International Law* (2004), 247-275, at 263.
79. Request of an Authoritative Interpretation pursuant to Article IX:2 of the Treaty Establishing the WTO, 25 January 1999, WT/GC/W/133.
80. Ehlermann and Ehring, *supra* note 77, at 814.
81. For general discussion of the decision-making in the WTO, *see* Kuijper, 'WTO institutional aspects', in Bethlehem, Van Damme, McRae and Neufeld (Eds), *The Oxford Handbook of International Trade Law* (OUP, 2009), pp. 80-128; Footer, *An Institutional and Normative Analysis of the World Trade Organization* (Martinus Nijhoff, 2006), pp. 181-270.

In the former case, the AB found that paragraph 5.2 of the Doha Ministerial Decision on Implementation-Related Issues and Concerns constitutes a 'subsequent agreement between the parties' within the meaning of VCLT Article 31(3)(a).[82] The AB held that the measure allowing only three months between the publication and the entry into force of the technical regulation at issue was inconsistent with Technical Barriers to Trade Agreement (TBT) Article 2.12 because paragraph 5.2 required a minimum of six months in that situation.[83] In the AB's view, a Ministerial Decision may qualify as a 'subsequent agreement between the parties' if '(i) the decision is, in a temporal sense, adopted subsequent to the relevant covered agreement; and (ii) the terms and content of the decision express an agreement between Members on the interpretation or application of a provision of WTO law'.[84] In the more recent example of *Australia-Tobacco Plain Packaging*, the panel qualified the Public Health Declaration, which 'was adopted by a consensus decision of WTO Members, at the highest level, on 14 November 2001 on the occasion of the Fourth Ministerial Conference of the WTO', as a 'subsequent agreement between the parties'.[85] To support its analysis, the panel referred to the *US-Clove Cigarettes* AB report.[86]

The idea that Ministerial Decisions or Declarations may substitute for authoritative interpretations to clarify WTO rules seems to gain support from *EC – Bananas III (Article 21.5 – Ecuador II) / EC – Bananas III (Article 21.5 – US)*. In these cases, the AB stated that 'in the WTO context, multilateral interpretations adopted pursuant to Article IX:2 of the WTO Agreement are most akin to subsequent agreements within the meaning of Article 31(3)(a) of the Vienna Convention'.[87] In other words, once Ministerial Decisions or Declarations are found to constitute subsequent agreements, they might function as authoritative interpretations.

5 CONCLUSIONS

This contribution first argues that a complete dismissal of the precedential value of the AB's decisions is undesirable. In practice, WTO members, including the US, have frequently cited AB reports in their submissions in what amounts to a clear recognition of their precedential value in ensuring that clarifications remain consistent. As correctly noted by the EU as a third participant in *US-Stainless Steel (Mexico)*, 'in practice most international tribunals do give certain weight to precedents when dealing with similar legal issues'.[88] That being said, however, '[t]he cult of the precedent is

82. Appellate Body Report, *United States-Measures Affecting the Production and Sale of Clove Cigarettes*, WT/DS406/AB/3, adopted on 4 April 2012, paras 241-275.
83. *Ibid.*, paras 241-247.
84. *Ibid.*, para. 262.
85. Panel Report, *Australia-Certain Measures Concerning Trademarks, Geographical Indications and Other Plain Packaging Requirements Applicable to Tobacco Products and Packaging*, WT/DS441/R, WT/DS458/R, WT/DS467/R, adopted on 28 June 2018, para. 7.2409.
86. *Australia-Tobacco Plain Packaging*, fn. 5010.
87. Appellate Body Report, *European Communities-Regime for the Importation, Sale and Distribution of Bananas*, WT/DS27/AB/RW/ECU/Corr.1, adopted on 11 December 2008, para. 390.
88. Panel Report, *US-Stainless Steel (Mexico)*, para. 7.20. The EU referred to the practice of the ECtHR, the ICTY, the International Tribunal for the Law of the Sea (ITLOS), the ICTY, the

thus just as dangerous as the rejection of precedent'.[89] This contribution offers judicial and political options to inject valuable flexibility into the WTO's de facto precedent system. The relevant practice of the ICTY, the ICJ, the ECtHR, and the CJEU suggests that the AB may also straightforwardly alter a previous decision, especially if the precedent was adopted a long time ago.[90] Of course, if a tribunal overrules a very recent decision, it could generate confusion and raise doubt about the direction and decisiveness of the tribunal. In this case, the AB may choose to distinguish a previous decision.[91] The use of distinguishing has limitations: although a tribunal could use distinguishing to amend a precedent by adding conditions, these conditions should be based on a material distinction between the precedent and the present dispute. When the facts of a precedent are materially identical or highly similar to those of the case at hand, it would be challenging to distinguish them on the basis of materially irrelevant facts. Such situation could be dealt with by the proposed political option, namely Ministerial Decisions or Declarations within the meaning under Article IV:1 of the WTO Agreement.

The proposed judicial or political options need support from WTO members. One possible way is to increase the relevance of the WTO by engaging private parties. In this regard, Bronckers' early academic work is still inspiring.[92]

International Criminal Tribunal for Rwanda, the International Criminal Court (ICC) and the International Centre for Settlement of Investment Disputes(ICSID). Moreover, former ICJ President Guillaume following precedents is very common in international jurisdictions even if these international tribunals are in fact not formally obliged to comply with precedent; *see* Guillaume, *supra* note 22, at 12.

89. Guillaume, *supra* note 22, at 23.
90. It is noteworthy that *Goodwin* overruled the previous judgments that were made more than 15 years ago. This long period of time provides the Grand Chamber with good reasons to update its case-law in order to reflect 'societal changes'. Moreover, in *US-Shrimp*, the AB adopted an evolutionary interpretation to update the meaning of 'exhaustible natural resources', which, as particularly noted by the AB, was 'actually crafted more than 50 years ago'. AB Report, *US-Shrimp*, para. 129.
91. The AB once appeared to distinguish its long-established sequence of analysis under GATT Article XX in *Indonesia-Import Licensing Regimes*.
92. Bronckers and Baetens, 'Reconsidering financial remedies in WTO dispute settlement', 16 *Journal of International Economic Law* (2013), 271-311; Bronckers, 'Private appeals to WTO law: An update', 42 *Journal of World Trade* (2008), 245-260; Bronckers and van den Broek, 'Financial compensation in the WTO: Improving the remedies of WTO dispute settlement', 8 *Journal of International Economic Law* (2005), 101-126.

CHAPTER 9

A New Approach to Rules of Origin in Services in the Era of Servicification: The Operationalization of the 'Substantial Input Test'

Daniela Gómez Altamirano

Today, most of the production of goods and services occurs via Global Value Chains (GVCs), in which different firms in different countries undertake different segments of the process. At the multilateral and regional level, however, rules of origin in services developed in a defective way. The issue is that the real origin of a service can only be identified when the legal and economic suppliers coincide. The General Agreement on Trade in Services (GATS)-based rules tend to consider only the origin of the legal supplier rather than the economic supplier. Proposals to overcome the defects in the current rules are put forward by mainly importing concepts from trade in goods to trade in services but in a limited way, for example, via the 'substantial input test' based on a value-added criterion. This paper examines rules of origin in services to better understand which approach would be more accurate in determining the real origin of the service. This will help develop a methodology to identify the segments of services in a value chain to then determine the value addition for the operationalization of the 'substantial input test'.

1 INTRODUCTION

World trade is changing, nowhere more so than in the services sector. Most of this trade occurs via Global Value Chains (GVCs), in which different firms in different countries undertake different parts of the process of producing a service in networked or fragmented arrangements. This new economic context raises the question of whether the existing 'rules of the game' as codified in the international legal trade regime are adequate to be applied in trade in services.

At the multilateral level, rules of origin in services can be found in Article XXVIII of the General Agreement on Trade in Services (GATS). In the GATS, the origin of a service is determined in accordance with its mode of supply. For cross-border supply (Mode 1), the country 'from' which a service is supplied to the consumer is deemed as the country of origin of that service. For consumption abroad (Mode 2), the country 'in' which a service is supplied to the consumer will confer the origin status to that service. As for services supplied through the presence of a corporation or an individual (Mode 3 and Mode 4), the nationality of one service's supplier is considered as the origin of these services.

The criticism of this rather simplistic approach is that the real origin of a service can only be identified when the legal and economic suppliers coincide. The GATS-based rules tend to consider only the origin of the legal supplier rather than the economic one (e.g., place of incorporation). Most regional trade agreements (RTAs) follow the same approach as GATS with the same limitation.

While rules of origin in trade in goods have been thoroughly discussed in the literature, much less attention has been given to the increasingly important issue of rules of origin for trade in services. The current scholarship on the topic is limited to identifying flaws in the current system and proposing approaches that might not be fully applicable either at the multilateral level or through RTAs. More importantly, these works have focused on the issue of 'servicification' of manufacturing (i.e., services rendered around the production of goods) rather than on service networks. The notions of 'imported intermediated inputs' and 'domestic value added' are not as well-developed in services as they are in the goods context. One reason is that this form of trade has, so far, been largely unrestricted. However, in view of the rapid growth of cross-border trade in services, the imposition of trade barriers may well be conceivable in the future.[1]

Proposals to overcome the defects in the current rules of origin for services have been put forward in a limited way. The proposals include the incorporation of the 'substantial input test' based on a value-added criterion, a 'substantial transformation' approach focusing on the process via which services are supplied, and through a bottom-up and sector-specific approach where reform should come first from RTAs and through the elaboration of sector-specific rules.

This chapter examines rules of origin for trade in services at the level of the World Trade Organization (WTO) and RTAs in order to better understand which approach

1. Mattoo and Wunsch-Vincent, 'Pre-empting protectionism in services: The GATS and outsourcing', 7 *Journal of International Economic Law* (2004), 765-800.

would not only be more accurate in determining the 'real' origin of the service but would also help in the development of GVCs for both traders and investors in exporting and importing countries. This chapter does not aim at evaluating the level of restrictiveness of rules of origin in services, but rather, attempts to offer policymakers a methodology aligned with the current fragmentation of trade in services to better serve their policy goals.

Following this introduction, section 2 provides conceptual considerations of rules of origin in trade in services as developed in the GATS and RTAs, elaborating on the limitations of the current rules and their implications in the determination of origin. Section 3 discusses the current proposals for rules of origin in services while pointing out the possible ways forward to build on such approaches. Within this context, this section puts forward a methodology to determine value addition to be conducted when implementing the 'substantial input test'. Section 4 presents a discussion on how this methodology could be applied in a simulation case study for networked-based services in the offshore industry. Finally, section 5 provides concluding remarks and thoughts to consider going forward.

This piece is included in Marco Bronckers' *liber amicorum* with great honour and enormous gratitude for his legacy. In 2009, Bronckers was teaching a module on trade remedies in the LLM on International Economic Law and Policy (IELPO) at the University of Barcelona. I was lucky enough to be one of his students. I remember the entire class waiting with enormous expectations for his lecture given his reputation of being not only a leading scholar but also an outstanding practitioner. All our expectations were exceeded. We witnessed his academic and professional credentials but what moved us even more was his sense of sharing knowledge, teaching his passion to younger generations and his unconditional commitment to make a better world through trade law.

2 RULES OF ORIGIN IN SERVICES: CONCEPTUAL CONSIDERATIONS

The need to define the origin of services arises in trade agreements providing for differential treatment between parties and non-parties. Unlike trade in goods where, most often, the preferential treatment takes the form of tariffs, in trade in services, the preference is exercised through a class of non-tariff measures, ranging from market access and quantitative limitations to regulatory restrictions and access to dispute settlement. Despite the differences, rules of origin in both goods and services pertain to the same objective, that is, to avoid the dilution of preferences and the 'free rider' dilemma.

The determination of origin in services is not only relevant for trade preferences under multilateral and bilateral Free Trade Agreements (FTAs) but also for many other reasons in the domestic regulation of trade, *inter alia*, jurisdiction of tribunals, law enforcement, trade statistic collection, taxation, regulatory responsibilities, technical standards implementation, qualification recognition (including licenses and certificates), government procurement, subsidies, emergency safeguards measures implementation, and balance of payments.[2]

To better illustrate the relevance of rules of origin in trade in services, let's consider two scenarios. First, suppose a company from country A establishes a commercial presence in country B to supply services to country C. In this situation, under what circumstances would the subsidiary of the company from country A established in country B benefit from trade preferences under the FTA between country B and country C? Second, a company established in country B provides offshore services to country C. The service exported from country B to country C is segmented in various services lines that are imported from various third countries. Would the cumulation of service lines benefit from trade preferences under the FTA between country B and country C since the final point of export is country B?

Although the first scenario seems to be less problematic and to some extent the determination of origin based on 'ownership' or 'control' requirements could be appropriate, when it comes to services that are segmented into different services lines, the current rules under multilateral, regional, and bilateral trade agreements prove to be inadequate to clearly determine the origin of the service and therefore the access to a preferential treatment.

2.1 Rules of Origin Determination under the GATS

Rules of origin in services were initially negotiated in connection with the rule of origin in goods.[3] It was only when the GATS was drafted that, at the multilateral level, countries made tentative[4] efforts to establish the criteria of origin determination for services to be applied in the trade relationship between Contracting parties. During the Uruguay Round, when the GATS was being drafted, the General Agreement on Tariffs and Trade (GATT) Secretariat recognized the importance of rules of origin for services to encompass a criterion to determine the 'nationality' of a product or a producer but translated to services and service providers.[5] The text of the GATS does not specify the

2. Wang, 'WTO origin rules for services and the defects: Substantial input test as one way out', 44 *Journal of World Trade* (2010), 1083-1108.
3. GATT Trade Negotiations Committee, Draft Final Act Embodying the Results of the Uruguay Round of Multilateral Trade Negotiations, MTN.TNC/W/FA.
4. According to trade experts, the origin rules of services, particularly those for the mode of commercial presence, appear to be one of the most complicated issues in the GATS; *see* Zdouc, 'WTO dispute settlement practice relating to the GATS', 2 *Journal of International Economic Law* (1999), 295-346.
5. Regarding the importance of rules of origin in services, the following are GATS disciplines where its determination becomes relevant: Article I (Scope of Definition); Article II (MFN); Article V (Economic Integration); Article XXI (Balance of Payments); Article XI (Subsidies); Article XVI (Market Access); Article XVII (National Treatment); Article XXIII (Dispute Settlement and Enforcement); Article XXX (Non-application); and Article XXXI (Denial of Benefits). GATT Secretariat, 'Rules of Origin in Services: Conceptual Issues', MTN.GNS/W/140, 15 October 1991, para. 3.

procedure to be followed when determining the origin of a service or service provider.[6] Rules of origin are not addressed explicitly in GATS Article XXXIV (Definition of Terms), which is limited to defining the natural and legal persons of a Member.

Generally speaking, the criteria used to determine the origin of a producer or corporation can be divided into two categories: the first set focuses on the nationality of the producer as reflected in the geographic location of assets or activity, that is: (i) place of incorporation; (ii) nationality of control; (iii) nationality of ownership; (iv) principal place of business; and (v) location of headquarters or centre of management or decision making. The second category looks at the product that is produced/sold and is frequently based on product content, that is: (vi) origin of value added; and (vii) origin of material and/or intangible inputs.

Taking into consideration the differences between trade in goods and trade in services, and the specific characteristics of services, the GATS incorporates an adaptation of rules of origin stipulated in the GATT. To this purpose, the GATS uses the words 'from'[7] or 'in'[8] the territory of one Member, or 'by'[9] a service provider of one Member, replacing the term 'originating in' found in the GATT.

GATS Article XXVIII provides the basis for the determination of rules of origin in services which will vary from one mode of supply to another.[10] For mode of cross-border supply (Mode 1), the service is supplied 'from' the territory of one Member to the territory of another Member, that is, the 'service of another Member' refers to a service provided 'from' the territory of that other Member. This means that the origin of services under Mode 1 is the place from which the service is provided. How to define such place is left to the discretion of each Member. As for the mode of consumption abroad (Mode 2), the service is supplied 'in' the territory of one Member to the service consumer of another Member, that is, the 'service of another Member' refers to a service provided 'in' the territory of that other Member. Therefore, the origin of services provided under this mode of supply is the place of consumption. For these two modes of supply, even if the geographic location is accurately found, it does not necessarily represent the origin of the actual service supplier.

For the supply of services through commercial presence (Mode 3) and presence of natural persons (Mode 4), the 'service of another Member' refers to a service supplied by a service supplier of that other Member. GATS also defines 'service

6. In the context of trade in goods, the text of the GATT does not specify a rule of origin for purposes of the agreement. Instead, it is left up to each Member to decide on the rules to determine the origin of goods entering its territory. Unlike rules of origin in goods where the Agreement on Rules of Origin was adopted, for services, no separate agreement was concluded after the Uruguay Round.
7. Article I(2)(a) GATS 'the supply of a service "from" the territory of one Member into the territory of any other Member'; and Article XXVIII(f)(i) GATS 'services supplied "from" the territory of that other Member'.
8. Article I(2)(b) GATS 'the supply of a service "in" the territory of one Member to the service consumer of any other member'; and Article XXVIII(f)(i) GATS 'services supplied "in" the territory of that other Member'.
9. Article I(2)(c) GATS 'the supply of a service "by" a service supplier of "by" vessel registered ... or "by" a person of that other Member'.
10. There are four modes of supply in GATS, cross-border supply (Mode 1), consumption abroad (Mode 2), commercial presence (Mode 3), and movement of natural persons (Mode 4).

supplier' as either a natural person or a legal person providing the service.[11] The origin of a natural person is determined by both a residence requirement, and the status as national or permanent resident.[12] A legal person is to be considered as such in two circumstances:[13] (i) if constituted or otherwise organized under the law of that other Member, as is engaged in substantive business operations in the territory of that Member or any other Member; or (ii) in the case of the supply of a service through commercial presence, owned or controlled by natural persons of that Member or legal persons of that other Member.[14] The concepts of ownership and control have been elaborated further under the GATS: a legal person is 'owned' by persons of a Member if more than 50% of the equity interest in it is beneficially owned by persons of that Member. It is 'controlled' by persons of a Member if such persons have the power to name a majority of its directors or otherwise to legally direct its actions.[15]

In addition to the general rules of origin, the GATS provides for special situations in case of denial of benefits (Article XXVII) and economic integration (Article V). As for the first scenario, Members may refuse to grant GATS benefits to the service supplier if the services are provided from or in a non-Member or a Member to which the denying Member does apply the WTO Agreements. In a similar way, a service provider that is a legal person might be denied benefits if it is not a service provider of a Member or when the services provider is from a Member to which the denying Member does apply the WTO Agreement. As for economic integration situations, a service supplier of another Member could enjoy the treatment under the economic integration agreement, if it is a legal person constituted under the laws of a party to the agreement and engages in 'substantial business operations' with the parties of such agreement.

While there have been few WTO cases analysing the issue of rules of origin determination in trade in services,[16] the complexities and defects of the current rules have been highlighted in the literature.[17] In particular, issues arise if the service supplier is a legal person under the commercial presence mode where the origin of service depends on the service supplier, and the latter's nationality is in turn decided by that of its owner or controller. Four main elements are considered in the implementation of the ownership or control requirement test for determining origin in services: (1) nationality of legal persons with equal or scattered shareholding structure; (2) services jointly supplied by multiple providers; (3) economic ownership of the services

11. Articles XXVIII(j) and XXVIII(g) GATS.
12. Article XXVIII(k) GATS.
13. The relationship between sub-paras (i) and (ii) of Article XXVIII GATS remains unclear as to whether these two requirements are mutually exclusive or interchangeable in the application. Given the express mentioned of 'commercial presence' in sub-para. (ii), sub-para. (i) probably does not apply to commercial presence mode. *See* Wang, *supra* note 2, at 1083.
14. Article XXVIII(m) GATS.
15. Article XXVIII(n)(i) and (ii) GATS.
16. On the determination of rules of origin in commercial presence mode, *see* Appellate Body report, *European Communities – Regime for the Importation, Sale and Distribution of Bananas (EC – Bananas III)*, WT/DS27, adopted on 27 September 1997, and Appellate Body report, *Canada – Certain Measures Affecting the Automotive Industry (Canada – Autos)*, WT/DS139, adopted on 19 June 2000.
17. *See, e.g.*, Zdouc, *supra* note 4, at 327; Wang, *supra* note 2, at 1083.

supplied vis-à-vis the legal ownership in situations where the economic and the legal ownership do not coincide; and (4) ultimate owner or controller of the legal person.

These four elements, however, encounter flaws. The underlying reason for such flaws is the fact that the ownership or control requirement test focuses on the supplier of the service in legal terms while ignoring the economic nature of both the service supplier and the service itself. In the services sector, the 'legal' service provider will not necessarily be the same as the one actually producing the service and, therefore, the origin of the service. Moreover, more trade in services occurs via GVCs in which different firms in different countries undertake different parts of the production process. This new configuration of services industry leaves the GATS rules of origin obsolete as the ownership or control requirement test may be misleading, as explained above, by not taking into account the origin of all service suppliers in the value chain.

2.2 Rules of Origin in Regional Trade Agreements

As reviewed in the previous section, the GATS offered a basic understanding of rules of origin in trade in services which in this chapter it is argued is inadequate for the fast-growing trade in services. The limited willingness of Member States to multilateral commitments in services has prevented WTO Members from making significant progress in the direction of modernizing the system to adapt it to the new needs and realities of today. The consequence of this phenomenon has been the realization of countries to negotiate and undertake WTO-plus commitments under RTAs.[18]

When discussing rules of origin in trade in services under RTAs, there are important considerations to consider based on economic and bargaining implications.[19] First, from the viewpoint of the importing RTA party, even though a liberal rule of origin does not fully eliminate discrimination against non-party countries, it does away with some discrimination and therefore enlarges the pool of foreign suppliers competing for access to the domestic market. Contrary, for countries aiming to protect their infant-stage industries, a restrictive rule of origin may be a policy option for governments to commit to market access limiting the immediate exposure to global competition.[20] From the viewpoint of the exporting RTA party, a restrictive rule of origin would limit export and associated employment gains to national suppliers. A more liberal rule of origin may attract new foreign investment from outside the RTA, that is, a country with liberal entry conditions for suppliers from outside the RTA may specially seek to become a hub for companies to access markets within the free trade area.[21] Second, countries have seen a way to avoid 'free riding' in multilateral negotiations by negotiating market access in RTAs with a limited number of countries.

18. From the total of 284 RTAs in force (and ratified to the WTO), almost half cover both goods and services. The most recent ones include Korea-Colombia, Korea-China, and Mexico-Panama. WTO Regional Trade Agreements Information System, RTA Database, http://rtais.wto.org.
19. Fink and Nikomborirak, *Rules of Origin in Services: A Case Study of Five ASEAN Countries* (World Bank, 2007).
20. Mattoo and Fink, 'Regional agreements and trade in services: Policy issues', 19 *Journal of Economic Integration* (2004), 742-779.
21. Fink and Nikomborirak, *supra* note 19.

For countries to have a bargaining power allowing access to their market in exchange for same concession, it makes sense to adopt a restrictive rule of origin for 'free rider' problems to be less severe. Liberal rules of origin in RTAs might create a scenario where, for example, for sequential negotiations, if the first RTA commits to liberal market access with liberal rules of origin, the trade partner in the second RTA would find it unproductive to give additional connections. In this scenario, the country adopting the liberal rule of origin will lose bargaining power to negotiate further deals with other partners.

As in trade in goods, the rules of origin for services in each bilateral or RTA may differ, depending on the particular interest of the signatories or their relative bargaining power if interests are divergent. At the same time, in crafting rules of origin in a RTA, Members of the WTO are bound by the disciplines of GATS Article V, as discussed above.

In most RTAs, the rules of origin normally appear in the 'denial of benefit' clause. They range from the narrowest rule which defines the origin of a service supplier by the nationality of the person who owns or controls the service supplier,[22] to the requirement of domestic ownership and control including the substantial business operation requirement,[23] and the most developed rule, for example, requiring that the majority of the ultimate beneficial owner are indeed of the nationality of the country claiming benefits under the RTA.

Rules of origin for service suppliers can be defined along a number of criteria. However, little guidance on how to determine the actual origin is offered in existing treaties. An exception is the China-Hong Kong Closer Economic Partnership Agreement (CEPA), which provides detailed rules of origin. In its annex on the definition of service suppliers, it is stipulated that for Hong Kong companies to enjoy preferential treatment, they must have had substantive business operations for three to five years in Hong Kong for the services they intend to provide in the mainland; they must have paid profit tax in Hong Kong; they must own or rent premises for business operations in Hong Kong; and more than 50% of employees must be Hong Kong residents (or Chinese people staying in Hong Kong on a one-way permit).[24]

From the review of 47 RTAs in the Asia-Pacific region,[25] it is clear that most RTAs have liberal services rules of origin provisions on natural persons. Some RTAs, for example, the Korea-US FTA, require the nationality test to fall under domestic laws. Others, like the EFTA-Singapore FTA, require natural persons to be at least permanent

22. For example, the Thailand-Australia FTA stipulates that either Party may deny the benefits of pre-establishment national treatment to 'an investor of the other Party that is a juridical person of such Party and to investments of such an investor where the Party establishes that the juridical person is owned or controlled by person of a non-Party'.
23. For example, the Treaty of Amity between Thailand and the United States.
24. Give the specific context of the CEPA negotiations just before the liberalization schedule to which China committed as part of its accession package to the WTO and the highly liberal market of Hong Kong, this agreement is a very unique one concluded with the purpose of promoting deeper integration between Hong Kong and Mainland. Full explanation provided in Fink and Nikomborirak, *supra* note 19.
25. Khumon, 'Rules of origin for services in Asia-Pacific Trade Agreements', 10 *Asian Journal of WTO & International Health Law and Policy* (2015), 591-618.

residents. More restrictive rules are found in most RTAs involving Japan,[26] requiring nationality as the only means to benefit from the RTA.

The study also found that for legal persons, the rule of origin clause varies from a restrictive to a more liberal approach. The vast majority of RTAs have adopted liberal rules or origin, for example, the Malaysia-Australia FTA[27] which requires a service supplier of a party to include a non-party supplier who establishes business under laws of either party and has a substantial business operation in the territory of an FTA member. Another example is the ASEAN Framework Agreement on Services (AFAS)[28] that allows benefits of the agreement to be extended to non-party legal persons who are incorporated in one of the parties and carry out substantial business operations in a territory of an AFAS party country.

A more restrictive rule of origin can be found in the Japan-Philippines Economic Partnership Agreement[29] requiring the benefits of the agreement to extend to a non-party whose country has a diplomatic relation with an FTA party in addition to meeting the incorporation and substantial business operations test. Probably the most restrictive rule of origin is the one found in the Thailand-Australia FTA[30] where benefits are denied to non-party services owned or controlled by a non-party even if they incorporate their business and have substantial business operations in any RTA party's territories.

In sum, there are three types of rules of origin in trade in services ranging from the more liberal to the more restrictive: (i) incorporation of non-party business in the country of an RTA party with substantial business operations; (ii) incorporation of non-party business in the country of an RTA party with substantial business operation plus diplomatic relationship with a country of non-party business; and (iii) only non-party business owned or controlled by a natural or legal person of one of the parties.

RTAs provide for the basic rules of origin in services but lack explicit guidance as to how the specific requirements are to be met. For legal persons, however, some insights can be drawn from these basic rules. For 'incorporation', a first requirement may simply be for a service supplier to be incorporated under the laws of the exporting RTA member. 'Substantive business operations' could be defined by the possession of a business or service license in the exporting RTA party, although this would say little about the scale of a service supplier's activities. Additional options include the payment of local profit taxes, the owning or renting of premises, a minimum sales requirement, a minimum number of years of establishment, and a requirement that the

26. For example, the Japan-Vietnam Economic Partnership Agreement and the Japan-Switzerland Economic Partnership Agreement.
27. Malaysia-Australia FTA, Article 8.2(d). *See also*, ASEAN-Korea FTA, Article 17; China-Panama FTA, Article 10.14; ROC-El Salvador and Honduras FTA, Article 10.14; Singapore-Peru FTA, Article 11.12.
28. AFAS, Article VI (Denial of benefits).
29. Japan-Philippines Economic Partnership Agreement, Article 105 (Denial of Benefits). *See also*, China-Costa Rica FTA, Article 99; Japan-Chile Economic Partnership Agreement, Article 86.
30. Thailand-Australia FTA, Article 103(p). *See also*, India-Singapore Comprehensive Economic Cooperation Agreement (CECA), Article 7.23.

export of services within the RTA territory be of the same nature as the services supplied in the exporting RTA party.

Regarding the 'domestic ownership and control' rest, eligibility of preferences may be confirmed to firms that are owned and/or controlled by persons of the exporting RTA party. This is usually defined through the equity share in a company or the voting rights controlled by domestic shareholders. In RTAs involving more than two parties, it is also possible to introduce a more liberal cumulated ownership and control criterion, that is, eligibility for preferences would be widened to service providers that are majority owned or effectively controlled by persons from RTA parties. Finally, 'domestic employment' requires a minimum share of employees consisting of national or residents.[31]

Although the requirement to apply the 'ultimately control' test is rarely found in RTAs, the Canada-United States-Mexico Agreement (CUSMA) presents an example of this more restrictive rule.[32] Such restrictive rule implies difficulties as identifying the ultimate control of a service supplier with multi-layered and multi-national shareholdings is not an easy task. Despite the difficulties, it is, perhaps, the most accurate way of determining origin.

As for natural persons, most RTAs use a criterion streamlined in the following way.[33] 'Nationality' can be determined by the passport of the service supplier. 'Residency' would be broader than the nationality test and will consider the forms of residency available in the specific country. 'Centre of economic interest' can be defined by a minimum number of years of residency, the payment of local income taxes, or the owning or renting of a dwelling.

3 TOWARDS A VALUE-ADDED APPROACH

As in the case of the GATS, it is also true that RTAs focus on the service supplier, natural or legal, rather than on the service itself for the determination of origin. This can be explained given that the notion of imported intermediates inputs and domestic value added are not as well-developed in services as they are in the goods context. This, as discussed above, may create problems in determining the real origin of services. The challenge of origin determination accentuates when the service under examination is not a single service exported by a single service supplier but a network-based service where multiple segmented services and service suppliers are part of a GVC in the supply of a given service.

Given the unique nature of services, it is widely accepted that the dissimilarity between goods and services makes it unfeasible to import origin concepts from the field of goods into that of services. However, there have been a few attempts that revisit the current rules of origin looking no more into the different characteristics between goods and services but instead to focus on the common characteristics between the two which would allow for an interpretation of rules of origin for goods in conformity to the

31. Fink and Nikomborirak, *supra* note 19.
32. United States-Canada-Mexico Agreement (USMCA), Ch. 15: Cross-Border Trade in Services.
33. Fink and Nikomborirak, *supra* note 19.

context of services.[34] This section reviews the proposals put forward by scholars by identifying some of their limitations. Further, this section develops a new approach based on value addition that might shed light on a more sophisticated methodology to determine the origin of services in the context of network-based services in GVCs.

3.1 The Suggested New Approaches and Their Limitations

There is limited literature on rules of origin in services, even fewer are the suggestions for a new interpretation of the current rules in the GATS and RTAs or ideas on how to construct a more accurate determination of origin for trade in services. Scholars have highlighted the importance of this topic in particular in today's trade dynamics and have also pointed out the defect of the current use and interpretation of the rules. Two research work put forward suggestions for a new determination of rules of origin in services by importing certain concepts from the sphere of goods into that of services.

In this context, Wang proposes a 'substantial input test' as a way forward.[35] This test is based on the value-added criterion to be used to interpret the ownership or control requirement under the mode of commercial presence. The legal grounds for such test are found in the GATT Secretariat, 'Rules of Origin and Services: Conceptual Issues', MTN.GNS/W/140 document[36] taken as supplementary means of interpretation according to Article 31 of the Vienna Convention on the Law of Treaties (VCLT). The use of this test will help to determine the real origin of services in all circumstances but in particular when dealing with legal persons of equal or scattered shareholder structure, joint provisions of services, and service outsourcing.

According to Wang, the substantial input test would not only focus on where the value is added but also how substantial such added value is. Following this approach, the country from where the substantial input is added to the service would be the origin of the service. The amount of input is evaluated according to the value that such input adds to a service. Factors including the shareholding structure of the legal person are no longer the focus; although relevant in some instances, series suppliers would be considered but only as a secondary factor.

---

34. Wang, *supra* note 2, at 845-862.
35. Wang's argument is that the only approach that appears feasible to apply to services is origin criterion based on nationality or value added. A nationality-based origin rule, such as location of incorporation, is perhaps the simplest and most transparent procedure and can be used to determine the origin of both products and providers. While a value-added criterion can also be used for both purposes, it is much more complex to implement. Indeed, in the services context it is likely to lead to greater arbitrariness and offer more discretion. Wang, *supra* note 2.
36. The document W/140 summarizes the usual rules of origin as follows: 'the origin of producers (corporations) is usually decided on the basis of one or more of the following criteria: (1) place of incorporation; (2) nationality of control; (3) nationality of ownership; (4) principal place of business; (5) location of headquarters or center of management/decision making; (6) origin of value added; and (7) origin of material and/or intangible inputs'. The first five of these criteria are related in that the focus is on the nationality of the producer/firm as reflected in the geographic location of assets or activity. The last two criteria focus on the product that is produced/sold and are frequently based on product content. GATT Secretariat, 'Rules of Origin and Services: Conceptual Issues', MTN.GNS/W/140, 15 Oct. 1991.

How to identify the different inputs when dealing with services considering their intangible nature? Wang gives some clues as to the valuable inputs, for example, that the biggest added value may come from the personnel who are most crucial to the service provision, such as haircutters, designers, and pilots. The important intellectual input may lead to the added value.

A major concern in operationalizing the substantial input test, as identified by Wang, is that the added value criterion is much more complex to implement and may lead to greater arbitrariness and offer more discretion to the government since the invisibility of the production process often inhibits an objective determination of how much value was added in a specific location. Given such concerns, Wang opted not to provide specific rules as to the substantial input test arguing that the excessive specific rules could be rigid and may be abused or evaded in particular given the fast-changing service industries and technological innovations. Instead, a flexible test should be applied on a case-by-case basis.

Due to such challenges, the key point is probably to strike a proper balance between utilizing the substantial input test to the determination of real origin and preventing its restrictive or distorting effects on trade, while serious efforts are needed to make the test more operational.

Building on Wang's proposal, Dinh advocates for the 'substantial transformation' approach and argues that the importation of the substantial transformation criterion from the field of goods into that of services should not be transferred exactly as it is applied in goods, but needs to go through a process of adaptation.[37] Rather than proposing a methodology to deal with rules of origin in services, he provides a possible way to promote reforms of the current rules by adopting a 'bottom-up' approach. It is more feasible for preferential trade agreements (PTAs) to adjust the current rules and adopt a more modern approach than for the GATS to be amended or new approaches incorporated through WTO panels and Appellate Body interpretations.

Dinh complements this argument by suggesting that rules of origin based on the substantial transformation criterion should be sector specific.[38] This idea follows to some extent the approach in trade in goods through the sectorial classification list, where rules of origin are sector specific.

Perhaps the more significant contribution of Dinh in proposing a new test to rules of origin in services is in the operationalization of such rules. The decision to grant benefits to a subsidiary service supplier may be *ex ante* based on its parent company's nationality, but the continuance of denial of benefits should be *ex post* depending on its own activities. That is a dual approach where the current rules which focus on the country 'in' or 'from' which the service is supplied, and the nationality of supplier are used *ex ante* for the grating of the concession, but a more sophisticated determination based on 'substantial transformation' be applied *ex post* when dealing with the 'denial of benefits' test. Although an innovative approach, this will bring inconsistency in the

37. Dinh, 'The standstill of rules of origin for services: Towards a "substantial transformation" approach', 19 *Journal of International Economic Law* (2016), 845-862.
38. A sectorial approach is also suggested by Wang noting that it is also possible to develop specific substantial input test for particular services or service sector. Wang, *supra* note 2.

application of the rules of origin and the concessions granted creating legal uncertainties as, given the already mentioned defects of the current rules, it is probably that the determination of origin under the traditional approach will not be the same as the determination using a 'substantial transformation' or 'substantial input' test.

Both Wang and Dinh advocate for the use of the 'substantial input' test as applied to rules of origin in services. However, none of them gives a more comprehensive response as to how to determine where the value is added and how substantial the value added is. Wang acknowledges such limitation but argues that a specific rule in determining value added could be risky as it will create arbitrariness from policymakers. Although these proposals advance the discussion of the defects of the current rules of origin, they do not shed much light on the way forward. Perhaps the most valuable contribution of both authors is the focus no longer on the service supplier but on the service as such which is a significant switch from the traditional thinking rooted in the GATS and in RTAs.

3.2 Suggested Methodology to Determine Value Addition for the 'Substantial Input Test'

To assess more fully the legal and economic implications of alternative rules of origin in services, it is necessary to obtain a better empirical understanding of the issues outlined in the preceding discussion. In doing so, this section aims at elaborating further on the already existing proposals looking into more specific ways to determine value addition and to simulate, through an empirical case, what would be the implications of using such methodology.

The proposed approach builds on the notion that the rules of origin in GATS and RTAs are defective as they are constructed around the service supplier, rather than on the service. Due to the nature of services, the criteria utilized in rules of origin in trade in goods cannot be transferred to the services arena. The arguments backing up such assumption range from the intrinsic characteristics of services to the lack of availability of services data. For example, Kingston argues that most service sectors differ from goods since one cannot evaluate the different components that make up a service. In particular, the substantial transformation test and change in tariff heading will not be workable. First, insufficient information is available regarding the structure of production for most services, and, more fundamentally, most traded services will be 'substantial transformations' of whichever inputs are used, simply because the service will not have existed before it was sold. That is, the non-storability of services frequently makes these traditional merchandise trade approaches irrelevant.[39]

Although the challenges to use a 'substantial transformation' approach are valid, the way the world currently operates in the trade arena is rapidly changing, prominently in the services sector where more trade occurs via GVCs. Data suggest that

39. Kingston, 'The economics of origin', in Vermulst, Bourgeois and Waer (Eds), *Rules of Origin in International Trade: A Comparative Study* (University of Michigan Press, 1994), pp. 7-25.

services industries are increasingly produced in networked or fragmented arrangements.[40] Services appear in the production cycle of products in different manners. They can be inputs to the production of goods as intermediate services (servicification of goods)[41] or can be outputs of networked production systems. Departing from the traditional view of services as compared to goods, modern services can now be unbundled and splintered into value chains just like goods and they can be electronically transported internationally through satellite and telecom networks.[42]

Given the intrinsic nature of services and the lack of available data and in the effort to use the 'substantial input' test to determine the origin of services, significant questions arise. How can services value chains or networks be analysed and measured? Is it possible to measure the supply of services in a kind of supply chain adding value at each step? According to the literature, there are different approaches to classify services analytically, from production services to consumption services or in statistical frameworks from transformation to margin services. Transformation services include services that refer to changes in the condition of consumer's goods, to the physical condition of persons or mental conditions of persons. Margin services relate to wholesaling or retailing, merchanting or financial institutions.[43]

The determination of intermediate inputs for goods in GVCs has been comprehensively analysed, but can the same methodology be applied to trade in services? The Broad Economic Categories (BEC) classification has been used to identify imported goods for their end-use, i.e., intermediate consumption vis-à-vis final use. A revised version of the BEC extends this classification to include services, although in a very early stage. Suggestions have also been put forward to measure intermediate inputs in services by looking at domestic and international transactions through the four modes of international service supply. Statistics on trade in services by mode of supply could allow for a better measurement of such network-produced services.[44]

Although the BEC classification and the approach looking at modes of service supply may help to identify the segmentation of intermediate inputs in services, another question is how to assess the value addition in each of the inputs or segments of production. In the GVC literature, value is generally determined by examining the transformation of inputs to outputs at each stage. In product-based industries, value is measured by the price of the inputs and outputs at each stage of a product's assembly. In services, measuring value is complicated by the lack of reliable company-level data and trade statistics for services. As pointed out by Wang, this can be done by simply looking at the price of the service; however, as argued by Dinh, this methodology can

40. Rainer and Maurer, 'Services and global value chains: Some evidence on servicification of manufacturing and services networks', *WTO Staff Working Paper*, No. ERSD-2015-03 (2015).
41. As enablers, services contribute to the manufacturing production that, by using trade in value added statistics to show the servicification of manufacturing, it is shown as substantial specially in developed economies where services account for about a third of manufacturing exports. As already noted, the servicification of manufacturing is not the focus of this paper rather the networked production system.
42. Ghani, Grover and Kharas, 'Can services be the next growth escalator?' *VoxEU*, 12 December 2011, voxeu.org/article/can-services-be-next-growth-escalator.
43. Rainer and Maurer, *supra* note 40.
44. *Ibid*.

be misleading. This will be the case when the value in price of the service would not entail that the value added is in that service.

Industry analysis shows that participation in different stages of the GVC depends on two key factors: labour costs and expertise.[45] Human capital has been found to be a key determinant of value creation.[46] Value is thus determined by using human capital requirements as a proxy, that is, the approximate employee education and experience level required to perform different service functions for each stage. For example, usually employees located in the lower part of the value chain have less education and experience, while employees in the upper section of the value chain are more educated and have more years of experience.

By indicating the human capital required at different levels of the offshore services value chain, this classification scheme helps in the identification of the value addition for the determination of origin while deploying the 'substantial transformation' test. For such calculation of the value added in labour costs and expertise, evidence shows that higher average exports per employee are a reliable indicator of greater added value. Such analysis uses average export revenue per employee to compare the value of the countries' services exports. The average revenue per employee is thus calculated by dividing the total value of exports per segment by the number of workers in that segment.

4 SIMULATION FOR NETWORKED-BASED SERVICES: THE OFFSHORE INDUSTRY

The offshore service industry, encompassing the trade of services performed in one country and consumed in another, is a good example of network-based services where this separation of production and consumption has permitted both developed and (more prominently) developing countries to contribute significantly to the world's services industry.[47]

Looking through value chains, the offshore service industry can be subdivided into two main segments: horizontal services provided across all industries and vertical services specific to particular sectors. The activities included in horizontal services support generic business functions and rely on process expertise. These services range from repetitive transactional processes to transformational operations that depend on analytical skills. Vertical services require specific industry knowledge. These services may be so highly specialized that they have limited applicability in other industries.[48]

45. Fernandez-Stark, Bamber and Gereffi, 'The offshore services global value chain: Economic upgrading and workforce development', in Gereffi, Fernandez-Stark and Psilos (Eds), *Skills for Upgrading: Workforce Development and Value Chains in Developing Countries* (Duke Center on Globalization, Governance & Competitiveness, 2011), pp. 132-189.
46. *See, e.g.*, Chadee, Raman and Michailova, 'Sources of competitiveness of offshore IT service providers in India: Towards a conceptual framework', 15 *Competition & Change* (2011), 196-220; Nyhoho, 'Determinants of comparative advantage in the international trade of services: An empirical study of the Heckshер-Ohlin Approach', 10(1) *Global Economy Journal* (2010), No. 3.
47. Fernandez-Stark, Bamber and Gereffi, *supra* note 45.
48. Fernandez-Stark, Bamber and Gereffi, *Engineering Services in the Americas* (Centre on Globalization, Governance & Competitiveness, 2010).

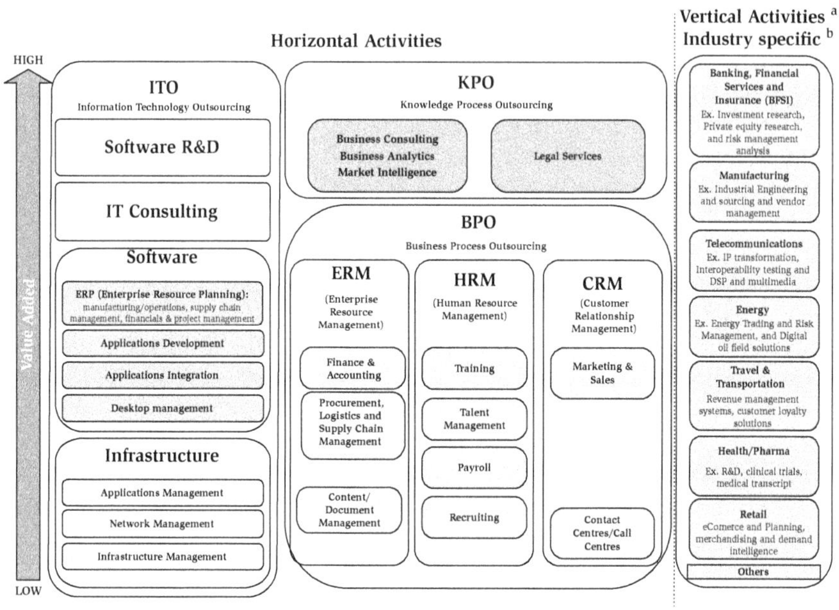

In the offshore industry, the general services provided across sectors are mainly Information Technology Outsourcing (ITO), Business Process Outsourcing (BPO), and Knowledge Process Outsourcing (KPO). ITO is the basic building block for the offshore services value chain and is centred around the production and use of software. It encompasses services such as network management, applications development, information technology (IT) consulting, and software research and development (R&D). ITO services span the low-, mid- and high-value segments of the chain. BPO is a highly diverse category that contains activities related to the management of enterprise resources (ERM), human resources (HRM), and customer relationships (CRM). Specific BPO services include call centres, payroll, finance, and accounting. Human resources (HR) activities are present in the low- and mid-value segments. KPO refers to specialized activities that often require professional licensing (such as in the medical, legal, and accounting fields). KPO services include market intelligence, business analytics, and legal services, which are the high-value-added general segment of the chain.

Noting that in the offshore services industry certain segments (ITO, BPO, and vertical services) contain high-, medium-, and low-value activities, the value of services can, thus, be related to skills levels and work experience, i.e., the human capital inputs of offshore services. Therefore, one could think that the value added for these services can be calculated by the wages paid to employees for different activities within industry segments. These relative wages reflect the required employee education and experience levels and will provide the best indication of 'low' and 'high' value-added activities.[49]

Consider a company from country A whose subsidiary established operations in country B with the objective of providing offshore services to country A. The subsidiary that is incorporated under the legal framework of country B outsources segments of the service from third countries. From the general services provided only those related to BPO are done by the company established in country B. KPO and ITO services are outsourced from third countries. What is then the origin of the offshore service in question?

Under the GATS Article XXVIII, if considered a cross-border supply, the origin of the service would be the place from which the service is provided. In this case, the origin under GATS would probably be country B. Such determination would not be entirely accurate given that the service exported from country B to country A involves segments of services produced by third countries. In a similar scenario where there is an RTA to which countries A and B are parties but not the third countries, the question would focus on the 'incorporation' and 'substantial business operations'. Could country A deny the benefits of the agreement considering that the company in country B does not meet the 'substantial business operation' test? That could be possible if country A is able to identify the 'substantial business operations' in the offshore service exported. Turning to the 'substantial input test' while developing the methodology of determining value addition used in the context of GVCs, the value-added segments of the offshore service exported from country B to country A are not produced in country B and its origin cannot be attached to it but rather to the third country where the higher value is added.

As noted, this methodology to identify the segment of the service which adds more value is difficult to implement given the lack of firm-level data, for which a determination will have to be undertaken on a case-by-case basis and be sector specific. As the research on services industry advances, more information will become available for policymakers to undertake the assessment of value addition and thus a better determination of 'rule of origin' will be possible.

5 CONCLUSION

Rules of origin in trade in services have been neglected in literature and policy making although services industries have gained momentum and relevance for development purposes both in developed and developing countries. As governments continue negotiating trade deals in bilateral and regional agreements covering trade in services and investment, attention should be put on the design of the rules of origin as they will determine the preferential treatment offered to trade partners as well as the bargaining power countries would like to retain in negotiating further agreements with other countries.

49. Fernandez-Stark, Bamber and Gereffi, *supra* note 45.

As things stand today, there appears to be a lack of consensus as to the ideal approach towards setting out rules of origin in services: arguments can be found in favour and against not only the current way of determining these rules but their restrictiveness (being liberal or more stringent). What is certain is that rules of origin regardless of whether being for goods or services should be 'objective, understandable and predicable', 'coherent' and 'based on a positive standard'.[50] In practice, however, only few countries apply a uniform rule of origin. Whatever rule is used, policymakers should make a conscious decision that the rule applied will be as accurate as possible and that it attains the intended policy goal. While a few studies[51] conducted on this topic reveal insights on an understudied topic, more empirical research is needed to provide better guidance to policymakers on the benefits and costs of different rules of origin in services trade.

The rules of origin in the GATS and RTAs clearly do not serve the purpose and show defects that merit review. The focus on the service supplier rather than on the service that is being supplied is the most important defect of the current rules. The use of concepts such as 'ownership' or 'controlled' is clearly a very basic test that leads to absurd conclusions of service suppliers being nationless or with double nationalities. The problem is aggravated when dealing with services being jointly supplied by providers of different nationalities or the service being outsourced.

Few attempts to revisit the current approach have been put forward by trying to import concepts from the trade in goods arena to one of the services. The 'substantial input test' and the 'substantial transformation test' seem to have some logic in identifying the real origin of the service not by looking at the service supplier but at the service itself. Although a step forward, the proposals limit themselves to the possible approach to be followed and give little guidance on how to apply the test, which is the real challenge.

There is a shared view that to avoid arbitrariness, the determination should be conducted on a case-by-case basis and be sector specific. Although this approach can be costly for governments. In theory, the determination will prove to be more accurate helping countries achieve more precisely their policy goals. Less clear is how to determine the value addition for the 'substantial transformation' test. A first attempt to address this issue is developed in this paper. The argument is that by using the methodology on GVCs, one can identify the segments of the service and put some value, in numbers, to each of them to determine where in the value chain the higher value is added. This could help determining where the service suffered the substantial transformation and, therefore, the origin of the service supplied.

50. WTO Agreement on Rules of Origin, Article 9.

51. *See*, *e.g.*, Mattoo and Wunsch-Vincent, *supra* note 1 and Fink and Nikomborirak, *supra* note 19.

CHAPTER 10

WTO Law's Balance Between Trade and Global Climate and Environmental Interests: The Case of the European Union and Some Aspects of Its Green Deal

Ben Smulders[*]

> *Occasionally, States leverage their markets to create regulatory incentives for others to follow, claiming that otherwise, their efforts to pursue a non-economic public interest will fail. The paradigm current example of this process is the European Union (EU) proposal for a Carbon Border Adjustment Mechanism (CBAM), on which Council and European Parliament have reached a political agreement and that is likely to be formally adopted in Mayy 2023. CBAM requires that all of the products, whether domestic or imported, have paid a carbon price commensurate with the carbon emissions generated during production. If, for an imported product, a carbon price has been paid in the third country, no adjustment will be required upon import to the EU. If not, an adjustment must be made, equivalent to the carbon price that would have been paid if the product had been produced in the EU. The purpose of the measure is to address climate change by giving effect to the polluter pays principle; that is, by internalizing the otherwise exogenous environment costs of carbon emissions. CBAM is designed to prevent so-called carbon leakage, that is, the risk that as the EU raises its environmental ambitions, the industry simply shifts offshore, continuing to serve the EU market*

* The author is employed by the European Commission but all views expressed herein are his own and do not bind in any way the institution he works for. The author is immensely indebted to his colleague James Flett for his invaluable ideas on the subject.

from a third country or other less regulated markets without diminishing its carbon emissions. Specifically, CBAM is quite particular because credit is given for any carbon price already paid in the third country, and this is central both to establishing its exclusive climate and environmental credentials and to understanding the very specific regulatory nudge created for third countries. It would also involve contingent support for exports, which is generally considered to be particularly trade-restrictive. CBAM is therefore of particular interest because it provides, in the current circumstances, the best available model for propelling us down the evolutionary track towards sustainable global governance of public goods.

1 INTRODUCTION

In the context of the implementation of the European Green Deal,[1] discussions are held about regulating production processes that are considered to be harmful from a climate and/or environmental protection perspective, including in third countries. Two sets of stakeholders tend to find themselves in counterpoints to each other: those advocating for the benefits of trade and those advocating for the climate and the environment. Each is, understandably, susceptible to presenting World Trade Organization (WTO) law in a manner that reflects their own interests. This chapter develops a few reflections in an attempt to assimilate those different interests. In doing so, it takes the policy objective that there is an urgent need for action on certain climate and environmental issues as a given. It then employs reasoning, as yet largely untested in litigation, in an attempt to explain how such action might best be defended as a matter of WTO law.

2 THE KEY POINT

The key point, it is submitted, is that achieving a level playing field between domestic and imported products is not a permissible end in itself but may be, in certain circumstances and under certain conditions, an indispensable part of achieving the overarching environmental objective.[2]

This is a horizontal point, potentially relevant to different climate and environmental issues, as well as to other legitimate policy objectives, such as human, animal or plant life or health, or public morals, or security of supply in a genuine case under the security exceptions of Article XXI of the General Agreement on Tariffs and Trade (GATT) 1994. It is also potentially relevant with respect to both taxation and regulation, which are therefore dealt with together. The rich complexity of the legal situation

1. *See* COM(2019)640 final, 'The European Green Deal', 11 December 2019.
2. *See, e.g.*, Bacchus, 'Legal issues with the European Carbon Border Adjustment Mechanism', Cato Institute, 9 August 2021, available at cato.org/briefing-paper/legal-issues-european-carbon-border-adjustment-mechanism (last visited June 2022).

is well-documented,[3] and it is well-understood that the legal analysis will ultimately depend on the particular objectives being pursued and the precise nature of the measure. However, this chapter aims to eschew such complexity in an attempt to shed light on the key point.

3 THE EU'S CONCEPTION OF THE WTO AND NON-ECONOMIC PUBLIC INTERESTS

The European Union (EU), itself an international organization, is committed to the rule of law, both internally and internationally. It is part of its DNA, as follows from Article 2 of the Treaty on European Union (TEU).[4] This continues to be the case notwithstanding the present blockage of WTO Appellate Body appointments, also in light of the Multi-Party Interim Arbitration Arrangement[5] it concluded in 2020 with some other WTO members pursuant to Article 25 of the WTO Dispute Settlement Understanding.[6]

The EU joined the WTO on the basis of an understanding that the WTO Agreement creates a framework within which a reasonable balance may be found between, on the one hand, encouraging international trade in the interests of all members, whilst, on the other hand, preserving the rights of Members to tax or regulate autonomously within certain limits.[7] From this perspective, extreme propositions should be rejected, for instance, the proposition that Members are free to tax or regulate as they wish: they must, in particular, generally ensure that any measures are even-handed and eventually necessary, that is, that there is no less trade-restrictive alternative that equally contributes to the legitimate policy objective. At the same time, the proposition should be rejected that Members pursuing a higher level of ambition

3. *See*, by way of illustration but not necessarily endorsement: Pauwelyn, 'Carbon leakage measures and border tax adjustments under WTO law', in Van Calster and Prévost (Eds), *Research Handbook on Environment, Health and the WTO* (Edward Elgar, 2013), pp. 448-506; Wilke, 'Feed-in tariffs for renewable energy and WTO subsidy rules', ICTSD Issue Paper No. 4 (2011); Condon, 'Climate change and unresolved issues in WTO law', 12 *Journal of International Economic Law* (2009), 895-926; Tran, 'Using GATT, Art XX to justify climate change measures in claims under the WTO Agreements', 27 *Environmental and Planning Law Journal* (2010), 346-359; Fatah and Cima, 'The WTO and renewable energy subsidies', 27 *Georgetown International Environmental Law Review* (2015), 515-537; Valeriani, 'Renewable energy subsidies and WTO law', *Ius In Itinere*, 13 July 2019, at 12; Rubini, 'Ain't wastin' time no more: Subsidies for renewable energy, the SCM Agreement, policy space, and law reform', 15 *Journal of International Economic Law* (2012), 525-579; Spiegel Feld and Switze, 'Whither Article XX? Regulatory autonomy under non-GATT Agreements after *China – Raw Materials*', 38 *Yale Journal of International Law Online* (2012), 16-30; Ahmad, *WTO Law and Trade Policy Reform for Low-Carbon Technology Diffusion: Common Concern of Humankind, Carbon Pricing, and Export Credit Support* (Brill | Nijhoff, 2021).
4. Article 2 TEU: 'The Union is founded on the values of respect for human dignity, freedom, democracy, equality, the rule of law and respect for human rights, including the rights of persons belonging to minorities. These values are common to the Member States in a society in which pluralism, non-discrimination, tolerance, justice, solidarity and equality between women and men prevail.'
5. WTO document JOB/DSB/1/Add.12, 30 April 2020.
6. For a discussion of the current difficulties experienced by the WTO, *see* Bronckers, 'Trade conflicts: Whither the WTO?', 47 *Legal Issues of Economic Integration* (2020), 221-244.
7. *See* in particular the various matters referred to in the recitals of the WTO Agreement.

when it comes to human, animal or plant life or health, or the environment are effectively prevented from doing so by the unconstrained economic risk that capital will re-locate offshore, to less costly jurisdictions, making the regulating Member a driver of a 'race to the bottom' and a social (at least in the sense of public health) or environmental dumper (a specific example of which is so-called carbon leakage). Instead, reflecting on its own origins, values and experiences, the EU searches for a third way: it searches for co-existence, and in doing so, it aims to show leadership.[8]

4 THE CASE OF REGULATION OF PRODUCT-RELATED PROCESS AND PRODUCTION METHODS

Regulation often relates to process or production methods (PPM) in the country of regulation that may have a negative impact on the environment, health or animal welfare or because they raise ethical issues. Therefore, when such regulatory standards are imposed on imported products, they de facto 'regulate' the production process abroad. In addition, PPM often, but not always, affect the physical characteristics of the final product as imported. However, sometimes they do not (and these are known as non-product related PPM regulations).

Two well-known examples of such extraterritorial measures introduced in order to protect the environment are the United States (US) measures imposing a ban on shrimp harvested in third countries with fishing methods that could pose a threat to sea turtles and the measures imposing labelling requirements on tuna imported from third countries and having the effect of excluding (Mexican) tuna products from the major distribution channels as long as the fishing methods did not protect dolphins. Both measures were challenged before the WTO, and the rulings have contributed to significant developments in WTO jurisprudence addressing the interface between trade and the environment.[9]

Due to their 'extraterritorial' nature, any measures taken in this area, even if in full respect of WTO rules, might still be controversial and sensitive for third countries. At the same time, national regulatory systems are increasingly being confronted with serious and growing threats linked to damage to the global environment that respect no

8. For a discussion of the increased profile of sustainability issues in EU free trade agreements, *see* Bronckers and Gruni, 'Retooling the sustainability standards in EU free trade agreements', 24 *Journal of International Economic Law* (2021), 25-51.
9. Appellate Body Report, *United States – Import Prohibition of Certain Shrimp and Shrimp Products*, WT/DS58, adopted on 21 November 2001, para. 121: '... whether exporting Member comply with, or adopt, a policy or policies unilaterally prescribed by the importing Member may, to some degree, be a common aspect of measures falling within the scope of one or another of the exceptions(a) to (j) of Article XX ... It is not necessary to assume that requiring from exporting countries compliance with, or adoption of certain policies (although covered in principle by one or another of the exceptions) prescribed by the importing country, renders a measure a priori incapable of justification of Article XX. Such an interpretation renders most, if not all, of the specific exceptions of Article XX inutile, a result abhorrent to the principles of interpretation we are bound to apply'. This paragraph has to be read in conjunction with the conclusions reached in Appellate Body Report (Article 21.5-Mexico), *United States – Measures Concerning the Importation, Marketing and Sale of Tuna and Tuna Products*, WT/DS381, adopted on 3 December 2015.

borders and transcend national jurisdictions. Consumers are also becoming aware of environmental, health, social and ethical aspects of food production and want to be empowered to choose sustainable food. Accordingly, various aspects related to environmental or ethical rules applied to imported products are gaining attention.

Unlike health standards (which generally focus on product characteristics in order to protect consumers in the EU), EU environmental or animal welfare standards do not apply systematically to imported products. There are currently no general provisions in EU law referring to environmental or - more generally - sustainability requirements applicable to agrifood products, including imported products, though certain specific PPM already apply to EU imports.[10] This may well change now that the EU is gradually moving towards more stainable food systems, as follows from its Farm to Fork Strategy[11] published together with its Biodiversity Strategy[12] in May 2020 as part of the European Green Deal. The Farm to Fork Strategy sets out an agenda for a fair, healthy and environmentally friendly food system, which requires efforts of all actors, including consumers, to adapt to new and stricter health and environmental, including animal welfare, standards. The transformation should result in a system where competition will be driven by sustainability considerations and criteria and where sustainable production becomes the logical choice. Moreover, the EU's new Common Agriculture Policy has been designed to guide and support European farmers - including small farmers - in these efforts.[13] The Farm to Fork Strategy also has a global dimension. It sets out the EU's ambition to become a global leader in food sustainability through its international cooperation on food research and innovation, by building partnerships, by promoting standards supporting sustainable practices at international level, and - finally - by its trade policy.[14]

The overarching obligations and rights concerning trade in goods are set out in the GATT 1994. Whether a regulatory measure affecting imported goods such as those described above is caught by the GATT depends on whether it is:

(i) discriminatory, meaning that it is either caught by:
   - Article I on most-favoured-nation treatment, which requires that products from one WTO Member must be treated no less favourably than the like products from any other country; or
   - Article III on national treatment, according to which imported products cannot be treated less favourably than domestic-like products; or

10. *See, e.g.*, Council Regulation (EC) No 1099/2009 of 24 September 2009 on the protection of animals at the time of killing, O.J. 2009, L 303/1; Council Regulation (EC) No 1/2005 of 22 December 2004 on the protection of animals during transport and related operations, O.J. 2005, L 3/1.
11. COM(2020)381 final, 'A Farm to Fork Strategy for a fair, healthy and environmentally-friendly food system', 20 May 2020.
12. COM(2020)380 final, 'EU Biodiversity Strategy for 2023: Bringing nature back to our lives', 20 May 2020.
13. *See*, notably COM(2022)226 final, 'Application of EU health and environmental standards to imported agricultural and agri-food products', 3 June 2022.
14. COM(2020)381 final, cited *supra* note 11.

(ii) a quantitative restriction which limits the quantity of a product being imported or exported (Article XI).

According to Article III GATT, only products that are not 'like' may be treated differently. Whether products are 'like' must generally be determined on a case-by-case basis by examining relevant factors, including the product's end-uses in a given market; consumers' tastes and habits; and the product's properties, nature and quality.

Firstly, different processes or production methods used for agrifood products may, in certain cases, render these products 'unlike' in terms of physical characteristics and nutritional properties (e.g., between organic and non-organic products).

Secondly, it would seem plausible to assume that the degree to which process and production methods, even if non-product related, frustrate or promote the attainment of the UN Sustainable Development Goals[15] increasingly determines the perception and behaviour of consumers, and thus the nature and extent of the competitive relationship between products. Accordingly, two products having the same physical properties and end-uses but differing in the degree of sustainability of their PPM may not be 'like' following this line of argument.

A measure is discriminatory when it constitutes either (1) de jure discrimination, that is, when the measure expressly differentiates between products on the grounds of origin; or (2) de facto discrimination, that is, when the measure is origin neutral on its face, but it has a detrimental impact on the conditions of competition between like products from different WTO members. De facto discrimination may exist, for instance, if domestic products can more easily meet a certain standard or requirement than imported products.

If none of the above provisions is breached, further analysis is generally not necessary because the measure is considered compatible with GATT. If the above provisions are breached, the measure can still benefit from the general exceptions to the GATT rules pursuant to its Article XX.[16] If it can, the measure can be maintained and considered overall GATT compatible.

To benefit from justification under Article XX GATT, a measure needs to genuinely pursue one or more of the policy objectives listed in Article XX ('provisional justification'). The most recurrent grounds in relation to non-product related PPM regulations concern the protection of human, animal, or plant life or health (Article

---

15. An overview of the 17 UN SDGs is available at: sdgs.un.org/goals.
16. Article XX(a), (b), (e) and (g) GATT reads:

> Subject to the requirement that such measures are not applied in a manner which would constitute a means of arbitrary or unjustifiable discrimination between countries where the same conditions prevail, or a disguised restriction on international trade, nothing in this Agreement shall be construed to prevent the adoption or enforcement by any contracting party of measures:
>
> (a) necessary to protect public morals;
> (b) necessary to protect human, animal or plant life or health; ...
> (e) relating to the products of prison labour; ...
> (g) relating to the conservation of exhaustible natural resources if such measures are made effective in conjunction with restrictions on domestic production or consumption ... .

XX(b)), the protection of (living and non-living) exhaustible natural resources (Article XX(g)), public morals (Article XX(a)); and prison labour products (Article XX(e)).

The measure must also satisfy the so-called necessity or related to test, which requires a balancing of various elements. These include consideration of the importance of the objectives pursued by the regulating member. If the objective is the protection of children - an important value in a given society - imposing a ban on imports may be a necessary measure, compared to, e.g., a labelling requirement. In this respect, the WTO upheld the EU ban on the import of seal products as it was based on strong societal concerns.[17] In the same vein, the EU bans the import and marketing of cat and dog fur on moral and ethical grounds.[18] This measure has never been challenged by trade partners and is believed to be fully compatible with WTO law. It is also necessary to consider the contribution of the measure to the objectives, meaning the measure must be suitable to achieve or contribute to the stated objectives. There should not be an alternative measure available that would be less trade-restrictive but make an equal or better contribution to achieving the stated objectives, taking into account technical and economic feasibility. For example, voluntary measures are generally considered less trade-restrictive than mandatory measures and labelling as less trade-restrictive than a ban on imports. Finally, the measure must meet the conditions of the chapeau of Article XX, which requires that there should be no arbitrary or unjustifiable discrimination in the design, structure and application of a measure between countries where the same conditions prevail or a disguised restriction on international trade.

In essence, to be justified under Article XX GATT, a measure must be necessary or related to achieving one or more of the covered policy objectives, be even-handed in design and not have protectionist elements. The measure should take into account any relevant international rules or standards. If the measure departs from these standards, the reasons must be provided, such as the existence of additional information or the decision to provide for a higher level of protection.

The measure should be based on science or other technical information where available and relevant (ideally from a relevant international body, and may include reports, decisions etc.). It should provide a rational basis for the measure, which is evident from an appropriate assessment. If the measure is based on the concept of precaution (on the grounds that certain information is not yet available), it should be based on all the available pertinent information, provide for the acquisition of the information necessary for a more complete assessment, and accommodate the possibility of review.

The above rules of the GATT are further developed in the WTO Agreement on Technical Barriers to Trade (TBT), which contains rules relating to discrimination (Article 2.1) and necessity (Article 2.2). It specifies that technical standards must not be

17. Appellate Body Report, *European Communities - Measures Prohibiting the Importation and Marketing of Seal Products*, WT/DS400 and WT/DS401, adopted on 18 June 2014.
18. Regulation (EC) No 1523/2007 of the European Parliament and of the Council of 11 December 2007 banning the placing on the market and the import to, or export from, the Community of cat and dog fur, and products containing such fur, O.J. 2007, L 343/1.

more trade-restrictive than necessary to fulfil legitimate objectives such as national security requirements; the prevention of deceptive practices; protection of human health or safety, animal or plant life or health, or the environment. When developing their technical standards, WTO members are expected to consider, among other elements, available scientific and technical information.

The TBT Agreement has been found not to apply to so-called non-product related PPM regulations (because the definition in Annex 1 refers to 'product characteristics or *their* related processes and production methods'). However, it does apply to measures that deal with terminology, symbols, packaging, marking or labelling as they apply to a product, PPM. If a measure falls within the scope of the TBT Agreement, it will be analysed under that framework. Article XX GATT does not apply in case of a breach of the TBT Agreement as the elements of Article XX GATT are already effectively integrated into Articles 2.1 and 2.2 of the TBT Agreement.

The GATT rules, and in particular its Article XX(b), are similarly further developed in the Agreement on the Application of Sanitary and Phytosanitary Measures (SPS Agreement), which also contains provisions relating to unjustified discrimination (Articles 2.3 and 5.5) and necessity (Articles 2.2 and 5.6). However, according to its Annex A, the SPS Agreement only applies to certain specific risks arising *within the territory* of the regulating Member.

To conclude, regulatory proposals such as the above must each be carefully considered on their facts, nature and design in order to assess and achieve compliance with WTO rules. In making this legal assessment, it is important to consider that the sustainability of food systems is a *global* issue, and *the EU, acting alone,* cannot successfully address the global threats related to the way food is produced and consumed. This characteristic is also very relevant when analysing the compatibility with WTO law of regulations of *non*-product related processes and production methods, as explained below.

5 THE CASE OF REGULATION OF NON-PRODUCT RELATED PROCESS AND PRODUCTION METHODS

Taxation or regulation of so-called non-product related PPMs is an even more sensitive matter for the EU's trading partners, just as their taxation or regulation of such matters would be a sensitive matter for the EU. In the regulatory context, it should be noted that the WTO Agreement on SPS, as stated in its Annex A.1, only applies to measures that protect human animal or plant life or health on the territory of the regulating Member, and the TBT Agreement, as confirmed in the *EC – Seal Products* case,[19] does not in principle apply to measures concerning non-product related PPMs. However, this does not imply that such measures are unregulated by the WTO Agreement or simply prohibited. Rather, they are subject, notably, to the provisions of Articles I (most-favoured-nation treatment), II (customs duties and other charges on imports), III

19. *EC – Seal Products*, WT/DS400 and WT/DS401.

(national treatment), XI (general elimination of quantitative restrictions) and XX (general exceptions) of the GATT 1994.

In searching for co-existence, measures should, where relevant, be based on science or other available technical information, that is, on the facts and evidence. At the same time, sometimes, the concept of precaution may justify temporary measures whilst more information is sought. Sometimes regulations require a standard to be set essentially just because it is necessary to have a standard. However, this aspect of the debate is not the heart of the matter. Even when the science is very clear, Members may simply have differently weighted policy priorities, leading them to different conclusions about the level of protection they deem appropriate with respect to specific matters - and it is this that lies at the heart of the problem.

In the search for co-existence, WTO Members should aim to engage with their respective trading partners in international, regional and bilateral fora in the search for agreement or compromise (as indicated in the *US – Shrimp* case).[20] Indeed, a full and frank exchange in which each side not only explains its own legitimate policy objectives to the other but, at the same time, shows itself able and willing to understand the legitimate policy objectives of the other and assimilate them in the search for a joint outcome is in everyone's interest. At the same time, unlike the situation within the EU, such compromises usually require consensus, and therefore there may come a point at which the issue has been exhaustively discussed without those discussions bearing timely fruit.

In the search for co-existence, careful consideration should also be given to the possibility of mutual recognition. However, this would only be possible in circumstances where the measures of the trading partner reflect an equivalent regulatory ambition. Furthermore, it is well understood that, where the cost bases of the different regimes are significantly different, also having regard to international transport costs, mutual recognition does not, in any event, provide a stable solution. Rather, it results in social or environmental dumping, internal pressure to de-regulate or internal resistance to further measures, none of which are acceptable outcomes for the Member with higher regulatory ambitions.

In the search for co-existence, very careful consideration should also be given to the position of least-developed and developing countries. A values-based EU[21] does not aim to frustrate comparative advantages. Rather, it aims to proactively address how it can create synergies between sustainable development on the one hand and the pursuit of higher regulatory ambitions by the EU on the other hand.

However, ultimately, if, having explored all the options, it appears not possible to agree on a basis for co-existence, WTO law does not intend a Member such as the EU to allow its higher regulatory ambitions to be indefinitely frustrated. What is there in WTO law that prevents it from pursuing those ambitions, including by enshrining a 'first mover disadvantage' (that is, by effectively penalising Members at the vanguard of addressing pressing global issues, eventually preventing them from pursuing their

20. *US – Shrimp*, WT/DS58.
21. *See, e.g.*, the EU's objectives in relation to developing countries set out in Article 3(5) TEU.

legitimate objectives)? There should indeed be no problem with WTO law compatibility as long as such a member intends to exercise its rights to tax or regulate within the framework provided by WTO law and, in doing so, sets out what it considers to be a reasonable basis for co-existence, taking into account the reasonable interests of its trading partners, whom it aims to treat in an even-handed manner unless there are specific objective justifications for differentiation.

6 THE EXAMPLE OF THE EU CARBON BORDER ADJUSTMENT MECHANISM

Some issues of public interest are clearly of broader concern and are clearly more pressing than others. For instance, the situation regarding climate change necessitates urgent action. The available scientific information overwhelmingly demonstrates that there is a need to internalize otherwise exogenous environmental costs associated with carbon emissions. This is clearly something that concerns all of us globally. The EU continues to take steps to achieve this objective internally whilst trying to be consistent with its international commitments. A typical example is the European Commission's recent proposal for a carbon border adjustment mechanism (CBAM)[22] as part of the so-called Fit for 55 package,[23] which also includes a proposal to revise the EU's current Emission Trading System (ETS) to which CBAM is closely connected, as will be explained below.[24]

Under CBAM, EU importers will buy carbon certificates corresponding to the carbon price that would have been paid had the goods been produced under the EU's carbon pricing rules set by ETS (although producers in third countries and importers are always entitled to provide actual data in order to establish their carbon emissions and the actual carbon price paid). Furthermore, once a non-EU producer can show that they have already paid a price for the carbon used in the production of the imported goods in a third country, the corresponding cost can be fully deducted from the EU importer. The CBAM will help reduce the risk of carbon leakage by encouraging

22. COM(2021)564 final, 'Proposal for a regulation of the European Parliament and of the Council, establishing a carbon border adjustment mechanism', 14 July 2021. Council and EP reached a political agreement on the proposal in December 2023 (see for the text, which is still subject linguistic revision and not expected to be formally adopted before May 2023: For CBAM, this still seems to be in lawyer linguist process, the trilogue compromise is on the Council website: https://data.consilium.europa.eu/doc/document/ST-16060-2022-INIT/en/pdf. See for a commentary: J. Flett, "The European Carbon BorderAdjustment Mechanism and its consistency with World Trade Organization Law", in "70 Years of EU Law – A Union for its citizens" Luxembourg, Publication Office of the European Union, 2022, pp. 268-291.
23. Fit for 55 is a package of proposals to make the EU's climate, energy, land use, transport and taxation policies fit for reducing net greenhouse gas emissions by at least 55% by 2030, compared to 1990 levels and is available at ec.europa.eu/commission/presscorner/detail/en/IP_21_3541.
24. COM(2021)551 final, 'Proposal for a directive of the European Parliament and of the Council amending Directive 2003/87/EC establishing a system for greenhouse gas emission allowance trading within the Union, Decision (EU) 2015/1814 concerning the establishment and operation of a market stability reserve for the Union greenhouse gas emission trading scheme and Regulation (EU) 2015/757', 14 July 2021.

producers in non-EU countries to green their production processes. CBAM are already in place in some regions around the world, such as California, where an adjustment is applied to certain imports of electricity. A number of countries, such as Canada and Japan, are planning similar initiatives. In addition, the International Monetary Fund (IMF) and the Organisation for Economic Co-operation and Development (OECD) have recently carried out work to study how such measures could support international efforts to reduce greenhouse gas emissions. G20 Finance Ministers also mentioned the need for closer international coordination on the use of carbon pricing mechanisms.

The EU's ETS is the world's first international emissions trading scheme and the EU's flagship policy to combat climate change. It sets a cap on the amount of greenhouse gas emissions that can be released from industrial installations in certain sectors within the EU. Allowances must be bought on the ETS trading market, though a certain number of free allowances is distributed to prevent carbon leakage. That system has been effective in addressing the risk of leakage, but it also dampens the incentive to invest in greener production at home and abroad. Therefore, CBAM will progressively become an alternative to this. Under the Commission's new proposal for a revised ETS, however, the number of free allowances for all sectors will decline over time so that the ETS can have maximum impact in fulfilling its ambitious climate goals. Furthermore, for the CBAM sectors, the free allowances will gradually be phased out as of 2026. More particularly, in order to complement the ETS, the CBAM will be based on a system of certificates to cover the embedded emissions in products being subsequently imported into the EU. The CBAM departs from the ETS in some limited areas, however, in particular since it is not a 'cap and trade' system. Instead, the CBAM certificates mirror the ETS price. Finally, as a potential EU own resource, revenues from CBAM will contribute to the EU's budget, as laid out in the December 2020 Interinstitutional Agreement between the Council, the European Parliament and the European Commission on budget and own resources.[25]

In sum, the European Commission considers its CBAM proposal essential in order to address the issue of carbon leakage; ensure that the exogenous costs of carbon emissions are properly internalised; enable the EU to raise its own internal ambitions still further; and assist in encouraging the EU's trading partners to join it in this historic enterprise of together responding to the present climate emergency. According to the European Commission, the mechanism is crafted in a manner consistent with Articles II and III of the GATT 1994 and, in any event, justified by the general exceptions in Article XX.[26] It claims that, in adopting such measure, the objective is not to safeguard

25. Interinstitutional Agreement between the European Parliament, the Council of the European Union and the European Commission on budgetary discipline, on cooperation in budgetary matters and on sound financial management, as well as on new own resources, including a roadmap towards the introduction of new own resources Interinstitutional Agreement of 16 December 2020 between the European Parliament, the Council of the European Union and the European Commission on budgetary discipline, on cooperation in budgetary matters and on sound financial management, as well as on new own resources, including a roadmap towards the introduction of new own resources, O.J. 2020, L 433 I/28.

26. For a recent discussion of the main policy issues, *see*: Englisch and Falcao, 'EU Carbon Border Adjustments for imported products and WTO law' (9 June 2021), available at ssrn.com/abstract = 3863038 or dx.doi.org/10.2139/ssrn.3863038.

the EU's domestic industries or ensure a level playing field as an end in itself; its objective, as an actor on the international stage, is to assume, in an effective manner, its share of the global responsibility for addressing climate change, and encourage others to do so, whilst recognising that it would be no solution to the problem at all to simply dump it on someone else's doorstep.

More concretely, why would the CBAM proposal be consistent with the balance of the EU's international trade obligations and rights, and in particular with WTO law? By its own terms, the exclusive objective of the measure is to address climate change by addressing (and eventually reducing) carbon emissions in the EU and globally. Indeed, as indicated above, CBAM is one element of the EU's 'Fit for 55' package, the purpose of which is to allow the EU to achieve climate neutrality by 2050. There is no doubt that this is a legitimate policy objective, having regard, in particular, to Article XX(g) of the GATT 1994, which refers to the conservation of exhaustible natural resources (commonly referred to as the 'environmental' exception).[27] For many people, this would also appear to have become, moreover, a moral question. More precisely, the measure aims to prevent so-called carbon leakage, that is, the risk that higher EU domestic environmental regulatory ambition would have the effect of shifting industry (or production) offshore to countries with less strict environmental rules, where it would continue polluting in order to serve the EU market. However, on further reflection, preventing carbon leakage is not an end in itself but only a necessary means of achieving the EU's overarching environmental objective. An ancillary consequence of the measure, at least in the medium term, will be to generate revenue; that is, like many such measures, there is both a revenue-raising and a behaviour-changing expectation. Revenue raising is not per se prohibited or problematic as a matter of WTO law, but, in any event, the fundamental purpose of the measure is behaviour-changing. In sum, the objective(s) of the measure are certainly *legitimate* as a matter of WTO law.

As the proposal explains, the particular environmental concern addressed by the proposal is a *global one*, a stable climate with limited average global temperature increases compared to pre-industrial levels being what is generally referred to as a 'common good'. That is, it can only reasonably be viewed as an indivisible whole, of concern to all. Climate change and its effects are not generally circumscribed by particular boundaries or regions, and devastating effects can occur in places that have very low carbon emissions. Accordingly, the EU and its citizens are legitimately concerned about climate change as a whole. To put it differently, the particular environmental concern or 'crisis' addressed by the proposal is an urgent, global, and indeed accelerating one, and this has certain specific legal consequences, as recalled below.

---

27. One cannot rule out the relevance of other provisions, such as, for example: Article XX(b) ('human, animal or plant life or health'); Article XX(a) ('public morals'); and/or Article XX(d) ('measures ... necessary to secure compliance with laws or regulations which are not inconsistent with the provisions of [the GATT 1994]'). For a discussion of the important and general nature of the environmental exception, *see* Bronckers and Maskus, '*China–Raw Materials*: A controversial step towards evenhanded exploitation of natural resources', 13 *World Trade Review* (2014), 393-408.

Legally, the first point to note is that the proposal regulates obviously a *non-product related PPM*, that is, a PPM (also in the third country) that, in this case, cannot be discerned in the characteristics of the resulting product. Whilst WTO Members commonly regulate product characteristics, they regulate non-product related PPMs also with respect to third countries less frequently because of the implications this may have for comparative advantage, the policy calculi of their trading partners and reciprocity. In this particular case, such measures are *necessary* and do not impose any *regulatory burden* regarding the manner in which third countries produce for their own domestic markets or their other export markets, only with respect to the manner in which they produce for the EU market.

Importantly also, the proposal can only reasonably be assessed together with, or at least in the context of, the EU ETS since, as the proposal explains, the two share a common objective and are designed to work together in an integrated fashion. In terms of *proportionality*, it is important to note that CBAM/ETS is always calibrated to the carbon footprint of the relevant product, taking into account any carbon price that may already have been paid: everyone/all products produced or sold in the market must pay an appropriate carbon price, but only once. In other words, consistent with its environmental objective, it is non-discriminatory and eventually even-handed amongst all WTO Members and relevant products. Consequently, when assessed under Articles I, III:4, and eventually XX of the GATT 1994, one can reasonably argue that it is consistent with the balance of the EU's WTO obligations and rights.[28]

In terms of necessity, there are certain differences between ETS (which is a so-called cap and trade system) on the one hand and CBAM on the other hand, not least because the proposal refrains from imposing any quantitative restrictions on imports. However, the European Commission claims that, for all such differences, there are reasonable explanations that flow exclusively from the legitimate policy objective(s) being pursued, having regard to what is reasonably available and taking into account technical and economic feasibility. This includes, in particular, the use of default values in case actual data is unavailable and other rules necessary to ensure compliance with the system introduced by the Proposal. Significantly, producers/importers are, in all cases, given the opportunity to demonstrate that they perform better than such default values based on their actual emissions.

CBAM, moreover, is the *least trade-restrictive measure available* capable of achieving the legitimate policy objective(s) of the EU; there is no alternative, less trade-restrictive measure that would make at least an equivalent contribution to the EU's legitimate policy objective(s), and that would be reasonably available, taking into account technical and economic feasibility. In particular, careful note is taken of the affirmation by some that a carbon tax based on the destination principle would be preferable, but it is questionable that such a measure would make an equivalent contribution to the legitimate policy objective(s) of the EU. Both measures would condition access to the EU market on the imposition of an appropriate environmental burden or tax. However, CBAM, unlike a carbon tax based on the destination principle,

28. Articles II, III:2 and XI of the GATT 1994 do not appear particularly apt, but in any event, a consideration of these provisions does not change the overall conclusion.

additionally *encourages or incentivizes* the EU's trading partners to consider carbon pricing arrangements of their own because it gives *credit* to any carbon price paid in the third country. This encouragement or incentive is a legitimate part of the EU's overarching objective because, as recalled above, the climate is a common good, of legitimate concern to all. Furthermore, we consider that CBAM/ETS may also reasonably be viewed as *less trade-restrictive* given the arrangements on both the import and the export side, including, in particular, the absence of any export rebate.

In that respect, it is to be noted that, with the introduction of CBAM, the existing free allowances under the ETS system will be abolished, and this does seem to be consistent with the balance of the EU's WTO obligations and rights since there will be no subsidies contingent in law or in fact upon export (a type of measure that would be prohibited and that would not benefit from the general exceptions in Article XX of the GATT 1994, as a matter of law or as a matter of fact). Furthermore, supporting exports would not be consistent with, and would undermine, the environmental objective of our non-product-related PPM regulation.

One could argue that WTO law obliges the EU to integrate its development objectives in CBAM/ETS. However, the term 'conditions' in the chapeau of Article XX of the GATT 1994 does not refer to all conditions (no two countries are identical in all respects); it refers to the conditions that are relevant in light of the legitimate policy objective(s) being pursued by the relevant measure, which in this case are environmental. Nothing in Article XX of the GATT 1994 obliges regulating members to integrate their development objectives in a measure that they adopt pursuant to one or more of the sub-paragraphs of Article XX. That is not to say that the EU is not concerned by such matters; there is a wide range of flanking measures in place designed to assist least-developed countries and developing countries to cope with climate change and adapt to EU regulations. However, where the balance might lie between environmental and developmental considerations is a matter of domestic policy and, by extension, international negotiation. WTO adjudicators have neither the mandate nor the means to address or resolve such questions.

Finally, the EU has engaged in very extensive efforts over a very long period of time at the international level in an effort to forge the consensus required to properly address the urgent matter of climate change and continues to do so. Also, this well-illustrates that the CBAM proposal would be fully consistent with the balance of the EU's WTO obligations and rights.

7 OTHER EXAMPLES OF EU REGULATION OF NON-PRODUCT RELATED PROCESS AND PRODUCTION MECHANISMS

The EU is also considering other regulations on PPMs, which, if adopted, will undoubtedly raise questions about WTO compatibility. First, the Commission has proposed a regulation on deforestation-free products[29] based on a system of mandatory

29. COM(2021)706 final, 'Proposal for a Regulation of the European Parliament and of the Council on the making available on the Union market as well as export from the Union of certain

due diligence rules. The proposal aims to prevent deforestation and forest degradation associated with products and commodities placed on the EU, such as soy, beef, palm oil, cocoa, coffee and wood. The objective is to minimize consumption of products coming from supply chains associated with deforestation or forest degradation – and to increase EU demand for and trade in legal and 'deforestation-free' commodities and products. The proposal addresses illegal deforestation, forest degradation, as well as deforestation due to agricultural expansion caused by the production of the commodities. Authorities will be able to check whether products or commodities are deforestation-free by using geolocation coordinates and remote monitoring via satellite images. Furthermore, the European Green Deal states that 'imported food that does not comply with relevant EU environmental standards is not allowed on EU markets'.[30] Furthermore, the Farm to Fork Strategy announces that 'environmental aspects [will be taken into account] when assessing applications for import tolerances for pesticides that are no longer allowed in the EU, while respecting WTO standards and obligations'.[31]

Import tolerances are maximum residue levels (MRLs) for pesticides that are based on uses authorized outside the EU.[32] This may include setting MRLs for substances no longer approved in the EU (for reasons other than public health reasons), which may be needed because producers in third countries face production conditions and pest pressures different from those in the EU. Uses may be different for the same substance on the same crop. Import tolerances can also relate to crops that are not grown in the EU (e.g., certain exotic fruits or coffee), and therefore no MRL based on EU uses is established. The purpose of setting import tolerances is to facilitate trade, and therefore, import tolerances will continue to be granted when they are found acceptable, i.e., if they are safe for EU consumers. Until now, the focus when setting MRLs for pesticides, including for import tolerances, has been only on the protection of EU consumers, and this requirement will continue to apply. In addition, in line with the commitments in the European Green Deal and the Farm to Fork Strategy, some environmental concerns, such as the worldwide decline of pollinators or the contamination of the environment with bioaccumulative, toxic and persistent chemicals, may also be considered in the process of setting MRLs.

Finally, as announced in the Farm to Fork Strategy, the Commission is preparing a revision of the EU animal welfare legislation, with legislative proposals planned for the end of 2023. As mentioned in the Commission's reply to the 'End of Cage Age' European citizens' initiative,[33] the Commission intends to include in these legislative proposals provisions to phase out and finally prohibit the use of cages, stalls and pens for farming pigs, laying hens, calves, rabbits, pullets, broiler breeders, layer breeders,

commodities and products associated with deforestation and forest degradation and repealing Regulation (EU) No 995/2010', 17 November 2021.

30. COM(2019)640 final, cited *supra* note 1, at 12.
31. COM(2020)381 final, cited *supra* note 11, at 18.
32. Article 3(2)(g) of Regulation 396/2005 of the European Parliament and of the Council of 23 February 2005 on maximum residue levels of pesticides in or on food and feed of plant and animal origin, O.J. 2005, L 70/1.
33. Available at europa.eu/citizens-initiative/initiatives/details/2018/000004_en.

ducks, geese and quail. The proposal will also consider options to address the EU citizens' demands to be able to choose products not derived from caged animals and, more generally, products fulfilling EU animal welfare standards. Such options could include the introduction of rules requiring that imported products were obtained under conditions that are equivalent to the EU's animal welfare rules, or some of them, and/or a labelling requirement also for imported products (either focusing on the housing conditions or covering more animal welfare criteria), in compliance with WTO rules.

In all these cases, there is scientific information available pointing at a situation that can be fairly described as urgent, indeed as an emergency, of a global nature. As in the case of CBAM and the need for reduction of carbon dioxide (CO_2) emissions, also in these cases, it can therefore be reasonably claimed that an appreciation of the underlying problems cannot be sensibly limited to the precise boundaries of the EU. Rather, it is at least a regional, if not an international, problem that demands a response tailored to that fact. For instance, the global reservoir of pollinating insects is a common good that, in the long term, if decimated, would likely never fully recover. The EU, for instance, is also a significant importer of certain foodstuffs and therefore has a long-term interest in ensuring that essential pollination processes are not disrupted. Consequently, subject to the foregoing reflections, it may well consider extending, at least on a temporary basis, its existing legislation on plant protection products to all products sold in the EU, not just those produced domestically, a reasoning that is valid *mutatis mutandis* in the other cases discussed in this article and therefore relevant for any assessment to be made under WTO law.

8 FINAL CONSIDERATIONS

All the measures discussed above are matters that can only reasonably be assessed in light of the *urgency*. That is, it is clear that urgent measures are necessary in order to prevent a further irreversible deterioration in the situation.

It is submitted that EU Membership of the WTO does not mean it must stand by whilst a common good, such as the climate, is permitted to irreversibly deteriorate because of the inability to reach an agreement at the international level as to how the costs of addressing climate change should be distributed, also from a historical perspective. On the contrary, EU Membership of the WTO does not preclude the EU and its citizens from assuming their fair share of the burden of addressing climate change *now* by ensuring that all the products they consume or produce *today* pay an appropriate carbon price without prejudice to the development aspect of the discussion. That is precisely what, e.g., CBAM/ETS seeks to achieve. In addition, unlike a carbon tax based on the destination principle, CBAM/ETS encourages and incentivizes our trading partners to adopt similar measures, and this is entirely consistent with the legitimate policy objective(s) being pursued. For all of these reasons, there seem to be good reasons to conclude that CBAM is consistent with the balance of the EU's WTO obligations and rights.

Unsurprisingly, the February 2021 Trade Policy Review[34] puts sustainability at the heart of the EU trade strategy for the coming years, setting a course for an open, sustainable and assertive trade policy that will be better able to shape global change and reflect EU strategic interests and values, in compliance with the WTO rules.

34. COM(2021)66 final, 'Trade Policy Review - An Open, Sustainable and Assertive Trade Policy', 18 February 2021.

CHAPTER 11

The Unsung Feet of Steel: Of Internal Markets, Regional Integration and (Un)fair Trade

Armin Cuyvers & Tom Ottervanger

This contribution firstly argues that, despite all challenges, the European Union's (EU) internal market functions and continues to produce significant benefits. Second, it is argued that it is largely the success of the internal market that actually empowers the EU to engage with its global challenges, including geo-political shifts and the increasing need for 'hard power'. Third, it is argued that both the EU and other regional organizations should learn from the evolving insights into the different costs and benefits of internal markets. Internal markets are flexible instruments that can serve multiple purposes, and the EU's internal market only provides one source of inspiration. Jointly, these claims lead to the conclusion that the internal market remains a vital and solid foundation for the EU and other forms of regional integration: the feet of steel on which the EU rests and must increasingly rest as the rule-based multilateral order around it is gradually eroded by nationalist forces.

1 AN INTERNAL MARKET AS A DRIVING FORCE

The European Union (EU) faces a wide variety of tremendously challenging political and socio-economic threats, both internally and externally. Among these are the invasion of Russia into Ukraine, Brexit (including subsequent conflicts on, *inter alia*, fishing rights, migrants and the position of Northern Ireland), severe tensions with countries such as Turkey, terrorism, cybercrime, immigration, the COVID-19 pandemic and climate change. Threats that play around the background of the rise of China, the relative withdrawal of the United States (US) as the guarantor of a rules-based multilateral order and the geo-political rebalancing caused by these shifts.[1]

These challenges raise vital questions about the future of the EU. Internally, choices loom on solidarity between Member States and the nature and ultimate limit of EU competences, *inter alia,* as the EU considers a health union, unprecedented joint spending on the Green Deal and COVID recovery, which may or may not become endemic features of the EU, as well as the urgent redesign of the fiscal and monetary framework supporting the euro. Externally, questions about hard power and autarky arise, which sit uneasily with the institutional set-up and historical DNA of the EU. Many of these issues touch upon the future of the role of the EU in the multilateral order to which the recipient of this Liber has devoted most of his career.

Meeting these challenges is further complicated by the unprecedented conflict with Member States that refuse to respect multiple foundational EU values and legal principles including the 'rule of law', primacy of EU law and direct effect. Some of these legal principles have always been the subject of intense scholarly and jurisprudential debate.[2] Yet never before have they been so openly and nakedly challenged by political actors and national (constitutional) courts as in recent years.

Precisely at a time when the EU seems required to act and evolve, it is therefore hampered by attacks on the legal and constitutional foundations that allow it to do so. Some observers see all this turmoil as signalling the demise of the Union. As with the ubiquitous and so far incorrect predictions of the euro's demise, however, this contribution argues these predictions of impending EU doom are wrong. For amidst the turmoil, one tends to forget that in many respects the EU has been and still is a success story, as well as a prerequisite for national success in the times to come.

To support this claim, we focus on the internal (single) market, which comprises, *inter alia,* the free movement of goods, services, capital and persons as well as a common competition policy and State aid regime. The internal market has been and remains crucial for the process of integration. Many of the key legal principles of Union law, including those on primacy and direct effect, have been largely developed in the context of internal market law and still play an essential role in the realization of the internal market as part of the wider goal of economic integration. Yet the internal market appears to be too easily overlooked and discarded these days as either no longer relevant or as part of the boring legal furniture of European regional integration.

We aim to reemphasize the ongoing relevance and potential of an internal market, both for the EU and for other areas in the world engaged in forms of regional integration. First, and most basically, we argue that in the grand scheme of things, the functioning of the EU internal market is not in danger, not even as a result of the current disputes with some Member States or the other challenges facing the EU. On the whole, the internal market functions and continues to produce significant benefits. Second,

1. Cf. Bronckers, 'Trade conflicts: Whither the WTO?', 47 *Legal Issues of Economic Integration* (2020), 221-244.
2. *See, e.g.*, Kirchhof, 'The European Union of States', in von Bogdandy and Bast (Eds), *Principles of European Constitutional Law*, 2nd ed. (Hart Publishing, 2010), pp. 737-762.

and related, we argue that the success of the internal market actually empowers the EU to engage with several of the global challenges listed above, including geo-political shifts and globalization, as only proven by Brexit. Third, building on these two findings, we claim that both the EU and other regional organizations should learn from the evolving insights into the different costs and benefits of internal markets. By doing so, they can avoid the pitfall of simply equating an internal market with allowing completely unfettered trade. Instead, internal markets are much more flexible instruments that can serve multiple purposes, with the EU's internal market only providing one possible model and source of inspiration.

Jointly, these claims lead to the conclusion that the internal market remains a vital and solid foundation for the EU and other forms of regional integration: the feet of steel on which the EU rests and must increasingly rest as the rule-based multilateral order around it is gradually eroded by nationalist forces. For, as Brexit ironically shows, well-regulated internal markets may well be the best political reply to globalization. After all, globalization, despite having led to rapid growth in the past, today is also linked to many undesirable outcomes such as unemployment, social and economic inequality, supply chain disturbances, climate change, environmental damage and tax avoidance.[3] Yet regional integration is not part of this problem. Instead, it is part of the solution. For collaboration offers our best chance to curtail unfettered 'hyperglobalization', especially when compared with futile attempts to reclaim absolute national sovereignty.

To this end, the next section first shows the overall success of the EU's internal market and how this success actually enables the EU to respond to some of the key crises facing it. Section 3 subsequently draws some of the lessons from these insights for other regional blocks, before a brief conclusion is drawn in Section 4.

2 A SUCCESS WITH NEW-FOUND RELEVANCE: THE INTERNAL MARKET, TRADE POLICY AND INDUSTRIAL STRATEGY

Sometimes it appears as if the internal market, like the EU more generally, suffers from the so-called oxygen effect: one rarely reflects, with sufficient gratitude, on the presence of oxygen in the air, until it is no longer there. Similarly, the EU's internal market, and the concrete benefits it brings, often appear to be taken for granted. It is, therefore, important to stress the success and robustness of the EU internal market. For, although far from perfect, and always a work in progress, its unique level of economic integration makes the EU the second largest trading block in the world, having lost first place to China after Brexit. And that is quite an achievement in itself. What is more, even during the COVID-19 pandemic, the economic heart of the internal market proved resilient, with logical temporal restrictions on free movement of persons and some medical supplies. Similarly, where the rule of law crisis might or should affect some forms of mutual recognition, especially in the context of criminal law, core

3. *See, e.g.*, Stiglitz, *Globalization and Its Discontents Revisited* (Penguin, 2017).

economic dimensions of the internal market still remain intact despite this crisis as well.[4]

The importance, magnitude and resilience of EU internal market achievements have only been emphasized by Brexit. Disproving disingenuous claims from Brexiteers about global Britain and the benefits of 'free trade' on World Trade Organization (WTO) terms, Brexit clearly demonstrates the enormous difference between relatively tariff-free trade and a real internal market.[5] The negative economic impact for the United Kingdom (UK) of leaving the EU internal market is already estimated at double that of the COVID pandemic (–4% of gross domestic product (GDP) as to COVID's –2%) and will only increase in the future. These statistics, shocking in themselves, are made more tangible by the supply chain problems in the UK, including empty shelves in supermarkets and UK companies being advised by their own government to create a secondary establishment in the EU to avoid the negative impact of Brexit and retain at least some of the benefits of the EU internal market. As these statistics and real-world effects of 'non-tariff barriers' show, an internal market provides tangible benefits, including lowering the costs of living for those who need it most.[6]

This conclusion of course in no way detracts from the fact that an internal market also raises crucial issues about the subsequent (re)distribution of the benefits created by that market, the need to balance trade and non-trade interests, or the need to ensure the democratic legitimacy of the rules underpinning the internal market and its distributional effects. Yet these remaining challenges do not detract from the major success of the EU internal market.

In fact, the success of the internal market has only become *more* important in our current climate of crises and shifting geo-political realities. Being one of the largest global trading blocks is proving to be a key source of 'hard' power for the EU, both internally and externally. For as long as traditional sources of hard power, such as the military, remain largely national, economic power remains of vital importance to the EU.[7] And economic power may of course be used for multiple purposes, including non-economic ones, or to counter other parties' hard power. The economic power the internal market generates may not be a silver bullet, but it remains the best bullet in the EU's arsenal.

Now the area of external relations of the EU is a complex one and we do not intend to discuss in any detail the institutional intricacies and other legal issues relating to the (implied) competences of the Union concerning foreign (economic) policy. This is best left to the outstanding expertise of the recipient of this Liber. What we do want to highlight are several recent developments in EU law, especially in trade policy and

4. *See, e.g.*, Joined Cases C-354/20 PPU and C-412/20 PPU, *L. and P.*, ECLI:EU:C:2020:1033.
5. Of course this fact had already been made more than clear by the experts in the field, *see* for a strong example Baetens, '"No deal is better than a bad deal?" The fallacy of the WTO fall-back option as a post-Brexit safety net', 55-SI *Common Market Law Review* (2018), 133-174.
6. *See, e.g.*, already Molle, *The Economics of European Integration: Theory, Practice and Policy* (Dartmouth, 2006).
7. *See* on the apparent confederal limits of the EU constitutional foundation Cuyvers, 'The confederal come-back: Rediscovering the confederal form for a transnational world', 19 *European Law Journal* (2013), 711-738.

industrial strategy, that demonstrate the increasing relevance of the EU's economic power, and hence the internal market on which it rests, also in the external dimension.

For this purpose, it suffices to say here that the Common Commercial Policy (CCP), which includes all trade in goods and services and foreign direct investment, is an exclusive competence of the EU and rests directly on the internal market.[8] Without a strong internal market, there cannot be an effective CCP. Yet, as is well known, Union law currently struggles to translate the EU's economic power into effective protection against unfair trade policies or practices of third countries.[9] In part, this is because EU law is geared towards *removing* barriers to trade, which historically was in the EU's interest, as opposed to creating barriers specifically targeting unwanted or harmful trade. In addition, the institutional set-up of the EU, including frequent unanimity requirements, does not always allow the EU to effectively bring to bear its economic force. For example, Union legislation concerning anti-dumping and protection against subsidized imports in the framework of the WTO, and its application in practice, is tricky and of limited use to prevent and remedy what is considered 'unfair trade'. Moreover, global institutions such as the WTO are facing existential threats, meaning that the EU is also less able to rely on other rule-based systems to protect it against unfair practices.[10]

The limited legal operationalization of the internal market as a protective tool, moreover, has been exacerbated by the historical reluctance of the EU to develop an active industrial policy, unlike in some Member States such as France. Be it due to principled resistance, lack of necessity or the impossibility of agreeing on what such a single industrial policy should look like, the lack of an active industrial policy further opened the EU up to active and well-funded industrial policies of others as well as unfair trade practices.

Recent developments, however, have launched new initiatives to further harness the power of the internal market to protect the EU from unfair trading practices and drive sustainable growth in the EU. Important in this respect was the economic and financial crisis as well as, among other things, the disruption brought by new technologies and climate change. Yet as indicated above, this development has been particularly triggered by the emergence of new global players who do not necessarily play by the same rule book, or long-standing global players that try to tear up the rule book. China and the US here of course form the most important examples. Where other governments actively support industry, directly or indirectly, through subsidies, contracts, low levels of labour costs and environmental standards as well as various (other) forms of protectionism, the protective potential of the internal market must be

8. *See, e.g.*, Cremona, 'External relations of the European Union: The constitutional framework for international action', in Craig and De Búrca (Eds), *The Evolution of EU Law*, 3rd ed. (OUP, 2021), pp. 431-479; Hillion, 'Conferral, cooperation and balance in the institutional framework of EU external action', in Cremona (Ed.), *Structural Principles in EU External Relations Law* (Hart Publishing, 2018).
9. *See* for an early analysis already Bronckers and Goyette, 'The EU's responses to foreign subsidies: An overview', in Matsushita, Ahn and Chen (Eds), *The WTO Trade Remedy System: East Asian Perspectives* (Cameron May, 2006), 145.
10. Bronckers, *supra* note 1.

developed. Yet this must be done without undermining the fundamental nature of a market or violating the core principles underpinning the EU and its legal order.[11]

As observed in the Commission's 2020 Communication on 'A new Industrial Strategy for Europe', therefore, new powers and competitors are emerging, and global competition, protectionism, market distortions and trade tensions pose new challenges that need a response.[12] Most importantly, the Communication states that 'The EU must leverage the impact, the size and the integration of its single market.' At the same time, it wishes to update its antitrust, merger and State aid policy and rules.[13]

To do so, various measures have recently been adopted or proposed. For example, in 2019, Regulation 2019/17 on safeguarding competition in air transport was adopted.[14] This instrument empowers the Commission, following a complaint by a Member State or air carrier or upon its own initiative, to conduct an investigation and take measures where third-country practices distort competition and cause injury to Union air carriers. Although the procedure is complicated and success far from certain, it is to be applauded that the EU is at least seriously attempting to translate its internal State aid rules to the international arena in this manner, and in a way that might be used as a source of inspiration for other sectors.

This is even more true for the May 2021 proposal for a far-reaching Regulation to control foreign subsidies that distort the internal market creating an uneven playing field for competition.[15] This proposal addresses third-country benefits through subsidies or other financial contributions that provide recipients with unfair advantages in M&A transactions, in public procurement procedures or, more generally, affect operations in the EU. This measure, building upon the Union's economic strength and hence its internal market, creates a strong link between industrial policy and competition policy and raises numerous issues of enforcement.[16] The Commission expects almost 100 cases a year. However, the most important effect of this reactive instrument, if adopted, may be that it triggers a dialogue with third countries.

Another reactive and politically more sensitive tool under the CCP, proposed by the Commission in December 2021, is the so-called Anti-Coercion Instrument, or the

11. In this context, it would be interesting to see if the new prohibition on backsliding could then also be used against the EU, and what position the Court of Justice of the European Union (CJEU) would take in such a scenario in comparison to its position in Case C-64/16, *Associação Sindical dos Juízes Portugueses*, ECLI:EU:C:2018:117 and especially Case C-896/19, *Repubblika*, ECLI: EU:C:2021:311.
12. COM(2020)102 final, 'A New Industrial Strategy for Europe'.
13. *Ibid.*, section 2.1.
14. Regulation (EU) 2019/712 of the European Parliament and of the Council of 17 April 2019 on safeguarding competition in air transport, and repealing Regulation (EC) No 868/2004, O.J. 2019, L 123/4.
15. COM(2021)223 final, 'Proposal for a regulation of the European Parliament and of the Council on foreign subsidies distorting the internal market', 5 May 2021. This proposal was based on the earlier COM(2020)253 final, 'Commission White Paper on levelling the playing field as regards foreign subsidies', 17 June 2020.
16. Cf. also the Communication from the Commission, COM(2021)350 final 'Updating the 2020 New Industrial Strategy: Building a stronger Single Market for Europe's recovery', 5 May 2021.

hammer.[17] The proposal would offer protection against economic coercion, for example, the introduction by a third country of a boycott, border controls, import duties or other formal or informal measures deliberately designed to put pressure on the EU to adjust its policy in areas such as climate change, safety or taxation. This legal instrument is potentially more far-reaching in its effect than the anti-subsidy proposal. It explicitly aims at a diplomatic dialogue and negotiations as a first step. Countermeasures in the form of tariffs or import or investment restrictions are considered only as a last resort, yet any prior dialogue will of course take place under the shadow of such measures.

In all of these examples, and this is the point we wish to make, the strength of the internal market provides the Union with its relative best source of power to act and protect the interest of its citizens, businesses and Member States. We focussed here on trade policy measures, where the internal market gives the Union enormous advantages vis-à-vis third countries compared to the position of individual Member States. Yet the internal market, and the financial means it provides, similarly provide the EU with at least some clout to deal with the aggression by Russia, or open challenges to key EU values, such as in the case of Poland and Hungary. So far, in fact, money and economic power seem to be the most powerful tool in the armoury of the EU and are likely to remain so for at least some time.[18]

Of course, this might also be fitting for a new order of international law, which cannot assume all the hard powers of a State in its current form and perhaps should not even strive to do so if it wants to retain its unique complementary and symbiotic relation to the State instead of simply replacing it.[19]

In turn, the central place of the internal market in the foundation of EU authority also raises the additional question if the EU should take more steps to further cement and harness its economic power. One option in this regard would be the creation of a more developed EU industrial policy. This could include adjusting the EU rules on State aid and merger control, to allow for the development of 'European Champions' able to compete on the global stage.[20] Another option is to more actively project EU values and interests through a European Road and Belt alternative, or impose climate norms,

17. COM(2021) 775 final, 'Proposal for a regulation of the European Parliament and of the Council on the protection of the Union and its Member States from economic coercion by third countries', 8 December 2021. For an example of a context where such an instrument may be needed, *see* the Chinese economic pressure on Lithuania, where China is severely pressuring undertakings not to source from Lithuania. *See* politico.eu/article/china-trade-attack-on-lithuania-exposes-eu-powerlessness/.
18. This despite plans, largely spearheaded by France, to boost EU strategic autonomy. Cf. the speech by French President Macron to the European Parliament on the opening of the French presidency of the Council, available at presidence-francaise.consilium.europa.eu/en/news/french-president-emmanuel-macron-s-speech-at-the-european-parliament-strasbourg-19-january-2022/.
19. *See* for more detail on this point Cuyvers, *The EU as a Confederal Union of Sovereign Member Peoples, Exploring the Potential of American (Con)federalism and Popular Sovereignty for a Constitutional Theory of the EU* (Wöhrmann, 2013).
20. Report cited *supra* note 16.

either directly or indirectly through a border adjustment tax.[21] These options are beyond the scope of this chapter, yet further illustrate the increasing relevance of a stable and effective EU internal market as the foundation on which further EU ambitions rest.

3 IF THE STEEL SHOES FIT: ECONOMIC REGIONAL INTEGRATION IN OTHER REGIONAL ORGANIZATIONS?

Based on the previous section, the question of course arises if other regions should want an internal market as well, and if so, if they should use the EU model. For who would not want a foundation of sturdy steel feet? And indeed, we see that many regions in Africa, Asia and Latin America aspire or have aspired to create an internal market. ASEAN forms an interesting example. Despite its historically more political and intergovernmental nature, ASEAN has developed several highly ambitious blueprints for an ASEAN internal market with clear inspiration from the EU.[22] Although the precise legal tools remain unspecified, these blueprints envision rather deep forms of economic integration and an internal market, albeit with some clear limits as to, for example, non-skilled labour. In Africa, the East African Community (EAC) provides a clear example of an internal market project, strongly based on the EU model up to and including plans for a common currency.[23]

Considering the importance of the internal market for the EU, the clear interest in internal markets in other regions, and the lifelong contribution of the recipient of this *Liber* to not just EU law but trade law globally, this section aims to make three core observations on the pros and cons of creating an internal market, and the preliminary questions that require a well-considered answer before initiating and designing one. The first observation concerns the significant and broad potential of an internal market, even though this potential is context-dependent. The second observation concerns the very real costs of an internal market, also in the longer run, which should be openly discussed and included in the cost-benefit analysis. The third observation concerns the aim and focus of the market, which might often benefit from deviating from the EU model.

21. *See* for an important insight on this issue, also including the complex internal reality in China: Jiang, *'Greening' the WTO Ban on China's Export Duties: Should WTO Law Allow China to Use Export Duties to Protect the Environment and, If So, in What Manner?* (PhD thesis, Leiden University, 2020).
22. *See, e.g.*, the ASEAN Secretariat 'ASEAN Economic Community Blueprint' of 2008 and the updated 2015 'ASEAN Economic Community Blueprint 2025', available at asean.org/book/asean-economic-community-blueprint-2025/. On feasibility and legal requirements, *see, inter alia*, Laursen, 'Requirements for regional integration: A comparative perspective on the EU, the Americas and East Asia', in Laursen (Ed.), *Comparative Regional Integration: Europe and Beyond* (Routledge, 2010), pp. 239-270.
23. *See* Gastorn and Masinde, 'The EAC Common Market', in Ugirashebuja, Ruhangisa, Ottervanger and Cuyvers (Eds), *East African Community Law: Institutional, Substantive and Comparative EU Aspects* (Brill | Nijhoff, 2017), pp. 285-292.

3.1 The Internal Market as a Swiss Army Knife

As indicated above, the EU internal market has contributed significantly to economic growth and prosperity in the EU.[24] Logically, therefore, one tends to focus on the *economic* upside of an internal market. And these upsides can indeed be significant and a logical driver to create an internal market. At the same time, the concrete internal economic benefits of an internal market also largely depend on contextual elements, including the structure of the national economies involved, existing infrastructure networks and resulting trade patterns. For example, if all members of a regional organization primarily export the same raw materials or foodstuffs to third countries, intra-regional trade may not offer many benefits. Similarly, where the combined GDP and trade of a region are relatively low, the gains of an internal market, in absolute terms, will also be smaller. For example, the combined GDP of all members of the Economic Community of West African States (ECOWAS) together is USD 687 billion dollars, smaller than the GDP of the Netherlands alone, at USD 912 billion, or only slightly higher than the annual turnover of Walmart in 2021, which stood at USD 559 billion. Hence, the absolute internal benefits of economic integration in ECOWAS will of course also be more limited.

As seen above, however, an internal market may also contribute significantly to *external* economic objectives, non-economic objectives, or more long-term objectives of an economic or non-economic nature. As to the external objectives, for example, the world is increasingly divided into regional blocks. This makes it harder for all but the largest of States to influence external events, including trade-related events. Even for States who have limited intra-community trade, therefore, the external bargaining power offered by an internal market, if used credibly and wisely, could offer economic benefits. For example, a joint front can be beneficial in the scenario where most members export the same products, or trade primarily with the same third States, or require similar concessions in trade agreements.[25]

A legal complexity here concerns the overlap in membership between different regional blocks.[26] After all, unless properly dealt with, if one territory is a member of two internal markets or even custom unions, goods could freely move between these blocks, even if product norms and custom rates are very different.[27] Especially where there is significant overlap in block membership, like in Africa and Latin America, or

24. *See, e.g.*, in 't Veld, 'The economic benefits of the EU Single Market in goods and services', 41 *Journal of Policy Modeling* (2019), 803-818. For the concrete example of Brexit, *see* Cuyvers, 'Balancing sovereignty, trade and Northern-Irish peace: Free movement of goods post-Brexit', in Kainer and Repasi (Eds), *Trade Relations after Brexit* (Nomos / Hart, 2019), pp. 181-212.
25. Cf. in this regard the relative failure of the EAC-EU Economic Partnership Agreement, finalized in 2014 but still not entered into force because of internal disagreement and doubts as to the internal fairness of the agreement. *See* the Economic Partnership Agreement between the East African Community partner states, of the one part, And the European Union and its Member States of the other part, annexed to COM(2016)64 final; available at: trade.ec.europa.eu /doclib/docs/2015/october/tradoc_153845.pdf.
26. *See* Article XXIV:5 General Agreement on Tariffs and Trade.
27. *See also* Aloo, 'External Relations and the EAC', in Ugirashebuja, Ruhangisa, Ottervanger and Cuyvers (Eds) *East African Community Law: Institutional, Substantive and Comparative EU Aspects* (Brill | Nijhoff, 2017), pp. 182-195.

where continental initiatives connect multiple regional systems, as with the African Continental Free Trade Agreement (ACFTA), this may undermine both the internal and external effectiveness of an internal market.

In addition to external *economic* benefits, an internal market may also offer *non-economic* benefits. Again as illustrated by the EU, economic power created by an internal market can sometimes be applied in other geo-political arenas. Clearly, the feasibility of such attempts depends on the level of economic strength and the capacity for effective collective application of this economic strength for other purposes. Yet in a reality where the rule-based multilateral order is increasingly under strain, and hence relative power becomes even more important, any such increase in bargaining power may be welcome. What is more, such an increased collective bargaining position may be especially valuable where a region may have to carefully navigate between several global powerhouses, such as ASEAN between China and the US.

Lastly, an internal market may also contribute to more long-term objectives, both of an economic and a non-economic nature. As to economic objectives, an internal market may be used to create and stimulate intra-community trade and investment. In the longer run, this strengthens the internal economy and increases the benefits of the internal market. On the non-economic side, an internal market may be a stepping-stone towards regional stability and institutional capacity building. Famously, for example, the EU internal market was also intended to decrease the risk of military conflict between its members by increasing the economic costs of such a conflict and creating a practice of negotiation and communication.[28] In this vein, an internal market, even if focussed on limited sectors or of limited scope, can help create regional institutions and a culture of collaboration and regional rule following. In turn, these benefits may later be used to collaborate in other areas, such as health, education, or external relations. Such more long-term objectives of course also overlap with the underlying aim and objectives of an internal market project, and hence will be discussed in more detail in section 3.3.

Before we do so, however, it is important to highlight some of the very real costs and downsides of an internal market, which should of course also be taken into account when designing a regional system.

3.2 From Feet of Steel to Ball of Lead?

An internal market comes with real costs, which may snowball over time. These costs should not be underestimated and must be taken into account when designing the internal market as well as the national and regional constitutional foundations of that market. If we take the EU model, for example, there are significant sovereignty costs involved. Extensive legislative and judicial powers have to be transferred to the regional level. In the EU, moreover, we increasingly see executive powers following

28. Cf. Duchêne, *Jean Monnet: The First Statesman of Interdependence* (W.W. Norton, 1994) and Van Middelaar, *De passage naar Europa: Geschiedenis van een begin* (Historische Uitgeverij, 2009).

suit as well.[29] The regional level, for example, has to be able to harmonize national legislation. A central court is highly practical in ensuring uniform and consistent interpretation of regional law.[30] In addition, the effectiveness of the regional system may require some form of primacy and direct effect doctrines, seeing how national law must be prevented, at least to a certain level, from violating or avoiding regional law.[31] As a result, effective regional integration may challenge national conceptions of sovereignty, democracy and national identity.[32] The EU has so far managed to appease such challenges, *inter alia,* through creative and flexible dialogue between national and EU courts. Yet no structural, ultimate solution has yet been found, and in our current period of crisis this legal fontanel of the EU legal order is coming under increasing and dangerous level of stress.[33]

An effective internal market, moreover, also requires extensive flanking regulation to work. For example, an effective competition policy, including the regulation of State aid, is necessary to ensure the functioning of an internal market.[34] Again this not only requires the transfer of certain competences, but may also lead to a clash between regional integration and sensitive national interests. For instance, in regions where the State may be closely involved in business, enforcing cartel rules or prohibitions on abuse of dominance may lead to sensitive clashes, as may the enforcement of State aid rules. Unless such flanking measures are also geared towards, for example, an active regional industrial policy, clashes may develop between State measures intended to promote national champions or the national economy and regional competition rules. The long, painful and not exceptionally successful negotiations on the so-called level-playing field rules post-Brexit illustrate just how complex it can be to agree on such rules, or to find an effective middle ground between a fully regionalized

29. Cf. already the development from Curtin, *Executive Power of the European Union* (OUP, 2009) to Van Middelaar, 'The Lisbon Treaty in a decade of crises: The EU's new political executive', in Södersten (Ed.), *The Lisbon Treaty Ten Years On: Success or Failure?* (SIEPS, 2019), pp. 17-44.
30. *See, e.g.,* in relation to the external Case C-284/16, *Achmea,* ECLI:EU:C:2018:158 and the internal context, Case C-585/18, *A.K. (Independence of the Disciplinary Chamber of the Supreme Court),* ECLI:EU:C:2019:982.
31. Cuyvers, 'The scope, nature and effect of EU law', in Ugirashebuja, Ruhangisa, Ottervanger and Cuyvers (Eds) *East African Community Law: Institutional, Substantive and Comparative EU Aspects* (Brill | Nijhoff, 2017), pp. 161-181.
32. Cf. Cuyvers, 'Brexit and the real democratic deficit: Refitting national and EU democracy for a global reality', in Ellian and Blommestijn (Eds), *Reflections on Democracy in the European Union* (Eleven International Publishing, 2020), pp. 105-126.
33. *See* in addition to the 'first generation' of challenges in Czech Constitutional Court judgment of 31 January 2012, *Landtova* Pl. ÚS 5/12, Case no. 15/2014 *Dansk Industri (DI) acting for Ajos A/S v. The estate left by A,* and BVerfGE, 2 BvE 123,267, 2 BvE 2/08 (2009) *Lissabon-Urteil,* the further challenge in BvR 859/15 (2021) *Weiss,* judgment of 5 May 2021 and of course the qualitatively different escalation in Polish Constitutional Tribunal of 7 October 2020, Assessment of the conformity to the Polish Constitution of selected provisions of the Treaty on European Union, case K 3/21. Even if in many ways the recent Polish challenge is more political than legal, this challenge is enabled buy and formulated in the language of this conundrum at the heart of EU constitutional law.
34. *See* in the African context, for example, Karanja-Ng'ang'a, 'EAC Competition Law', in Ugirashebuja, Ruhangisa, Ottervanger and Cuyvers (Eds) *East African Community Law: Institutional, Substantive and Comparative EU Aspects* (Brill | Nijhoff, 2017), pp. 433-453.

competition policy and rather weak rules that do not add that much to WTO standards.[35]

Another potential cost of an internal market concerns the distribution of benefits, both at the Member State and the citizen level. Neither the benefits nor the burdens of an internal market will automatically be equally or equitably distributed. In other words, some States and some individuals will gain more than others, and some will lose more than others. Even if economic integration leads to a net benefit, this unequal distribution will lead to difficulties. At the State level, this dynamic is illustrated by the fate of the first East African Community. In this first Community, the perception was that Kenya was reaping an excessive part of the benefits of integration. It is commonly accepted that this perceived imbalance was an important factor in the eventual collapse of the first EAC.[36] At the level of unequal benefits on the citizen level, the EU provides a valuable example. In the EU, popular resistance against integration seems at least in part based on the resistance by those who are sometimes called 'the losers of globalization', or in this case regionalization.

In itself, this unequal distribution of costs and benefits need not be that problematic: after all, almost any policy or intervention will have winners and losers. The additional challenge for regional integration is that to compensate for such unequal distribution, it may be necessary to transfer *even more* competences to the regional level, in turn increasing the challenge of legitimizing regional governance and sufficiently protecting national democracy and sovereignty.

After all, addressing inequality may involve redistribution of benefits, and redistribution between States or citizens quickly becomes complex. Just look at the horror that the term 'transfer union' elicits in Germany or the Netherlands. In the EAC, the signatories tried to address this challenge through Article 6(e) of the Treaty establishing the second East Africa Community. This provision explicitly defines 'equitable distribution of benefits' as one of the fundamental principles of the Community. Of course, stating this principle is one thing, but effectively operationalizing it is quite another. Yet it is already valuable in itself to explicitly recognize this challenge and to formulate the general values and principles that should inform the regional response.

In the EU, the challenge of redistribution and solidarity was always present but roared to near existential importance during the euro crisis.[37] With the asymmetric shocks of the financial and sovereign debt crises, some Member States and EU citizens were affected much more negatively than others. This led to the need for financial assistance between Member States to save the euro, which is an integral part of the internal market. COVID-19 and climate change then only deepened the need for

35. *See* the Trade and Cooperation Agreement between the European Union and the European Atomic Energy Community, of the one part, and the United Kingdom of Great Britain and Northern Ireland, of the other part, O.J. 2021, L 149/10, specifically Title XI.

36. *See* the EAC Treaty Article 6(e) as well as Masinde and Omolo, 'The road to East African integration', in Ugirashebuja, Ruhangisa, Ottervanger and Cuyvers (Eds) *East African Community Law: Institutional, Substantive and Comparative EU Aspects* (Brill | Nijhoff, 2017), pp. 1-21.

37. *See* for a thorough analysis Borger, *The Currency of Solidarity: Constitutional Transformation During the Euro Crisis* (CUP, 2020).

solidarity and redistribution, leading to an unprecedented level of financial redistribution with NEXTGEN EU.[38] So far, the gap between the need for solidarity and the resistance to solidarity has only been bridged by creative borrowing techniques and central bank interventions, not a stable model for the future at all.

Once States are interconnected through an internal market, therefore, especially when this entails a common currency, the need for redistribution and solidarity may increase. In turn, this may require even deeper integration and further increases in the sovereignty cost of an internal market. Similar self-deepening dynamics of an internal market can also be observed in other domains, such as social security, health care, criminal law or marriage law.[39] As with pushing a snowball down a snowy slope, therefore, it is wise to anticipate the future accruing costs of an internal market, as well as to consider ways of controlling or managing those costs once the project is underway. Doing so also requires exploring lighter versions of internal market integration than the EU model. For if this is not done, an internal market may come to feel more like a lead ball dragging States into a certain direction than a solid foundation for effective collaboration.

Most fundamentally, however, to ground and create a really effective internal market its 'Member States' and 'member peoples' must develop or accept a more modern or updated conception of sovereignty. Such a concept must fit with the current global realities, including intense interconnectedness, just as the original concept of sovereignty as designed by Bodin fitted the realities of a French monarchy under attack.[40] For any outdated, absolute conception of sovereignty, which labels any limitation of State power as anathema, is not just incompatible with an effective internal market, but with our present reality, and as such can only lead to failure. Consequently, the creation of an internal market can also be seen as a small part of a larger, and even more vital exercise: to adjust our political and economic models to a globalized, interconnected reality.[41] Of course, that deeper and more fundamental potential of an internal market also brings us to our third observation on the variable aims and objectives of an internal market.

3.3 Internal Markets as Tools and Not Ends

Internal markets are logically associated with liberalization and unfettered market forces. The EU model can strengthen this association. Yet internal markets are not inherently the same as full trade liberalization or neoliberalism. The tool of an internal market, and more specifically the legal tools developed in internal market law, can equally be used for very different purposes. Let us give three brief examples.

38. *See, e.g.*, Crowe, 'The European budgetary galaxy', 13 *EuConst* (2017), 428-452 and De Witte, 'The European Union's COVID-19 recovery plan: The legal engineering of an economic policy shift', 58 *Common Market Law Review* (2021), 635-682.
39. *See, e.g.*, Case C-440/05, *Commission v. Council (Ship Source Pollution)*, ECLI:EU:C:2007:62 or Case C-673/16, *Coman*, ECLI:EU:C:2018:385.
40. Franklin, *Bodin: On Sovereignty* (CUP, 2007).
41. *See* for a small attempt Cuyvers, 'What chimpanzees can teach the EU: Or why the EU should embrace sovereignty as part of human nature', 6 *European Papers* (2021), 1229-1254.

Firstly, opening up one's economy to global competition may indeed be devastating where undertakings in the region are not yet competitive with global players. Of course, the idea of a market is partially that, by being exposed to competition, businesses in the region will adapt and become more competitive. Yet where the gap is too big, this may simply be impossible. Similarly, global trade rules and trade patterns may lock certain States or businesses into the lowest rung of the value-added ladder. Africa provides a clear case. For many African States, the focus remains heavily on the export of raw materials and foodstuffs. As a result, they only get a very small percentage of the total value added in later stages of the value chain, preventing more structural economic development.

Instead of opening up and liberalizing, however, an internal market may also *protect*. If designed properly, an internal market may provide a green-house environment where, within the internal market, undertakings can grow and become competitive enough to face external competition and boost structural economic development. Where individual States may not be able to offer sufficient protection and a sufficient market to grow, internal markets may be able to do so, also providing undertakings in the region with the chance to move into goods or services with a higher percentage of added value, and developing a pool of skilled labour along the way. As we saw above, moreover, the EU itself is of course also increasingly discovering the capacity of its internal market to protect. Other internal market projects may learn from this approach, and develop tailor-made protective elements from the start. For where the EU may consider some third State tactics unfair, other regions just might consider the prolongation of historically skewed trade relations with the EU unfair, and justification enough for some compensatory hammers and anvils on their side.

Second, internal markets may be more limited or choose a different order of development as compared to the EU model. Market integration in the EU started with goods, as trade in goods constituted more than 70% of the economy in the 1960s.[42] Gradually, the EU internal market developed to increasingly cover (digital) services, capital, more and more categories of persons and a common currency. As this demonstrates, several elements of the EU internal market developed at different stages, and are not necessarily mutually dependent. Indeed the claim that all of the freedoms underlying the EU internal market are inextricably linked and cannot be separated only emerged rather late, and was especially boosted by the Brexit negotiations. Consequently, they rather represent the current legal-political reality in the EU rather than any inherent truth about internal markets.[43]

The logical consequence is that other internal market projects can also choose focus on only some of the freedoms underlying the EU internal market. In any event, they can opt for a different order of developing these freedoms. For instance, a region could focus first on digital services, or movement of capital, instead of starting with

42. Van den Bogaert, Cuyvers and Antonaki, 'Free movement of services, establishment and capital', in Kuijper et al. (Eds) *The Law of the European Union* (Wolters Kluwer, 2018), pp. 539-586.
43. *See* Van den Bogaert and Cuyvers, 'Brexit Blues: They still haven't found what they're looking for …', 94 *Nederlands Juristenblad* (2019), 1388-1397 and Cuyvers, *supra* note 24.

goods. This could be especially useful where there are limited goods to trade or not sufficient infrastructure, whereas focussing on modern technologies might allow these regions to leapfrog ahead. The relative focus of the *ANDEAN* community, and its Court of Justice on intellectual property rights offers an example of such a narrower focus.[44] One other example, and potentially interesting alternative, can be seen in ASEAN. Here the suggestion has arisen to focus economic integration on specific value chains. So instead of targeting all goods or services, one could try to support the free movement of those production factors used within a specific value chain, say textiles or electronics. Another example from the ASEAN blueprints is a reduced focus on free movement of persons. After all, free movement of persons is especially complex: unlike people, most goods tend not to marry, get sick, have children or need social security. Reducing free movement of persons may, therefore, also reduce the need for harmonization and the impact of the internal market on sensitive areas such as social security, public health and criminal law.

Such alternative approaches clearly raise challenges as well. Yet they are worth exploring. For if feasible, one could create a more limited internal market, and hence one with lower sovereignty costs, which might also fit better in the less legalized and institutionalized nature of other regions.[45] Consequently, internal markets, and even the different legal building blocks of internal markets, can be modified and redesigned, using the EU experience as a modular toolkit.

Third, and as indicated above, internal markets are not just about the economy or trade liberalization, but may also serve vital, non-economic aims. As indicated, internal markets may provide protection in a new global reality which is becoming less rule-based and more multi-polar. Of course, the level of protection depends on the economic size and operational unity of the market, yet it remains true that it is better to hang together than to hang alone. What is more, as again illustrated by the EU developments, economic power can sometimes be converted or leveraged into other form of geo-political power that might benefit or protect a region. This may be particularly relevant for those regions that may not be able to develop other sources of hard power. Conversely, an effective regional collaboration and internal market may also allow a region to convert other sources of external leverage, be they, for example, certain resources, strategic location or migration, into concrete economic advantage, boosting long-term growth and economic development.

Because markets involve market actors, moreover, an internal market may also be seen as a way of engaging private actors and civil society in the process of regional integration. One risk of regional integration is that it remains elite driven and is not informed or supported by civil society. Especially if combined with some form of direct effect, and strengthened by proper channels of consultation, for example, with the social partners, an internal market can engage such private actors, broadening the basis for regional integration.

44. Cf. Cerda Silva, 'Copyright convergence in the Andean Community of Nations', 20 *Texas Intellectual Property Law Journal* (2012) 429-470.
45. Cf. Jetschke and Katada, 'Asia', in Börzel and Risse (Eds) *The Oxford Handbook of Comparative Regionalism* (OUP, 2016), pp. 225-248.

A last alternative objective of an internal market we want to stress here, as it may be overlooked, is its capacity to act as an incubator and stabilizer for regional collaboration more generally. An internal market may allow States and relevant actors to get used to the practice of regional collaboration and help in gradually growing or designing the formal and informal practices and institutions required for effective regional integration. Such a process may especially occur where the internal market remains focused on specific sectors or challenges, ideally well below the level of political hot-button issues. Here, of course, the example of the European Coal and Steel Community can be given. Although coal and steel were far from politically or militarily irrelevant, this specific focus, and the many technical and technocratic questions that accompanied it, allowed for a more sheltered beginning than if the EU had tried to create a full-blown internal market from the start. If an internal market is indeed to serve this additional or alternative objective as an incubator of integration, it may therefore be wise to look for economic sectors that are particularly suitable for this purpose, even if they may not be the sectors where economic integration will provide the highest economic benefits in the short run. Indeed the economic benefits of a full-blown internal market may then become more long-term, as such benefits can only be reaped after the necessary groundwork for more full-scale economic integration has been put into place.

4 CONCLUSION: THE ENDURING RELEVANCE OF INTERNAL MARKETS

Internal markets, including their flanking measures such as those relating to competition policy and an industrial strategy, remain solid and vital building blocks for the EU and many other areas in the world engaged in forms of regional economic integration. Global challenges have only made these building blocks more relevant. The potential of a well-designed and effective internal market is increasingly needed to achieve a broad array of economic as well as non-economic purposes in the international arena. Sadly, this need is partially driven by the gradual dismantling of the global rule-based order. We would conclude by encouraging regions to further develop, cherish and regularly update their integration efforts inspired by the lessons that can be learned from the EU, as well as from the writings and wisdom of Marco Bronckers.

CHAPTER 12

Is There a Future for the WTO Appellate Body and WTO Dispute Settlement?

Peter Van den Bossche[*]

The World Trade Organization (WTO) dispute settlement system, which for long was hailed as the pearl in the crown of the WTO, is in an existential crisis. This crisis, which had been looming for many years, became acute in December 2019 due to the refusal of the United States (US) to appoint new appellate judges and the ensuing paralysis of the Appellate Body. This contribution discusses: first, the underlying causes of the current crisis of WTO dispute settlement; second, how WTO Members have unsuccessfully tried to address this crisis to date; and third, whether binding, two-stage dispute settlement in the WTO can be restored. It is submitted that there is a future for the Appellate Body and WTO dispute settlement, but that in the current political setting, it would be wise not to seek reform in haste and without careful consideration of what kind of appellate review and dispute settlement will serve the rules-based, multilateral trading system best. For now, the use of the Multi-Party Interim Appeal Arbitration Arrangement (MPIA) may allow Members to experiment with new approaches to appellate review and dispute settlement in general and thus prepare the ground for future reform.

* This contribution is partly based on Chapter 3 of Van den Bossche and Zdouc, *The Law and Policy of the World Trade Organization*, 5th ed. (CUP, 2022), and a contribution made in November 2021 to a webinar on *The Appellate Body Crisis and Dispute Resolution: What is the Future of the WTO's Crown Jewel?*, organized by the Business and Government Professional Interest Council, Harvard Kennedy School. I owe thanks to Yuliia Kucheriava and Gabriela Garcia Merchan for their able assistance.

1 INTRODUCTION

It is with great pleasure that I contribute to this *liber amicorum* for Marco Bronckers, a long-time friend and *companion de route* in advocating for a rules-based multilateral trading system. I first heard of Marco in 1985 when I was a student of John Jackson at the University of Michigan Law School. A few years earlier, Marco had also studied under Jackson and had raised expectations of excellence which I struggled to meet. Over the years, I had the pleasure of interacting with Marco on numerous occasions at conferences or in bilateral contact. These were always moments of learning for me. My contribution to this *liber amicorum* deals with a topic which I know to be close to Marco's heart, WTO dispute settlement. He appeared before panels and the Appellate Body in several cases. While I did not have the pleasure of hearing Marco plead before me when I served on the Appellate Body in the 2010s, I very well remember his clever and passionate advocacy on behalf of his client in *Korea – Alcoholic Beverages* in 1998 when I was part of the Appellate Body Secretariat. Marco, I wish you all the best and hope that our paths will continue to cross.

One of the principal achievements of the General Agreement on Tariffs and Trade (GATT) Uruguay Round of Multilateral Trade Negotiations (1986-1994), which resulted in the establishment of the World Trade Organization (WTO), was the creation of a ground-breaking system for the resolution of trade disputes between WTO Members.[1] This system, which replaced the dysfunctional GATT dispute settlement system, is in many respects unique among international, State-to-State dispute resolution systems. The WTO dispute settlement system has compulsory jurisdiction, provides for appellate review and results in legally binding rulings, compliance with which can be enforced. For more than two decades, this dispute settlement system has served WTO Members very well and was commonly referred to as the jewel in the crown of the WTO. To date, developed and developing-country Members alike have brought, in total, more than 600 disputes to the WTO for resolution.[2] The Appellate Body, the WTO's standing appellate tribunal, rendered since 1995 twice as many judgments ('reports', in WTO speak) as the International Court of Justice and was often called upon to settle disputes on politically sensitive issues relating to, for example, public health, environmental protection, consumer safety, public morals and national security.[3] In 9 of 10 disputes in which the responding party had to bring the challenged measure or legislation into conformity with WTO law, it has done so.[4] Over the past two decades, the WTO dispute settlement system made an important contribution to the objective that within the WTO, 'right prevails over might'. As the legendary Julio Lacarte Muró, the first Chair of the Appellate Body, remarked, the WTO dispute settlement system works to the advantage of all Members, but it especially gives

1. *See* Understanding on Rules and Procedures Governing the Settlement of Disputes (Dispute Settlement Understanding or DSU), Annex 2 to the Marrakesh Agreement on the Establishment of the World Trade Organization, O.J. 1994, L 336/234.
2. *See* worldtradelaw.net/databases/searchcomplaints.php (last visited June 2022).
3. For an overview, *see* worldtradelaw.net/databases/abreports.php/ (last visited June 2022).
4. *See* Van den Bossche and Zdouc, *The Law and Policy of the World Trade Organization*, 5th ed. (CUP, 2022), p. 215.

security to developing-country Members that, in the past, often lacked the political or economic clout to enforce their rights and to protect their interests.[5]

The WTO's dispute settlement system is currently, however, in an existential crisis. This crisis was triggered by the United States (US), which has blocked since 2017 the process of (re-)appointment of members of the Appellate Body. As a result of this blockage, the number of Appellate Body members, normally seven, dropped on 11 December 2019 below the minimum of three needed to hear and decide new appeals from first instance panel reports.[6] Since 11 December 2019, all but two panel reports have been appealed by the losing party to the now-paralyzed Appellate Body.[7] These appeals 'into the void' leave disputes in legal limbo because as long as the appellate review is pending, there is no legally binding resolution of the dispute.[8] There are currently 21 unresolved disputes pending before the Appellate Body.[9] The paralysis of the Appellate Body has severely undermined the effectiveness and credibility of the WTO dispute settlement system. Not surprisingly, in 2020 and 2021, there has been a drastic drop in the number of disputes brought to the WTO for resolution.[10]

2 FROM A LOOMING TO AN ACUTE CRISIS

While the current crisis of WTO dispute settlement was triggered by the US's blockage of the process of (re-)appointment of Appellate Body members, this crisis has been looming for a long time and for several reasons. *First*, over the years, the workload of the dispute settlement system grew steadily, in particular, due to the increasing number of claims of WTO inconsistency raised in each dispute and the rising complexity of the measures challenged and the legal arguments made. However, the resources made available did not keep track of this growing workload. *Second*, the institutional imbalance between the successful quasi-judicial branch of the WTO and its ineffective legislative/negotiating branch became ever more apparent. This prompted WTO Members to seek solutions to their trade disputes and concerns about insufficient or missing legal standards through litigation rather than negotiation. This

5. *See* Lacarte and Gappah, 'Developing countries and the WTO legal and dispute settlement system', 3 *Journal of International Economic Law* (2000), 395-401, at 400. Ambassador Lacarte Muró served as the Deputy Executive Secretary of the GATT in 1947-1948, and as Permanent Representative of Uruguay to the GATT in the 1960s, 1980s and early 1990s. He was the Chair of the Uruguay Round committee that negotiated the DSU.
6. Of the 13 appeals pending on 11 December 2019, the Appellate Body was still allowed - under Rule 15 of the Working Procedures for Appellate Review - to complete three appeals, including the appeal in *Australia - Tobacco Plain Packaging* (2020). The other 10 appeals were left uncompleted.
7. The panel reports in *Australia - Anti-Dumping Measures on A4 Copy Paper* (2020) and *United States - Anti-Dumping and Countervailing Duties on Ripe Olives from Spain* (2021) were not appealed and thus adopted by the DSB by reverse consensus.
8. Pursuant to Article 16.4 of the DSU, appealed panel reports cannot be adopted by the WTO Dispute Settlement Body, and thus become legally binding, until after completion of the appeal.
9. Note that once the Appellate Body is operational again, it will take years to work through this backlog before any new appeals can be heard.
10. In 2020 and 2021, merely 5 and 9 disputes were brought to the WTO for resolution, compared to 39 and 19 disputes in 2018 and 2019. *See* worldtradelaw.net/databases/complaintcount.php (last visited June 2022).

development resulted in the resolution of sensitive trade issues through adjudication, which led to the perception in some quarters of judicial activism by WTO panels and, in particular, the Appellate Body. Already in 2001, Claude Barfield of the Washington-based American Enterprise Institute suggested that the WTO dispute settlement system is 'substantively and politically unsustainable'. Barfield suggested that governments may only continue to obey its rulings if the powers of the WTO dispute settlement system are curbed.[11] While strongly disagreeing with Barfield's prescription, others have also warned against excessive reliance by WTO Members on adjudication instead of seeking political agreement on new rules to resolve problems arising in trade relations.[12] *Third*, certainly, since 2010, some Members, and in particular the US, adopted an ever more antagonistic discourse against the Appellate Body whenever the latter's rulings were unfavourable. The US began criticizing vigorously the Appellate Body's jurisprudence, especially in the areas of safeguards, subsidies, countervailing and anti-dumping duty measures. *Fourth*, the US began to undermine the independence and impartiality of WTO adjudicators by, *inter alia*, blocking the reappointment of Appellate Body Members in 2007, 2011 and again in 2016.[13] The current crisis of the WTO dispute settlement system was thus already looming for some time. However, it became acute when, as mentioned above, the US blocked the process of (re-)appointment of Appellate Body members each time a vacancy arose in June, July and December 2017, in September 2018 and in December 2019.[14] In justification of this blockage, the US stated that it had, and has, serious 'concerns' regarding the functioning of the Appellate Body. The US criticizes the Appellate Body for alleged 'judicial overreach' as well as 'blatant disregard' for certain procedural and institutional rules.[15]

As to the so-called judicial overreach, the US accuses the Appellate Body, *first*, of judicial activism, that is, of creating, through erroneous interpretations of WTO provisions, obligations the US had never agreed to; *second*, of rendering 'advisory opinions' on issues that were not strictly necessary to rule upon to resolve the dispute at hand; *third*, of reviewing factual findings of the panels and in particular findings on

11. *See* Barfield, *Free Trade, Sovereignty, Democracy: The Future of the World Trade Organization* (American Enterprise Institute Press, 2001), pp. 1-68.
12. *See* Ehlermann, *Some Personal Experiences as Member of the Appellate Body of the WTO*, Policy Papers, RSC No. 02/9 (European University Institute, 2002), p. 14.
13. The examples of Jennifer Hillman (US) in 2011 and Seung Wha Chang (Korea) in 2016 were highly publicized.
14. The last time new Appellate Body members were appointed was in late 2016. Hyun Chong Kim (Korea) and Zhao Hong (China) were appointed by the DSB as of 1 December 2016. Mr Kim resigned July 2017 to become Korea's Minister of Trade; Ms Zhao's term ended on 30 November 2020.
15. *See* US President's 2018 Trade Policy Agenda, pp. 22 et seq., available at ustr.gov/about-us/policy-offices/press-office/reports-and-publications/2018/2018-trade-policy-agenda-and-2017 (last visited February 2022); and United States Trade Representative, 'Report on the Appellate Body of the World Trade Organization', February 2020, at ustr.gov/sites/default/files/Report_on_the_Appellate_Body_of_the_World_Trade_Organization.pdf (last visited February 2022). *See also* the statement by the US at the DSB meetings on 22 June 2018 concerning Article 17.5 DSU and the 90-day timeframe for appellate review, on 27 August and 26 September 2018 concerning Article 17.6 DSU and appellate review of panel findings of fact, including on the meaning of domestic law; and on 29 October 2018 concerning the issuance of advisory opinions on issues not necessary to resolve a dispute.

the meaning of domestic law, because they fall outside the Appellate Body's mandate under Article 17.6 of the Understanding on Rules and Procedures Governing the Settlement of Disputes (DSU); and, *fourth*, of considering past Appellate Body reports as having binding precedential value. As to the alleged disregard for procedural and institutional rules, the US objects in particular, *first*, to the Appellate Body exceeding the mandatory 90-day timeframe for appellate review without the explicit agreement of the parties and, *second*, to allow, pursuant to Rule 15 of the Working Procedures for Appellate Review, outgoing Appellate Body Members to complete the disposition of appeals, which were assigned to them before their term in office ended. It should be noted that with the exception of the last concern (regarding the completion of the disposition of appeals by outgoing Appellate Body members), the US had also, under the Obama and G.W. Bush administrations, voiced the same or very similar concerns regarding the functioning of the Appellate Body. However, the Trump administration, by blocking the (re-)appointment of Appellate Body members, transformed these 'concerns' into an existential crisis of the Appellate Body. As mentioned above, on 11 December 2019, the number of Appellate Body members in office fell below the minimum of three required to hear an appeal, and the resulting paralysis of the Appellate Body has severely undermined the effectiveness and credibility of the whole WTO dispute settlement system. Unless an agreement is reached on how to address the US' concerns regarding the functioning of the Appellate Body, the WTO's unique experiment with binding international adjudication will sadly come to an end.

3 2019 DRAFT GENERAL COUNCIL DECISION ON THE FUNCTIONING OF THE APPELLATE BODY

In search of an agreement to overcome the current crisis, no less than 22 WTO Members, as well as the WTO's African Group, have, in late 2018 and in 2019, tabled, either individually or jointly, position papers with proposals to address the US concerns regarding the functioning of the Appellate Body.[16] Some of these position papers, such as the Communication from the European Union (EU), China, Canada, India, Norway, New Zealand, Switzerland, Australia, the Republic of Korea, Iceland, Singapore, Mexico and Montenegro on 10 December 2019, were rather 'sceptical' about the legitimacy of the concerns raised by the US and made proposals which safeguarded the

16. Communication from the EU, China, India and Montenegro to the General Council, WT/GC/W/753, dated 26 November 2018 and WT/GC/W/753/Rev.2, dated 11 December 2018; Communication from the Separate, Customs Territory of Taiwan, Penghu, Kinmen and Matsu to the General Council, WT/GC/W/763 Rev., dated 8 April 2019; Communication from Thailand to the General Council, WT/GC/W/769, dated 26 April 2019; and Communication from the African Group to the General Council, WT/GC/W/776, dated 26 June 2019. *See also*, more generally, European Commission, *Concept Paper on WTO Modernisation*, Part 3 on Future EU Proposals on Dispute Settlement, dated 20 September 2018; and Communication from Canada, *Strengthening and Modernizing the WTO: Discussion Paper*, Theme 2: Safeguarding and Strengthening WTO Dispute Settlement, JOB/GC/201, dated 21 September 2018.

key features of WTO appellate review.[17] Other position papers, such as the Communication by Japan, Australia and Chile, dated 18 April 2019 and the Communication from Brazil, Paraguay and Uruguay of 25 April 2019, were much more sympathetic to the US concerns and proposed to alter some key features of WTO appellate review.[18] Finally, communications like those of Thailand, dated 26 April 2019, and Honduras, dated 21 and 29 January and 4 February 2019, respectively, tried to strike a middle ground.[19] However, almost all WTO Members were, and still are, of the view that whatever legitimate concerns the US might have regarding the functioning of the Appellate Body, these concerns did not justify the obstruction of the appointment process, which resulted in the paralysis of the Appellate Body. WTO Members repeatedly, and in growing numbers, called upon the US to allow for the appointment of new Appellate Body members. At the meeting of the Dispute Settlement Body (DSB) on 27 October 2021, no less than 121 WTO Members requested the DSB to take immediately the decision to unblock the appointment process.[20] In response to this request, the US stated, as it had done in response to numerous similar requests in the past, that it was not in a position to support the proposed decision as it 'continued to have systemic concerns with the Appellate Body'. According to the US, 'Members had to undertake fundamental reform if the system was to remain viable and credible'. The US stated that it 'looked forward to ... constructive engagement with Members at the appropriate time'.[21]

In December 2018, the WTO General Council appointed Ambassador David Walker of New Zealand as 'Facilitator' to resolve the differences among WTO Members on the functioning of the Appellate Body.[22] Over the next 10 months, Walker met with WTO Members in small groups and in open-ended informal meetings to discuss the proposals for reform tabled and seek a way out of the crisis. The US, however, did not table any reform proposal and, reportedly, did not actively engage in the informal meetings but only sent note-takers to meetings. Based on the proposals made by Members and the extensive discussions on these proposals, Walker submitted on 15 October 2019 to the General Council a Draft Decision on the Functioning of the

17. *See* Communication from the EU, China, Canada, India, Norway, New Zealand, Switzerland, Australia, Republic of Korea, Iceland, Singapore and Mexico and Montenegro to the General Council, WT/GC/W/752/Rev. 2, dated 11 December 2018. On the US reaction to the Communication from the EU, China, Canada, India and others, *see* Statements by the United States at the Meeting of the WTO General Council on 12 December 2018 (agenda items 7 and 8). geneva.usmission.gov/2018/12/12/statements-items-7-and-8-by-the-united-states-at-the-meeting-of-the-wto-general-council/ (last visited June 2022).
18. Communication from Japan, Australia and Chile to the General Council, WT/GC/W/768, dated 18 April 2019, and WT/GC/W/768/Rev., dated 26 April 2019; and Communication from Brazil, Paraguay and Uruguay to the General Council, WT/GC/W/767/Rev. dated 25 April 2019.
19. Communication from Thailand to the General Council, WT/GC/W/769, dated 26 April 2019; and Communications from Honduras to the General Council, WT/GC/W/758, dated 21 January 2019, WT/GC/W/759, dated 21 January 2019, WT/GC/W/760, dated 29 January 2019, and WT/GC/W/761, dated 4 February 2019.
20. Dispute Settlement Body, Minutes of the meeting held on 30 August 2021, WT/DSB/M/455, dated 27 October 2021, paras 8.1-8.27. Included in this number are the EU Members States on whose behalf the EU spoke.
21. *Ibid.*, para. 8.23.
22. Ambassador Walker served as DSB chair and later as General Council chair.

Appellate Body.[23] The Draft Decision aimed at 'seeking workable and agreeable solutions to improve the functioning of the Appellate Body' in the hope of avoiding the paralysis of the Appellate Body as of December 2019.[24]

The Draft Decision, *inter alia,* addressed: *first*, the US concern regarding judicial activism, by stating that, pursuant to Articles 3.2 and 19.2 of the DSU, Appellate Body rulings 'cannot add to or diminish the rights and obligations provided in the covered agreements'; *second,* the US concern regarding binding precedent, by stating that precedent is 'not created through WTO dispute settlement proceedings', but that consistency and predictability in the interpretation of WTO law is 'of significant value to Members'; *third,* the US concern regarding advisory opinions rendered by the Appellate Body, by stating that the latter may only address issues raised by the parties and to the extent necessary to resolve the dispute; *fourth,* the US concern regarding appellate review of panel findings on the meaning of municipal law, by stating that the meaning of municipal law is to be treated as a matter of fact and therefore, pursuant to Article 17.6 of the DSU, not subject to appellate review; *fifth,* the US concern regarding the 90-day timeframe for appellate review, by stating that, pursuant to Article 17.5 of the DSU, the Appellate Body is obligated to issue its report within 90 days of the notice of appeal and that this timeframe can only be extended with the agreement of the parties; and *sixth,* the US concern regarding Rule 15 of the Working Procedures for Appellate Review, by providing that only the DSB can authorize an outgoing Appellate Body member to complete the disposition of an appeal after the expiry of her/his term in office, provided that the hearing in the appeal took place prior to the expiry of the term. The Draft General Council Decision was a carefully constructed compromise between the Members engaged in the discussions on the functioning of the Appellate Body, which preserved the core features of WTO appellate review while at the same time addressing US concerns.

However, the hope that the Draft Decision would allow the WTO to avoid the paralysis of the Appellate Body as of 11 December 2019 was very short-lived. On the same day as it was submitted to the General Council, the US rejected the Draft Decision as insufficient to address its concerns. According to the US, 'the fundamental problem was that the Appellate Body was not respecting the current, clear language of the DSU' and that some Members 'appeared willing to tolerate - or even encourage - those actions'.[25] For the US, the fundamental question, which Members failed to address, was why the Appellate Body felt free to disregard the clear text of the DSU and other WTO agreements.[26] In response to this question, the US suggested that the failure of the WTO negotiating function led 'to unchecked institutional creep by the Appellate Body as Members pushed to achieve through litigation what they had not achieved or could

23. General Council, Informal Process on Matters related to the Functioning of the Appellate Body - Report by the Facilitator, H.E. Dr David Walker (New Zealand), JOB/GC/222, dated 15 October 2019, Annex.
24. *Ibid.*, para. 1.22.
25. General Council, Minutes of Meeting, held on 15 and 16 October 2019, WT/GC/M/180, dated 3 December 2019, para. 4.51.
26. *Ibid.*, paras 4.51 and 4.52. *See also* General Council, Minutes of Meeting, held on 9 December 2019, WT/GC/M/181, dated 24 February 2021, para. 5.103.

not achieve at the negotiating table'.[27] The US observed that some Members apparently considered the Appellate Body to be an independent international court which 'inherently had more expansive authority than what was provided in the DSU, for example, to create jurisprudence and fill gaps in the WTO Agreements'.[28] The US also noted that 'some Appellate Body members viewed themselves as 'appellate judges' serving on a 'World Trade Court' that was the 'centrepiece' of the WTO dispute settlement system, rather than one component of it'.[29] The US argued that 'such an expansive vision of the Appellate Body was not reflected in the DSU and had not been agreed to by the United States'.[30] The US's position on the functioning of the Appellate Body arguably reflects: *first,* its strong disagreement with especially those parts of the Appellate Body jurisprudence which, in its view, restricts the ability of the US to protect its domestic industry from import competition by using trade remedy measures; and *second,* its wish to return to a pre-WTO situation in which a binding dispute settlement mechanism with quasi-judicial features would not interfere with US sovereignty, and it could use its economic and other power to 'resolve' trade disputes with trading partners.[31]

In sharp contrast with the very critical assessment by the US of the functioning of the Appellate Body, the EU stated at the General Council meeting on 9 December 2019, two days before the Appellate Body was paralyzed by the US, that the Appellate Body 'had served well all Members in an independent, highly professional and, given the circumstances, very efficient manner' and that it 'therefore commended all the present and past members of the Appellate Body on their work as well as the staff working on the Appellate Body's secretariat'.[32] The EU argued that: 'Members should remedy the current situation by boosting the WTO's negotiating arm rather than chopping off its dispute settlement arm'.[33] Other WTO Members, including China, made similar

27. *Ibid.*, para. 4.52. *See also* General Council, Minutes of Meeting, held on 9-10 December 2019, WT/GC/M/181, dated 24 February 2021, para. 5.106.
28. *Ibid.*, para. 4.53. *See also* General Council, Minutes of Meeting, held on 9-10 December 2019, WT/GC/M/181, dated 24 February 2021, para. 5.107.
29. *See, e.g.*, Ehlermann, 'Six years on the bench of the "World Trade Court": Some personal experiences as member of the Appellate Body of the World Trade Organization', 36 *Journal of World Trade* (2002), 605-639; Van den Bossche, 'The making of the "World Trade Court": The origins and development of the Appellate Body of the World Trade Organization', in Yerxa and Wilson (Eds), *Key Issues in WTO Dispute Settlement: The First Ten Years* (CUP, 2005), pp. 63-79; and Van den Bossche, 'From afterthought to centerpiece: The Appellate Body and its rise to prominence in the world trading system', in Sacerdoti, Yanovich and Bohannes (Eds), *The WTO at Ten: The Contribution of the Dispute Settlement System* (CUP, 2006), pp. 289-325.
30. General Council, Minutes of Meeting, held on 15 and 16 October 2019, WT/GC/M/180, dated 3 December 2019, para. 4.53. *See also* General Council, Minutes of Meeting, held on 9-10 December 2019, WT/GC/M/181, dated 24 February 2021, para. 5.107.
31. On 17 June 2020, during briefings to the US House Ways and Means Committee and Senate Finance Committee, Amb. Robert Lighthizer, the United States Trade Representative, reportedly said that 'he would be content if the Appellate Body (AB) is never restored, arguing that the WTO members need to talk about a new dispute settlement system' and that 'he believes the original (GATT) non-binding system that encouraged countries to work out their disputes was better'. *See* Washington Trade Daily, 18 June 2020, washingtontradedaily.net.
32. *See* General Council, Minutes of Meeting, held on 9-10 December 2019, WT/GC/M/181, dated 24 February 2021, para. 5.140.
33. *Ibid.*, para. 5.138.

statements of strong support for the WTO dispute settlement system in general and the Appellate Body in particular.[34] Those WTO Members disagreed with the US that the Appellate Body had systematically engaged in judicial overreach and demonstrated consistent disregard for procedural and institutional rules.[35]

4 2020 MULTI-PARTY INTERIM APPEAL ARBITRATION ARRANGEMENT

In the wake of the failure to adopt the Draft General Council Decision on the Functioning of the Appellate Body, 17 WTO Members announced on 24 January 2020 that, while they remain committed to finding a solution to the Appellate Body crisis, they would work together 'towards putting in place contingency measures that would allow for appeals of WTO panel reports in disputes among themselves'.[36] At the initiative of the EU, they instructed their officials to 'expeditiously finalize work' on a multi-party arrangement for appeal arbitration under Article 25 of the DSU. This DSU article provides for 'arbitration within the WTO as an alternative means of dispute settlement'.

On 27 March 2020, 16 WTO Members announced that they had reached an agreement on the *Multi-Party Interim Appeal Arbitration Arrangement under Article 25 of the DSU*, commonly referred to as the Multi-Party Interim Appeal Arbitration Arrangement (MPIA). This MPIA became effective on 30 April 2020, when it was notified to the DSB.[37] The MPIA is an interim arrangement intended 'to preserve, in disputes among Members participating in the MPIA, a functioning and two-step dispute settlement process, as envisaged by the DSU'.[38] It is designed to remain in place only until a lasting improvement to the Appellate Body situation is found.[39] The MPIA

34. *Ibid.*, paras 5.176-5.183.
35. *See, e.g.*, Statement by Amb. Zhang Xiangchen (China) at the WTO General Council meeting on 15 & 16 October 2019 on wto2.mofcom.gov.cn/article/chinaviewpoins/201910/20191002905004.shtml.
36. *See* trade.ec.europa.eu/doclib/docs/2020/january/tradoc_158596.pdf. In 2019, the EU had already concluded bilateral arrangements for appeal arbitration under Article 25 of the DSU with Canada and Norway, under which former Appellate Body Members would serve as appeal arbitrators. *See, e.g.*, for the EU/Canada Arrangement trade.ec.europa.eu/doclib/docs/2019/july/tradoc_158273.pdf.
37. Statement on a Mechanism for Developing, Documenting and Sharing Practices and Procedures in the Conduct of WTO Disputes, Addendum, JOB/DSB/1/Add. 12, dated 30 April 2020, trade.ec.europa.eu/doclib/docs/2020/april/tradoc_158731.pdf. Note that out of the 17 WTO Members which in January 2020 committed themselves to working towards an appeal arbitration arrangement, only Korea did not become, and still is not, a party to the MPIA. When the MPIA was notified to the DSB on 30 April 2020, 19 WTO Members had signed up to this arrangement.
38. *See* EU Statement at the Regular DSB meeting – 29 June 2020, Agenda point 13, available at eeas.europa.eu/delegations/world-trade-organization-wto/81752/eu-statement-regular-dsb-meeting.
39. Statement on a Mechanism for Developing, Documenting and Sharing Practices and Procedures in the Conduct of WTO Disputes, Addendum, JOB/DSB/1/Add. 12, dated 30 April 2020, paras 1 and 15 and Annex 1, para. 2.

applies to all disputes between participating WTO Members.[40] Parties to the MPIA commit not to appeal panel reports to the paralyzed Appellate Body, i.e., agree not to appeal panel reports into the void but will resort to appellate arbitration under Article 25 of the DSU.[41] As explicitly stated in the MPIA, appeal arbitrations under this arrangement are to a large extent governed, with any necessary adjustments, by the provisions of the DSU and other rules and procedures applicable to appellate review under the DSU, such as the Working Procedures for Appellate Review.[42]

At the same time, the MPIA contains some procedural innovations to enhance procedural efficiency and streamline the proceedings.[43] In this regard, note that the MPIA States that 'the parties *request* the arbitrators to issue the award within 90 days following the Notice of Appeal' (emphasis added)[44] and that 'to that end, the arbitrators may take appropriate organizational measures to streamline the proceedings, without prejudice to the procedural rights and obligations of the parties and due process'.[45] Such organizational measures may include decisions on page limits, time limits and deadlines, as well as on the length and number of hearings required.[46] To issue awards within the 90-day timeframe, the MPIA arbitrators 'may also *propose* substantive measures to the parties' (emphasis added).[47] In this regard, explicit reference is made to 'an exclusion of claims based on the alleged lack of an objective

40. *See ibid.*, para. 9 and Annex 1, para. 6. With exception of those where the interim panel report has already been issued by the date the MPIA enters into force or by the date of its enforcement by a new participant.
41. However, if neither party appeals under this appeal arbitration procedure, the panel report is circulated and adopted by the DSB in the usual way. The MPIA is to be put into practice in specific disputes through individual appeal arbitration agreements based on the model annexed to the arrangement.
42. Statement on a Mechanism for Developing, Documenting and Sharing Practices and Procedures in the Conduct of WTO Disputes, Addendum, JOB/DSB/1/Add. 12, dated 30 April 2020, Annex 1, para. 11.
43. *See ibid.*, Annex I, para. 12.
44. *Ibid.* However, Annex 1, para. 14 suggests that this is more than a mere 'request'. Para. 14 states: 'On a proposal from the arbitrators, the parties may agree to extend the 90-day time-period for the issuance of the award'. Party consent may thus be required to exceed the 90-day timeframe. Note that the Draft General Council Decision on the Functioning of the Appellate Body of 15 October 2019 stated: 'Consistent with Article 17.5 of the DSU, the Appellate Body *is obligated* to issue its report no later than 90 days from the date a party to the dispute notifies its intention to appeal' (emphasis added) and 'In cases of unusual complexity or periods of numerous appeals, the parties may agree with the Appellate Body to extend the time-frame for the issuance of the Appellate Body report beyond 90 days'. Neither the Draft Decision nor the MPIA address the issue of the legal value of a report or award issued after 90-day timeframe without the parties' consent.
45. *Ibid.* Query whether these measures will be helpful. *First*, in 2015, the Appellate Body already consulted WTO Members on the possibility of imposing page limits. At the time, most WTO Members consulted were less than enthusiastic about the imposition of page limits. *Second*, the Working Procedures for Appellate Review already provide for many time limits and deadlines, which are (too) demanding. *Third*, with the exception of the original and compliance proceedings in *EC and certain member States – Large Civil Aircraft (2011, 2019)* and *US – Large Civil Aircraft (2nd complaint) (2012, 2019)*, there has always been only one hearing and the duration of these hearings seldom exceeded two days.
46. *See ibid.*
47. *Ibid.*, Annex 1, para. 13.

assessment of the facts pursuant to Article 11 of the DSU'.[48] The MPIA also circumscribes the mandate of the appeal arbitrators. Appeal arbitrators are to review only issues of law, may only address the issues necessary to resolve the dispute, cannot add to or diminish the rights and obligations provided in the WTO agreements and are to provide consistency and predictability in the interpretation of these rights and obligations.[49] Note, however, that mandate of appeal arbitrators under the MPIA does not in any meaningful way differ from the mandate of Appellate Body members under Article 17 of the DSU. According to the MPIA, appeals are dealt with by three arbitrators selected randomly from a pool of 10 standing arbitrators.[50] The pool of arbitrators is made up of persons of recognized authority and demonstrated expertise.[51] In July 2020, the parties to the MPIA notified the DSB that they had agreed on the composition of the pool of arbitrators.[52] The appeal arbitrators will be provided with appropriate administrative and legal support, subject to the necessary guarantees of quality and independence.[53] Pursuant to Article 25 of the DSU, the appeal arbitration awards are final and binding on the parties, and the panel reports will be attached to the awards.[54] Article 21 of the DSU, regarding the surveillance of implementation, including compliance proceedings, as well as Article 22 of the DSU, regarding compensation and arbitration on the suspension of concessions, apply to arbitration awards emanating from Article 25 procedures.[55]

In its statement at the DSB meeting of 29 June 2020, when the MPIA was introduced by its proponents, the US underlined that it does not object to WTO Members utilizing Article 25 of the DSU or other informal procedures to help resolve disputes.[56] If any Member considers that use of the arbitration provision in Article 25 may assist it in securing a positive solution to a dispute, as foreseen under Article, the

48. *Ibid.* It is difficult to imagine that the party which considers that the panel failed to make an objective assessment of the facts will ever be willing and/or able to accept the arbitrators' proposal to drop its Article 11 DSU claim(s) of error.
49. *See ibid.*, Preamble and Annex 1, paras 9-10.
50. Paragraph 5 of the MPIA states: 'In order to promote consistency and coherence in decision-making, the members of the pool of arbitrators will discuss amongst themselves matters of interpretation, practice and procedure, to the extent practicable'. To give effect to this provision, para. 8 of Annex 1 of the MPIA provides that arbitrators '*may* discuss their decisions relating to the appeal with all of the other members of the pool of arbitrators ...' (emphasis added). It is unclear whether there will be an 'exchange of views' in each appeal arbitration, as is the case in appellate proceedings under Article 17 of the DSU.
51. *See ibid.*, paras 4-6, and Annex 1, para. 7.
52. *See* trade.ec.europa.eu/doclib/docs/2020/august/tradoc_158911.12-Suppl.5%20(002).pdf. The MPIA Pool includes: Mateo Diego-Fernández Andrade (Mexico), Thomas Cottier (Switzerland), Locknie Hsu (Singapore), Valerie Hughes (Canada), Alejandro Jara (Chile), José Alfredo Graça Lima (Brazil), Claudia Orozco (Colombia), Joost Pauwelyn (European Union), Penelope Ridings (New Zealand), and Guohua Yang (China).
53. *See ibid*, para. 7. The MPIA envisages that the support structure will be entirely separate from the WTO Secretariat staff and its divisions supporting the panels and be answerable, regarding the substance of their work, only to appeal arbitrators. The MPIA parties requested the Director General to ensure the availability of a support structure meeting these criteria.
54. *See also ibid.*, Annex 1, para. 15 and footnote 10.
55. *See ibid.*, Annex 1, para. 17.
56. *See* Statements by the United States at the Meeting of the WTO Dispute Settlement Body Geneva, 29 June 2020, Multi-Party Interim Appeal Arbitration pursuant to Article 25 of the DSU

US, in principle, supports such efforts. The US objected, however, to any arrangement that would 'perpetuate the failings' of the Appellate Body. According to the US, the MPIA 'incorporates and exacerbates some of the worst aspects of the Appellate Body's practices', and it does so by: *first,* weakening the mandatory deadline for completing Appellate Body reports; *second,* contemplating appellate review of panel findings of fact; *third,* failing to reflect the limitation on appellate review to those findings necessary to resolve the dispute; *fourth,* promoting the use of precedent by identifying 'consistency' (regardless of correctness) as a guiding principle for decisions; and *fifth,* encouraging arbitrators to create a body of law through litigation.[57] For the US, the real goal of the MPIA is not to help the participants resolve disputes but to create an ersatz Appellate Body that would, at best, 'perpetuate the failings' of the original Appellate Body.[58] The US has made it known that it objects to using any WTO financial or staff resources in support of appeal arbitration under the MPIA.[59]

On 1 January 2022, 26 WTO Members were a party to the MPIA, including Brazil, Canada, China, the EU and Mexico, i.e., 5 of the 10 most frequent users of the WTO dispute settlement system. The number of parties to the MPIA is expected to increase further. At present, the parties in seven disputes have notified the DSB that they have agreed – under the terms of the MPIA – to Procedures for Arbitration under Article 25 of the DSU.[60] It is expected that the appeal, if any, in *Costa Rica – Measures Concerning the Importation of Fresh Avocados from Mexico* (DS524), will, in early 2022, be the first appeal heard and decided by an MPIA tribunal. Others will definitely follow. However, the MPIA is but an interim and partial 'solution' to the current crisis of WTO dispute settlement.

5 POSSIBLE WAYS TO OVERCOME THE CURRENT CRISIS

To preserve the rules-based multilateral trading system, it is imperative that the Appellate Body crisis and its destructive impact on the effectiveness and credibility of the WTO dispute settlement system are addressed. While the MPIA is at present, and perhaps for some time, all that is possible to address the crisis, the WTO requires an

(JOB/DSB/1/ADD. 12), Agenda item 13, available at geneva.usmission.gov/wp-content/upload/sites/290/Jun29.DSB_.Stmt_.as-deliv.fin_.public13218.pdf (last visited June 2022).

57. *Ibid.*
58. *Ibid.*
59. *See* news.bloomberglaw.com/international-trade/u-s-pledges-to-block-funding-for-eus-wto-appellate-body-proxy.
60. *See* ielp.worldtradelaw.net/dsu-25-interim-appeals/. *See, e.g., Canada – Measures Concerning Trade in Commercial Aircraft* (complaint by Brazil), Agreed Procedures for Arbitration under Article 25 of the DSU, WT/DS522/20, dated 3 June 2020; *Colombia – Anti-Dumping Duties on Frozen Fries from Belgium, Germany and the Netherlands* (complaint by the European Union, Agreed Procedures for Arbitration under Article 25 of the DSU, WT/DS591/3, dated 15 July 2020; *Costa Rica – Measures Concerning the Importation of Fresh Avocados from Mexico* (complaint by Mexico), Agreed Procedures for Arbitration under Article 25 of the DSU, WT7524/5/Rev.1, dated 2 December 2021; *China – Anti-Dumping and Countervailing Duty Measures on Wine from Australia* (complaint by Australia), Agreed Procedures for Arbitration under Article 25 of the DSU WT/DS602/3, dated 20 December 2021.

effective dispute settlement system involving all its Members, including the US. While the US has been very clear about what it considers to be the errors of the Appellate Body, it has been quite vague regarding what kind of dispute settlement system it would want the WTO to have. Merely stating that this system should be the system provided for in the DSU is not helpful when Members differ fundamentally as to what that system is. What gives hope, however, is that other WTO Members have shown considerable willingness to address the concerns of the US regarding the functioning of the Appellate Body, even though they do not share (all of) these concerns. The 2019 Draft General Council Decision on the Functioning of the Appellate Body is the best example of this. Future negotiations, if and when the US is willing and able to engage in them, could and should build on this Draft Decision, which preserves the core features of binding, two-stage, independent and impartial dispute resolution. However, these future negotiations should not be limited to 'fixing' the Appellate Body but also address the known shortcomings of the other stages of WTO dispute settlement. WTO Members have been discussing these shortcomings in the consultation, panel and implementation stages since 1998, first in the context of the DSU review discussions and subsequently in the context of the Doha Development Round negotiations on DSU reform. In the course of the years, there has been a large number of useful proposals for improvement of the WTO dispute settlement system.[61]

In reflecting on the WTO dispute settlement system of the future, the first question that needs to be answered is whether WTO dispute settlement really needs appellate review. In a paper published in 2020, Bernard Hoekman and Petros Mavroidis argue that it does not, but that what is needed, instead, is the establishment of a permanent panel body of 15 panellists – full-time adjudicators with no affiliation with any government and appointed for eight years, non-renewable.[62] This is by no means a new idea. The EU already tabled a proposal for such a permanent panel body in 1998.[63] The establishment of a permanent panel body does, however, not make appellate review redundant. There is no doubt that, if wisely selected, permanent panellists would produce high-quality panel reports, which arguably may not need review. Also, to the extent that the permanent panel body would hear important cases *in plenum* and would have exchanges of views among all panellists in other cases, there would arguably be no need for appellate review to ensure the consistency of the case law. However, the need for an appellate review remains. In many disputes, the key issues and interests at stake are too important to be decided in a one-stage dispute

61. All publicly available documents relating to the DSU reform negotiations can be found on the WTO website as TN/DS documents.

62. *See* Hoekman and Mavroidis, 'To AB or Not to AB? Dispute Settlement in WTO Reform', 23 *Journal of International Economic Law* (2020), 703-722.

63. *See* Dispute Settlement Body, Special Session, Contribution of the European Communities and its Member States to the Improvement of the WTO Dispute Settlement Understanding, TN/DS/W/1, dated 13 March 2002. Note that this proposal, first made in the context of the DSU review discussions, and repeated in 2002 in the context of the Doha Development Round negotiations on DSU reform, got very little support from other WTO Members. *See also* Cottier, 'The WTO Permanent Panel Body: A Bridge too Far?', 6 *Journal of International Economic Law* (2003), 187-202.

settlement system. Also, parties often have more focused and detailed legal argumentation on appeal than they had before the panel. This has allowed the Appellate Body to come to better-motivated decisions. In general, the decisions reached by a two-stage dispute settlement system have more legitimacy and authority than decisions reached by a single-stage dispute settlement system. Hoekman and Mavroidis see single-stage WTO dispute settlement as a solution to the current crisis.[64] But is this so? Would a final, binding finding of WTO inconsistency by a permanent panel body be more acceptable to the US (and others) than a finding of inconsistency by the Appellate Body? At present, most WTO Members are strongly in favour of a two-stage dispute settlement system. President Trump's United States Trade Representative (USTR), Robert Lighthizer, clearly was not, but where does the Biden administration stand on this?

If it is agreed that WTO dispute settlement needs appellate review, i.e., that the WTO needs the Appellate Body, the next question is what the proper role of the Appellate Body in WTO dispute settlement is. In a paper published in 2021, Thomas Cottier argues that any reform of the WTO dispute settlement system should put panels at the heart of the system and that the role of the Appellate Body should be recalibrated.[65] While the Appellate Body has, over the past two decades, reviewed legal findings of panels in full and *de novo*, Cottier proposes that the Appellate Body should, in most cases, adopt a much more deferential standard of review. He proposes that the Appellate Body would apply a standard of reasonableness when reviewing most legal findings of a panel. The Appellate Body would limit itself to determine whether the panel finding appealed is properly argued and substantiated. If a panel's legal finding is based on a reasonable and legitimate interpretation of the law, the Appellate Body should, according to Cottier, uphold the panel's finding. In most appeals, the Appellate Body would therefore not develop its own line of legal argumentation on the issues on appeal, which is how the Appellate Body has understood its task in the past. While the standard of reasonableness would be the Appellate Body's principal standard of review of legal findings, it would not be its only standard. Cottier suggests that for panel findings concerning, what he refers to as 'constitutional issues' of WTO law, the proper standard of appellate review would still be full and *de novo* review. Such 'constitutional issues' would include the interpretation of fundamental principles and exceptions, special and differential treatment, issues relating to the rule of law, governance and transparency, and issues relating to the relationship between WTO law and other areas of international law. Situations in which panels have adopted conflicting interpretations of WTO law would, according to Cottier, also justify full and *de novo* review. This is a very interesting line of thinking, but how is the Appellate Body to distinguish between findings on 'constitutional issues', which warrant full and *de novo* review, and findings on other issues, which would be subject to only a review of their reasonableness? Does a finding on the legality of the zeroing methodology raise a 'constitutional issue'? Arguably not, but this is nevertheless a politically very sensitive

64. *See* Hoekman & Mavroidis, *supra* note 62, at 705 and 718.
65. Cottier, 'Recalibrating the WTO dispute settlement system: Towards new standards of appellate review', 24 *Journal of International Economic Law* (2021), 1-23.

and controversial issue for some WTO Members. Does a finding on the meaning of the concept of 'public body' raise a 'constitutional issue'? Probably yes, as it concerns the fundamental question of whether the WTO system accommodates State-capitalist as well as market-capitalist economic systems. Generally speaking, many of the appeals heard by the Appellate Body raise important questions about the policy space left to a WTO Member under WTO law and, thus, questions regarding the extent to which WTO law limits national sovereignty. Do these questions not raise issues of a constitutional nature, and do panel findings on such issues not warrant full and *de novo* appellate review? Cottier himself recognizes the problem of distinguishing between 'constitutional issues' and other issues and writes that: 'there is no formal difference between fundamental principles and technical or plain rules in treaty law. Often they are overlapping'.[66] In determining the appropriate standard of appellate review, a differentiation between findings raising 'constitutional issues' or other issues may not be helpful. However, Cottier's call for more deference by the Appellate Body to panel findings deserves careful consideration. Such deference may be warranted if and when the current *ad hoc* panels are replaced by a permanent panel body of the kind already proposed by the EU in 1998. The establishment of a permanent panel body would, however, constitute a further 'judicialization' of WTO dispute settlement, and it is doubtful that this is acceptable to the US.

6 CONCLUSION

As long as there is no agreement on the reform of the Appellate Body, appellate review of panel findings will only be available under the MPIA and only to the parties to the MPIA. This state of affairs, while obviously far from ideal, does offer a welcome opportunity for MPIA tribunals to experiment with approaches to appellate review different from the approach taken by the Appellate Body. While the appeal arbitration procedure under the MPIA is based on the substantive and procedural aspects of appellate review pursuant to Article 17 of the DSU, the MPIA also allows - as noted above - for flexibility, and room for experimentation, in order to improve appellate review. MPIA tribunals could and should experiment with a more deferential standard of appellate review, possibly by drawing a distinction between findings on 'constitutional issues' and findings on other issues, as suggested by Thomas Cottier. MPIA tribunals could and should also experiment with different ways of addressing other problems which have haunted the Appellate Body and are high on the list of concerns the US has with the Appellate Body, such as judicial activism, advisory opinions, the 90-day timeframe for appellate review, the role of precedent, and the review of factual findings of the panel. Adopting a more deferential standard of appellate review - if it can be consistently applied - may mitigate some of these concerns but will not make them disappear. MPIA tribunals will be confronted with the same realities and constraints as the Appellate Body struggled with for over two decades. Experimentation by MPIA tribunals with different approaches to appellate review may result in a

66. *Ibid.*, at 16-17.

better understanding of, and appreciation for, the approach taken by the Appellate Body. However, experimentation with different approaches to appellate review may also prepare the ground for the reform of the Appellate Body and, more broadly, WTO dispute settlement. Carefully preparing that ground for reform through experimentation by MPIA tribunals is better than now rushing into reform negotiations which - in the current political context - may result in a new WTO dispute settlement system not worth having. There is a future for the Appellate Body and WTO dispute settlement, but it would be wise not to seek reform in haste and without careful consideration of what kind of appellate review and dispute settlement will serve the rules-based multilateral trading system best.

PART III Interaction Between Legal Systems

CHAPTER 13

EU-, EEA- or WTO-Style Dispute Resolution in the EU-Swiss Relations?

Christa Tobler[*]

While the European Union (EU) rejects World Trade Organization (WTO)-style trade sanctions and remedies in the relations between its Member States, such measures are very much part of the dispute settlement mechanism in the EU's external relations. The contribution focuses on the mechanism reflected in the draft text for an institutional agreement between the EU and Switzerland, and it analyses the nature of the remedies provided in this context from a comparative perspective. While the draft institutional agreement has been shelved by the Swiss Federal Government, the issues underlying it will remain relevant.

1 INTRODUCTION

In his book *In Place of Inter-State Retaliation: The European Union's Rejection of WTO-style Trade Sanctions and Trade Remedies*, Phelan notes that the European Union (EU) forbids the use of inter-State retaliation to enforce obligations between its Member States.[1] Indeed, even in the rarely used variation of the infringement procedure where a Member State goes after another Member State, it must first bring the matter before the Commission, and retaliation by the Member State itself is not possible (Article 259

* For feedback on earlier drafts, I would like to thank Fengan Jiang (China University of Political Science and Law, Beijing), Matthias Oesch (University of Zurich) and Benedikt Pirker (University of Fribourg).

1. Phelan, *In Place of Inter-State Retaliation: The European Union's Rejection of WTO-style Trade Sanctions and Trade Remedies* (OUP, 2014).

Treaty on the Functioning of the European Union (TFEU)).[2] However, while there is a rejection of such retaliation *inside* the EU, it is very much part of the dispute settlement mechanisms in the EU's *external* relations, a fact that also appears in Marco Bronckers's academic work.[3]

The present contribution in his honour is a modest 'legal miniature' related to the Swiss-EU relations, and more specifically to the dispute settlement model provided for in the draft for a so-called Institutional Agreement ('Draft InstA').[4] In the Swiss public debate, this mechanism has led to a heated and sometimes confused debate. For example, it has been argued among those vehemently opposed that the new rules would allow the EU to impose 'fines' on Switzerland and to 'dictate their level'.[5] But is that really so? What types of remedies does the Draft InstA envisage and are these more EU-style or World Trade Organization (WTO)-style – or something different? In order to answer this question, the present contribution begins with a brief sketch of the EU-Swiss legal relations, the Draft InstA and dispute settlement. This is followed by a discussion of the model chosen for dispute settlement in the Draft InstA. Against that backdrop, the text turns to the issue of remedies and in doing so employs a comparative perspective that includes in particular European Economic Area (EEA) law, WTO law and the Brexit Withdrawal Agreement (WA). This is followed by a brief conclusion.

In the course of the research done for this contribution, the Swiss Federal Government decided to shelve the Draft InstA,[6] much to the consternation of the EU Commission.[7] Arguably, this does not mean that the issue of a new dispute settlement mechanism is off the table. Eventually, Switzerland will have to find a solution with the EU for a more stable framework of their legal relationship. The present contribution, therefore, sticks to its topic.

2. This particular version of the EU infringement procedure has been said to resemble the WTO dispute settlement procedure; Thorbjørn, 'Dispute Settlement', in Olsen, Steinicke and Sørensen (Eds), *WTO Law From a European Perspective* (Wolters Kluwer, 2012), pp. 37-63, at p. 56.
3. For example, Bronckers and Gruni, 'Retooling the sustainability standards in EU free trade agreements', 24 *Journal of International Economic Law* (2021), 25-51; Bronckers and Gruni, 'Taking the enforcement of labour standards in the EU's free trade agreements seriously', 56 *Common Market Law Review* (2019), 1591-1622.
4. Accord facilitant les relations bilatérales entre l'Union Européenne et la Confédération Suisse dans les parties du marché intérieur auxquelle la Suisse participle, official draft text of November 2018, eda.admin.ch/dam/europa/fr/documents/abkommen/Acccord-inst-Projet-de-texte_fr.pdf.
5. For example, Minder, 'Das institutionelle Rahmenabkommen hat gravierende Mängel', 3 April 2019, minder.sh/das-institutionelle-rahmenabkommen-hat-gravierende-maengel/: 'Wir können zwar Nein sagen, werden dafür aber bestraft. Die Höhe der Busse diktiert die EU.' Further Kompass/Europa, 'Das Rahmenabkommen (InstA): Der falsche Weg für die Schweiz!', 21 December 2020, kompasseuropa.ch/wp-content/uploads/2020/12/Kurz-Argu-1.pdf, p. 1.
6. eda.admin.ch/eda/en/fdfa/fdfa/aktuell/news.html/content/eda/en/meta/news/2021/5/26/83705.
7. Commission Statement on the decision by the Swiss Federal Council to terminate the negotiations of the EU-Swiss Institutional Framework Agreement, 26 May 2021, https://ec.europa.eu/commission/presscorner/detail/en/statement_21_2683.

2 EU-SWISS LEGAL RELATIONS, THE DRAFT InstA AND DISPUTE SETTLEMENT

2.1 EU-Swiss Agreements and the Draft InstA

Switzerland and the then European Communities began to conclude agreements from the 1950s onwards. So far, three phases can be distinguished:[8]

- In the first phase, agreements concerned issues such as consultations with the European Community on Coal and Steel (ECSC) and trade with the European Economic Community (EEC) in cheese and watches.
- A second phase began with the conclusion of two general trade agreements in 1972, with the ECSC and with the EEC, respectively. Today, the latter is the only surviving agreement of a group of free trade agreements (FTAs) concluded by the EEC with the then Member States of the European Free Trade Association (EFTA). According to the European Commission, the EU-Swiss FTA[9] is the cornerstone of the EU-Swiss legal relations.[10]
- The third phase followed Switzerland's rejection, in a popular vote in 1992, of membership in the EEA. This phase began with the conclusion of seven mostly economic agreements in 1999 (in Switzerland, commonly termed 'Bilaterals I'). This was followed by a second package of a broader nature in 2004 ('Bilaterals II') and thereafter by a number of further agreements on various issues.

Today, the list of agreements compiled by the Swiss Federal administration fills 30 pages.[11] Different types of agreements can be distinguished, including notably agreements on the cooperation of authorities and other bodies, the participation of Switzerland in EU programmes, the association of Switzerland to the EU's Schengen and Dublin systems and – of particular interest for present purposes – the movement of goods, persons and services. These so-called market access agreements are very largely based on EU rules that are thus incorporated into the EU-Swiss legal relationship.

The EU conceives of the market access agreements as part of the larger picture of 'the extended internal market', which next to Switzerland includes notably the EEA EFTA States Iceland, Liechtenstein and Norway and (in the future) also the so-called

8. For this systematic, *see* Łazowski, 'Switzerland', in Blockmans and Łazowski (Eds), *The European Union and Its Neighbours: A Legal Appraisal of the EU's Policies of Stabilisation, Partnership and Integration* (T.M.C. Asser Press, 2006), pp. 147-184, at 151 et seq.; further, following the systematic suggested by Łazowski, e.g., Tobler and Beglinger, *Grundzüge des bilateralen (Wirtschafts-)Rechts: Systematische Darstellung in Text und Tafeln*, vol. 1 (Dike, 2013), Tafel 28. More generally for the historical perspective, *see* Grin, *Suisse – Europe: Une perspective historique* (Fondation Jean Monnet pour l'Europe, 2020).
9. Agreement between the European Economic Community and the Swiss Confederation, O.J. 1972, L 300/189 (as amended).
10. *See* policy.trade.ec.europa.eu/eu-trade-relationships-country-and-region/countries-and-regions/switzerland_en (last visited February 2023).
11. *See* eda.admin.ch/dam/europa/de/documents/publikationen_dea/accords-liste_de.pdf (last visited February 2022) (in the German language).

AMS States (Andorra, Monaco and San Marino).[12] The EU's long-standing wish for homogeneity in the extended internal market forms the background to the negotiations with Switzerland on a renewed institutional set-up for selected market access agreements. The negotiations began in 2014. They focussed notably on the interpretation of the agreements in line with relevant European Court of Justice (ECJ) case law, their updating in the light of new EU law and the settlement of disputes between the parties to the agreements. At some point, the issue of modernized State aid rules also found its way into the negotiations. The negotiations resulted in the draft text mentioned in the introduction.

The now shelved Draft InstA relates to five market access agreements of the 'Bilaterals I', on the free movement of persons (FMP),[13] air transport,[14] land transport,[15] agricultural products[16] and the mutual recognition of conformity assessments.[17] The model developed for the InstA was also meant to be used for future market access agreements and for an overhaul of the various existing agreements on the trade in goods, among them notably the FTA of 1972. The modernized State aid rules in the Draft InstA relate specifically to the Air Transport Agreement; at least on the EU side they were also meant to serve as a model for a future overhaul of the agreements on the free movement of goods.[18]

2.2 The Dispute Settlement Mechanism at Present and in the Draft InstA

As they stand, the five market access agreements to which the Draft InstA relates entrust the task of dispute settlement to the respective Joint Committees that are in charge of managing the agreements and that are composed of representatives of both

12. For example, Council conclusions on a homogeneous extended internal market and EU relations with non-EU Western European countries, 11 December 2018.
13. Agreement between the European Community and its Member States, of the one part, and the Swiss Confederation, of the other, on the free movement of persons, O.J. 2002, L 114/6 (as amended).
14. Agreement between the European Community and the Swiss Confederation on Air Transport, O.J. 2002, L 114/73 (as amended).
15. Agreement between the European Community and the Swiss Confederation on the Carriage of Goods and Passengers by Rail and Road, O.J. 2002 L, 114/128 (as amended).
16. Agreement between the European Community and the Swiss Confederation on trade in agricultural products, O.J. 2002, L 114/132 (as amended).
17. Agreement between the European Community and the Swiss Confederation on mutual recognition in relation to conformity assessment, O.J. 2002, L 114/369 (as amended).
18. Generally on the InstA in the English language Kaddous, 'Switzerland and the EU: Current issues and new challenges under the Draft Institutional Framework Agreement', in: Gstöhl and Phinnemore (Eds), *The Proliferation of Privileged Partnerships between the European Union and Its Neighbours* (Routledge, 2019), pp. 68-83; Kaddous 'The Failure of the Institutional Agreement from a Legal Perspective', in: Maresceau and Tobler (Eds), *Switzerland and the European Union. A Challenging Relationship* (Brill, 2023, forthcoming), pp. 310-336, Schwok, 'The Shelved Institutional Agreement EU-CH from a Political Science Perspective', in: Maresceau and Tobler (Eds), *Switzerland and the European Union. A Challenging Relationship* (Brill, 2023, forthcoming), pp. 281-309.

parties. If a dispute is brought to a Joint Committee, this body will consult on the matter with a view to finding a commonly agreed solution. In the history of EU-Swiss relations, there have been but few instances where this approach did not succeed. For such cases, the agreements generally do not provide for any further means to settle the dispute. Two examples stand out:

- First, the dispute regarding the corporate tax rules of some Swiss Cantons which the Commission at the time considered to be State aid contrary to the FTA of 1972,[19] a view that Switzerland rejected. This particular dispute was eventually solved in view of new tax rules of the Organisation for Economic Co-operation and Development (OECD), i.e., outside the legal framework of the FTA.[20]
- Second, the EU institutions consider certain labour protection measures under Swiss law to be contrary to the FMP Agreement.[21] It has not been possible to solve this dispute over the years.

In view of such problems, the negotiations on the InstA aimed, among other issues, to add a *judicial* element to the hitherto merely diplomatic-technical dispute resolution mechanism. The negotiations went through different stages, starting from a model where a party could unilaterally turn to the ECJ once the Joint Committee had failed to find a solution[22] and resulting eventually in a mechanism based on what is sometimes called the 'Ukraine model' (*see* further below 3). In the framework of the latter, if a dispute cannot be settled in the Joint Committee, an arbitration procedure can be requested. Where the dispute concerns Union law incorporated into the bilateral agreement, the arbitration panel is obliged to seek guidance from the ECJ before deciding on the dispute. The arbitration panel is also obliged to apply the Court's interpretation to the dispute before it.

The contours of the new dispute settlement mechanism are outlined in Article 10 Draft InstA; details can be found in a protocol. Article 10 provides:

> (1) In the event of difficulty in the interpretation or application of this Agreement or of one of the agreements concerned or of a legal act referred to in it, the Contracting Parties shall consult each other within the Sectoral Committee in order to find a mutually acceptable solution. To this end, all necessary information shall be provided to enable a thorough examination of the

19. Commission Decision of 13 February 2013 on the incompatibility of certain Swiss company tax regimes with the Agreement between the European Economic Community and the Swiss Confederation of 22 July 1972, COM(2007)411 final.
20. For example, Tobler, 'State aid under Swiss-EU bilateral Law: The example of company taxation', in Bulterman. Hancher, McDonnell and Sevenster (Eds), *Views of European Law from the Mountain: Liber Amicorum Piet Jan Slot* (Wolters Kluwer, 2009), pp. 195-205.
21. *See, e.g.*, ec.europa.eu/commission/presscorner/detail/en/MEMO_16_3185.
22. Tobler, 'One of many challenges after "Brexit": The institutional framework of an alternative agreement – lessons from Switzerland and elsewhere?', 23 *Maastricht Journal of European and Comparative Law* (2016), 575-594, at 587.

situation. If the Sectoral Committee fails to find a solution, either Contracting Party may request that the matter be formally placed on the agenda of the Sectoral Committee for resolution. The Sectoral Committee shall examine all possibilities to maintain the proper functioning of the agreement concerned.

(2) If the Sectoral Committee fails to find a solution to the difficulty referred to in paragraph 1 within three months of the date on which the difficulty was brought before the Sectoral Committee, Switzerland or the EU may request that an arbitral tribunal settle the dispute in accordance with the Protocol on the Arbitral Tribunal.

(3) Where the dispute raises a question concerning the interpretation or application of a provision referred to in the second paragraph of Article 4 of this Agreement, and if its interpretation is relevant to the settlement of the dispute and necessary to enable the arbitral tribunal to give its decision, the arbitral tribunal shall refer the matter to the Court of Justice of the EU. The judgment of the Court of Justice of the EU shall be binding on the arbitral tribunal.

(4) Switzerland shall enjoy the same rights as the Member States and institutions of the EU and shall be subject to the same procedures before the Court of Justice of the EU, mutatis mutandis.

(5) Each party shall take all necessary measures to comply in good faith with the decision of the arbitral tribunal. The Party found by the arbitral tribunal not to have complied with this Agreement or a relevant agreement shall inform the other Party and the Sectoral Committee of the steps it has taken to comply with the decision of the arbitral tribunal.

(6) If the Party which has been found by the arbitral tribunal not to have complied with this Agreement or a relevant agreement does not, within a reasonable period of time (within the meaning of Article X of the Protocol on the Arbitral Tribunal), communicate the measures it has taken to comply with the decision of the arbitral tribunal, or if the other Party considers that the measures communicated are not in conformity with the decision of the arbitral tribunal, that other Party may take compensation measures up to and including the suspension of all or part of an agreement or agreements concerned in order to remedy any imbalance.

(7) The Party affected by the measures referred to in paragraph 5 may submit its observations to the Sectoral Committee for a ruling on the proportionality of these measures. If the Sectoral Committee has not reached a decision within six months of being seized, either Party may refer the question of the proportionality of the compensation measures to arbitration in accordance with the Protocol on the Arbitral Tribunal.

(8) Where the application of all or part of one or more of the agreements concerned is suspended, the rights and obligations already acquired by individuals and economic operators shall be preserved.

Article 4(2) Draft InstA, referred to in paragraph 3 above, reads:

Insofar as their application involves concepts of EU law, the provisions of this Agreement and the agreements concerned, and the legal acts of the EU to which reference is made therein, shall be interpreted and applied in accordance with the case law of the Court of Justice of the EU either before or after the signature of the agreement concerned.

3 THE MODEL CHOSEN FOR DISPUTE SETTLEMENT IN THE DRAFT INSTA

Brown has noted that over time the EU has developed a consistent approach as regards dispute settlement provisions in FTAs concluded by it, an approach that is now used in an essentially identical manner in different agreements: as a first step consultations, which may be followed by arbitration, which may lead to the possibility of suspension of concessions.[23]

To this, it must be added that where an agreement includes concepts or provisions that are derived from Union law, the model also includes a role for the ECJ, as reflected in Article 10(6) of the Draft InstA. This particular approach is not unique to that agreement: previously, it was used in a group of EU association agreements with Eastern European countries, and subsequently, it was employed, among others, in the context of Brexit.

In 2014, the EU concluded particularly ambitious association agreements with Ukraine,[24] Moldova[25] and Georgia.[26] These agreements contain notably provisions on a Deep and Comprehensive Free Trade Area (DCFTA) which include legally binding legislative or regulatory approximation commitments.[27] As noted in academic writing,[28] the dispute settlement mechanism that applies in this particular context departs from the traditional diplomatic approach, such as applicable in the non-DCFTA part (and also reflected in most of the EU-Swiss agreements to date), and instead provides for a 'quasi-judicial' mechanism.[29] Insofar, it is modelled upon the WTO dispute

23. Brown, 'WTO dispute settlement and dispute settlement in EU FTA Agreements', in Bourgeois, Bronckers and Quick (Eds), *WTO Dispute Settlement: Time to Take Stock* (P.I.E. Peter Lang, 2017), pp. 107-115.
24. Association Agreement between the European Union and its Member States, of the one part, and Ukraine, of the other part, O.J. 2014, L 161/3.
25. Association Agreement between the European Union and the European Atomic Energy Community and their Member States, of the one part, and the Republic of Moldova, of the other part, O.J. 2014, L 260/4.
26. Association Agreement between the European Union and the European Atomic Energy Community and their Member States, of the one part, and Georgia, of the other part, O.J. 2014, L 261/4.
27. On this issue *see* Van Elsuwege and Petrov (Eds), *Legislative Approximation and Application of EU Law in the Eastern Neighbourhood of the European Union: Towards a Common Regulatory Space?* (Routledge, 2014), and regarding Ukraine in particular Van der Loo, *The EU-Ukraine Association Agreement and Deep and Comprehensive Free Trade Area: A New Legal Instrument for EU Integration Without Membership* (Brill, 2016), at 247 et seq.
28. Notably Van der Loo, *supra* note 27, at 292 et seq.; further e.g., Rudyuk, 'How the trade disputes between EU and Ukraine will be settled under the EU Ukraine Association Agreement', 4 *Lex Portus* (2017), 37-50, at 40.
29. With respect to the Ukraine Agreement, there is a first application of this mechanism: Final Report of the Arbitration Panel on the 'Restrictions applied by Ukraine on exports of certain wood products to the European Union', 11 December 2020, available at trade.ec.europa.eu/doclib/docs/2020/december/tradoc_159181.pdf. For general information on this dispute *see* policy.trade.ec.europa.eu/enforcement-and-protection/dispute-settlement/bilateral-disputes/ukraine-wood-export-ban_en.

settlement mechanism, though with a special element where regulatory approximation to EU law is concerned: where the dispute concerns a question of interpretation of a concept or provisions of EU law as incorporated into the agreement, the arbitration tribunal is obliged to request the ECJ to give a ruling on the question, which will be binding (Article 322 Ukraine Agreement; Article 267 Georgia Agreement, Article 403 Moldova Agreement).

The same mechanism, often referred to as the 'Ukraine model', was subsequently included in the EU-Armenia Enhanced Partnership Agreement (Article 342),[30] in the Draft InstA EU-Switzerland[31] and in the EU-UK WA for matters arising after the transition period (Article 174).[32]

One particularly vocal critic, former president of the EFTA Court Carl Baudenbacher, has argued that the Ukraine model is not suitable for countries such as Switzerland or the United Kingdom (UK) as it was developed for 'ex-Soviet' States.[33] Senti in an article on the development from power-oriented to rule oriented-dispute settlement in FTAs points to the trade imbalance between the partners and the financial support of East-European States by the EU as reasons why the EU was able to insist on the new model and in particular on the role of the ECJ in that model.[34] According to Van der Loo, the reason why Ukraine accepted this far-reaching mechanism was its strong political will to be integrated into the EU.[35] Views differ with respect to the suitability of the ECJ as a court for such matters: while according to Baudenbacher, the ECJ by definition cannot be not neutral towards third States,[36] a study by Oesch and Speck on the ECJ case law in relation to the EU-Swiss relations has found otherwise.[37]

From an EU law point of view, it is the nature of the relevant agreements as agreements that incorporate EU law that has led to the development of the Ukraine

30. Comprehensive and enhanced Partnership Agreement between the European Union and the European Atomic Energy Community and their Member States, of the one part, and the Republic of Armenia, of the other part, O.J. 2018, L 23/4.
31. For example, Tobler, *supra* note 22, at 388 et seq. For a general comparison Ukraine Agreement - EEA - EU-Swiss bilateral agreements, *see* Schwok and Naiy, 'Le traité historique entre l'Union européenne et l'Ukraine: au-delà des controverses, la réalité du texte', 585 Rev, de l'UE (2015), 93-101.
32. Agreement on the withdrawal of the United Kingdom of Great Britain and Northern Ireland from the European Union and the European Atomic Energy Community, O.J. 2020, L 29/7.
33. In the English language e.g., Baudenbacher, 'Why did EU-Swiss negotiations on a Framework Agreement fail?' *Brussels Report*, 27 May 2021, brusselsreport.eu/2021/05/27/why-did-eu-swiss-negotiations-on-a-framework-agreement-fail/, as well as Baudenbacher, 'The UK's Brexit deal leaves it no better than ex-Soviet states on its own road to vassaldom', *The Telegraph*, 14 January 2019, telegraph.co.uk/politics/2019/01/14/mrs-mays-brexit-deal-leaves-uk-no-better-ex-soviet-states-road/.
34. Senti, 'Streitschlichtung und regionale Freihandelsabkommen. Von der 'power oriented' zur 'rule oriented' Schlichtung', 20 *Zeitschrift für Europarecht* (2018) 146-160, at 154.
35. Van der Loo, *supra* note 27, at 300.
36. Baudenbacher, 'The ECJ used to be a neutral court for the UK: It no longer is', *LSE Blog*, 9 March 2021, blogs.lse.ac.uk/brexit/2021/03/09/the-ecj-didnt-used-to-be-a-foreign-court-it-is-one-now /.
37. Oesch and Speck, 'Das geplante institutionelle Abkommen Schweiz-EU und der EuGH', in Epiney and Hehemann (Eds), *Schweizerisches Jahrbuch für Europarecht 2016/2017* (Schulthess/Stämpfli, 2017), pp. 257-273.

model, seen against the background of the autonomy of the Union legal order and its consequences for the institutional set-up of agreements with third States, as elaborated by the ECJ since its Opinions on the EEA Agreement.[38] Under this case law, the ECJ itself claims the final authority over the interpretation of EU law-derived provisions of external agreements. In the case of the Ukraine model, this happens through a mechanism that resembles the preliminary ruling according to Article 267 TFEU as far as interpretation questions are concerned.[39] As noted in academic writing, this mechanism aims to ensure a uniform interpretation and application of the Agreement's annexed EU legislation without jeopardizing the exclusive jurisdiction of the ECJ to (authoritatively) interpret EU law.[40] According to Van der Loo, the Ukraine model has found the right equilibrium.[41]

In relation to the EU-Swiss relations, it is interesting to note that outside the agreements that were meant to be covered by the InstA, two old agreements (which predate the Court's EEA Opinions) provide for arbitration models that give the arbitration panel a broader jurisdiction than is compatible with the Union's modern autonomy doctrine.[42] In contrast, one younger agreement limits the jurisdiction in line with that doctrine (predating the Ukraine model, this agreement is not based on that particular model).[43] Today, the former approach would no longer be acceptable under EU law.[44] Seen against the background of the history of dispute settlement mechanisms in external EU Agreements that incorporate EU law, the Ukraine model presents itself as the EU's modern standard in that respect. An approach where the EU institutions are directly in charge – i.e., a 'one pillar model' – is reportedly discussed in relation to an encompassing internal market association to be entered by the AMS States, and is due

38. Opinion 1/91, *EEA I*, ECLI:EU:C:1991:490; Opinion 1/92, *EEA II*, ECLI:EU:C:1992:189; more recently in particular Case C-284/16, *Slovak Republic v. Achmea*, ECLI:EU:C:2018:158. In academic writing instead of many Kochenov, 'EU law without the rule of law: Is the veneration of autonomy worth it?', 34 *Yearbook of European Law* (2015), 74-96; Nic Shuibhne, 'What is the autonomy of EU Law, and why does that matter?', 88 *Nordic Journal of International Law* (2019), 9-40; and Lenaerts, Gutiérrez-Fons and Adam, 'Exploring the autonomy of the European Union legal order', 81 *ZaöRV* (2021), 47-88. In the context of the Draft InstA, *see* Pirker, 'Zum Schiedsgericht im Institutionellen Abkommen', *Jusletter*, 3 June 2019, paras 22 et seq.
39. This term is expressly used by Van der Loo, Van Elsuwege and Petrov, 'The EU-Ukraine Association Agreement: Assessment of an Innovative Legal Instrument', *EUI Working Papers LAW* 2014/09, p. 20; subsequently also Van der Loo, *supra* note 27, at 297, as well as Van der Loo, 'The institutional framework of the Eastern Partnership Association Agreements and the Deep and Comprehensive Free Trade Areas', in Gstöhl and Phinnemore, *supra* note 18, pp. 102-120, at p. 114.
40. Instead of many: Emersen and Movchan, *Deepening EU-Ukrainian Relations: What, Why and How?*, 2nd ed. (Centre for European Policy Studies, 2018), p. 268.
41. Van der Loo, *supra* note 27, at 297.
42. Article 17 of the Cooperation Agreement between the European Atomic Energy Community and the Swiss Confederation in the field of controlled thermonuclear fusion and plasma physics, O.J. 1978, L 242/2; Article 38 of the Agreement between the European Economic Community and the Swiss Confederation on direct insurance other than life assurance, O.J. 1991, L 205/3.
43. Article 29(3) of the Agreement between the European Community and the Swiss Confederation on the simplification of inspections and formalities in respect of the carriage of goods and on customs security measures, O.J. 2009, L 199/24.
44. Tobler, 'Schiedsgerichte im bilateralen Recht?', *SZIER* (2012), 1-6, with further references.

to the very small size of these countries.[45] A special role for the Commission and the ECJ is also provided for in the EU-Swiss Agreement on Air Transport.[46]

Baudenbacher has argued that in practice there are now only two options left: namely the Ukraine model or the EEA model.[47] The latter was developed for the EEA with its special institutional pillar for the EEA EFTA States, including notably the EFTA Court which has jurisdiction over EEA law matters arising in the EEA EFTA States. Under the EEA Agreement,[48] judicial homogeneity is based on the obligation of the EFTA Court to follow ECJ case law within the framework of Article 6 EEA.[49] Baudenbacher himself has been a long-standing advocate of the EEA model for Switzerland, i.e., a model where Switzerland, for the purposes of a new institutional set-up, would be 'docking on' to the EFTA Court.[50] It should be noted, however, that under EEA law the EFTA Court is in charge only for the EEA EFTA variations of the infringement and preliminary ruling procedures, as well as for the settlement of disputes among EEA EFTA States (Articles 31, 34 and 32 ESA/Court Agreement,[51] respectively). In contrast, disputes between the EU and the EFTA sides that cannot be solved in the EEA Joint Committee can be taken to the ECJ, though *only* if both parties agree to this course of action (Article 111(3) EEA). From the perspective of the EEA EFTA States, this is a psychological plus as they cannot be forced to appear before the ECJ.[52]

The same mechanism can be found in Article 20 of the Agreement on the Establishment of a European Common Aviation Area (ECAA).[53] In these cases, therefore, a dispute can go directly to the ECJ, rather than indirectly through an arbitration panel as is the case in the Ukraine model. Finally, it should be noted that the EEA model predates the Ukraine model. It is open whether the EU at present would be willing to extend it to other States or arrangements. In the case of the Draft InstA, the Swiss Government was opposed to the EEA model; it rather preferred the Ukraine model.

45. Maiani, '"Unique, yet archetypal" Relations between the European Union and Andorra, Monaco and San Marino', in Gstöhl and Phinnemore, *supra* note 18, pp. 84-101, at p. 96.
46. *See* Case C-547/10 P *Switzerland v. Commission*, ECLI:EU:C:2013:139.
47. Baudenbacher, 'The choice Britain faces if it wants an EU trade deal: Either EFTA, or the Ukraine model', *LSE Blog*, 21 June 2020, blogs.lse.ac.uk/brexit/2020/07/21/the-choice-britain-faces-if-it-wants-an-eu-trade-deal-either-efta-or-the-ukraine-model/.
48. Agreement on the European Economic Area, O.J. 1994, L 1/3.
49. The EFTA Court does not always follow ECJ case law. An interesting example concerns return cases in the framework of the movement of persons; *see, e.g.*, Tobler, 'Free movement of persons in the EU v. in the EEA: Of effect-related homogeneity and a reversed *Polydor* principle', in Cambien, Kochenov and Muir (Eds), *European Citizenship under Stress: Social Justice, Brexit and Other Challenges* (Brill, 2020), pp. 482-507.
50. For example, Baudenbacher, *supra* note 33, at the end. On this option, *see* Joelle de Sépibus, 'Ein institutionelles Dach für die Beziehungen zwischen der Schweiz und der Europäischen Union – Wie weiter? Ein Überblick über Vor- und Nachteile unterschiedlicher Optionen', *Jusletter* 14 July 2014, paras 16 et seq.
51. Agreement between the EFTA States on the Establishment of a Surveillance Authority and a Court of Justice, O.J. 1994, L 344/1.
52. Tobler, 'Dispute resolution under the EEA Agreement', in: Baudenbacher (Ed.), *The Handbook of EEA Law* (Springer, 2015), pp. 195-207, at p. 199.
53. Agreement on the Establishment of a European Common Aviation Area (ECAA), O.J. 2006, L 285/3.

4 REMEDIES UNDER THE DRAFT INSTA

4.1 Introductory Remarks

Article 10(6) Draft InstA describes the remedies that can be taken by the aggrieved party where a panel ruling is not observed as 'compensation measures up to and including the suspension of all or part of an agreement or agreements concerned in order to remedy any imbalance.' The wording of the provision indicates that the essential aim of the remedies is to re-establish the balance in the legal relationship between the parties that have been disturbed by the breach of obligations by the defaulting party. Oesch notes that in practice remedies can also be used to exercise pressure in order to induce compliance.[54] According to Oesch, it is not entirely clear from the text whether the remedy must relate specifically to the agreement(s) where the breach occurred of whether it could also relate to other EU-Swiss agreements. Pirker concludes from the reference to 'agreement or agreements *concerned*' - in my opinion convincingly - that the possibility of cross-retaliation is not foreseen in Article 10(6) Draft InstA.[55] If so, this marks an important difference with the Brexit WA (*see* further below section 4.3.3).

Against this backdrop, it remains to be discussed what is meant both by 'suspension' and by 'compensation up to suspension'.

4.2 Suspension 'EEA Style' as the Most Extreme Remedy

According to Article 10(6) Draft InstA, suspension is the most extreme form of remedy in this particular framework. As Pirker observes, this excludes cancellation used specifically as a remedy (though independent of that, cancellation is always possible).[56]

On the point of suspension, the Draft InstA differs from the Ukraine model that informed the dispute settlement mechanism as such. For example, the EU-Ukraine Agreement contains specific rules on remedies in relation to regulatory approximation: Article 5(6) of Annex XVII provides that if no agreement can be reached on the inclusion of the new law, the EU may decide to suspend the granting of *internal market treatment* in the sector concerned (which is a WTO law element in the framework of the hybrid nature of the Agreement which combines a WTO law approach with an EU law approach).

Conversely, under Article 10(6) Draft InstA, suspension concerns *legal provisions* ('all or part of an agreement or agreements concerned'). While similar in terms of its effect, from a technical point of view the approach is different. In this respect, the Draft InstA follows the model of EEA law: The EEA Agreement provides for a dynamic system of updating the annexes of the Agreement in the light of new and relevant EU

54. For this and the following Oesch, *Schweiz – Europäische Union. Grundlagen, Bilaterale Abkommen, Autonomer Nachvollzug* (EIZ Publishing, 2020), para. 111.
55. Pirker, *supra* note 38, fn. 14.
56. *Ibid.*

law. Where a party in the EEA Joint Committee refuses to agree to an amendment, Article 102(4) EEA provides that in a first step the EEA Joint Committee shall examine all further possibilities to maintain the good functioning of this Agreement and take any decision necessary to this effect, including the possibility to take notice of the equivalence of legislation. In a second step, if the EEA Joint Committee has not taken a decision on an amendment of an Annex to the Agreement, Article 102(5) EEA provides that 'the affected part thereof ... is regarded as provisionally suspended, subject to a decision to the contrary by the EEA Joint Committee'. This last step has never been taken so far in the practice of EEA law; in fact, the parties to the EEA agree that it is not in the interest of the good functioning of the agreement and should be avoided.[57]

4.3 Lesser Remedies: WTO- or EU-Style? And What about Financial Sanctions?

4.3.1 Introductory Remarks

While the most extreme form of a remedy is explicitly named in Article 10(6) Draft InstA (namely suspension), it remains open to what 'compensation *up to* suspension' could entail. The explanations published by the Swiss Federal Government on the Draft InstA are silent on this point,[58] and there is particularly little academic writing on the matter. A rare exception, Oesch mentions the following potential examples that relate to different agreements that were meant to be covered by the InstA: the raising of customs duties on agricultural products, the refusal of free movement rights under the FMP Agreement (though acquired rights are protected), the refusal to recognize conformity assessments and the raising of the fees for heavy lorries crossing the Swiss Alps.[59]

EEA law does not provide for this type of remedy and neither does internal EU law. As will be seen in the next section, the examples given by Oesch reflect WTO-style remedies. In this context, the issue of financial sanctions – as suggested among others by Bronckers – will also be touched upon, followed by some remarks on the rather particular approach used in the context of the UK's withdrawal from the EU.

4.3.2 Remedies under WTO Law and Bronckers's Suggestion for Financial Sanctions

Van den Bossche and Zdouc note that the WTO Dispute Settlement Understanding (DSU) provides for one *final* remedy in the case of a breach of obligations, namely the withdrawal or modification of the WTO-inconsistent measure (Article 3.7 DSU), and

57. Fjeld Dystland, Böckmann Finstad and Sórebó, 'Art. 102 EEA', in Arnesen et al. (Eds), *Agreement on the European Economic Area: A Commentary* (Nomos, 2018), paras 41 et seq.
58. Erläuterungen zum Institutionellen Abkommen Schweiz-EU, 16 January 2019, https://www.eda.admin.ch/dam/europa/de/documents/abkommen/InstA-Erlaeuterungen_de.pdf.
59. Oesch, *supra* note 54, para. 111

for two *temporary* remedies pending a final solution of the problem, namely mutually acceptable compensation (Article 22.2 DSU) and retaliation (Articles 3 and 22.3 DSU).[60] The first of the latter category is rare. In the case of retaliation, the aggrieved State may request the dispute settlement body to authorize it to retaliate proportionately through the suspension of obligations in the same sector or, if that party considers that this is not practicable or effective, in other sectors under the same agreement or, again if that party considers that it is not practicable or effective and the circumstances are sufficiently serious, under another covered agreement (cross-retaliation).

This system is reflected in many external agreements of the EU, among them also the general dispute settlement rules in the DCFTA part of the Ukraine Agreement: according to Article 315(2), the complaining party is entitled to suspend obligations under the DCFTA to a level equivalent to the nullification or impairment caused by a Party failing to bring itself into compliance with the panel's findings. It seems logical that this is also the idea that underlies Article 10(6) Draft InstA for so far as remedies less than suspension are concerned (though, as argued convincingly by Pirker, minus the possibility of cross-retaliation).

Article 315(3) of the Ukraine Agreement specifically mentions increases in tariff rates. Indeed, the raising or imposition of customs duty appears to be the most typical retaliation measure under WTO law. However, depending on the part of WTO law at issue, other measures are also conceivable, e.g., the suspension of obligations relative to licensing requirements on imports.[61] But could such measures also include fines imposed by the aggrieved party on the defaulting party, even where they are not specifically mentioned? Obviously, retaliation measures have financial implications but they must be distinguished from financial sanctions such as the imposition of fines in the form of a lump sum and of penalty payments in the EU infringement procedure (Article 260(2) and (3) TFEU). It is submitted that there are a number of differences:

- First, the EU law financial sanctions are imposed not by another Member State, as are retaliation measures under WTO law, but rather by the Court of Justice.
- Second, the money to be paid by the defaulting Member State goes to the EU,[62] rather than benefitting the aggrieved State, as is the case with customs duties under WTO law (at least in theory - it has been noted in academic writing, including that of Bronckers, that in practice such retaliation is not always feasible).[63]

60. Van den Bossche and Zdouc, *The Law and Policy of the World Trade Organization. Text, Cases and Materials*, 4th ed. (CUP, 2017), p. 199.
61. *See* www.wto.org/english/res_e/publications_e/ai17_e/dsu_art22_jur.pdf, pp. 8 and 10 et seq.
62. For example, Case C-70/06, *Commission v. Portugal*, ECLI:EU:C:2008:3, operative part of the judgment ('Orders the Portuguese Republic to pay to the Commission of the European Communities, into the account 'European Community own resources', a penalty payment ...'). *See also* AG Jääskinen in his Opinion in Case C-292/11, P *Commission v. Portugal*, ECLI: EU:C:2013:321, paras 67 et seq. - Thank you to my colleague from Leiden University, Armin Cuyvers, for helping me find this information!
63. Van den Bossche and Zdouc, *supra* note 60, pp. 206 et seq., note that in particular for developing countries, applying retaliation measures is often not a genuine option as their own economy will also suffer; *see also* the writing of Bronckers and colleagues listed in *infra* notes 67 and 68.

- Third, based on the ECJ case law, the two types of financial sanctions mentioned in Article 260 TFEU can be imposed simultaneously due to their different aims: while a lump sum is intended to punish the Member State for its breach of EU law, a penalty payment is intended to induce the Member State to comply with the Court's judgment.[64] In contrast, the nature of WTO retaliation measures is never punitive.[65] The WTO itself notes that there is some debate on 'whether the purpose of the suspension of obligations is to enforce recommendations and rulings, or merely to rebalance reciprocal trade benefits (at a new and lower level). Irrespective of the answer, it is clear that the suspension of obligations has the effect of rebalancing mutual trade benefits. It is also clear that the complainants who suspend obligations often do so with the intention of inducing compliance.'[66]

In academic writing, those who have discussed the introduction of new types of remedies in order to make the WTO system more effective also include Bronckers, together with colleagues van den Broek[67] and Baetens.[68] Bronckers and Baetens have compared the WTO remedies to the EU law system with its sophisticated combination of public and private enforcement elements. In the most recent version of their argument, they expressly mention both financial sanctions under Article 260 TFEU and Member State liability. With their suggestion for a new type of financial remedy under WTO law, they essentially follow the latter path by advocating the introduction of monetary damages to be paid by the defaulting WTO State to the aggrieved WTO State in order to repair the injury caused by the illegal trade measure.

4.3.3 The Brexit WA: A Combination of EU-Style Financial Sanctions and EEA-Style Suspension

While financial sanctions EU-style are as of yet missing in WTO law, they can be found - mutatis mutandis - in the dispute settlement procedure under the UK WA. Interestingly, here such measures are combined with suspension EEA-style. Article 178(1) and (2) WA provide:[69]

---

64. Case law beginning with Case C-304/02, *Commission v. France*, ECLI:EU:C:2005:444.
65. Thus, the Dispute Settlement Body in the case WT/DS27/ARB, *EC – Bananas III (US) (Article 22.6 – EC)* (1999), para. 6.3. *See* further www.wto.org/english/res_e/publications_e/ai17_e/dsu_art22_jur.pdf, p. 5.
66. *See* www.wto.org/english/tratop_e/dispu_e/disp_settlement_cbt_e/c6s10p1_e.htm. In academic writing, *see, e.g.*, Spamann, 'The myth of "rebalancing" retaliation in WTO dispute settlement practice', 9 *Journal of International Economic Law* 2006, 31-79.
67. Bronckers and van den Broek, 'Financial compensation in the WTO: Improving the remedies of WTO dispute settlement', 8 *Journal of International Economic Law* (2005), 101-126.
68. Bronckers and Baetens, 'Reconsidering financial remedies in WTO dispute settlement', 16 *Journal of International Economic Law* (2013), 281-311; as well as Bronckers and Baetens, 'Financial Payments as a Remedy in WTO Dispute Settlement Proceedings: An Update', in Bourgeois, Bronckers and Quick, *supra* note 23, pp. 67-98.
69. *See also* House of Commons, 'The UK-EU Withdrawal Agreement: dispute settlement and EU powers', Briefing Paper No. 9016, https://commonslibrary.parliament.uk/research-briefings/cbp-9016/, p. 5.

> (1) If the arbitration panel rules in accordance with Article 177(2) that the respondent has failed to comply with the arbitration panel ruling referred to in Article 173, at the request of the complainant it may impose a lump sum or penalty payment to be paid to the complainant. In determining the lump sum or penalty payment, the arbitration panel shall take into account the seriousness of the non-compliance and underlying breach of obligation, the duration of the non-compliance and underlying breach of obligation.
>
> (2) If, 1 month after the arbitration panel ruling referred to in paragraph 1, the respondent has failed to pay any lump sum or penalty payment imposed on it, or if, 6 months after the arbitration panel ruling referred to in Article 177(2), the respondent persists in not complying with the arbitration panel ruling referred to in Article 173, the complainant shall be entitled, upon notification to the respondent, to suspend obligations arising from:
> (a) any provision of this Agreement other than those contained in Part Two; or
> (b) parts of any other agreement between the Union and the UK under the conditions set out in that agreement.
>
> The notification shall specify the provisions which the complainant intends to suspend. Before deciding to suspend parts of an agreement referred to in point (b) the complainant shall first consider whether the suspension of the provision of this Agreement in accordance with point (a) would be an appropriate response to the breach. Any suspension shall be proportionate to the breach of obligation concerned, taking into account the gravity of the breach and the rights in question and, where the suspension is based on the fact that the respondent persists in not complying with the arbitration panel ruling referred to in Article 173, whether a penalty payment has been imposed on the respondent and has been paid or is still being paid by the latter. ...

Conversely, the remedies provided for in the dispute settlement mechanism in the EU-UK Trade and Cooperation Agreement (TCA)[70] do not include financial sanctions but are limited to the traditional WTO approach of retaliation by suspending obligations (Article 749 TCA). According to Peers,[71] this difference means that retaliation can occur more quickly under the TCA than under the WA, i.e., there is an advantage in terms of time.[72]

When the Commission in March 2021 acted in response to a perceived failure of the UK to comply with obligations under the WA regarding checks on goods traded from Great Britain into Northern Ireland,[73] it decided to pursue a twofold avenue, namely infringement proceedings as well as the dispute settlement procedure under

70. Trade and Cooperation Agreement between the European Union and the European Atomic Energy Community, of the one part, and the United Kingdom of Great Britain and Northern Ireland, of the other part, O.J. 2021, L 149/10.
71. Peers, 'Analysis 4 of the Brexit deal: Dispute settlement and the EU/UK Trade and Cooperation Agreement', *EU Law Analysis*, 8 January 2021, eulawanalysis.blogspot.com/2021/01/analysis-4-of-brexit-deal-dispute.html.
72. In the particular context of labour, social, environmental and climate protection, there is the possibility of far-reaching 'rebalancing measures' (Article 411 TCA), considered by Bronckers and Gruni, *supra* note 3 (2021) a fundamental break with the EU's traditional, softer approach to handling violations of sustainability obligations by its trading partners.
73. For the facts, *see* the letter from Vice-President Šefčovič to Lord Frost of 15 March 2021; ec.europa.eu/info/publications/letter-vice-president-maros-sefcovic-david-frost-15-march-2021_en.

the WA.[74] Lock has argued that the combination in the latter of financial sanctions and the suspension of parts of the WA under Article 178(2) makes the dispute settlement procedure stronger than the infringement procedure in the particular context of Brexit due to the possibility of cross-retaliation, i.e., there is an advantage in terms of actual enforcement:

> While it mirrors Article 260 TFEU in first relying on penalty payments or lump sum payments, it goes a crucial step further if these are not made. It allows for suspension of parts of the WA or – crucially – 'parts of any other agreement between the Union and the United Kingdom under the conditions set out in that agreement'. This is a thinly veiled reference to the agreement on the future relationship between the EU and the UK, the TCA, which itself contains a clause reflecting this. ... says that where 'a Party persists in not complying with a ruling of an arbitration panel established under an earlier agreement concluded between the Parties, the other Party may suspend obligations under the covered provisions ...'. The covered provisions ... are all provisions of the TCA with a few exceptions. Notably, it includes all provisions on trade in goods with only minor exceptions. This would for instance allow the EU to suspend tariff free trade in certain goods, should the UK not comply with the ruling of an arbitration panel in this case.[75]

5 CONCLUSION

The above comparative discussion can be summarized as follows. First, dispute settlement under the Draft InstA follows the Ukraine model, which adds to the WTO-style mechanism the twist of a preliminary ruling-type of role of the ECJ. This is different from the EEA model, which predates the Ukraine model. Second, in terms of remedies in cases where a ruling of the arbitration panel is not respected, the Draft InstA combines different approaches, namely EEA-style suspension of (part of) the bilateral law in question, on the one hand, and WTO-style retaliation, on the other hand, though in the latter context arguably without the possibility of cross-retaliation.

Article 10(6) Draft InstA does not mention financial sanctions. It is submitted that against the background of the above discussion, it cannot be interpreted as including such sanctions. Indeed, it may be argued that so far, financial sanctions EU-style such as fines in the shape of a lump sum as well as penalty payments are linked to EU Membership – be it directly (Article 260 TFEU) or indirectly as in the case of Brexit, in view of certain post-membership obligations (Article 178 WA). In that context, it is telling that there are no financial sanctions in the EEA EFTA variation of the infringement procedure that applies to the EEA EFTA States (Article 108 EEA, Article 31 ESA/Court Agreement). Arguably, the nature of remedies will not change if and when EU-Swiss talks about a new institutional framework will resume.

74. European Commission, press release, 15 March 2021, Withdrawal Agreement: Commission sends letter of formal notice to the United Kingdom for breach of its obligations under the Protocol on Ireland and Northern Ireland, ec.europa.eu/commission/presscorner/detail/en/ip_21_1132.
75. Lock, 'A tricky move: EU legal action and the Northern Ireland Protocol', *Verfassungsblog*, 19 March 2021, verfassungsblog.de/a-tricky-move/.

CHAPTER 14

Is There an EFTA Legal Culture?

Carl Baudenbacher

European Free Trade Association's (One of EFTA) task is to conclude and maintain free trade agreements (FTAs) with countries outside the European Union (EU). Under the 1994 European Economic Area (EEA) Agreement, the EFTA Court distinguished itself early on with liberal case law, e.g., on trade in fortified foodstuffs, the international exhaustion of trademark rights or the repackaging of pharmaceuticals. Competition-friendly rulings were rendered on the applicability of competition law to collective agreements and industrial action, the scope of judicial review of fining decisions or the right of audience of in-house counsel. In internet and life insurance law, the Court relied on a liberal conception of man and a liberal contract model, and in landmark cases on financial market law and procurement law, it emphasized the principle of liability and the need to avoid moral hazard. Overall, free trade orientation is the main feature of EFTA's culture. However, since 2018, case law has tended to favour governments. National courts have reacted by reducing the number of references. The European Court of Justice has stopped the once flourishing judicial dialogue with the EFTA Court.

1 INTRODUCTION

Legal culture is an iridescent term. It often refers to 'living law' or, in the language of legal realism, 'law in action'. Sometimes, however, the notion is also related to legal families or legal traditions. One speaks of the culture of civil law and common law, of the German or the French legal circle etc. In the sociology of law, legal culture is understood as the values, ideas and attitudes that a society has with regard to the law.[1] At the European level, common European legal culture and European legal culture must be distinguished. Common European law refers to 'the common body of legal norms and legal principles in the member states of the EU, the EEA and other European states such as Switzerland'.[2]

Such norms can be found in all areas of the law: constitutional law, private law, administrative law and criminal law. As far as European law is concerned, the focus is usually on the EU's own legal culture. The dynamic character of EU law, its sector-specific structure and its market-based legitimacy are said to be style-forming.[3] Of course, not only the fact that the EU has the competence to legislate plays a role but also the existence of a supranational supervisory authority, the European Commission, and a supranational European Court of Justice (ECJ).

In the present contribution, the European concept of legal culture is, on the one hand, understood as a concept of economic law, including the coordination mechanism and image of man, on which the applicable law is based. On the other hand, the question of whether there is a European legal culture is asked with regard to the European Free Trade Association (EFTA). This article is dedicated to Marco Bronckers, a grandee of European and international economic law, both as a practitioner and as a scholar, and a dear friend. He has not only mastered World Trade Organization (WTO) law like no other but is also at home in EU law. And he has always followed closely what is happening in EFTA and the European Economic Area (EEA).

2 EFTA IN A NUTSHELL

2.1 Prehistory and Establishment

On 23 July 1952, the Treaty establishing the European Coal and Steel Community (ECSC), concluded by France, Germany, Italy and the three Benelux countries Belgium, the Netherlands and Luxembourg, entered into force. The six subsequently worked towards the creation of the European Economic Community (EEC), which would establish a customs union based on common supranational institutions. A customs union is a trading bloc consisting of a free trade area internally with a common external tariff and a common external trade policy. From 1956 onwards, the United Kingdom (UK), together with Switzerland, tried to prevent a division of Western Europe by promoting the idea of creating a large free trade area within the Organization for European Economic Cooperation (OEEC). However, the negotiations failed due to French resistance.[4] In 1956, during the Suez Crisis, which was to end badly for both countries, French Prime Minister Guy Mollet proposed to the UK the formation of a

1. Michaels, 'Rechtskultur', hwb-eup2009.mpipriv.de/index.php/Rechtskultur (last visited January 2022).
2. Laura M. Baudenbacher, *Vom gemeineuropäischen zum europäischen Rechtsmissbrauchsverbot* (Nomos, 2016), p. 21 (tr. CB).
3. Michaels, *supra* note 1.
4. *See* Baudenbacher, 'Swiss economic law facing the challenges of international and European law', 131 *Zeitschrift für Schweizerisches Recht* (2012), 419 et seq., at 522 et seq.

union called 'Frangleterre'. British Prime Minister Anthony Eden rejected this.[5] A year later, on 5 March 1957, the six Member States of the ECSC concluded the Treaties of Rome, the Treaty establishing the EEC and the Treaty establishing the European Atomic Energy Community (EURATOM). The two treaties entered into force on 1 January 1958.

EFTA was established in Stockholm on 4 January 1960 under British leadership as a counter-model to the EEC. Besides the UK, the founding members were the Scandinavian States of Denmark, Norway and Sweden, the Alpine republics of Austria and Switzerland, and Portugal. The UK, Denmark, Norway and Portugal were North Atlantic Treaty Organization (NATO) States, Austria, Sweden and Switzerland were neutral.

EFTA's aims were much more modest than those of the EEC. The EEC, based on supranational structures including common supervision and a common court of justice, aimed to create a common market, which was seen as a means to the political goal of unifying Europe. EFTA was (and still is) a free trade area which abolished customs duties on industrial products and part of the processed agricultural products within it. However, each EFTA State retained its foreign trade sovereignty and therefore has its own customs regime vis-à-vis third countries. The Free Trade Association has no legislative competence, there is no common surveillance and no common court. The sovereignty of the Member States is therefore protected to a large extent.[6]

2.2 Chequered History

EFTA's membership has changed frequently. Finland became an associate EFTA State in 1961 and a full member in 1986. Iceland joined on 1 March 1970. Denmark and the UK left EFTA on 31 December 1972 to join the EEC. Portugal did so on 31 December 1985. Liechtenstein became an EFTA member on 22 May 1991. Before that, the country had been included in EFTA indirectly through a customs union with Switzerland. A fundamental realignment became necessary after 1995, when the association was reduced to four Member States as a result of the accession of Finland, Austria and Sweden to the EU. Three of them, Iceland, Liechtenstein and Norway, were (and are) linked to the European Union (EU) through the multilateral EEA Agreement and participate fully in the Single Market.[7] The fourth EFTA State, Switzerland, has concluded numerous sectoral bilateral agreements with the EU that give its industry partial privileged access to the Single Market. According to the conclusions of the EU Council of 19 February 2019, Switzerland has not only entered into a bilateral relationship through its participation in significant parts of the EU's internal market

5. lemonde.fr/idees/article/2007/01/17/frangleterre-par-robert-sole_856464_3232.html (last visited January 2022).
6. Baudenbacher, *supra* note 4, at 523.
7. efta.int/eea/eea-agreement (last visited January 2022).

and policies, but participates in a 'common economic area'.[8] This holds true for industry. However, other sectors, especially banks and insurance companies, do not have this access.

A new EFTA Convention was signed in Vaduz on 21 June 2001 and entered into force on 1 June 2002. The main innovation was the integration of rules and principles of the EEA and the bilateral agreements between the EU and Switzerland into the EFTA Convention.[9]

EFTA maintains a worldwide system of bilateral free trade agreements (FTAs). In many cases, it has been able to conclude such treaties before the EU. In certain cases, where the four EFTA States Switzerland, Norway, Iceland and Liechtenstein had different interests, Switzerland entered into such agreements outside EFTA. The most important examples are the FTAs with Japan and with China.

As far as dispute settlement is concerned, Article 31 of the original EFTA Convention only provided for a general consultation and complaint procedure before the EFTA Council. Only six issues were submitted to the Council under this procedure. According to Article 47 of the Vaduz Convention, the EFTA Council, in which the Member States are represented by ministers or officials, has the task of seeking an amicable solution. If the matter cannot be settled, it may be referred to a tripartite arbitration tribunal. If the losing EFTA State does not implement the award of the arbitral tribunal, compensatory measures may be taken. Private individuals and companies do not have access to dispute resolution. There are no known cases in which arbitration proceedings have been initiated.

3 EFTA STATES' FTAs WITH THE EEC

3.1 Conclusion

After the UK's accession to the EEC in 1973, EFTA was increasingly drawn into the EEC's wake. Along with the UK and Denmark, non-aligned Ireland also joined the EU. The remaining EFTA States each concluded bilateral FTAs with the EEA, which mainly related to industrial products. This created a large free trade area in Western Europe. The content of the various FTAs was largely based on EEC law. There were no supranational bodies. In the EEC, the national courts of the Member States and the ECJ were responsible for the interpretation, in the EFTA States, the respective national courts. Conflicts were resolved by joint committees. Today, only the EEC-Switzerland agreement has kept its full relevance.[10]

8. 'Council conclusions on EU relations with the Swiss Confederation', Council Press Release 116/19 of 19 February 2019, consilium.europa.eu/en/press/press-releases/2019/02/19/council-conclusions-on-eu-relations-with-the-swiss-confederation/pdf (last visited January 2022).
9. efta.int/Legal-Text/EFTA-Convention-1152 (last visited January 2022).
10. Agreement between the European Economic Community and the Swiss Confederation, O.J. 1972, L 300/189; on the relevance of the Free Trade Agreement for EEA/EFTA States *see* Case E-2/03, *Ákæruvaldið v. Ásgeirsson and others*, judgment of 12 December 2003.

3.2 Case Law

In case law, two basic questions played a preeminent role: whether provisions of the FTAs were capable of direct application and whether FTA law, which was identical in content to EEC law, was to be interpreted in the same way as the latter. Six rulings were (and still are) of particular importance in this context: In two landmark cases, *Stanley Adams* (1978) and *Omo* (1979), the Swiss Federal Supreme Court refused to allow private parties in Switzerland to invoke the competition and free movement of goods rules of the FTA.[11] In the 1979 *Austro-Mechana* case, the Austrian Supreme Court in essence took the same stand as the Swiss Federal Supreme Court in *Omo* but was much more cautious in its reasoning.[12]

The misguided rulings of the Swiss Federal Supreme Court gave rise to far-reaching reactions by the ECJ in the *Kupferberg* and *Polydor* judgments, both on the EEC-Portugal FTA. In its *Kupferberg* decision, the ECJ held that private individuals in the EEC could very well rely on provisions of the EEC-Portugal FTA.[13] This obviously also applied to the other FTA's concluded by the Community. The Swiss Federal Supreme Court looked bad after this. In the *Polydor* case, however, which also concerned the EEC-Portugal FTA, the ECJ ruled that provisions in FTAs which were identical in content to those of Community law, but had a different context, might have to be interpreted differently.[14] This too was a response to the narrow approach of the Swiss Federal Court in *Omo*.

4 EEA AGREEMENT

4.1 General

The multilateral EEA Agreement, which entered into force on 1 January 1994, binds the three EFTA States, Iceland, Liechtenstein and Norway to the EU Single Market. Originally, the treaty was intended for all seven States that were part of EFTA at the time, but Switzerland opted out after a negative referendum on 6 December 1992 and Finland, Austria and Sweden joined the EU on 1 January 1995 after belonging to the EEA for one year on the EFTA side. Liechtenstein became an EEA Contracting Party on the EFTA side on 1 May 1995.

---

11. Bundesgericht (Federal Supreme Court, Switzerland), *Adams v. Staatsanwaltschaft des Kantons Basel-Stadt*, judgment of 3 May 1978, 104 IV 175; Bundesgericht, *Bosshard Partners Intertrading AG v. Sunlight AG*, judgment of 25 January 1979, 105 II 49.
12. OGH (Supreme Court, Austria), judgment of 10 July 1979, 4Ob302/79, ECLI:AT:OGH0002:1979:0040OB00302.79.0710.000.
13. Case 104/81, *Hauptzollamt Mainz v. C.A. Kupferberg & Cie KG a.A.*, ECLI:EU:C:1982:362.
14. Case 270/80, *Polydor Limited and RSO Records Inc. v. Harlequin Records Shops Limited and Simons Records Limited*, ECLI:EU:C:1982:43; *see* Leigh and Bronckers, 'Transposing the interpretation of EEC treaty concepts to agreements between the EEC and the third countries: Exhaustion of industrial and intellectual property rights', 76 *American Journal of International Law* (1982), 857-862, at 858; Baldi, 'Zur Rechtsnatur des Freihandelsabkommens Schweiz/EWG', 36 *Wirtschaft und Recht* (1984), 83-103.

The EEA Agreement is based on a two-pillar model with an EU and an EFTA pillar. The substantive law originates in the EU pillar. The EEA/EFTA States have a co-determination right in its creation. The law in both pillars is, therefore, largely identical in substance. Two features are particularly important: the EU's common policy on foreign trade is not part of EEA law. The EEA/EFTA States can therefore conclude FTAs – as stated either together with Switzerland in the framework of EFTA or individually – as they see fit. And the EEA/EFTA States are not subject to monitoring by the Commission and judicial control by the ECJ. They have their own watchdog, the EFTA Surveillance Authority (ESA), and their own EFTA Court. The EFTA Court is in principle required to follow the relevant case law of the ECJ in the interest of homogeneity. But this homogeneity requirement is not a one-way street. First, in many cases, the EFTA Court has to answer novel legal questions that have not yet arisen before the ECJ (so-called going first constellation). It then has the 'first mover advantage'. Second, the EFTA Court has sometimes gone its own way precisely where EFTA culture was in question. And third, the ECJ has followed the EFTA Court in many cases.[15] In 2014 the then ECJ President Skouris described the concept of homogeneity in his contribution to the *Festschrift* marking the EFTA Court's 20th anniversary. He declared:

> The long lasting dialogue between the EFTA Court and the ECJ has allowed the flow of information in both directions. 'Ignoring EFTA Court precedents would simply be incompatible with the overriding objective of the EEA Agreement which is homogeneity.' The symbiotic nature of the relationship has contributed to the successful development of the EEA Single Market. Both courts stand as examples for each other thus depicting mutual respect, strengthening the rules of homogeneity and representing a high level of appreciation. Cooperation between the two was built on strong foundations which have stood the test of time.[16]

Homogeneity had thus developed into a process-oriented concept. My former Head of Cabinet at the EFTA Court, Philipp Speitler, now a judge in Germany, elaborated on this. He wrote in 2017:

> [I]n a dynamic EEA, homogeneity cannot demand the permanent identical interpretation of EEA law by both courts. If this were the case, this concept would reach its limits: it should not be overlooked that the courts never decide cases in parallel. Neither do they have to answer the same questions, nor do they have to decide the same cases at the same point in time. Both courts, however, have to take all the circumstances of the question or the case at hand into consideration; and invariably the circumstances differ. Furthermore, it is a necessity for both courts to be able to take account of developments in science, including economic theories, and changes in technology and society. The decisions about the interpretation of the EEA Agreement are often made after long intervals. So over the years the circumstances, and indeed how to interpret the provisions of the EEA Agreement, may change. Consequently, when the courts give different answers to similar

15. *See, e.g.*, Baudenbacher, *Judicial Independence: Memoirs of a European Judge* (Springer, 2019), Ch. 21.
16. Skouris, 'The role of the Court of Justice of the European Union in the development of the EEA Single Market. Advancement through collaboration between the EFTA Court and the CJEU', in *The EEA and the EFTA Court: Decentred Integration* (Hart Publishing, 2014), pp. 3-12, at 12.

questions about EEA law, these differences may by no means entail a breach of the principle of homogeneity.[17]

4.2 Free Trade

From the outset, EFTA and the EFTA States have been committed to the idea of free trade. The EFTA Court for its part has rendered landmark decisions in which this orientation was decisive and which have also influenced the case law of the ECJ. I want to mention three.

4.2.1 Nutritional Need and Precautionary Principle in Food Law

Kellogg's cornflakes were produced in Denmark, fortified with several vitamins and some iron. They were freely marketed and sold throughout Europe. However, the Norwegian health authorities prohibited their sale. ESA brought an infringement action on the grounds that this was an unlawful restriction on the free movement of goods. Norway, supported by the governments of Denmark (as intervener), France and the Netherlands, argued that according to a 1983 ECJ precedent[18] the marketing of fortified goods could be prohibited if there was no nutritional need for the fortification. Specifically, the Norwegian government argued that there was no nutritional need in its country because the population's diet contained sufficient iron. We, the state, the government representatives said, make sure they get the iron they need by giving them a piece of iron-fortified goat cheese –'brunost' – every morning at school until they are 15 years old, after which they have enough iron in their bodies for the rest of their lives. The EFTA Court rejected the nutritional need argument.[19]

Second, the Norwegian government invoked the precautionary principle, and the EFTA Court essentially accepted this. According to this maxim, a national government is entitled to take measures even if there is no definitive proof that a product is dangerous, as long as qualified scientists in the field share the same view. However, this approach presupposes that the government has carried out a comprehensive risk assessment. It cannot rely on purely hypothetical considerations and may only attempt to achieve zero risk in the rarest of cases. In addition, the government's actions must be transparent, proportionate and non-discriminatory, and the overall fortification policy must be coherent. Norway's policy to promote the fortification of products with iron by giving away iron-fortified cheese to all school children was inconsistent. The country had, moreover, allowed or mandated the fortification of other products with

17. Speitler, 'Judicial homogeneity as a fundamental principle of the EEA', in Baudenbacher (Ed.), *The Fundamental Principles of EEA Law: EEA-ities* (Springer, 2017), pp. 19-33, at 29.
18. Case C-174/82, *Criminal proceedings against Sandoz BV*, ECLI:EU:C:1983:213.
19. Case E-3/00, *EFTA Surveillance Authority v. Kingdom of Norway*, judgment of 5 April 2001; *see* Alemanno, 'The precautionary principle', in Baudenbacher (Ed.), *The Handbook of EEA Law* (Springer, 2015), pp. 839-851; Bronckers, 'Exceptions to liberal trade in foodstuffs: The precautionary approach and collective preferences', in Baudenbacher, Tresselt and Örlygsson (Eds), *The EFTA Court: Ten Years On* (Hart Publishing, 2005), 105-119.

vitamins. Thus, Norway lost the case, but could successfully invoke the precautionary principle in a future case if it complied with the said conditions.

The Commission had supported ESA's claim that a national ban on the marketing of foodstuffs could not be justified on the grounds of lack of nutritional need in the population. In the ECJ's *Danish Vitamins* case,[20] the facts were very similar to *Kellogg's*. The Commission buttressed its infringement action against Denmark with the argument that the EFTA Court's *Kellogg's* judgment ought to be followed because it was 'an element in the development of the law' which reflected the considerable changes in the methods used to determine health risks over the past 20 years. The ECJ referred to the EFTA Court's *Kellogg's* ruling six times and found in favour of the Commission.

4.2.2 International Exhaustion of Trade Mark Rights

The commitment to free trade also shaped the EFTA Court's *Maglite* ruling.[21] In this case, the Court found that under the Trade Mark Directive,[22] the EEA/EFTA States had retained the right to opt for the international exhaustion of trade mark rights. All three EEA/EFTA States had done so. Under the principle of international or worldwide exhaustion, a trade mark owner may not hinder the import of goods bearing the mark if they have been put on the market by the owner himself or by somebody else with his consent somewhere in the world. The Maglite flashlights had been imported into Norway by a non-authorized dealer from California. Since the EEA is a free trade area and not a customs union, it was clear that the flashlights could not be imported into the EU from Norway if the ECJ did not favour international exhaustion. The EFTA Court knew that the same question was pending before the ECJ in the *Silhouette* case. That case involved a parallel importer, who had purchased Silhouette spectacle frames in Bulgaria and marketed them in Austria.

The Governments of Liechtenstein and Norway as well as ESA argued that the EEA/EFTA States retained the power to opt for international exhaustion. The Governments of France, Germany and the UK and the Commission claimed that if individual Member States were allowed to determine freely whether holders of rights are able to object to imports from third countries, this could lead to a situation where the same products may be subject to parallel imports into one Member State, but not into another. The result would be internal disparities in the market. Therefore, the principle of free movement of goods had to be the same in all Member States and that principle had also to apply to the EEA.

The EFTA Court rejected the latter argumentation holding that unlike the European Community (EC) Treaty, the EEA Agreement has not established a customs union, but a free trade area. According to the rules of origin of the EEA Agreement, the

20. Case C-192/01, *Commission v. Denmark*, ECLI:EU:C:2003:492.
21. Case E-2/97, *Mag Instrument Inc. v. California Trading Company Norway (Exhaustion of trade mark rights)*, advisory opinion of 3 December 1997.
22. First Council Directive 89/104/EEC of 21 December 1988 to approximate the laws of the Member States relating to trade marks, O.J. 1989, L 40/1.

principle of free movement of goods applies only to goods originating in the EEA, while in the Community a product is in free circulation once it has been lawfully placed on the market in a Member State. Since the Maglite flashlights were manufactured in the United States (US) and imported into Norway, they were not subject to the principle of the free movement of goods within the EEA.

The EFTA Court mentioned that the Commission's first proposal for a Trade Mark Directive had provided for international exhaustion. However, this plan was defeated in the European Parliament. The amended proposal limited the exhaustion rule to goods that had been put on the market 'within the Community'. However, we also pointed to the fact that some Member States, both in the Community and in EFTA, either retained international exhaustion or left the question open for interpretation by the national courts. In substance, the EFTA Court pointed out that: (i) international exhaustion is in the interests of free trade and competition and thus in the interests of consumers; (ii) parallel imports from countries outside the EEA lead to a greater supply of goods bearing a trade mark on the market; and (iii) price levels of products will be lower than in a market where only importers authorized by the trade mark holder distribute their products. Furthermore, the principle of international exhaustion was said to be in line with the main function of a trade mark, which is to allow the consumer to identify with certainty the origin of the products. Finally, the EFTA Court stated that its interpretation of the Trade Mark Directive in the EEA context was also in line with the WTO Agreement on Trade-Related Aspects of Intellectual Property Rights (TRIPS), where the issue was left open for the Member States to regulate.

In his opinion, in *Silhouette* of 29 January 1998, Advocate General Jacobs advised the ECJ to rule that in the Community international exhaustion was no longer possible.[23] He cited the above-mentioned passages from *Maglite verbatim* and distinguished the two cases in the same way as the EFTA Court had done. Six months after *Maglite*, the ECJ held that the EU Member States were in fact prevented from opting for international exhaustion. It held that this was:

> the only interpretation which is fully capable of ensuring that the purpose of the Directive is achieved, namely to safeguard the functioning of the internal market. A situation in which some Member States could provide for international exhaustion while others provided for Community exhaustion only would inevitably give rise to barriers to the free movement of goods and the freedom to provide services.[24]

Maglite and *Silhouette* were intensely discussed in academic literature, and free traders from all over the world commended the EFTA Court on its stand. On 9 March 1998, i.e., between the delivery of the Opinion of AG Jacobs in *Silhouette* and the handing down of the judgment, the US Supreme Court had signalled its willingness to take a liberal

23. Case C-355/96, *Silhouette International Schmied v. Hartlauer Handelsgesellschaft*, Opinion of AG Jacobs, ECLI:EU:C:1998:33.
24. Case C-355/96, *Silhouette International Schmied v. Hartlauer Handelsgesellschaft*, ECLI: EU:C:1998:374, para. 27.

stand on the matter of international exhaustion in its judgment in the copyright law case *Quality King Distributors*.[25]

4.2.3 *Repackaging of Pharmaceuticals and Adding Own Design*

The parallel importer *Paranova* had repackaged pharmaceuticals and moved the colour stripes from the middle of the box to the edges. In its judgment, the EFTA Court rejected *Merck's* argument that the necessity test, as developed by the ECJ, also applied to the change of design and that there was no necessity for the parallel importer to add new design elements in order to gain market access. It held that once the right to repackage and to depict the original trade mark is established, and market access is thereby assured, the necessity test would no longer apply. The interests involved had to be balanced and the function of the parallel importer for the regulation of prices had to be taken into account.[26] We thereby followed a different approach than the Supreme Courts of Germany, Austria and Denmark. This prompted the England and Wales Court of Appeal to refer a fresh case to the ECJ and to ask, *inter alia*, the following question:

> [D]oes the first condition set out in Bristol-Myers Squibb ...., namely that it must be shown that it is necessary to repackage the product in order that effective market access is not hindered, apply merely to the fact of reboxing (as held by the Court of Justice of the European Free Trade Association in Case E-3/02 *Paranova v. Merck*) or does it also apply to the precise manner and style of the re-boxing carried out by the parallel importer, and if so how?

The English judge in charge of the case indicated that he was sympathetic to the EFTA Court's position. AG Sharpston and the ECJ agreed with the EFTA Court's approach and made ample reference to *Paranova v. Merck*.[27] The German Supreme Court for its part overruled its previous case law on the matter and based itself on our judgment in cases *STILNOX*, *Micardis* and *Lefax/Lefaxin* without making a request for a preliminary ruling to the ECJ.[28]

4.3 Competition Law[29]

Articles 53 and 54 EEA reproduce the cartel prohibition and the abuse prohibition of Articles 101 and 102 Treaty on the Functioning of the European Union (TFEU). Under Article 55 EEA, Articles 53 and 54 EEA are enforced by the Commission and ESA. According to the allocation of competences in Article 56 EEA, the Commission is responsible in most cases.

25. *Quality King Distributors v. L'anza Research Int'l, Inc.*, 523 U.S. 135 (1998).
26. Case E-3/02, *Paranova AS v. Merck and others*, judgment of 8 July 2003.
27. Case C-348/04, *Boehringer Ingelheim KG and Others v. Swingward Ltd and Dowelhurst Ltd*, Opinion of AG Sharpston, ECLI:EU:C:2006:235; judgment of the Court, ECLI:EU:C:2007:249.
28. *STILNOX*, I ZR 173/04 (2007); *Micardis*, I ZR 89/05 (2007); *Lefax/Lefaxin*, I ZR 30/05 (2008).
29. *See* Baudenbacher, 'EFTA Surveillance Authority (ESA) & Court', *Global Dictionary of Competition Law*, concurrences.com/en/dictionary/efta-surveillance-authority-esa-court (last visited January 2022).

4.3.1 *Collective Bargaining*

In C-67/96 *Albany*, the ECJ held that collective agreements aimed to improve the working conditions and thus were beyond the scope of European competition law. The limits of such immunity were not examined.[30] AG Jacobs had concluded that in virtually all legal systems, including US law, collective agreements were to some extent sheltered from competition law, but that such immunity was not unlimited.[31] The ECJ did not follow Jacobs' opinion, but the EFTA Court chose to base its *LO*[32] ruling on it. It held in paragraph 75 of the judgment that provisions of collective agreements prima facie fall outside the scope of Article 53 EEA. If, however, the national court finds that they do not, in fact, pursue the apparent objectives, 'they may, in light of the objectives actually pursued, fall within the scope of Article 53 EEA'.

In *Holship*, the EFTA Court in essence declared the dockworkers' priority right to load and unload vessels in Norwegian ports illegal because it was incompatible with EEA competition law and infringed the right of freedom of establishment. The Court pointed to the negative freedom of association and referenced the *Sørensen and Rasmussen* judgment of the ECtHR's Grand Chamber.[33] In *Katoen Natie Bulk* and *Middlegate Europe* which were referred by the Council of State and the Constitutional Court of Belgium, the ECJ's Grand Chamber found a closed shop system for Belgian dockworkers to be incompatible with EU law.[34] The Council of State had cited the EFTA Court's *Holship* ruling in its order for reference. The Norwegian Supreme Court followed the EFTA Court's *Holship* judgment and an application of the Norwegian unions to the European Court of Human Rights had no success.[35]

4.3.2 *Scope of Judicial Review*

In *Norway Post*, the EFTA Court upheld a decision by ESA that *Posten Norge AS* ('Norway Post') had abused its dominant position in the market for business-to-consumer parcel services with over-the-counter delivery in Norway by pursuing an exclusivity strategy with preferential treatment when establishing and maintaining its Post-in-Shop network. However, the fine imposed on Norway Post was reduced from EUR 12.89 million to EUR 11.112 million. With regard to the scope of judicial review,

---

30. Case C-67/96, *Albany International BV v. Stichting Bedrijfspensioenfonds Textielindustrie*, ECLI:EU:C:1999:430.
31. *Ibid.*, Opinion of AG Jacobs, ECLI:EU:C:1999:28.
32. Case E-8/00, *Landsorganisasjonen i Norge and Norsk Kommuneforbund v. Kommunenes Sentralforbund and others*, judgment of 22 March 2002.
33. Case E-14/15, *Holship Norge AS v. Norsk Transportarbeiderforbund*, judgment of 19 April 2016; ECtHR, *Sørensen and Rasmussen v. Denmark*, Appl. Nos 52562/99 and 52620/99, judgment of 11 January 2006.
34. Joined Cases C-407/19 and C-471/19, *Katoen Natie Bulk Terminals NV and General Services Antwerp NV v. Belgische Staat* and *Middlegate Europe NV v. Ministerraad*, ECLI:EU:C:2021:107.
35. ECtHR, *Norwegian Federation of Trade Unions (LO) and Norwegian Transport Workers' Union (NTF) v. Norway*, Appl. No. 45487/17, judgment of 10 September 2021; *see also* Ellingsen, 'Reconciling fundamental social rights and economic freedoms: The ECtHR's ruling in *LO and NTF v. Norway* (the *Holship* case)', 59 *Common Market Law Review* (2022), 583-604.

the EFTA Court referenced the ECtHR's *Menarini* judgment[36] and held in paragraph 100 that:

> Article 6(1) ECHR requires that subsequent control of a criminal sanction imposed by an administrative body must be undertaken by a judicial body that has full jurisdiction. Thus, the Court must be able to quash in all respects, on questions of fact and of law, the challenged decision.... Therefore, when imposing fines for infringement of the competition rules, ESA cannot be regarded to have any margin of discretion in the assessment of complex economic matters which goes beyond the leeway that necessarily flows from the limitations inherent in the system of legality review.[37]

In paragraph 101, the EFTA Court found that although it:

> may not replace ESA's assessment by its own and, accordingly, it does not affect the legality of ESA's assessment if the Court merely disagrees with the weighing of individual factors in a complex assessment of economic evidence, the Court must nonetheless be convinced that the conclusions drawn by ESA are supported by the facts.

The EFTA Court's approach to the review of fining decisions of competition authorities thus goes beyond a 'manifest error' test. Barbier de La Serre observed that '[in] abandoning the "margin of appreciation" standard in *Posten Norge* [the EFTA Court] made a very significant contribution to the improvement of the right to a fair trial'.[38] Other eminent competition lawyers such as Temple Lang, Forrester and Freeman concurred.[39] In the given context, it must be emphasized that Marco Bronckers wrote, together with Anne Vallery, a marvellous annotation of *Posten Norge* under the title 'The EFTA Court advances the debate on human rights and administrative competition law enforcement.'[40]

4.3.3 Right of Audience of In-House Counsel

In *Abelia*, the EFTA Court had to deal with the question of whether in-house attorneys may represent their own company. According to Article 17 of the Court's Statute, other parties than the EFTA States, ESA, the EU and the European Commission must be represented before the Court by a 'lawyer'. In *Prezes*, the ECJ had held that the parallel

36. ECtHR, *A. Menarini Diagnostics s.r.l. v. Italy*, Appl. No. 43509/08, judgment of 27 September 2011.
37. Case E-15/10, *Posten Norge AS v. EFTA Surveillance Authority*, judgment of 18 April 2012, para. 100.
38. Barbier de la Serre, 'A lesson on judicial review from the other European Court in Luxembourg', competitionlawblog.kluwercompetitionlaw.com/2012/04/27/a-lesson-on-judicial-review-from-the-other-european-court-in-luxembourg (last visited January 2022).
39. Temple Lang, 'Competition law: The Brussels perspective', in Baudenbacher (Ed.), *The Handbook of EEA Law* (Springer, 2016), pp. 523-545; Forrester, 'The style of the EFTA Court', in *The EEA and the EFTA Court: Decentred Integration* (Hart Publishing, 2014), pp. 21-42, at 35.
40. Bronckers and Vallery, 'E-15/10 Norway Post: The EFTA Court advances the debate on human rights and administrative competition law enforcement', European Law Review (2012), 105-113.

provision in its Statute precluded employed lawyers from acting on behalf of their employer. The ECJ found that:

> the concept of independence of lawyers is determined not only positively, that is by reference to professional ethical obligations, but also negatively, that is to say, by absence of an employment relationship.[41]

The EFTA Court decided, however, that whether an in-house attorney is sufficiently independent must be assessed on a case-by-case basis in light of the circumstances.[42] It held that:

> the requirement that a party be represented before the Court by an independent third party is not a requirement designed generally to exclude representation by employees of the principal or by those who are financially dependent upon it. The essence of the requirement imposed by EEA law is to prevent private parties from bringing actions in person without recourse to an appropriate intermediary. So far as legal persons are concerned, the requirement of representation by a third party thus seeks to ensure that they are represented by someone who is sufficiently detached from the represented legal person. Whether this is so has to be addressed by the Court on a case by case basis.[43]

In the matter at hand, one lawyer was the head of the Business Legislation Department of the Confederation of Norwegian Enterprise (NHO). Her independence was found not to be affected as the Court had not been provided with information demonstrating that the interests of NHO were largely the same as those of the applicant. The other lawyer was an employee of an independent law firm, which paid her salary, regardless of a contract between NHO and the law firm for the temporary provision of her services. She was also deemed to be sufficiently independent of the applicant. The applicant was thus found to be properly represented before the EFTA Court.

Denying the right of audience to an in-house attorney would amount to a simple restriction of competition and even – as former ECJ President *Skouris* wrote as early as 1975 when he was a university assistant in Germany – a discrimination.[44] One must also not overlook the fact that the exclusion of in-house attorneys from the right of audience was introduced in Germany in 1934 in light of the fact that a high proportion of them were Jews.[45] Finally, it should be noted that on 14 September 2010, the ECJ in *Akzo Nobel* also denied in-house attorneys the client-attorney privilege.[46] It would therefore be consequent for the EFTA Court to also apply the case-by-case test in this context in the future.

41. Case C-422/11 P, *Prezes and Republic of Poland v. Commission*, ECLI:EU:C:2012:553, para. 24.
42. Case E-8/13, *Abelia v. EFTA Surveillance Authority*, order of 29 August 2014.
43. *Ibid.*, para. 46.
44. Skouris, 'Die Diskriminierung des Syndikusanwalts (§ 46 BRAO) aus verfassungsrechtlicher Sicht', (1975) BB, 1230 et seq.
45. Baudenbacher and Speitler, 'Der Syndikus der Gegenwart – Interessensvertreter oder Anwalt des Rechts?', (2015) NJW, 1211-1515; Hellwig, 'Der Syndikusanwalt – Neue Denkansätze', (2015) *Anwaltsblatt*, 2-12.
46. Case C-550/07 P, *Akzo Nobel Chemicals Ltd and Akcros Chemicals Ltd v. European Commission*, ECLI:EU:C:2010:512.

In 2020, the ECJ's Grand Chamber in *Uniwersytet Wrocławski* held, without referencing the EFTA Court's *Abelia* ruling, that a lecturer who legally represents a university with which he or she is associated, is an independent legal counsel.[47]

4.3.4 *Private Plaintiff as 'Private Attorney General'*

The EFTA Court has developed extensive case law on access to documents and thus on the principle of transparency.[48] The most important judgment is *DB Schenker I*. There, the EFTA Court held that the only explicit restriction on disclosure of documents in EEA law is the obligation of professional secrecy under Article 122 EEA and Article 14(4) EFTA Surveillance and Court Agreement (SCA). The rules on access to documents are an embodiment of the principles of transparency and good administration, which reflect the democratic traditions of the EEA/EFTA States. Private enforcement of the EEA competition rules through damages actions in national courts should be encouraged, as it can make a significant contribution to maintaining effective competition in the EEA. By pursuing its private interests, a plaintiff simultaneously contributes to the protection of the public interest, which also benefits consumers.[49] This view was shared by Advocate General Kokott in her Opinions in Cases *Schenker und Co AG* and *KONE*.[50]

4.3.5 *Restriction of Competition by Object*

In *Ski Taxi*, two cab companies had submitted a joint bid in response to a tender by Oslo University Hospital. The Norwegian Competition Authority found a violation of the prohibition of cartels in the Norwegian Competition Act, which corresponds to Article 53 EEA, and imposed fines. The Supreme Court referred questions to the EFTA Court.

The EFTA Court considered that certain forms of coordination between undertakings affect competition to a sufficient extent that it is unnecessary to examine their effects. In order to determine the degree to which competition is affected, account must be taken of the content of the provisions of the agreement, its objectives and the economic and legal context in which it is placed. In determining this context, an account must also be taken of the nature of the goods or services concerned and the actual conditions for the functioning and structure of the market or markets in question. Although the intention of the parties is not a necessary factor in determining whether an agreement between undertakings is restrictive of competition, nothing

47. Case C-515/17 P, *Uniwersytet Wrocławski v. REA*, ECLI:EU:C:2020:73.
48. *See* Baudenbacher and Clifton, 'Opticks: The refractive index of transparency in EEA law', *Concurrences* No. 2 (2014), at 5 et seq.
49. Case E-14/11, *Schenker v. EFTA Surveillance Authority*, judgment of 21 December 2012.
50. Case C-681/11, *Bundeswettbewerbsbehörde and Bundeskartellanwalt v. Schenker & Co. AG and Others*, Opinion of AG Kokott, ECLI:EU:C:2013:126, para. 78; Case C-557/12, *Kone AG and Others v. ÖBB-Infrastruktur AG*, ECLI:EU:C:2014:45, footnote 36.

precludes competition authorities, national courts or the Court of Justice from taking this factor into account. This was in line with ECJ case law.

However, on one crucial point, the EFTA Court did not follow the reasoning of the ECJ, but relied on the opinion of Advocate General Wahl in *CB v. Commission*. In paragraph 61 of the judgment, we refer to his comments in paragraph 56 of his Opinion, according to which only conduct whose harmful nature is proven and easily identifiable in light of experience and economics is to be considered as a restriction of competition by an object whose harmful character is readily apparent in light of experience and economics.[51]

4.3.6 Guaranteeing Fair and Effective Competition

Under the Airport Slot Regulation 95/93 EEC, time slots for the take-off and landing of aeroplanes are allocated to airlines according to a system of 'grandfather rights'. If an air carrier is able to show that he operated the slots for at least 80% of the time during the scheduling period for which they have been allocated, he is entitled to the same series of slots in the subsequent equivalent scheduling period. This renders market entry for newcomers rather difficult. In practice, an incumbent airline could keep a slot forever. A dispute before the Reykjavík District Court concerned the interpretation of the regulation at Keflavík International Airport for the year 2014. On 22 September 2014, that court submitted a request for a preliminary ruling in *Wow Air*. The EFTA Court's President granted the accelerated procedure under Article 97a of the Court's Rules of Procedure on the basis of the economic sensitivity of the case. The potential effects of the judgment on slot allocations in the near future were deemed to be such as to constitute a matter of exceptional urgency. The order stated in that regard:

> To guarantee fair and effective competition is one of the most important goals of the EEA Agreement. Effective competition benefits both consumers and competitors and contributes to the common good. In the case at hand, Iceland's special geographic situation must be taken into account with Keflavík essentially being the only international airport in the country.[52]

I am not aware of any presidential order in the EU that granted the accelerated procedure based on this kind of reasoning. Judgment was rendered on 10 December 2014, within less than three months. The EFTA Court provided support to the independent coordinator who is competent for the initial allocation of the time slots, holding that:

> [i]n order for the system to be effective, the coordinator has to be independent from any vested interests and has to have the necessary financial resources to accomplish the tasks assigned to him by the Regulation. It must be ensured that

51. Case E-3/16, *Ski Taxi and others v. Norwegian Government*, judgment of 22 December 2016; Case C-67/13 P, *Groupement des cartes bancaires (CB) v. European Commission*, ECLI: EU:C:2014:1958.
52. Case E-18/14, *Wow air ehf v. Samkeppniseftirlitið and others*, order of the president of 30 September 2014, para. 7.

> neither the authorities of the EEA State concerned nor any other party can unduly influence the coordinator before, during and after the allocation process.[53]

This presupposes that there is:

> a clear separation of tasks between the coordinator, the coordination committee and the EEA State so as to avoid any conflict of interest at any time in the allocation and monitoring procedure. In other words, the coordinator must have the expertise and the integrity necessary to contribute to the objectivity, transparency and efficiency of time slot allocation.[54]

This was important because coordinators are often former employees of the big flagship carriers. Second, the EFTA Court ruled that the national competition authorities have the right to give direct instructions to the undertakings when it comes to transferring time slots after the initial slot allocation, if this is found to be required under national or EEA competition law.[55] Thereby the system of grandfather rights has, to a certain extent, been opened up to competition.

4.4 Image of Man

In *Inconsult*, the EFTA Court had to answer the novel legal question of whether a website could constitute a 'durable medium' within the meaning of the Insurance Mediation Directive 2002/92/EC and whether it was sufficient for an insurance company to make insurance contracts available only on its website without handing out a printed copy to customers. The concept of 'durable medium' is contained in a number of directives.

The EFTA Court held that a website can be a durable medium provided that several criteria are met: first, it must enable the customer to store the information in question. Second, it must allow the customer to keep the information accessible for as long as it is relevant for him/her to protect his interests vis-à-vis the insurance intermediary. Third, the website must allow the unchanged reproduction of the information stored. It is important that the information is stored in such a way that the insurance intermediary cannot unilaterally change it.[56]

In the case of sophisticated websites, the EFTA Court distinguished between those that serve as a portal for the provision of information on another instrument that can be classified as a durable medium and those that can themselves constitute a durable medium. The first type allows the user to access information, for example, in the form of an e-mail with an attachment, which he can copy and store on his own computer. For this method to constitute the transmission of information to the customer in a durable medium, the website must contain features that are reasonably likely to encourage the customer either to save the information on paper or to store it

53. Case E-18/14, *Wow air ehf v. Samkeppniseftirlitið and others*, judgment of 10 December 2014, para. 37.
54. *Ibid.*, para. 38.
55. *Ibid.*, para. 73.
56. Case E-4/09, *Inconsult Anstalt v. Financial Market Authority*, judgment of 27 January 2010.

on another durable medium. The second type contains a secure storage area for individual users, accessed by a user code and password. Provided that any possibility of alteration of the information by the insurance intermediary is excluded, this type of storage can be compared to the user's own hard drive. This type of sophisticated website meets the requirement of ensuring unaltered reproduction necessary for classification as a durable medium.

In *Content Services*,[57] the ECJ cited *Inconsult* in relation to the concept of 'durable medium', but concluded, in line with AG Mengozzi, that the consumer may remain entirely passive in the transmission of the information. Information on the seller's website that is merely accessible via a link sent to the consumer was said to neither be 'given' to nor 'received' by the consumer. *Paolo Mengozzi* stated in paragraph 33 of his Opinion that:

> even though clicking on a hyperlink is an entirely commonplace action, within the capability of any internet user, not all users are in a position to understand, when the contract is concluded, that they need to click on the link in order to be able, should the need arise, to protect their own rights better in the future.' To find otherwise 'would risk opening the gates to possible abuses'.[58]

It may be added that the German Supreme Court also referenced *Inconsult* in its *Holzhocker* judgment.[59] But it took a similar approach as the ECJ, holding that in light of EU law consumers must receive instruction concerning the right of withdrawal without needing to take any action themselves. In *BAWAG*,[60] the ECJ, following AG Bobek, moved in the direction of the EFTA Court's *Inconsult* judgment. Both AG Bobek and the ECJ cited *Inconsult*. In a judgment of 29 May 2018, the Austrian Supreme Court followed EFTA Court *Inconsult* to the letter.[61]

4.5 Model of Contract

4.5.1 Working Time Directive

In *Matja Kumba*, the EFTA Court was concerned with the interpretation of the Working Time Directive 2003/88/EC. The Norwegian non-profit foundation Fossumkollektivet offered treatment to young people with alcohol or drug problems. The therapists lived with the patients to create a family-like situation. The working day started at 7 am and ended at 11 pm. In addition to the time between 11 pm and 7 am, workers received two hours of rest each day. The workers slept in flats at the workplace. They were entitled to three months of paid leave every three years. During the period in question, a '3-7-4-7 rotation system' was applied; therapists worked three days, had seven days off

57. Case C-49/11, *Content Services Ltd v. Bundesarbeitskammer*, ECLI:EU:C:2012:419.
58. Case C-49/11, *Content Services Ltd v. Bundesarbeitskammer*, Opinion of AG Mengozzi, ECLI: EU:C:2012:126, para. 56.
59. BGH (Supreme Court, Germany), *Holzhocker*, judgment of 29 April 2010, I ZR 66/08 (2010).
60. Case C-375/15, *BAWAG PSK AG v. Verein für Konsumenteninformation*, ECLI:EU:C:2017:38.
61. OGH (Supreme Court, Austria), judgment of 29 May 2018, 4Ob58/18k, ECLI: AT:OGH0002:2018:0040OB00058.18K.0529.000.

and then worked four days followed by seven days off. The average working time was 56 hours per week.

The Working Time Directive 2003/88/EC required Member States to ensure that weekly working time including overtime did not exceed 48 hours. However, the Directive allowed Member States to set a maximum working time of more than 48 hours, provided that the general principles of the protection of the safety and health of workers were respected. There was greater scope for exceptions if the worker agreed. Exceptions to mandatory rest periods were also possible. Member States could lay down special rules for admission, treatment and/or care in hospitals or similar establishments. Norway had transposed the Directive for the professions concerned in such a way that the maximum working time was 9 hours out of 24 hours per day and 40 hours in 7 days. Exceptions were provided, but no more than 13 hours per day and no more than 48 hours per week were allowed. Other solutions were possible in special cases. According to a decree of the Ministry of Labour, the maximum weekly working time for assisted living was 48 hours, but the individual worker could commit in writing to a maximum working time of 60 hours. Workers living in the facility were allowed to work more than 60 hours. Workers could only be dismissed if there was an objective reason based on the circumstances of the company, the employer or the worker. Due to losses in 2009, 2011 and 2012, Fossumkollektivet Foundation decided to switch from a '3-7-4-7 rotation' to a '7-7 rotation'. Seven working days (i.e., 84 hours per week) were followed by seven rest days. This allowed for significant cost savings. The plaintiffs did not accept the proposed change in working hours. The employer issued a notice of dismissal, accompanied by an offer of re-employment on different terms.

The EFTA Court found that the '7-7 rotation' was compatible with the Directive in the circumstances, provided that a worker had made an express, voluntary and individual commitment to work 84 hours per week and that the general principles of the protection of workers' health and safety were respected. If these conditions were met, the parties could exercise their contractual freedom. The question also arose whether a worker could withdraw his consent to work more than 60 hours per week. The EFTA Court found that the Directive did not contain such a provision. The issue had, therefore, to be resolved under national law – within certain limits set by the Directive. A national law provision which did not allow a worker to withdraw his consent to work more than 60 hours a week in an establishment such as the one at issue – without giving reasons – was therefore considered to be compatible with the Directive, provided that the general principles of the protection of workers' health and safety were respected. The EFTA Court underlined the importance of a fair balance between the interests of workers and employers.

From an economic law perspective, another important question was whether dismissal and an offer of reinstatement on new terms and conditions constituted a discrimination – prohibited by the Directive – against the worker. As in German law, the EFTA Court distinguished between a dismissal due to urgent operational requirements and a dismissal without the existence of such reasons. Urgent operational needs exist if there are reasons that are completely independent of the employee's refusal to consent to the change. If this is the case, a dismissal does not constitute a disadvantage within the meaning of the Directive. It should be added that there was a third group involved in the case whose legitimate interest had to be taken into account, namely the patients.

The Commission and ESA had unsuccessfully argued that: (i) a working plan amounting to an average weekly working time of 84 hours in a cohabitant care arrangement offering treatment for young people with drug and/or alcohol problems was incompatible with the directive; and (ii) a provision of Norwegian law under which employees who do have housing in or attached to a cohabitant care institution might not be allowed to revoke their previous consent to a working time of more than 48 hours were incompatible with the directive and that a dismissal due to a failure to consent to a working time arrangement of more than 48 hours over a seven-day period always constitutes a detriment to the worker.

With this judgment, the EFTA Court upheld a fundamental principle of contract law: the sanctity of contracts. This means that an agreement that has duly been entered into is binding on the parties unless there is an exception recognized by law. The parties must honour their obligations by performing their contractual duties.

4.5.2 *Purchase of Second-Hand Life Assurance Policies*

The cases *Vienna Life and Swiss Life* concerned the question whether certain consumer protection rules of the Life Assurance Directive 2000/83/EC[62] should apply to the purchase of second-hand life assurance policies. The purchase of second-hand life assurance policies is a specific form of investment. The buyer has no apparent relation to the insured person(s), meaning he or she is not seeking the insurance aspect of the contracts. This kind of business is motivated by tax considerations and buyers speculate on the lives of people whose drinking and smoking habits they are not aware of. Both ESA and the Commission argued that certain EEA consumer protection rules applied in such a case. Since it found the business in question to be a tax motivated form of investment, the EFTA Court came to the opposite conclusion.[63] In such a situation, the classical liberal contractual model applies. Negotiating the terms of a contract between businesses must be left to the market forces. Since equal partners face each other, the thesis of the 'guarantee of fairness' (*Richtigkeitsgewähr*) of the contract put forward by Schmidt-Rimpler[64] comes to bear. From an economic perspective, contracts concluded between such partners are a tool for the optimal allocation of resources. Freedom of contract is essential to the operation of a market economy. In *Vienna Life* and *Swiss Life*, the EFTA Court has based itself on the same idea of man as in *Inconsult*. For the sake of completeness, it may be added that the image of man underlying the EFTA Court's case law is the one prevailing in the UK and in Switzerland. In both countries, courts base themselves on the assumption that human

62. Directive 2001/83/EC of the European Parliament and of the Council of 6 November 2001 on the Community code relating to medicinal products for human use, O.J. 2001, L 311/67.
63. Joined Cases E-15/15 and E-16/15, *Franz-Josef Hagedorn v. Vienna-Life Lebensversicherung AG* and *Rainer Armbruster v. Swiss Life (Liechtenstein) AG*, judgment of 10 May 2016.
64. Schmidt-Rimpler, 'Grundfragen einer Erneuerung des Vertragsrechts' 147 AcP (1949), 130-197.

beings are reasonable in the sense of 'normal'. They are not stupid or careless, nor are they overly cautious.[65]

4.6 Principle of Liability (Avoiding Moral Hazard)

4.6.1 Economic Function of Liability

Walter Eucken, one of the leading figures of the German ordoliberal school, has dealt with the maxim of liability in his ground-breaking book on principles of economic policy (*Grundsätze der Wirtschaftspolitik*), which was published in 1952, two years after his death.[66] According to Eucken, the fundamental principle of a competition economy is a workable price system. That means that measures such as state subsidies, the establishment of compulsory state monopolies, general price cuts, import bans, and the like are to be avoided. In addition, Eucken called for an active competition policy that aimed to establish a market form that is as close as possible to the ideal type of complete competition. Further constitutive and regulatory principles of a competition economy are, in Eucken's view, open markets, private property, freedom of contract, the principle of liability and the consistency of economic policy. Eucken attached great importance to the principle of liability. Only market players who can also be held liable for their actions will act responsibly.

4.6.2 Liability of a State in a Systemic Crisis

In October 2006 and May 2008 respectively, Landsbanki Íslands hf ('Landsbanki') launched branches in the UK and in the Netherlands, which provided online savings accounts under the brand name Icesave. The Icesave programme offered market-beating interest rates of 6%. It attracted 300,000 depositors in the UK and 100,000 in the Netherlands. As a consequence of the American subprime crisis, Landsbanki collapsed in October 2008. The Icelandic Deposit Guarantee Fund was unable to pay the minimum amount of 20,000 Euros prescribed by EEA law to British and Dutch depositors. Agreements negotiated by the Icelandic government with the UK and the Netherlands, which provided for payment by Iceland, failed in two referenda.

On 15 December 2011, ESA, supported by the European Commission as an intervener, brought an action seeking a declaration that by failing to ensure payment of the minimum amount of compensation (EUR 20,000) to Icesave depositors in the Netherlands and the UK, Iceland had failed to comply with the obligations resulting from EEA law. Iceland asked the EFTA Court to dismiss the application. The UK and the Netherlands submitted observations supporting ESA's position, whereas Liechtenstein and Norway sided with the Icelanders.

65. *See* Greer LJ in *Hall v. Brooklands Auto-Racing Club*, [1933] 1 KB 205; Baudenbacher, *Lauterkeitsrecht. Kommentar zum Gesetz gegen den unlauteren Wettbewerb (UWG)* (Helbing Lichtenhahn, 2001), Article 3(b), pp. 15 et seq.
66. Eucken, *Grundsätze der Wirtschaftspolitik*, 7th ed. (UTB, 2004).

On 13 January 2013, the EFTA Court dismissed ESA's application on legal grounds. However, the EFTA Court added that in recital 16 of the preamble to the Deposit Guarantee Directive, the European legislature stated that deposit insurance 'might in certain cases have the effect of encouraging the unsound management of credit institutions'.

The EFTA Court then held:

> This points to the concept of moral hazard. In economic literature the lesson of moral hazard has been described with the words that 'less is more'. Professor Joseph E. Stiglitz has formulated in this respect: '[T]he more and better insurance that is provided against some contingency, the less incentive individuals have to avoid the insured event, because the less they bear the full consequences of their actions'. ...
>
> It is recalled that, in a crisis of a magnitude such as the one experienced in Iceland, an EEA State would have very limited options to ensure compensation to depositors that is, first, it could provide a State guarantee for a loan taken out by the scheme itself, or, second, it could directly fund the scheme or its depositors. Thus, moral hazard would also occur in the case of State funding, serving to immunize a deposit-guarantee scheme from the costs which have, in principle, to be borne by its members.[67]

As regards Professor Stiglitz, a Nobel laureate in economics, some commentators said that quoting an economist in a judgment was inappropriate. These people have not understood what economic law is about. In the *Icesave* case, the author of this contribution was not only the presiding judge, but also the judge rapporteur. He hereby discloses that when his wife Doris Baudenbacher-Tandler wrote her PhD thesis at the University of Bern on 'Protection against new investor risks' in the mid-1980s, she explained to him why it was so important to avoid 'moral hazard' in financial matters. I mention this not only because intellectual honesty dictates it but also because Marco's friendship, relates not only to me, but also to Doris.

4.6.3 Award of a Public Contract to the Wrong Bidder

In *Fosen-Linjen*, the EFTA Court held that a simple breach of European public procurement law may in itself be sufficient to trigger the liability of the contracting authority under the Remedies Directive 89/665/EEC, to compensate the person harmed for the damage incurred, provided that the other conditions for the award of damages were met, such as, in particular, the existence of a causal link.[68] This went against the *Nucleus* case law of the Supreme Court of Norway, according to which damages for the positive contract interest could only be awarded if there was a material breach. Material is a synonym of sufficiently serious within the meaning of the ECJ's and the EFTA Court's case law on State liability. It is clear that this standard involves the

67. Case E-16/11, *EFTA Surveillance Authority v. Iceland*, judgment of 28 January 2013, paras 166-167.
68. Case E-16/16, *Fosen-Linjen AS v. AtB AS*, judgment of 31 October 2017.

possibility of discriminating against foreign bidders without fear of grave consequences. It also requires no justification, that such a standard of liability which privileges the state leads to moral hazard.

5 LUGANO CONVENTION

5.1 General

In connection with the Brussels Regulation and the Lugano Convention, there has been talk of a fifth freedom of the market. Just as goods, persons, services and capital are recognized in the internal market, judgments in civil and commercial matters should also be able to circulate freely. In this respect, both the Brussels Regulation and the Lugano Convention have a free trade component to a certain extent.

5.2 Brexit: EFTA States Favouring a Free Trade Solution

This is relevant in the present case because the UK applied for readmission to the Lugano Convention as an independent contracting party on 2 April 2020. This was readily possible and the three Lugano/EFTA States, Switzerland, Norway and Iceland, agreed to the request. However, Articles 70 and 72(3) of the Convention require unanimous acceptance by the Contracting States. Such accession falls within the external competence of the EU, so the EU therefore had to decide on the UK's application for accession.

5.3 EU Protectionism Blocks a Free Trade Solution

On 1 July 2021, Switzerland, the depositary of the Lugano Convention, notified the contracting parties of the EU's refusal to give its consent to the UK's accession. The European Commission's refusal of the UK's request is based on the untenable thesis that the Lugano Convention is intended for States with close regulatory integration with the EU, i.e. States that are fully (like the EU States and the EEA/EFTA States Iceland and Norway) or partially (like the EFTA State Switzerland) part of the internal market. This contention is untenable.

The Lugano Agreement predates the establishment of the Single Market. When Switzerland was unable to join the EEA Agreement as a result of the negative vote on 6 December 1992, no one spoke of leaving the Lugano Convention. Even if, following its refusal to sign the unequal Institutional Framework Agreement with the EU,[69] Switzerland were to creep out of the internal market in which it partially participates, as threatened by the EU, its Lugano membership could not be called into question.

69. brusselsreport.eu/2021/05/27/why-did-eu-swiss-negotiations-on-a-framework-agreement-fail (last visited January 2022).

In fact, the Commission's action is a politically motivated tit-for-tat for Brexit. In doing so, the Commission has also violated procedural rules. In fact, it is a matter of tangible economic interests, specifically France's desire to divert legal services from London to Paris. In the debate in the *Assemblée Nationale*, this was admitted with a frankness that only French protagonists can afford:

> More generally, Brexit is an opportunity to strengthen the attractiveness of the Paris legal market and we are very vigilant in this regard. The UK wants to maintain its international influence in this area, but we have advantages that we need to bring to bear now. The UK has indicated its intention to accede to the Lugano Convention on Jurisdiction and the Enforcement of Judgments in Civil and Commercial Matters; we oppose this. The recognition of judgments is an additional incentive for EU member states, which we must use.[70]

The fact that the weakest and most vulnerable on the continent as well as in the UK are being harmed in the process[71] is of no concern to France and the Commission.

6 CONCLUSIONS

6.1 Free Trade Orientation of EFTA

The answer to the question posed in the title of this essay is yes. There is an EFTA legal culture. As far as its content is concerned, however, things have been complicated in the last four years by the fact that a paradigm shift has taken place at the EFTA Court.

The idea of free trade has shaped EFTA at Four's DNA from the very beginning. It is the most significant feature of EFTA's legal culture. The current four EFTA States Iceland, Liechtenstein, Norway and Switzerland consequently entertain a worldwide network of FTAs which is continuously expanded.[72] For the sake of completeness, it may be added that the belief in free trade is, *mutatis mutandis*, also an essential feature of the UK and of the 'New Hanseatic League', the group of the fiscally conservative northern EU countries Denmark, Estonia, Finland, Ireland, Latvia, Lithuania, the Netherlands and Sweden.[73] Austria, the Czech Republic and Slovakia are close to the new group whose name is derived from the Hanseatic League, a northern European trade and defence alliance that existed until the 16th century.

70. *See* the declaration of Dupond-Moretti in the Assemblée Nationale on 11 February 2021, available at vie-publique.fr/discours/280374-eric-dupond-moretti-11022021-ue-royaume-uni (last visited January 2022).
71. corporatejustice.org/news/ngos-and-legal-experts-call-on-eu-to-allow-uk-accession-to-lugano-convention (last visited January 2022).
72. For an overview, *see* twitter.com/EFTAsecretariat/status/1473302120904417284 (last visited January 2022).
73. Available at vm.fi/documents/10623/6305483/Position+EMU+Denmark+Estonia+Finland+Ireland+Latvia+Lithuania+the+Netherlands+and+Sweden.pdf (last visited January 2022).

6.2 Contributions of the EFTA Court

6.2.1 1994-2017: Free Trade and Market Orientation

The EFTA Court has over almost a quarter of a century made important contributions to a system of free trade and effective competition in the EEA. This approach aimed to protect the actors of a market, producers, workers, consumers, traders and investors. In *Deveci* the EFTA Court held that '[t]he EEA Agreement has linked the markets of the EEA/EFTA States to the single market of the EU. The actors of a market are, *inter alia*, undertakings.'[74]

The EFTA Court's legal policy involved the defence of fundamental freedoms and fundamental rights, of the freedom of competition, a liberal image of man, and a liberal model of contract. Consequently, the EFTA Court also spoke out against setting wrong incentives by facilitating moral hazard. All in all, this case law was highly appreciated by its big sister institution on the other side of Avenue Kennedy in Luxembourg, the Court of Justice of the EU.

6.2.2 Setback: Abandonment of International Exhaustion of Trade Mark Rights

In October and November 2008, the *L'Oréal* cases were referred to the EFTA Court by the Follo District Court and the Oslo District Court. Both Norwegian courts wanted to know, in essence, whether Article 7(1) of the Trade Mark Directive was to be understood to the effect that international exhaustion was permitted in light of *Maglite*, on the one hand, and of *Silhouette*, on the other. Given my strong beliefs in this matter, I recused myself from the cases. The European Commission, which originally had favoured international exhaustion as the general standard, asked the EFTA Court to overrule *Maglite* and to align itself with the ECJ's *Silhouette* ruling. ESA, the Norwegian, Icelandic and Liechtenstein Governments invited the EFTA Court to confirm *Maglite*. On 8 July 2008, the Court overruled *Maglite*. Unlike in *Maglite*, where the Court had elaborated on the advantages of international exhaustion for competition and consumers, no substantive reasons were given. The EFTA Court simply genuflected before its sister court. That was difficult to understand, in particular since, similarly to *Maglite*, the goods in question originated from the US. The case could and should thus have been distinguished from *Silhouette*. There is no better witness for this than the long-time President of the ECJ, Vassilios Skouris. In the Court's first *Festschrift*, in 2005, he wrote on the relationship between *Maglite* and *Silhouette* that the ECJ did not follow the EFTA Court's approach and that: 'Advocate General Jacobs

74. Case E-10/14, *Enes Deveci and Others v. Scandinavian Airlines System Denmark-Norway-Sweden*, judgment of 18 December 2014, para. 74.

explained quite convincingly in his opinion why the differences in scope between the EEA Agreement and the EC Treaty justified that result.'[75]

The late Judge Pierre Pescatore, one of the great trade law specialists on the ECJ bench, stated on the occasion of the EFTA Court's Tenth Anniversary in 2004 that he was very much concerned with the protectionist tendencies in the ECJ's jurisprudence and that he considered *Silhouette* 'a disgrace in the EC case law'. He added in view of a possible future EFTA Court case:

> So, what should the EFTA Court do, in view of this basic difference of principles and approach, if it finds itself either in the situation that it has to cope with a problem which is new and which has, so far, not be tackled by the EU Court, because it is defensive and protective in contradiction to the basic principles of EFTA? What would I do, if I had the privilege of being in President Baudenbacher's place? I would go to the extreme limit of EFTA's own mission by fostering free trade and try my best to dissuade the EC Court from indulging further protectionist tendencies.[76]

The EFTA Court did not even discuss these issues. Its judgments were based on a mechanical and thus inaccurate understanding of homogeneity.

With *L'Oréal*, the fortress Europe, which had been built in this field with the ECJ's *Silhouette* ruling, was perfected. That the ECJ in *Silhouette* added that the Community authorities could always extend the exhaustion in question by entering into international reciprocity agreements, is not comforting. This was, at the end of the day, a fig leaf that aimed to conceal the protectionist direction the EU had taken in this field. The US is more liberal. On 30 May 2017, the Supreme Court even held that patent rights are subject to international exhaustion in the case *Impression Products v. Lexmark International*.[77] As everybody knew when *Silhouette* was decided, a reciprocity agreement that could be concluded between the two large Western trading blocs is not in sight. In Europe, the only Supreme Court that sticks to international exhaustion both in trade mark law and in copyright law is the Swiss Federal Supreme Court. In trade mark law, this was decided in *Chanel* and in copyright law in *Nintendo*.[78]

6.3 2018-...: EFTA Court's Partial Change of Paradigm

In connection with the resignation of the author of this essay from the EFTA Court and the election of the Icelandic Judge Páll Hreinsson as the new President on 1 January 2018, the leading Norwegian international law scholar Mads Andenæs, speaks of a

75. Skouris, 'The ECJ and the EFTA Court under the EEA Agreement: A paradigm for international cooperation between judicial institutions', in Baudenbacher, Tresselt and Örlygsson (Eds), *The EFTA Court: Ten Years On* (Hart Publishing, 2005), pp. 123-129, at 126.
76. *See* his remarks in Utgård, 'Procedural aspects of homogeneity: International coordination and harmonisation in the area of civil procedure, particularly within the European Economic Area (EEA)', in Baudenbacher, Tresselt and Örlygsson (Eds), *The EFTA Court: Ten Years On* (Hart Publishing, 2005), pp. 131-144, at p. 143.
77. *Impression Products v. Lexmark International*, ___ U.S. 581 (2017), 137 S.Ct. 1523 (2017).
78. Bundesgericht (Federal Supreme Court, Switzerland), *Chanel S.A. Genève et Chanel S.A. v. EPA AG*, judgment of 23 October 1996, 122 III 469; Bundesgericht, *Imprafot AG v. Nintendo Co. Ltd. und Waldmeier AG*, judgment of 20 July 1998, 124 III 321.

'rupture'.[79] His diagnosis is understandable.[80] The principle of proportionality has been misapplied in the case of the Norwegian ski star Henrik Kristoffersen,[81] and the Norwegian government has tried to have two landmark cases from the time before the rupture reversed. In one case the attempt succeeded, in the other it did not. The EFTA Court's track record in recent rulings concerning the Norwegian NAV scandal is a mixed one. NAV is the Norwegian welfare authority. For decades it has made the payment of benefits dependant on physical presence on Norwegian soil, in clear violation of EEA law and the European Human Rights Convention.[82] Moreover, President Hreinsson regularly acts as a paid advisor to the Icelandic government, to which he owes his nomination and re-nomination. Thus, he lacks the independence mandated by Article 30 paragraph 1 ESA/Court Agreement. The EFTA Court is thus unlawfully composed and any ruling in which Mr Hreinsson has participated may be challenged as invalid.[83]

Since 2018, Norway, the superpower of the EFTA pillar, has been able to push its unlawful 'Room for Manoeuvre' (RFM) concept largely unhindered. The most important elements of the 'RFM' programme are the stacking of the ESA and the EFTA Court with a safe pair of hands, i.e. with political appointees, the refusal to establish an entity on the model of the Article 255 TFEU panel with the task of scrutinizing nominees for judgeship, the permanent claiming of the presidency of ESA by Norway, the systematic disregard of the duty of loyalty laid down in Article 3 EEA (the provision mirroring Article 4(3) Treaty on European Union (TEU)), the denial of the existence of EEA fundamental rights, the undermining of fundamental freedoms by asking Norwegian courts to settle for a mere plausibility test instead of the proportionality test required under EEA law, and, last but not least, guided teaching and research at Norwegian universities.[84] In addition, there is the policy of systematically arguing against the reference of cases to the EFTA Court, unless it is a matter of judicial revisionism which may end in favour of the Norwegian Government. All this has led to a paradigm shift from the protection of citizens and economic operators to a pronounced state-friendliness.

The Norwegian Government did not like the pre-rupture EFTA Court's public procurement law judgment in *Fosen*.[85] By opting for strict liability, the ruling took away RFM from the Norwegian authorities. Two prominent Norwegian RFM protagonists,

79. Andenaes, 'Two Opinions on free movement and unemployment benefits in the EFTA Court: A Bit of a Dog's Breakfast', *EU Law Live*, 9 July 2021, eulawlive.com/op-ed-two-opinions-on-free-movement-and-unemployment-benefits-in-the-efta-court-a-bit-of-a-dogs-breakfast-by-mads-andenaes/ (last visited January 2022).
80. Baudenbacher, 'The decline of the EFTA Court', *Brussels Report*, 9 September 2021, brusselsreport.eu/2021/08/09/the-decline-of-the-efta-court/ (last visited January 2022).
81. Case E-8/17, *Henrik Kristoffersen v. Norwegian Ski Federation*, judgment of 16 November 2018.
82. Andenaes, *supra* note 79.
83. See Case E-21/16, *Pascal Nobile v. DAS Rechtsschutz-Versicherung AG,* decision of 14 February 2017; Case E-21/16, *Pascal Nobile v. DAS Rechtsschutz-Versicherung AG*, order of the president of 20 February 2017.
84. *See* in particular the 'Ruhrgas' commentary on the EEA Agreement of 2018, whose most important parts were dealt with by prominent RFM-authors: Arnesen et al. (Eds), *Agreement on the European Economic Area: A Commentary* (Beck / Hart / Nomos, 2018).
85. *See supra*, 4.6.3.

Professors Arnesen and Fredriksen, first successfully asked the referring Trondheim Court of Appeal not to follow that ruling.[86] When the *Fosen* firm appealed, the two asked the Supreme Court to re-refer the case to the EFTA Court. The Norwegian EFTA Court Judge Christiansen then flew to Oslo and invited the President of the Supreme Court to make a second reference.[87] This was a clear breach of his oath to maintain the secrecy of deliberations (Article 4 Rules of Procedure 2018). The Supreme Court followed his advice. The President of the EFTA Court subsequently announced publicly that *Fosen* would be overruled, he steered the composition of the Court toward the desired outcome, motions of bias were defeated in secret resolutions.[88] In the end, the EFTA Court allowed the Norwegian Supreme Court to maintain its state-friendly *Nucleus* jurisprudence.[89] The Supreme Court did so, and the Government Attorney had the delicacy to express his satisfaction. It was a textbook example of case-fixing. ESA played along. The Commission pointed out that to give states a leeway would lead to moral hazard, but had no comments on the obvious bias of Mr. *Hreinsson*.[90]

Again at the instigation of the Government Attorney, the Norwegian Supreme Court made a second attempt in Case E-4/19 *Campbell*[91] to have a pre-rupture judgment (the 2016 ruling in Case E-28/15 *Jabbi*[92] concerning the scope of the Union Citizenship Directive 2004/38/EC) revised, but this time without success. Hreinsson, at the time the EFTA Court's junior judge, had at least indirectly violated his oath to keep the secrecy of the deliberations in a speech at the EFTA Court's Spring Conference 2016.[93]

After the *Fosen* charade, Norwegian courts which consist to a large percentage of former bureaucrats have started to disregard EFTA Court preliminary rulings, in particular from the time before 2018, at will. All this is steered by the Norwegian Government Attorney, who advises the Government and the administration on all EEA law matters, represents the Government in all EEA-related court cases and has close connections with RFM-friendly scholars, and the Prime Minister's Office. The separation of powers no longer functions in EEA law cases. This is a rule of law issue.

86. Arnesen and Frederiksen, 'Erstatningsansvar ved brudd på anskaffelsesreglene – etter EFTA-domstolens tolkningsuttalelse i Fosen-Linjen', 23 *Tidsskrift for forretningsjus* (2018), 169-195.
87. vg.no/nyheter/innenriks/i/0nWKL0/efta-dommer-diskuterte-omstridt-sak-med-hoeyesterett-kan-ha-gjort-seg-inhabil (last visited January 2022).
88. Baudenbacher, 'Fosen and NAV – "room for manoeuvre"', *Anbud365*, 13 November 2019, anbud365.no/internasjonalt/eu/fosen-and-nav-room-for-manoeuvre/ (last visited January 2022); Baudenbacher, 'Fosen Fiasco – Now the ball is in the Norwegian Supreme Court's field', *Anbud365*, 5 July 2019, anbud365.no/regelverk/fosen-fiasco-now-the-ball-is-in-the-norwegian-supreme-courts-field/ (last visited January 2022).
89. Case E-7/18, *Fosen-Linjen AS*.
90. Baudenbacher, 'Fosen is about public procurement law, but also about the integrity of the EEA judicial system', *Anbud365*, 3 June 2019, anbud365.no/regelverk/fosen-is-about-public-procurement-law-but-also-about-the-integrity-of-the-eea-judicial-system/ (last visited January 2022).
91. Case E-4/19, *Campbell v. Immigration Appeals Board*, judgment of 13 May 2020.
92. Case E-28/15, *Yankuba Jabbi v. Immigration Appeals Board*, judgment of 26 July 2016.
93. eftacourt.int/press-publications/the-eea-single-market-2016-efta-court-spring-conference/ (last visited January 2022).

Moreover, Norwegian legal philosopher Rune Slagstad speaks of an 'erosion of democracy'.[94]

The Norwegian-dominated ESA does not have the strength to oppose this development. But other players have drawn consequences. Icelandic courts have become very reluctant to refer cases since the rupture of 2018. In 2021, the EFTA Court, a full-time institution with a manning table of 20 persons, registered four cases. Three were references, two from Norwegian courts and one from a Liechtenstein court. Moreover, EU courts are scaling back judicial dialogue with the EFTA Court. From 1994 to 2017, the ECJ, its Advocates General and the General Court of the EU referred to EFTA Court case law 238 times in 151 cases.[95] AG Trstenjak described the dialogue between the ECJ and the EFTA Court as 'unique' in *Marques Almeida*.[96] Skouris, then President of the ECJ, wrote in 2014:

> The long lasting dialogue between the EFTA Court and the ECJ has allowed the flow of information in both directions. 'Ignoring EFTA Court precedents would simply be incompatible with the overriding objective of the EEA Agreement which is homogeneity.' The symbiotic nature of the relationship has contributed to the successful development of the EEA Single Market. Both courts stand as examples for each other thus depicting mutual respect, strengthening the rules of homogeneity and representing a high level of appreciation. Cooperation between the two was built on strong foundations which have stood the test of time.[97]

The EFTA Court has in the past been the only court of general jurisdiction whose case law was regularly taken into account by EU courts when interpreting EU law. Since 2018, the EFTA Court's jurisprudence has been referenced 24 times by Advocates General and EU courts, but only two citations on minor points relate to a post-2018 judgment.[98] The change of paradigm from the protection of citizens and economic operators to the preference for state interest is incompatible with both the will of the Contracting Parties and the traditional EFTA culture.

6.4 Final Remarks

EFTA these days comes in three formations: EFTA at four, consisting of Iceland, Liechtenstein, Norway and Switzerland; EFTA at three, consisting of the EEA/EFTA States Iceland, Liechtenstein and Norway; and the Lugano-EFTA at three, consisting of Iceland, Norway and Switzerland. EFTA at four will continue its free trade policy, basically staying on the traditional line. Lugano-EFTA has also made its presence felt in a positive sense by supporting the UK's accession to the Lugano Convention. Disappointed 'remainers' and some commentators outside the UK have said, not without

94. dagogtid.no/feature/utholing-av-demokratiet-6.23.24010.9a02cef642 (last visited January 2022).
95. *See* Baudenbacher, *supra* note 15, Ch. 21.
96. EU:C:2012:414, footnote 25.
97. Skouris, *supra* note 16, at 12.
98. Case C-637/17, *Cogeco Communications Inc.*, Opinion of AG Kokott, ECLI:EU:C:2019:32, notes 45 and 46 (citing Case E-10/17, *Nye Kystlink AS v. Color Group AS and Color Line AS*, judgment of 17 September 2018).

glee, that it is only logical that the British should be punished and that it is hard to see why the British legal market should retain its advantages. This falls short. British advantages are based on merit, while France relies on protectionism. This is not compatible with the EU's repeatedly invoked commitment to competition and open borders.

However, the development of the EEA/EFTA is of great concern. Due to the two pillar model, the European Commission cannot take action against an EEA/EFTA State. But it could raise the problems described above in the EEA Joint Committee. Norway pays a lot of cohesion money, but since EU actors are also affected by the situation of the EFTA pillar, the Commission will not be able to look the other way all the time. As the author of these lines has stated many times, the structures of the EEA Agreement are good, but the institutions of the EFTA pillar are too small and too inhomogeneous. With three members in each ESA and the EFTA Court, too much hangs on chance.[99] If two of them are State-oriented, the protection of citizens and economic operators becomes secondary. If Switzerland and maybe even the UK changed their position towards the EEA, the problem would be solved.[100] Whether this will happen is, of course, an open question. If it does not occur, ESA and the EFTA Court would have to be enlarged to five members each. However, the chances that the EFTA pillar superpayer and superplayer Norway will agree to this are rather slim.

99. *See also* Bekkedal, review of Baudenbacher, 'Restoring the balance in the European Economic Area', 58 *Common Market Law Review* (2021), 1922-1924.

100. Pisani-Ferry et al., 'Europe after Brexit: A proposal for a continental partnership', 9 May 2017, bruegel.org/2016/08/europe-after-brexit-a-proposal-for-a-continental-partnership/ (last visited January 2022); Baudenbacher, 'Two souls in Europe's breast: the attractions of EFTA for the UK', 5 June 2018, blogs.lse.ac.uk/brexit/2018/06/05/two-souls-in-europes-breast-the-attractions-of-efta-for-the-uk/ (last visited January 2022).

CHAPTER 15

The EU-Mercosur FTA and the Protection of the Environment: True Ambition or Just Enough to Get It Ratified?*

Giovanni Gruni

After 20 years of negotiations, the European Union (EU) concluded a free trade agreement (FTA) with Argentina, Uruguay, Brazil and Paraguay, being the countries composing the Mercado Comun del Sur (MERCOSUR) which is the largest organization of economic integration in South America. This chapter looks at the section of the FTA on environmental standards and shows how it has substantive and procedural shortcomings that weaken the relevance of the section for the protection of the environment. The last part of the contribution proposes some amendments to improve the legal significance of the environmental section of the EU-MERCOSUR FTA.

It isn't what we say or think that defines us, but what we do. (Jane Austen)

1 INTRODUCTION

After 20 years of negotiations, the European Union (EU) concluded a free trade agreement (FTA) with Argentina, Uruguay, Brazil and Paraguay, being the countries composing the Mercado Comun del Sur (MERCOSUR), the largest organization of economic integration in South America.[1] This FTA is part of a wider policy of the EU to

* This contribution was submitted in March 2022.

1. *See* ec.europa.eu/trade/policy/countries-and-regions/regions/mercosur/index_en.htm.

conclude trade deals outside the World Trade Organization (WTO) to regulate trade relations with third countries.[2] Other large deals are already (partially) in force with Canada, Japan and other countries, while negotiations are ongoing with other countries around the world. The EU-Mercosur FTA would strengthen economic cooperation between the EU and some of the most vibrant South American economies. Yet more than two years after its conclusion, the EU-Mercosur FTA is still on hold with the European Parliament expressing scepticism about its content[3] and France explicitly opposing its ratification.[4] Notably, the FTA is attracting criticism for its alleged lack of environmental obligations. In 2020, nine Member States symbolically wrote to the Trade Commissioner Dombrovskis asking for a solution to the stalemate and the ratification of the deal.[5] The European Commission has attempted to reassure the detractors of the deal by concluding a side document on the environment with Mercosur that would strengthen the environmental protection already present in the FTA.

This chapter looks at the part of the EU-Mercosur FTA dedicated to the protection of the environment and submits that the present version of the EU-Mercosur FTA indeed has substantive and procedural shortcomings that considerably weaken its capacity to ensure that the contracting parties respect the environment and fight climate change. It then proposes a number of amendments that would provide the environment with the same quality of legal protection that the FTA offers to trade and intellectual property rights. This chapter is a spin-off of the research I conducted with Marco Bronckers between 2018 and 2021. On the occasion of his retirement, I want to express my profound gratitude for the opportunity of working with him as this has greatly influenced my understanding of world trade law. Omissions and mistakes contained in this chapter remain of course only mine.

Section 2 presents the relevant provisions of the EU-Mercosur FTA dealing with environmental obligations; section 3 explains how such obligations could be enforced in case of non-compliance. Section 4 highlights the main shortcomings of the present version of the FTA; section 5 proposes a number of reforms of the FTA and EU law more broadly that would provide environmental obligations with the same level of protection already provided to trade rules and intellectual property rights.

2 SUBSTANTIVE OBLIGATIONS

The Members of the WTO are allowed under certain conditions to conclude FTAs outside the WTO context. The EU-Mercosur FTA is an example of such type of FTA

2. For an overview of the FTA policy of the EU *see* Gruni, *The EU, World Trade Law and the Right to Food* (Hart Publishing, 2018), at 78-81.
3. Amendment 36 to the 2018 Annual Report on the Implementation of the Common Commercial Policy, A9-0160/36, available at europarl.europa.eu/doceo/document/A-9-2020-0160-AM-036-036_EN.pdf.
4. *See* euractiv.com/section/climate-environment/news/france-says-opposes-eu-mercosur-trade-deal-over-deforestation-concerns/ and batimes.com.ar/news/economy/macron-says-france-will-continue-to-oppose-eu-mercosur-trade-deal.phtml (both last visited 5 August 2022).
5. *See* politico.eu/article/eu-countries-corner-macron-on-mercosur-trade-deal/ (last visited 5 August 2022).

going beyond WTO rules agreed between a smaller group of countries.[6] Accordingly, the EU-Mercosur FTA builds on most traditional areas of WTO law such as free movement of goods and services and intellectual property rights. The EU-Mercosur FTA also contains rules specifically dedicated to the protection of the environment that do not exist in the WTO.[7] These rules share similar substantive characteristics and enforcement with the part of the FTA protecting labour standards. In fact, in the EU policy jargon, both the environmental and labour standards form part of the EU's effort to include sustainable development concerns in its FTAs.

Accordingly, the EU-Mercosur FTA contains a chapter dedicated to the protection of the environment which includes a number of environmental standards. These standards fall into three different groups: obligations based on existing international agreements, obligations related to existing domestic legislation and more aspirational clauses referring to higher levels of protection.

The first group of obligations is based on existing international standards. In particular, the EU-Mercosur FTA commits the parties to *effectively implement* the multilateral environmental conventions they ratified. Some articles also refer to specific conventions the parties must implement. Notably, the EU-Mercosur FTA contains the obligation to implement the Paris Agreement on climate change[8] as well as parts of the Convention on Biological Diversity (CBD),[9] the Convention on International Trade of Endangered Species of Wild Fauna and Flora (CITES)[10] and the International Treaty on Plant Genetic Resources for Food and Agriculture.[11] In a dedicated section on the sustainable management of fisheries and aquaculture, the FTA mandates the implementation of relevant parts of the UN Convention on the Law of the Sea and the Food and Agriculture Organization code of conduct on responsible fisheries.[12] Notably, the section on sustainable management of forests does not contain any references to specific international standards but rather an obligation to 'implement measures to combat illegal logging and related trade'.[13]

The second type of obligations refers to existing domestic legislation. The EU-Mercosur FTA, like most recent EU FTAs, contains a non-regression clause mandating that Member States do not weaken environmental obligations. This obligation is conditioned on an intended effect on trade or investment.[14] This means that in addition to the regression in the levels of protection to activate the clause, an intention to lower the levels of protection to attract trade or investment is required. In addition,

6. Van den Bossche and Zdouc, *The Law and Policy of the World Trade Organization* (CUP, 2017), at 671.
7. EU-Mercosur FTA, Chapter on Trade and Sustainable Development, available at trade.ec.europa.eu/doclib/html/158166.htm (hereinafter cited as EU-Mercosur TSD Chapter).
8. Article 6.2 EU-Mercosur TSD Chapter.
9. Article 7 EU-Mercosur TSD Chapter.
10. Article 7 EU-Mercosur TSD Chapter.
11. Article 7 EU-Mercosur TSD Chapter.
12. Article 9 EU-Mercosur TSD Chapter.
13. Article 8 EU-Mercosur TSD Chapter.
14. Article 2 EU-Mercosur TSD Chapter.

the EU-Mercosur FTA Members are obliged to enforce domestic environmental protection.[15] This obligation is conditioned to an actual effect on trade and investment in addition to 'a recurring course of action or inaction'. The difference between intended and actual effect is that in the second case, it has to be demonstrated that lowering the levels of protection attracted trade or investment in practice. We will examine the legal consequences of these specifications below.

A third category includes a range of vaguer provisions to raise the standards of environmental protection. It is common in EU FTAs that some sections on the protection of the environment contain clauses which barely have any legal significance.[16] This happens, for instance, when the FTAs simply *reaffirm* vaguer principles or ideas related to sustainable development. Some also include vague references to cooperation on environmental protection without any reference to any specific objective to achieve or legal obligation to respect. An example is Article 1(3) of the Trade and Sustainable Development (TSD) Chapter, where the parties reaffirm 'their commitment to promoting sustainable development of international trade in such a way to contribute to the objective of sustainable development [...]'.

3 THE ENFORCEMENT MECHANISM

World trade law is an area of public international law which is generally considered to benefit from particularly effective enforcement. This is due mainly to the extremely successful dispute settlement mechanism of the WTO which provides for two levels of adjudication after mandatory consultations. In addition, the Panel or Appellate Body Reports[17] can be followed by the authorization of trade sanctions to push the Member towards compliance. On top of this international enforcement procedure, the EU has a domestic mechanism that allows companies to file a complaint to the EU Commission to flag illegal trade barriers and violations of intellectual property protection contained in world trade law. This mechanism is contained in the Trade Barrier Regulation.[18]

EU FTAs follow a mechanism of enforcement with regard to the sections on economic rules and intellectual property rights. They contain a dispute settlement mechanism that can be activated by States in case of alleged non-compliance of another Member to the FTA. Such mechanism is a simplified version of the WTO dispute settlement which in the EU-Mercosur FTA provides only for one level of adjudication and the creation of a panel on the basis of a roster of trade experts. The panel proceeding in the FTA is preceded by mandatory consultations. To enforce economic

15. Article 2.5 EU-Mercosur TSD Chapter.
16. Bronckers and Gruni, 'Retooling the sustainability standards in EU free trade agreements', 24 *Journal of International Economic Law* (2021), 25-51, at 28.
17. The Appellate Body mechanism is suspended at the moment of writing; *see, e.g.*, csis.org/programs/scholl-chair-international-business/world-trade-organization-appellate-body-crisis (last visited June 2022).
18. Regulation (EU) 2015/1843 of the European Parliament and of the Council of 6 October 2015 laying down Union procedures in the field of the common commercial policy in order to ensure the exercise of the Union's rights under international trade rules, in particular those established under the auspices of the World Trade Organization (codification), O.J. 2015, L 272/1.

clauses, EU FTAs provide for the possibility of withdrawing preferences to put pressure on the non-complying country.

The EU-Mercosur FTA, like all recent EU FTAs, provides for a separate mechanism of enforcement for disputes related to environmental protection. This mechanism has some similarities with the general enforcement of the FTA but also some important differences. In both mechanisms, the dispute is referred to independent experts who are supposed to make findings on the compatibility of the disputed measure (or lack thereof) with the treaty standard. In both mechanisms, an infringement of the relevant international standards does not require a showing of trade effects. The key difference is what happens after the experts have made their findings. An infringement finding in respect of sustainability standards is not binding, but merely an element in the parties' ongoing attempts to conciliate their dispute. Another difference with regular dispute settlement is that, if the defendant country refuses to bring itself into compliance with the sustainability standards, no sanctions are envisaged. These important differences between the enforcement of economic obligations and of environmental protection create a two-track system where environmental obligations have considerably weaker procedural guarantees. This is in line with the idea that the EU is utilizing a more 'promotional' approach in its FTAs with regard to environmental protection in contrast with the traditional binding and enforceable approach for economic rules and the protection of intellectual property.

4 ANALYSIS OF ENVIRONMENTAL PROTECTION IN THE EU-MERCOSUR FTA

Environmental clauses in EU FTAs are not the only area of world trade law that refers to other sources of international law. There is a longstanding practice in international intellectual property law, for instance, to utilize the WTO and FTAs to make international obligations binding and enforceable.[19] On the contrary, environmental protection in the EU-Mercosur still leaves space for States to circumvent obligations. Moreover, often the EU-Mercosur FTA has sections that barely contain legal obligations or do not contain obligations at all. This section highlights the main shortcomings of the present version of the section on the protection of the environment of the EU-Mercosur FTA.

4.1 Obligations Based on International Standards

4.1.1 The Paris Agreement on Climate Change

We can consider first the obligation to '*effectively implement*' the Paris Agreement on Climate Change contained in Article 6.2 of the TSD section. There are reasons to believe that its value in terms of obliging the State to take steps towards solving climate change would be at least contested. This is partly related to the nature of the obligations in the

19. Prevost and Van den Bossche, *Essentials of WTO Law* (CUP, 2021), at 195.

Paris Agreement itself. This Agreement is generally considered not to contain a result obligation beyond a requirement for States to report the actions taken to achieve nationally determined contributions (NDCs).[20] According to some, the achievement of the NDCs themselves remains voluntary.[21] Yet others have affirmed that in this respect, States have assumed an obligation of conduct, to engage in their best efforts to achieve the goals they have set themselves in the NDCs.[22] This subsection shows that even if we accept the more binding interpretation of NDCs, the present version of the FTA provides limited legal protection.

In a situation where the legal value of NDCs is contested, a reference to them in an FTA could increase their legal significance. There are, however, doubts that this is the case. As an example, in its NDC, Brazil recorded its intention to achieve, in the Brazilian Amazonia, zero illegal deforestation by 2030, and to restore and reforest 12 million hectares of forests by 2030.[23] In the EU-Mercosur FTA, there is an obligation to 'effectively implement' the Paris Agreement. What does this FTA language add to the intentions Brazil expressed under the Paris Agreement? To begin with, by virtue of the FTA, any doubt has been removed that Brazil's compliance with its NDC might be considered voluntary. The commitment in the Paris Agreement has been firmed up by the FTA. In respect of the EU, Brazil would unambiguously accept that its NDC represents a binding commitment (and, vice versa, of course). While the nature of that commitment is probably not a result obligation, the obligation to effectively implement its NDC would at least require Brazil to make its best efforts to achieve its goals under the Paris Agreement. That would give Brazil some margin to argue by 2030 that the result of reforestation, for example, could not be achieved because of certain unforeseen or external obstacles. Brazil also has a choice in the means to achieve this goal. However, the best-efforts obligation arguably imposes an ongoing obligation on Brazil to demonstrate that it is moving towards its stated goal for 2030. Furthermore, no matter how one reads Brazil's commitment to implement the Paris Agreement towards the EU, it does not depend on whether or not Brazil's environmental policies have an effect on trade with the EU. Accordingly, it is conceivable that the EU, once Mercosur is ratified, could challenge Brazil's policies under the FTA's bilateral dispute settlement mechanism, claiming that Brazil is not working towards its stated goal and, therefore, not meeting its best-efforts obligation.[24] This is unlikely, however, especially if we consider how best-effort obligations are treated in the context of EU FTAs.

In fact, a recent dispute on labour standards under the EU-South Korea FTA does contain an analysis of best-effort obligations that suggests that they can be challenged

20. Article 4(2) Paris Agreement to the United Nations Framework Convention on Climate Change, 21st Conference of Parties, 12 December 2015, O.J. 2016, L 282/4.
21. Article 4.2 Paris Agreement ('Parties shall pursue domestic mitigation measures, with the aim of achieving the objectives of such contributions'). *See* further Bodansky, 'The Legal Character of the Paris Agreement', 25 *Review of European, Comparative & International Environmental Law* (2016), 142-150; Crawford, 'The Current Political Discourse Concerning International Law', 81 *Modern Law Review* (2018), 1-22, at 21.
22. Meyer, 'Obligations of conduct in the international law on climate change: A defence', 27 *Review of European, Comparative & International Environmental Law* (2018), 130-140.
23. Brazil's NDC is available through unfccc.int/NDCREG (last visited 5 August 2022).
24. Bronckers and Gruni, *supra* note 16.

in a dispute under an FTA.[25] The same case, however, showed how difficult it is to prove the violation of a best-effort obligation in an international procedure. In this case, it proved impossible to demonstrate a violation of the obligation of conduct notwithstanding the reticence of South Korean national institutions to respect the obligation. The case provides an analysis of the obligation to make *continued and sustained efforts towards ratifying* a number of international conventions. This is an obligation of conduct similar to the one of respecting NDCs in the Paris Agreement. The Panel observed that:

> 291. Overall, the Panel is mindful of the fact that Korea has not committed to a specific timeframe for the ratification of the four outstanding International Labour Organization (ILO) Conventions. The Panel also finds that Korea's efforts are less than optimal, and that there is still much to be done.
>
> 292. Nonetheless, it is the view of the Panel that the less-than-optimal effort of Korea, in and of itself, does not fall below the legal standard set out in the last sentence of Article 13.4.3 of the EU-Korea FTA.[26]

Notwithstanding the relevance of including an obligation to implement the Paris Agreement, the threshold for finding a violation of an obligation of conduct as identified in the EU-South Korea case seemed to require a high level of inaction and possibly an act of the State that goes explicitly against the obligation. This might prove even more difficult in the EU-Mercosur FTA since the obligation of conduct to respect NDCs is not explicit in the FTA but would be derived from the general reference to effectively implement the Paris Agreement on Climate Change. In other words, in the EU-Mercosur FTA itself it is not clarified that NDCs become legally binding as a consequence of the reference to the Paris Agreement. Arguably, in the absence of clear rules in this regard, this would be a contested legal issue in a potential dispute under the EU-Mercosur FTA. An alternative interpretation would be in fact that the obligation to *effectively implement* the Paris Agreement on Climate Change does not change the legal nature of NDCs as a consequence of the inclusion of the environmental agreement in the FTA. All these elements significantly reduce the legal relevance of the obligation to implement the Paris Agreement. Notably, there are other parts of the FTA where States accepted unequivocally binding obligations that can provide some inspiration on how to make this clause more legally significant (*see* section 5.1).

4.1.2 Other Environmental Conventions

There are other parts of the environmental section of the EU-Mercosur FTA which contain references to international standards but most of these references barely create any obligations on the State parties. An example is Article 8 on protecting forests. The entire article is written in a mild, promotional language with the sole exception of paragraph 2(c) which does create an obligation to combat illegal logging and illegal

25. Report of the Panel of experts proceeding constituted under Article 13.15 of the EU-Korea Free Trade Agreement, 20 January 2021, paras 259-293.
26. Report cited *supra* note 25, paras 291-292.

trade. Similar weaknesses affect Article 7 on trade and biodiversity which refers to the CBD, the CITES, and the International Treaty on Plant Genetic Resources for Food and Agriculture. But the Article only goes on to say that the Parties to the EU-Mercosur FTA 'recognize their importance', an expression that does not create obligations related to those international treaties. Article 7(2) would have created an obligation to 'implement effective measures leading to a reduction of illegal trade in wildlife', but the following 'consistent with international agreements to which it is a party' means that the EU-Mercosur does not create new obligations in that respect beyond what the parties already have under other treaties. This means that the entire section on biodiversity and most of the section on forests (with the only exception of Article 8(2)c) are either of a promotional and non-binding nature or a repetition of obligations that the parties already have under international law.

4.2 Obligations Related to Domestic Law

The sustainability chapter of the EU-Mercosur FTA also contains clauses stipulating that each party is obliged not to lower the level of domestic environmental protection. This is expressed in two ways: FTA parties must not weaken environmental laws (non-regression clause), and parties must not fail to enforce these laws (non-enforcement clause). Both these obligations are conditioned on intended or actual effects on trade and investment.[27] What the non-regression and non-enforcement clauses add is that also the lowering of domestic protection, even when this does not conflict with a party's international commitments, can be prohibited under the FTA. But then a link with trade or investment is required. Why a link with trade or investment was chosen in respect of non-regression and non-enforcement clauses in a particular FTA is inexplicable. In fact, having to prove that a lowering of environmental protection actually has trade or investment effects may appear so formidable a condition as to render the disciplines of the non-regression and non-enforcement clauses illusory.

One is reminded here of the unsuccessful challenge brought by the United States (US) against Guatemala under the Central America Free Trade Agreement (CAFTA).[28] The US complained notably that Guatemala did not effectively protect the rights of association, among others, by failing to protect trade union leaders and members against violence. In a ruling issued in 2017, the panel in that case did fault Guatemala on various counts. Yet the panel ultimately found no infringement of CAFTA. The US had not proven that Guatemala had failed to enforce its labour laws 'in a manner affecting trade' between the parties.[29] According to the panel, the US should have shown that Guatemala's disputed practices had conferred 'some competitive

27. *See* above, section 2.
28. Dominican Republic – Central America – United States Free Trade Agreement.
29. Article 16.2.1(a) CAFTA – Dominican Republic FTA with the United States.

advantage on an employer or employers engaged in trade with the United States'.[30] Yet the CAFTA panel found no evidence that any cost savings that might have accrued to Guatemalan exporters as a result of the alleged enforcement failures provided a competitive advantage.[31] There is no guidance yet on how the trade or investment effects test in the non-regression and non-enforcement clauses of the EU's FTAs is to be interpreted (note that the aforementioned EU-Korea labour dispute did not involve a violation of the FTA's non-regression clause, but of that agreement's international commitments).[32]

4.3 Provisions Lacking of Prescriptive Value

The EU-Mercosur FTA contains numerous passages of exhortatory or purely aspirational nature. Such sections do not create any obligations on the State parties and have barely any legal significance. In addition, they pollute the text of the FTA and make the sections on environmental standards excessively convoluted watering down their overall prescriptive content and opening the door to questions as if these are more political statements rather than legal obligations. An example of this is Article 1(3) of the TSD Chapter stating that:

> The Parties recognize that the economic, social and environmental dimensions are interdependent and mutually reinforcing dimensions of sustainable development, and reaffirm their commitment to promoting the development of international trade in such a way as to contribute to the objective of sustainable development, for the welfare of present and future generations.

4.4 Shortcomings of the EU-Mercosur FTA Approach to Enforcement

As mentioned above, the EU enforces its FTAs via a domestic procedure included in the Trade Barrier Regulation in addition to the enforcement procedures included in the FTA itself. The trade barrier regulation (TBR) is not available at the moment to enforce environmental obligations and the enforcement mechanism of the EU-Mercosur FTA is not the same as the one that can be used to enforce the parts of the FTA on trade and intellectual property. This section highlights the weaknesses of both approaches.

The present version of the Trade Barrier Regulation does not allow complainants to bring a case on the basis of allegations of violations of environmental standards. As I showed in a piece written with Marco Bronckers,[33] (to which I refer the reader), the present Regulation also lacks rules on legal standing, for instance, with regard to trade unions and environmental non-governmental organizations (NGOs), and it would

30. Dominican Republic – Central America – United States Free Trade Agreement, Arbitral Panel Established Pursuant to Chapter 20, Guatemala – Issues Relating the Obligations Under Article 16.2.1(a) of the CAFTA-DR, para. 190.
31. CAFTA panel, para. 463.
32. Report cited *supra* note 25, para. 92.
33. Bronckers and Gruni, 'Taking the enforcement of labour standards in the EU's free trade agreements seriously', 56 *Common Market Law Review* (2019), 1591-1622.

need a number adaptations in order to accommodate complaints on environmental standards. A recent initiative[34] of the European Commission attempted to accommodate private complaints at the EU level also on violations of the obligations related to the environment in EU FTAs. The Chief Trade Enforcement Officer created a new procedure allowing private parties to flag to the Commission situations of alleged non-compliance of obligations contained in FTAs. The procedure works on the basis of Single Entry Points allowing private stakeholders but also Member States to complain about violations, among other things, of environmental and labour standards contained in EU FTAs. The procedure is not based on secondary legislation and leaves wide discretional space to the European Commission on how to assess alleged violations of the labour standards obligations, including those related to forced labour. In a set of guidelines published in November 2020 and updated in June 2022,[35] the European Commission explains that the complainant will be kept informed of whether the complaint leads to enforcement action by the Commission utilizing the instruments available under international law. This new development attempts to fill a gap in the enforcement of labour standards contained in trade agreements via EU law even if it lacks the legal guarantees of the TBR which remains inaccessible for these kinds of complaints. The complaining party, for instance, is not able, under this new, more flexible procedure, to appeal the decision taken by the Commission in front of the Court of Justice of the European Union (CJEU). Overall the new procedure lacks the formal requirement and legal strength of the TBR.

Concerning the dispute settlement contained in the FTA, as mentioned above, the choice made was not to allow State parties to use the general dispute settlement for violations of the environmental standards included in the FTA. Instead, the FTA has a dedicated system of consultations and the possibility to ask for the creation of a panel of environmental law experts to assess the alleged violation. Some of the procedures of the dispute settlement system for environmental standards are similar to those utilized for the general dispute settlement of the FTA.

After the dispute settlement in case of persistent non-compliance by the State party, there are no additional explicit steps that can be taken under EU FTAs. In fact, different from Canada and the US trade agreements, the EU's FTAs do not allow economic or trade sanctions with regard to environmental standards. This remains one of the main features of the promotional approach of the EU Commission when it comes to the enforcement of environmental standards in its FTAs. During the negotiations of the Comprehensive Economic and Trade Agreement (CETA), for instance, the EU refused to include a system of financial sanctions which Canada was ready to adopt.[36]

34. *See* trade.ec.europa.eu/doclib/docs/2021/november/tradoc_159907.pdf (last visited 5 August 2022).
35. 'Operating guidelines for the Single Entry Point and complaints mechanism for the enforcement of EU trade agreements and arrangements', 22 June 2022, available at trade.ec.europa.eu/access-to-markets/en/form-assets/operational_guidelines.pdf (last visited 5 August 2022).
36. Araujo, 'Labour provisions in EU and US mega-regional trade agreements: Rhetoric and reality', 67 *International & Comparative Law Quarterly* (2018), 233-253, at 242; Fritz, *Analysis and Evaluation of the Comprehensive Economic and Trade Agreement (CETA) Between the EU and Canada* (Hans-Böckler-Foundation Project No. 2014-779-1, 26 January 2015), at 29, available at

Finally, the EU-Mercosur FTA does not contain obligations requiring State parties to create specific procedural instruments at the domestic level to enforce via domestic courts the obligations on environmental standards contained in the FTA. This is in stark contrast with the sections of the EU-Mercosur FTA on intellectual property rights which are precise and detailed on the obligations of domestic courts when enforcing intellectual property rights, listing a number of specific procedural requirements.[37]

5 REFORMING THE EU-MERCOSUR FTA ENVIRONMENTAL CLAUSE

Environmental obligations in the EU-Mercosur FTA show that there is increasing awareness about the role that world trade law can play in solving global environmental issues. However, as the previous sections showed, the EU-Mercosur FTA does not have the same legal precision with regard to the obligations on the environment as those related to free trade and intellectual property rights. Environmental obligations also lack the enforcement instruments that have been in the toolbox of world trade law for decades and that in the WTO context have proved extremely valuable in enforcing obligations contained in trade agreements. This last section summarizes possible directions for reform of the present system to strengthen how EU FTAs can contribute to the fight against climate change and to the protection of the environment.

First, environmental obligations in EU's FTAs can be written in a clearer and more precise way. Whenever an international convention is referred to, the FTA should at least state clearly that the convention shall be ratified, implemented and enforced domestically by the State party. Alternatively, the FTA could include obligations related to the environment directly in the FTA itself. Obligations should not rely on additional conditions that are too difficult to demonstrate, like the one that the FTA is violated only if the environmental violation affects trade between the parties. These types of conditions have already been proved in the US experience to make the treaty obligations insignificant. In addition, the array of aspirational clauses that lack prescriptive content pollutes the FTAs without providing a contribution to the protection of the environment. They should be either reformulated to add prescriptive content or taken away altogether. The FTA could clarify what are the legal consequences of a treaty's inclusion in the FTA, for example, with regard to the Paris Agreement on Climate Change. The first step could be stating that NDCs become binding under the FTA or even turning them into obligations of result to be achieved by a specific deadline.

Second, the gap in enforcement still present at the EU level with obligations on environmental standards excluded from the issues that can trigger a complaint under the trade barrier regulation can be fixed by reforming the relevant EU legislation in order to accommodate complaints based on such standards. In addition to my 2019

thomas-fritz.org/english/analysis-and-evaluation-of-the-comprehensive-economic-and-trade-agreement-ceta-between-the-eu-and-canada.

37. *See* below section 5.

proposal mentioned above,[38] there are alternative ways to create a legal procedure to allow private complaints at the EU level based on violations of environmental obligations, for instance, an ad hoc legislative instrument inspired by the TBR. The mentioned solution found by the European Commission of creating a more flexible mechanism under the supervision of the Chief Trade Enforcement Officer can be a temporary response to this enforcement gap but this system retains some elements of informality. Accordingly, it cannot be considered a substitute for a full-fledged procedure similar to the TBR or for a reform of the TBR itself to accommodate violations of the obligations related to the protection of the environment.

Thirdly, the protection of the environment is still treated in EU FTAs as an issue that does not deserve the same level of ambition with regard to enforcement as the obligations on free trade or intellectual property. To change this and to provide binding obligations related to the environment with stronger legal enforcement in case of non-compliance, the EU should learn from the experiences of other countries which already utilize the general dispute settlement of their FTAs to enforce environmental standards. This is the case, for instance, under the recently concluded Comprehensive and Progressive Agreement for Trans-Pacific Partnership (CPTPP) where no separate procedure is envisaged to settle disputes on environmental standards, but only the appointment of environmental experts instead of trade experts as panel members is required.[39] This different approach would avoid the present situation where Panels assessing violations of the obligations related to the environment rely on a procedure which is more tentative and less precise than the one utilized for the general enforcement of the FTA.

Fourthly, at the moment, the text of the EU-Mercosur FTA does not provide for any kind of sanctions or penalty in case of persistent non-compliance. This remains one of the core elements of the EU Commission promotional approach with regard to labour and environmental obligations in FTAs. Notwithstanding the absence of an explicit system of sanctions in case of violations related to the environment in EU's FTAs there are options available under international law. The EU can terminate or suspend the trade liberalization provided by the FTA in case of violations of FTA obligations, including those related to the environment. This possibility, which was mentioned by the CJEU when assessing the EU-Singapore FTA[40] appears, however, rather unlikely to happen in practice. Overall, the Commission had shown itself reluctant to take enforcement actions with regard to labour standards even when they were explicitly available.[41] An example is the Generalized System of Preference Plus (GSP+), an arrangement on the basis of which selected developing countries to receive additional

38. Bronckers and Gruni, 'Improving the enforcement of labour standards in EU's free trade agreements', in Prevost, Alexovicova and Pohl (Eds), *Restoring Trust in Trade: Liber Amicorum in Honour of Peter Van den Bossche* (Hart Publishing, 2019), pp. 157-172.
39. CPTPP Article 28.8(5).
40. Opinion 2/15, *Singapore FTA*, ECLI:EU:C:2017:376, para. 161 (referring to Article 60(1) Vienna Convention on the Law of Treaties (VCLT)).
41. *See* Depaigne, 'Protecting fundamental rights in trade agreements between the EU and third countries', 42 *European Law Review* (2017), 562-576; Vogt, 'A little less conversation: The EU and the (non) application of labour conditionality in the Generalized System of Preferences', 31 *International Journal of Comparative Labour Law and Industrial Relations* (2015), 285-304.

tariff preferences when ratifying a list of international instruments protecting human rights, labour standards and the environment. In case of violations of those international conventions, the EU can suspend the tariff preferences.

More realistically, in order to provide a system of sanctions to be used in case of non-compliance those sanctions should be mentioned explicitly in the text of the FTA itself, which is not the case today. The question then is what kind of sanctions could be included in the EU FTAs, which would work to promote compliance with a set of environmental obligations. One possibility would be designing a system of financial sanctions on the basis of which the violating country shall pay a pecuniary amount until it complies with the obligation. Canada, for instance, includes a system of fines in case of infringements of the sustainability chapters in its FTAs. The EU also has experience with this mechanism of enforcement since the Commission can request the CJEU to impose fines against the Member States in case of violations of EU law.[42] Notably, the amount of the fine is calculated considering factors such as the severity of the infringement, its duration, and the ability to pay off the offending country. The CPTPP also provides for the possibility of paying a monetary penalty in lieu of trade sanctions. All these, already operational, instruments could be used as inspiration to design a system of penalties tailored to violations of the obligations related to the environment. The amount paid by the offending country could contribute to a fund controlled by an independent body.

This does not mean that trade sanctions should not also be available in case of persistent violations of environmental obligations. The general remedies available under the FTA dispute settlement system could be extended to these types of violations at least if the country is refusing to make financial payments or does not bring itself into compliance. This would be done as *extrema ratio* since the preference would be to avoid the economic damage caused by trade sanctions also to the imposing country. This already happens in EU FTAs with regard to violations of free trade obligations and intellectual property rights where after a reasonable period of time the party can suspend obligations in case the offending party does not respect the Report of the panel. While by no means this should be the preferred instrument of enforcement, the fact that potential trade sanctions are available can deter from violating the obligations.

Finally, we should consider the FTA obligations related to domestic enforcement of environmental laws. The EU-Mercosur FTA fails to detail the procedural guarantees that should be present at the domestic level to enforce environmental standards. This is an extremely weak approach to domestic enforcement which does not clarify the procedures that should be available at domestic level. Clear guidance on how to reform this can be found in the section of the EU-Mercosur FTA on intellectual property rights which contains a well-detailed list of measures to be taken to enforce intellectual property rights at the domestic level. Accordingly, the EU-Mercosur FTA could clarify that provisional and precautionary measures, remedies, injunctions and damages are also available to enforce environmental laws domestically.

42. *See* Falkner, 'Fines against Member States: An effective new tool in EU infringement proceedings?', 14 *Comparative European Politics* (2016), 36-52.

6 CONCLUSIONS

The ratification of the EU-Mercosur FTA is being delayed partly because of its perceived lack of environmental protection. In turn, this is delaying the economic benefits that the FTA would create once it enters into force. This chapter showed that even if the EU-Mercosur FTA contains a section dedicated to climate change and the protection of the environment, it falls considerably short of what world trade law could achieve in terms of enforcing substantive environmental obligations. Such shortcomings could be corrected if the same approach used with trade obligations and intellectual property rights were to be applied to the environmental rules of the EU-Mercosur FTA. This would mean imposing clear and precise obligations supported by an enforcement mechanism with all the elements generally used by the EU to enforce world trade law (TBR, consultations, dispute settlement and sanctions).

With regard to substantive obligations, more clarity would be needed on the legal effects of the reference to the Paris Agreement on Climate Change since that environmental agreement barely contains binding obligations in itself. If that reference means that the NDCs become binding either in the form of an obligation of conduct or even of result, this would have to be clarified. In the present formulation, this remains unclear and open to interpretative disputes in case of non-compliance. There is already case law in the area of labour standards in EU FTAs showing how obligations of conduct are difficult to enforce even when explicitly stated. This is not even the case in the EU-Mercosur FTA which only contains a general reference to the Paris Agreement. The EU-Mercosur FTA also refers to other international conventions on the environment, mainly restating existing international law or not creating any legal obligation and choosing instead to use promotional language. These sections too could be clarified always referring at least to the three basic obligations of ratifying the referred conventions, implementing them via domestic law and enforcing them via domestic courts. Notably, the section on forests and the one on biodiversity are particularly vague and have limited legal significance in their present form. In addition to references to international standards, the FTA also contains a non-regression clause. The clause is, however, dependent on the requirement of demonstrating a link with trade which proved to be an unsurmountable hurdle in a case between the US and Guatemala under the CAFTA.

With regard to the enforcement of the obligations on the protection of the environment, the EU-Mercosur FTA creates a two-track system on the basis of which such obligations are excluded from a substantial part of the enforcement procedures utilized to enforce the rest of the FTA. This means that after consultations and a Report from a Panel of experts, no further steps can be taken in terms of withdrawal of preferences or sanctions. The chapter commented on how this could be amended while still maintaining trade sanctions as *extrema ratio* in case of persistent non-compliance. The EU-Mercosur FTA also fails to create clear obligations on the enforcement of environmental laws via domestic courts as it does, for instance, with regard to intellectual property rights. A possibility would be to state that precautionary measures, remedies, injunctions and damages should also be available at domestic level with regard to the protection of the environment. The recently created Contact Points can be considered an informal temporary fix which, however, does not have the same legal guarantees the TBR offers to the enforcement of economic obligations and intellectual property rights.

CHAPTER 16

Prochain Arrêt: *Arts-Loi* – European Human Rights Law and the Protection of the Freedom of Artistic Expression

Mielle Bulterman & Rick Lawson

To what extent does the law protect art, or, to be more precise, the freedom of artistic expression? This question brings together two themes that have always been dear to Marco Bronckers. Until the turn of the century, the European Court of Human Rights did not intervene if controversial works of art triggered indignant reactions from the authorities or influential sectors of society. The Court's traditional emphasis on the importance of pluralism, tolerance and broadmindedness did not result in a high level of protection for the freedom of artistic expression. In the last two decades, however, the Strasbourg Court became bolder, especially when artistic expressions were essentially political in nature. This development is to be welcomed, especially in authoritarian environments. Recently the Court of Justice of the European Union (EU) delivered its first judgments on artistic expression, and it will be interesting to see how it will develop its potential.

1 INTRODUCTION

The metro station *Arts-Loi* is in the centre of Brussels, only a few blocks away from Marco Bronckers' house. *Arts-Loi*, or in Dutch *Kunst-Wet*, derives its name from the intersection of two streets: the rue de la Loi/Wetstraat and the avenue des Arts/Kunstlaan. Although most commuters will take the name for granted, the metro station is a standing invitation to reflect on the relationship between the arts and law.

It is often said - mostly by lawyers though - that law is actually a form of art: *ius est ars boni et aequi*. The art of striking a fair balance between competing interests; the art of not only applying the law and respecting its formalities but also looking beyond appearances and identifying the issues that are genuinely at stake; the art of doing justice to the specific circumstances of the individual without losing sight of the wider picture and the legitimate needs of society as a whole.

In this chapter, we want to reflect on the relationship between law and art from a different perspective: to what extent does the law protect art, or, to be more precise, the freedom of artistic expression? This seems an appropriate way to honour our colleague and friend, Marco, as it brings together two of the themes that have always been dear to him. There is no need to expand on Marco's qualities as a lawyer: both in academia and in legal practice, he has built himself a formidable reputation. But there was always art, too. Anyone who has enjoyed the hospitality of Marco and Dominique will be aware of the central place that art has to them and to their house: the paintings, photographs and sculptures leave the visitor with a sense of awe and delight. Marco's library of art books, in which Picasso occupies a special place, shows that he takes the study of art at least as seriously as the study of the law. So what is more logical than to explore the interface between the two?

Indeed, when Leiden Law School organized a symposium on law and art in 2016, it was clear that Marco should play a central role.[1] The reason for organizing the symposium was a special donation to the Law School: an artwork by the Syrian artist Rabi Koria. It was entitled *Homs*, named after the historic city in Syria that was virtually destroyed in 2014-2015 during the civil war. The donor was an alumnus from Leiden Law School, Jan Maarten Boll - coincidentally Marco's first mentor when he started to practice law. Or maybe it was not a coincidence: both men developed a life-long passion for art.[2]

At the symposium, Marco interviewed both the artist and the donor, and then moderated the discussion. Under his direction, the event focussed on the relationship between art, law and justice. Cultural heritage in Syria was seriously under threat; to what extent can the law protect this heritage? Marco invited Rabi Koria to reflect on the question of how an artist can give substance to his freedom of expression in a situation of war. What is the impact of being uprooted, which is inextricably linked to fleeing from one's country of origin, on the development of an artist? And to his old mentor, Jan Maarten Boll, Marco put the question of what role art can play in conveying the horrors of war and injustice. Can art help us, Marco asked, in our endeavours to impress upon new generations of students the crucial role of the law and the rule of law?

1. For a brief description of the event, *see* universiteitleiden.nl/en/events/2016/05/kunst-en-recht-kunst-en-onrecht, and the article 'Leidse rechtenfaculteit geeft "asiel" aan kunstwerk Homs', *De Volkskrant*, 14 May 2016, volkskrant.nl/cultuur-media/leidse-rechtenfaculteit-geeft-asiel-aan-kunstwerk-homs~b482445e.
2. For his work *Homs* Koria had received the Royal Award for Modern Painting from King Willem-Alexander in 2015. Jan Maarten Boll was also the driving force behind the establishment at Leiden University, in 2019, of the Uytenbogaert Chair on Tolerance. He passed away in November 2020.

It seems fair to assume that Marco when reflecting on *Homs*, was reminded of Picasso, his long-time favourite artist, and his famous painting *La Guernica.* With all the differences in style and context, both works of art were triggered by the cruelty and destruction of war. Both works were conceived in exile: Koria painted *Homs* in Amsterdam, Picasso painted *La Guernica* in Paris. For many years, the latter painting could not be displayed in Spain. It was only in 1981 after the dictatorship was brought to an end, that the painting arrived in Spain. And even then, it was not secure: it was displayed behind bullet-proof glass screens out of fear of vandalism. It took more than a decade before it was considered safe to liberate *La Guernica* from its high-security environment. The painting was taken to the Museo Reina Sofía in Madrid, where it was exhibited without extreme precautions. But even then, controversy remained, with Basque nationalists arguing that the picture should be brought to the Basque Country.

Here we have in a nutshell a number of elements that make it worthwhile to explore the protection of the freedom of artistic expression. Like books, sculptures, music and performances, paintings can have a strong societal impact. And they raise emotions. They may be admired; they may provoke hostile reactions. Works of art may be considered immoral. Even if the artist wants to stay clear from politics, his work may be claimed for a cause, or rejected as politically flawed – when *La Guernica* was first exhibited, it was criticized by some Marxist groups for lack of political commitment.[3] Authorities may ban art, they may prosecute artists, they may criminalize possession of *entartete Kunst.*

Now clearly, all this is something of a dark past. Or is it? What to think of Anna Sinkova and her frying pan? It is not too long ago that Anna took a frying pan, broke some eggs into it and fried them – over the Eternal Flame at the Tomb of the Unknown Soldier. Two others fried sausages on skewers over the flame while the final member of the group filmed the scene. Anna was caught and charged with desecrating the Tomb of the Unknown Soldier. What to think of this? Does it matter that Anna belonged to an artistic group? That they went to a World War II Memorial in order to make an 'act of performance'? That Anna herself posted the video on the Internet on behalf of the group, with an accompanying statement condemning the burning of natural gas to maintain the Eternal Flame at the taxpayers' expense? To the domestic courts, all this did not matter: Anna was found guilty and sentenced to three years' imprisonment, suspended for two years. All her appeals were dismissed. What mattered more to these courts, perhaps, was that all this took place in Ukraine, a country that finds itself in a state of war with Russia.[4]

So domestic law and practice may or may not offer artists and their works a degree of protection. In our contribution, we will explore how much protection *European* human rights law has to offer. In doing so we will focus, as Marco would like us to do, on the *visual* arts: paintings, sculptures, films, performances. Books, novels

3. When it comes to Picasso, our library is definitely less extensive than Marco's. So here we rely on Wikipedia.
4. The facts come from ECtHR, *Sinkova v. Ukraine*, Appl. No. 39496/11, judgment of 27 February 2018. The *Sinkova* case obviously predates the disastrous Russian invasion of 24 February 2022. Yet the horrors that were inflicted upon Ukraine in World War II may have influenced the position of the Ukrainian courts when reviewing the *Sinkova* case.

and the like will be mostly left aside. For obvious reasons, most attention will go to the European Convention of Human Rights (ECHR) since this is the traditional source of protection of our fundamental freedoms. The case law of the European Court of Human Rights is an inexhaustible treasure trove full of remarkable cases, and in passing, we will also come across some decisions of the European Commission of Human Rights – which existed until 1998 and supervised compliance with the Convention in tandem with the Court. But our explorations will not be limited to Strasbourg. We will also have a glimpse at the law of the European Union (EU). Unlike the ECHR, the Charter of Fundamental Rights of the EU specifically states that 'the arts shall be free of constraint', and it will be interesting to examine what this adds to the protection of artistic expressions.

2 ARTISTIC EXPRESSION AND THE ECHR

2.1 The Frame: Article 10 ECHR

The obvious starting point for our explorations is Article 10 ECHR, which enshrines the right to freedom of expression. This right consists of three elements: the freedom to hold opinions, the freedom to impart information and ideas, and the freedom to receive such information and ideas. The special significance of free speech was acknowledged already in the early days of the Strasbourg case law. In the famous case of *Handyside* (1976), which concerned the British ban on *The Little Red Schoolbook*, the European Court of Human Rights observed:

> Freedom of expression constitutes one of the essential foundations of such a [democratic] society, one of the basic conditions for its progress and for the development of every man. Subject to paragraph 2 of Article 10, it is applicable not only to 'information' or 'ideas' that are favourably received or regarded as inoffensive or as a matter of indifference but also to those that offend, shock or disturb the State or any sector of the population. Such are the demands of that pluralism, tolerance and broadmindedness, without which there is no 'democratic society'.[5]

These words are rightly famous. The Court's call for pluralism, tolerance and broad-mindedness seemed to resonate with the general mood prevailing in Europe at the time.

Usually most attention goes to the second part of the quote, with its reference to expressions that 'offend, shock or disturb'. The Court's logic is undeniable: there is little point in protecting mainstream ideas only. But at the same time, it is clear that offensive or shocking expressions are controversial by definition and, hence, that there will always be calls to suppress them. Perhaps this is all the more true for works of art, given art's inherent tendency to transcend everyday realities.[6] By announcing that it will offer protection to expressions that 'offend, shock or disturb', the Court might be

5. ECtHR, *Handyside v. United Kingdom*, Appl. No. 5493/72, 12 December 1976, para. 49.
6. *See* in this respect also the observation of Frank La Rue, the UN Special Rapporteur on the promotion and protection of the right to freedom of opinion and expression: 'art may be used to

said to make a promise: it will act *deliberately counter-intuitive*, it will seek to counterbalance the intuitive reactions of 'the State or any sector of the population'. That is, as an Englishman would put it, a courageous idea. Any such endeavour is destined to be disputed.

The first line of the quote merits some reflection as well. It suggests that there are several dimensions to the freedom of expression. On the one hand, the collective interest is served by the existence of a public space where matters of common interest can be discussed freely, so as to foster 'progress' of society. On the other hand, there is an individual dimension as well – individuals need the opportunity to speak out, to share their feelings and opinions with others. There is a link here with the right to the free development of one's personality.

The Court has traditionally granted a high level of protection to the press and to those who seek publicity in order to address issues of general importance. There is very little scope for restrictions on political speech. In this contribution, we will try to find out if similar considerations apply to art. But we may note already at this stage that the Court has held as regards journalists that the methods of reporting 'may vary considerably, depending, among other things, on the media in question. It is not for this Court, nor for the national courts for that matter, to substitute their own views for those of the press as to what technique of reporting should be adopted by journalists'; Article 10 protects 'not only the substance of the ideas and information expressed, but also the form in which they are conveyed'.[7] Indeed, freedom of the press covers possible recourse to 'a degree of exaggeration or even provocation'.[8] Clearly, these are statements that artists will read with great interest.

That does not mean, however, that anything goes. Opinions may differ as regards the borders between what is still acceptable and what is not, but most commentators will agree that the freedom of expression is not unlimited. Indeed, Article 10 states that the exercise of the freedom of expression 'carries with it duties and responsibilities' – it is the only provision in the Convention to do so. In line with this, the second paragraph of Article 10 provides that the freedom of expression may be subject to formalities, conditions, restrictions or penalties. At the same time, the drafters of the Convention were aware of the danger that these restrictions might undermine the freedom of expression. Therefore they stipulated that any interference has to meet three requirements: it has to be prescribed by law; it has to serve a legitimate aim (such as the protection of national security, the reputation of others, or morals); and the interference has to be 'necessary in a democratic society' in order to protect the stated aim.

---

provoke strong feelings without the intention of inciting violence, discrimination or hostility' (Report of 7 September 2012, UN doc. A/67/357, para. 46).

7. For an early example *see* ECtHR, *Jersild v. Denmark*, Appl. No. 15890/89, judgment of 23 September 1994, para. 31.
8. *See, e.g.*, ECtHR, *Stoll v. Switzerland*, Appl. No. 69698/01, judgment of 10 December 2007, para. 148.

These conditions have been the subject of extensive case law.[9] For present purposes, we do not need to go into great detail. Suffice it to say that the Court ruled, already in its *Handsyide* judgment, that the domestic authorities have a certain latitude when assessing the need to limit the freedom of expression. This is all the more so if they seek to protect morals – a situation that is not unlikely to occur when works of art cause controversy:

> it is not possible to find in the domestic law of the various Contracting States a uniform European conception of morals. The view taken by their respective laws of the requirements of morals varies from time to time and from place to place, especially in our era which is characterized by a rapid and far-reaching evolution of opinions on the subject. By reason of their direct and continuous contact with the vital forces of their countries, State authorities are in principle in a better position than the international judge to give an opinion on the exact content of these requirements as well as on the 'necessity' of a 'restriction' or 'penalty' intended to meet them.
>
> ... it is for the national authorities to make the initial assessment of the reality of the pressing social need implied by the notion of 'necessity' in this context. Consequently, Article 10 § 2 leaves to the Contracting States a margin of appreciation.[10]

This does not mean a *carte blanche* for the domestic authorities, though. The margin of appreciation 'goes hand in hand with European supervision', as the Court put it poetically in *Handyside*. Its supervision embraces both the legislation and the decisions applying it, even those given by the domestic court. The Court is therefore empowered to give the final ruling on whether an interference is reconcilable with Article 10. In doing so, the Court will determine whether the interference in the issue was proportionate to the legitimate aims pursued and whether the reasons adduced by the national authorities to justify it were relevant and sufficient. Another point of reference is whether the national authorities applied standards which were in conformity with the principles embodied in Article 10 and, moreover, that they based themselves on an acceptable assessment of the relevant facts.

The key question is, of course, how all this plays out in practice. On the one hand, the Court promises that it will offer protection to expressions that 'offend, shock or disturb'; on the other hand, it leaves a margin of appreciation to domestic authorities seeking to protect morals. It is high time to see what this means for artistic expressions.

2.2 Rough Sketch: The *Müller* Case, Article 10 ECHR and Artistic Expression

It was Josef Felix Müller, a Swiss sculptor, graphic artist and painter, who introduced the Court to the world of art.

9. For a recapitulation of the case law over the years *see, e.g.*, ECtHR, *Zana v. Turkey*, Appl. No. 18954/91, judgment of 25 November 1997, para. 51, and ECtHR, *Bédat v.* Switzerland, Appl. No. 56925/08, judgment of 29 March 2016, paras 48-54.
10. *Handyside*, para. 48.

It all started in 1981, five years after the *Handyside* judgment was delivered. An exhibition of contemporary art, entitled *Fri-Art 81*, was organized in Fribourg, Switzerland, in a former seminary building that was due to be demolished. The organizers invited several artists to take part, each of whom was allowed to invite another artist of his or her own choosing. The artists were meant to make free use of the space allocated to them; they created their works on the spot. One of them was Mr Müller. In the space of three nights, he produced three large paintings entitled *Drei Nächte, drei Bilder*. They were on the show already a few days before the official opening of the exhibition - but not for long.

We will leave it to the reader's imagination to visualize what was in the three nocturnal pictures.[11] What is clear is that, as soon as the doors were opened, a girl reacted so violently to the paintings, that her father lodged a formal complaint. Meanwhile, another visitor threw down one of the paintings, trampled on it and crumpled it. Alarmed by the consternation, the principal public prosecutor of the Canton of Fribourg descended to the exhibition. He entertained no doubts: Mr Müller's paintings qualified as obscene within the meaning of the Criminal Code. He reported the matter to the investigating judge and required that the paintings be destroyed.

As a result, events took a dramatic turn. The investigating judge arrived at the official opening of the exhibition, accompanied by a small army of police officers. The pictures were immediately removed and seized. Mr Müller and the organizers were each sentenced to a fine of 300 Swiss francs for publishing obscene materials. 'Not without misgivings' the trial court decided *not* to order the destruction of the three works: they were confiscated and deposited for safekeeping. In its judgment, the trial court did not mince its words:

> Mr. Müller's three works ... are undoubtedly repugnant at the very least. The overall impression is of persons giving free rein to licentiousness and even perversion. The subjects - sodomy, fellatio, bestiality, the erect penis - are obviously morally offensive to the vast majority of the population. Although allowance has to be made for changes in the moral climate, even for the worse, what we have here would revolutionize it. Comment on the confiscated works is superfluous; their vulgarity is plain to see and needs no elaborating upon.[12]

Mr Müller had invited an art expert, the curator of the *Kunsthalle* in Basle, to explain the artistic qualities of his work. But the Swiss courts were not impressed by his 'learned-seeming but wholly unpersuasive remarks':

> Nor can a person of ordinary sensitivity be expected to go behind what is actually depicted and make a second assessment of the picture independently of what he can actually see. To do that he would have to be accompanied to exhibitions by a procession of sexologists, psychologists, art theorists or ethnologists in order to have explained to him that what he saw was in reality what he wrongly thought he saw.

11. The curious will find a detailed description in ECtHR, *Müller v. Switzerland*, Appl. No. 10737/84, judgment of 24 May 1988, para. 16.
12. *Müller*, para. 14.

If ever someone was looking for a concrete example of expressions that 'offend, shock or disturb', then Mr Müller's paintings seemed to tick the boxes. He lost his case in all instances. Yet he secured one legal success: after eight years, he managed to recover his paintings. 'With some hesitation' the court ordered the return of the paintings, noting that Mr Müller 'had achieved a certain repute' in the intervening period and expressing the pious hope that 'he may find it unnecessary to shock by resorting to vulgarity'.

Mr Müller finally applied to the European Court of Human Rights. This being the first case of its kind to reach Strasbourg, Mr Müller pleaded for recognition of the freedom of artistic expression. Banning a work or convicting the artist struck at the very essence of the right guaranteed in Article 10, he submitted and had damaging consequences for a democratic society. Mr Müller was prepared to admit that his paintings reflected a conception of sexuality that was at odds with the prevailing social morality of his days, but their symbolical meaning had to be considered – these were works of art. Freedom of artistic expression would become devoid of substance, Mr Müller argued, if paintings like his could not be shown to people interested in the arts as part of an exhibition of experimental contemporary art.

The Court seized the opportunity and clarified that, indeed, freedom of artistic expression does come within the ambit of Article 10 ECHR. The freedom of expression extends to 'cultural, political and social information and ideas of all kinds' and 'those who create, perform, distribute or exhibit works of art contribute to the exchange of ideas and opinions which is essential for a democratic society'.[13]

But in the end, that did not help Mr Müller a lot. The Court noted dryly that 'artists are certainly not immune from the possibility of limitations' as provided for in Article 10 § 2. It reminded Mr Müller that whoever exercises his freedom of expression undertakes 'duties and responsibilities'; their scope will depend on his situation and the means he uses. The Court took into account that while Mr Müller's paintings depicted sexual scenes in a crude manner, the general public had free access to the exhibition.

In that context, the Court accepted that the Swiss authorities intended to protect morals when taking the impugned measures against Mr Müller. Recalling its relativist finding in *Handyside* that morals may vary from one place to the other, the Court noted:

> having inspected the original paintings, the Court does not find unreasonable the view taken by the Swiss courts that those paintings, with their emphasis on sexuality in some of its crudest forms, were 'liable grossly to offend the sense of sexual propriety of persons of ordinary sensitivity' (...). In the circumstances, having regard to the margin of appreciation left to them under Article 10 § 2, the Swiss courts were entitled to consider it 'necessary' for the protection of morals to impose a fine on the applicants for publishing obscene material.

And so the Court found by a large majority (6 votes 1) that no violation of Article 10 had occurred. From the artist's perspective, that was no doubt a disappointing outcome. What would be the explanation? Was the Court – to remain in the style of Mr Müller's

13. *Müller*, paras 27 and 33.

paintings – only paying lip service to the freedom of artistic expression? Or did the Court exercise restraint since it was just entering a new domain, and would it be more assertive in later cases? Was it appropriate for the Court to 'inspect' the original paintings and perform, implicitly, a quality control so as to differentiate between 'good' and 'bad' art?

Or was it a mere combination of factual circumstances that led to this outcome? The exhibition had been widely advertised and was open to all, without any charge being made for admission. That element did play a decisive role in a case that was rejected, a few months later, by the European Commission of Human Rights.[14] Perhaps things might have been different if the exhibition was more ... discrete?

2.3 Adding Colour, but Not Too Bright: Otto Preminger and the Protection of Religious Feelings

In the next case, the exhibition *was* more discrete. An association, the Otto-Preminger-Institut, intended to show a film in its cinema in Innsbruck, Austria. The cinema was not a private club and as such the showing of the film was accessible to the general public. It appears, however, that the cinema usually showed 'art house' films that would attract a relatively small section of the public. At any rate, an admission fee was charged, an age limit of 17 applied, and the timing of the showings (at 10:00 p.m.) further diminished the risk of unsolicited exposure to the film.

One can easily spot the differences with the *Müller* case. The exhibition in Fribourg was open to the general public; it actually sought to attract the public at large; the entrance was free; there was no 'warning' about the nature of the exhibition – so it was conceivable that an unsuspecting passer-by would run into Mr Müller's rather explicit paintings. All this was different in *Otto Preminger*; the cinema even made sure that information on the film was provided in its programme announcements. Ironically, this was held *against* the organizers: because the film had been advertised, it was sufficiently 'public' to cause offence.

Cause offence? The film in question was *Das Liebeskonzil* – based on a book that had been banned as blasphemous immediately upon publication in Germany in 1894. One century later, *Das Liebeskonzil* still caused controversy. At the request of the Roman Catholic diocese, the authorities seized the film; later its forfeiture was ordered. The measures were said to be necessary to ensure religious peace in the region: the authorities pointed out that a large majority of the local population (about 87%) was Roman Catholic.

When the *Otto Preminger* case came before the European Court of Human Rights, the Austrian authorities argued that they had acted in order to protect the rights of

14. Referring to *Müller*, the Commission rejected a complaint by a British sculptor who was convicted for 'outraging public decency'. The sculpture in question consisted of a model's head which had attached to each of its ears an earring made out of a freeze-dried human foetus, of three to four months' gestation. The Commission noted expressly that the sculpture was displayed in an exhibition which was open to, and sought to attract the public. It declared the application inadmissible, as a result of which the case never came before the Court. *See* ECommHR, *S. & G. v. United Kingdom*, Appl. No. 17634/91, dec. of 2 September 1991.

others, that is, the freedom of religion as protected by Article 9 ECHR. The Court accepted that indeed their purpose was to protect 'the right of citizens not to be insulted in their religious feelings by the public expression of views of other persons'. One might object that the risk that coincidental visitors would be confronted with offensive material unwittingly was small. If indignation were to arise among the Roman Catholic part of the population, it was rather caused by the mere knowledge that *Das Liebeskonzil* was being seen by others. But the Court followed the same cautious approach as it did in *Müller*:

> as is borne out by the wording itself of Article 10 § 2, whoever exercises the rights and freedoms enshrined in the first paragraph of that Article undertakes 'duties and responsibilities'. Amongst them – in the context of religious opinions and beliefs – may legitimately be included an obligation to avoid as far as possible expressions that are gratuitously offensive to others and thus an infringement of their rights, and which therefore do not contribute to any form of public debate capable of furthering progress in human affairs.
>
> This being so, as a matter of principle it may be considered necessary in certain democratic societies to sanction or even prevent improper attacks on objects of religious veneration, provided always that any 'formality', 'condition', 'restriction' or 'penalty' imposed be proportionate to the legitimate aim pursued.
>
> As in the case of 'morals' it is not possible to discern throughout Europe a uniform conception of the significance of religion in society (see *Müller* ...); even within a single country such conceptions may vary. For that reason it is not possible to arrive at a comprehensive definition of what constitutes a permissible interference with the exercise of the right to freedom of expression where such expression is directed against the religious feelings of others. A certain margin of appreciation is therefore to be left to the national authorities in assessing the existence and extent of the necessity of such interference.[15]

And so the Court found – with a majority of six votes to three – that no violation had occurred.

One of the more generous interpretations of the judgment is that it should be read as an incitement to the authorities of the Member States of the Council of Europe to grant effective protection to religious minorities. If that indeed was the central message (although in this case, it was the religious *majority* that was protected), then its importance could not, and cannot, be over-estimated in an era that is marked by identity politics and religious intolerance.

But other than that, the judgment was mostly criticized. Space does not allow us to go into detail.[16] For present purposes, we may limit ourselves to stating the rather obvious: the Court was again very cautious. It mentioned the freedom of artistic expression only in passing.[17] Moreover, it exercised a very limited review: 'The content

15. ECtHR, *Otto-Preminger-Institut v. Austria*, Appl. No. 13470/87, judgment of 20 September 1994, para. 50.
16. For a discussion (by two co-authors who could agree on everything, but not on this case) *see* Lawson and Schermers, *Leading Cases of the European Court of Human Rights* (Ars Aequi Libri, 1997), pp. 572-573.
17. *Otto-Preminger-Institut*, para. 56, noting that the Austrian courts 'had due regard to the freedom of artistic expression'.

of the film cannot be said to be incapable of grounding the conclusions arrived at by the Austrian courts'. The same caution prevailed two years later, in the case of *Wingrove*.[18]

2.4 A Change of Perspective: *Karataş*, the *Künstler* and *Pussy Riot* – Political Art

So by the turn of the century, the picture was rather pale. The Court did recognize the freedom of artistic expression, but at the same time, it was not prepared to overrule the balance struck by domestic authorities in individual cases. Referring to the margin of appreciation, it did not find any violations.

Interestingly, in each of the cases discussed so far, the European Commission of Human Rights had taken a much more assertive position.[19] In *Müller* it had found, by 11 votes to 3, that the confiscation of the paintings was in breach of Article 10. When the Court ruled otherwise, the Commission gave it another try in *Otto Preminger:* by a majority of 13 to one it took the position that a breach of Article 10 had occurred. Again the Court saw it differently. History repeated itself in *Wingrove:* the Commission found a violation, this time by 15 votes to 2; the Court said no. The Commission never managed to persuade the Court: a change in its case law would occur only about a decade later, long after the Commission was abolished.

There is one exception though. In the case of *Karataş*, a Turk of Kurdish origin published an anthology of poems entitled *The song of a rebellion – Dersim*, referring to a region with a long history of violent clashes between Kurdish clans and government forces. The poet was prosecuted for disseminating separatist propaganda. The trial court found that he glorified the insurrectionary movements in the Kurdish region and sentenced Mr Karataş to over one-year imprisonment and a fine.

When his case came to Strasbourg, the roles were reversed: the European Commission of Human Rights did *not* find a violation of Article 10, but this time the Court did. In essence, the Court was not convinced by the Turkish argument that the conviction was necessary for the protection of national security and territorial integrity. The Court accepted that, taken literally, the poems might be construed as inciting readers to hatred, revolt and the use of violence. But, the Court continued, it had to be borne in mind that the case concerned poetry, 'a form of artistic expression that appeals to only a minority of readers'.[20] Unlike the mass media, poetry 'by definition is addressed to a very small audience', a fact which limited its potential impact on national security.[21]

18. ECtHR, *Wingrove v. United Kingdom*, Appl. No. 13470/87, judgment of 25 November 1996, para. 50. This case concerned the refusal by the British Board of Film Classification to grant a distribution certificate for a video that the applicant, a film director, had recorded. The video, entitled *Visions of Ecstasy*, portrayed St Teresa of Avila in acts of an overtly sexual nature.
19. But *see* the case of *S. & G. v. United Kingdom*, mentioned above.
20. ECtHR, *Karataş v. Turkey*, Appl. No. 23168/94, 8 July 1999, para. 49.
21. *Karataş*, para. 52. For a similar approach, *see* ECtHR, *Alinak v. Turkey*, Appl. No. 40287/98, judgment 29 March 2005, paras 41-45 (concerning a fictional novel; the Court entertained equally low expectations as to the impact of fiction).

To this backhand argument, the Court added a consideration of a different nature: the publication also had 'an obvious political dimension'. The poems expressed deep-rooted discontent with the fate of the Kurdish people. That was a crucial aspect of the case: there is little scope under Article 10 ECHR for restrictions on political speech or debate on matters of public interest. Also taking into account the severity of the penalty imposed on Mr Karataş the Court found that his conviction was disproportionate and so there had been a violation of the Convention.

Unlike the cases discussed so far, *Karataş* did not really revolve around the concept of artistic freedom. For the Court,[22] the case was rather part of a series of 13 similar Turkish cases, all decided at the same time, concerning convictions for pro-Kurdish statements that were seen by the authorities as a threat to national security. Some cases concerned newspaper articles, others a book.[23] Mr Karataş happened to write poetry, and for the Court that mainly meant that he was destined not to make a significant impact on anything, let alone national security.

And yet, with its emphasis on the political overtones of a work of art, the *Karataş* judgment foreshadowed the case of *Vereinigung Bildender Künstler v. Austria*, decided in 2007.[24] In this case too, the Court found a violation of Article 10 ECHR. It was a narrow vote - four votes to three - but it was a breakthrough: the first time that a breach of the freedom of artistic expression was found.

At first sight, the case resembled *Müller*: a painting with images of quite acrobatic sexual activities, controversy. But there was a difference that would play a crucial role: a political dimension. The work in question was entitled *Apocalypse*. It had been produced by the Austrian painter Otto Mühl, himself an outspoken character.[25] The huge painting, measuring over 16 m^2, featured a collage of some 30 public figures - including Mother Teresa, an Austrian cardinal and the former head of the Austrian Freedom Party (FPÖ) Jörg Haider - all naked and involved in sexual undertakings. The bodies of these figures were painted in a cartoon-like fashion, but photos that were taken from newspapers were used for their heads. The eyes of some were hidden by black bands. The painting was displayed by the *Vereinigung Bildender Künstler*, an association of artists celebrating its 100th anniversary with an exhibition entitled *The century of artistic freedom*.

Among those portrayed was a certain Mr Meischberger, an FPÖ politician who, at the time of the exhibition, was a member of the National Assembly. Mr Meischberger

22. It is worth noting that *Karataş* was decided by the 'new' Court. On 1 November 1998 Protocol 11 entered into force, as a result of which the existing Commission and Court - both part-time bodies - were merged into the new, full-time Court. Its judges were newly elected. The series of Turkish cases decided in the summer of 1999 were among the first judgments of the new Court.
23. *See, e.g.*, ECtHR, *Sürek v. Turkey (No. 1)*, Appl. No. 29982/95, judgment of 8 July 1999, and *Polat v. Turkey*, Appl. No. 23500/94, judgment of 8 July 1999.
24. ECtHR, *Vereinigung Bildender Künstler v. Austria*, Appl. No. 68354/01, judgment of 25 January 2007.
25. According to Wikipedia, Mr Mühl founded a commune in 1972, the declared aim of which was the destruction of bourgeois marriage and private property. It was viewed by some as an authoritarian sect. In 1991 he was convicted of sexual offences with minors and drugs offences and sentenced to seven years' imprisonment.

was shown while engaging in sexual activities with Mr Haider, two other FPÖ politicians and Mother Teresa.

The painting did not fail to raise controversy. A visitor threw red paint at it, covering the part which happened to show Mr Meischberger, among others. Meanwhile, Mr Meischberger brought proceedings against the *Vereinigung*. He argued that the painting debased him and his political activities. In the end, he was successful: the painting could no longer be exhibited and compensation was awarded.

Importantly, when the *Vereinigung* brought the case in *Strasbourg*, the Court found that the aim of the interference was *not* to protect public morals, as had been the case in *Müller* – rather the Austrian courts had intervened to protect Mr Meischberger's reputation. This opened the door to an essentially political assessment of the situation. The Court noted that various members of the Austrian Freedom Party had strongly criticized Otto Mühl's work in the past. Hence his painting could be understood to constitute some sort of counter-attack against the FPÖ. Consequently, the Court found that the scene that depicted Mr Meischberger – admittedly 'in a somewhat outrageous manner' – did not concern his private life, but rather his public standing as a politician.

Adding insult to injury, the Court noted that Mr Meischberger was 'certainly one of the less well known of all the people appearing on the painting' and 'nowadays, since his retirement from politics, [he] is hardly remembered by the public at all'.[26] The Court also observed that, even before Mr Meischberger brought proceedings, 'his' part of the painting was covered by red paint. As a result, his portrayal was certainly diminished, if not totally eclipsed, by the portrayal of all the others, 'mostly more prominent', who were still completely visible.

In a similar vein, the Court drew attention to the satirical nature of the work. Satire, the Court remarked, is a form of artistic expression and social commentary and, 'by its inherent features of exaggeration and distortion of reality, naturally aims to provoke and agitate. Accordingly, any interference with an artist's right to such expression should be examined with particular care'.[27]

The Court lastly noted that the Austrian courts' injunction was not limited either in time or in space. It, therefore, prevented the exhibition of the painting, 'irrespective of whether Mr Meischberger was known, or was still known', at the place and time of a potential exhibition in the future. The Court concluded that the Austrian courts' injunction was disproportionate and, therefore, in violation of Article 10.

As was already mentioned, it was a narrow vote – four votes to three. But of the three dissenters, two agreed that the State's margin of appreciation should be particularly limited, 'or indeed practically non-existent', where its interference affects artistic freedom.[28]

26. *Vereinigung Bildender Künstler*, para. 35.
27. *Ibid.*, para. 33.
28. *Vereinigung Bildender Künstler*, joint dissenting opinion of Judges Spielmann and Jebens, para. 6. The two dissenters found, however, that the painting in question interfered excessively with the fundamental personal dignity of Mr. Meischberger. They referred with approval to an order of the German Federal Constitutional Court (3 June 1987; BVerfGE 75, 369) which they summarized as follows: 'where there was a conflict with human dignity, artistic freedom (*Kunstfreiheit*) must always be subordinate to personality rights'.

In the years that followed, the Court was confronted increasingly with cases that featured an amalgam of art and politics. More often than not, these cases concern 'artistic protests' in countries with authoritarian regimes. The cases differed from *Vereinigung* in that the protests were addressed directly against the authorities, and that they sometimes led to very high penalties. In response to this trend, the Court granted a high level of protection to 'expressive acts' that qualify as 'artistic and political at the same time'.[29]

This brings us to the end of our tour through the Strasbourg case law. The final note will come from the Russian feminist punk rock band *Pussy Riot*. The group gained fame - or notoriety - with its progressive stance and provocative actions. In 2012 it tried to stage a performance inside a cathedral in Moscow. The idea was to perform the song *Punk Prayer – Virgin Mary, Drive Putin Away* from the altar, in order to voice the group's protest against the support of the Orthodox Church for Mr Putin's election campaign. The band had invited journalists and media to the performance to gain publicity. The show did not last long, though. Although no service was taking place at the time, cathedral guards managed to force the band out within a minute. Afterwards, three group members were convicted of 'hooliganism motivated by religious hatred' and sentenced to two years' imprisonment.

When the Strasbourg Court reviewed the case, its starting point was that the performance constituted 'a mix of conduct and verbal expression' which amounted to 'a form of artistic and political expression covered by Article 10 ECHR'.[30] The Court accepted that the action could be seen as a breach of the accepted rules of conduct in a place of religious worship. Therefore, the imposition of certain sanctions might in principle be justified by the demands of protecting the rights of others. One can sense a trace of *Otto Preminger* here, but the Court seems less driven by deference for the dominant religion than by the wish not to be seen as condoning anti-religious hate speech. However, the Court noted that the group had not disrupted any religious services, nor had they caused any injuries or any damage to church property. In those circumstances, the punishment imposed on the group members was very severe.

Turning to the artistic side of the events, the Court noted that the Russian courts had not paid attention to the context of the performance. They had not examined the lyrics of the song which *Pussy Riot* had intended to perform: the conviction was based primarily on the group's conduct. Yet their actions neither contained elements of violence nor stirred up or justified violence, hatred or intolerance of believers. Against that background, the Court found a breach of Article 10.

29. *See* ECtHR, *Tatár and Fáber v. Hungary*, Appl. No. 26005/08, judgment of 12 June 2012, para. 41 (public display of dirty clothing near Parliament, meant to represent the 'dirty laundry of the nation'). *See also* ECtHR, *Murat Vural v. Turkey*, Appl. No. 9540/07, judgment of 21 October 2014, paras 40-56 (pouring paint on statues of Ataturk: an 'expressive act'); ECtHR, *Shvydka v. Ukraine*, Appl. No. 17888/12, judgment of 30 October 2014, paras 37-38 (detaching a ribbon from a wreath laid by the President of Ukraine at a monument: an 'act of political expression'); ECtHR, *Mătăsaru v. Moldova*, Appl. No. 69714/16, judgment of 15 January 2019, para. 31 (exposing sculptures of an obscene nature in front of the Prosecutor General's Office and attaching to them pictures of a politician and several senior prosecutors).
30. ECtHR, *Alekhina and others v. Russia*, Appl. No. 38004/12, judgment of 17 July 2018, para. 206.

2.5 Artistic Expression and the ECHR: *Prochain Arrêt*?

There is a risk that all these individual case descriptions add up to a dazzling sort of pointillism. So let's take a step back and ask ourselves which picture emerges. Clearly, the Court's case law on artistic expression has been the subject of quite a development.

If we stick to the metaphor of the Brussels metro system that was used in the introduction, the Court took off at high speed. It promised to protect expressions that 'offend, shock or disturb' (*Handyside*, 1976) and confirmed, as soon as the opportunity arose, that freedom of artistic expression falls within the ambit of Article 10 ECHR (*Müller*, 1988). But then the metro train immediately slowed down: the Court was not prepared to offer a high level of protection to controversial works of art. Acknowledging that different standards prevail in Europe when it comes to morals, it left a wide margin of appreciation for the authorities. As a result, no violations were found (*Müller*, 1988; *Otto Preminger*, 1994; *Wingrove*, 1997).

It was only at the turn of the century that the metro gained speed again: the Court found a breach of Article 10 in the case of the *Karataş* (1999), followed by the cases of *Vereinigung Bildender Künstler* (2007) and *Pussy Riot* (2018). Interestingly these cases concerned 'expressive acts' (a poem, a painting, a performance) that qualified as artistic *and political* at the same time. It wasn't so much *l'art pour l'art* that was granted protection: with a bit of exaggeration, it could be said that the Court protected political speech adorned with an artistic layer. Did the Court really increase its level of protection to artistic freedom as such? It is an open question. We will have to wait for an answer until the Court is confronted with an 'old-fashioned' case in which the artist shocks his environment without any political intention.[31]

From the metro station *Arts-Loi*, it is only two stops to *Schumann*. If we leave the metro there, we find ourselves in the heart of the EU – a convenient starting point for a short exploration of the position of artistic freedom in EU human rights law. We do not allow ourselves to be discouraged by the fact[32] that, unlike most other metro stations in Brussels, *Schumann* does not contain any works of art.

3 ARTISTIC EXPRESSION AND THE EU CHARTER OF FUNDAMENTAL RIGHTS

Indeed the first impression is promising. Unlike the ECHR, the Charter of Fundamental Rights of the EU specifically covers the concept of artistic freedom. Article 13 of the Charter explicitly states that 'the arts and scientific research shall be free of constraint. Academic freedom shall be respected'. This provision follows the example of, among

31. For instance in the case of ECtHR, *Samodurov and others v. Russia*, Appl. Nos. 22081/11 and 59476/12, communicated on 19 October 2017, one of at least nine cases about artistic expression that are currently pending before the Court and communicated to the respondent governments.
32. As this contribution was written at a time that the COVID-19 pandemic made travelling difficult, we have to resort to Wikipedia once more. The Dutch page on Schumann metro station mentions that one of the walls features a timeline ('Why did Brussels become the capital of Europe?'). However, according to the transport company Brussels Intercommunal Transport Company (MIVB) this 'qualifies as "cultural dynamics" rather than art'.

others, post-war German constitutional law, where the freedom of the arts (*Kunstfreiheit*) is specifically protected by Article 5(3) of the *Grundgesetz*.

The official explanations of Article 13 of the Charter are short and not very helpful.[33] No clarification of the term 'the arts' is offered, nor are we told how artistic and academic freedom relate to one another. Instead, it is pointed out that 'this right' (without specifying which right is meant) is deduced primarily from the freedoms of thought and expression. It is to be exercised having regard to Article 1 (human dignity) and is subject to the limitations set out in the case law on Article 10 ECHR. That does not bring us much further.

The field of application of the Charter is circumscribed by the scope of EU law. And since the EU does not have wide competencies in the area of culture, it does not come as a surprise that, so far, Article 13 of the Charter has featured in only a few cases before the Court of Justice of the EU. A recent high-profile case concerned the so-called *Lex CEU* which effectively forced the Central European University out of Budapest. This law triggered an infringement procedure against Hungary. In this case, Article 13 of the Charter played a role, but the emphasis was, understandably, on academic, not artistic, freedom.[34]

The main case to report here reminds us in the way of the adventures of Pussy Riot in Moscow: it is about music. But this is where the commonalities end. In 1977, the German band Kraftwerk recorded the song *Metall auf Metall*. Twenty years later, the artist Sabrina Setlur recorded a different song, entitled *Nur mir* - a different song, but it contained a rhythm sequence from the Kraftwerk song. The sequence, of about 2 seconds, had been sampled and included in a continuous loop that ran throughout *Nur mir* (which was perhaps not a very adequate title). Kraftwerk felt that this was a violation of their copyrights and went to court. This was the beginning of a long legal battle - a continuous loop, one might say - that would last well over 20 years.[35] Since intellectual property is a matter regulated by EU law, namely Directive 2001/29 on the harmonization of certain aspects of copyright and related rights in the information society,[36] the proceedings included a preliminary reference to the Court of Justice.[37]

The question before the Court was, essentially, whether the use of the sample was a 'reproduction' in the sense of Article 2(c) of Directive 2001/29 and thus a breach of the exclusive rights owned by Kraftwerk. The Luxembourg Court started by acknowledging that the use of a sound sample, even if very short, must, in principle, be regarded as a reproduction in part. However, an exception had to be made 'where a user, *in exercising the freedom of the arts*, takes a sound sample in order to use it, in a

33. For the official explanations *see* O.J. 2007, C 303/17, or, for instance, the helpful site of the EU Fundamental Rights Agency, fra.europa.eu.
34. Case C-66/18, *Commission v. Hungary*, ECLI:EU:C:2020:792, paras 222-228.
35. *See* Dobusch, 'Nächste Runde im Sample-Streit um "Metall auf Metall": Kein Sieger, nur Verlierer - BGH entschied zum dritten Mal über Remixfreiheit', in *Netspolitik.org*, 30 April 2020.
36. Directive 2001/29/EC of the European Parliament and of the Council of 22 May 2001 on the harmonization of certain aspects of copyright and related rights in the information society, O.J. 2001, L 167/10.
37. Case C-476/17, *Pelham GmbH and Others v. Ralf Hütter and Florian Schneider-Esleben*, ECLI:EU:C:2019:624.

modified form unrecognizable to the ear, in a new work'.[38] Of course, intellectual property rights deserve protection, but:

> A balance must be struck between that right and other fundamental rights, including freedom of the arts, enshrined in Article 13 of the Charter, which, in so far as it falls within the scope of freedom of expression, enshrined in Article 11 of the Charter and in Article 10(1) of the [ECHR], affords the opportunity to take part in the public exchange of cultural, political and social information and ideas of all kinds (*see*, to that effect, ECtHR, 24 May 1988, *Müller and Others v. Switzerland*, ..., § 27, and ECtHR, 8 July 1999, *Karataş v. Turkey*, ..., § 49).[39]

The Court felt that it would not be acceptable if the owner of the copyrights could always prevent each and every use of 'his' sound bites, even if it concerned a new artistic work that contained very short, modified and unrecognizable samples.

So the case led to an interpretation of intellectual property law. But what matters more for present purposes is the end of the quote. Of course, the *Müller* and *Karataş* judgments were not exactly leading authorities on the issue of sampling. But the reference may be seen as a signal that the Luxembourg Court is well aware of the Strasbourg jurisprudence and, arguably, is willing to take it into account. That is an important observation because a consistent approach by the two courts, each within its own domain, can contribute to a strong protection of fundamental rights in Europe.

4 CONCLUSION

Although it is unlikely that Marco would be personally attracted by the paintings and other artistic expressions that were discussed in this contribution, we do not exclude that he will be disappointed by the low level of protection that they received.

Despite its rhetoric about pluralism, tolerance and broadmindedness, the Strasbourg Court has been mostly deferent to the indignant reactions that controversial artworks triggered. Until the turn of the century, the Court was apparently not willing to go against the grain when artistic expressions 'offended, shocked or disturbed' the authorities or influential sectors of the population. Some lip service was paid to the 'poet's prerogative',[40] but that did not entail an impressive degree of protection.

In the last two decades, however, the European Court of Human Rights has become bolder, especially when artistic expressions were actually political in nature. This development is to be welcomed. One must expect that there will be increasing pressure on expressions that are artistic and political at the same time, and therefore extra vigilance is needed to preserve the space for free speech. Europe has entered an era where strong political forces are committed to everything but pluralism, tolerance and broadmindedness – the core values of democracy, according to the Strasbourg Court in *Handyside*. In a direct response to this development, the Court has acknowledged that the States are under a positive obligation to create an environment that

38. Case C-476/17, *Pelham*, para. 31. Emphasis added.
39. *Ibid.*, para. 34. ECLI numbers omitted.
40. ECommHR, *Karataş v. Turkey*, Appl. No. 23168/94, report of 11 December 1997, para. 49.

allows for a free exchange of opinions and ideas.[41] In order to establish the extent to which States comply with this obligation, art will be the litmus test. Art has this inherent capacity to provoke strong feelings, and in an environment where 'civic space' is shrinking and where identity politics create a climate of division and hostility, it seems inevitable that less tolerance will be displayed towards artistic expressions.[42] Seen from that perspective, the freedom of artistic expression may well become one of the front lines between liberal and illiberal forces in Europe in the not-so-distant future.

There is a distinct yet closely related development. In this context of polarization, one can imagine that those who wish to make their opinions known will be forced to be creative and voice their dissent in veiled, artistic ways.[43] Or, conversely, they will have recourse to exaggerations, crude symbolic acts, provocations and disturbing demonstrations: these 'rough' forms of expression are more likely to attract attention than conventional forms of protest. Inevitably, such an escalation will lead to hard cases for the courts to decide. One such hard case involved Anna and her frying pan at the Tomb of the Unknown Soldier. When she was sentenced to three years' imprisonment, she was not too sure if she could count on the Strasbourg Court. She could not: the Court found that her conviction was not disproportionate.[44] It was a split vote though, four votes to three. This is not much of a consolation to Anna, but the fact that the Court was so divided, as it had been in most of the cases under review here, illustrates how judges still struggle to agree on the right approach.

Amidst all this political turmoil, one should of course not forget the 'pure' artistic expressions. There must still be artists who shock their environment without any political intention, and they deserve protection too. In other words, one may hope that the Strasbourg Court will be prepared to meet its promise of the 1970s: to counterbalance the intuitive *or* deliberate reactions of 'the State or any sector of the population'. Recently the Court of Justice of the EU has joined the fray, and it will be interesting to see how it will develop its potential.

This journey started at the metro station *Arts-Loi* in the centre of Brussels. We passed several stations, engrossed in a conversation about the relationship between the arts and law. Time to get out now, even though the metro has not yet reached the end of the line. But already, one thing is clear: it is high time for lawyers to take art seriously. As Marco has always done.

41. ECtHR, *Dink a.o. v. Turkey*, Appl. No. 2668/07, judgment of 14 September 2010, para. 137.
42. *See* EU Fundamental Rights Agency, *Protecting Civic Space in the EU*, Vienna 2021, esp. p. 33.
43. Indeed on 3 May 2022 the new 'Kofi Annan Courage in Cartooning Award' was awarded to Ukrainian and Hungarian press cartoonists. On the same day the Human Rights Foundation (HRF) announced the three recipients of the 2022 Václav Havel International Prize for Creative Dissent.
44. ECtHR, *Sinkova v. Ukraine*, Appl. No. 39496/11, 27 February 2018, para. 111, noting that Anna was given only a suspended sentence; 'she did not serve a single day of it'.

CHAPTER 17

The Right to Regulate and Investor-State Dispute Settlement: Renewable Energy and the Fair and Equitable Treatment Standard

Robert Howse & Sarah Levin[*]

In order to address climate change, governments in the European Union (EU) and elsewhere have created markets for renewably generated electricity through subsidies, price supports and related measures. Over time, as governments learn from their experience with incentivizing green energy through such schemes, and also cope with other budgetary priorities, it is understandable that the nature and amount of support would be adjusted (especially since costs of renewables generation have fallen remarkably). When Spain, however, attempted such adjustments, it was faced with an avalanche of claims by investors in the renewables market under the Energy Charter Treaty (ECT). This essay explores how in Investor-State Arbitration under the ECT, arbitrators have responded to investors' arguments that they are entitled to compensation in damages because regulatory changes (for legitimate policy reasons) negatively impacted the economic value of their investments. While in some cases (e.g., Charanne), tribunals have rightly held that such changes are, in fact, to be expected in an experimental regulatory scheme and cannot attract liability under the fair and equitable treatment (FET) standard in the ECT, others (such as Eiser) have held Spain liable in damages for economically rational policy adjustments. Overall, these

* For several years, Howse served as an advisor to the Renewable Energy and International Law Project of REEP, a consortium of private sector and other actors. In this version of the chapter, Howse takes sole responsibility for the section on *Eiser*.

cases create uncertainty about the scope for experimentation in devising climate change policies that are economically viable. This uncertainty is bad for climate policy and for economic efficiency generally.

1 INTRODUCTION: INTERNATIONAL ECONOMIC LAW AND SUSTAINABILITY

An essential theme in the scholarship and advocacy of Marco Bronckers is that international economic law should promote sustainable economy-strong environmental and social standards.[1] Marco has explored how basic provisions of the central World Trade Organization (WTO) treaty on trade in goods, the General Agreement on Tariffs and Trade (GATT), should be interpreted to provide appropriate space for domestic social and environmental regulation. In this regard, his 2000 article with McNelis stands as a seminal study of the concept of likeness in the non-discrimination obligation of GATT that concerns domestic regulations (National Treatment).[2] The Appellate Body (AB) of the WTO, through incorporating elements of the approach sketched by Marco and a range of other doctrinal moves, evolved a jurisprudence according to priority to what the AB would refer to as the 'right to regulate,' the policy space of WTO Members to engage in non-discriminatory regulation of non-trade concerns, allowing for States' divergent judgments about policy priorities and regulatory policy tools.[3]

In the case of the investment regime (a decentralized international legal system consisting of numerous bilateral investment treaties and other agreements, such as the Energy Charter Treaty), in contrast with the WTO, the protection for the 'right to regulate' is, generally speaking, highly precarious. There is no *jurisprudence constante* in the investment regime (ad hoc arbitral tribunals regularly contradict each other on basic doctrinal choices). A significant number of arbitral awards seem indifferent to the need of States for policy space to regulate concerns such as the environment or climate change. Other tribunal decisions show greater sensitivity to regulatory autonomy. But uncertainty as to what a tribunal might do in terms of imposing liability in monetary damages for non-discriminatory policies that harm the economic interests of investors has led to justified worries about regulatory chill. Criticisms are particularly severe involving the fair and equitable treatment (FET) norm, a concept absent in WTO law.

1. Bronckers and Gruni, 'Retooling the sustainability standards in EU free trade agreements', 24 *Journal of International Economic Law* (2021), 25-51.
2. Bronckers and McNelis, 'Rethinking the "like product" definition in GATT 1994: Anti-dumping and environmental protection', in Cottier (Ed.), *Regulatory Barriers and the Principle of Non-Discrimination in World Trade Law: Past, Present, and Future* (University of Michigan Press, 2000), pp. 345-386.
3. Howse, 'The World Trade Organization 20 years on: Global governance by judiciary', 27 *European Journal of International Law* (2016), 9-77.

2 FAIR AND EQUITABLE TREATMENT AND REGULATORY STABILIZATION

Beginning with the notorious *Tecmed* award, several arbitral tribunals have suggested that, even apart from contractual or other specific commitments to investors, FET includes an obligation to stabilize the regulatory framework, at least to some extent, in order to avoid economic harm to existing foreign investors and investments. Some tribunals have been reluctant to read such an obligation into FET, though they have been prepared to find a violation where specific commitments or representations have been made. Still other decisions have focused either on the procedures of regulatory change (transparency, notice, consultation with the investor, due process of law) or, less explicitly, on the motivation for regulatory change (discrimination, political games, opportunism versus legitimate policy reasons). The inconsistent approaches arbitrators have taken have led to an enormous amount of unpredictability and make the *regulatory chill* hypothesis highly plausible: a risk-averse host State might well avoid otherwise socially efficient regulatory changes given the uncertainty as to whether an investor-State dispute settlement (ISDS) tribunal will adopt a narrow approach to FET that allows States to make changes without specific commitments or representation or very expansive approach, essentially requiring stabilization. The latter approach would lead democratic governments to avoid important regulatory changes, which in turn would have dire consequences for the constituents of those governments. ISDS tribunals are not the only international judicial instances that impose limits on democratic decision-making, of course. So do regional human rights courts, for example. However, ISDS carries the risk of liability in damages that can rise to billions of dollars. That is a uniquely high cost to impose on public decision-making.

There are a number of possible solutions to this problem. For some critics, experience with FET is an important ingredient in advancing the case that investment protection with ISDS should be eliminated in order to preserve regulatory democracy. Another option would be to remove the standard FET language from investment agreements while preserving perhaps obligations on transparency and national treatment. A third possibility would be to rewrite FET clauses to limit strictly the scope of application to situations of procedural unfairness or impropriety, discriminatory intent, or cases of specific commitments or inducements on which the investor reasonably relied. And finally, the FET obligation could be subject to a general public policy exception, like Article XX GATT or the updated Indian model investment agreement.

In this essay, we use the context of the ISDS litigation avalanche against changes to host States' regulatory frameworks for renewable energy as a case study to illuminate these issues and possible solutions, focusing particularly on one award against Spain under the Energy Charter Treaty, the *Eiser* case, where (unlike some other awards addressing the same overall regulatory regime for renewable energy) the tribunal found Spain liable in damages for changes to its regulatory framework, without any evidence of discrimination nor of the breach of a specific commitment or representation to the investor by the Spanish government.

3 POLICY-MAKING EXPERIMENTATION TO MITIGATE CLIMATE CHANGE: GOVERNMENT-CREATED MARKETS FOR CLEAN ENERGY

Governments have created markets for electricity from renewable energy sources (RES), mostly wind and solar, but also, in some cases, geothermal, in order to change the energy mix. The intent of governments in doing was to mitigate climate change by shifting away from energy sources with high carbon emissions. These markets are relatively new. Governments, responding to the high price of generating electricity from renewable sources, created regimes offering a mix of subsidies and price supports to incentivize generation. With little experience in creating these types of programmes, particularly in the renewable energy space, in the initial phases of these programmes, governments made huge assumptions regarding technology, potential capacity, balances and imbalances on the grid. Governments have faced challenges of asymmetrical information in evaluating the likely behaviour of private firms in response to the different incentive structures. For these reasons, one would expect a steep learning curve from the actual operation of these programs, and therefore that governments would end up changing, perhaps multiple times, and indeed substantially, the regulatory framework in light of information revealed by the actual experience of operating these markets.

It would not be surprising, however, if investors bargained for some degree of stabilization to manage the uncertainty about these markets and to protect large investments at the front end. In the absence of such a bargain, one would imagine a strong presumption that regulatory change would occur as a normal matter, adjusting to these neophyte markets as they actually evolve.

This chapter takes guidance from scholars, such as Joseph Stiglitz, who argue that it is generally inefficient for the government to compensate private actors for a State's regulatory change.[4] This view is supported by law and economics scholarship, including that of Louis Kaplow[5] and Richard Revesz.[6]

Promises to stabilize regulation in specific cases could, of course, be understood as a form of investment incentive, especially where the foreign investor makes a large 'captive' up-front investment and the host State can, through regulatory change, capture down the road more of the rents from the venture than anticipated *ex ante*, leaving the investor trapped with sizeable sunk costs. This is sometimes understood as

4. Stiglitz, 'Regulating multinational corporations: Towards principles of cross-border legal frameworks in a globalized world balancing rights with responsibilities', 23 *American University International Law Review* (2008), 451-558.
5. Kaplow, 'An economic analysis of legal transitions', 99 *Harvard Law Review* (1986), 509-617. Kaplow shows that firms can manage the risk of regulatory change through a variety of market mechanisms; there is no convincing case of market failure that suggests the need for the government to intervene.
6. Nash and Revesz, 'Grandfathering and environmental regulation: The law and economics of new source review', *NYU Law and Economics Working Papers* (2007) No. 07-10, at 47: 'Rules of legal transition relief are inadvisable because they give rise to poor incentives: They discourage actors from anticipating changes in legal rules, and they encourage actors to seek economic rents from transition relief regimes.'

the 'obsolescing bargain' or the 'hold up' concept. However, the economic case against compensation for regulatory change as a general principle provides us with a sceptical presumption of FET that provides a general stabilization guarantee to all foreign investors covered by the treaty in all circumstances, regardless of the business and financial judgments investors have made and absent any clearly bargained for specific commitments.

4 REGULATORY STABILIZATION, FAIR AND EQUITABLE TREATMENT, AND THE PROTECTION OF INVESTOR 'EXPECTATIONS': INCONSISTENT APPROACHES BY ISDS TRIBUNALS

The varying approaches tribunals have taken to determine a violation of FET are apparent from contrasting two frequently cited foundational cases. In *Técnicas v. Mexico*, the tribunal held that the Mexican government's refusal to renew Tecmed's licence was non-transparent, contradictory and unreasonably inconsistent such that it affected Tecmed's basic expectations and therefore a violation of FET under Article 4 of the Spain-Mexico bilateral treaty (BIT). The tribunal based its reasoning of FET on principles of good faith and an investor's legitimate, reasonable expectations and found that the Mexican government's actions lacked due process, transparency and a reasonable amount of certainty.[7]

By contrast, the tribunal in *Waste Management, Inc. v. Mexico* posits a drastically different standard, holding that FET is violated by a lack of due process, which results in impropriety. The tribunal describes the standard as follows:

> the minimum standard of treatment of FET is infringed by conduct attributable to the State and harmful to the claimant if the conduct is arbitrary, grossly unfair, unjust or idiosyncratic, is discriminatory and exposes the claimant to sectional or racial prejudice, or involves a lack of due process leading to an outcome which offends judicial propriety – as might be the case with a manifest failure of natural justice in judicial proceedings or a complete lack of transparency and candour in an administrative process. In applying this standard it is relevant that the treatment is in breach of representations made by the host State which were reasonably relied on by the claimant.[8]

The *Waste Management* tribunal put forward a standard of FET that maintains customary law's minimum standard of treatment under the North American Free Trade Agreement. The standards and rationales provided by the *Waste Management* and *Tecmed* tribunals illustrate the competing narratives of the meaning of FET and how these variances in standards ultimately shape the differences in outcomes.

7. *Técnicas Medioambientales Tecmed, S.A. v. United Mexican States*, ICSID Case No. ARB (AF)/00/2, award of 29 May 2003.
8. *Waste Management Inc. v. Mexico*, ICSID Case No. ARB(AF)00/3, award of 30 April 2004, para. 98, quoted in *Mobil Investments Canada Inc. & Murphy Oil Corporation v. Canada*, ICSID Case No. ARB(AF)/07/04, decision on liability and on principles of quantum of 22 May 2012, para. 141, and in *Cargill, Incorporated v. United Mexican States*, ICSID Case No. ARB(AF)/05/2, award of 18 September 2009, para. 282.

5 REGULATORY CHANGE AND RENEWABLE ENERGY IN SPAIN: *EISER V. SPAIN*

The *Eiser* decision was preceded by an arbitral award addressing Spain's renewable energy programme that took into account in a sensitive way the regulatory interests in question and the justification Spain had for altering its program, *Charanne v. Spain*.[9] As with *Eiser*, the claimants made capital investments under a federal government scheme of subsidies to incentivize investment in the renewable energy sector. Once investments had been made by each claimant, market changes and realized maintenance costs led the government to make legitimate public policy decisions to alter the subsidy schemes. International law leaves no doubt that a sovereign State has the power to make legitimate public policy decisions, and many investment treaties recall this explicitly through non-precluded measures or essential security provisions.

At the time the investments were made by the ISDS claimants, Spain had regulations that incentivized investment through '[a] system of premiums and regulated tariffs to remunerate electricity production originating from photovoltaics'.[10] The process by which Spain enacted these regulations was important to the investor safeguards, particularly with respect to receiving notice and having a platform to air grievances to the government as a result of any regulatory changes. There are three types of laws and regulations in the Spanish legal system:

> Laws and Royal Decree-laws have the force of law and are superior to Royal Decrees. Royal Decrees, having a regulatory status and being subordinate to Laws, are implemented and supplemented by Ministerial Orders and Resolutions, which are at a lower rank than Royal Decrees. One of the distinctions between a Royal Decree and a Royal Decree-Law is that the former involves a mandatory hearing procedure for those affected by the regulation, whereas this procedure does not apply to Royal Decree-Laws. Another distinction is that Royal Decrees may be subject to challenge and review by organs of administrative jurisdiction, whereas Royal Decree-Laws may not.[11]

The Spanish Government enacted the 2007 Royal Decree in May 2007 to 'regulate the energy activities under the special regime' and provide a 'new regulatory framework for the electricity production under the special regime'.[12] The Decree 'guarantee[d] the facility owners operating under the special regime reasonable compensation for their investment' with 'lesser administrative intervention in fixing the electricity prices' and 'a better and more efficient attribution of the costs of the system'.[13] The Decree set forth the rights of producers and established three categories of tariffs, dependent on the working capacity of the facility – a producer with a smaller working capacity received higher compensation.[14] Each category has 'two fixed regulated

9. *Charanne B.V. and Construction Investments S.A.R.L. v. Kingdom of Spain*, SCC Case No. V 062/2012, award of 21 January 2016.
10. *Ibid.*, para. 79.
11. *Ibid.*, paras 90-91.
12. *Ibid.*, para. 110.
13. *Ibid.*, para. 111.
14. *Ibid.*, para. 122.

tariffs: a higher applicable rate for the first 25 years of the lifespan of the facility, and a lower applicable rate starting from the 26th year'.[15]

The Decree provides revision procedures for the tariffs, premiums, supplements and also sets a limit up to which facilities are entitled to benefit under the special regulatory regime. Article 44 of the Decree sets forth the terms of revision of the tariffs:

> During 2010, in view of the outcome of the monitoring reports on the compliance degree with the Renewable Energy Plan (PER) 2005-2010 Strategy for Energy Saving and Efficiency in Spain (E4), as well as new objectives in the following PER for 2011-2020, a revision will be undertaken regarding tariffs, premiums and supplements, as well as lower and higher applicable rate limits defined in this Royal Decree, taking into account costs associated with each of these technologies, the level of involvement of the special regime in the overage of the demand and its impact on the technical and economic management of the system, always guaranteeing rates of reasonable return with reference to the cost of currency in the capital market. Every four years thereafter, a new review will be carried out in accordance with the above criteria.[16]

In addition, the tribunal notes several promotional materials, incentives and opportunities that the Spanish government used to market the renewable energy sector from 2005 to 2007.[17] The 2008 Royal Decree was enacted for facilities that were not able to benefit under the 2007 Decree as a result of registration timing.[18] Whether a facility was regulated by the 2007 Decree or 2008 Decree turned on whether the facility was registered after 29 September 2008.[19] In 2008, a report of the National Energy Commission noted that '[u]nder Article 22 of RS 661/2007 and Resolution CNE of 27 September 2007, the facilities registered after 29 September 2008 could no longer benefit from the regime established in RD 661/2007'.[20] However, the 2008 report reaffirmed the legal certainty and protection of legitimate investor expectations for the initial and new regimes, stating that 'periodic reviews every four years have been planned solely for the newly established facilities', not for those regulated by the 2007 Decree.[21] Facilities subject to the 2007 Decree were regulated and revised according to 'establish[ed] transparent mechanisms consisting of annual updates of such mechanisms' with the purpose of providing certainty to investments and significantly limiting regulatory risk.[22]

Under the 2008 Royal Decree, the Spanish Government established a new regime for the same type of facilities and maintained a regulatory scheme based on incentives and subsidies to continue to promote the photovoltaic sector in Spain. However, the 2008 Decree reduced the incentives from the 2007 Decree, particularly around compensation.

15. *Ibid.*
16. *Ibid.*, para. 125.
17. *Ibid.*, paras 95-107.
18. *Ibid.*, para. 136.
19. *Ibid.*
20. *Ibid.*, para. 129.
21. *Ibid.*, para. 131.
22. *Ibid.*, para. 132.

While the 2007 Decree provided for fixed compensation, the 2008 Decree 'provide[d] for quarterly tenders by quotas... which would be reduced to the extent that the tenders are filled'.[23] The 2008 Decree likely adapted to the fact that fixed compensation is arguably economically inefficient because it provides a rate of return that is, in effect, risk free. The Decree also set a maximum time period of 25 years for a 'tariff applicable to a facility ... [starting] from the latest commissioning date of the facility or the date of registration'.[24] In addition, the 2008 Decree allowed for revisions to the regulated rates 'from 1 January of the second year following the tender in which it was assigned'.[25] These changes were significant.

Under the 2010 Decree, the Spanish government again modified its 'support framework for renewable energy projects by cutting financial support, especially to photovoltaic electricity production, improving the technical integration of renewable energy installations and easing administrative procedures'.[26] Once a generator hit a particular threshold, additional energy was not eligible for government support and 'excess electricity generated by that particular installation during that particular year [would] not be supported and [would] be sold at the wholesale electricity market price'.[27]

Despite these changes, the government also implemented some stabilizing aspects as a part of the Decree in order to mitigate the impact of the changes on generators. For example, '[b]etween 2011 and 2013, the share of equivalent hours remain[ed] as established in the PER 2005-2010 and concerned power stations ... enjoy[ed] three extra years of Government support, scaling up the support period from 25 to 28 years'.[28]

In December 2010, the Spanish government again sought to shrink 'the tariff deficit in the electricity sector'.[29] This Royal Decree-Law placed a 'limit on operating hours of photovoltaic facilities' and essentially taxed economic actors in the renewable energy sector by establishing 'an obligation to pay charges for the use of the transportation and distribution network'.[30]

The Government nonetheless maintained the guarantee that facilities registered under the 2007 and 2008 Decrees would 'continue receiving compensation in the form of payment on account in accordance with the scheme applicable under the new methodology' until remuneration could be determined.[31] This allowed for the facilities registered under the 2007 and 2008 Decrees to avoid some, but not all, of the new taxes and fees placed on more recently registered facilities.

However, in 2012, Spain imposed further changes. The Government placed new taxes on the electricity sector, had 'a complete reversal of the philosophy of special

23. *Ibid.*, para. 140.
24. *Ibid.*, para. 141.
25. *Ibid.*, para. 142.
26. *See* iea.org/policiesandmeasures/pams/spain/name-24874-en.php (last visited February 2022).
27. *See* iea.org/policiesandmeasures/pams/spain/name-24874-en.php (last visited February 2022).
28. *See ibid.*
29. *Charanne*, para. 156.
30. *Ibid.*, para. 158.
31. *Ibid.*, para. 183.

regime remuneration ... enacted under RD-Law 1/2012 ... applied [new regulations] to all new facilities and abolishe[d] the economic regime regulated under RD 661/2007 (the FIT feed-in tariff scheme)'.[32] The Spanish government declared its concerns and rationale in the preamble to the legislation:

> The preamble to this urgent Decree refers to the high tariff deficit that could jeopardise the sustainability of the electricity system; the complex economic and financial situation for maintaining the incentives to renewable facilities; the excess installed generating capacity sufficient to ensure that demand is met; the fact that in 2010 a number of technologies (wind power, solar photovoltaic and solar thermal power) had exceeded the targets of Spain's PER 2005-2010, and achieving Europe's renewable energy targets for 2020 was possible.[33]

5.1 Policy Space for Regulatory Change Prior to *Eiser*: *Charanne v. Spain*

The *Eiser* decision was preceded by an arbitral award addressing Spain's renewable energy programme that took into account in a sensitive way the regulatory interests in question and the justification Spain had for altering its program, *Charanne v. Spain*. As with *Eiser*, the claimants made capital investments under a federal government scheme of subsidies to incentivize investment in the renewable energy sector. Developing a renewable energy sector in both countries required these heavy capital investments, which were undertaken in reliance on these subsidy schemes. Once investments had been made by each claimant, market changes and realized maintenance costs led the governments to make legitimate public policy decisions to alter the subsidy schemes. International law leaves no doubt that a sovereign State has the power to make legitimate public policy decisions, and many investment treaties recall this explicitly through non-precluded measures or essential security provisions.

In *Charanne*, the two claimants were Dutch and Luxembourg companies who were shareholders of a limited liability company called Grupo T-Solar Global SA ('T-Solar'), whose activities include 'generation and sale of electricity produced by photovoltaic solar plants'.[34] The claimants attained their investment in T-Solar through an acquisition of Grupo Isolux Corsan Concesiones SA and Grupo Isolux Corsan SA. 'At the time of the notification of the dispute, T-Solar owned, via certain companies, 34 production facilities generating electricity by means of solar photovoltaic technology under the special regime.'[35]

5.2 The Legal Standard for FET Applied by the *Charanne* Tribunal

In *Charanne*, based on the regulatory changes summarized in section 5 above, the claimants alleged that 'after attracting their investments in the photovoltaic generation

32. European Parliament, Petition No. 2520/2014, 29 February 2016, at 2.
33. *Ibid.*
34. *Charanne*, para. 4.
35. *Ibid.*, para. 5.

sector', the Spanish Government 'unlawfully amended the special regime regulating the industry, causing various losses'.[36] The aforementioned changes served as the basis of the claimant's accusations. Legal and administrative challenges were brought to Spain and were heard by the nation's highest court. In 2012, the Spanish Supreme Court held that the 2010 Royal Decree 'was consistent with the law and did not violate investors' legitimate expectations in accordance with the Spanish law'.[37]

The tribunal analysed both expropriation and FET claims on the merits of the dispute. Article 26(6) of the Energy Charter Treaty (ECT) States that 'a tribunal ... shall decide the issues in dispute in accordance with this Treaty and applicable rules and principles of international law'.[38] The tribunal found that there was no direct or indirect expropriation on the part of the Spanish Government and that Spain had met its obligation to provide effective means for claimants' claims.[39]

In analysing the FET claims related only to the 2010 Decree and laws, the tribunal focused on the Spanish government's actions and the claimant's reasonable and legitimate expectations. The tribunal wrote, 'in the absence of a specific commitment toward stability, an investor cannot have a legitimate expectation that a regulatory framework such as that at issue in this arbitration is to not be modified at any time to adapt to the needs of the market and to the public interest'.[40]

5.3 The *Eiser* Tribunal's Interpretation of the Regulatory Facts

Contrary to claimant's allegations, the tribunal found that alteration of the regulatory framework did not infringe on the claimant's legitimate expectations because there was no specific commitment made to them by the government. The tribunal used an objective test to find that promotional materials encouraging investors to make investments within the renewable energy sector in Spain were not enough to entail a specific commitment. Promotional materials '[did] not include any language from which it can be reasonably inferred that the regulated tariff would remain untouched for the rest of the regulatory lives of the plants'.[41] The tribunal went further in stating that the broad applicability of these regulatory changes, even if narrowed considerably, would not serve as a specific commitment. The tribunal held that 'in absence of a specific commitment, an investor cannot have a legitimate expectation that existing rules will not be modified'.[42]

However, the tribunal analysed the modifications to see whether they were so substantial or disproportionate, arbitrary, non-transparent, unreasonable or inconsistent that by themselves they violated FET. The tribunal concluded that the Spanish government continued to provide regulatory stability through transparent and non-ambiguous, reasonable regulatory changes, reserving its right to amend the legislation

36. *Ibid.*, para. 80.
37. *Ibid.*, para. 173.
38. *Ibid.*, para. 16.
39. *Ibid.*, paras 455-467.
40. *Ibid.*, para. 510.
41. *Ibid.*, para. 497.
42. *Ibid.*, para. 499.

in this way. In agreement with the Respondent, the tribunal argued that the claimants should have been more diligent in their investment research. Furthermore, the claimants did not establish that the regulatory changes were 'unfair or inconsistent' or that they were 'adopted in violation of Spanish legislative and regulatory due process'.[43]

Although required to register, the tribunal did not agree with the claimants that the registration requirement gave them an 'acquired right to determined compensation'.[44] The tribunal stated that 'there is no principle of international law prohibiting a State to take regulatory measures with immediate effect in situations in progress except when there are specific commitments as those resulting from a contract'.[45] The tribunal concluded that the registration requirement was purely administrative and that without a specific commitment, the Spanish government, under both the treaty and international law, did not have liability for these regulatory changes in 2010.

Acknowledging that Spain did, in fact, amend an essential element of the regulations governing photovoltaic operators and facilities, the tribunal found that Spain acted reasonably, consistently, proportionally and within the public interest (and therefore, the tribunal found, within international law).[46] The tribunal found that the Government's actions were reasonable in aiming to 'prevent[] the technical collapse of the system and contribute to ensure better security and management'.[47] The tribunal found Spain's justifications for the policies persuasive and not in breach of FET.

Finally, the tribunal found that the 2010 changes were reasonable and distinct from the cases in Argentina because they were not retroactive.[48] The tribunal states that the situation addressed here vastly differs from the case in *CMS v. Argentina* and provides two reasons. First, in this case, there was no contractual commitment as there was in *CMS*. Here, the court writes, 'Here the issue is to determine to what extent the State can modify and immediately apply regulatory measures of general application.'[49] Second, claimants argue that the case here was similar to the situation in *CMS* because both governments effectuated retroactive regulatory change. The tribunal again disagreed and stated that 'the claimants' argument on retroactivity is simply a different formulation of the argument that the State did not have any possibility to alter the legal framework benefiting the claimant's plants'.[50] Furthermore, the tribunal explained, 'the obligation to accord FET does not mean that the regulatory framework should remain the same for all eligible plants throughout their lifespans. In fact, such an approach would amount to freezing the regulatory framework, limiting any change of the regulation to new generation plants that would settle after such changes'.[51]

43. *Ibid.*, para. 539.
44. *Ibid.*, para. 510.
45. *Ibid.*, para. 548.
46. *Ibid.*, paras 539-541.
47. *Ibid.*, para. 538.
48. *Ibid.*, paras 543-549.
49. *Ibid.*, para. 545.
50. *Ibid.*, para. 546.
51. *Ibid.*

In sum, the *Charanne* tribunal sought to articulate within the concept of FET a version of the 'right to regulate' – the notion that, even if a regulatory action caused unexpected economic disadvantage to the investor that, if non-discriminatory, reasonable and proportionate, to a legitimate public policy objective, the regulatory action does not violate the FET standard, at least not unless some other legal principle is undermined, such as non-retroactivity or reliance on specific representations or promises.

5.4 *Eiser*: A Huge Leap in the Wrong Direction

The *Eiser* award stands in stark contrast to *Charanne*. The *Eiser* tribunal found that there is an obligation of stabilization regardless of whether a specific commitment or representation was made to the investor. Under the *Eiser* doctrine, the host State assumes per se liability for a change to any 'essential characteristic' of a regulatory scheme on which the investor may have relied under FET, regardless of the rationality of the change and the importance of the public policy goals being advanced. As will be seen, the *Eiser* tribunal finesses its departure from *Charanne* by characterizing the regulatory change introduced by Spain as a complete overturning of the entire legal and regulatory framework, in contrast to the purportedly more modest changes in *Charanne*. The *Eiser* tribunal also sometimes misrepresents its own doctrine as based on the reasonableness of regulatory change, at one point characterizing the regulatory change at issue as 'total and unreasonable'.[52] Of course, large or fundamental changes in a regulatory scheme could be reasonable. In fact, the tribunal never identified *anything* unreasonable about the regulatory change and admitted elsewhere in the award that in fact the goal of fiscal savings was a reasonable one[53] and that the regulatory change achieved this purpose.[54]

5.5 Information Asymmetries and Efficient Incentive Regulation

Indeed even if the *Eiser* tribunal had gone beyond the mere assertion that the regulatory change challenged by the investor was 'unreasonable' and sought to give *reasons* for a finding of unreasonableness, it would not likely have succeeded. Based on sound regulatory economics that takes into account information asymmetries, the change was eminently reasonable. The regulatory change at issue came on the heels of a change of government in Spain and the determination of the new government to introduce fiscal responsibility into the programme of State aid for renewable energy. Instead of setting State aid in such a manner as to guarantee a fixed rate of return to investors, regardless

52. *Eiser Infrastructure Limited and Energía Solar Luxembourg S.à.r.l. v. Kingdom of Spain*, ICSID Case No. ARB/13/36, award of 4 May 2017, para. 363.
53. *Ibid.*, para. 371: 'Respondent faced a legitimate public policy problem with its tariff deficit, and the tribunal does not question the appropriateness of Spanish authorities adopting reasonable measures to address the situation.'
54. *Ibid.*, para. 150: 'The new measures were intended to, and did, accomplish the objective of significantly reducing the level of subsidies paid to CSP and other renewables generators.'

of the cost structure of the investor's operation, now the benchmark would be established based on a hypothetical facility that achieved a certain minimum level of efficiency in its costs.

A common problem when a State uses a subsidy instrument to induce a private economic actor to achieve a certain outcome (here providing renewable energy to the grid) is to determine the amount of the subsidy. A common way of doing this is to set the subsidy so as to guarantee the private economic actor a certain rate of return over costs. As has been widely explored in the regulatory economics literature – most profoundly by the Toulouse School economists Laffont and Tirole[55] – straightforward rate of return regulation greatly reduces incentives for cost reduction: the private economic actor is guaranteed the same rate of return regardless of whether it has high costs or low costs.

One solution to this is to provide a lump-sum subsidy, but due to information asymmetries, this approach can be problematic; the government cannot know exactly how much of a lump sum is needed to induce an efficient firm to achieve a given outcome. Firms have a strong incentive not to reveal the minimum level of subsidization that would induce them to produce the outcome because they would like to pocket maximize the subsidy. Unless the government can find a way to induce firms to reveal their cost structures, the lump sum risks being too large or too small relative to what would be required to induce the outcome in question. Thus, it is understandable that, first, given the extreme information asymmetries about costs in the first instance, Spain launched its renewable energy programme with the rate of return regulation, which virtually assures that the outcome will be achieved since the firm is given a reward regardless of its costs; and second, once information about costs of different firms was revealed through the application of rate of return regulation, Spain would seek to reward cost efficient firms by limiting the subsidy so that a firm must have a certain level of cost efficiency to earn the required rate of return.

This was exactly the function of the measure attacked in *Eiser*. Spain's regulatory trajectory from rate-of-return regulation to a more calibrated approach that sought to incentivize cost reduction in light of information revealed about firms' costs was entirely predictable. Regulatory economics suggests that this is how a rational State would proceed in creating a new market in an area where to start with, there is little revealed information about firms' costs.

The *Eiser* tribunal could not deny that the motive for the new government's regulatory changes was a legitimate one, although it disparaged, for no apparent good reason other than the novelty of the regulatory approach, the new methodology as if its economic logic were unclear. In a highly tendentious manner, the tribunal sought to besmirch the new regulatory approach by indicating that it was controversial and heavily debated.[56]

55. Laffont and Tirole, 'Using cost observations to regulate firms', 94 *Journal of Political Economy* (1986), 614-641; Laffont and Tirole, *Theory of incentives in procurement and regulation* (MIT Press, 1993).
56. *Eiser*, para. 407.

However, most regulatory changes that affect different governmental and private interests in various ways are heavily contested in liberal democracies. This says nothing about their intrinsic merits. For the tribunal, 'sweep and novelty'[57] in regulation are inherently suspicious or questionable. Yet, this is merely a conservative prejudice of sorts, a bias against change. Policy challenges may merit or not, as the case may be, a more modest or a more radical change in regulatory approach. Especially in a novel area such as renewable energy, as noted earlier in this paper, it would be extremely odd to make a working assumption that social welfare maximizing regulatory change would necessarily be marginal or minor as opposed to the original regulatory framework needing significant overhaul. While the tribunal was obviously ignorant of regulatory economics and incapable of critiquing the specific cost formulas in the changed regulatory scheme, it appeared to find in some way suspicious or questionable that the costs of a hypothetical plant, extrapolating from revealed information about actual costs of specific elements, were used as a benchmark rather than the costs structures of existing firms.[58]

However, since these costs structures would precisely have reflected the lack of incentive for cost minimization in the historical rate of return approach, using the historical data of actual firms as a benchmark would have undermined Spain's very objective of introducing an appropriate incentive for cost efficiency in the amount of its subsidy. Be that as it may, the tribunal could not point to any issue of procedural fairness or impropriety; in fact, the legality of the regulatory changes was upheld by Spain's highest court.[59] The tribunal, at one point in its award, suggested that it was a failing of Spain not to have taken into account the circumstances of the particular investor, but a careful reading of the award suggests that this is in fact a red herring; it is another way of stating that if Spain had acted in such a way as to protect the interests of the particular investor in question, it would not have moved to a methodology that takes into account efficiency. Further, this goes to the fundamental reason why Spain's regulatory change negatively impacted the claimant; it had an inefficient cost structure. The claimant had decided to take a risky bet: it would invest heavily at the outset in order to have large capacity available to go online down the road instead of taking more of a wait-and-see approach to how this fledging market would develop. Thus, claimant's venture was heavily leveraged; and much of its borrowing had to be done on terms shaped by the financial crisis. Nothing short of preposterous, and perhaps disingenuous, is the tribunal's insinuation that, because some of Spain's officials were aware of the claimant's financing practices,[60] this represented some sort of endorsement of these practices or assumption of responsibility to ensure that Eiser would remain viable despite the vulnerable financial structure in question.

57. *Ibid.*, para. 407.
58. *Ibid.*, paras 393 and 398.
59. *Ibid.*, para. 372.
60. *Ibid.*, para. 415.

5.6 The *Eiser* Tribunal's Focus on the Investor's Interests and Avoidance of Regulatory Economics

At numerous points in its award, the tribunal indicates that the *sole* perspective from which it, in fact, views the issue of the 'fairness' of the regulatory change is that of the investor. It was simply false for the tribunal to imply that Spain's regulatory scheme was totally or completely changed: the regulatory framework remained an incentive-based one to obtain the outcome of supplying renewable energy to the grid and changing Spain's energy mix in a green direction. From the perspective of this particular investor, though, arguably, everything had changed due to the cost structure of that particular investor. For the claimant, its business was changed from a profitable one to an unviable one. But this merely begs the question of in what sense 'fairness' requires that the State maintain a regulatory scheme that allows every existing investor to continue making a profit, regardless of considerations such as cost efficiency. That is almost like writing moral hazard into the very idea of FET.

This goes to a fundamental difference between *Charanne* on the one hand and *Eiser* on the other. In *Eiser*, the tribunal purports to construct a reliance interest of the investor independently of any specific representation or guarantee of stabilization.[61] This really amounts to a return to *Tecmed* and the notion that FET contains a per se guarantee that the regulatory framework at the time the investment was made will not change in a way that fundamentally affects negatively the value of the investment. To disguise the fundamental difference in approach with *Charanne*, the *Eiser* tribunal, however, thought it necessary to make false or at least completely unsubstantiated assertions concerning the unreasonableness of the regulatory change or to falsely assert that the entire or complete regulatory framework was changed.

Furthermore, the tribunal slanted or manipulated the facts so as to produce at least some sort of illusion that Spain's government had made specific representations of stability. For example, the tribunal asserts: 'The 1997 Electricity Law guarantees to investors in the energy sector a reasonable return.'[62] Yet the reference to reasonable return in the statute that is cited by the tribunal in no way takes the form of a guarantee: the provision in question merely states a reasonable rate of return as the *objective* to be sought or borne in mind when calculating the subsidy. The tribunal, through sleight of hand, tries to bootstrap a statement of regulatory objective into an entitlement.

A similar move is evident where the tribunal cites a certain document that says that the investor's plants are granted a right to operate subject to the applicable special regulatory regime for renewable energy. The tribunal makes it appear that this statement implies that the regulatory regime is frozen for the investor. But that is a leap of logic of monumental proportions. To take a hypothetical example, a motorist may be granted a licence to operate a vehicle pursuant to the highway traffic act, but this says nothing about what the motorist may expect will be the content of the rules to which she is subject as a licensed driver under the highway traffic act at any future point in time. Somehow realizing it is taking a leap of logic, the tribunal leaves matters at

61. *Ibid.*, paras 382 and 386.
62. *Ibid.*, para. 102.

saying: '[t]he Parties disagreed whether these documents constituted binding commitments'.[63] The tribunal doesn't take an explicit position on binding commitments but hints that, in any case, some sort of reliance interest is established.

6 A COMPARATIVE PERSPECTIVE: *WIRTGENS V. CZECH REPUBLIC*

Decided not long after *Eiser*, an arbitral award involving renewable energy incentives in the Czech Republic illustrates a route to protecting the right to regulate in sharp contrast to the approach of the *Eiser* tribunal. Not dissimilar to *Charanne*, but with greater explicitness, the Wirtgens tribunal establishes that the right to alter the regulatory framework establishes a *default*: the presumption under FET is that investors may be subject to regulatory changes subsequent to making the investment, whether or not such changes alter in a negative way the economic situation of the investment. There is no need for the host State to *prove* that its regulation is rational or objectively justifiable to a tribunal with little concept of climate or regulatory economics (the *Charanne* award, by contrast, has language suggesting that even where there is no specific commitment, there must be a determination that the regulatory change meets some standard of objective or substantive rationality). The *Wirtgens* tribunal makes it very clear that it is for the *investor* to overcome the default by establishing that the host State made specific commitments to the investor to stabilizations that objectively establish a reliance interest. The investor must overcome the general rule that FET affords no stabilization of the regulatory framework. *Alternately*, of course, the investor may argue (in the manner of the *Waste Management* award discussed in the introduction to this essay) that the manner or regulatory intervention violates some norm of legal fairness - that it is arbitrary, inconsistent, discriminatory, lacking the possibility of administrative or judicial review, etc.

In *Wirtgens*, the host State *had* made specific commitments to the investor. The tribunal noted that whatever regulatory changes were made, those specific commitments had been fulfilled by the Czech Republic. Namely, the government had explicitly and specifically guaranteed claimants a 15-year payback of capital expenses and a 7% rate of return over that same 15-20 years in subsection 6(1)(b) of Act 180.[64] The tribunal's approach seems to suggest that by undertaking specific commitments to investors, a host State *limits* its liability for regulatory change under a FET clause that falls outside the scope of those commitments.

The background of this dispute is much more politically complex than the *Charanne* case. The Czech Republic was established in 1993 and joined the European Union (EU) in 2004. As a condition of joining the EU, the Czech Republic was required to incorporate many aspects of EU law into its domestic legal system, including laws governing the renewable energy sector. The EU set binding renewable energy targets in 2001 and then again in 2009. By 2010, EU members were required to produce 8% of

63. *Ibid.*, para. 126.
64. *Ibid.*, para. 469.

their energy consumption from RES; but by 2020, each was required to produce 13% of total energy from renewable sources.

6.1 The Evolving Czech Regulatory Regime

It was in this context that in 2005, the Czech Republic enacted legislation governing the renewable energy sector with the purpose of achieving these stated targets. The law (hereafter known as 'Support Scheme') broadly consisted of two parts: (1) the continuation of existing tax incentives and (2) the enactment of Act 180 entitled 'On the Support of Electricity Generation from Renewable Energy Sources' ('Act 180').[65]

The claimants invested in 3 solar plants in the Czech Republic: Struharov, Svetlá and Vemérov.[66] For all three plants, the claimants opted to be compensated through feed-in tariffs ('FITs'). One important point is that the Act only contemplated compensating RES producers, not grid operators, for FITs, which 'were funded through a compulsory surcharge set by the ERO in its yearly price decisions and invoiced to all electricity consumers by the grid operators as part of the electricity bill'.[67] FITs were based on investment costs but were limited by a 5% brake rule, such that when in 2009 and 2010, a significant drop in the market price of solar panels led to lower investment costs, it created 'windfall profits [for the producers] at the expense of the Czech consumers'.[68]

This predicament led the Czech Republic to amend the Support Scheme in 2009 and 2010 in four ways. First, the government abolished the brake rule so that 'ERO could reduce the FIT by more than 5% for plants connected in the following year'.[69] The tribunal states that this amendment did not affect the claimants. Second, the government limited 'the Support Scheme to small PV plants that had an installed capacity of up to 30kWh'[70] but only affected plants connected after 2011. This also did not affect the claimants because their plants went became operational in 2010 and 2011. Third, in November 2010, the government abolished the tax incentives, claiming it was 'no longer justified'.[71] Fourth, the government 'limited the contribution of consumers to the RES subsidies' and instead put the burden of the subsidies on the State budget.[72] This is referred to as a Solar Levy. These latter amendments were applicable to claimant's plants.

The Solar Levy and the elimination of the tax incentives were challenged in domestic courts and went up to the nation's highest court. The Czech Republic's Constitutional Court ruled on two key points. The State's actions were legitimate given the public interest, and 'under Act 180 RES producers were at most entitled to expect

65. *Wirtgen and JSW Solar (zwei) GmbH & Co. KG v. Czech Republic*, PCA Case No. 2014-03, award of 11 October 2017, para. 15.
66. *Ibid.*, para. 29.
67. *Ibid.*, para. 21.
68. *Ibid.*, para. 42.
69. *Ibid.*, para. 385.
70. *Ibid.*, para. 46.
71. *Ibid.*, para. 47.
72. *Ibid.*, para. 48.

that their investment would be paid back in 15 years, which time was maintained despite the Solar Levy'.[73] The Court also required a forum for investors that were harmed in a 'disproportionate manner' by the change in regulations to prove that 'the measures had a 'strangling effect' on their business' and seek judicial or tax redress.[74]

Most of the cases brought by individual investors as a result of this requirement were dismissed. The Supreme Administrative Court dismissed cases where investors argued that they had 'expectations beyond the 15-year payback guarantee'.[75] The Court 'confirmed that the guarantee under Act 180 did not include a guarantee of sufficient cash flow or of certain level of profitability'.[76] It also defined 'strangling effect' to mean essential liquidation or a similar effect but granted tax relief where it could be shown that producers were suffocating from the Solar Levy.

6.2 The Claimants' Case for Compensation and the Czech Republic's Response

The claimants alleged that the Czech Republic breached Article 2(1), the FET provision of the Treaty between Germany and the Czech Republic ('the Treaty'). They argued that Article 2(1) forbids a State from 'deliberately caus[ing] damage to foreign investors' and must 'protect their legitimate expectations relied on when investing'.[77] The claimants argue that Article 2(1) was breached for several reasons: the Czech Republic attracted and then deliberately harmed solar investors; claimants had relied on the Support Scheme and had legitimate expectations of benefits since the Support Scheme was specific enough to meet the threshold of a 'specific guarantee or representation' made to investors and therefore support a violation of FET; the Solar Levy effectively ended the FITs; claimants had a legitimate expectation of the tax incentives, the 15-year payback and windfall profits; the legislative changes made by the Czech Republic were not foreseeable, and therefore, there was no amount of due diligence that the investor could have done to avoid this harm.[78]

The Czech Republic disputed that it made specific guarantees or representations through the Support Scheme or tax incentive programme and argued that 'the claimants' only legitimate expectation could have been to receive a 15-year return on their investment, an expectation which was met'.[79] The Government also argues that the Solar Levy did not effectively end the FITs. Had the claimants had experience in the solar industry or conducted proper due diligence, the Czech Republic argues, 'they would not have formed the expectation that they would continue to benefit from excessive profits without any regulation limiting these profits' and 'claimants would

73. *Ibid.*, para. 58.
74. *Ibid.*, para. 63.
75. *Ibid.*, para. 65.
76. *Ibid.*, para. 65.
77. *Ibid.*, para. 274.
78. *Ibid.*, paras 274-286.
79. *Ibid.*, para. 325.

have also discovered that the Support Scheme was out of balance with its underlying objectives, and that significant changes were thus likely'.[80]

Therefore, the Czech Republic argued that regulatory amendments were foreseeable, and the State's actions were reasonable in response to the public interest and domestic financial stability. The Government asserted that a State measure is reasonable where 'it bears a reasonable relationship to some rational policy'[81] and that, as such, the Czech Republic's actions were reasonable.

6.3 The Legal Standard for FET Applied by the *Wirtgens* Tribunal

Article 2(1) of the Treaty states: 'Each Contracting State shall in every case accord investment fair and equitable treatment.'[82] In line with the claimants, the tribunal holds that 'claims under Article 2(1) of the Treaty are based on "the protection of claimants' legitimate expectations" and on "the obligation not to deliberately cause harm to claimants' investments"'.[83] In analysing whether the Czech Republic violated FET, the tribunal examines Act 180, the withdrawal of the income tax incentives, the introduction of the Solar Levy within the context of claimants' legitimate expectations and any deliberate harm on the part of the Czech Republic.

In interpreting the disputed section 6 of Act 180, the tribunal concludes that 'it is clear that the language "amount of revenue stays unchanged" ... was not an absolute guarantee of revenues to solar PV plants ... [T]here is no abstract promise of "revenues" to investors'.[84] The tribunal found that the withdrawal of the tax incentives was a reasonable and foreseeable decision made in the public interest.

Elaborating on reasonability, the tribunal noted that the rate of return guaranteed was 'reasonable and in line with the renewable support schemes of other EU Member States'.[85] Furthermore, the Czech Republic took care to ensure continued and promised reasonable profit of 7%.[86] The tribunal concluded that in order for a claimant to establish that a State action breached FET, the expectations on which the investor relies must be objectively reasonable 'at the time when the investor makes the investment'.[87]

The tribunal went to great lengths to discuss the economic and policy context within which the Czech Republic modified its regulatory scheme to respond to the foreseeability question. The tribunal stated that 'an investor can have no legitimate expectation that the host State's laws will not change. Indeed, as observed by the tribunal in *Micula*: "The State has a right to regulate, and investors must expect that the legislation will change, absent a stabilization clause or other specific assurance giving

80. *Ibid.*, paras 331 and 333.
81. *Ibid.*, para. 347.
82. *Ibid.*, para. 354.
83. *Ibid.*, para. 356.
84. *Ibid.*, para. 367.
85. *Ibid.*, para. 373.
86. *Ibid.*, para. 406.
87. *Ibid.*, para. 407, quoting *Duke Energy Electroquil Partners and Electroquil S.A. v. Republic of Ecuador*, ICSID Case No. ARB/04/19, award of 18 August 2008, para. 340.

rise to a legitimate expectation"'.[88] Through this analysis, although not explicitly stated, the tribunal inferred that it was foreseeable that the Czech Republic would undertake some regulatory change and especially so within the economic circumstances.

With regard to the Solar Levy, the Czech Republic was careful 'not to alter the framework of Act 180' in its introduction and 'ensure that the initial payback period of 15 years for capital expenses and the reasonable profit of 7% promised through Act 180 would be retained'.[89] The tribunal also noted that the domestic court system provided for due process and an opportunity for relief should a company be substantially and disproportionately impacted by the regulatory changes.

The tribunal noted that 'the FET obligation is breached when the legitimate expectations of an investor are not met. These expectations *must* arise from representations made by the State, on which the investor relied at the time of its investment. They must be objectively reasonable and must take into account all relevant circumstances'.[90]

In a sense, the tribunal is concluding that all regulatory changes are foreseeable absent a specific commitment of the State not to undertake them. The default, as it were in FET, is the State's right to regulate: regulatory change is, per se, legitimate and ought to be the basis of the investor's expectations. Only where the State makes specific promises to stabilize aspects of the regulatory framework would FET be engaged, and only where breaches of those specific promises can be established by the investor.

To determine whether a State has given a specific representation or guarantee on which an investor relied, the tribunal must look at each circumstance and context, 'content and clarity of the alleged promise are of critical relevance'.[91] The tribunal concluded that specific representations were not made either with regard to the regulatory amendments. The claimants relied on no statutory promise or contract with the Czech Republic to provide more than what was upheld. There were no representations that the tax incentives apply for the duration of the plant's life.

The tribunal found no impropriety and contrasted this present case with the concept left open in *Waste Management* that a deliberate act meant to frustrate or coerce an investor could be a violation of FET. The claimants did not establish that they were discriminated against or that Act 180 was even designed to promote foreign investment. The Czech Republic had legitimate public policy reasons to amend the Support Scheme regulating renewable energy. No evidence was presented to persuade the tribunal that the resulting harm caused to investors was improper or deliberate. Thus, the tribunal found that there were no violations and consequently dismissed the claimants' FET claims.

The tribunal concluded that the Czech Republic made two guarantees: (1) 'A return of investors investment or payback of capital expenses in 15 years and (2) a

88. *Ibid.*, para. 408, quoting *Micula et al. v. Romania*, ICSID Case No. ARB/05/20, award of 11 December 2013, para. 666.
89. *Ibid.*, para. 399.
90. *Ibid.*, para. 407.
91. *Ibid.*, para. 409.

return on investment or profit of at least 7% p.a. over 15 and later 200 years.'[92] Both guarantees were met for the claimants in this case.

7 CONCLUSION: REPEATING THE MISTAKES OF *EISER* – SUBSEQUENT CASE LAW

While the record is mixed and awards are still coming down, many of the subsequently decided cases on Spain's renewable energy programme (at least those that are publicly available) imitate the same mistakes and arbitrator sleight of hand as *Eiser*.[93] The least troubling of these awards rely heavily on findings of fact that, at the time the investment was made, Spain had been undertaking specific commitments to the stability of incentives to induce investment. At least those decisions are, in theory, compatible with the kind of right to regulate established by the *Wirtgens* tribunal in the Czech case. As discussed above: in theory, the kinds of representations relied on in some of the later Spain cases fall short of the burden of proof to establish a promise from the state of stabilization that was required by the *Wirtgens* tribunal.

An exception is *Cube Infrastructure Fund SICAV v. Spain*, where the tribunal pointed to a press release in 2007 that was tied to RD661/2007: while not attempting to construct RD661/2007 as itself containing a specific commitment, the tribunal held that the press release was the kind of instrument on which an investor could rely, giving 'assurances that transcended assurances that are set out or are implicit in legislation'.[94] The relevant words in the press release were: '[t]he revisions carried out in the future of the tariffs will not affect those installations already in operation. This guarantee provides legal safety for the producer, affording stability to the sector and fostering its development'.[95]

This is the strongest case that can be made for the existence of a specific commitment to foreign investors under the original Spain renewable energy scheme. However, it is limited to installations already in operation' and thus would be hard to characterize as an *inducement* to foreign investment. In *Cuba Infrastructure Fund*, there was also a partial dissent by Arbitrator Tomuschat, who questioned whether any commitments of this character entitled the investor to more than the general legislative provision for a 'reasonable return'. By contrast, *9REN Holding v. Spain* is even worse than *Eiser* in its complete dismissal of the economically rational new regime as 'entirely uncertain, unreasonable, and future remuneration impossible to predict'.[96] Again, here, we see the dangers to climate policy where the adjudicators have abject ignorance of regulatory economics.

92. *Ibid.*, para. 469.
93. Power, 'Solar Wars Part X: The Force is strong with investors', bilaterals.org, 20 August 2019, bilaterals.org/?solar-wars-part-x-the-force-is.
94. *Cube Infrastructure Fund SICAV and others v. Kingdom of Spain*, ICSID Case No. ARB/15/20, decision on jurisdiction, liability and partial decision on quantum of 19 February 2019, para. 275.
95. Cited in *Cube Infrastructure Fund*, para. 266.
96. *9REN Holding S.a.r.l. v. Kingdom of Spain*, ICSID Case No. ARB/15/15, award of 31 May 2019, para. 314.

CHAPTER 18

The (Private) Legal Person in Public International Law: More Than a Question of Legal Subjectivity

Christian Tietje[*]

This contribution in honour of Marco Bronckers deals with the legal status of the juridical or legal person in international law. Even though there is a long-standing discussion on the responsibility of companies in international law with regard to environmental concerns, human rights and other regulatory areas (corporate social responsibility (CSR)), there is still legal uncertainty about the theoretical foundation of the status of the legal person in the international legal system. In this regard, it will be demonstrated that it is necessary to differentiate between legal capacity as such and individual subjective rights. This differentiation has been applied with regard to the human being, but not yet to legal persons. Applying it to legal persons enables us to strike an appropriate balance of responsibility structures and guaranteed rights of freedom of the legal person in the international system.

* Parts of this chapter have been published in German language some years ago in: Delbrück et al. (Eds), *Aus Kiel in die Welt: Kiel's Contribution to International Law: Festschrift zum 100-jährigen Bestehen des Walther-Schücking-Instituts für Internationales Recht* (Duncker & Humblot, 2014), pp. 671-691.

1 INTRODUCTION

Marco Bronckers has addressed the legal position of the individual economic actor in the international system in numerous publications.[1] In this short contribution in honour of Marco, we will take a look at a specific category of private economic actors: the legal person under private law (*Juristische Person des Privatrechts*). Legal persons under private law are the most economically significant private actors in the international economic system, regardless of how they are legally organized. In international economic law, the legal status of legal persons under private law has been discussed time and again since the 1970s with regard to transnational corporations and international law.[2] This discussion continues to this day under the heading of Corporate Social Responsibility (CSR).

With the Supreme Court of Canada's decision of *Nevsun Resources Ltd. v. Araya*,[3] the discussion regarding the binding effect of customary international law on private law entities has taken on a fascinating new dimension. In that decision, the Canadian Supreme Court, by a five-to-four majority, came out in support of a potentially binding effect of customary international law on corporations.[4] This is in sharp contrast to the US Supreme Court's decision in *Jesner v. Arab Bank*[5] – also a five-to-four decision, in which the Supreme Court famously rejected a binding effect of customary international law on private corporations.[6]

The *Nevsun* and *Jesner* decisions will not be analysed in detail here. The starting point for the following considerations is rather the realization that the discussion indicated above has so far always revolved around the question of whether and, if so, to what extent, the legal person under private law can be a subject of international law.[7] This contribution will rather ask how international law deals with the legal person of private law as such, ultimately independent of the question of international legal subjectivity. As a successful lawyer, Marco Bronckers has certainly had to deal with countless legal persons of private law. As a scholar, he has repeatedly dealt extensively with international law. The combination of both points of view in the following reflections will hopefully be of interest to him.

1. *See, e.g.*, Bronckers, 'Is Investor-State Dispute Settlement (ISDS) superior to litigation before domestic courts? An EU view on bilateral trade agreements', 18 *Journal of International Economic Law* (2015), 655-677; Bronckers, 'From "direct effect" to "muted dialogue": Recent developments in the European Courts' case law on the WTO and beyond', 11 *Journal of International Economic Law* (2008), 885-898.
2. For a detailed account *see, e.g.*, Nowrot, *Normative Ordnungsstruktur und private Wirkungsmacht: Konsequenzen der Beteiligung transnationaler Unternehmen an den Rechtssetzungsprozessen im internationalen Wirtschaftssystem* (Berliner Wissenschafts-Verlag, 2006).
3. Supreme Court of Canada, *Nevsun Resources Ltd. v. Araya*, Case No. 37919, 28 February 2020.
4. For details *see* Walton, '*Nevsun Resources Ltd. v. Araya*', 115 *American Journal of International Law* (2021), 107-114.
5. *Jesner v. Arab Bank, PLC*, No. 16-499, 584 U.S. ___ (2018).
6. For details *see* Hamilton, '*Jesner v. Arab Bank*', 112 *American Journal of International Law* (2018), 720-727.
7. For the discussion *see* Nowrot, *supra* note 2, at 528 et seq.

2 SOME HISTORICAL ASPECTS ON THE STATUS OF THE LEGAL PERSON IN INTERNATIONAL LAW

While national legal orders for the last 150-plus years have learned how to legally deal with juridical person,[8] there is hardly any historical starting point or development in international law one could point to. In the international system, companies initially understood in general terms as economic actors in the form of groups of persons, have played an important role since the Middle Ages, initially through the Hanseatic League and the Fuggers, among others, and later the international trading companies such as the East India Company. However, a special feature was that for many centuries the predecessors of today's actors in cross-border economic trade referred to as transnational or multinational enterprises, acted with only very limited private autonomy; they were primarily active based on State-granted privileges, either directly, or indirectly as envoys or in other State-related functions.[9]

Apart from the special phenomenon of economic actors operating across borders, which today are referred to as transnational corporations, legal persons historically played a role in international law only to the extent that international law relegated all questions of the legal status of legal persons to the regulatory jurisdiction of domestic law. The international court of justice (ICJ) summarized this legal situation in 1970 in its *Barcelona Traction* judgment as follows:

> International law has had to recognize the corporate entity as an institution created by States in a domain essentially within their domestic jurisdiction. This in turn requires that, whenever legal issues arise concerning the rights of States with regard to the treatment of companies and shareholders, as to which international law has not established its own rules, it has to refer to the relevant rules of municipal law.[10]

It is difficult to find rules on legal persons in international law that go beyond this from a historical perspective. When the Treaties of Friendship, Commerce, and Navigation, which in their present form regularly also refer to 'societies',[11] entered into force in great numbers in the 19th century, they only included natural persons in their personal scope of application in many areas.[12] This corresponds with the historical significance and the dogmatic conception of diplomatic protection. Particularly in the 19th century, diplomatic protection was used very intensively and largely without restriction by States, especially for the protection of economic interests, including those of legal persons, with often warlike consequences. However, the preconditions for the exercise

8. *See, e.g.*, for the German legal system Dietmair, *Die juristische Grundrechtsperson des Art. 19 Abs. 3 GG im Licht der geschichtlichen Entwicklung* (Decker Verlag, 1988), at 9 et seq.
9. For details on the development, *see* Nowrot, *supra* note 2, at 99 et seq.
10. *Barcelona Traction, Light and Power Company, Limited (Belgium v. Spain)*, ICJ Rep. 1970, 3, para. 38.
11. *See, e.g.*, Articles I(1), VI, VII and other provisions of the Treaty of Friendship, Commerce and Navigation between the Federal Republic of Germany and the United States of America of 29 October 1954, 273 UNTS 105.
12. Bayer, *Das System der deutschen Handelsverträge von 1853 bis 1914* (Berliner Wissenschafts-Verlag, 2004), 175.

of protection were hardly standardized by international law. In particular, the requirement under international law that domestic legal remedies be exhausted before protection can be exercised is only developed later.[13] If international law dealt directly with legal persons in this respect, it was ultimately only in confirmation of their complete mediatization by the domestic legal order. Another example of this is the numerous treaties of the 19th century on the mutual recognition of the legal capacity of foreign legal persons concluded by the German Empire.[14]

The comprehensive 'shield of sovereignty' thus given[15] did not allow the legal person to be seen as an independent legal entity in international law. However, this was not primarily conceptual in the sense of the mediatization of the individual as it was known with regard to the natural person. Regarding the natural person, it was clear that it could not be reached by international law, since international law, in the classic words of Heinrich Triepel:

> can only apply to the relations of coordinated States among themselves. This sentence ... decides on the nature of the position accorded to the individual. This cannot be that of a legal subject. The individual is incapable, from the point of view of a legal community uniting States as such, of being the bearer of own rights and duties emanating from the legal order of this community.[16]

Regarding the legal person, there was no need for such a fundamental consideration. It was clear that a legal person could only be created by domestic law - whether as a fiction or as a real association personality - and thus could only be assigned to domestic law. The legal person was, therefore, by definition, exclusively a domestic legal person. This has basically remained the case until today, although the observed relativization of the historical concept will be discussed in a moment. At this point, however, it should be pointed out that the well-known discussion on the subjectivity of transnational or multinational companies under international law has so far had no effect on the finding that the legal person in the broader sense, even if it is not a transnational company, is a phenomenon only of domestic law, not of international law. It is necessary to come back to this.

3 CONTEMPORARY INTERNATIONAL LAW AND THE LEGAL PERSON

The sobering finding that the legal person is largely disregarded in international law, which was presented from a historical perspective, must be put into perspective today. International law and international economic law turn to the legal person in numerous

13. Dugard, 'Diplomatic Protection', in *Max Planck Encyclopedia of Public International Law* (2009), para. 3.
14. von Liszt, *Das Völkerrecht*, 10th ed. (Springer, 1915), 117.
15. The image of 'sovereignty armour or shield' (Souveränitätspanzer) was coined by Bleckmann, 'Zur Funktion des Art. 24 Abs. 1 Grundgesetz', 35 ZaöRV (1975), 79-84, at 82.
16. Triepel, *Völkerrecht und Landesrecht* (C.L. Hirschfeld, 1899), 20 et seq.; on this also Peters, 'Das subjektive internationale Recht', 59 *Jahrbuch des öffentlichen Rechts der Gegenwart* (2011), 411-456, at 416; Peters, *Beyond Human Rights: The Legal Status of the Individual in International Law* (CUP, 2016).

regulatory areas. Far beyond the question of the subjectivity of transnational corporations under international law, which is still a matter of dispute today, the legal person is increasingly being assigned rights and obligations that are unmediated by international law and thus recognized under international law. However, this does not apply comprehensively; in part, there are also considerable regulatory gaps.

3.1 World Trade Law

World trade, as an actual phenomenon, is carried out by private economic entities. Accordingly, the rationale of the legal order of the World Trade Organization (WTO) also includes private economic entities in its scope of application. Individual activities generate economic and thus global welfare gains. Individuals are, therefore, the actual subjects of protection of the WTO legal order. This was expressed clearly in the decision of a WTO panel in *United States – Sections 301-310 of the Trade Act of 1974*. The Panel expressly stated:

> Many of the benefits to Members which are meant to flow as a result of the acceptance of various disciplines under the GATT/WTO depend on the activity of individual economic operators in the national and global market places. The purpose of many of these disciplines, indeed one of the primary objects of the GATT/WTO as a whole, is to produce certain market conditions which would allow this individual activity to flourish.[17]

The Panel then elaborated on these points of view and summarized them to the effect that one could speak of a 'principle of indirect effect' in favour of private economic entities.[18] However, this also makes it clear that private economic entities, and thus also legal persons, are not initially assigned any 'direct' rights in the sense of an independent legal entity by WTO law. As is well known, this corresponds to the consistent case law of the European Court of Justice (ECJ) on the legal effect of WTO law in Union law.[19]

Regardless of the disputed question of the direct applicability of WTO law, one set of rules of world trade law is particularly significant for legal persons. Specifically, this concerns the question of whether WTO law protects the existence of a legal person in the event of a cross-border transfer of their seat. The starting point for this consideration is provisions in numerous Treaties on Friendship, Commerce, and Navigation that require mutual recognition of the legal capacity of companies. In a 2003 judgment, the Federal Supreme Court (BGH) of Germany, with explicit reference to the ECJ's well-known *Überseering* decision,[20] granted direct applicability to the corresponding clause in the German-American Treaty of Friendship, Commerce, and Navigation of 1954, with the consequence that the personal statute of the Florida company concerned

17. *United States – Section 301-310 of the Trade Act of 1974*, Report of the Panel, WT/DS152/R, para. 7.73.
18. *Ibid.*, para. 7.78.
19. For a detailed discussion, *see, e.g.*, Bronckers, *supra* note 1.
20. Case C-208/00, *Überseering v. Nordic Construction Company Baumanagement*, ECLI: EU:C:2002:632.

had to be determined according to United States (US) law.[21] In doing so, the BGH made the following central statement, following the ECJ case law on the effect of freedom of establishment as a subjective right of legal persons (Article 54 Treaty on the Functioning of the European Union (TFEU)):

> If national treatment, most-favoured-nation treatment and freedom of establishment have been agreed and a company is accordingly allowed to do business in another country, it cannot be denied there the legal personality to which it is entitled under the law of the State in which it was established. In particular, the freedom of establishment includes the full recognition of legal capacity and capacity to sue and be sued.[22]

This finding by the BGH has direct consequences for what is probably the most significant international treaty restricting the application of the so-called seat theory, the General Agreement on Trade in Services (GATS) of the WTO. According to the provisions of the GATS, in service sectors for which liberalization commitments have been assumed by WTO members, there is, among other things, a right for foreign companies to have commercial presence. Commercial presence is defined as 'any type of business or professional establishment, including through the constitution, acquisition or maintenance of a juridical person' (Article XXVIII(d)(i) GATS). A legal person is defined as a 'legal entity duly constituted or otherwise organized under applicable law' (Article XXVIII(m)(i) GATS). From these provisions, which can be summarized as a right of establishment (cf. Article XVI GATS) and which are backed up by the guarantees of national treatment (Article XVII GATS) and most-favoured-nation treatment (Article II GATS), it follows directly in the sense of the cited BGH ruling that a company effectively established in a WTO member must be recognized in its legal capacity. This is the case at least in Germany - and under WTO law ultimately also in every other WTO member - as far as the provision of services is concerned.[23] However, the BGH itself did not take this consistent step. In its 'Trotting track' decision in 2008, the BGH held:

> Nor can an obligation to recognize Swiss companies with their administrative seat in Germany be derived from the General Agreement on Trade in Services .... This Agreement, the sole purpose of which is to promote trade in services, is addressed only to the Member States and does not establish any subjective rights of the nationals of these States. An interpretation of national law that is friendly to international law ... in the sense of also guaranteeing freedom of establishment for companies already fails because the Agreement is not understood in this way internationally ....[24]

21. BGH (Supreme Court, Germany), judgment of 29 January 2003, VIII ZR 155/02.
22. BGH, judgment of 29 January 2003, cited *supra* note 21.
23. Likewise Hoffmann, 'Annex to Art. 12 EGBGB', in Dauner-Lieb et al. (Eds), *Anwaltkommentar BGB*, vol. 1 (Deutscher Anwaltverlag, 2005), paras 146 ff.; more reserved Lehmann, 'Fällt die Sitztheorie jetzt auch international? - Zur Vereinbarkeit der kollisionsrechtlichen Anknüpfung an den Geschäftssitz mit dem GATS', (2004) RIW, 816-841; different Kindler, in Sonnenberger and Bieber (Eds), *Münchener Kommentar zum BGB: Internationales Handels- und Gesellschaftsrecht*, 4th ed. (C.H. Beck, 2006), para. 482.
24. BGH, judgment of 27 October 200, II ZR 158/06.

The BGH does not offer any justification in an actual legal sense for its view. In this respect, it sticks with the unsatisfactory statement that specific rights of the legal person under international law are supposed to follow from bilateral friendship and trade treaties, but not from the multilateral services agreement, which is comparable in terms of regulation.

Incidentally, the legal challenge posed here is further exacerbated if one takes into account that the free trade agreements (FTAs) currently being negotiated, or in some cases those already concluded, by the European Union (EU) with numerous States regularly guarantee freedom of establishment and define this, among other things, as the 'continuation of a legal entity'.[25] Since international rules on the freedom to provide services have fallen under the exclusive competence of the EU since the Lisbon Treaty (Article 207(1) TFEU) and the ECJ has, at least so far, granted bilateral FTAs far-reaching direct applicability in the sense of subjective rights with priority of application over domestic law,[26] there is far-reaching potential here for the guarantee of legal existence through international law. However, the explicit denial of direct effect in recent FTAs, such as in the EU-UK Trade and Cooperation Agreement,[27] Comprehensive Economic and Trade Agreement (CETA),[28] and the EU-Iraq Partnership and Cooperation Agreement[29] puts this conclusion in question.

3.2 International Investment Protection Law and Arbitration

The most far-reaching subjective legal guarantees for legal persons under international law probably arise from international investment protection law. The legal sources of international investment protection law are primarily found in close to 3,000 bilateral investment treaties (BITs), as well as multilateral agreements such as the Energy Charter Treaty. These are increasingly supplemented by FTAs with regulations on investment promotion and protection.

International investment protection is thus initially investment protection under international law, in a purely intergovernmental relationship. Just a few years ago, the Federal Constitutional Court (BVerfG) concluded from this that the investor only receives protection in this relationship as a legal reflex, not on the basis of his own rights. According to the court, rights and obligations under BITs are only established in

25. *See, e.g.*, Article 7.9 of the Free trade Agreement between the European Union and its Member States, of the one part, and the Republic of Korea, of the other part, O.J. 2011, L 127/6: 'For the purposes of this Section: (a) establishment means: (i) the constitution, acquisition or maintenance of a legal person'; *see also* Mathis and Laurenza, 'Services and investment in the EU-South Korea free-trade area: Implications of a new approach for GATS V agreements and for bilateral investment treaties', 13 *Journal of World Trade* (2012), 157-185.
26. *See* in particular Case C-265/03, *Igor Simutenkov v. Ministerio de Educación y Cultura and Real Federación Española de Fútbol*, ECLI:EU:C:2005:213.
27. Article 5(1) of Trade and Cooperation Agreement between the European Union and the European Atomic Energy Community, of the one part, and the United Kingdom of Great Britain and Northern Ireland, of the other part, O.J. 2021, L 149/10.
28. Article 30.6 of Comprehensive Economic and Trade Agreement (CETA) between Canada, of the one part, and the European Union and its Member States, of the other part, O.J. 2017, L 11/23.
29. Article 77(2) Partnership and Cooperation Agreement between the European Union and its Member States, of the one part, and the Republic of Iraq, of the other part, O.J. 2012, L 204/20.

the inter-State relationship between the home and host State.[30] This legal view is hardly tenable and is not widely shared in international arbitration.[31] If it is correctly assumed that rights from an investment protection treaty under international law are rights of the investor directly deriving from international law,[32] this also explains the comprehensive procedural possibilities that investors have today as direct rights of action against States. The ICJ already laid the conceptual foundation for this in *Barcelona Traction*:

> States ever more frequently provide for such protection, in both bilateral and multilateral relations, either by means of special instruments or within the framework of wider economic arrangements. Indeed, whether in the form of multilateral or bilateral treaties between States, or in that of agreements between States and companies, there has since the Second World War been considerable development in the protection of foreign investments. The instruments in question contain provisions as to jurisdiction and procedure in case of disputes concerning the treatment of investing companies by the States in which they invest capital. Sometimes companies are themselves vested with a direct right to defend their interests against States through prescribed procedures.[33]

In today's arbitration practice, these seminal statements of the ICJ are summarized as follows, citing as an example the arbitral tribunal in *BG Group Plc. v. Argentina:*

> The proliferation of bilateral investment treaties has effected a profound transformation of international investment law. Most significantly, under these instruments investors are entitled to seek enforcement of their treaty rights by directly bringing action against the State in whose territory they have invested. Investors

30. BVerfG, Order of the Second Senate of 8 May 2007, 2 BvM 1/03, ECLI:DE:BVerfG:2007:ms20070508.2bvm000103, para. 51: 'From an international-law point of view, the specific feature of the arbitration of disputes before the International Centre for Settlement of Investment Disputes is that private individuals are able to complain as claimants of the violation of an international agreement concluded between states. In terms of content, therefore, the violation of an obligation is complained of which is owed not directly to the private applicant, but to his or her home state, although the protective purpose of the agreement targets the interests of private investors. Rights and obligations of the opposing state emerge in such case constellations from an international agreement which as a rule contain a separate necessity clause; thus, such rights and obligations emerge from a relationship governed by international law.' Critically Tietje and Szodruch, 'Staatsnot bei Staatsinsolvenz: Individualrechte und Gemeinwohlverpflichtung im transnationalen Wirtschaftsrecht', 19 *Zeitschrift für Bankrecht und Bankwirtschaft* (2007), 498-503, 501.
31. The attribution of direct subjective legal positions becomes clear, *inter alia*, in *BG Group Plc. v. Argentina*, UNCITRAL Arbitration, Award of 24 December 2007, para. 145; *Corn Products International, Inc. v. Mexico*, ICSID Case No. ARB(AF)/04/01, Decision on Responsibility of 15 January 2008, paras 167 et seq.; *Republic of Bulgaria*, ICSID Case No. ARB/03/24, Decision on Jurisdiction of 8 February 2005, para. 141; in detail Arb. Rovine, Concurring Opinion in *Archer Daniels Midland Company and Tate & Lyle Ingredients Americas, Inc. v. United Mexican States*, ICSID Case No. ARB (AF)/04/5 (NAFTA), Award of 21 November 2007, paras 17 et seq.
32. In detail Braun, 'Investitionsschutz durch internationale Schiedsgerichte', TranState Working Papers No. 89 (2009), at 13 et seq.; on the investor as a partial subject of international law, comprehensively Braun, *Ausprägungen der Globalisierung: Der Investor als partielles Subjekt im Internationalen Investitionsrecht. Qualität und Grenzen dieser Wirkungseinheit* (Nomos, 2012), pp. 162 et seq.
33. *Barcelona Traction, Light and Power Company, Limited*, para. 90.

may seek redress in arbitration without securing espousal of their claim or diplomatic protection.[34]

This already indicates the dogmatic consequences of the direct legal entitlement of investors through investment protection treaties: first, the own investor rights lead to the fact that the conceptually purely inter-State legal institute of diplomatic protection, in which natural and legal persons only act as the object, not the subject, of the right, is displaced. This is connected to the fact that the purely intergovernmental legal institution of reprisal is not excluded in principle in the area of investment protection, but instead is subject to considerable restrictions due to the investor rights involved. As the International Law Commission (ILC) articles on State responsibility show, not all individual rights as third-party rights are likely to be grounds for exclusion of a countermeasure (reprisal).[35] Rather, Article 50(1)(b) ILC articles show that only 'obligations for the protection of fundamental human rights' have such an exclusion effect, not economic rights.[36] Of course, this does not change the character of individual investor rights, nor does it change the fact that the impairment of these rights must be taken into account within the framework of the necessary proportionality assessment in the case of reprisal.[37] From a dogmatic point of view, this is not a surprising result, since economic rights of the legal person in international law are also rights dependent on the State. This leads to the fact that the economic rights of investors do not exclude the purely inter-State right of reprisal, but nevertheless subject it to considerable restrictions in its exercise.

In a somewhat different dimension, the interplay of national and international law on legal persons also becomes apparent in the determination of State affiliation, and thus in the question of the right to sue in investment protection law. The State itself determines who an investor is in the respective home State as a legal person under international investment protection law. Investment protection treaties regularly refer to domestic law to determine the nationality of legal persons. However, international law increasingly restricts the freedom of States to determine the nationality of a legal person through their domestic law.[38] In addition to the case law of the ECJ on the freedom of establishment, provisions in friendship and trade treaties and, where applicable, the GATS, denial of benefits clauses are increasingly being considered in investment protection law. They serve to set limits on the legal freedoms of States,

34. *BG Group Plc. v. Argentina*, UNCITRAL Arbitration, Award of 24 December 2007, para. 145.
35. For a discussion, *see* Braun, *Ausprägungen*, *supra* note 32, pp. 151 et seq. with further references.
36. For the majority, *see* Braun, *Ausprägungen*, *supra* note 32, p. 53 fn. 492; Dahm, Delbrück and Wolfrum, *Völkerrecht. Band I/3: Die Formen des völkerrechtlichen Handelns; Die inhaltliche Ordnung der internationalen Gemeinschaft*, 2nd ed. (Walter de Gruyter, 2002), 989.
37. Braun, *Ausprägungen*, *supra* note 32, pp. 154 et seq. with further references.
38. For a detailed discussion of the relevant provisions, *see* Perkams, 'The determination of nationality of investors in international investment agreements (IIAs) – Taking stock of the criteria used in modern investment law', in Tietje, Kraft and Lehmann (Eds), *The Determination of the Nationality of Investors under Investment Protection Treaties*, Beiträge zum Transnationalen Wirtschaftsrecht, vol. 106 (Institute of Economic Law, Transnational Economic Law Research Center, 2011), pp. 13-24.

especially in cases of so-called letterbox or shell companies.[39] This also applies to the practice of arbitral tribunals, according to which the prohibition of abuse of rights sets limits on the permissible determination of the nationality of a legal entity for States.[40] In this respect, there is at least an approach, albeit controversial, which approximates the considerations of the ICJ in the Nottebohm proceedings.[41] Just as with the nationality of natural persons, the law of the legal person is also given a further determinant under international law.

All in all, international investment protection law shows that the legal person is not only recognized as a legal entity by international law, but that it is also directly vested with its own rights under international law.

3.3 Human Rights

Human rights are the most important category of subjective rights under national and international law. They apply per se to the natural person. Their applicability to legal persons depends on an explicit or implicit attribution of rights. Domestically, this is the function, as shown in Article 19(3) of the German Constitution (*Grundgesetz*) ('The basic rights shall also apply to domestic legal persons to the extent that the nature of such rights permits'). In the international sphere, for example, the first sentence of Article 1 of the First Additional Protocol to the European Convention on Human Rights (ECHR) makes such an attribution of rights to the legal person. It states: 'Every natural or legal person has the right to respect for his or her possessions.'

Beyond the 1st Additional Protocol, the ECHR does not contain any substantive statements on the legal person. However, Article 34 of ECHR grants the right of individual application to the European Court of Human Rights (ECtHR) to any 'natural person, non-governmental organisation or group of persons'. From this, as well as from the nature of the ECHR rights, the ECtHR has consistently held that legal persons and other groups of persons are directly entitled to Convention rights insofar as the nature of the corresponding rights does not preclude this. The autonomy of the legal entity's legal personality recognized by the ECtHR is only broken in exceptional cases, namely if the legal entity is incapable of acting in regard to the assertion of a human rights

39. *See, e.g.*, Happ, 'Denial of benefit clauses and any other mechanisms that limit the scope of BITs for investors', in Tietje, Kraft and Lehmann, *supra* note 38, pp. 61-68.
40. *Tokio Tokelés v. Ukraine*, ICSID Case No. ARB/2/18, Decision on Jurisdiction, 29 April 2004, Dissenting Opinion, para. 5; *Vacuum Salt Products Ltd. v. Republic of Ghana*, ICSID Case No. ARB/92/1, Award, 16 February 1994, para. 54; *TSA Spectrum de Argentina, S.A. v. Argentine Republic*, ICSID Case No. ARB/05/5, 19 December 2008, para. 162; *Mobil v. Venezuela*, ICSID Case No. ARB/07/27, Decision on Jurisdiction, 10 June 2010, para. 205; *Libananco Holdings Co. Limited v. Republic of Turkey*, ICSID Case No. ARB/06/8, Award, 2 September 2011, para. 516; iareporter.com/articles/20110905_2/ (last visited February 2022); c.f. *Saluka Investments BV (the Netherlands) v. The Czech Republic*, UNICITRAL, Partial Award of 17 March 2006, para. 241; *Tokio Tokelés v. Ukraine*, ICSID Case No. ARB/2/18, Award, 29 April 2004, para. 54.
41. Tietje and Bering, 'Beyond formal criteria: Determining nationality of corporations in "hard cases"', in Tietje, Kraft and Lehmann (Eds), *General Public International Law and International Investment Law – A Research Sketch on Selected Issues*, Beiträge zum Transnationalen Wirtschaftsrecht, vol. 105 (Institute of Economic Law, Transnational Economic Law Research Center, 2011), pp. 31-43.

violation and, therefore, a piercing of the corporate veil appears necessary in the interest of the natural persons participating in the legal entity.[42]

Apart from the ECHR, there are hardly any explicit or implicit attributions of human rights to legal persons or groups of persons in international law. Rather, it is settled treaty practice under the International Covenant on Civil and Political Rights that legal persons have no right of appeal under the Optional Protocol, nor do the substantive legal guarantees of the Covenant apply to legal persons. The Commission on Human Rights, for example, stated the following in a 1989 communication:

> The present communication is submitted on behalf of a company incorporated under the laws of Trinidad and Tobago. While counsel has indicated that Mr. D. C., the company's managing director, has been duly 'authorized to make the complaint on behalf of the company', it is not indicated whether and to what extent his individual rights under the Covenant have been violated by the events referred to in the communication. Under article 1 of the Optional Protocol, only individuals may submit a communication to the Human Rights Committee. A company incorporated under the laws of a State party to the Optional Protocol, as such, has no standing under article 1, regardless of whether its allegations appear to raise issues under the Covenant.[43]

In addition to this purely procedural statement on the lack of appealability of legal persons, the dogmatic construction of the international covenant's relationship to legal persons is clearly shown in the 29 March 2004 General Comment No. 31 of the Commission on Human Rights. Comment No. 31 on 'The Nature of the General Legal Obligation Imposed on States Parties to the Covenant' states:

> The beneficiaries of the rights recognized by the Covenant are individuals. Although, with the exception of article 1, the Covenant does not mention the rights of legal persons or similar entities or collectivities, many of the rights recognized by the Covenant, such as the freedom to manifest one's religion or belief (article 18), the freedom of association (article 22) or the rights of members of minorities (article 27), may be enjoyed in community with others. The fact that the competence of the Committee to receive and consider communications is restricted to those submitted by or on behalf of individuals (article 1 of the Optional Protocol) does not prevent such individuals from claiming that actions or omissions that concern legal persons and similar entities amount to a violation of their own rights.[44]

A similar legal situation exists under the American Convention on Human Rights (ACHR). Although according to Article 44 ACHR '[a]ny person or group of persons, or any nongovernmental entity legally recognized in one or more Member States of the Organization' may lodge a complaint with the Inter-American Commission on Human Rights, the substantive rights of the Convention are not considered to be own rights of

42. For a detailed analysis of the case law of the ECtHR, *see* Emberland, *The Human Rights of Companies: Exploring the Structure of ECHR Protection* (OUP, 2006), pp. 76 et seq.
43. *A newspaper publishing company v. Trinidad and Tobago*, Communication No. 360/1989, U.N. Doc. CCPR/C/36/D/360/1989 (1989), para. 3.2.
44. General Comment No. 31, Nature of the General Legal Obligation Imposed on States Parties to the Covenant, 26 May 2004, Doc. CCPR/C/21/Rev.1/Add.13, para. 9.

legal persons. The Commission on Human Rights has stated the following in this regard:

> The Commission ... considers that the Convention grants its protection to physical or natural persons. However, it excludes from its scope legal or artificial persons, since they represent a legal fiction. This interpretation is confirmed when the true meaning attributed to the phrase 'person means every human being' is seen in the text of the Preamble to the Convention, which establishes that the essential rights of man 'are based upon attributes of the human personality' and reiterates the need to create conditions that will enable all persons to achieve 'the ideal of free men enjoying freedom from fear and want.'[45]

The decision-making practice of the African Human Rights Commission is somewhat less clear. As a result, the Commission has repeatedly declared complaints by legal persons or groups of persons admissible and well-founded; however, this was probably done primarily in the interest of objective human rights protection. It is unclear whether a legal person is truly entitled to independent rights under the African Charter. The concept of the African Charter, which is primarily based on the idea of collective rights,[46] as well as the decision-making practice of the Human Rights Commission, which as a rule is not dogmatically but rather pragmatically oriented, hardly allows for reliable statements.[47]

The overview of selected human rights instruments and their treatment of legal persons makes it clear that the international human rights regime conceptually dates to a time when, as coined by Savigny,[48] among others, the idea prevailed that a legal person per se *is* not entitled to human rights. Apart from the right to property, the validity of which is still disputed under customary law today,[49] hardly any explicit economic freedom rights are standardized in international human rights protection. Thus, the dogmatic point of contact for rights of the legal person is comprehensively missing. In simplified terms, it can also be said that international human rights protection, in a broader social sense, is based more on human dignity and less on individual freedom.

45. Inter-American Commission on Human Rights, *Bendeck-Cohdinsa v. Honduras*, Report No 106/99, Petition, 27 September 1999, para. 17.
46. On this, e.g., Schaarschmidt, 'Gruppenrechte als Menschenrechte? Erkenntnisse aus dem afrikanischen Völkerrecht', *Kollektivität – Öffentliches Recht zwischen Gruppeninteressen und Gemeinwohl* (Nomos, 2012), pp. 97-112; Kriesel, *Peoples' Rights: Gruppenrechte im Völkerrecht. Theorie und Praxis des kollektiven Menschenrechtsschutzes in Afrika, Amerika und Europa* (Mohr Siebeck, 2020).
47. van Kempen, 'The recognition of legal persons in international human rights instruments: Protection against and through criminal justice?', in Pieth and Ivory (Eds), *Corporate Criminal Liability: Emergence, Convergence, and Risk* (Springer, 2011), pp. 355-389, at p. 361 et seq. with further references.
48. von Savigny, *System des heutigen Römischen Rechts* II (1840), p. 236.
49. For discussion, e.g. Ohler, 'Der Schutz privaten Eigentums als Grundlage der internationalen Wirtschaftsordnung', 61 JZ (2006), 875-883 with further references.

4 CONCEPTUAL CHALLENGES: INTERNATIONAL LEGAL SUBJECTIVITY AND INTERNATIONAL SUBJECTIVE RIGHTS

The findings of this short study are so far ambivalent. On the one hand, the legal person is increasingly recognized as a subject of international law, especially in the economic sphere, and as a legal entity endowed with rights directly deriving from international law. On the other hand, the protection of human rights under international law remains, at least in part, in legal categories in which the legal person under private law does not actually exist. Apart from conceptual considerations, which will be discussed in a moment, this is particularly problematic when it comes to aspects of corporate responsibility or, in a narrower sense, corporate criminal liability. The need for effective human rights protection for corporations in the light of potential criminal prosecution on the basis of international law is obvious and poses major regulatory challenges.[50] It must be realized that corporate criminal liability was deliberately not included in the Statute of the International Criminal Court.[51] Yet, in the EU, the Organisation for Economic Co-operation and Development (OECD) and the UN, there are numerous regulatory efforts aimed at obliging States under international law to provide for corporate criminal offences in the domestic sphere with regard to corruption and terrorist financing, among other things.[52] In addition, international human rights covenants can be used to derive obligations for States to hold companies criminally responsible for human rights violations.[53]

The actual conceptual challenge that arises from the previous analysis, however, is to find starting points for a system-shaping explanation of the legal status of the legal person in international law. The starting point here, as is advocated for in recent international law scholarship, should be the realization that a distinction must be made in principle between international legal subjectivity and international subjective rights. In this respect, subjectivity under international law is to be understood as capacity under international law, i.e., as the potential of legal entity in general. In the case of international subjective rights, as in the domestic sphere, it is a matter of the legal power to which the individual is entitled to demand concrete action.[54] It is thus also clear that international subjective rights can also exist beyond the human rights sphere. The legal situation in international law corresponds here to the domestic legal situation, which also knows subjective public rights standardized in fundamental rights and statutory law below the Constitution.

While the differentiation of subjectivity under international law and international subjective rights has so far only been applied to the natural person, the human being,

50. In detail van Kempen, *supra* note 47, at 355 et seq.
51. On the history of the origins, *see* Blakesley, 'Jurisdiction *ratione personae* or the personal reach of the Court's jurisdiction', in Doria, Gasser and Bassiouni (Eds), *The Legal Regime of the International Criminal Court: Essays in Honour of Professor Igor Blishchenko* (Martinus Nijhoff, 2009), pp. 421-458, at p. 428 et seq.
52. For an overview of this, *see*, e.g., Köck, *Wirtschaftsstrafrecht: Eine systematische Darstellung*, 2nd ed. (Facultas-WUV, 2010), at 295 et seq.
53. For a detailed overview, *see* van Kempen, *supra* note 47, at 379 et seq.
54. Peters, *supra* note 16, at 526 et seq. and *passim* for details.

this study has shown that there is considerable potential for application to the legal person as well. The subjectivity of international law, such as the international legal capacity of the legal person under private law, can hardly be denied today. In international economic law, legal persons as 'born' subjects of cross-border economic transactions in today's international legal order are directly or indirectly legally integrated into existing regulatory structures to a large extent. This can partly be seen as a development in special legal regimes and therefore does not necessarily always have an impact on the design of traditional institutions of international law, as the ICJ advocated in the *Diallo* judgment.[55] In any case, however, the aforementioned developments are about the recognition of the international legal capacity of legal persons in the international legal order as such. At the same time, it follows that international law studies that focus on the content and scope of concrete individual rights of companies, as in investment protection law, and draw conclusions from this given subjectivity under international law, are methodologically problematic.[56] Legal capacity and legal entity are inadmissibly confused here. Whether, and to what extent, the legal person is entitled to individual subjective rights in individual regulatory areas of international law is independent of the realization that the legal person, just like the natural person has legal capacity as such under international law.

Legal capacity does not necessarily imply certain rights under international law, of which the legal person is the bearer. However, it is clear that the recognition of legal capacity expresses that the international legal order respects the legal person's capacity as a subject. It would be incompatible with this to leave, as it were, the fate of the legal person entirely to domestic law. How domestic law deals with the legal person is, therefore, also a question of international law, at least in the sense of the prohibition of arbitrariness.

The allocation of individual subjective rights to the legal person is initially reserved for the structuring of specific legal regimes of international law. In this respect, limits to the freedom to regulate must be named, at least with a view to the development of legal policy. The rule of law requirement under international law demands an appropriate balance of individual rights and obligations. This must also apply to the legal person. In concrete terms, it follows that, for example, a discussion on corporate responsibility in international investment protection law, which includes far-reaching subjective rights of legal persons, is legitimate and necessary.[57] At the same time, however, it is also necessary *de lege ferenda* to discuss improved human rights protection for legal persons. Corporate responsibility and, where applicable, even corporate criminal liability, are matters of international law that per se call for a basic set of defensive rights of the legal person. Only through an appropriate balance of

55. *See*, e.g., Schmalenbach, 'Ahmadou Sadio Diallo Case (Republic of Guinea v. Democratic Republic of the Congo)', in *Max Planck Encyclopedia of Public International Law* (OUP, 2019).
56. For such an approach, *see, e.g.*, Braun, *Ausprägungen, supra* note 32.
57. On this, e.g., Tietje, 'Individual rights in human rights and investment protection – Coherence of State and corporate responsibility', in Hanschel et al. (Eds), *Mensch und Recht: Festschrift für Eibe Riedel zum 70. Geburtstag* (Duncker & Humblot, 2013), pp. 271-288.

responsibility structures and guaranteed rights of freedom of the company is it possible to realize the rule of law under international law in relation to the legal person under private law.

CHAPTER 19

Assistance from an Unexpected Corner?: International Trade Law's Contribution to Combatting Pandemics

Freya Baetens & James Crawford[*]

International trade law contains several mechanisms that can facilitate measures to mitigate the effects of a pandemic and contribute to its prevention in the future. Restrictive measures on trade in goods, services and intellectual property protection have a high chance of succeeding against challenges at the World Trade Organization (WTO) or under Preferential Trade Agreements (PTAs) when their necessity is supported by scientific evidence and they are applied in a non-discriminatory manner. Outright bans on exports may be more difficult to defend. Review panels may have to balance the need for such measures against their potential risk: preventing access to indispensable products and services in neighbouring countries. Two questions remain, one procedural and one substantive. The procedural question is: how long can trade-restrictive pandemic measures be maintained? This question might not be difficult to answer, since it is heavily fact-based and there is case law precedent. The substantive question is more difficult: particularly with regard to intellectual property protection and States' duty to cooperate, do we need to rethink established trade rights and obligations?

* This work was partly supported by the Research Council of Norway through its Centres of Excellence funding scheme (project number 223274) and the FRIPRO Young Research Talents (project number 274946). Freya Baetens is grateful for the feedback of Roger O'Keefe, organiser of the Bocconi webinar *COVID-19 and International Law: Novel Strain or Old Wine in New Test Tubes* (15 December 2020), the webinar participants, Stefaan Van den Bogaert, Reinhard Quick, Petros Mavroidis, Niall Moran, Lothar Ehring, Veronica Lavista and Hiroki Yamada.

1 PROLOGUE

James – I became well-acquainted with Marco's work when I was appearing as counsel for the appellant (China) in *US – Anti-Dumping and Countervailing Duties*,[1] in my first World Trade Organization (WTO) case. In this case, the WTO Appellate Body had to interpret the term 'public body' under the Agreement on Subsidies and Countervailing Measures (SCM Agreement).[2] Under this provision, a subsidy is deemed to exist if 'there is a financial contribution by a government or any public body within the territory of a Member' and a benefit is thereby conferred. In its examination, the Appellate Body applied the International Law Commission's Articles on State Responsibility to decide whether 'public body' included 'any entity controlled by a government'.[3] Not only were Marco's writings in that case (and later) my first port of call in WTO matters, but also I am glad to be able to call him my friend.

Freya – As a newly minted assistant professor at Leiden University, I received an invitation from Marco Bronckers to have lunch in Café De Vriend. He had heard someone had been hired who was, among other things, interested in international trade law so he wanted to have a closer look at the newcomer who was dabbling in 'his' field. He discovered that I was trying to build up a legal practice as well as an academic career so with his characteristic kindness and generosity, he provided me with good advice, recommendations and introductions – and he has continued to do so to this day. Shortly thereafter, I joined his law firm in Brussels and we became 'confrères' at the Brussels Bar. For more than a decade now, we frequently cooperate: few people have taught me as much as Marco about what it means to be a lawyer (first rule: clients wish to receive advice to solve a concrete problem, they are not asking for long-winded academic *exposés*). In the meantime, I have also been fortunate to get to know Dominique, Marco's wife. Over the course of 2021, an *annus horribilis* for many, and in particular, for our family, the support of Marco, Dominique and Kenza (their granddaughter) helped us to survive – I will be forever grateful.

2 INTRODUCTION

The current global health crisis is reshaping the world as we know it – including the international legal world, or is it not? In spite of grand statements about a major turning point, international law already contains several mechanisms that facilitate or permit measures to adjust our legal systems to a pandemic, mitigating its effects and ideally also contributing to its prevention in the future. The rules on international responsibilities of States and international organizations provide a framework within which

1. Appellate Body Report, *United States* – Definitive Anti-Dumping and Countervailing Duties on Certain *Products from China* WT/DS379/AB/R, adopted 25 March 2011.
2. Article 1.1(a)(1) of the SCM Agreement which forms part of Annex 1A (containing the multilateral agreements on trade in goods) to the WTO agreement. *See* WTO, *The Legal Texts – The Results of the Uruguay Round of Multilateral Trade Negotiations* (CUP, 1999).
3. ILC, Articles on Responsibility of States for Internationally Wrongful Acts, Supplement No. 10 (A/56/10), Ch. IV.E.1.

allegations of wrongful actions by, for example, China or the World Health Organization (WHO) can be examined.[4] The question remains which rules of international law would be breached by these countries or international organizations.[5] Human rights rules may help to determine the legality of emergency domestic measures restricting rights relating to them, such as free movement including travel, demonstration, professional activity, property, physical integrity, asylum applications, migration, etc.[6] Transnational financial agreements contribute to the legal review of emergency financial measures, such as State aid for companies (government-supported loans) or stimulus packages issued by the European Central Bank.[7]

In response to the COVID-19 pandemic, international trade law has seen an avalanche of measures that derogate from its main tenet: free trade. The WTO and the rules under various Preferential Trade Agreements (PTAs) are at times being stretched to their limits.[8] Due to a variety of exceptions built into the system, such measures can not only be consistent with the existing legal regime, but even contribute to 'solving' the pandemic (or the legal issues it raises), which is not to say, of course, that there is no room for improvement.[9] This chapter looks at the three 'pillars' of the international trading system: trade in goods, services, and intellectual property protection – mapping what works to combat pandemics and suggesting reform where deficiencies can be identified. More attention is given to trade in goods because of the primary focus on goods in the WTO agreements and most PTAs, and the resulting availability of case law precedents. This analysis is not meant to be exhaustive: for example, possible violations of the SCM Agreement through pandemic-related government subsidies supporting specific industries, or of the Agreement on Government Procurement through measures favouring domestic producers of certain medical supplies,[10] fall beyond the scope of this chapter.

---

4. For example, in October 2021, the US Office of the US Director of National Intelligence (ODNI) released a declassified Intelligence Community assessment on COVID-19 origins, stating that an animal-to-human transmission and a lab leak in China were both plausible hypotheses for how COVID-19 spread, available at dni.gov/index.php/newsroom/reports-publications/reports-publications-2021/item/2263-declassified-assessment-on-covid-19-origins (last visited 3 July 2022); in May 2021, the Independent Panel for Pandemic Preparedness and Response (set up by the World Health Organization) released a report (*Covid-19: Make It the Last Pandemic*) found serious failures in the WHO and States' responses to the pandemic, available at theindependentpanel.org/wp-content/uploads/2021/05/COVID-19-Make-it-the-Last-Pandemic_final.pdf (last visited 3 July 2022).
5. This is addressed, for example, in Bergkamp, 'State liability for failure to control the COVID-19 epidemic: International and Dutch law', 11 *European Journal of Risk Regulation* (2020), 343-349.
6. *See, e.g.*, Pelliconi, 'COVID-19: Italy is not a "place of safety" anymore: Is the decision to close Italian ports compliant with human rights obligations?', *EJIL:Talk!*, 23 April 2020, available at: ejiltalk.org/covid-19-italy-is-not-a-place-of-safety-anymore-is-the-decision-to-close-italian-ports-compliant-with-human-rights-obligations (last visited 3 July 2022).
7. For example, bankingsupervision.europa.eu/home/search/coronavirus/html/index.en.html (last visited 3 July 2022).
8. Gruszczynski, 'The COVID-19 pandemic and international trade: Temporary turbulence or paradigm shift?', 11 *European Journal of Risk Regulation* (2020), 337-342.
9. Arato, Claussen and Heath, 'The perils of pandemic exceptionalism', 114 *American Journal of International Law* (2020), 627-636.
10. The US proposed to modify its commitment by excluding essential medicines/critical outputs from the GP Agreement. This US proposal to the GP Committee was later withdrawn so this did

3 COVID AND TRADE IN GOODS

Trade in goods is the basic staple of the WTO regime as well as virtually all PTAs – and this trade has generally suffered during the COVID-19 crisis. This was not the case, however, in all sectors: trade has increased in certain areas such as personal protective equipment (PPE). For example, China supplied 92% of the EUR 14 billion worth of facemasks imported into the European Union (EU) in the first semester of 2020, representing an eighteen-fold increase compared to 2019.[11]

3.1 Under the WTO's General Agreement on Tariffs and Trade (GATT)

WTO Members (and other States) have taken a series of measures affecting trade in goods in the context of the COVID crisis. At the time of writing, a non-exhaustive list of no less than 347 packages of measures (of which 182 are still in force, at least in part) was compiled by the WTO Secretariat in an attempt to provide transparency with respect to trade and trade-related measures taken in response to the COVID-19 crisis. The Secretariat took care to emphasize that '[t]he list of measures does not pass judgment on or question the right of WTO Members to take such actions'.[12] This list contains liberalizing as well as restrictive measures. The former category includes measures which provide for the temporary elimination of import tariffs, licensing requirements and export duties, the suspension of anti-dumping duties and value-added tax (VAT) exemptions for certain imports. The latter category of measures includes those which provide for temporary export prohibitions (bans), export licensing requirements (schemes), the requirement of export authorization for certain products; non-commercial export restrictions (on PPE and sanitizer products), temporary export control requirements for statistical purposes and export quotas. In general, most liberalizing measures relate to imports (143/183 or 78%), whereas most restrictive measures relate to exports (143/165 or 86%).

Where WTO Members adopt measures that further liberalize trade in response to a pandemic, there is no problem under WTO law (except if such liberalization would be implemented in a discriminatory manner). Where WTO Members adopt restrictive measures, however, such as export bans on medical equipment, the question arises as to whether the pandemic could be used as a defence to justify such measures. Such a defence could either be invoked when defending a measure prior to a breach having been established, or where a prima facie violation of the agreement has already been found. For example, a measure could initially be argued to fall under the exceptions to GATT Article XI:2 ('general elimination of quantitative restrictions'), preventing the

not raise any concrete problem in the end, *see* wita.org/blogs/wto-government-procurement-on-medicine/ (last visited 3 July 2022).

11. *See* ec.europa.eu/eurostat/web/products-eurostat-news/-/DDN-20201006-1?inheritRedirect=true&redirect=/eurostat/home%3F (last visited 3 July 2022).
12. Not all of these measures were taken by WTO Members, e.g., four measures taken by Serbia are listed. wto.org/english/tratop_e/covid19_e/trade_related_goods_measure_e.htm (last visited 3 July 2022).

finding of a violation. In the alternative, should this not be accepted and an inconsistency were to be established, the general exceptions of GATT Article XX and (perhaps) the security exceptions of GATT Article XXI could justify the measure.

3.1.1 Non-tariff Restrictions under GATT Article XI

Let us consider the example of Ukraine, which has taken both liberalizing and restrictive measures in the area of trade in goods in response to the COVID-19 pandemic.[13] As far as liberalizing measures are concerned, Ukraine adopted one measure pertaining to the temporary elimination of import tariffs (including VAT) on medicines, medical goods and medical equipment. Only if this measure were to be applied in a discriminatory manner, rather than on a Most-Favoured-Nation (MFN) basis, would this fall foul of GATT Article I. Furthermore, Ukraine adopted two restrictive measures including a temporary export restriction for certain medical equipment and a similar restriction for ethyl alcohol and other spirits. Export prohibitions on essential medical items are prima facie breaches of the WTO agreements as they risk violating the prohibition on non-tariff restrictions. GATT Article XI:1 provides that '[n]o prohibitions or restrictions ... shall be instituted or maintained' on the exportation of products. GATT Article XI:2(a) stipulates that this shall not extend to '[e]xport prohibitions or restrictions temporarily applied to prevent or relieve *critical shortages* of foodstuffs or other *products essential to the exporting contracting party*' (emphasis added).

The Appellate Body in *China – Raw Materials* found that in order for GATT Article XI:2(a) to apply, the shortage must relate to foodstuffs or other products that are 'absolutely indispensable or necessary'.[14] During a pandemic, medical equipment may well fall into the category of 'essential' products so this exception is likely to apply in such cases, if there is a (threatened) critical shortage.[15] Export bans have also been enacted for products such as leguminous vegetables (pea family), which may be less likely to qualify as 'absolutely indispensable'[16] – and have been decried as such in a joint statement of the Directors-General of UN Food and Agriculture Organization

13. At the initial time of writing of this contribution, the war in Ukraine had not started yet so these measures are not resulting from any regulatory desire in that context. For general analysis, *see* Pauwelyn, 'Export restrictions in times of pandemic: Options and limits under international trade agreements', 54 Journal of World Trade (2020), 727-748.
14. Appellate Body Report, *China – Measures Related to the Exportation of Various Raw Materials*, WT/DS394/AB/R, adopted on 30 January 2012, para. 326: 'For Article XI:2(a) to apply, the shortage, in turn, must relate to "foodstuffs or other products essential to the exporting Member". Foodstuff is defined as "an item of food, a substance used as food". The term "essential" is defined as "[a]bsolutely indispensable or necessary". Accordingly, Article XI:2(a) refers to critical shortages of foodstuffs or otherwise absolutely indispensable or necessary products. By including, in particular, the word "foodstuffs", Article XI:2(a) provides a measure of what might be considered a product "essential to the exporting Member" but it does not limit the scope of other essential products to only foodstuffs.'
15. For an analysis of the terms 'essential products' and 'critical shortage' *see* Mavroidis, *The Regulation of International Trade* (MIT Press, 2016), at 100-101.
16. These temporary export bans have been enacted by Egypt, El Salvador and Honduras; e.g., Egypt's temporary export ban on leguminous vegetables and products thereof, with the

(FAO), WHO and WTO.[17] Finally, one could wonder to what degree WTO Members have discretion to manage anticipated risks of such a critical shortage (i.e., the level of precaution). If WTO Members start to address the risks much earlier than necessary, such measures could be merely protective and lead to the disruption of global supply chains.

However, as further explained below, restrictions on imports or exports that are not justified under Article XI:2 of GATT could still be justified under Article XX(b) of GATT if they meet the requirements of posing a threat to human health.[18] On the contrary, if the requirements of Article XI:2(a) are met, there is no scope for the application of Article XX.[19] Although Article XIII of GATT refers to non-discriminatory administration of quantitative restrictions, most of the Article refers to the imposition of import quotas. However, Article XIII:5 includes export quotas within the ambit of the exception as well, though it is unclear how export shares would be administered.

3.1.2 General Exceptions under GATT Article XX

Continuing with the Ukrainian example, were a breach of GATT Article XI to be found, Ukraine would likely defend its measures under GATT Article XX(b), which provides an exception for measures 'necessary to protect human, animal or plant life or health'.[20] The Panel in *US – Gasoline* presented a three-tier test in respect of this provision: first, the policy must fall within the range of health-related matters; second, the measure was necessary; and third, it complied with GATT Article XX's chapeau provisions.[21] Further, as established by the *China–Raw Materials* Appellate Body Report in interpreting the concept 'in short supply', the concept of 'critical shortages' in GATT Article XI:2(a) is narrower than the 'shortages' referred to in GATT Article XX(j), therefore 'there is more leeway to justify measures under Article XX(j) of GATT than under Article XI:2(a) of GATT'.[22]

Ukraine's restrictive measures may well satisfy the first criterion where they relate to medical equipment. In terms of whether the measures may also be deemed necessary, the Appellate Body found that this entails an analysis of 'all relevant

---

exception of: peanuts; fresh or chilled peas; fresh or chilled beans; frozen leguminous vegetables; white beans; and canned chickpeas (HS 0708; 0713; 1106; 2004; 2005), due to the COVID-19 pandemic. WTO documents G/MA/QR/N/EGY/1/Rev.1, 28 April 2020; and G/MA/QR/N/EGY/1/Rev.1/Add.1, 24 June 2020.

17. Joint Statement by Qu Dongyu, Tedros Adhanom Ghebreyesus and Roberto Azevêdo, Directors-General of the FAO, WHO and WTO, 31 March 2020, available at wto.org/english/news_e/news20_e/igo_26mar20_e.htm (last visited 3 July 2022).
18. Mavroidis, *supra* note 15, at 86.
19. *Ibid.*, at 103.
20. *Ibid.*, at 73 et seq.
21. Panel Report, *United States – Standards for Reformulated and Conventional Gasoline*, WT/DS2/R, adopted on 29 January 1996, para. 6.20.
22. Mavroidis, *supra* note 15, at 460; Appellate Body Report, *China – Measures Related to the Exportation of Various Raw Materials*, WT/DS394/AB/R, adopted on 30 January 2012, para. 325.

factors';[23] a rather empty reference. This analysis begins by weighing the extent of the measure's contribution to the achievement of its objective against the trade restrictiveness of that measure, in light of the importance of the interests or values at stake. Where this allows for a preliminary conclusion of necessity, alternatives to the measure may then be considered which must provide an equivalent contribution to public health but be less trade restrictive. It is for the complaining WTO Member to identify possible alternatives to the offensive measure: the responding Member does not have to show that there are no reasonably available alternatives to achieve its objectives.

In the context of a pandemic, measures that may be challenged before the WTO include export prohibitions and quotas, as well as the requirement for export licences and authorization. It would seem more difficult to show that a complete export ban is necessary compared to an export quota or licence requirement. Moreover, there is an interpretative question surrounding what constitutes a 'contribution to public health'. Does public health merely apply internally or do consequences beyond a WTO Member's own borders need to be taken into account? It would appear that 'necessary' would refer to 'inside a Member's borders' given its requirement of an analysis of trade restrictiveness. In the case of public health, however, the reality of the pandemic is that a WTO Member's public health situation can influence public health beyond its own borders. This weighing and balancing exercise is likely to be highly context specific.[24] However, if a measure banning the export of vital medical equipment is taken out of an abundance of precaution and has dire consequences in a neighbouring State, could this be described as contributing to public health, or as being necessary?[25]

Panels 'enjoy a certain latitude' in designing the appropriate methodology to use when determining the contribution of a measure to its objective.[26] The Appellate Body tends to back evidence-based decision-making when determining contributions to protecting health.[27] Lastly, the Appellate Body found that reasonably available alternative measures must allow Members to achieve their desired level of protection.[28] Once more, a distinction can be made between export prohibitions and export quotas or licence requirements. If a licence requirement would allow a Member to reach its objectives relating to safeguarding the supply of medical equipment, an export ban could be deemed to be disproportionate, particularly in cases where the public health of neighbouring countries is imperilled as a result of such a ban.

23. Appellate Body Report, *Brazil – Measures Affecting Imports of Retreaded Tyres*, WT/DS332/AB/R, adopted on 17 December 2007, para. 156.
24. *Brazil – Measures Affecting Imports of Retreaded Tyres*, para. 182.
25. Take the example of an export ban on ventilators where Country A is only using 50% of its capacity whereas its neighbour, Country B, has a demand for ventilators in ICUs that exceeds its current stock.
26. *Brazil – Measures Affecting Imports of Retreaded Tyres*, para. 145.
27. The AB has found that for a contribution to exist, there must be 'a genuine relationship' of ends and means and that this depends on 'the nature, quantity, and quality of evidence existing at the time the analysis is made'. *Brazil – Measures Affecting Imports of Retreaded Tyres*, para. 145.
28. '[A] measure or practice will not be viewed as an alternative unless it "preserve[s] for the responding Member its right to achieve its desired level of protection with respect to the objective pursued".' *Brazil – Measures Affecting Imports of Retreaded Tyres*, para. 170.

Finally, compliance with the chapeau of Article XX GATT needs to be considered, which requires that measures are only justified if they, in addition to falling under one of the listed exceptions, are not applied 'in a manner which would constitute a means of arbitrary or unjustifiable discrimination between countries where the same conditions prevail, or a disguised restriction on international trade'. Compliance with Article XX's chapeau would most likely not be an issue in terms of protecting public health, unless a measure was applied inconsistently among third countries. Discrimination occurs when countries with the same conditions are treated differently (and vice versa). The question is: what should count as the 'same conditions' vis-à-vis a pandemic? If certain countries such as Sweden fail to observe public health safeguards that are widely adopted in other counties, could WTO Members discriminate against them as a result of this, for example, by suspending flights to/from Sweden (and therefore blocking goods coming in via cargo planes)?[29] At the same time, is it not a State's prerogative to try new approaches, different from those taken by other States, in particular at the outset of a pandemic when there are so many unknowns? Would a WTO panel always have the competence to decide whether a certain measure contributes to public health? And to balance that measure against its economic costs? Based on the current WTO jurisprudence, it is not clear what a WTO panel would decide in such cases.

3.1.3 Security Exceptions under GATT Article XXI

Article XXI(b)(iii) GATT stipulates that:

> [n]othing in this Agreement shall be construed ... to prevent any contracting party from taking any action which it considers necessary for the protection of its essential security interests ... taken in time of war or other emergency in international relations.

The seminal dispute in which this provision was interpreted, is *Russia – Traffic in Transit*. This case concerned Ukraine's challenges to Russian bans and restrictions on traffic in transit by road and rail, from Ukraine, across Russia, destined for Kazakhstan and the Kyrgyz Republic, as well as to the alleged de facto extension of these bans and restrictions to Ukrainian traffic in transit destined for Mongolia, Tajikistan, Turkmenistan and Uzbekistan.[30] The Panel found that, while the chapeau of Article XXI(b) allows a Member to take action 'which it considers necessary' for the protection of its essential security interests, this discretion is limited to circumstances that objectively fall within the scope of the three sub-paragraphs of Article XXI(b).[31] Consequently, the Article is not entirely 'self-judging'.[32] Based on the particular circumstances affecting relations between Russia and Ukraine, the Panel determined that the situation between

29. ekathimerini.com/254202/article/ekathimerini/news/greece-says-it-will-not-allow-direct-flights-from-uk-sweden-until-july-15 (last visited 3 July 2022).
30. Panel Report, *Russia – Traffic in Transit*, WT/DS512/R, adopted on 5 April 2019.
31. *Russia – Traffic in Transit*, WT/DS512/R, paras 7.53-7.101.
32. *Ibid.*, paras 7.102-7.104.

Ukraine and Russia since 2014 qualified at least as an 'emergency in international relations' under sub-paragraph (iii) of Article XXI(b).[33] The Panel also found that the challenged transit bans and restrictions were enacted in 2014 and 2016, and therefore were 'taken in time of' this 2014 emergency.[34] Accordingly, Russia's actions were objectively 'taken in time of' an 'emergency in international relations' under Article XXI(b)(iii).[35]

The Panel interpreted the term 'essential security interests' as referring to those interests relating to the 'quintessential functions of the State', depending on the 'particular situation and perceptions of the State in question' which can be expected to vary with changing circumstances.[36] As a result, it falls within the discretion of every Member to define what it considers to be its essential security interests. Equally, and perhaps more controversially, the specific language 'which it considers' was held to imply that each Member individually can decide on the 'necessity' of its essential security measures.[37] In doing so, a Member is under the obligation to interpret and apply Article XXI(b)(iii) in good faith - and a WTO panel can review whether such good faith has indeed been exercised and whether the essential security measures were 'not implausible' as measures to protect the stated interests.[38] Importantly, a war or other emergency in international relations 'involves a fundamental change of circumstances which radically alters the factual matrix in which the WTO-consistency of the measures at issue is to be evaluated'.[39] Unlike assessments of whether measures are covered by the general exceptions under Article XX GATT (discussed above), an Article XXI(b)(iii) evaluation does not require a prior determination that the measures would be WTO-inconsistent had they been taken in 'normal times'.[40]

Applying these findings to the pandemic-context: could a WTO Member defend a trade-restrictive measure on the ground that it considers such measure 'necessary for the protection of its essential security interests' in time of a pandemic if this qualifies as an 'emergency in international relations'? A WTO panel would most likely find it has jurisdiction to review aspects of the Member's invocation of Article XXI(b)(iii) as such measures would fall under the Panel's terms of reference within the meaning of the Dispute Settlement Understanding (DSU): the Article is not entirely self-judging or non-justiciable. As a result, the Respondent would have to prove it has met the requirements to invoke this Article. Specifically, the Respondent would need to prove that the pandemic forms a circumstance that objectively falls within the scope of the sub-paragraphs of Article XXI(b).

Turning first to the terms of sub-paragraph (iii), the determination 'other emergency in international relations' could be held to cover the COVID-19 crisis. In this

33. *Ibid.*, paras 7.76 and 7.114-7.123.
34. *Ibid.*, paras 7.70 and 7.124-7.125.
35. *Ibid.*, para. 7.126.
36. *Ibid.*, paras 7.130-7.131.
37. *Ibid.*, paras 7.146-7.147.
38. *Ibid.*, paras 7.132-7.135 and 7.138-7.139.
39. *Ibid.*, para. 7.108.
40. For further analysis, *see* Heath, 'Trade and security among the ruins', 30 *Duke Journal of Comparative & International Law* (2020), 223-266.

sense, on the one hand, a pandemic could be considered an emergency in international relations as it creates tensions between countries in relation to the spread of the virus. On the other hand, one could argue that the pandemic, in itself, is a health emergency of international scope that is not related to tensions between two countries, though those may emerge in relation to due diligence in the spread of the virus (but then that would be the emergency in itself, not the pandemic). In any case, the existence of a pandemic could arguably be seen as an objective fact amenable to objective determination, to put it in the words of *Russia – Traffic in Transit* Panel.[41]

There are several points of contention in this regard. First, the pandemic would appear to be a situation 'of heightened tension or crisis or a general instability engulfing or surrounding a State'[42] – but unlike situations of armed conflict, the particular type of interest for the Member in question is not related to defence, but rather to public health as a subset of the public order.[43] Second, this could be argued to be an internal situation, which takes place simultaneously in all countries, but not necessarily a problem *between* those countries. Third, the public order reference is not included in GATT though it has been 'understood in practice with as synonymous' to public morals included in Article XX.[44] In this context, a panel may perhaps be guided by the European Court of Justice (ECJ) and the precedent in *Russia–Traffic*. That being said, the ECJ referred to provisions where there is an express reference to public policy *and* public health, so one could wonder how appropriate it would be to *extend* the concept of essential security interests, first to public order and second to public health per se. Moreover, the argument could be made that such extensive interpretation would violate the rule that adjudicatory mechanisms should not legislate.

Fourth, whether the measures were 'taken in time of' such an emergency: a Panel is like to understand this phrase to require that the measures are taken *during* the emergency. Unlike a war where an objective determination tends to be more easily achievable, the start and, more importantly, the end date of a pandemic is more difficult to determine. Would measures that are taken in August 2022 be viewed with as much leniency as similar measures taken in, say, April 2020? Could a measure initially be seen as WTO-consistent, only to lose such consistency later on as the pandemic draws to a close? Could measures endlessly lose and regain consistency as the pandemic abates and then gathers strength again when a new virus strain emerges? This is a battlefield where a potential legal bout might be fought.

Moving to the terms of the chapeau: on the one hand, a worldwide pandemic may arguably be seen as 'an essential security interest', and a WTO panel may accept a Member's assessment of whether a measure is necessary in this regard. On the other

41. *Russia – Traffic in Transit*, para. 7.70.
42. *Ibid.*, paras 7.76-7.77.
43. The categorization of 'public health' as an aspect of 'public order' has been recognized by the ECJ, for example, in Case C-50/06, *Commission v. The Netherlands*, ECLI:EU:C:2007:325 and Case C-170/04, *Klas Rosengren and Others v. Riksåklagaren*, ECLI:EU:C:2007:313 as discussed in Kessedjian, 'Public order in European law', 1 *Erasmus Law Review* (2007), 1-36; Davin, 'Epidemics and investment law: A host State's perspective', in Murase and Zhou (Eds), *Epidemics and International Law* (Brill, 2021), 475-497.
44. Mavroidis, *supra* note 15, at 428.

hand, the pandemic in itself may not be 'an essential *security* interest' as there is no 'security' at risk in its existence, and a WTO panel may deem it necessary to determine the good faith with which any such declaration was made. Applying *Russia–Traffic in Transit* criteria: adopting pandemic measures can be seen as part of the 'quintessential functions of the State, namely, the protection of … its population from external threats'[45] insofar as the State's exercise of its discretion when taking such measures would not extend beyond the boundaries of good faith. The question remains whether a pandemic is an external threat. It would be for the Member taking the pandemic measures to determine their 'necessity' for the protection of public health, that is, assuming that public health is an 'essential security interest', an interpretation which is arguable but not a given, as explained above.[46]

If a WTO panel were to accept that a State can enact COVID-19 measures as part of its essential security interests, it would furthermore need to assure itself that the specific measures at issue are not 'so remote from or unrelated to the emergency in international relations' that they become 'implausible as measures protective of those interests'.[47] Were a very low threshold (for the Respondent) to be accepted, this risks 'opening the floodgates' for unilateral measures' justifications.

3.2 Under Preferential Trade Agreements (PTAs)

Aside from potentially violating the WTO agreements, measures affecting trade in goods may infringe PTA provisions. Continuing with the Ukrainian example, restrictions on the export of medical equipment may infringe on the EU-Ukraine Association Agreement (AA) or the Free Trade Agreement (FTA) between the European Free Trade Area (EFTA) and Ukraine.[48] Article 35 of the EU-Ukraine AA provides that no party 'shall adopt or maintain any prohibition or restriction or any measure having an equivalent effect on the import of any good of the other Party or on the export or sale for export of any good destined for the territory of the other Party'.[49] GATT Article XI:1 (general elimination of quantitative restrictions) is incorporated and made 'an integral part of the Agreement'.[50]

While it is uncommon for export restrictions to give rise to disputes under PTAs, a dispute under Article 35 of the EU-Ukraine AA was decided in 2020 (the first-ever EU

45. *Russia – Traffic in Transit*, para. 7.130.
46. *Ibid.*, para. 7.146.
47. *Ibid.*, paras 7.138-7.139.
48. Article 2.6 EFTA-Ukraine FTA on 'Import and export restrictions' provides: 'The rights and obligations of the Parties in respect of export and import restrictions shall be governed by Article XI of the GATT 1994, which is hereby incorporated into and made part of this Agreement.'
49. Article 35 Import and export restrictions: 'No Party shall adopt or maintain any prohibition or restriction or any measure having an equivalent effect on the import of any good of the other Party or on the export or sale for export of any good destined for the territory of the other Party, except as otherwise provided in this Agreement or in accordance with Article XI of GATT 1994 and its interpretative notes. To this end, Article XI of GATT 1994 and its interpretative notes are incorporated into, and made an integral part of, this Agreement.'
50. Article 35 Import and export restrictions.

trade dispute under a bilateral agreement).[51] *Ukraine – Export prohibitions on wood products* (*Ukraine – Wood products*) related to two export prohibitions on wood products (the 2005 export ban on rare and valuable species and the 2015 temporary ban on all exports of unprocessed timber), which were alleged to have breached Article 35 (Import and Export Restrictions) of the Agreement.[52] While the facts of this dispute are removed from the context of the current pandemic, the arguments put forward by both parties may well be instructive for future cases relating to export bans taken under PTAs in the context of COVID-19-related measures.

In relation to its export bans on wood products, Ukraine sought to defend this measure in three main ways. First, Ukraine attempted to distinguish Article 35 of the EU-Ukraine AA from GATT Article XI:1 by claiming that the former only prohibits restrictions that have the 'actual effect' of restricting trade.[53] Second, Ukraine argued that a transition period would apply until 2025 allowing it to maintain restrictions in the meantime. Third, Ukraine claimed such bans fell within its right to regulate under Article 290(1) of the EU-Ukraine AA[54] as well as exceptions provided for in Article 36 of the EU-Ukraine AA, namely GATT Article XX(b) ('necessary to protect human, animal or plant life or health') as justification for the 2005 export ban and (g) ('relating to the conservation of exhaustible natural resources') as justification for the 2015 export ban.[55]

In relation to this first point, the EU responded that such an interpretation of Article 35 of the EU-Ukraine AA would result in 'WTO minus' treatment, whereby the EU reduced its rights under the PTA as compared to (and in breach of) the WTO rules. The latter stipulates that deviating from the non-discrimination rule through PTAs is only allowed if it creates further trade liberalization above and beyond the WTO standards. The EU also argued that trade statistics confirm beyond doubt that Ukraine's

51. Final Report of the Arbitration Panel, *Restrictions applied by Ukraine on exports of certain wood products to the European Union*, adopted on 11 December 2020, available at trade.ec.europa.eu/doclib/docs/2020/december/tradoc_159181.pdf. There is a general lack of litigation of trade matters under PTAs. Between 2007 and 2017, only two cases were successfully completed under PTAs. *See* Vidigal, 'Why is there so little litigation under free trade agreements? Retaliation and adjudication in international dispute settlement', *CTEI Working Paper* No. CTEI-2017-14 (2017), at 1; 'Ukraine wood export ban found illegal in independent panel ruling', 12 December 2020, trade.ec.europa.eu/doclib/press/index.cfm?id = 2223.
52. This Article, along with Article 34 (National Treatment), make up section 3 of the Agreement on Non-Tariff Measures.
53. *See Ukraine – Wood products*, Integrated Executive Summary of the EU, 7 October 2020, para. 8, available at trade.ec.europa.eu/doclib/docs/2020/october/tradoc_158969.pdf (last visited 3 July 2022).
54. Article 290: '1. Recognising the right of the Parties to establish and regulate their own levels of domestic environmental and labour protection and sustainable development policies and priorities, in line with relevant internationally recognised principles and agreements, and to adopt or modify their legislation accordingly, the Parties shall ensure that their legislation provides for high levels of environmental and labour protection and shall strive to continue to improve that legislation. 2. As a way to achieve the objectives referred to in this Article, Ukraine shall approximate its laws, regulations and administrative practice to the EU acquis.'
55. Article 36: 'Nothing in this Agreement shall be construed in such a way as to prevent the adoption or enforcement by any Party of measures in accordance with Articles XX and XXI of GATT 1994 and its interpretative notes, which are hereby incorporated into and made an integral part of this Agreement.'

measures have had the actual effect of halting trade in the products concerned.[56] Second, according to the EU, the transitional period does not apply to export bans but rather to the elimination of customs duties on imports and exports between the Parties, which is to be implemented gradually.[57] Third, the EU put forward that Article 290 of the EU-Ukraine AA 'cannot be construed as conferring an unlimited right to derogate' as this would defeat the purpose of the AA.[58] The EU claimed that the right to regulate must be exercised in accordance with the provisions that operationalize it, including Article 36 of the EU-Ukraine AA, which incorporates GATT Articles XX and XXI.[59]

Particularly the Parties' arguments relating to Article XX(b) defence ('necessary to protect human, animal or plant life or health') are relevant in the present context as pandemic-related defences would likely come under this sub-paragraph. The EU argued that Ukraine did not provide 'any evidence showing a risk to the specific habitat or population of the ten wood species covered by the 2005 export ban, nor that the 2005 export ban had any positive effects on the conservation'.[60] None of the species are classified as threatened under the International Union for Conservation of Nature's Red List. Ukraine did not demonstrate that the risk to these trees is linked to exports. Therefore, this measure cannot be considered to be 'necessary' as less trade-restrictive alternative measures are available.[61] The EU further pointed out that compliance with GATT Article XX's chapeau would also be an issue as discrimination between domestic consumers and those in the EU is 'arbitrary and unjustifiable'.[62]

The *Ukraine – Wood products* tribunal found that the legal truth lay somewhere in the middle, though the precedential value of the decision has been questioned because of its 'important shortcomings'.[63] More precisely, it found that Ukraine's 2005 export ban was incompatible with Article 35 of the AA, forbidding export prohibitions, but that it was justified under Article XX(b) of the GATT 1994, as made applicable to the Association Agreement by Article 36 of the AA (General Exceptions), as a measure

56. *Ukraine – Wood products* (EU integrated executive summary), paras 8 and 13.
57. *Ibid.*, para. 15.
58. *Ibid.*, para. 16.
59. In relation to the 2015 export ban, the EU describes how parliamentary documents explicitly confirm that the export ban was 'designed to promote Ukraine's own wood processing industry...by refocusing export from raw wood materials to processed wood products.' (para. 22). Thus it says any conservation achieved is incidental and not sufficient to comply with Article XX(g).
60. *Ukraine – Wood products* (EU integrated executive summary), para. 18.
61. *Ibid.*, para. 19: 'Therefore, on balance it cannot be considered as necessary under Article XX(b) of the GATT 1994, all the more so as there are less trade restrictive alternative measures that would allow Ukraine to achieve its objective to the same extent (such as a limitation of the quantity of trees/wood of the species covered by the 2005 ban that can be harvested or placed on the market each year, a moratorium on cutting trees of these wood species in the areas where illegal logging occurs the most, or a very low harvesting limit, the application of administrative controls on trading of wood from these areas and of course the forest management measures that Ukraine is in the process of finalising and that Ukraine has listed in its submissions).'
62. *Ukraine – Wood products* (EU integrated executive summary), para. 20.
63. *See also*, Polovets, 'Report of Arbitration Panel in Restrictions applied by Ukraine on Exports of Certain Wood Products to the European Union', 48 *Legal Issues of Economic Integration* (2021), 1-14; for an (overly) critical analysis *see* Pogoretskyy, 'The arbitration panel report in *Ukraine – Export Prohibition on Wood Products*: Lessons from the "Pegasus" of international adjudication', 22 *Journal of World Investment & Trade* (2021), 732-758.

'necessary to protect ... plant life', taking also into account relevant provisions of Chapter 13 of the AA on trade and sustainable development. In other words, the 2005 export ban was therefore not considered in breach of Article 35 of the AA (incompatible but justified). This is an interesting conclusion as it would appear to allow discriminatory environmental protection, permitting lower environmental protection for domestic sales. Ukraine's 2015 temporary export ban was also held to be incompatible with Article 35 of the AA, forbidding export prohibitions. This was not justified under Article XX(g) of the GATT 1994 because the export ban was not sufficiently related 'to the conservation of exhaustible resources [...] made effective in conjunction with restrictions on domestic production or consumption'.

The key difference between *Ukraine – Wood products* and any claim invoking the COVID-19 emergency (or a pandemic more broadly) as a defence is that the former relates to the protection of plants rather than human life. However, the disputes would likely proceed in a similar manner with a preliminary defence based on Article 35 of the EU-Ukraine AA (or an equivalent provision under another PTA), followed by a defence under GATT Article XX(b). What we can learn from an in-depth analysis of the award is that a Tribunal is likely to view a PTA rule on import and export restrictions as identical to the equivalent obligation under GATT Article XI:1. Respondents could, therefore, dispute the applicability of Article 35 of the EU-Ukraine AA or similar PTA provisions, on the basis that they incorporate GATT Article XI:1 and so do not apply to 'essential' products. If a pandemic measure were to be categorized as a de iure or de facto export prohibition, the complainant will not need to demonstrate actual effects in order for the Tribunal to find a violation.[64] Reference to the provisions of Chapter 13 (trade and sustainable development) would most likely not cure the incompatibility of the measures at issue.[65] The same would probably also apply to chapters on 'trade and labour' and 'trade and environment' included in more recent PTAs such as the EU-Canada Comprehensive Economic and Trade Agreement (CETA).[66]

With regard to the analysis of the justification clauses, the present analysis will focus on the Tribunal's findings on the 'necessary to protect human and plant life' exceptions under Article 36 of the EU-Ukraine AA, and not those on 'exhaustion of natural resources' as the former will more likely be invoked to defend COVID-19 measures. On this basis, we may anticipate that a future Tribunal will probably start by examining whether the objective of the measures is a 'human life or health' objective within the meaning of GATT Article XX(b) – in other words, whether the measures are designed to protect 'human life or health'.[67] More specifically, a Tribunal can be expected to examine the importance of the interests or values at stake,[68] the material

64. *Ukraine – Wood products*, Award, paras 182-218.
65. *Ibid.*, paras 241-253.
66. CETA Chapter-by-Chapter, available at: policy.trade.ec.europa.eu/eu-trade-relationships-country-and-region/countries-and-regions/canada/eu-canada-agreement/ceta-chapter-chapter_en; For a more extensive analysis, *see* Bronckers and Gruni, 'Retooling the sustainability standards in EU free trade agreements', 24 *Journal of International Economic Law* (2021), 25-51.
67. *Ibid.*, paras 283-297.
68. *Ibid.*, paras 307-309.

contribution of the measures at issue,[69] the trade restrictiveness of the measure[70] and the existence of alternative measures to reach the same goal.[71]

Applying this to the two particular Ukrainian measures (temporary export restriction for certain medical equipment and a similar restriction for ethyl alcohol and other spirits): the highly important interest at stake would be (global) public health; the material contribution of such restrictions to the curing (or managing) of the pandemic would require factual evidence (which would seem feasible to deliver); their trade restrictiveness is arguably limited due to the temporary character of the measures and to the fact that the medical equipment subjected to the measures is well-delimited. Though one might question whether temporary nature and product scope determine trade restrictiveness, they do impact the overall effect of the measures. The main point of contention could be whether alternative measures are available, but it must provide 'an equivalent contribution to the achievement of the objective pursued'[72] and it would be up to the complainant to identify such measures. Finally, moving to the chapeau: in our example, Ukraine would have to prove that its measures do not 'constitute a means of arbitrary or unjustifiable discrimination between countries where the same conditions prevail' or 'a disguised restriction on international trade'. Compliance with the chapeau would not be an issue in terms of protecting public health, unless a measure was applied inconsistently among third countries – which is not in the Ukrainian example.[73]

4 COVID AND TRADE IN SERVICES

As with trade in goods, States have taken a series of measures affecting trade in services in the context of the COVID-19 crisis. As of the time of writing, a non-exhaustive list of 115 packages of measures affecting the trade in services was compiled by the WTO Secretariat, taking again care to note that such a list should not be regarded as passing judgment on or questioning the right of WTO Members to take such actions.[74] This list contains both liberalizing and restrictive measures which mostly relate to financial services (capital, liquidity and reporting requirements). Liberalizing measures include those which promote ongoing lending to the economy; the use of telemedicine for medical services; the extension of temporary work visas in critical sectors; foreign investment support; and lifting restrictive conditions in the air transport industry. Restrictive measures provide for the reduction of commercial banks' foreign exposure; postponing 5G auction process (telecom); government-insured mortgage pools; foreign

69. *Ibid.*, paras 310-328.
70. *Ibid.*, paras 329-333.
71. *Ibid.*, paras 334-343.
72. *Brazil – Measures Affecting Imports of Retreaded Tyres*, para. 156.
73. In the analysis of *Ukraine – Wood products*, discrimination was mentioned in relation to conservation measures because selling to the Ukrainian domestic market undermines conservation. However, providing medical equipment to the domestic market does not undermine public health objectives.
74. wto.org/english/tratop_e/covid19_e/trade_related_services_measure_e.htm (last visited 3 July 2022).

investment screening; and lifting tax on tourism services. Interestingly, this list does not include travel restrictions imposed throughout the pandemic, including absolute restrictions and quarantine requirements, restrictions for infected persons and for unvaccinated persons.

Disputes under General Agreement on Trade in Services (GATS) are, perhaps, less likely to occur because Members have made more limited concessions in their Schedule with regard to sensitive sectors such as financial services. Nevertheless, it is not unthinkable that some of these might fall foul of, for example, GATS Article XVI, when they adopt limitations on market access. Due to the lack of case law, it is uncertain how a WTO panel would deal with this. GATS Article XVI does not contain any exception for the restriction of exportation on 'essential services', similar to GATT Article XI – but other GATS provisions do. For example, GATS Article XII dealing with restrictions to safeguard the balance of payments and, therefore, restrictions on services *imports*, stipulates that '[i]n determining the incidence of such restrictions, Members may give priority to the supply of services which are more essential to their economic or development programmes. However, such restrictions shall not be adopted or maintained for the purpose of protecting a particular service sector'.[75] The question of similar conditions may arise when considering restrictions on the supply of services under GATS Modes 3 and 4, i.e., supply of a service by a service supplier of one Member, through commercial presence in the territory of any other Member and by a service supplier of one Member, through the presence of natural persons of a Member in the territory of any other Member.[76]

In this sense, international healthcare workers are becoming increasingly mobile.[77] It seems to be a common understanding that health worker mobility would fall under GATS Mode 4, and the commitments made in this context for relevant (sub)sectors related to health workers seem to be significant both under GATS and PTAs. Of the 139 WTO Member's schedule of commitments, 69 are health-related services commitments.[78] Though this chapter referred principally to import restrictions limiting the practice of health care by foreigners, export restrictions with regard to healthcare workers (for example, in the context of the pandemic) could require a showing of necessity.

Should a departure from a GATS obligation exist, Article XIV provides for almost identically worded exceptions as GATT Article XX, including for measures 'necessary to protect human, animal or plant life or health' as well as a chapeau requiring such exceptions to be applied indiscriminately in countries 'where like conditions prevail' (not 'the same' as in GATT). Measures may be applied differently to different countries, but this may not result in discrimination where Members can show that the measures are necessary and applied in a non-arbitrary manner. The same is true for GATS Article XIV*bis* which sets out security exceptions in virtually identical terms as GATT Article

75. Article XII:3 GATS.
76. Article I:2 GATS.
77. For relevant statistical data *see* Carzaniga, Dhillon, Magdeleine and Xu, 'International Health Worker Mobility and Trade in Services', *WTO Staff Working Paper* ERSD-2019-13 (28 November 2019), at 8-9.
78. Carzaniga et al., *ibid.*, at 15.

XXI. Due to the high similarity between GATT and GATS in this respect, the analysis above with regard to GATT Articles XX and XXI applies also *mutatis mutandis* to GATS Article XIV and XIV*bis*, albeit that GATS Article XIV contains an express reference to public order, whereas GATT Article XX does not.

Similar provisions on services have been included in PTAs – the main difference being that, due to the 'positive listing' approach under GATS, trade liberalization under PTAs may encompass larger shares of the services market. The substantive rules, which govern the finding of breach and the application of exceptions, however, are generally speaking not significantly different from those under GATS, which again are highly similar to those under GATT, so again, the above analysis applies also to services under PTAs.

5 COVID AND INTELLECTUAL PROPERTY PROTECTION

As with trade in goods and services, States have taken a series of measures affecting the protection of trade-related intellectual property rights in the context of the COVID-19 crisis. As of the time of writing, a non-exhaustive list of 77 packages of measures affecting trade-related intellectual property rights was compiled by the WTO Secretariat.[79] However, particular problems may arise concerning intellectual property rights in the context of measures combating the pandemic, for example, relating to the affordability and scarcity of COVID-19 vaccines. Only Trade-Related Aspects of Intellectual Property Rights (TRIPS) is discussed in this section because of its significant similarities with PTA chapters on intellectual property rights.[80]

5.1 TRIPS Waiver Discussions

Arguably, a suspension of pharmaceutical monopolies, possibly of a temporary character, may be needed to avoid a 'debilitating vaccine apartheid', a description of the situation made by South Africa and India.[81] In response to such concerns, India and South Africa filed a request for a waiver from TRIPS for any medical product relating to the 'prevention, containment or treatment' of COVID-19 in October 2020.[82] This waiver

79. *See* wto.org/english/tratop_e/covid19_e/trade_related_ip_measure_e.htm (last visited 3 July 2022).
80. For further research on how a WTO waiver would simultaneously affect TRIPS-like obligations in PTAs *see* Ruse-Khan and Paddeu, 'A TRIPS-COVID waiver and overlapping commitments to protect intellectual property rights under international IP and investment agreements', *South Centre Research Paper* 144 (27 January 2022).
81. wto.org/english/tratop_e/covid19_e/trade_related_ip_measure_e.htm (last visited 3 July 2022).
82. IP/C/W/669, 'Waiver from certain provisions of the TRIPS Agreement for the prevention, containment and treatment of COVID-19', Communication from India and South Africa, 2 October 2020, available at docs.wto.org/dol2fe/Pages/SS/directdoc.aspx?filename=q:/IP/C/W669.pdf (last visited 3 July 2022); further analysis: Lester, 'Who will get the coronavirus vaccines and when? Waiving TRIPS rules to fight COVID-19', *IELP Blog*, 17 October 2020, ielp.worldtrade law.net/2020/10/who-will-get-the-coronavirus-vaccines-and-when-.html (last visited 3 July 2022).

would cover any intellectual property relating to gels and disinfectants, PPE, medical equipment including ventilators, testing agents and equipment, and vaccines. Several other Members including Egypt, Indonesia, Jordan, Bolivia and Venezuela supported the proposal.[83] The proposal also received the support of the WHO.[84] Others, including the EU, the United States (US) and the United Kingdom (UK) opposed the waiver, with the UK describing it as an 'extreme measure to address an unproven problem'.[85] The request was rejected by the TRIPS Council on 16 October 2020 but Members continued discussing the waiver in various formal and informal TRIPS Council meetings. In an attempt to reconcile positions, the co-sponsors submitted a revised proposal in June 2021.[86]

Following the agreement to engage in a text-based process, negotiations continued throughout June and July 2021. In that period, the EU also submitted a proposal for a Draft General Council declaration on the TRIPS Agreement and Public Health in the circumstances of a pandemic.[87] It called for limiting export restrictions, supporting the expansion of vaccine production, and facilitating the use of current compulsory licensing provisions in the TRIPS Agreement, particularly by clarifying that the requirement to negotiate with the right holder of the vaccine patent does not apply in urgent situations such as a pandemic, among other issues. The two texts (the proposed waiver and the Draft General Council declaration) discussed in the TRIPS Council reflect the diverging positions. While the common goal remains to provide 'timely and secure access to high-quality, safe, efficacious and affordable vaccines and medicines for all, disagreement persisted on the fundamental question of what is the appropriate and most effective way to address the shortage and inequitable access to vaccines and other COVID-related products'.[88] This disagreement focuses on the scope of products to be covered by the waiver and of intellectual property rights to be waived, as well as issues relating to the duration of the waiver, its implementation and the protection of undisclosed information. On 17 June 2022, the Ministerial Conference issued a Decision on the TRIPS Agreement making available a new waiver with respect to COVID-19 vaccines on the basis of the 'exceptional circumstances' of the COVID pandemic.[89] The Decision refers to the possibility of a Member authorizing the use of

83. The proposal has been co-sponsored by the delegations of Kenya, Eswatini, Mozambique, Pakistan, Bolivia, Venezuela, Mongolia, Zimbabwe, Egypt, the African Group, the Least Developed Countries Group, the Maldives, Fiji, Namibia, Vanuatu, Indonesia and Jordan. wto.org/english/news_e/news21_e/trip_20jul21_e.htm (last visited 3 July 2022).
84. *See* twitter.com/DrTedros/status/1317449471727407104 (last visited 3 July 2022).
85. UK statement to the TRIPS Council: Item 15, 16 October 2020, gov.uk/government/news/uk-statement-to-the-trips-council-item-15 (last visited 3 July 2022).
86. IP/C/W/669/Rev. 1, 'Waiver from certain provisions of the TRIPS Agreement for the prevention, containment and treatment of COVID-19', Revised decision text, 25 May 2021, docs.wto.org/dol2fe/Pages/SS/directdoc.aspx?filename=q:/IP/C/W669R1.pdf (last visited 3 July 2022).
87. IP/C/W/681, 'Draft General Council declaration on the TRIPS Agreement and Public Health in the circumstances of a pandemic', 18 June 2021, docs.wto.org/dol2fe/Pages/SS/directdoc.aspx?filename=q:/IP/C/W681.pdf (last visited 3 July 2022).
88. wto.org/english/news_e/news21_e/trip_20jul21_e.htm (last visited 3 July 2022).
89. Ministerial Decision on the TRIPS Agreement, adopted on 17 June 2022 (WT/MIN(22)/30), available at docs.wto.org/dol2fe/Pages/SS/directdoc.aspx?filename=q:/WT/MIN22/30.pdf.

a subject-matter patent required for the production and supply of COVID-19 vaccines without the consent of the right holder. However, it has different requirements from those in TRIPS Article 31 and 31*bis*. The Decision has been criticized from both sides, on the one hand by pharmaceutical companies, claiming that the waiver of intellectual property rights, is a 'dangerous signal ... to all innovative sectors',[90] as well as by the People's Vaccine Alliance, arguing that the Decision is insufficiently broad and that the opportunity was missed for a 'meaningful IP waiver'.[91]

Though the Decision has been flagged as a great success within the WTO,[92] its impact may be less significant than apparent at first glance given the vaccine-producing capacities of middle to low-income countries. Vaccine production was expanded across the globe by pharmaceutical companies in an attempt to thwart the limitations imposed by countries such as the US and UK to export until their own population was served.[93] The question remains whether patent waivers are capable of increasing the actual supply and distribution of vaccines.

5.2 TRIPs Compulsory License Discussions

WTO Members may issue compulsory licences in line with TRIPS Article 31. Ordinarily, such licences may only be issued where negotiations with the patent holder have failed. Where the medical system of a country is on the point of being overwhelmed by a pandemic, the 'reasonable period of time' for negotiations would likely be shortened. However, this requirement of trying to obtain a voluntary licence may be waived in the case of a 'national emergency'. Where a compulsory licence has been issued, the right holder has to receive 'adequate remuneration in the circumstances of each case, taking into account the economic value of the authorization'. The Doha Declaration on TRIPS and Public Health confirms that countries are free to determine the grounds for granting compulsory licences, what constitutes a national emergency, or other circumstances of extreme urgency.[94] The Protocol Amending the TRIPS Agreement entered into force on 8 December 2005 and permits derogations from TRIPS Article 31(f) ('any such use shall be authorized predominantly for the supply of the domestic market of the Member authorizing such use') and (h) ('the right holder shall be paid adequate remuneration in the circumstances of each case, taking into account

See also Watal, 'Analysis of the 12th WTO Ministerial Conference Decision on the TRIPS Agreement', *EJIL:Talk!*, 8 July 2022.

90. Mersh, 'WTO Ministerial Conference delivers TRIPS waiver to criticism', EURACTIV.com, 22 June 2022, euractiv.com/section/health-consumers/news/wto-ministerial-conference-delivers-trips-waiver-to-criticism/ (last visited 3 July 2022).
91. *Ibid.*
92. Heilprin and Fletcher, 'WTO agrees on limited IP waiver for COVID-19 vaccines and package to reduce harmful fishing subsidies', *Health Policy Watch*, 17 June 2022, healthpolicy-watch.news/wto-negotiators-agree-on-package-to-reduce-harmful-fishing-subsidies-and-limited-ip-waiver-on-covid-19-vaccines/ (last visited 3 July 2022).
93. Bown and Bollyky, 'How COVID-19 vaccine supply chains emerged in the midst of a pandemic', 45 *The World Economy* (2022), 468-522.
94. Doha WTO Ministerial 2001: TRIPS, WT/MIN(01)/DEC/2, 'Declaration on the TRIPS Agreement and public health', 14 November 2001, para. 5(c).

the economic value of the authorization').[95] As a result, a system of compulsory licences may hence have been a sufficiently feasible path forward, rather than a global waiver. This is not to say that such path would be easy: developing countries have argued that compulsory licenses may be ineffective as they entail cumbersome procedures and requirements, relating, for example, to packaging.[96] Moreover, there is no precedence for using compulsory licenses for intellectual property rights other than patents.

Further, given that the limitations on vaccine production exceed the issue of patents in itself, it is questionable whether the WTO has (or should have) the capacity to address supply problems in situations such as pandemics. Aside from allowing subsidies and waving patents in cases where other limitations to production have been resolved, in accordance with the Decision, it would seem questionable how much further a trade organization like the WTO could go without a clear mandate from its Members.

6 CONCLUSIONS

Ultimately, potentially restrictive measures with regard to trade in goods, services and intellectual property rights taken during a pandemic have a high chance of succeeding against challenges to them at the WTO or under PTAs where their necessity is supported by scientific evidence and they are applied in a non-discriminatory manner. In particular, this would likely be the case under the general exceptions of GATT Article XX. It seems unclear whether they could be conceived as consistent with the essential security exception. Outright bans on exports may be more difficult to defend, particularly where they are taken in an overly wide-ranging manner. Review panels may have to balance the need for such measures against their potential risk: preventing access to indispensable products and services in neighbouring countries.

Two questions remain, one procedural and one substantive. The procedural question is: how long can trade-restrictive pandemic measures be maintained? One would think only for as long as necessary, but how to determine that necessity? This might not be a very difficult question to answer, since it will be heavily fact-based and there is case law precedent. The substantive question is the more difficult one: particularly with regard to intellectual property protection and States' duty to cooperate, do we need to rethink established trade rights and obligations? Has the MC-12 Decision shown that the WTO is able to rise to the occasion, was it unnecessary in light of the companies' own actions, or was the decision too little, too late? The conclusion is counterfactual and would require a study of whether unlimited access to mRNA vaccine intellectual property would have made any real difference. On this occasion, it

95. 'WTO Analytical Index, TRIPS Agreement – Article 31', available at wto.org/english/res_e/publications_e/ai17_e/trips_art31_oth.pdf (last visited 3 July 2022).

96. *See, e.g.*, IP/C/W/672, 'Waiver from certain provisions of the TRIPS Agreement for the prevention, containment and treatment of COVID-19 – Responses to questions', 15 January 2021, paras 1-5 and 18, available at docs.wto.org/dol2fe/Pages/SS/directdoc.aspx?filename=q:/IP/C/W672.pdf (last visited 3 July 2022).

would appear that other limitations, such as capacity problems, might have meant that increased intellectual property access would not necessarily have resulted in increased production. In the future, it would appear that the world is better prepared to increase capacity, but only time will tell.

Index

D

www.ingramcontent.com/pod-product-compliance
Lightning Source LLC
Chambersburg PA
CBHW070251260926
51849CB00001BA/140
9789403548760